T0181529

Lecture Notes in Computer Science 14341

Founding Editors

Gerhard Goos
Juris Hartmanis

The series Lecture Notes in Computer Science (LNCS), including its subseries Lecture Notes in Artificial Intelligence (LNAI) and Lecture Notes in Bioinformatics (LNBI), has established itself as a medium for the publication of new developments in computer science and information technology research, teaching, and education.

LNCS enjoys close cooperation with the computer science R & D community, the series counts many renowned academics among its volume editors and paper authors, and collaborates with prestigious societies. Its mission is to serve this international community by providing an invaluable service, mainly focused on the publication of conference and workshop proceedings and postproceedings. LNCS commenced publication in 1973.

Weizhi Meng · Zheng Yan · Vincenzo Piuri
Editors

Information Security Practice and Experience

18th International Conference, ISPEC 2023
Copenhagen, Denmark, August 24–25, 2023
Proceedings

Editors
Weizhi Meng 🆔
Technical University of Denmark
Kongens Lyngby, Denmark

Zheng Yan 🆔
Xidian University
Xi'an, China

Vincenzo Piuri 🆔
University of Milan
Milan, Italy

ISSN 0302-9743   ISSN 1611-3349 (electronic)
Lecture Notes in Computer Science
ISBN 978-981-99-7031-5   ISBN 978-981-99-7032-2 (eBook)
https://doi.org/10.1007/978-981-99-7032-2

This Springer imprint is published by the registered company Springer Nature Singapore Pte Ltd.
The registered company address is: 152 Beach Road, #21-01/04 Gateway East, Singapore 189721, Singapore

Paper in this product is recyclable.

Preface

This volume contains the papers that were selected for presentation and publication at the 18th International Conference on Information Security Practice and Experience (ISPEC 2023), which was organized by SPTAGE Lab, DTU Compute, Technical University of Denmark on 24–25 August 2023. It is worth noting that ISPEC embraced a new conference logo from this year.

The main goal of the ISPEC 2023 conference was to promote research on new information security technologies, including their applications and their integration with IT systems in various vertical sectors. Previous ISPEC conferences have taken place in Singapore (2005), Hangzhou, China (2006), Hong Kong, China (2007), Sydney, Australia (2008), Xi'an, China (2009), Seoul, South Korea (2010), Guangzhou, China (2011), Hangzhou, China (2012), Lanzhou, China (2013), Fuzhou, China (2014), Beijing, China (2015), Zhangjiajie, China (2016), Melbourne, Australia (2017), Tokyo, Japan (2018), Kuala Lumpur, Malaysia (2019), Nanjing, China (2021), and Taipei, Taiwan (2022). For all editions, the conference proceedings were published by Springer in the Lecture Notes in Computer Science series. Note that ISPEC 2020 was postponed to 2021 due to the COVID-19 pandemic.

This year, we received 80 submissions in total. Each submission was carefully reviewed (double-blinded) by an average of 3.2 Program Committee members in terms of novelty, practical application, and technical quality to reach a common conclusion. Eventually, the Program Committee decided to accept 27 full papers with an acceptance rate of 33.8%. In addition, 8 short papers were accepted based on the quality and received reviews. The accepted papers cover multiple topics of cyber security and applied cryptography. In addition to the paper presentations, the program also featured two invited keynote: 1) titled "Enhancing Security in Software and AI" from Yang Xiang (Swinburne University of Technology, Australia), and 2) titled "Strengthening Machine Learning-based Intrusion Detection Systems in Adversarial Environments" from Wenjing Lou (Virginia Tech, USA).

For the success of ISPEC 2023, we would like to first thank the authors of all submissions and all the PC members for their great efforts in selecting the papers. We also thank all the organizing committee members and local chairs. Finally, we thank everyone else, student helpers and session chairs, for their contribution to the program.

August 2023

Weizhi Meng
Zheng Yan
Vincenzo Piuri

Organization

General Chairs

Robert H. Deng   Singapore Management University, Singapore
Steven Furnell   University of Nottingham, UK
Allen Man Ho Au   Hong Kong Polytechnic University, China

Program Chairs

Weizhi Meng   Technical University of Denmark, Denmark
Zheng Yan   Xidian University, China
Vincenzo Piuri   University of Milan, Italy

Publicity Chairs

Kuo-Hui Yeh   National Donghwa University, Taiwan RoC
Chunhua Su   University of Aizu, Japan
Qiang Tang   Luxembourg Institute of Science and Technology, Luxembourg

Publication Chairs

Wenxiu Ding   Xidian University, China
Wenjuan Li   Hong Kong Polytechnic University, China

Web Chairs

Wei-Yang Chiu   Technical University of Denmark, Denmark
Brooke Lampe   Technical University of Denmark, Denmark

Local Chair

Wei-Yang Chiu   Technical University of Denmark, Denmark

Program Committee

Xin Jin   Ohio State University, USA
Mingjun Wang   Xidian University, China
Lukasz Krzywiecki   Wroclaw University of Technology, Poland
Zheng Yan   Xidian University, China
Xinyi Huang   Fujian Normal University, China
Jun Shao   Zhejiang Gongshang University, China
Willy Susilo   University of Wollongong, Australia
Weizhi Meng   Technical University of Denmark, Denmark
Xingye Lu   Hong Kong Polytechnic University, China
Emmanouil Vasilomanolakis   Technical University of Denmark, Denmark
Rongxing Lu   University of New Brunswick, Canada
Edgar Weippl   University of Vienna, Austria
Aniello Castiglione   University of Salerno, Italy
Panayiotis Kotzanikolaou   University of Piraeus, Greece
Masoud Kaveh   Aalto University, Finland
Haiyang Xue   University of Hong Kong, China
Yaxing Chen   Northwestern Polytechnical University, China
Ioannis Mavridis   University of Macedonia, Greece
Dong-Seong Kim   National Institute of Technology, South Korea
Nikolaos Pitropakis   Edinburgh Napier University, UK
Nathan Clarke   University of Plymouth, UK
Francesco Flammini   Linnaeus University, Sweden
Steven Furnell   University of Nottingham, UK
Pierangela Samarati   Università degli Studi di Milano, Italy
Chunhua Su   University of Aizu, Japan
Wenjuan Li   Hong Kong Polytechnic University, China
Javier Lopez   University of Malaga, Spain
Dieter Gollmann   Hamburg University of Technology, Germany
Qianhong Wu   Beihang University, China
Noboru Kunihiro   University of Tsukuba, Japan
Xixun Yu   Hainan University, China
Yun-She Yap   Universiti Tunku Abdul Rahman, Malaysia
Bela Genge   University of Medicine, Pharmacy, Sciences and
                                    Technology of Targu Mures, Romania
Shujun Li   University of Kent, UK

Contents

Secure and Efficient Federated Learning by Combining Homomorphic Encryption and Gradient Pruning in Speech Emotion Recognition

Samaneh Mohammadi[1,2]([✉]), Sima Sinaei[1], Ali Balador[2],
and Francesco Flammini[2]

[1] RISE Research Institutes of Sweden, Västerås, Sweden
{samaneh.mohammadi,sima.sinaei}@ri.se
[2] Mälardalen University, Västerås, Sweden
{ali.balador,francesco.flammini}@mdu.se

Abstract. Speech Emotion Recognition (SER) detects human emotions expressed in spoken language. SER is highly valuable in diverse fields; however, privacy concerns arise when analyzing speech data, as it reveals sensitive information like biometric identity. To address this, Federated Learning (FL) has been developed, allowing models to be trained locally and just sharing model parameters with servers. However, FL introduces new privacy concerns when transmitting local model parameters between clients and servers, as third parties could exploit these parameters and disclose sensitive information. In this paper, we introduce a novel approach called Secure and Efficient Federated Learning (SEFL) for SER applications. Our proposed method combines Paillier homomorphic encryption (PHE) with a novel gradient pruning technique. This approach enhances privacy and maintains confidentiality in FL setups for SER applications while minimizing communication and computation overhead and ensuring model accuracy. As far as we know, this is the first paper that implements PHE in FL setup for SER applications. Using a public SER dataset, we evaluated the SEFL method. Results show substantial efficiency gains with a key size of 1024, reducing computation time by up to 25% and communication traffic by up to 70%. Importantly, these improvements have minimal impact on accuracy, effectively meeting the requirements of SER applications.

Keywords: Federated Learning · Privacy-preservation · Homomorphic Encryption · Speech Emotion Recognition

1 Introduction

Speech Emotion Recognition (SER) detects and classifies human emotions expressed in spoken language. SER benefits diverse domains like mental health diagnosis, education, and entertainment [9]. While analyzing speech data can

W. Meng et al. (Eds.): ISPEC 2023, LNCS 14341, pp. 1–16, 2023.
https://doi.org/10.1007/978-981-99-7032-2_1

unveil sensitive information, including biometric identity, personality traits, geographic origin, emotional state, age, gender, and health condition [10]. Ethical and privacy concerns arise when using such data. Regulations such as GDPR [18] have been introduced to protect personal data. Thus, privacy must be a priority in developing and implementing SER applications across domains.

Federated Learning (FL) offers a promising solution to maintain data privacy while enabling machine learning (ML) models to be trained on decentralized devices [14]. FL trains ML models on local client devices without transferring raw data to a central server, which preserves data privacy and ensures compliance with regulations such as GDPR. For SER, the initial processing of speech data and training perform on clients' devices, and only local model parameters are sent to the central server for model aggregation [11]. FL reduce the risk of privacy breaches while still achieving accurate outcomes for SER applications.

However, FL introduces new privacy concerns regarding the transmission of local model parameters between clients and servers, as this data could potentially be exploited by third parties to reconstruct speech data and disclose sensitive information [6]. Differential Privacy (DP) is a promising mechanism used in FL to protect individual data points. Applying DP to SER applications can introduce accuracy challenges due to the distortion of voice data caused by the addition of noise. It adversely affects the utility and output accuracy of the SER model by more than 10% reduction (depends on privacy budget and noise scale) [4]. Thus, SER applications face difficulties achieving desired accuracy levels [17].

An alternative approach to preserving privacy without compromising SER accuracy is using diverse homomorphic encryption methods, such as Paillier homomorphic encryption (PHE) [3]. PHE ensures privacy by encrypting local model parameters during communication and computation. However, using PHE in the FL setup may introduce challenges, including increased communication traffic and computation time [19], particularly in resource-constrained settings like edge devices. Therefore, carefully considering these challenges is crucial when implementing PHE in FL systems for SER applications.

In this paper, we propose a novel method for SER called Secure and Efficient Federated Learning (SEFL), which combines Paillier homomorphic encryption with a novel gradient pruning technique. This approach enhances privacy in FL setups for SER applications while reducing communication traffic and computation time with almost maintaining acceptable model accuracy. Gradient pruning is performed on the gradients of each client during every training round. This technique removes or prunes gradients with low magnitudes, as they contribute minimally to weight updates and have a limited impact on overall performance.

The SEFL method effectively reduces the size of encrypted local model parameters transmitted between the client and server, leading to decreased communication traffic. Additionally, gradient pruning reduces the number of parameters and floating point operations (FLOPs), shortening the encryption and decryption time and thus addressing the computation time associated with encryption methods.

The novel contributions of this paper can be summarized as follows:

- Develop a novel SEFL algorithm for SER applications that ensures privacy while enhancing efficiency in terms of reduced communication and computation overhead, as well as maintaining acceptable accuracy.
- Conduct a proof of concept implementation of Paillier homomorphic encryption in FL for SER applications to ensure the confidentiality of the client.
- Evaluate SEFL on a public SER dataset to demonstrate its considerable gains in efficiency, such as a reduction of computation time by 10–25% and communication traffic by 50–70%, depending on pruning percentage, while having a very limited impact on accuracy, in order to meet the requirements of SER applications.

The paper is structured as follows. Section 2 provides an overview of the background and related works on SER using FL, privacy-preserving techniques, and communication and computation-efficient FL. Section 3 describes the application of SEFL method for SER, including non-functional requirements, threat model, and the proposed SEFL algorithm. Section 4 presents experimental results obtained using SEFL in the SER reference application. Finally, Sect. 5 concludes the paper and provides insights for future developments.

2   Background and Related Works

This section reviews related work in SER using FL, explores homomorphic encryption techniques for privacy preservation in FL, and reviews work on efficient communication and computation in FL.

2.1   Speech Emotion Recognition Using Federated Learning

Speech emotion recognition (SER) uses ML algorithms to understand human emotions from audio signals. It requires large amounts of sensitive data, raising privacy concerns. FL offers a promising solution by collaborating on decentralized devices without sharing raw data [11]. Some studies propose FL-based approaches for building private decentralized SER models using federated self-training [16]. However, existing method rely on the FL framework for privacy preservation and do not apply additional privacy-preserving techniques in FL or consider various threat models.

2.2   Privacy-Preserving Federated Learning

Homomorphic encryption (HE) is used in FL to protect user privacy and enable secure aggregation [3]. With HE, data is encrypted before being sent to the central server for training, ensuring privacy. The server performs computations on the encrypted data without decrypting it, using homomorphic operations like addition and multiplication. The encrypted results are then returned to devices for decryption and aggregation [12]. Most prevalent among HE variants are Paillier, FV, and CKKS [1]. Paillier allows additions to encrypted data, whereas FV and CKKS allow additions and multiplications. It is possible to encrypt integers using the Paillier and FV schemes, but only approximate results can be obtained with the CKKS scheme. However, most HE variants add additional computational and communication overhead, making it more challenging to scale FL to large numbers of devices.

2.3   Communication and Computation-Efficient Federated Learning

During FL training, transmitting model parameters like DNN models between devices and a central server can cause high communication overhead and slow learning [3]. Compression techniques like gradient pruning help reduce model size [7]. However, weight pruning methods in FL may lead to accuracy loss [13]. Implementing privacy-preserving mechanisms like HE on edge devices with limited computational capabilities and communication bandwidth in FL systems introduces significant overhead and impractically long training times [8]. Existing solutions include batching multiple plaintexts into a single one to reduce computation overhead [19], but this approach still results in high communication overhead. Achieving a balance between communication, computation, and privacy remains an ongoing challenge in FL with HE.

3   Application of Secure and Efficient Federated Learning for Speech Emotion Recognition

In this section, we will provide an overview of the non-functional requirements for SER applications, describe the threat model for our system, and provide a detailed explanation of the proposed SEFL (Secure and Efficient Federated Learning) method for SER applications.

3.1   Non-functional Requirements of Speech Emotion Recognition Application

Non-functional requirements for SER applications encompass performance-related aspects rather than specific functionalities. Key requirements include privacy, efficiency and accuracy. Meeting these requirements is essential to fulfilling user needs, expectations, and legal obligations. A detailed explanation of non-functional requirements is presented in this section, with corresponding evaluations demonstrating compliance.

1. *Privacy:*
   (a) Personal speech data must be kept on local devices only [18].
   (b) The central server must not be able to access local model parameters to infer sensitive information.

(c) Communication between clients and servers should be protected from unauthorized access in order to keep SER parameters confidential.
2. *Efficiency:*
    (a) In order to reduce hardware costs and consider the typically resource-constrained edge devices, SER computation overhead must be minimized.
    (b) Communication overhead between SER clients and servers must be minimized in order to optimize network resource consumption when using limited bandwidth connections.
3. *Accuracy:*
    (a) The level of accuracy of SER applications must be kept high enough to reliably identify the correct emotions from speech samples. We can consider a baseline accuracy of a minimum 70% in detecting the four basic emotions - neutral, sad, happy, and angry [17].

It is essential to note that these requirements are often interdependent. For example, privacy-preserving methods can impact efficiency in terms of communication and computation overhead. Additionally, implemented SER in the FL setup show a slight drop in accuracy (up to 0–5%) [16]. Communication traffic is defined as the number of bits exchanged between clients and servers. In centralized SER training, the amount of speech data sent to the central server depends on factors like audio clip length, sampling rate, and pre-processing steps. For instance, CREMA-D dataset [2] used 7,442 audio clips, with each client sending around 8–10 MB to server in each training round.

3.2   Threat Model

In this paper, we consider the honest-but-curious (HBC) paradigm for the server, which implies that the server is not malicious but still retains curiosity about the clients' data or models. However, this assumption introduces certain potential threats. Specifically, the HBC server has the ability to infer sensitive information, such as the speaker's identity, by reconstructing speech data from the model parameters. By analyzing distinctive characteristics of the speaker's voice, such as pitch, tone, and accent, the server may potentially identify individuals. Moreover, HBC servers can analyze the reconstructed speech data to gather sensitive information about the speaker's emotional state. Indicators of emotions can reveal the speaker's emotional state or personality.

3.3   Proposed Method: SEFL

To address the privacy threat posed by an HBC server, as well as to meet the non-functional requirements of the SER application, we propose a new approach called Secure and Efficient Federated Learning (SEFL). SEFL combines Paillier homomorphic encryption with a novel gradient pruning method. The SEFL method ensures that the speech data remains on the end devices during training (Req. 1.a). Using Paillier homomorphic encryption, the HBC server can only access ciphertext data and cannot infer sensitive information from the model parameters (Req. 1.b). Additionally, the encrypted model parameters shared by clients ensure unauthorized parties cannot access the SER model without compromising the cryptosystem (Req. 1.c). Furthermore, SEFL incorporates gradient pruning based on the magnitude on the client side, aiming to prune gradients with low magnitudes, as they contribute less to weight updates and have a limited effect on overall performance. This approach reduces encryption computation and communication overhead, improving efficiency (Req. 2) while maintaining comparable accuracy to the initial model (Req. 3).

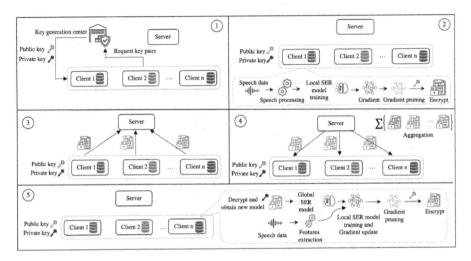

Fig. 1. An overview of secure and efficient federated learning for speech emotion recognition.

Figure 1 presents the overview of SEFL for SER application. In Step 1, the initial model is configured, the key generation center collects client requests, generates public-private key pairs, and returns them to the clients. Moving to Step 2, clients extract relevant features and train their SER models using a multilayer perceptron network locally on their devices. Gradients are calculated using backpropagation, which propagates them from the loss function backwards to help adjust the network parameters based on the gradient, reducing the error between the output value and the desired one. Each client then applies gradient pruning techniques which are based on magnitude aim to remove gradients with low magnitudes. Additionally, in this step, the PHE scheme is applied to encrypt the newly pruned gradients of each client.

Advancing to Step 3, each client transmits its encrypted gradient to the server. In Step 4, the server leverages homomorphic operations to aggregate all encrypted client gradients and generate a new encrypted gradient, which it distributes to all clients. Step 5 involves clients decrypting the received new encrypted gradient from the server and updating their local model. These steps continue to iterate until the desired model is achieved or the termination condition is met. For a more comprehensive understanding of the SEFL method, please refer to Algorithm 1, which outlines the steps and rules involved.

The parameters in the SEFL Algorithm 1 for SER and their descriptions are as follows: x: extracted speech features of clients dataset, w: parameters of the model, fp: feedforward process, $Label$: output label of SER in each iteration, f^*: activation function, $loss$: loss function, c: loss calculated by the loss function, e: minimum error, bp: backpropagation process, $grad$: gradient calculated by the backpropagation process, η: learning rate, T: total iterations, K: selected clients, B: local minibatch size and pp: pruning percentage.

Algorithm 1: SEFL for SER

Input: T, x, K, B, pp, η

1   Server broadcasts w_0^g

2   **for** $t \leq T$ **do**

3   **Key generation center:**

4   **while** *listening request from clients* **do**

5   **if** *receive requests from clients* **then**

6   Generate key pairs: Public key (pk), Private key (sk)

7   **Return** key pairs $\{(pk),(sk)\}$

8   **Clients-side:**

9   Request key pairs from **key generation center**

10   Initialize the model parameters w_i^t

11   **for** $i \in 1,2, ..., K$ **do**

12   Forward propagation: $label_i = fp(x_i, w_i^t)$

13   Compute loss: $c = \text{loss}(f^*(x_i), label_i)$

14   **if** $c < e$ **then**

15   Break

16   **else**

17   Back propagation: $grad_i = bp(x_i, w_i^t, c)$

18   Gradient pruning: $\tilde{grad}_i = (grad_i, pp)$

19   Encryption: $E_i = Enc(\tilde{grad}_i, pk)$

20   Send E_i to the server

21   Receive new aggregated encrypted model from server E_g^t

22   Decryption: $grad_i^{t+1} = Dec(E_g^t, sk)$

23   Update: $w_{i+1}^t = w_i^t - \eta \cdot grad_i^{t+1}$

24   **Server-side:**

25   Aggregation: $E_g^t = (E_i^t \bigoplus E_{i+1}^t \bigoplus ... \bigoplus E_K^t)$

26   Broadcast updated model parameters E_g^t

Paillier Homomorphic Encryption (PHE). Within SEFL, the PHE scheme developed as a promising solution to ensure the confidentiality and privacy of participants' speech data in the context of FL for the SER application. The Paillier cryptosystem, a partially homomorphic encryption scheme, allows the server to process and aggregate model parameters with the homomorphic property on the server without requiring decryption. One key advantage of the Paillier homomorphic cryptosystem is its resistance against attacks from the HBC server. It has been designed to protect against possible privacy breaches by ensuring that ciphertexts do not reveal any information about the plaintexts. This is proven through its resilience against the chosen plaintext attack (CPA) based on the decisional composite residue problem. Consequently, PHE emerges as the most efficient partially homomorphic encryption scheme available for FL settings [20].

Basically, Paillier encryption consists of three parts: key generation center, encryption, and decryption. Following is a more detailed discussion.

Key Generation Centre: Here we explain how to generate keys in more detail by referring to lines [3–7] of Algorithm 1. Select two primes p and q that are sufficiently large and equal in length and satisfy $gcd(p \times q, (p-1) \times (q-1)) = 1$. Then, calculate n, λ and lcm represents the least common multiple as:

$$n = p \cdot q \tag{1}$$

$$\lambda = lcm(p - 1, q - 1) \tag{2}$$

An integer g is a generator and satisfies $g \in Z_{n^2}^*$ so that n can divide the order of g. Then, define $L(x)$ to calculate μ as:

$$L(x) = \frac{(x - 1)}{n} \tag{3}$$

$$\mu = (L(g^\lambda \bmod n^2))^{-1}) \bmod n \tag{4}$$

Thus, the public and private key pair can be shown as $(pk, sk) = \{(n, g), (\lambda, \mu)\}$.

Encryption: The encryption process (line 19 of Algorithm 1) with the public key (pk) can be described as follows, assuming the plaintext is a gradient of the client in each iteration $grad$, the ciphertext is E, and for some random $r \in \{0, \ldots, n - 1\}$:

$$E = g^{grad} \cdot r^n \bmod n^2 \tag{5}$$

Decryption: Using a private key (sk), the ciphertext E and plaintext $grad$ can be decrypted as follows (line 22 of Algorithm 1):

$$grad = L(E^\lambda \bmod n^2) \cdot \mu \bmod n \tag{6}$$

Gradient Pruning. To enhance the efficiency of the SEFL method for SER on edge devices with limited resources, we propose a novel approach combining Paillier homomorphic encryption with gradient pruning. Gradient pruning removes or prunes gradients with low magnitudes, as they contribute less to weight updates. By selectively pruning these gradients, the computational and memory requirements are reduced. This reduces the size of encrypted local model

---

Algorithm 2: Gradient pruning

Input: $grad_i$, Pruning threshold: p_i, pp
Output: $\tilde{grad}_i$

1 **for** $l \in g_i$ **do**
2   N_l = Number of parameters in each layer
3   Pruning index = N_l * pp/100
4   p_i = Find pruning index-th value in l_{g_i}
5   **if** *Each amount in* $l <= p_i$ **then**
6   ⌊ Remove gradients below threshold in this layer and update l_{g_i}
7   Update gradient based on pruning in each layer: $\tilde{grad}_i$
8 Return pruned gradient $\tilde{grad}_i$

---

parameters, minimizing communication traffic. Additionally, gradient pruning reduces parameters and floating-point operations (FLOPs), resulting in faster encryption and decryption times and mitigating computation time.

The Algorithm 2 shows the gradient pruning techniques, which aim to remove or prune gradients with low magnitudes. The algorithm incorporates a flexible pruning threshold for each layer of the neural network, allowing it to adapt to the specific requirements of each client during every training round. This adaptive approach enhances the effectiveness of the pruning process. By customizing the pruning threshold to match the unique characteristics of each layer, we ensure that only weights with minimal influence on the continuity of the loss function are pruned. This selective pruning strategy preserves the accuracy of the model while effectively reducing computational and memory overhead.

To determine the pruning threshold for each layer, we consider the number of parameters and the desired pruning percentage specific to that layer, as shown in 2–4 lines of Algorithm 2. By analyzing the gradients of each weight, we assess the rate of change in their magnitudes and make decisions regarding whether to prune or not based on this information. To seamlessly integrate this algorithm, we incorporate it into line 18 of our overall SEFL Algorithm 1, ensuring that the pruning process is smoothly integrated into the larger training process.

4   Experimental Results

This section presents the industrial use case and simulation settings for evaluating the SEFL method. It covers the public dataset used, speech processing and feature extraction techniques, SER model architecture, and FL framework. We conduct a comprehensive evaluation of SEFL, assessing its privacy implications, effectiveness in reducing communication traffic and computation time, and comparing its accuracy with the original model.

4.1   Use-Case Description and Simulation Setting

DAIS[1] (Distributed Artificial Intelligent Systems) project aims to create a distributed edge intelligence system by combining IoT and AI, ensuring trustworthy connectivity and interoperability. Within this project, various industry-driven use cases are explored, including domains like digital life, smart manufacturing, and mobility. One important use-case in DAIS is SER in home entertainment recommendation systems. This use-case involves recommending digital content, such as movies, based on users' emotions. This requires a distributed, efficient, and privacy-preserving SER system: that was one essential motivation for exploring SEFL for SER.

We evaluated SEFL using the widely used CREMA-D dataset [2], which consists of 7,442 original clips from 91 actors. The dataset includes 48 male and 43 female actors of various ages, representing diverse races and ethnicities. The actors expressed 12 sentences, corresponding to six emotions: anger, disgust, fear, happy, neutral, and sad. For training the SER model, we focused on the four most frequent emotion labels: neutral, sad, happy, and angry.

For speech processing, we employed the OpenSMILE toolkit to generate the Emo-Base feature set. These features are designed to be highly discriminative and have achieved state-of-the-art performance in SER tasks. We utilized a multilayer perceptron (MLP) architecture for the SER model, comprising two dense layers with sizes [256, 128] and ReLU activation. To enhance convergence in the FedSGD algorithm, we set a local training batch size of 20 and a learning rate of 0.1. Additionally, we incorporated a 0.2 dropout rate to mitigate overfitting.

In FL training, each of the 91 distinct speakers in the dataset serves as a unique client. We used 80% of the data for local training at each client, reserving the remaining 20% for validation. We tested our approach on a laptop using a customized FL framework. To ensure robustness, we conducted five experiments with different test folds and reported the average results. The experiments were performed on a Windows 10 Pro environment with an Intel Core i7 CPU @1.80GHz processor and 16.0 GB RAM.

4.2   Privacy Considerations

The SEFL method ensures privacy in the SER application by preventing information leakage through the HBC server. It satisfies requirement 1.a by keeping speech data on end devices throughout the training process. To enhance client confidentiality and protect against breaches, the method incorporates PHE. This encryption technique ensures that the HBC server only accesses ciphertexts, maintaining the confidentiality of plaintexts. Thus, requirement 1.b is fulfilled, significantly reducing the risk posed by the threat model.

The SEFL method ensures that the private key remains accessible to authorized clients, preventing unauthorized access to the SER model without compromising the cryptosystem. This design feature fulfills requirement 1.c. Addi-

---

[1] DAIS Project Website: https://dais-project.eu/.

tionally, by altering the key pair during each iteration, even if an attacker manages to break a few training rounds, they would not be able to obtain the final result. It is important to note that breaking a cryptosystem is challenging but not impossible. Due to space limitations, we refer to the related work [15] for security analysis. Increasing the size of cryptographic keys improves privacy and security. However, larger key sizes generally result in longer execution times, as shown in Fig. 2. Thus, finding the right balance between privacy requirements and execution time is crucial for optimizing the SEFL method.

4.3 Efficiency in Terms of Communication Traffic

In centralized SER applications with the CREMA-D dataset, a single client typically transmits around 8–10 MB of speech data to the central server. However, the SEFL method in FL training for SER applications significantly reduces the data size transmitted. Instead of sending raw speech data, only the local model update is transmitted, resulting in a substantial reduction of approximately 70% in data size, as shown in Table 1. The SEFL method achieves this reduction by employing PHE and gradient pruning on the client side. The choice of key sizes and pruning percentages can influence the communication traffic between the client and the server.

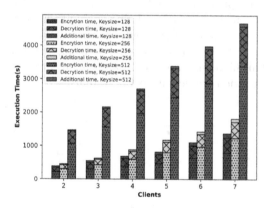

Fig. 2. Impact of key length and number of clients on total execution time.

In our experiments, we tested different key sizes (KS) of 128, 256, 512, and 1024 bits, combined with gradient pruning percentages (PP) of 20%, 40%, 60%, and 80%, to determine the optimal configuration. Table 1 provides an overview of the communication traffic for FL of SER messages in three modes: 1) plaintext, 2) ciphertext for PHE, and 3) ciphertext for SEFL. Based on our findings, setting the gradient pruning percentage to 80% allows for the use of a larger key size of 1024 bits, resulting in communication traffic of 11.3 MB, which is comparable to that of a centralized SER model. This configuration achieves an accuracy of

Table 1. Communication traffic of SER in FL using PHE, and SEFL based on different key sizes

Method	Type of Data	PP	Communication Traffic (MB)			
			$KS = 128$	$KS = 256$	$KS = 512$	$KS = 1024$
FL for SER	Plaintext	–	2.18	2.18	2.18	2.18
PHE	Ciphertext	–	7.96	14.4	27.3	53.8
SEFL	Ciphertext	20%	**6.55**	**11.7**	**22.2**	**43.4**
SEFL	Ciphertext	40%	**5.05**	**8.99**	**17.0**	**32.7**
SEFL	Ciphertext	60%	**3.55**	**6.20**	**11.4**	**22.2**
SEFL	Ciphertext	80%	**2.20**	**3.37**	**6.01**	**11.3**

69.89% (as shown in Table 3), close to the acceptable levels observed in SER application baselines. Using a key size of 512 bits and a pruning percentage of 60%, the communication traffic was 11.4 MB, comparable to that of a centralized SER model, while achieving an accuracy of 70.32%. Furthermore, with a key size of 128 bits and a pruning percentage of 80%, the communication traffic was reduced to approximately 3 MB, similar to FL training for SER applications. The corresponding accuracy achieved was 69.89%, which is close to the acceptable levels observed in SER application baselines. Figure 3-left side demonstrates that doubling the key size in both PHE and SEFL results in a linear increase in communication traffic. Notably, SEFL outperforms PHE by reducing clients' ciphertext message size by up to 80% when increasing the pruning percentage from 20% to 80%. This highlights the effectiveness of our proposed SEFL method in reducing communication traffic within FL systems.

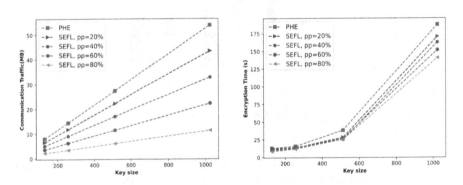

Fig. 3. Left: Communication traffic for PHE and SEFL with different key sizes. Right: Encryption times for PHE and SEFL with different key sizes.

4.4 Efficiency in Terms of Computation Time

The SEFL method reduces computation time for encryption and decryption, improving efficiency. Table 2 and Fig. 3-right side demonstrates the measured encryption and decryption times in PHE, comparing the SEFL approaches for SER applications. Our findings confirm a substantial increase in encryption and decryption time as the key size exponentially grows. Our findings, presented in Fig. 3-right side and Table 2, confirm that increasing the pruning percentage from 20% to 80% leads to a reduction of approximately 10% to 25% in encryption and decryption times for SEFL. This reduction becomes more significant when using a larger key size. Therefore, SEFL successfully decreases computation times while preserving user privacy in SER within FL systems.

Table 2. Encryption/decryption times of PHE and SEFL based on key sizes

Method	PP	Type of Computation	Computation Time (s)			
			$KS = 128$	$KS = 256$	$KS = 512$	$KS = 1024$
PHE	–	Encryption	12.9087	15.4075	38.3163	187.3240
		Decryption	3.6393	4.1267	10.9752	55.1653
SEFL	20%	Encryption	12.2097	13.9581	28.2548	170.359
		Decryption	3.5393	4.1433	10.1937	51.0521
SEFL	40%	Encryption	10.8051	13.2047	26.7844	162.3815
		Decryption	3.16783	4.0514	8.1276	48.44876
SEFL	60%	Encryption	9.3748	12.7632	25.3584	151.6185
		Decryption	2.6446	4.0597	7.70719	48.9399
SEFL	80%	Encryption	8.2718	11.4931	25.0631	140.4393
		Decryption	2.2468	3.9250	7.7071	47.2599

4.5 Performance Metrics: Accuracy, F1-Score, Precision, and Loss

The requirements section mentioned that centralized SER systems typically achieve a minimum baseline accuracy of 70%. Additionally, it has been observed that there may be a possibility of a 0–5% drop in accuracy when implementing SER in the FL setup [16]. Our initial SER model in the FL setup achieved an accuracy of 72.90%, which meets the requirements. To evaluate the performance of SER in the FL setup using PHE and SEFL, we measured accuracy, F1-score, precision, and loss function. Our analysis indicates that using PHE maintains accuracy and other metrics at the same level as SER performance in FL.

As shown in Fig. 4 and Table 3, SEFL has a limited impact on accuracy and other metrics due to using gradient pruning techniques. Despite this limitation, even with the highest pruning percentage, the accuracy remains close to 70%, still satisfying the SER application's requirements. Our experiments utilized a

Table 3. Performance comparison of SER in FL using PHE, and SEFL method.

Method	PP	Accuracy	F1-score	Precision	Loss
Initial SER model in FL	–	**72.90%**	**64.84%**	**67.49%**	**0.675**
PHE	–	**72.87%**	**64.81%**	**67.26%**	**0.678**
SEFL	20%	**71.82%**	**63.52%**	**65.99%**	**0.686**
SEFL	40%	**71.55%**	**62.54%**	**65.17%**	**0.689**
SEFL	60%	**70.32%**	**61.46%**	**65.04%**	**0.706**
SEFL	80%	**69.89%**	**58.39%**	**60.49%**	**0.740**

key size of 128, with 20 clients per training round and 200 total epochs. Pruning percentage was applied at levels of 20%, 40%, 60%, and 80%. The results indicate that even with 80% gradient pruning, SEFL's impact on accuracy and performance parameters is minimal. The achieved accuracy is still very close to the acceptable baseline for the SER application.

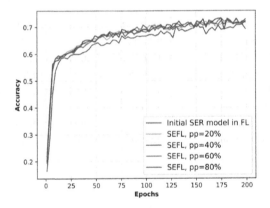

Fig. 4. Accuracy comparison of SER in FL and SEFL.

5   Conclusions and Future Work

This paper presents SEFL, a novel approach tailored for SER applications, combining Paillier homomorphic encryption and gradient pruning within FL. SEFL effectively addresses privacy concerns while reducing computation time and communication traffic while maintaining acceptable model accuracy. Experimental evaluations demonstrate that SEFL, with a key size of 1024, achieves a significant 25% reduction in computation time and an impressive 70% reduction in communication traffic compared to PHE without gradient pruning. The proposed method achieves a satisfactory model accuracy of approximately 69.89%, meeting the requirements of SER applications on resource-constrained edge devices. SEFL strikes a balance between privacy and performance, making it an effective solution for SER. With the increasing importance of trustworthy AI in supporting higher levels of autonomy [5], we believe that the proposed method can be extended to other domains with similar requirements. Future research aims to explore the potential of multi-key HE in FL for SER, preventing privacy leakage and collusion between devices and the server.

Acknowledgement and Disclaimer. This work was partially supported by EU ECSEL project DAIS which has received funding from the ECSEL JU under grant agreement No.101007273. The work reflects only the authors' views; the European Commission is not responsible for any use that may be made of the information it contains.

References

1. Acar, A., Aksu, H., Uluagac, A.S., Conti, M.: A survey on homomorphic encryption schemes: theory and implementation. ACM Comput. Surv. (CSUR) **51**(4), 1–35 (2018)
2. Cao, H., Cooper, D.G., Keutmann, M.K., Gur, R.C., Nenkova, A., Verma, R.: CREMA-D: crowd-sourced emotional multimodal actors dataset. IEEE Trans. Affect. Comput. (CSUR) **5**(4), 377–390 (2014)
3. Fang, C., Guo, Y., Hu, Y., Ma, B., Feng, L., Yin, A.: Privacy-preserving and communication-efficient federated learning in internet of things. Comput. Secur. **103**, 102199 (2021)
4. Feng, T., Peri, R., Narayanan, S.: User-level differential privacy against attribute inference attack of speech emotion recognition in federated learning. arXiv preprint arXiv:2204.02500 (2022)
5. Flammini, F., Alcaraz, C., Bellini, E., Marrone, S., Lopez, J., Bondavalli, A.: Towards trustworthy autonomous systems: taxonomies and future perspectives. IEEE Trans. Emerg. Top. Comput. 1–13 (2022). https://doi.org/10.1109/TETC.2022.3227113
6. Jere, M.S., Farnan, T., Koushanfar, F.: A taxonomy of attacks on federated learning. IEEE Secur. Priv. **19**(2), 20–28 (2020)
7. Jiang, Y., et al.: Model pruning enables efficient federated learning on edge devices. IEEE Trans. Neural Netw. Learn. Syst. (2022)
8. Jiang, Z., Wang, W., Liu, Y.: FLASHE: additively symmetric homomorphic encryption for cross-silo federated learning. arXiv preprint arXiv:2109.00675 (2021)
9. Khalil, R.A., Jones, E., Babar, M.I., Jan, T., Zafar, M.H., Alhussain, T.: Speech emotion recognition using deep learning techniques: a review. IEEE Access **7**, 117327–117345 (2019)
10. Kröger, J.L., Lutz, O.H.-M., Raschke, P.: Privacy implications of voice and speech analysis – information disclosure by inference. In: Friedewald, M., Önen, M., Lievens, E., Krenn, S., Fricker, S. (eds.) Privacy and Identity 2019. IAICT, vol. 576, pp. 242–258. Springer, Cham (2020). https://doi.org/10.1007/978-3-030-42504-3_16

11. Latif, S., Khalifa, S., Rana, R., Jurdak, R.: Federated learning for speech emotion recognition applications. In: 2020 19th ACM/IEEE International Conference on Information Processing in Sensor Networks (IPSN), pp. 341–342. IEEE (2020)
12. Liu, X., Li, H., Xu, G., Chen, Z., Huang, X., Lu, R.: Privacy-enhanced federated learning against poisoning adversaries. IEEE Trans. Inf. Forensics Secur. **16**, 4574–4588 (2021)
13. Ma, X., Lin, S., Ye, S., He, Z., Zhang, L., Yuan, G., Tan, S.H., Li, Z., Fan, D., Qian, X., et al.: Non-structured DNN weight pruning-is it beneficial in any platform? IEEE Trans. Neural Netw. Learn. Syst. **33**(9), 4930–4944 (2021)
14. McMahan, B., Moore, E., Ramage, D., Hampson, S., y Arcas, B.A.: Communication-efficient learning of deep networks from decentralized data. In: Artificial Intelligence and Statistics, pp. 1273–1282. PMLR (2017)
15. Park, J., Lim, H.: Privacy-preserving federated learning using homomorphic encryption. Appl. Sci. **12**(2), 734 (2022)
16. Tsouvalas, V., Ozcelebi, T., Meratnia, N.: Privacy-preserving speech emotion recognition through semi-supervised federated learning. In: 2022 IEEE International Conference on Pervasive Computing and Communications Workshops and other Affiliated Events (PerCom Workshops), pp. 359–364. IEEE (2022)
17. Tuncer, T., Dogan, S., Acharya, U.R.: Automated accurate speech emotion recognition system using twine shuffle pattern and iterative neighborhood component analysis techniques. Knowl.-Based Syst. **211**, 106547 (2021)
18. Voigt, P., Von dem Bussche, A.: The EU General Data Protection Regulation (GDPR). A Practical Guide, 1st edn., vol. 10, no. 3152676, p. 10–5555. Springer, Cham (2017). https://doi.org/10.1007/978-3-319-57959-7
19. Zhang, C., Li, S., Xia, J., Wang, W., Yan, F., Liu, Y.: {BatchCrypt}: efficient homomorphic encryption for {Cross-Silo} federated learning. In: 2020 USENIX Annual Technical Conference (USENIX ATC 2020), pp. 493–506 (2020)
20. Zhang, J., Chen, B., Yu, S., Deng, H.: PEFL: a privacy-enhanced federated learning scheme for big data analytics. In: 2019 IEEE Global Communications Conference (GLOBECOM), pp. 1–6. IEEE (2019)

FedLS: An Anti-poisoning Attack Mechanism for Federated Network Intrusion Detection Systems Using Autoencoder-Based Latent Space Representations

Tran Duc Luong[1,2] , Vuong Minh Tien[1,2] , Phan The Duy[1,2] ,
and Van-Hau Pham[1,2(✉)]

[1] Information Security Laboratory, University of Information Technology, Ho Chi
Minh city, Vietnam
{19521815,19522346}@gm.uit.edu.vn
[2] Vietnam National University, Ho Chi Minh city, Vietnam
{haupv,duypt}@uit.edu.vn

Abstract. The recent explosion in the number and advancement of cyberattacks induces the deployment of machine learning (ML)-based network intrusion detection systems (NIDS) in the network infrastructure of each corporation. However, there are plenty of difficulties for enterprise organization in training a conventional ML-based IDS, such as the data shortage, the privacy concerns about sensitive information, etc. Fortunately, federated learning (FL) has emerged as a decentralized training scheme that facilitates the collaboration of different parties in building a robust ML-based NIDS. As a result, this IDS model can learn new signatures of cyber threats from various data sources without the privacy breaches. Nonetheless, because of the server's blindness to the local training, the FL framework has to face the risks of poisoning attacks where the compromised clients intentionally inject adversarial data into their local dataset or directly manipulate the model weights before updating to the server for aggregation. Several anti-poisoning techniques have been proposed to mitigate the impact of poisoning attacks in FL, but these approaches regularly require some prior knowledge and do not work well in the case of non-Independently and Identically Distributed (non-IID) data environments. This paper introduces a new defensive mechanism for FL-based NIDS, named FedLS, by adopting penultimate layer representations (PLR) and Autoencoder (AE)-based latent space to filter malicious updates from the aggregation phase. The experimental results on CIC-ToN-IoT and N-BaIoT datasets have demonstrated the effectiveness of our FedLS in detecting advanced poisoning methods in both IID and non-IID cases. More specifically, the Accuracy and F1-Score metrics of FL-based NIDS witness a surge to over 99% after integrating our proposed defense in the best case.

© The Author(s), under exclusive license to Springer Nature Singapore Pte Ltd. 2023
W. Meng et al. (Eds.): ISPEC 2023, LNCS 14341, pp. 17–35, 2023.
https://doi.org/10.1007/978-981-99-7032-2_2

Keywords: Federated learning (FL) · network intrusion detection system (NIDS) · Penultimate Layer Representation (PLR) · Latent Space Representation (LSR) · Autoencoder (AE) · cyberattack

1 Introduction

In recent years, the growth of network traffic and connected devices has resulted in an exponential increase in the complexity of cyberattacks [6,12]. Network Intrusion Detection Systems (NIDS) are used to detect and alert on potential attacks and have become an essential component of network security. Traditional rule-based IDS solutions have limitations in detecting modern and sophisticated attacks due to the static nature of the rules. Whereas, machine learning (ML)-based IDS has emerged as a promising solution to overcome these drawbacks by learning and adapting to new threats without manual rule updates [25]. With the advancements in ML techniques and the increasing availability of large datasets, ML-based IDS has become an active area of research and development [19].

A traditional method to train ML-based models is centralized learning that involves collecting a vast amount of training data from different sources and centralizing it on a single server. This central server accounts for all the training processes, including model training and data preprocessing, based on the collected data. However, the centralized approach seems to be prone to privacy breaches and security concerns when sensitive information of raw data could be exposed during the data transmission and utilization. Also, the enormous volume of data makes a heavy burden of computational costs on the central server [2]. In contrast, Federated Learning (FL) is a novel approach to collaborative ML, enabling distributed training of ML models while keeping the data decentralized [18,24]. In other words, FL allows multiple parties to perform local training on their dataset and send only the model updates instead of raw data to the global server for aggregation, which preserves the data privacy and confidentiality. Besides, the resulting global model can take advantages of various data sources without the privacy leakage. Hence, FL can be considered as a promising training framework for building advanced ML-based NIDS in the context of cyberattacks [1,4,9,15].

However, FL is still vulnerable to poisoning attacks [17,20,30] originating from internal parties that can significantly degrade the performance of the learning algorithm. To be more specific, these attacks can be performed through different techniques, such as data poisoning and model poisoning. The former occurs at the data level, where malicious clients have their local models trained on intentionally manipulated data and then send them to the aggregation server. In the latter, adversaries manage to craft malicious updates based on the model parameter space before uploading them to the server. Compared to data poisoning, this model poisoning technique is easier to conduct and also often more detectable. The severity of poisoning attacks depends on the attacker's level of knowledge and the attack's sophistication.

As a result, various defense mechanisms and techniques, such as data sanitization, outlier detection, robust model aggregation, and so on, have recently been proposed in order to maintain the robustness of the FL-based model in the presence of poisoning attacks. Whereas the poisoning detection through data quality inspection [11, 29] might violate the privacy-preserving goal of FL, the approaches using outlier detection algorithm [3, 22] seem to be inefficient in non-IID setttings. Also, almost all previous defenses are conducted on the model parameters space, which increases an enormous computational cost on the FL training process.

In recent times, the definition of latent space representation (LSR) has received considerable critical attention from researchers in manufacturing new anti-poisoning mechanisms. To be more specific, the papers [10, 23] adopted the Penultimate Layer Representation (PLR) to reveal the important pattern in updated models, where benign weights follow a similar direction in contrast with those of anomalous models. Nonetheless, [23] needs an auxiliary server-side dataset to retrieve PLR vectors, which is hard to collect because it must adhere to the same distribution as local training datasets. Besides, the approach in [10] directly extracts PLR of each local updates without a common dataset, leading to the sense of uncertainty in PLR vectors when it comes to non-IID settings. In addition, both of the above works only focus on model poisoning techniques.

To overcome the aforementioned issues, in this work, we propose a latent space-based defensive framework against both data poisoning and model poisoning attacks, named FedLS, in the context of federated NIDS. Frankly speaking, FedLS makes use of Autoencoder (AE) to learn latent space representation (LSR) of each PLR's model, which reduces the instability of PLR as metioned in [10]. After that, the similarity level of each local LSR and the global one is computed via Center Kernel Alignment (CKA) algorithm before clustering them (CKA scores) as benign/attack groups. The benign cluster would then be transferred to the central server for the FedAvg aggregation.

Our main contributions are listed as follows:

- This work leverages the penultimate layer and Autoencoder-based latent space to design a new defensive mechanism, called FedLS, against poisoning attacks in federated learning. Our method does not require any knowledge or auxiliary datasets in advance as the previous schemes [23, 29].
- We provide an in-depth understanding of two types of poisoning attacks, including label flipping and untargeted-Med, via different experimental scenarios. The results on two ML-based NIDS datasets have proved that FedLS can work well when the number of adversaries accounts for 20% and 40% respectively.
- Our proposed method outperforms the FedCC [10] in differentiating benign non-IID models from malicious ones.

The structure of the study takes the form of five chapters, including this introduction. In Sect. 2, we outline related works about poisoning attacks as well as previous defense methods accordingly. The methodology chapter in Section 3 describes the threat model and a detailed design of our FedLS. Then, the experimental results and explanation are illustrated in Section 4. Finally, we conclude and propose some future works in Sect. 5.

Table 1. Defensive mechanisms proposed by the previous works

Work	Year	Method	Poisoning Attacks	Dataset	Data-level	Model-level
CONTRA [5]	2021	Cosine similarity, Clustering	Label Flipping, Backdoor	MNIST, CIFAR-10, Loan	–	x
LoMar [16]	2023	Outlier Detection	Label Flipping	Amazon, MNIST, KDDCup99, VGGFace2	–	x
FLDetector [28]	2022	Predict Model	Untargeted Attack, Scaling Attack, Distributed Backdoor Attack, A Little is Enough Attack	MNIST, CIFAR10, FEMNIST	–	x
Fed-IDS [22]	2021	Predict Model, Outlier Detection	Label Flipping Generative Adversarial Networks (GAN)-based Synthetic Data.	Kitsune	–	x
SecFedNIDS [29]	2022	Outlier Detection, Class Path Similarity	Label Flipping, Clean Label Attack	UNSW-NB15 CICIDS2018	x	x
Fltrust [7]	2020	Cosine similarity, Clustering	Label Flipping, Krum attack, Trim attack, Scaling attack, Adaptive attack	MNIST, Fashion-MNIST, CIFAR-10, Human activity recognition (HAR), CH-MNIST	–	x
DPA-FL [14]	2023	Outlier Detection	Label Flipping, Backdoor	CICIDS2017	–	x
FLARE [23]	2022	Latent Space Representations	+ Untargeted - Backdoor: Attack-Krum-Untargeted, Attack-TM-Untargeted + Targeted - Backdoor: Attack-Krum-Backdoor, Attack-Coomed-Backdoor	CIFAR-10, fMNIST, Kather	–	x
FedCC [10]	2022	Latent Space Representations	+ Untargeted: Attack-Krum, Attack-Med + Targeted - Backdoor	fMNIST, CIFAR-10, CIFAR-100	–	x
MCDFL [11]	2023	Latent Feature Space	Label Flipping	CIFAR-10, Fashion-MNIST	x	–
Fed-LSAE (Ours)	2023	Autoencoder-based Latent Space Representations	Label Flipping, GAN, Weight-scaling Model Poisoning, Untargeted-Med	CIC-ToN-IoT N-BaIoT	–	x

2 Related Work

Despite the privacy-enhancing benefits, FL remains susceptible to poisoning attacks which could undermine the integrity of FL training, thus devastating the accuracy of the learned model. Many recent studies [22, 26, 27] have demonstrated the effectiveness of poisoning attacks in significantly impacting the performance of FL. Specifically, Vy et al. [22] presented two types of poisoning techniques in the context of FL-based IDS, including label flipping and GAN-based attack. The experimental results on the Kitsune dataset witnessed a significant decrease from 99% to approximately 40% in Accuracy and F1-Score metrics of the global IDS performance when suffering from both aforementioned attack methods. The likewise results were demonstrated in the paper [26] in terms of label flipping and backdoor attacks.

As a consequence, a great deal of defense mechanisms [3, 22, 29] have been published in an effort to mitigate the risk of poisoning attacks against the FL framework. We summarize all of them in Table 1.

On the one hand, many previous studies focused on outlier detection to recognize poisonous updates from compromised agents. For instance, Zhao Zhang et al. [29] proposed a two-level method, namely SecFedNIDS, to defeat poisoning attacks in FL-based NIDS. Thereby, SecFedNIDS manages to sanitize local data through class path similarity extracted by the Layer-wise Relevance Propagation (LRP) algorithm and also detects malicious model updates as outliers by the Stochastic Outlier Selection (SOS) algorithm at the server-side. This approach, however, requires knowing the number of attackers in advance, which seems infeasible in real-world cases. In addition, other proposed methods [3,22] using the Local Outlier Factor (LOF) would encounter many obstacles in a non-IID environment.

On the other hand, plenty of defensive mechanisms based on latent space representation (LSR) have been released recently. Thereby, the FLARE framework [23] proposed by Ning Wang et al., is one of the very first works to adopt penultimate layer representation (PLR) to reveal malicious updates. More specifically, the Maximum Mean Discrepancy (MMD) is used to estimate the distance between pairwise PLR sequences, and then a trust score is defined for each local model via the softmax function. The following aggregation phase considers a trust score value as another scale factor for each local model in the FedAvg algorithm. Consequently, it can reduce the impact of poisoned models with low trust scores. However, FLARE requires a subset of raw data on the server-side to extract PLR from each updated model weight, which is tricky to collect and can disturb the data privacy standard of FL. In addition, Hyejun Jeong et al. [10] designed a latent space-based defensive scheme, namely FedCC, to maintain the robustness of FL-based image classifiers against model poisoning attacks. By comparing the similarity level of each local PLR vector and the global PLR via CKA scores, FedCC can cluster updated local models into two groups, where the smaller would be anomalous members because the number of adversaries does not exceed half of the total collaborative clients. Nevertheless, FedCC still has limitations in retrieving PLR without the same dataset, leading to the instability of PLR sequences. To resolve this issue, our FedLS implements Autoencoder (AE) as a component to acquire the most important features of PLR vectors.

3 Methodology

This section gives the overview of the threat model, which describes the knowledge as well as abilities of adversaries. A detailed design of our defensive approach is also illustrated, with the aim of building a robust federated NIDS.

3.1 Threat Model

To ensure the objectivity, we make the assumption that the quantity of adversarial parties m in the FL system is consistently less than half of the total number of clients, to be precise $m = 20\%$ and $m = 40\%$ respectively. The rest of the participating agents, including the server, are considered trustworthy parties throughout the global model training process. Meanwhile, the nodes controlled by attackers continuously execute poisoning attacks on the FL system by updating their malicious local models at all time.

Attacker's Knowledge and Goals. As a collaborative agent, the adversary has a thorough understanding of the global architecture which consists of the learning algorithm, training data, model hyperparameters such as batch size, learning rate, optimizer, etc. Therefore, attackers would conduct their poisoning techniques in a white-box manner. Their main goal is to severely damage the accuracy and performance of the federated NIDS by sending malicious model weights to the global aggregator. In other words, only untargeted poisoning techniques are focused on this work.

Attacker's Capabilities

- **Allowed.** The adversaries have full control over the local training procedure with their own dataset. Also, they can manipulate some of the hyperparameters of the model obtained from the global server to achieve the highest effectiveness of poisoning attacks.
- **Not allowed.** In the training setting, it is essential for each participant to follow the agreed-upon algorithms and does not interfere with other participants' training data or learning process. Moreover, the attackers could not compromise the aggregation phase of the central server.

Attacker's Strategies

- **Label Flipping (LF).** This is a type of data poisoning attack in which an attacker intentionally changes the true labels of a portion of the training data to mislead the ML model during the training process. As a result, the learned model classifies the testing samples into incorrect categories. Since our work relies on the binary classification tasks where considering label 0 as benign and 1 as attack, adversaries would flip all the benign samples into attack ones and vice versa.
- **Untargeted-Med.** This model poisoning attack is proposed in the paper [10] with the aim of breaking the Coordinate-wise Median [8] aggregation mechanism. Thereby, adversaries adjust the model parameters by using its maximum and minimum values to guide the coordinate-wise median values towards an opposite direction.

3.2   Robust Federated Learning for NIDS

In this paper, FL-based NIDS undergoes the training process as shown in Fig. 1. To be more precise, the following are the general steps to train a robust federated NIDS model:

- *Initialization*: A global NIDS model w is initialized at the central server, along with a total of n participating agents.
- *Model distribution*: In each round t, the server selects k out of n clients to join in the training step. A duplicate version of the current global model w_t is then sent to each participating client.
- *Local training*: The i-th client trains the model on their local dataset D_i for a fixed number of iterations. After the round t, the resulting model weights $w_{i,t}$ and the size of D_i are submitted to the central server for aggregation.
- *Model aggregation*: In this step, our FedLS module would be integrated to verify local models so that it can remove any anomalous updates from FL aggregation. The detailed mechanism of FedLS is described in Sect. 3.4. Based on the resulting list B of benign clients from FedLS, the central server then aggregates them into a new global NIDS model for round $t + 1$ by FedAvg algorithm as Eq. (1).

$$w_{t+1} \leftarrow \sum_{i=1}^{|B|} \frac{|D_i|}{|D|} w_{i,t} \tag{1}$$

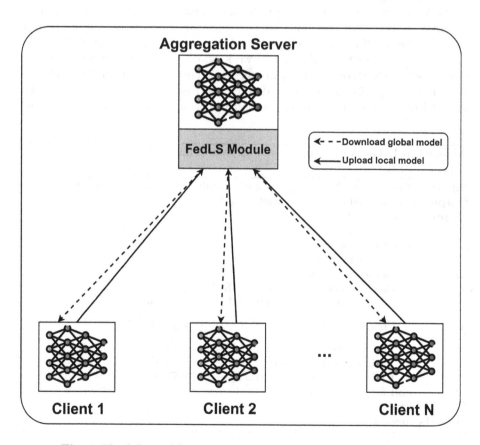

Fig. 1. The federated learning training mechanism for NIDS model.

where $|D_i|$ refers to the size of the dataset in the i-th benign client, and D is the total number of data samples from all benign agents in the list B, whose size is defined as $|B|$.

The aggregated version of the global model is then distributed to newly k clients in the next communication round. This training process is iterated until the NIDS model reaches the convergence point or peaks at a high level of detection rate as expected.

3.3 Autoencoder Pretraining Process

Before distributing a replicated copy of the global model to participating agents, the global model undergoes an internal collaborative training within a limited number of server-side organizations, utilizing their respective datasets over a single round. It is assumed that all such organizations are honest and harmless, which are under the control of the global server. Therefore, this is conducive for AE to learn the main characteristics of benign PLR vectors over E epochs, as described in Algorithm 1.

In Algorithm 1, θ_e and θ_d denote the parameters of the encoder and decoder networks, respectively. The function f_{θ_e} represents the encoder network, which maps the input PLR vector $\mathbf{x}$ to a latent space representation (LSR) $\mathbf{h}$. The function g_{θ_d} represents the decoder network, which maps the hidden representation $\mathbf{h}$ back to the reconstructed PLR vector $\hat{\mathbf{x}}$. The Mean Squared Error (MSE) loss function $\mathcal{L}(\mathbf{x}, \hat{\mathbf{x}})$ measures the difference across P parameters between the input PLR vector $\mathbf{x}$ and its reconstruction $\hat{\mathbf{x}}$. The algorithm updates the param-

---

Algorithm 1. The Autoencoder training process for learning important features of benign PLRs.

Input: N PLR vectors $\mathbf{X} = \{x_1, x_2, ..., x_N\}$, learning rate α, number of epochs E.
Output: Encoder and decoder parameters θ_e, θ_d.
1: **procedure** AE($\mathbf{X}$)
2:     Initialize θ_e and θ_d;
3:     **for** $e = 1$ **to** E **do**
4:         **for** $i = 1$ **to** N **do**
5:             Sample a PLR vector: $\mathbf{x}_i$;
6:             Compute encoder output as LSR: $\mathbf{h}_i = f_{\theta_e}(\mathbf{x}_i)$;
7:             Compute decoder output from LSR: $\hat{\mathbf{x}}_i = g_{\theta_d}(\mathbf{h}_i)$;
8:             Compute MSE loss: $\mathcal{L}(\mathbf{x}_i, \hat{\mathbf{x}}_i) \leftarrow \frac{1}{P} \sum_{p=1}^{P} (\mathbf{x}_{i,p} - \hat{\mathbf{x}}_{i,p})^2$;
9:             Compute gradients $\nabla \theta_e \mathcal{L}$ and $\nabla \theta_d \mathcal{L}$;
10:            Update encoder parameters: $\theta_e \leftarrow \theta_e - \alpha \nabla \theta_e \mathcal{L}$;
11:            Update decoder parameters: $\theta_d \leftarrow \theta_d - \alpha \nabla \theta_d \mathcal{L}$;
12:        **end for**
13:    **end for**
14: **end procedure**

---

eters of the encoder and decoder networks using stochastic gradient descent with learning rate α for a specified number of epochs E.

We choose AE because it is an unsupervised algorithm that works well even if there is a limited volume of training data. Also in this work, AE can learn the most important patterns of PLR vectors, especially when the internal server-side organizations suffer from the data heterogeneity. As a result, it is conducive to the exactness of the following RBF-CKA computation that minimizes the likelihood of misclassifying benign non-IID weight as abnormal ones.

3.4   Workflow of FedLS

The following Fig. 2 and Algorithm 2 describe the detailed design of our proposed method, FedLS, in excluding malicious updates from the FL system. The

---

Algorithm 2. The mechanism of FedLS for thwarting poisoning attacks.

Input: The global model weights W, a set of k local weights $L = \{w_1, w_2, ..., w_k\}$, a pretrained AE model.
Output: A list of benign models B
 1: **procedure** FEDLS(W, L)
 2:      ▷ **PLR Extractor for W and L**
 3:      **for** $i < k$ **do**
 4:          $L\_plr[i] \leftarrow L[i][penultimate\_layer]$;
 5:      **end for**
 6:      $W\_plr \leftarrow W[penultimate\_layer]$;
 7:      ▷ **Retrieve AE-based LSR of each PLR vector**
 8:      **for** $i < k$ **do**
 9:          $L\_lsr[i] \leftarrow AE.encoder(L\_plr[i])$;
10:      **end for**
11:      $W\_lsr \leftarrow AE.encoder(W\_plr)$
12:      ▷ **Compute CKA score between global LSR and each local LSR**
13:      **for** $i < k$ **do**
14:          $CKA\_scores[i] \leftarrow CKA(W\_lsr, L\_lsr[i])$;
15:      **end for**
16:      ▷ **Cluster CKA scores into 2 groups by KMeans algorithm**
17:      $kmeans = KMeans(n\_clusters = 2).fit(CKA\_scores)$
18:      $labels = kmeans.labels\_$
19:      ▷ **Select larger cluster as benign vectors B**
20:      **for** $i < 2$ **do**
21:          $cnt[i] \leftarrow sum(labels == i)$;
22:      **end for**
23:      **if** $cnt[0] < cnt[1]$ **then**
24:          $B \leftarrow list(labels == 1)$;
25:      **else**
26:          $B \leftarrow list(labels == 0)$;
27:      **end if**
28:      **return** B;
29: **end procedure**

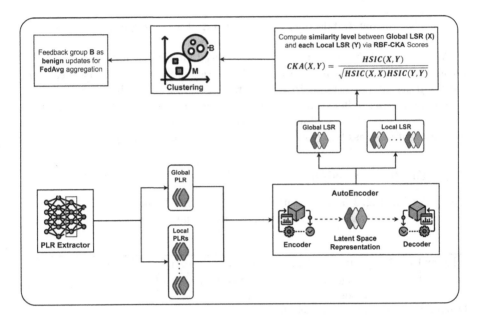

Fig. 2. FedLS module using Penultimate Layer Representation (PLR) and Autoencoder-based Latent Space Representation (LSR) in thwarting poisoning attacks.

desired output of FedLS is a list of benign weight vectors B, which gives feedback to the server for robust aggregation. Firstly, a total of k updated local model parameters from selected agents, along with the global weight, are directly fed into a PLR extractor (lines 3–6) to retrieve a set of k PLR vectors and a global PLR accordingly. In the next step (lines 8–11), the latent space representation (LSR) of each PLR is extracted from the bottleneck layer of the pretrained AE. As we said before, this helps to reduce the instability of PLR vectors resulting from local agents training their models on different data distributions. It can also minimize the computational costs, considering that the dimension of the PLR is still relatively large. Moreover, LSR vectors can reveal the most important features of the models, as well as the training data representation. As a consequence, poisoning attacks at both data and model level are likely to be detected. Later, we adopt the Radial Basis Function (RBF) CKA algorithm to compute the similarity level between the resulting global LSR and each local LSR (lines 13–15). In a normalized version, the CKA score is computed based on the Hilbert-Schmidt Independence Criterion (HSIC) as in Eq. (2).

$$CKA(X,Y) = \frac{HSIC(X,Y)}{\sqrt{HSIC(X,X)HSIC(Y,Y)}} \tag{2}$$

where X and Y are kernel matrices corresponding to the global LSR and each local LSR. Thereby, CKA values are in range of $[0, 1]$ where 0 means not similar at all and vice versa. The previous papers [13, 21] indicated that the CKA metric shows a high degree of consistency when it comes to evaluating the similarity between the representations of neural networks. Furthermore, the RBF-CKA algorithm can show that the similarity rate among benign models having both IID and non-IID data is higher than those of abnormal models and benign ones. Finally, the CKA values will be clustered into two groups by a clustering algorithm (lines 17–18). In this work, we choose K-means because CKA values are only one-dimensional data points. Based on two generated clusters, we consider the larger as a group of benign updates B while the other is malicious ones M (lines 20–27) since the ratio of attackers does not exceed 50%. The resulting list B is then sent to the global server for the FedAvg aggregation, as illustrated in Sect. 3.2.

4 Experiments

In this section, we describe experimental settings such as dataset, hardware configuration, training parameters, etc. which are used in our evaluation. Then, we give an overview of defensive FedLS against untargeted poisoning attacks via different experimental scenarios.

4.1 Dataset and Data Preprocessing

To build robust federated NIDS, we utilize two recent ML-based NIDS datasets in the context of Internet of Things (IoT), namely CIC-ToN-IoT and N-BaIoT. Both are network traffic collections containing cyberattacks against real-world IoT networks. The CIC-ToN-IoT dataset has over 5.3 milion records with 47% benign samples and 53% malicious ones relating to different categories such as Backdoor, DoS, DDoS, XSS, Ransomware, etc. Whereas, N-BaIoT focuses on several types of attacks on IoT devices, including Mirai, Gafgyt, and Bashlite botnet attacks. The proportion of normal traffic and attack traffic in N-BaIoT is 1:10. In this work, we only take a subset of both datasets to conduct our experiments, in which there are approximately 1.07 milion CIC-ToN-IoT samples and 800,000 network records in the N-BaIoT dataset.

Both datasets undergo the same preprocessing stage. To be more specific, we exclude non-functional features with unique values from the training dataset. Any samples with non-numeric (NaN) values or infinity (Inf) values are also removed. The resulting CIC-ToN-IoT samples then have 70 main features, while N-BaIoT consists of 115 features. Additionally, the Label column is used as the training target in both datasets, where label 0 is considered as normal traffic and label 1 as attack ones. Finally, the feature values on two datasets are normalized to the interval of [0,1] via a linear transformation called Min-Max normalization as in Eq. (3).

$$x' = \frac{x - \min(x)}{\max(x) - \min(x)} \tag{3}$$

where x' is the normalized version of feature value x. Besides, $\max(x)$ and $\min(x)$ are the maximum and the minimum values of this feature in the dataset, respectively.

In the FL training procedure, 75% of each dataset will be used as the training data, divided for local agents. The remaining data is separated into 2 parts, including 20% for the server-side testing data and 5% for the AE pretraining process.

4.2 Experimental Settings

Environmental Setup. In this work, we utilize Pytorch framework and scikit-learn library to build our FedLS on the hardware configuration of Intel® Xeon® E5-2660 v4 CPU (16 cores - 1.0 GHz), 100 GB RAM and the operating system of Ubuntu 16.04.

Performance Metrics. Since our work is based on binary classification tasks, we decided to assess our proposed method by the following four basic metrics:

- *Accuracy*: the proportion of correct predictions out of the total number of samples.
- *Precision*: the proportion of true positive predictions out of all positive predictions.
- *Recall*: the proportion of true positive predictions out of all actual positive samples.
- *F1-score*: the harmonic mean of *Precision* and *Recall*, which gives an overall measure of a model's accuracy in terms of both false positives and false negatives.

In this work, if there exists a dramatic increase in the above-mentioned metrics, we could confirm the high efficiency of our FedLS approach in detecting and removing poisoned models from the FL system.

Training Specification. The training process of FL involves 10 communication rounds ($R = 10$), with a total of $n = 10$ clients participating in the learning phase. In each round, solely k agents are selected based on a fraction factor C. In this study, C is set to 1.0, resulting in $k = C * n = 10$ agents in each round. During the training phase, all participants train their local models for 3 epochs using a batch size of 2048. The loss function used is the cross-entropy, and the stochastic gradient descent (SGD) optimizer with a learning rate of 0.001 and momentum of 0.9 is also employed.

Additionally, the ML-based NIDS is built based on a lightweight convolutional neural network structure named LeNet, whose architecture is depicted in Table 2. To construct the encoder and decoder for the AE, linear layers with bias are employed, as shown in Table 3. For each benign model's PLR, it is inputted into the AE model and trained for $E = 20$ epochs using the Adam optimizer with a learning rate of 0.001. The input and output dimensions of the AE are equivalent and represent the number of dimensions for each PLR vector, which is 128 in the below experiments.

Table 2. LeNet Architecture

Layer	In	Out	Kernel/Stride/Padding	Activation
conv2d_1	1	64	2×2 / 1 / 1	ReLU
batchnorm2d	64		–	–
maxpool2d			2×2 / 1 / 0	–
conv2d_2	64	128	2×2 / 1 / 0	ReLU
batchnorm2d	128		–	–
maxpool2d			2×2 / 1 / 0	–
flatten	–	–	–	–
fc_1	–	128	–	ReLU
fc_2	128	64	–	ReLU
fc_3	64	2	–	–

4.3   Evaluation Result

Baseline Performance of FL-Based NIDS. In this scenario, we aim to evaluate the benchmark performance of LeNet-based NIDS in the context of FL. Each local agent has the same data distribution as others, or IID data in other words. As depicted in Fig. 3, the detection rate of NIDS against cyberattacks on both datasets has achieved approximately 99% across four metrics after 4 communication rounds. The results have indicated the baseline effectiveness of federated NIDS in revealing the attack traffic in a network infrastructure.

Defensive Performance of Our FedLS Against Poisoning Attacks. The following experiments will focus on the robustness of FL-based NIDS in an IID environment with the support of our FedLS module when dealing with two aforementioned poisoning techniques. We assess our proposed FedLS in both $m = 20\%$ and $m = 40\%$, which means there are respectively 2 and 4 adversaries out of 10 local agents in this scenario. Additionally, A and dashed lines refer to metrics in case of poisoning attacks without FedLS, while D and solid lines describe the federated NIDS performance under attacks with our defense FedLS.

Table 3. Structure of Encoder and Decoder in AE architecture

Layer	Input	Output	Activation
Encoder			
Linear	128	512	ReLU
Linear	512	128	ReLU
Linear	128	64	ReLU
Linear	64	16	–
Decoder			
Linear	16	64	ReLU
Linear	64	128	ReLU
Linear	128	512	ReLU
Linear	512	128	Tanh

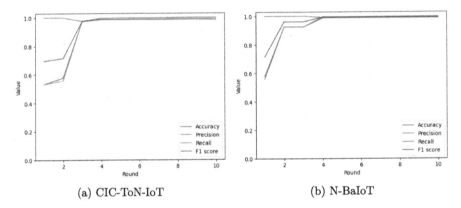

(a) CIC-ToN-IoT   (b) N-BaIoT

Fig. 3. The baseline performance of federated NIDS on *(a)* CIC-ToN-IoT and *(b)* N-BaIoT datasets.

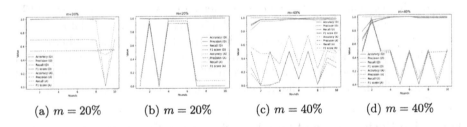

(a) $m = 20\%$ (b) $m = 20\%$ (c) $m = 40\%$ (d) $m = 40\%$

Fig. 4. The FedLS performance in thwarting Label Flipping attacks in case of $m = 20\%$ and $m = 40\%$ on *(a, c)* CIC-ToN-IoT and *(b, d)* N-BaIoT datasets respectively.

In terms of Label Flipping (LF) attacks, Fig. 4 has illustrated an upward trend in FL-based NIDS performance after integrating with our FedLS. More specifically, LF causes considerable fluctuations in the global detection rate around the level of 50% across all metrics. Some communication rounds even witness a value of 0% in Precision, Recall and F1-Score, for example round 8 in case of $m = 40\%$ on the CIC-ToN-IoT dataset. However, the presence of FedLS module has prompted the detection performance of federated NIDS to increase to approximately 99% and 98% in both cases of $m = 20\%$ and $m = 40\%$, respectively. The results imply the great capability of FedLS in learning data representation through LSR so that almost all flipped samples are detected and filtered out.

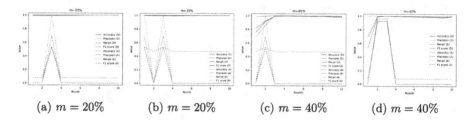

(a) $m = 20\%$ (b) $m = 20\%$ (c) $m = 40\%$ (d) $m = 40\%$

Fig. 5. The FedLS performance in thwarting untargeted-Med attacks in case of $m = 20\%$ and $m = 40\%$ on *(a, c)* CIC-ToN-IoT and *(b, d)* N-BaIoT datasets respectively.

A likewise trend is shown in Fig. 5 when it comes to untargted-Med attacks. Frankly speaking, the global NIDS model has been completely damaged by untargeted-Med techniques when 3 out of 4 metrics achieve 0% only after 4 training rounds in all cases. We can see that this kind of untargeted model poisoning attacks is not only easier to conduct but also more effective than data poisoning techniques because it directly manipulates each parameter in the updated model. In addition, the global NIDS reaches a peak of roughly 99% across all metrics after being defensed by FedLS. Thanks to AE-based LSR, our proposed defense mechanism has shown its perfect performance against untargeted model poisoning techniques.

Defensive Performance of Our FedLS Compared to other Methods in Non-IID Settings. This section aims to show the superior performance of our FedLS compared to a previous defensive mechanism, FedCC [10] in a heterogeneous data environment when it comes to the untargeted-Med poisoning technique. We select LeNet model and the untargeted-Med attack as in FedCC to maintain the objectivity of comparison. Additionally, the CIC-ToN-IoT dataset is used for this evaluation instead of N-BaIoT, since the ratio of normal and attack samples in the former is more balanced than in the latter. The data distribution among collaborative agents is illustrated in Fig. 6, where clients 2 and 3 refer to the adversaries in $m = 20\%$ case while clients 2–5 are considered as compromised agents given that $m = 40\%$. The reason we choose this data distribution is to clarify the ability of FedLS to differentiate clearly between benign clients having non-IID and the real attackers. All the following metrics are averaged over the federated training process to show the stability of the global model in both poisoning attacks and non-IID settings.

Table 4. Performance comparison between FedLS and FedCC when integrating into FL-based NIDS in a non-IID environment.

Scheme	m=20%				m=40%			
	Accuracy	Precision	Recall	F1-Score	Accuracy	Precision	Recall	F1-Score
FedCC	0,6949	0,6803	0,8205	0,7138	0,5937	0,5704	0,8550	0,6591
FedLS	**0,7032**	**0,7689**	**0,8705**	**0,7748**	**0,7148**	**0,7173**	**0,9933**	**0,8123**

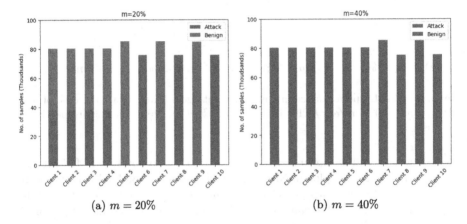

(a) $m = 20\%$ (b) $m = 40\%$

Fig. 6. The data distribution among clients on CIC-ToN-IoT datasets in case of non-IID.

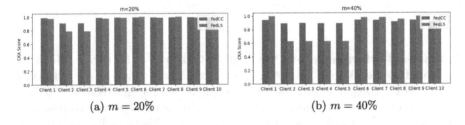

(a) $m = 20\%$ (b) $m = 40\%$

Fig. 7. Comparison of similarity level between the global LSR and each local LSR via CKA scores between FedLS and FedCC.

The statistics from Table 4 has indicated that our FedLS achieves a better performance than FedCC in exactly removing anomalous agents, instead of benign non-IID clients, from the FL training process. The federated NIDS model with FedLS witnesses a stable trend in its intrusion detection performance, with over 70% in Accuracy and 77% in F1-Score in both cases. In contrast, the NIDS model defended by FedCC still comes across obstacles when only obtaining a level of 59.3% in Accuracy and 57% in Precision. To explain those results, we can look at the differences in the CKA scores between the two schemes in Fig. 7. As we can see, the CKA scores of malicious updates seem to be distinct from others in FedLS while those of FedCC are still obscure. For example, in the case of FedLS with $m = 40\%$, local models from adversaries (Clients 2–5) achieves 0.6 CKA scores, which means they are only 60% similar to the global one. As a result, FedLS easily recognizes them as malicious entities and discarded them from the aggregation phase. Also, non-IID clients are considered as benign ones since they follow the same pattern and retain a high similarity level of over 90% compared to the global LSR. In contrast, there is only a slight difference by roughly 0.05 among CKA scores of clients in FedCC scheme throughout the FL process, leading to the misclassification of benign non-IID clients as attackers. Consequently, in some communication rounds, the aggregated model guarded by FedCC might suffer from the presence of some poisoned updates. The likewise result is presented in the event of $m = 20\%$.

5   Conclusion

This study proposes a robust aggregation mechanism for detecting and preventing poisoning attacks against a federated network intrusion detection system. More specifics, we leverage a combination of Autoencoder and latent space inspection to reveal malicious updates from local agents. The experimental results on CIC-ToN-IoT and N-BaIoT datasets have demonstrated the high-quality effectiveness of FedLS in defeating untargeted poisoning attacks such as Label Flipping and untargeted-Med. Also, our FedLS presents a better performance than FedCC [10] in non-IID case. We desire that our research provides a new aspect of developing robust FL-based systems in the real world. In the future, FedLS will be examined in the context of advanced poisoning strategies (such as backdoor, adversarial attacks, etc.) and homomorphic encryption-based models. Another anti-poisoning approach using knowledge distillation should also be considered.

Acknowledgement. This research is funded by the University of Information Technology - Vietnam National University Ho Chi Minh City under grant number D1-2023-16.

References

1. Agrawal, S., et al.: Federated learning for intrusion detection system: concepts, challenges and future directions. Comput. Commun. **195** (2022)
2. Aleesa, A., Zaidan, B., Zaidan, A., Sahar, N.M.: Review of intrusion detection systems based on deep learning techniques: coherent taxonomy, challenges, motivations, recommendations, substantial analysis and future directions. Neural Comput. Appl. **32**, 9827–9858 (2020)

3. Andreina, S., Marson, G.A., Möllering, H., Karame, G.: Baffle: backdoor detection via feedback-based federated learning. In: 2021 IEEE 41st International Conference on Distributed Computing Systems (ICDCS), pp. 852–863 (2021)

4. Arisdakessian, S., Wahab, O.A., Mourad, A., Otrok, H., Guizani, M.: A survey on IoT intrusion detection: federated learning, game theory, social psychology and explainable AI as future directions. IEEE Internet Things J. **10**, 4059–4092 (2022)

5. Awan, S., Luo, B., Li, F.: CONTRA: defending against poisoning attacks in federated learning. In: Bertino, E., Shulman, H., Waidner, M. (eds.) ESORICS 2021. LNCS, vol. 12972, pp. 455–475. Springer, Cham (2021). https://doi.org/10.1007/978-3-030-88418-5_22

6. Bout, E., Loscri, V., Gallais, A.: How machine learning changes the nature of cyberattacks on IoT networks: a survey. IEEE Commun. Surv. Tutor. **24**(1), 248–279 (2022)

7. Cao, X., Fang, M., Liu, J., Gong, N.Z.: Fltrust: byzantine-robust federated learning via trust bootstrapping. arXiv preprint arXiv:2012.13995 (2020)

8. Fang, M., Cao, X., Jia, J., Gong, N.Z.: Local model poisoning attacks to byzantine-robust federated learning (2021)

9. Ghimire, B., Rawat, D.B.: Recent advances on federated learning for cybersecurity and cybersecurity for federated learning for internet of things. IEEE Internet Things J. **9**(11), 8229–8249 (2022)

10. Jeong, H., Son, H., Lee, S., Hyun, J., Chung, T.M.: FedCC: robust federated learning against model poisoning attacks (2022)

11. Jiang, Y., Zhang, W., Chen, Y.: Data quality detection mechanism against label flipping attacks in federated learning. IEEE Trans. Inf. Forensics Secur. **18**, 1625–1637 (2023)

12. Kaloudi, N., Li, J.: The AI-based cyber threat landscape: a survey. ACM Comput. Surv. (CSUR) **53**(1), 1–34 (2020)

13. Kornblith, S., Norouzi, M., Lee, H., Hinton, G.: Similarity of neural network representations revisited (2019)

14. Lai, Y.C., et al.: Two-phase defense against poisoning attacks on federated learning-based intrusion detection. Comput. Secur. **129**, 103205 (2023)

15. Lavaur, L., Pahl, M.O., Busnel, Y., Autrel, F.: The evolution of federated learning-based intrusion detection and mitigation: a survey. IEEE Trans. Netw. Serv. Manag. **19**(3), 2309–2332 (2022)

16. Li, X., Qu, Z., Zhao, S., Tang, B., Lu, Z., Liu, Y.: Lomar: a local defense against poisoning attack on federated learning. IEEE Trans. Dependable Secure Comput. **20**, 1 (2021)

17. Liu, P., Xu, X., Wang, W.: Threats, attacks and defenses to federated learning: issues, taxonomy and perspectives. Cybersecurity **5**, 1–19 (2022)

18. Lo, S.K., Lu, Q., Wang, C., Paik, H.Y., Zhu, L.: A systematic literature review on federated machine learning: from a software engineering perspective. ACM Comput. Surv. (CSUR) **54**(5), 1–39 (2021)

19. Mishra, P., Varadharajan, V., Tupakula, U., Pilli, E.S.: A detailed investigation and analysis of using machine learning techniques for intrusion detection. IEEE Commun. Surv. Tutor. **21**(1), 686–728 (2019)

20. Mothukuri, V., Parizi, R.M., Pouriyeh, S., Huang, Y., Dehghantanha, A., Srivastava, G.: A survey on security and privacy of federated learning. Futur. Gener. Comput. Syst. **115**, 619–640 (2021)

21. Son, H.M., Kim, M.H., Chung, T.M.: Compare where it matters: using layer-wise regularization to improve federated learning on heterogeneous data (2021)

22. Vy, N.C., Quyen, N.H., Duy, P.T., Pham, V.-H.: Federated learning-based intrusion detection in the context of IIoT networks: poisoning attack and defense. In: Yang, M., Chen, C., Liu, Y. (eds.) NSS 2021. LNCS, vol. 13041, pp. 131–147. Springer, Cham (2021). https://doi.org/10.1007/978-3-030-92708-0_8
23. Wang, N., Xiao, Y., Chen, Y., Hu, Y., Lou, W., Hou, Y.T.: Flare: defending federated learning against model poisoning attacks via latent space representations. In: ACM ASIACCS 2022, pp. 946–958 (2022)
24. Zhang, C., Xie, Y., Bai, H., Yu, B., Li, W., Gao, Y.: A survey on federated learning. Knowl.-Based Syst. **216**, 106775 (2021)
25. Zhang, C., Jia, D., Wang, L., Wang, W., Liu, F., Yang, A.: Comparative research on network intrusion detection methods based on machine learning. Comput. Secur. **121**, 102861 (2022)
26. Zhang, J., Chen, B., Cheng, X., Binh, H.T.T., Yu, S.: PoisonGAN: generative poisoning attacks against federated learning in edge computing systems. IEEE Internet Things J. **8**(5), 3310–3322 (2021)
27. Zhang, J., Chen, J., Wu, D., Chen, B., Yu, S.: Poisoning attack in federated learning using generative adversarial nets. In: 2019 18th IEEE International Conference On Trust, Security And Privacy In Computing And Communications/13th IEEE International Conference On Big Data Science And Engineering (TrustCom/BigDataSE), pp. 374–380 (2019)
28. Zhang, Z., Cao, X., Jia, J., Gong, N.Z.: Fldetector: defending federated learning against model poisoning attacks via detecting malicious clients. Assoc. Comput. Mach. 2545–2555 (2022)
29. Zhang, Z., Zhang, Y., Guo, D., Yao, L., Li, Z.: Secfednids: robust defense for poisoning attack against federated learning-based network intrusion detection system. Futur. Gener. Comput. Syst. **134**, 154–169 (2022)
30. Zhou, X., Xu, M., Wu, Y., Zheng, N.: Deep model poisoning attack on federated learning. Futur. Internet **13**(3), 73 (2021)

Mitigating Sybil Attacks in Federated Learning

Ahmed E. Samy[✉] and Šarūnas Girdzijauskas

Software and Computer Systems, KTH, Royal Institute of Technology, Kistagången 16, 16440
Stockholm, Sweden
{aesy,sarunasg}@kth.se

Abstract. Federated learning (FL) is a distributed learning paradigm that facilities a basic data-privacy level, as the clients do not have to share their raw data.
Since the clients send local model updates, it increases the attack surface of FL—
with possible attackers sharing poisoning updates with the aggregation server. In
this work, we focus on the Sybil attacks, a type of poisoning attack where attackers can have multiple identities to overpower the honest clients in the system. In
particular, we define a cosine-similarity-based measurement to track the clients'
behavior. To mitigate the Sybil attacks, we propose *FedSybil*, a behavior-based
defense with a reputation mechanism for FL under independent and identically
distributed (IID) and non-IID data settings. In extensive experiments, we demonstrate the effectiveness of our approach with an improved *model accuracy* over
the state-of-the-art approaches reaching over 50% improvement under attacks.

Keywords: Federated learning · neural networks · poisoning attacks · security

1 Introduction

Large amounts of training data are often required and shared with a central server to
train powerful machine learning (ML) models, particularly deep learning models. In
doing so, the training process at the server can be computationally expensive, compromising the user's data privacy. Modern distributed learning paradigms, i.e., Federated
Learning (FL) [1–3], promise essential solutions to the latter, especially over resource-
constrained settings such as learning over Internet-of-Things (IoT) [4]: data is held with
the clients, and only the local model updates are shared with the server during training.
The server in FL aggregates the uploaded model updates into a single global update in
an iterative training process.

Despite providing basic privacy over the user data, from a security perspective, the
local clients have more control over the learning process; they may contribute maliciously by sharing poisoning model updates. Thus, federated learning suffers from an
increased attack surface. One popular attack, i.e., Sybil attack [5], has been studied
recently in FL [6,7]. In Sybil attacks, the malicious client aims to subvert the distributed
system by creating multiple aliases with *similar intent* to outweigh the honest clients. In
the SoTA for defending against Sybil attacks [8,9], the authors have proved that Sybil
poisoning attacks may cause a drastic reduction in model accuracy in FL.

Furthermore, the local data of the clients are likely to exhibit skewed distributions
over the clients in real-life applications [10,11]. Nevertheless, most existing defenses

© The Author(s), under exclusive license to Springer Nature Singapore Pte Ltd. 2023
W. Meng et al. (Eds.): ISPEC 2023, LNCS 14341, pp. 36–51, 2023.
https://doi.org/10.1007/978-981-99-7032-2_3

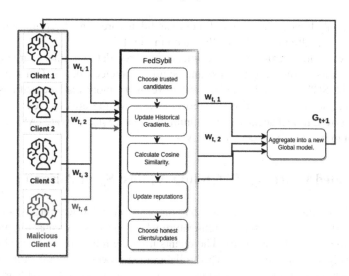

Fig. 1. An overview of FL and FedSybil located at the aggregation server. FedSybil consists of three components: accumulating updates, computing cosine similarities over updates, and getting the least similar (honest) clients. Through FedSybil, the malicious (red) clients are detected, and their updates are discarded. (Color figure online)

against poisoning attacks, such as Krum [12], are ineffective under non-independent and identically distributed (non-IID) data scenarios. During experiments, we observed that for the clients with the same targeted malicious objective, their model updates are the most similar in IID and non-IID settings [8]. Subsequently, [8,9] have proposed a similarity-based weighted aggregation. The weights are defined based on the overall similarity of each client with the others. Our study on these methods shows that these approaches may penalize honest clients, reducing their learning rates by mistake. *With many clients regarded as malicious, model learning gets hindered, causing a drastic reduction in the model accuracy, as shown in our experiments.*

Motivated by those mentioned above, we first define a cosine-similarity-based measurement to track the client's behavior in the system. Our core insight is that clients with the same adversarial objective will likely exhibit similar model updates. Concretely, a shared adversarial objective is to classify the same feature-space pattern into the same targeted class, e.g., misclassifying malicious software, not to detect it as malware. Thus, the server tracks the clients' behaviors by computing how similar the accumulated model updates of the clients in the system are.

Second, to mitigate Sybil attacks, we propose *FedSybil*, a federated learning mechanism resilient against poisoning attacks under both IID and non-IID settings. *FedSybil* is a behavior-based defense where the proposed cosine-similarity-based measurement defines behavior. Furthermore, we introduce a reputation mechanism and a clustering-based detection based on the defined behaviors. At every iteration, the reputation mechanism helps in probabilistically selecting potentially trusted clients, while the clustering ensures that only honest clients out of those candidates are considered for aggregation. An overview of FedSybil and FL is illustrated in Fig. 1

Third, we conduct extensive experiments on three datasets under targeted label-flipping, backdoor poisoning attacks, and Sybil untargeted attacks. Our experiments show that the SOTA methods can be ineffective under more realistic settings, with a drastic model accuracy reduction. Moreover, we prove the effectiveness of *FedSybil* with an improved model accuracy and minimum Attack Success Rate (ASR), reaching over 50% improvement in model accuracy.

2   Federated Learning: Defending Against Sybil Poisoning Attacks

Federated Learning (FL) is a standard paradigm for machine learning on distributed datasets [1–3]. It is a client-server architecture where the server creates the model and shares the weights with the clients. The clients train the model on their local data and share the weights with the server. This collaborative process continues till the model training reaches a (sub)optimal convergence state. In doing so, federated learning provides the collaborators a basic level of privacy as the data never leaves the clients' side.

Concretely, in each round $t \in [1, T]$, a fraction C of the clients are chosen to update the weights of the global model w_t locally as $w_{t+1}^k = w_t - \mu \Delta_{t+1}^k$ where μ is a fixed learning rate, Δ_{t+1}^k and w_{t+1}^k are the model update and weights produced by client k at round $t + 1$. Consequently, the aggregation server averages the weights into a new global model w_{t+1} at iteration $t + 1$ as follows:

$$w_{t+1} = w_t + \sum_{k=1}^{K} \frac{n_k}{n} \Delta_{t+1}^k, \tag{1}$$

$$\Delta_{t+1}^k = w_t - w_{t+1}^k \tag{2}$$

where K is the number of selected clients, n is the total number of data points, n_k is the number of data points of the kth client. Δ_{t+1}^k and w_{t+1}^k are the model update and weights produced by client k at round $t + 1$. The latter method is called FedAVG.

There are two main settings of federated learning: FedSGD and FedAVG [1]. In FedSGD, clients share each local update with the server that should do the aggregation. For FedAVG, clients may do many local updates first before sharing the updates with the server. FedAVG, by design, is more communication-efficient.

Algorithm 1. The FedSybil algorithm

Input: Initial model w_0; H are the historical updates, with starting values as the initial random weights (of the clients' local models); β is mini-batch size; E is the number of local epochs; S_{pop} is the client population; C is the fraction of the clients for local training; initial reputation scores r are set to 1.

1: **procedure** SERVER(w_0, β, E, C)
2:     **for** each round $t = 1, 2, \ldots$ **do**
3:         $S_t \leftarrow$ select top $\lceil C|S_{pop}| \rceil$ clients for local training with probability $p_i \propto r_i$.
4:         **for** each client $i \in S_t$ **in parallel do**
5:             $\delta^i_{t+1} \leftarrow$ CLIENTUPDATE(j, w_t)
6:             $H_i \leftarrow \frac{2H_i + \delta^i_{t+1,\text{output}}}{2}$ ▷ Aggregated (historical) updates of the output layer
7:         **end for**
8:         **for** each client $i \in S_t$ **do**
9:             **for** each client $j \in S_t$ **do**
10:                 **if** $i \neq j$ **then**
11:                     $cs_{ij} \leftarrow$ COSINESIMILARITY(H_i, H_j)
12:                 **end if**
13:             **end for**
14:             $\iota_i \leftarrow \max_j(cs_i)$ ▷ Compute the alignment score
15:             **if** $\iota_i > t$ **then**
16:                 $r_i \leftarrow r_i - \Delta$ ▷ Δ is set to 0.1
17:             **else**
18:                 $r_i \leftarrow r_i + \Delta$
19:             **end if**
20:         **end for**
21:         $S_{honest}, S_{malicious} \leftarrow$ CLUSTER($\iota, S_{pop}, n\_cluster = 2$)   ▷ Cluster clients based on the alignment score ι
22:         $\hat{S}_t \leftarrow$ select K clients from $S_t \cap S_{honest}$.
23:         $w_{t+1} \leftarrow$ AGGREGATE(w_t, δ^i_{t+1}), $\forall i \in \hat{S}_t$
24:     **end for**
25: **end procedure**

Algorithm 2. CosineSimilarity(H_i, H_j)

Input: Historical update vectors H_i and H_j for the clients i and j, respectively.

1: **procedure** COSINESIMILARITY(H_i, H_j)
2:     **for** each label $l = 0, 1, \ldots, L$ **do**
3:         $cs^l_{ij} \leftarrow \frac{H^l_i \cdot H^l_j}{\|H^l_i\| \|H^l_j\|}$
4:     **end for**
5:     $L_{\text{top}} \leftarrow$ select ℓ labels with top cosine similarities.
6:     $cs_{ij} \leftarrow \sum_{l \in L_{top}} cs^l_{ij}$
7: **end procedure**

2.1   FedSybil Design

Our central insight is that in Sybil-based attacks, the malicious clients exhibit more similar learning behaviors than the honest clients. These similarities result from the fact that the malicious clients in these attacks tend to drive model updates towards one or similar (Sybil) malicious objectives that are typically different from the objective of the honest client. In doing so, the similarities between a pair of two malicious Sybil attackers are often observed in our experiments to be higher than with a pair of honest clients or between an honest and malicious client. The variance between two honest clients is due to the stochastic nature of the gradient-based learning method, namely SGD, that the clients rely on for optimization. This phenomenon can be observed in both IID and non-IID settings. Based on these findings, we next present *FedSybil*.

In Algorithm 1, we illustrate *FedSybil* where the training between the clients and the server unfolds synchronously. The learning process leverages the following main components:

Similarity Scores. In line 9, Algorithm 1, The angles between every two clients have been defined as the cosine similarity cs_{ij} between their updates δ_{output}. As the cosine similarity ranges from -1 to 1, it defines how much close the client pairs are. We compute the cosine similarity based on the gradients of the output layer, as they are critical to any targeted attacks. In detail, as shown in Algorithm 2, the cosine similarity between two clients is computed as the *sum* of the *top* cosine similarities over the labels (between the gradient vectors of the corresponding labels in the output layer). Intuitively, the labels with the maximum cosine similarities are the labels that are impacted by the attack. For scalability, we calculate the cosine similarities for a fraction C of the clients at each iteration (Algorithm 1, line 3).

For deeper neural networks, we do not consider the weights of the non-output layers when computing the cosine similarities, as they do not map directly to the output probabilities. However, more work on feature importance in neural networks may be necessary to capture Sybil attacks based on these weights [13, 14]; we consider this as part of our future work.

Alignment Score is the overall similarity score per client ι_i calculated as the maximum of his similarity scores with the other clients. An alignment score defines the overall behavior of each client in the system. A high alignment score (approaching a value of 1) means that the client is very similar to others, hence bad behavior. Based on our experiments, we recommend two aggregation methods: *max*, or the *average* over top similarity scores per client to avoid missing a malicious client only because they happen to have low similarity scores with honest clients.

Historical Model Updates. Model updates may diverge at a given iteration due to the variance of the Stochastic Gradient Decent (SGD) - even for clients with the same malicious objective. To have a more accurate estimate of the client's intent, we normalize the divergence (line 6, Algorithm 1) by calculating the similarity scores over the updates produced by the client in the past iterations. Precisely, we choose the mean operation over the past updates to ensure that the aggregated updates follow the same distribution regardless of how often the clients are selected.

Reputation and Detection Mechanism. In Algorithm 1, Lines 11–14, we introduce a reputation mechanism where the trust scores of the clients are maintained and initialized to 1's. The trust score is updated accordingly by comparing the client's alignment score with a given threshold at each iteration. Thus, based on the clients' behaviors, reputations are maintained during training and used to select potential candidates for local training.

Upon aggregation, to differentiate between the honest and malicious clients from the candidate clients in an unsupervised manner, we employ Kmeans [15]. Specifically, we divide all clients based on their alignment scores into honest and malicious groups. The clustering is not applied directly to the model updates, so it is effective under non-IID data distribution. We choose the cluster with the smaller center to identify the honest clients. As in Lines 22 and 21 in Algorithm 1, we choose K clients from the honest clients at each round for aggregation. Therefore, K will always have the total number of honest clients in the system as an upper bound.

Aggregation Rule. The aggregation rule can be any of the federated learning aggregation methods such as FedAVG, FedSGD, FedProx [16]. In this work, we use the FedAVG aggregation rule in Eq. 1. As *FedSybil* is agnostic to the aggregation rule. Secure aggregations such as multi-Krum [12] can be also used. We demonstrate that multi-Krum and *FedSybil* can be combined with no conflict. More details are later discussed in the evaluation section.

3 Security Analysis

3.1 Threat Model

Attacker Capability. Data are assumed to be private for each client. The malicious clients cannot access the local data of the other clients. We also assume that the server and the honest clients cannot be compromised, similar to [8]. On the other hand, malicious clients can observe the global model. They can affect the state of other models by sharing malicious model updates. The attackers also may access the system with multiple aliases to organize Sybil attacks. Finally, the privacy of the model updates is not accounted for in this work.

Attacker Objective. Attackers aim to reduce the quality of the models being learned by sharing poisoning model updates. To do so, they organize untargeted or targeting poisoning attacks. A targeted attack can be label-flipping [17] where the attackers change the label of a given class. Alternatively, they can inject a specific pattern in the data (backdoor attacks [18]). In the evaluation, we demonstrate how federated learning can be particularly vulnerable in the case of Sybil attacks.

Data Distribution. The data can be independent and identically distributed (IID) or non-IID. To imitate the real-world scenarios, we choose the Dirichlet distribution [18] to control how the class labels are distributed over the clients. We include the data distribution in the threat model, as most of the existing defenses in the literature, such as multi-Krum [12], do not perform well under non-IID settings [9].

Table 1. Evaluation datasets.

Dataset	Classes	Training samples	Test samples	Features	Model	Learning rate	Reporting fraction	Clients
MNIST	10	$6 \cdot 10^4$	10^4	784	Softmax	0.01	20%	100
Fashion-MNIST	10	$6 \cdot 10^4$	10^4	120	CNN	0.0001	20%	100
Cifar	10	$5 \cdot 10^4$	10^4	512	CNN	0.01	30%	100

3.2 Attacks and Mitigations

Label Flipping. It is a type of Sybil based targeted poisoning attack where attackers cooperate to encourage a specific source label to be classified as a target label of their choice. As our proposed methods run on the assumption that clients are dissimilar enough, having similar objectives among this type of Sybil attackers lead to high similarity scores, thereby being distinguishable by our algorithms. The same assumption holds regardless of IID or non-IID data. If the attackers try to produce dissimilar updates to avoid being detected, their attacks lose effectiveness. We demonstrate the effectiveness of our algorithms in keeping high accuracy and reducing the attack rates in the evaluation.

Backdoor Attacks. It is another type of targeted poisoning attack. In this attack, the attackers encourage the training examples with a specific embedded pattern to be classified into a target label of their choice. Similarly, Sybil clients must work together to over-weigh the honest clients in the system. In doing so, they essentially exhibit similar behaviors. Compared to honest clients' alignment scores, these attackers' high alignment scores capture such similarities. Accordingly, the server does not consider these updates in the aggregation. We prove these findings in our experiments.

Untargeted Attacks. attackers in this attack do not target a particular class. They aim to push the model into high-class error rates on all labels. Attackers can submit random weights or flip the actual class labels to execute this attack. This attack type can be coordinated (Sybils) or individual attacks. In the case of the Sybil attack, attackers instead work together to send arbitrary model updates. Because the attackers coordinate similar Sybil attacks in this scenario, they are distinguishable by our defenses. On the other hand, for individual attacks, *FedSybil* becomes less effective, as it relies on the similarity among the attackers. To mitigate a such attack, *FedSybil* can be augmented with secure aggregation methods such as multi-Krum [12]. In the next section, we address the possibility of combining *FedSybil* with multi-Krum.

4 Evaluation and Discussion

4.1 Experiment Setup

Datasets. We evaluate *FedSybil* on three real-life classification datasets: MNIST [19], Fashion-MNIST, [20] and Cifar [21]. Every dataset has been chosen in our experiments for specific reasons. First, we choose MNIST as a standard digit classification task widely used for evaluation in federated learning [1]. Cifar is chosen as a color image classification. Cifar and Fashion-MNIST are chosen for more complex deep learning models and difficult datasets. We believe the choice of datasets reflects different learning experiences for testing our methods and baselines. The details of the datasets are listed in Table 1. The distribution of the class labels over clients is decided by a Dirichlet distribution. The Dirichlet hyperparameter varies between 0.05 and 100, where 0.05 and 100 represent non-IID and IID settings, respectively.

Training Details. For all datasets, we train for 100 rounds and five local epochs with a local batch size of 50, except for Cifar, where it is 32. The SGD is the default optimizer with a momentum of 0.9 on MNIST. At each round, 20–30% of the clients are chosen for aggregation. To calculate the cosine similarities, we consider all clients and set the hyperparameter ℓ to 30% of the labels for MNIST and Cifar, while all labels are considered for Fashion-MNIST.

Baselines and Metrics. We choose FedAVG(FL), FoolsGold (FG) [8], and Contra [9] as baselines for *FedSybil*. We compare the four algorithms with different adversary rates in {33%, 50%, 90%} at different data distributions ϕ in {0.05, 100} on label flipping and backdoor pattern attacks, as well as Sybil untargeted attacks. We use the model accuracy and Attack Success Rate (ASR) for metrics. Attack success rates are calculated as the ratio between the number of (correct) source labels classified into (adversary) target labels and the total number of testing examples. An attacker succeeds when he/she manages to flip a right label to a target wrong label correctly.

4.2   FedSybil Evaluation

Tables 2 to 5 show the results of the proposed *FedSybil* with comparison to Contra, FoolsGold and the vanilla FedAVG as baselines under Backdoor (Table 2), Sybil untargeted (Table 3) and label flipping attacks (Table 4). To simulate the backdoor attack, we inject a white pixel in the bottom right part of the images, then assign them labels of 1. For the untargeted attack, all labels are flipped to 0. We flip labels 1 to 7 on all datasets for label-flipping attacks.

Viewing the results, we observe that *FedSybil* outperforms on all attacks under mostly all the different settings. Contrarily, FoolsGold performs less, sometimes even less than federated learning, with no defense. Despite being state-of-the-art, FoolsGold was evaluated in unrealistic settings: with only ten clients and unrealistic synthesized data distribution of "sort-and-partition" [1] with an extreme case of non-identicalness. Under our settings, FoolsGold shows a high false positive rate, penalizing honest clients and decreasing their learning rates. In doing so, the aggregated global model does not get enough contributions from the clients, thereby the lower model accuracy. We guess that the reduced learning rates slow down the training process. As a result, FoolsGold may need a higher number of iterations to reach the convergence (as reported by the authors); For Contra, having a reputation mechanism increases the chances of choosing trusted clients with higher learning rates; therefore, the better results. However, Contra is essentially similar to FoolsGold; both have adaptive learning rates when aggregating. Viewing Table 4, we see lower model accuracy due to falsely penalizing honest clients. Based on these findings, we conclude that the cosine similarities may not provide enough guarantee, so the learning rates can be manipulated accordingly.

On the other hand, *FedSybil* defense relies on reputation-based selection and cluster-based detection mechanisms. Clustering the clients is primary in filtering out the malicious clients from the selected candidates upon aggregation. In contrast, high reputations ensure that the selected clients are potentially honest. Without the reputation mechanism, a random pool with many malicious clients may be initially selected. Accordingly, a few honest clients can only pass through the detection, slowing down the training process. At the same time, relying on reputations alone does not provide enough guarantees against malicious clients. Furthermore, as shown in the results tables, *FedSybil* consistently performs better regardless of the data distribution and attack percentage. As our defense becomes more confident about the Sybil clients with higher attack percentages, the performance of the *FedSybil* becomes better.

Finally, the results highlight the differences between the attack types. From Tables 2 and 3, the targeted backdoor and untargeted attacks have the most impact on `FedAVG` and FoolsGold. That is because all classes are targeted and flipped in both attacks. However, being such impactful, they are more distinguishable by *FedSybil*.

On the other hand, viewing Table 4, the label flipping attack has the most negligible impact having one specific label flipped to a target adversarial label. As it is a more sub-

Table 2. Backdoor attacks - Accuracy results.

% Attack	Non-IID	MNIST				Fashion-MNIST				Cifar			
		FL	FG	Contra	FedSybil	FL	FG	Contra	FedSybil	FL	FG	Contra	FedSybil
50%	0.05	69.0	70.6	59.8	**84.1**	70.7	62.1	73.4	**75.6**	10.0	16.0	**36.8**	31.2
	100	85.4	89.3	89.6	**90.4**	78.6	80.3	80.3	**83.0**	13.2	35.6	33.7	**39.0**
70%	0.05	34.7	52.9	57.1	**81.0**	61.2	40.0	73.9	**77.3**	10.0	19.8	**36.0**	36.4
	100	74.1	88.2	88.9	**90.3**	76.1	77.7	72.0	**82.8**	10.0	16.6	36.7	**37.4**

Table 3. Sybil Untargeted attacks - Accuracy results on Fashion-MNIST.

% Attack	Non/IID	FL %	FG %	Contra %	FedSybil
50%	0.05	23.0	32.4	70.4	**74.3**
	100	56.8	66.7	79.6	**83.0**
70%	0.05	10.1	30.6	58.7	**76.9**
	100	10.0	62.0	76.7	**82.8**

Table 4. Label-flipping attacks - Accuracy results%.

% Attack	Non-IID	MNIST				Fashion-MNIST				Cifar			
		FL	FG	Contra	FedSybil	FL	FG	Contra	FedSybil	FL	FG	Contra	FedSybil
50%	0.05	83.1	56.6	80.5	**84.5**	58.2	31.5	34.3	**63.2**	28.4	20.3	**32.4**	32.1
	100	81.1	84.1	79.5	**90.3**	67.9	72.3	64.0	**74.1**	33.6	10.2	34.1	**37.0**
70%	0.05	76.9	67.0	83.0	**87.4**	58.2	31.7	34.4	**63.2**	28.4	20.3	**31.8**	31.6
	100	79.0	78.2	78.1	**90.3**	65.0	63.4	60.4	**74.3**	32.4	10.2	34.0	**36.5**

Table 5. Label-flipping attacks - comparison with the reported accuracy results from [9] on MNIST

% Attack	Non/IID	FG %	Contra %	FedSybil
33%	0.05	69.3	72.8	**87.0**
	100	78.3	83.9	**91.0**
50%	0.05	66.6	70.4	**84.9**
	100	76.1	81.6	**91.1**

tle attack, it is more challenging for our defenses to detect them compared to the other attacks. For more insights, Table 5 reports the results of *FedSybil* on MNIST compared to Contra under the same original settings provided by [9] with label-flipping attacks.

4.3 FedSybil Under Non-IID Settings

The core assumption of the *FedSybil* is that the clients' local models are sufficiently dissimilar. This dissimilarity is due to the stochastic gradient descent's stochastic nature and the local data's dissimilarity. Thus, the attackers participating in the same Sybil attacks should exhibit more similarity than the honest clients as they learn the same adversarial objective. This insight has been observed under both non-IID and IID settings.

To verify our insight, Fig. 2 shows the normalized pairwise cosine similarities for ten clients with IID (on the left) and non-IID (on the right) settings. The cosine similarity matrix has been calculated on MNIST data under a backdoor poisoning attack. The first four clients are Sybil clients, while the bottom six are chosen to be honest.

For the training data, we vary the distribution using the Dirichlet distribution [18]. Particularly, for N classes, we draw the training examples for each client independently with class distribution parameterized by the Nth vector q, drawn as $q \sim Dir(\phi p)$ where p is the class prior distribution and ϕ is a concentration parameter. When $\phi \to 0$, each client has data with only one class, while the data is fully IID as $\phi \to \infty$.

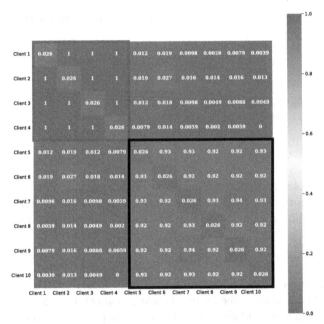

(a) IID where the smallest values are between client 10 (honest) and client 4 (malicious). The diagonal is set to ϵ.

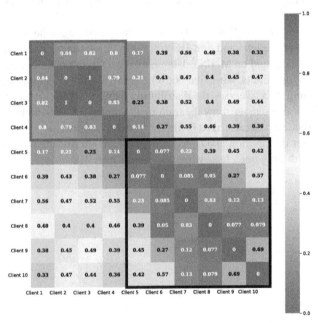

(b) Non-IID where the smallest values are the diagonal between the client and itself.

Fig. 2. Heatmap charts of the normalized cosine similarities between the clients. The top 4 clients are malicious clients and the bottom 6 are **honest** clients. The malicious clients with the same objective are the most similar to each other compared to the honest clients. (Color figure online)

In Fig. 2(a), the data is IID with $\phi = 100$, and non-IID in Fig. 2(b), with $\phi = 0.05$. Viewing the figures, in the case of IID, all clients show high similarity (small angle) due to similar distributions. The Sybil clients have exact similarities and highly similar updates. We can also observe that the angle between one honest client and another malicious client is maximum.

On the other hand, in the case of non-IID, the angle between two honest clients in the system is the maximum. In both cases, the Sybil clients are distinguishable by their highest similarity, demonstrating our earlier insight about the Sybil attackers. Be noted that two honest clients may still have high similarity such as clients 7 and 8. However, they have smaller overall alignment scores compared to the malicious ones.

Finally, if the attackers know about *FedSybil*, they may change the data distribution or craft other updates to achieve more dissimilarity. However, for their Sybil attacks to remain effective, they must approach the same adversarial objective, keeping their updates similar.

4.4 Single Client Attacks

There are attacks such as the single-shot replacement attack [18] where attackers do not have to do Sybils. As these attacks are conducted only by a single attacker, similarity-based defenses (e.g., *FedSybil*) are not enough to subvert them. To simulate this attack, we implement a 70% label flipping attack with another single untargeted attack that flips all labels to 0 on Fashion-MNIST. Viewing Table 6, we can see that each defense independently is not effective (in terms of ASR) to mitigate both attacks happening concurrently; Multi-Krum fails to mitigate the label-flipping attack, while *FedSybil* fails to mitigate the single attack. Although *FedSybil* can mitigate the 70% label-flipping attack, having the single untargeted attack causes the clustering-based detection in *FedSybil* to assign the single attacker to a separate cluster while keeping all other honest and malicious clients in the other group, thus subverting our defense. Be noted that *FedSybil* here was used without the reputation mechanism. To mitigate both attacks, we unit *FedSybil* with multi-Krum with $f = 1$; together, both can defend against the 70% attack, proving that both defenses can augment each other to provide a better defense.

Table 6. Single untargeted attack that flips all labels to zero with 70% 1 to 7 label-flipping Attack on Fashion-MNIST

	Multi-Krum	FedSybil	FedSybil+Multi-Krum
Accuracy %	65.0	10.0	**74.2**
ASR %	11.5	90.0	**2.57**

4.5 Coordinated Attacks

The attackers may collude to introduce intelligent perturbations where noises are added intentionally to similar updates to create dissimilarity. For example, two malicious clients can submit two update vectors such that $v_1 = x_1 + \alpha$ and $v_2 = x_2 - \alpha$, where

x_1, x_2 are malicious updates, and α is a shared perturbation vector. When these two vectors are aggregated together, the result is the sum $x_1 + x_2$. Adding perturbation to the poisoning updates, they become dissimilar and may go undetected. For this attack to be successful, the same perturbations must be added by the colluding clients to features relevant to the model's correctness. However, the perturbations must also be orthogonal to the non-relevant features to increase the dissimilarity. To mitigate this, the similarity can be computed on only the relevant features whose importance is estimated, similar to [1]. That last trick we have not mentioned in the paper.

Another synchronized attack is a poisoning attack with adaptive updates proposed by [8]. In this attack, the Sybil clients send poisoning updates when their similarity scores are low. However, this attack takes much work to achieve. First, it requires the Sybil clients to work together to calculate their cosine similarities. Second, to avoid being detected, the updates must be sent in a frequency below a certain threshold but still sent often enough so the attacks remain effective. Defining the threshold requires knowledge about how many honest clients are in the system, the distribution of the client's training data, and the defense of *FedSybil*.

4.6 Scalability

Our system currently computes the cosine similarity between all clients over all the labels. The time complexity of calculating the cosine similarity at every iteration is $\mathcal{O}(|S_{\text{pop}}|^2 ld)$ where $|S_{\text{pop}}|$ is the number of clients, l is the number of labels, and d is the number of features in the output layer. The cosine similarity can be, however, computed on a random subset S_t of clients, with time complexity $\mathcal{O}(|S_t|^2 ld)$. Empirically, We did not observe a noticeable drop in the performance compared with the baselines. The reason is likely that training requires many iterations; therefore, sampling different clients at each iteration for similarity calculations seems sufficient to cover enough clients eventually.

5   Related Work

In poisoning attacks, the clients aim to reduce the global model accuracy by submitting adversarial updates to the aggregation server. Subsequently, they can change the future states of the global and local honest models. As in FL, there is no access to the data or the training process, the defenses are done in the aggregation process at the server. Next, we provide an overview of the current defenses.

Defences Against Untargeted Attacks. For byzantine attackers in FL, instead of relying on averaging the weights, some approaches have proposed more robust estimates of the mean for robust aggregations [12,22]. [22], have introduced the *multi-Krum* secure aggregation. At each iteration, the smallest $n - f - 2$ distances are calculated for each client with the other clients. Upon aggregation, the f clients with the highest distances are disregarded. Also, *trimmed mean* and *median* aggregations have been proposed in [12]. With the median aggregation, the global model update is the median of the clients' model updates. In trimmed mean, the highest and lowest β values for each feature are trimmed before averaging. Despite effectively mitigating the untargeted poisoning attacks, the latter aggregation rules work only in IID settings. Furthermore, they assume a known and bound maximum number of malicious clients that they fail with many Sybil attacks [8].

Defences Against Targeted Attacks. To address targeted attacks, behavior-based approaches [23,24] have been proposed. The idea is to measure the similarities between the clients' past local updates to detect malicious clients who systematically share adversarial updates with the aggregation server. In [23], the authors calculate the cosine similarities between each local and aggregated model update. Based on the mean, the median, and the standard deviation of the similarities (guaranteed by the honest majority), the bad updates are determined prior to the aggregation. While in [24], as the global model is trained on a small root dataset, it is used as a reference to compute the local models' cosine similarities (and trust scores). Accordingly, a trust-based weighted average of the local updates is computed to update the global model. Similar to the previous approaches, behavior-based approaches are effective under IID settings. With different distributions between clients and the server, honest clients are expected to be penalized by mistake for being dissimilar.

Defences Against Sybil Attacks. In Sybil attacks, malicious clients exhibit more behavioral similarities than honest clients. Thus, the defenses compute pairwise similarities. More relevant to our approach, In [8], based on the cosine similarities, the learning rate of the similar clients are reduced; therefore, their contribution to the global model. [9] extended the latter approach by computing trust scores to choose the trusted clients for aggregation probabilistically. However, both approaches may penalize honest clients, reducing their learning rates by mistake. With many clients regarded as malicious, model learning gets hindered, causing a drastic reduction in the model accuracy, as shown in our experiments. On the other hand, a recent approach has been proposed in [25], where the author employs a maximum spanning tree to differentiate between honest and malicious clients. However, in contrast to our approach, they assume that the number of malicious clients can not be more than that of honest clients.

More recent attacks have been introduced in [26] such as LIE, MIN-MAX, MIN-SUM, and AGR-Tailored. However, these attacks assume either IID settings to work or require that malicious clients know other clients' updates which are out of the scope of our defined threat model in this work.

6 Conclusion

Federated Learning is a distributed multi-party machine learning system where the clients keep their raw data private and only share the local model updates with an aggregation server. However, that opens the door to different poisoning attacks where the attackers send poisoning updates to the server. In this work, we have focused on Sybil attacks, where an adversary can create multiple identities or control multiple devices to overpower the honest clients in the system. In particular, We defined a cosine-similarity-based measurement to track the historical behavior of the clients. To defend against the Sybil attacks, we introduced *FedSybil*, a behavior-based approach with a reputation mechanism for robust federated learning. Furthermore, we demonstrated the effectiveness of *FedSybil* against the Sybil attacks in terms of better model accuracy and lower attack success rates than the state-of-the-art defenses. Finally, we presented some research challenges, emphasizing coordinated attacks as potential future research directions.

References

1. McMahan, B., Moore, E., Ramage, D., Hampson, S., Arcas, B.A.: Communication-efficient learning of deep networks from decentralized data. In: Artificial Intelligence and Statistics, pp. 1273–1282 (2017)
2. Bonawitz, K., et al.: Towards federated learning at scale: system design. Proc. Mach. Learn. Syst. **1**, 374–388 (2019)
3. GoogleAI, F.: Collaborative machine learning without centralized training data (2017)
4. Silvano, W.F., Marcelino, R.: Iota tangle: a cryptocurrency to communicate Internet-of-Things data. Future Gener. Comput. Syst. **112**, 307–319 (2020). https://doi.org/10.1016/j.future.2020.05.047
5. Douceur, J.R.: The sybil attack. In: Druschel, P., Kaashoek, F., Rowstron, A. (eds.) IPTPS 2002. LNCS, vol. 2429, pp. 251–260. Springer, Heidelberg (2002). https://doi.org/10.1007/3-540-45748-8_24
6. Bhagoji, A.N., Chakraborty, S., Mittal, P., Calo, S.: Analyzing federated learning through an adversarial lens. In: International Conference on Machine Learning, pp. 634–643 (2019)
7. Fung, C., Yoon, C.J., Beschastnikh, I.: Mitigating sybils in federated learning poisoning. arXiv preprint arXiv:1808.04866 (2018)
8. Fung, C., Yoon, C.J., Beschastnikh, I.: The limitations of federated learning in sybil settings. In: 23rd International Symposium on Research in Attacks, Intrusions and Defenses (RAID 2020), pp. 301–316 (2020)
9. Awan, S., Luo, B., Li, F.: Contra: defending against poisoning attacks in federated learning. In: European Symposium on Research in Computer Security, pp. 455–475 (2021)
10. Zhao, Y., Li, M., Lai, L., Suda, N., Civin, D., Chandra, V.: Federated learning with non-iid data. arXiv preprint arXiv:1806.00582 (2018)
11. Hsieh, K., Phanishayee, A., Mutlu, O., Gibbons, P.: The non-iid data quagmire of decentralized machine learning. In: International Conference on Machine Learning, pp. 4387–4398 (2020)
12. Blanchard, P., El Mhamdi, E.M., Guerraoui, R., Stainer, J.: Machine learning with adversaries: byzantine tolerant gradient descent. In: Advances in Neural Information Processing Systems, vol. 30 (2017)
13. Leino, K., Sen, S., Datta, A., Fredrikson, M., Li, L.: Influence-directed explanations for deep convolutional networks. In: 2018 IEEE International Test Conference (ITC), pp. 1–8 (2018)
14. Datta, A., Sen, S., Zick, Y.: Algorithmic transparency via quantitative input influence: Theory and experiments with learning systems. In: 2016 IEEE Symposium on Security and Privacy (SP), pp. 598–617 (2016)
15. Kodinariya, T.M., Makwana, P.R.: Review on determining number of cluster in k-means clustering. Int. J. **1**(6), 90–95 (2013)
16. Li, T., Sahu, A.K., Zaheer, M., Sanjabi, M., Talwalkar, A., Smith, V.: Federated optimization in heterogeneous networks. Proc. Mach. Learn. Syst. **2**, 429–450 (2020)
17. Barreno, M., Nelson, B., Joseph, A.D., Tygar, J.D.: The security of machine learning. Mach. Learn. **81**(2), 121–148 (2010)

18. Bagdasaryan, E., Veit, A., Hua, Y., Estrin, D., Shmatikov, V.: How to backdoor federated learning. In: International Conference on Artificial Intelligence and Statistics, pp. 2938–2948 (2020)
19. LeCun, Y., Bottou, L., Bengio, Y., Haffner, P.: Gradient-based learning applied to document recognition. Proc. IEEE **86**(11), 2278–2324 (1998)
20. Xiao, H., Rasul, K., Vollgraf, R.: Fashion-MNIST: a novel image dataset for benchmarking machine learning algorithms. CoRR abs/1708.07747 (2017)
21. Krizhevsky, A., Hinton, G., et al.: Learning multiple layers of features from tiny images (2009)
22. Yin, D., Chen, Y., Kannan, R., Bartlett, P.: Byzantine-robust distributed learning: towards optimal statistical rates. In: International Conference on Machine Learning, pp. 5650–5659 (2018)
23. Muñoz-González, L. Co, K.T., Lupu, E.C.: Byzantine-robust federated machine learning through adaptive model averaging. arXiv preprint arXiv:1909.05125 (2019)
24. Cao, X., Fang, M., Liu, J., Gong, N.Z.: Fltrust: byzantine-robust federated learning via trust bootstrapping. arXiv preprint arXiv:2012.13995 (2020)
25. Ranjan, P., Corò, F., Gupta, A., Das, S.K.: Leveraging spanning tree to detect colluding attackers in federated learning. In: IEEE INFOCOM 2022-IEEE Conference on Computer Communications Workshops (INFOCOM WKSHPS), pp. 1–2 (2022)
26. Shejwalkar, V., Houmansadr, A.: Manipulating the byzantine: optimizing model poisoning attacks and defenses for federated learning. In: NDSS (2021)

Privacy-Preserving Authentication Scheme for 5G Cloud-Fog Hybrid with Soft Biometrics

Jiahui Wang[1], Yulong Fu[1,2(✉)], Mengru Liu[1], Jin Cao[1,2], Hui Li[1,2], and Zheng Yan[1,3]

[1] School of Cyber Engineering, Xidian University, Xi'an, Shaanxi, China
`ylfu@xidian.edu.cn`
[2] State Key Laboratory of Integrated Services Networks, Xi'an, Shaanxi, China
[3] Aalto University, Espoo, Finland

Abstract. The feature of Enhanced Mobile Broadband (eMBB) and Cloud-Fog hybrid architecture in 5G significantly enhance the communication and computation capabilities of 5G devices, and make the biometric traits collection, recognition and authentication become possible. However, since biometrics such as face ID, fingerprint, etc. are belonging to user's privacy, by considering the curiosity of cloud server and the law of General Data Protection Regulation (GDPR), we can't use biometrics directly in 5G cloud-fog hybrid scenarios. To solve this problem, in this paper, we propose a privacy-preserving authentication scheme based on soft biometric traits (PPA-SBT). In our scheme, soft biometrics without privacy attributes are designed to protect the biometrics with privacy attributes through encryption, and improve the recognition speed and accuracy rate. We conducted the theoretical security analysis of the proposed scheme with formal method and also conducted experiments with real dataset and public datasets respectively, the experimental results demonstrate the feasibility and convenience of PPA-SBT.

Keywords: 5G Security · Soft Biometric Traits · Biometric Recognition · Cloud-Fog Hybrid Architecture · Formal Verification

1 Introduction

The advent of 5G has ushered in a new era of mobile networks, offering higher speeds, increased capacity, and lower latency compared to 4G. This has enabled the Internet of Everything (IoT) [13] expanding the possibilities of the mobile Internet. However, many IoT devices such as sensors, camera, etc., are less of the ability of computation. To address those limitations, the 5G cloud-fog hybrid

This work was supported by National Key R&D Program of China No.2022YFB2902205 and the Key Research and Development Program of Shaanxi (No.2020ZDLGY08-08).

architecture has been proposed and widely adopted. This architecture combines the computing power and storage capacity of the cloud with the capabilities of fog nodes, which are connected to IoT and terminal devices, aiming to overcome challenges such as high latency and bandwidth waste (see Fig. 1).

User authentication plays a crucial role in ensuring security in 5G network applications, particularly in scenarios involving massive Machine Type Communications (mMTC), where a large number of smart terminal devices are connected. Biometric recognition is widely recognized for its convenience and reliability, with applications in domains such as medical [6] and payment [24] sectors. In the 5G cloud-fog hybrid environment, where terminals and IoT devices connect directly to fog nodes, leveraging fog computing services and accessing cloud services through fog, biometric recognition becomes increasingly advantageous, improving the overall user experience.

However, using single biometrics presents certain challenges, including issues related to data quality that can affect system accuracy [30]. Moreover, transmitting highly sensitive biometric data between cloud and fog raises concerns about privacy breaches, potentially leading to identity theft and security risks. It should be noted that we consider the scenario based on 5G network and following the centralized settings in the 3GPP standards. This paper mainly focuses on centralized authentication mechanisms, and does not discuss distributed authentication and privacy protection methods such as blockchain.

To address these challenges, we propose a privacy-preserving authentication scheme based on soft biometric traits. Soft biometric traits, such as height, weight, gender, and hair color, are non-identifying and readily collectible features. They can be used to generate encryption keys for protecting biometric data while improving the efficiency and accuracy of biometric recognition as auxiliary information.

With regard to the issue of privacy protection, several privacy protection schemes have been proposed for biometric recognition. Zhu et al. [37] introduced an online fingerprint authentication scheme based on outsourced data, utilizing an improved homomorphic encryption technique for matching encrypted fingerprint data in outsourcing scenarios. Zhang et al. [36] designed a data encryption and secure outsourcing matching algorithm that employs random matrices and vectors for data encryption and matching, while introducing perturbations to protect privacy before encryption. Although these schemes protect biometric characteristics as privacy assets, the accuracy of matching encrypted biometrics may be reduced compared to traditional methods due to increased error rates.

Compared with above schemes for privacy protection of biometric recognition, the biggest difference of our scheme is that we make use of soft biometric traits, which are easy to collect, as the key to protect users' privacy. There are low-cost devices everywhere in our lives such as smart bracelets, mobile phones, computers, surveillance cameras, weighing scale and so on, soft biometric traits can be collected and extracted from these devices. Therefore, the authentication is more natural and convenient without complex operations in our scheme.

Contribution. We proposed a privacy-preserving authentication scheme based on soft biometric traits (PPA-SBT). User biometric and soft biometric data are collected by IoT and terminal devices and transmitted to nearby fog computing centers. Fog computing center generates the secret key using the extracted soft biometrics traits, encrypt the collected biometric data, and send it to a trusted authentication center for decryption and biometric recognition. By separating the cloud server from biometric functions and only using it for soft biometric data filtering, the privacy of users' data is safeguarded. Our scheme leverages the advantages of soft biometric traits to ensure accurate and efficient authentication while preserving privacy during transmission. The key contributions of our paper include:

- We proposed a privacy-preserving authentication scheme based on soft biometric traits.
- We used Tamarin to formalize our scheme and prove the security of the solution.
- We established the real dataset and did experiments to analyze the experimental results under the real scenario. We also established the 552 users' artificial dataset using public datasets to analyze the experimental performance better.

The remainder of the paper is organized as follows. Section 2 provides an overview of the background and related works relevant to our research. Section 3 presents our proposed scheme in detail. Section 4 analyzes the performance of the scheme, briefly describes the formal tool used, and verifies the proposed scheme. Section 5 introduces the experiments conducted and presents the experimental results. Finally, Sect. 6 concludes the paper.

2   Background and Related Works

2.1   Background

Cloud-Fog Hybrid Architecture. The evolution of mobile communication technology and IoT applications have led to increased demands for data storage and processing. In 2006, Google CEO Eric Schmidt introduced the concept of "cloud computing" [27]. Cloud computing is a two-tier network architecture, consisting of a front tier (mobile network) and a back tier (cloud devices and servers), connected via the Internet [28]. Cloud computing offers reliable and cost-effective support to various entities. However, challenges arise due to constant Internet connection requirements and the increased demand for wireless data transmission. These challenges include high bandwidth pressure, latency, and compromised data transmission.

To overcome these challenges, fog computing has emerged as a complementary paradigm to cloud computing. Fog nodes serve as facilities or infrastructures that provide resources for widely distributed services at the edge of the network [35]. By leveraging resources from nearby fog nodes, fog computing

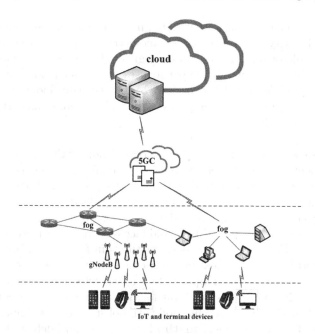

Fig. 1. Cloud-Fog Hybrid Architecture.

enables substantial storage and computation with reduced communication costs. Cloud and fog computing each offer their own advantages. While the cloud has ample resources to host various applications, it can introduce latency and waste bandwidth. On the other hand, fog computing can provide faster response times but lacks sufficient computing power for complex tasks [34]. The cloud-fog hybrid architecture is applied in various fields, including 5G network user identity authentication.

Biometric Authentication. Authentication plays a crucial role in ensuring system and data security, especially in the context of cloud-fog hybrid architectures. Biometric recognition utilizes human body characteristics, offers distinct advantages over traditional authentication methods like passwords and tokens. These characteristics, including physical and behavioral traits, are unique, secure, and difficult to lose or forget. Consequently, biometric recognition provides higher convenience, reliability, and security. With the increasing use of sensors and mobile devices, biometric recognition technology is emerging as a mainstream trend in future 5G cloud-fog hybrid architectures. The biometric recognition system encompasses two phases: enrollment/registration, involving the extraction and storage of users' biometric features in a database, and recognition, where biometric recognition is performed.

Specifically, Biometric recognition can be divided into two categories: verification and identification. Verification matches an individual's biometrics against a specific index, such as a user identify ID, in a 1:1 matching system to validate their claimed identity. Identification uses biometric comparison to determine the identity of an unknown individual among registered users in a database, employing a 1:N matching system. This paper focuses on biometric identification.

Next, we provide a brief overview of mainstream biometric technologies, namely face recognition, fingerprint recognition, and voiceprint recognition/speaker recognition.

Face Recognition. This is a popular biometric technology that uses human facial features for identification. Generally, the face recognition system consists of four modules: face acquisition and detection, face pre-processing, feature extraction and face recognition [26]. Pre-processing involves tasks like grayscale correction, noise filtering, light compensation, and geometric correction. Feature extraction extracts a feature vector from the face, and face recognition performs verification or identification. There are several basic methods in face recognition. **Feature-based method** utilizes local features of the face such as eyes, lips, etc., for face segmentation and uses them as input data for face detection. **Holistic method** considers the entire face as a single unit for detection and recognition. **Hybrid method** combines feature-based method with holistic method. Another popular method is the **Template-based method**, recognizes and detects human faces by computing the correlation of the input image to the standard face pattern using whole facial features.

Fingerprint Recognition. Fingerprints are identifiable, immovable, stable and unique for everyone, their basic properties will never change over time, so it can be as a reliable means of recognition. Fingerprint matching techniques are classified into three categories [26].

- Pattern based/image based matching: It compares the basic fingerprint patterns between the user to be identified and the stored fingerprint templates.
- Minutiae-based method: It identifies minutiae points and their relative positions on finger. First, the minutiae features of fingerprints are extracted from the images, and then the minutiae features of the two fingerprint images are matched for verification or identification.
- Correlation-based methods: It is based on rich gray scale information. It can handle poor quality data.

Generally, the fingerprint recognition system consists of four modules: fingerprint acquisition, fingerprint pre-processing, feature extraction and fingerprint matching [2]. In the acquisition module, the fingerprint image is captured using a sensor. The pre-processing module then eliminates unwanted data, such as noise and reflection, through segmentation, binarization, noise removal, smoothing, and thinning. Next, the feature extraction module extracts fingerprint features. Finally, these acquired features are compared with templates in the database for verification or identification.

Voiceprint Recognition/Speaker Recognition. Voiceprint recognition, also known as speaker recognition, identifies individuals based on unique voice characteristics. It takes advantage of physiological differences in vocal tract shapes, larynx sizes, and other voice production organs [29]. Speaker recognition offers the following advantages [17]:

- It overcomes the "perceived intrusion" barrier in other biometric systems by not requiring direct physical contact.
- It utilizes the ubiquity of microphones found in portable devices like mobile phones and laptops, eliminating the need for additional hardware.

Speaker recognition systems (SRS) can be categorized as text-dependent or text-independent. Text-dependent SRS requires speakers to utter specific known phrases, while text-independent SRS allows flexibility in spoken phrases [12].

The speaker recognition system comprises two key modules: feature extraction and pattern recognition. The feature extraction module transforms the high-dimensional speech signal into a lower-dimensional feature subspace, retaining the speaker's discriminative information. Common methods for pattern recognition include template matching, nearest neighbor, neural networks, hidden Markov models and so on [29].

Soft Biometrics. Soft biometrics encompass various physical, behavioral, and adhered human characteristics that provide partial information about an individual but lack distinctiveness and permanence to differentiate any two individuals [11,15]. Examples of soft biometric traits include anthropometric measurements, eye and hair color, notable marks (scars, tattoos, birthmarks), and characteristics like gender and age [7,32].

While lacking distinctiveness and permanence, soft biometrics offer advantages such as minimal computational requirements, convenient collection, and privacy preservation. They can be employed to filter large biometric databases [23] or enhance the performance of traditional biometrics [22]. Tome et al. [31] described people as soft biometrics in terms of global traits and head features. They found that soft biometrics can maintain the robustness of face recognition and improve the performance in scenarios at a distance. Lyle et al. [19] proposed to use gender and ethnicity features extracted from the periocular region images using the SVM classifier to improve the accuracy and performance of periocular recognition. Yang et al. [33] verified the combination of width measurement and finger vein recognition improves recognition accuracy and speed. Ailisto et al. [1] used weight and fat percentage as soft biometrics. Niinuma et al. [21] demonstrated the effectiveness of continuous user authentication by combining soft biometrics with traditional authentication schemes.

2.2   Related Works

User authentication in the cloud environment is crucial to ensure access to services, resources, and sensitive data is limited to legitimate users who have undergone authentication [25]. Biometric recognition, as a proof of characteristics, offers advantages including non-lost, non-intrusive, and difficult-to-forge characteristics, making it a suitable replacement for traditional authentication [4]. However, protecting biometric data during communication and transmission is essential due to privacy risks and potential hacking.

To protect biometric images, two main methods are commonly employed: information hiding and encryption [9]. Existing techniques encrypt biometric images using various domains such as chaotic, fractional, and combined domains to enhance transmission security. Khan et al. [16] utilized the fractional Fourier transform (FRT) for secure transmission of biometric images by employing FRT scaling factors and random phase masks as encryption keys. Bhatnagar et al. [8] proposed a chaotic encryption framework based on fractional wavelet packet transform (FrWPT) to safeguard palmprint data. Mehta et al. [20] introduced an encryption-based solution for iris biometric template security, employing multiple 1-D chaos and 2-D Arnold chaotic maps. Chen et al. [10] utilized a chaotic cryptosystem based on electrocardiogram (ECG) signals to generate encryption keys for securing text or images. Ali et al. [3] proposed an edge-centric multimodal authentication system that encrypts face images and speech signals using chaotic sequences generated by a chaotic system, ensuring confidentiality and security during transmission. However, the data processed by these methods are often large, and the encryption process is complex and time-consuming.

In addition, to the best of our knowledge, there is no existing work that specifically considers the privacy protection of identity authentication in the cloud-fog hybrid architecture of 5G network.

3   Proposed Scheme

We propose a privacy-preserving authentication scheme based on soft biometric traits (PPA-SBT) to protect privacy and ensure authentication accuracy. PPA-SBT consists of two phases: Registration and Authentication.

In the Registration phase, users collect their biological characteristics and soft biometric traits using sensors and submit them along with their identification Nickname to the Trusted authentication center (AUC) for storage.

In the Authentication phase, users send authentication requests to AUC through the fog computing center (FCC) and the cloud server (Cloud). AUC selects the required features and sends them to Cloud for storage while instructing the user to collect additional data. This process ensures privacy and security even if Cloud is honest but curious. After that, Users collect the required features and send them to FCC. The fusion calculation of the user's soft biometric traits is outsourced to FCC. After normalization, the soft biometric traits of different dimensions are fused and transformed to generate the secret key K_{SBC}' by FCC, and $K_{SBC}/K_{SBC+1}/K_{SBC-1}$ by AUC respectively. AUC can attempt to decrypt the user's biological characteristics using these keys, as the real-time collected soft biometric data in the Authentication phase may deviate slightly from the data stored in AUC during the Registration phase. A successful decryption confirms the user's identity.

Table 1. Notations and definition

Notation	Definition
FCC	Fog computing center
Cloud	The cloud server
AUC	Trusted authentication center which has the database storing all users' registration data
SBC_List	Total soft biometric traits(the total capacities of all sensors)
BC_List	Total biological characteristics
Fid/Sid/uid	Identity identifier of FCC/session/user
SBC_Q	Soft biometric traits to be transmitted used for filtering in Cloud
BC_Q	Biological characteristics to be transmitted which is used to identity authentication
V_SBC	AUC-generated vectors from SBC Q content of eligible UEs sent to Cloud for filtering storage
V_Nickname$_i$	Hash of the user's Nickname
V_SBC'	Soft biometric traits collected by UE corresponding to SBC_Q contained in SBC_List
K_SBC'	Soft biometric traits collected by UE corresponding to content other than SBC_Q in SBC_List used to generate encryption key
K_SBC	Soft biometric traits corresponding to K_SBC'storaged in AUC to generate decryption keys
V_BC'	Biological feature collected by UE
K_{SBC}'	The key used to encrypt V_BC' based on soft biometric traits generated by FCC
$K_{SBC/SBC+1/SBC-1}$	The key used to decrypt biometric ciphertext using soft biometric traits generated by AUC
K	The pre-shared key used to encrypt the key information between Cloud and FCC
S_Vnickname'	The set of V_Nickname of matching users

The notations and definition of PPA-SBT are listed in Table 1. Then we give a detailed introduction to PPA-SBT.

3.1 Registration Phase

In the scheme, the specific process of the registration phase is shown in Fig. 2. Before performing the biometric recognition, the users must register, so that both the biological characteristics and the soft biometric traits of the users are stored in AUC. The specific steps are as follows:

– UE sends its unique identity Nickname to AUC, while Nickname is named by UE and confirmed by AUC.

- AUC sends SBC_List and BC_List to UE in order to prompt UE to submit the corresponding data.
- UE collects the corresponding data in real time and sends them together with Nickname to AUC.
- AUC adds the characteristic data, Nickname and automatically generated index collected by UE to its local database (or disk) after receiveing the data. Then AUC sends the successful registration message to UE.
- After UE receives the successful registration message sent by AUC, it can initiate the authentication phase process.

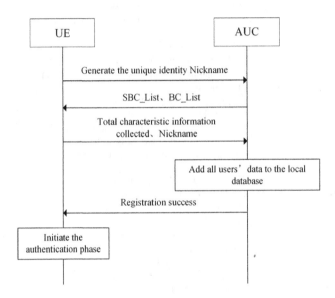

Fig. 2. Registration Phase Process.

3.2   Authentication Phase

In the scheme, the specific process of the authentication phase is shown in Fig. 3. The authentication process can be carried out between UE and AUC after the registration is performed, the specific steps are as follows:

- First, UE sends the authentication request to FCC, which includes SBC_List and BC_List. Then FCC forwards the authentication request and its own identifier Fid to Cloud.
- After receiving the message from FCC, Cloud randomly selects SBC_Q and BC_Q to be transmitted from SBC_List and BC_List, and determines the session identifier S_id of this time, and then sends them to AUC together. Please note that soft biometric data corresponding to SBC_Q are used to filter the database, and other soft biometric data are used to generate the encryption key. And biometric data corresponding to BC_Q is used to recognition.

- AUC generates a set of vector V_SBC_i from the content corresponding to SBC_Q of all UEs in the database, and performs a hash operation on the identity Nickname$_i$ of UEs to generate V_Nickname$_i$. After that, all the V_SBC_i, V_Nickname$_i$ and session identifier Sid of UEs are sent to Cloud together.
- Cloud saves the V_SBC_i and V_Nickname$_i$, and then sends SBC_Q, BC_Q, Sid, and Fid to the FCC according to the previously received Fid. Then FCC sends SBC_Q, BC_Q and Sid to UE.
- UE collects the characteristics corresponding to SBC_List and BC_Q, and records the soft biometric characteristics corresponding to SBC_Q contained in the SBC_List as V_SBC', the remaining soft biometric characteristics as K_SBC' which is used to encrypt, and the biological characteristics as V_BC'. And then V_SBC', K_SBC' and V_BC' are sent to FCC.
- FCC uses K_SBC' to generate the soft biometric key K_{SBC}', and uses the key to encrypt the biometric information V_BC' to generate the biometric ciphertext c. Then FCC uses the key K pre-shared with Cloud to encrypt the biometric ciphertext c, V_SBC', Sid and Fid and then sends the ciphertext to Cloud.
- Upon receiving the message, Cloud decrypts it using the pre-shared key K with FCC. It compares V_SBC' with the vector group V_SBC_i to obtain the vector group V_SBC_j containing potential soft biological characteristics of the same person. Cloud extracts the V_Nickname of users in V_SBC_j to generate the user identity set S_Vnickname'. Cloud sends S_Vnickname', the ciphertext c, and Sid to AUC. AUC generates the soft biometric key K_{SBC} using the remaining soft biometric characteristics K_SBC. It attempts to decrypt the ciphertext using K_{SBC}, K_{SBC+1}, and K_{SBC-1}. If the decryption fails, it indicates that the submitted identity by the user equipment (UE) does not belong to the same person. Otherwise, they may belong to the same person. AUC obtains the decrypted biometrics V_BC' and the set S_Nickname containing potential identities of the same person. AUC compares V_BC' with the user templates in V_BC_j using specified thresholds for similarity. If the similarity exceeds the threshold, the authentication is successful, and Auth_success is returned by AUC. Otherwise, the authentication fails, and Auth_fail is returned.

3.3 Key Agreement

During the authentication phase, FCC and AUC generate the same key to encrypt and decrypt the biological characteristics data. Considering the slight variations between the submitted traits during registration and authentication, we set a reasonable error range for each trait. If the difference exceeds this range, the traits are likely from different users. We also assign weights to each trait for fusion using weighted summation to generate the key. To ensure security and privacy, FCC and AUC operate in a non-interactive manner to prevent key leakage during transmission. The key generation process is carried out separately in FCC and AUC.

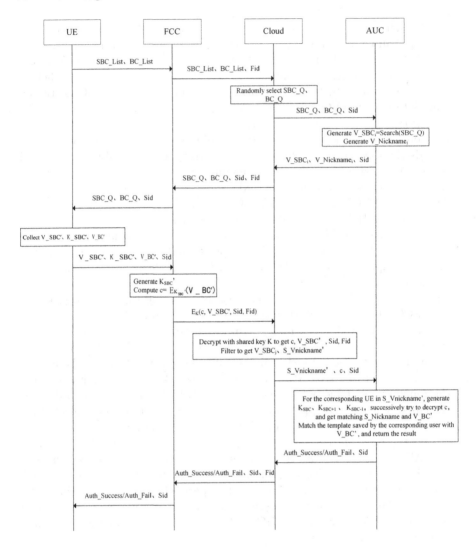

Fig. 3. Authentication Phase Process.

- For FCC, it uses the soft biometric traits K_SBC' collected by UE during the authentication phase to fuse and generate the soft biometric key K_{SBC}', the specific formulas are as follows:

$$SBC' = \sum_{i=1}^{n} w_i \times K\_SBC'_i \qquad (1)$$

where SBC' represents the value after weighted fusion, $K\_SBC'_i$ is the value of the i-th soft biometric trait during authentication, w_i is the corresponding weight, and n represents the total number of soft biometric traits.

$$\Delta = \sum_{i=1}^{n} w_i \times \Delta_i \tag{2}$$

where Δ represents the total soft biometric error range, and Δ_i represents the i-th soft biometric trait's error range.

$$K'_{SBC} = Hash\left(\left\lfloor \frac{SBC'}{\Delta} \right\rfloor\right) \tag{3}$$

where $\lfloor x \rfloor$ represents the result of x rounding down. And K'_{SBC} is the final result of key after fusion. Then FCC uses K'_{SBC} to encrypt the private data such as the face and fingerprint of UE and generate the ciphertext.

- For each user in S_Vnickname', AUC fuses the soft biometric traits from the registration phase to generate the soft biometric keys K_{SBC}, K_{SBC+1}, and K_{SBC-1}. These keys are used for attempting to decrypt the ciphertext. If decryption is successful, the user is added to the set S_Nickname, indicating a potential match with the user being authenticated. The fusion formula is:

$$SBC = \sum_{i=1}^{n} w_i \times K\_SBC_i \tag{4}$$

where SBC represent the value after weighted fusion, K_SBC_i represent the i-th soft biometric trait's value submitted in registration phase, and the meanings and values of w_i and n are the same as in equal (1).

$$K_{SBC} = Hash\left(\left\lfloor \frac{SBC}{\Delta} \right\rfloor\right) \tag{5}$$

$$K_{SBC+1} = Hash\left(\left\lfloor \frac{SBC}{\Delta} \right\rfloor + 1\right) \tag{6}$$

$$K_{SBC-1} = Hash\left(\left\lfloor \frac{SBC}{\Delta} \right\rfloor - 1\right) \tag{7}$$

- For AUC, there is:

$$\frac{SBC}{\Delta} = \frac{SBC' + x}{\Delta} = \frac{SBC'}{\Delta} + \frac{x}{\Delta} \tag{8}$$

where x is the deviation of SBC and SBC'. We assume that for the same user, the absolute value of x will not exceed the total error range Δ. So there is $\left|\frac{x}{\Delta}\right| \leq 1$. When $\frac{SBC}{\Delta}$ and $\frac{SBC'}{\Delta}$ are rounded down, the difference between the rounded results is at most 1, so the value of K'_{SBC} is equal to the value of one of K_{SBC}, K_{SBC+1} and K_{SBC-1} if the two soft biometric traits used by FCC and AUC may belong to the same person, that is, the absolute value of x does not exceed Δ. This decryption process is also the process of further filtering and reducing the space of verified users which can significantly improve the overall efficiency by shortening the execution time of the authentication phase process.

4   Analysis of Our Scheme

4.1   Performance Analysis

Our scheme leverages low-cost sensors to provide convenient and natural authentication. Soft biometric traits are used not only for privacy protection but also to narrow down the search space for biometric matching, resulting in faster user identification. The computational complexity is kept low due to the small amount of computation required for soft biometric traits. This ensures that fog computing, with its limited compute capacity, can handle the authentication process efficiently. Additionally, the combination of biological characteristics and soft biometric traits prevents impersonation by non-living entities, adding an extra layer of security.

4.2   Security Analysis

Analysis Tool. The Tamarin prover is a powerful automated tool for formal verification [14]. The input of tamarin includes the actions that the protocol initiators, responders, and trusted servers may take, the specification of the adversary and the desired security properties of the protocol. It uses parallel interleaving of multiple instances in the protocol to prove whether the protocol can achieve specified properties [5]. The multiset rewriting used to describe the action of protocol and adversary consists of three sequences of facts that define the transition of the system. A single fact represents the state of protocol and adversary. The Tamarin prover can use an efficient and fully automated mode to construct proofs.

Attacker Model. In the security analysis, we consider the attacker model used in formal analysis. The Dolve-Yao model assumes that the attacker cannot break the cryptographic algorithm and needs the correct key to decrypt encrypted data. The attacker's abilities include eavesdropping on network messages, intercepting and storing messages, forging and sending messages, and participating in protocol operations as a legitimate participant.

For a stronger security analysis, we adopt the eCK model [18]. This model assumes that the attacker can obtain the long-term private key, temporary private key, and session key of a participant. The attacker can expose the private keys and secrets of individual participants but not the entire secret of a party. The model also considers the impact of compromised keys on subsequent sessions.

In our scheme, the privacy protection focuses on the users' biometric characteristics. Since the distance between sensors and FCC is very close, it is assumed that they trust each other and the message transmission between them is secure. The secure communication between Cloud and AUC relies on processed user identities via hashing. And, the ciphertext of private data is transmitted from FCC to AUC, ensuring decryption capability only by AUC. The encrypted users' biometrics are transmitted to Cloud by FCC, requiring verification against potential biometric interception.

Proof Process. We assume secure communication between the user and the fog computing center, as well as between the Cloud and AUC. We analyze the communication security between these entities by considering them as a whole, denoted as U and S respectively. The proof process involves the following steps:

1. Modeling the authentication scheme using the Tamarin language, including functions and rules of the protocol and its environment. The formal model is depicted in Fig. 5.
2. Adding the necessary security goals to the model, as shown in Fig. 4. These goals ensure that the attacker cannot obtain the biological characteristics at any point, and that S believes the authentication message was sent by U only when it was indeed sent by U.
3. Performing the analysis of the model using the command line and obtaining the result, as depicted in Fig. 6.

```
//security goals
lemma executable:
  exists-trace
"Ex u s m #i #j. Send(u,m) @i & Recv(s,m) @j & i<j"

lemma secrecy_of_key:
  "All u s k #i. Secret_k(u, s, k) @i ==> not (Ex #j. K(k) @j)"

lemma secrecy_of_vbc:
  "All m #i. Secret_m(m) @i ==> not (Ex #j. K(m) @j)"

lemma auth_by_vbc:
  exists-trace
"Ex u m #i #j. Authentic(u, m) @i & Send(u, m) @j & j<i"
```

Fig. 4. Security Goals.

Result of Analysis. In the formal analysis, the main security goals we choose are that the attacker cannot get the user's biometrics, and the user can realize the authentication between it and AUC by its biometrics. The premise is that FCC and Cloud pre-share the key K to encrypt and decrypt the transmitted data including soft biometrics, and FCC and AUC encrypt and decrypt the private data based on K'_{SBC} and one of K_{SBC}, K_{SBC+1} and K_{SBC-1}. The result of the analysis shows that PPA-SBT can meet these security goals. Because the intruder can not get the key generated by the soft biometric traits, the biological characteristic encrypted by the key will not be leaked. Besides, soft biometric traits do not reveal privacy. Therefore, the privacy data of the user will be protected. Our scheme is security and feasible.

5   Experiments and Results

Table 2 describes the soft biometrics considered along with their corresponding instances(different values that a soft biometric may have) used in our expriments, and the quantified value of binary and discrete instances is included in

```
builtins: symmetric-encryption
functions: f/1[private]

//U and S share some secret
rule Key_shared:
    [ Fr(~secret) ]
  -->
    [ !Sharedkey($U, $S, ~secret) ]

// U sends auth request
rule U_1:
    [ Fr(~sn)]
  -->
    [ Out(<$U, ~sn>) ]

// S responds
rule S_1:
    [ In(<$U, ~sn>), Fr(~sq) ]
  -->
    [ Out(<$U, ~sq>) ]

// U sends features
rule U_2:
    [ In(<$U, ~sq>), Fr(~vbc), Fr(~vsbc), !Sharedkey($U, $S, ~ksbc), !Sharedkey($U, $S, ~keyUS) ]
  --[ Secret_k($U, $S, ~ksbc), Secret_k($U, $S, ~keyUS), Secret_m(~vbc), Send($U, ~vbc) ]->
    [ Out(senc(<$U, ~vsbc, senc(~vbc, f(~ksbc))>, ~keyUS)) ]

// S matchs features and authenticates identity
rule S_2:
    [ !Sharedkey($U, $S, ksbc), !Sharedkey($U, $S, keyUS), In(senc(<$U, vsbc, senc(vbc, f(ksbc))>, keyUS)) ]
  --[ Recv($S, vbc), Secret_k($U, $S, ksbc), Secret_k($U, $S, keyUS), Secret_m(vbc), Authentic($U, vbc) ]->
    []
```

Fig. 5. Formal Model.

```
/* All well-formedness checks were successful. */

end

==============================================================================
summary of summaries:

analyzed: softbiometrics.spthy

  executable (exists-trace): verified (8 steps)
  secrecy_of_key (all-traces): verified (22 steps)
  secrecy_of_vbc (all-traces): verified (18 steps)
  auth_by_vbc (exists-trace): verified (8 steps)

==============================================================================
```

Fig. 6. Results Summarized by Tamarin.

parentheses. We collected information regarding weight, height, facial golden triangle number, gender, mole, skin spots, acne, dark circle, eye pouch, glasses, eyebrow shape, eyes shape, nose shape and lip shape. In terms of the type of value, weight, height and golden triangle number are continuous, gender, mole, skin spot, acne, dark circle and eye pouch are binary, and the rest of them are discrete. In terms of the category, height, weight, gender belong to body traits, and the rest of them belong to face traits. The reason we do not choose clothing traits is that they often change, and key generation requires a certain degree of stability and durability. The biometric characteristics we chose were face and fingerprint because of their widely acceptance and use. We conducted experiments on our real dataset and public datasets respectively.

Table 2. Soft biometrics extracted from expriments

Soft biometrics	Value
Weight	Continuous value
Height	Continuous value
Golden triangle number	Continuous value
Gender	Female(0) Male(1)
Mole	No(0) Yes(1)
Skin spot	No(0) Yes(1)
Acne	No(0) Yes(1)
Dark circle	No(0) Yes(1)
Eye pouch	No(0) Yes(1)
Glasses	No glasses(0) Dark glasses(0.5) Ordinary glasses(1)
Eyebrow shape	Bushy eyebrows(0) Eight eyebrows(1) Raise eyebrows(2) Straight eyebrows(3) Round eyebrows(4) Arch eyebrows(5) Thin eyebrows(6) Else(7)
Eyes shape	Round eyes(0) Thin eyes(1) Big eyes(2) Small eyes(3) Normal eyes(4) Else(5)
Nose shape	Normal nose(0) Thick nose(1) Thin nose(2) Else(3)
Lip shape	Thin lip(0) Thick lip(1) Smile lip(2) Upset lip(3) Normal lip(4) Else(5)

5.1 Experiments and Results Based on Real Dataset

In our schema, soft biometric traits are used to generate the encryption key for privacy protection, and the error range between soft biometric traits obtained from UE in registration phase and in authentication phase will affect the correctness and consistency of key generation, encryption and decryption for the same user. So we need to set the reasonable error range for each soft biometric trait based on collected data.

Dataset. We collected biometric and soft biometric data from 20 individuals on two occasions with a one-week interval. The data included high-definition face images, fingerprint images, height, weight, and other soft biometric traits extracted from face images using the face++ API. Observing the data fluctuations, we found that weight deviated by less than 3 kg, height deviated by less than 3 cm, and the golden triangle number deviated by less than 10 for the same person under normal circumstances. Based on these findings, we set reasonable parameters for generating consistent keys in our experiments.

Recognition Methods. For face recognition, we use the dlib-based deep learning face recognition library: face_recognition For fingerprint recognition, we use Professor Raffaele's OpenCV-based Python fingerprinting program.

Experiment Environment. Our experimental environment are Windows10, VMware Workstation15.5, Ubuntu18.04. The programming language is Python3.7. The experimental topology is shown in Fig. 7.

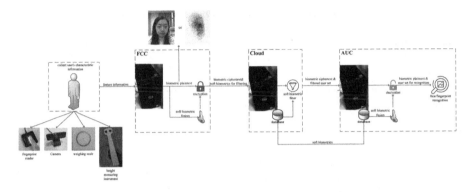

Fig. 7. Experimental Topology.

Experimental Results. We tested each user in our real dataset multiple times with and without soft biometric encryption&decryption for face and fingerprint authentication. The results shown in Table 3 indicate that using soft biometric encryption&decryption for face authentication introduces a small time cost in exchange for higher security during transmission. Similarly, using soft biometric encryption&decryption for fingerprint authentication reduces the total authentication time. This is due to the varying efficiencies of the face recognition and fingerprint recognition algorithms employed in our experiments.

Table 3. Comparison results using real dataset

Comparison term	Average authentication time without soft biometric encryption & decryption(s)	Average authentication time with soft biometric encryption& decryption(s)
Face authentication	2.833	3.7
Fingerprint authentication	3.4	1.65

5.2 Experiments and Results Based on Public Datasets

Due to the small size of our real dataset, our results were limited. Therefore, we also conducted experiments on larger public datasets. Besides, the recognition methods and experiment environment were are same as above.

Experiment Datasets. For facial images, we used a subset of the Color FERET Database. It contains over 10,000 photos of more than 1,000 individuals, capturing variations in expressions, lighting, posture, and age. For fingerprints, we used NIST Supplemental Fingerprint Card Data (SFCD) published by National Institute of Standards and Technology (NIST). It contains 5520 fingerprint images of 552 individuals. Then we artificially generated height and weight data for 552 individuals to match the SFCD fingerprint dataset and the Color FERET face dataset, and we got other soft biometric traits data from face images through open source API interface such as Face++. In this way, we established an artificial dataset of 552 individuals containing one-on-one face, fingerprint and all soft biometric data.

Table 4. Comparison results of authentication time using public datasets

Methods	Biometric authentication without soft biometric encryption & decryption	Biometric authentication with soft biometric encryption & decryption
The time AUC attempts to decrypt	0	$x \cdot T_{singer\_decryption}$ $(x \leq 552)$
The time AUC performs biometric recognition	$552 \cdot T_{singer\_recognition}$	$y \cdot T_{singer\_recognition}$ $(y \leq x \leq 552)$
The total authentication time	$552 \cdot T_{singer\_recognition}$	$x \cdot T_{singer\_decryption} +$ $y \cdot T_{singer\_recognition}$

Table 5. Comparison results of face recognition using public datasets

Comparison term	The minimum value	The maximum value	The average value
x	10	552	124
y	2	354	70
The total authentication time	$0.5 \cdot T_{face}$	$11 \cdot T_{face}$	$2.5 \cdot T_{face}$

Table 6. Comparison results of fingerprint recognition using public datasets

Comparison term	The minimum value	The maximum value	The average value
x	10	552	116
y	2	353	65
The total authentication time	$0.007 \cdot T_{fingerprint}$	$0.86 \cdot T_{fingerprint}$	$0.5 \cdot T_{fingerprint}$

Experimental Results.

Comparison of Authentication Time Using and Not Using Soft Biometric Encryption&Decryption When Using All 552 Public Dataset Users as the Experimental Database. We conducted 2000 experiments separately for face recognition and fingerprint recognition in order to obtain reliable results. We mainly analyzed the soft biometric encryption&decryption results and the total authentication time.

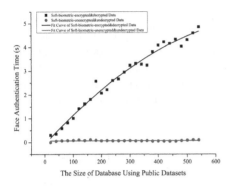

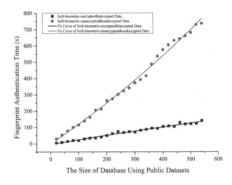

Fig. 8. Trend of Face Authentication Time.

Fig. 9. Trend of Fingerprint Authentication Time.

- For the soft biometric encryption&decryption results, in all experiments, the user set decrypted by Cloud contain the authenticated user, that is, the user set recognized by AUC contains the authenticated user. Therefore, soft biometric encryption&decryption will not affect the final biometric recognition results.

- For the total authentication time, we compared the authentication time using and not using soft biometric encryption&decryption. The time can be divided into AUC's decryption attempts and biometric recognition. By analyzing the experimental data, we found that the decryption time and the biometric recognition time differed between the two cases. The results are shown in Table 4. The number of decryption attempts, represented by x, depends on Cloud's database filtering. The number of biometric recognitions, represented by y. $T_{singer\_recognition}$ represents the single biometric comparison time of AUC, and $T_{singer\_decryption}$ represents the single decryption time of AUC.

Since the number of times AUC attempts to decrypt depends on the result of Cloud filtering database by using of a part of soft biometric at firsts, x is less than or equal to the total number of database users 552. Since the process of AUC's attempt to decrypt is equivalent to secondary filtering, and the subset of database users that have been successfully decrypted by AUC is used for biometric recognition, the number of times that AUC performs biometric recognition which is y is less than or equal to the number of times that AUC attempts to decrypt which is x.

However, since FCC generates soft biometric keys using soft biometric traits, Cloud randomly selects traits to instruct fog to generate keys and encrypt the data. And then Cloud uses soft biometric traits to filter, generate soft biometric keys. This randomness leads to variations in the number of decryption attempts and biometric recognitions, resulting in varying total authentication times. So we analyzed the results obtained from multiple experiments and got the shortest time, the longest time and the average time for comparison. The results for face and fingerprint recognition are shown in Tables 5 and 6 respectively, where T_{face} and $T_{fingerprint}$ respectively represents the total time of face and fingerprint authentication not using soft biometric encryption&decryption. Therefore, Using soft biometric filtering, encryption, and decryption greatly reduces the total authentication time for fingerprint authentication. However, for face authentication, it may slightly increase the authentication time due to differing efficiencies of the recognition algorithms used.

Comparison of Authentication Time Using and Not Using Soft Biometric Encryption&Decryption When Using Part of the 552 Public Dataset Users as the Experimental Database. The trend graphs obtained from multiple experiments show that as the size of the database increases exponentially, the authentication time for face authentication without soft biometric encryption&decryption does not increase significantly, while the increase in authentication time using soft biometric encryption&decryption gradually becomes slower. The trend graph of face authentication obtained is shown in Fig. 8, and the trend graph of fingerprint authentication obtained is shown in Fig. 9. For fingerprint authentication, using soft biometric encryption&decryption significantly reduces the authentication time compared to not using it. However, it is important to note that the results may vary when using public datasets compared to real datasets, as the quality of face and fingerprint images can affect the authentication time.

6 Conclusion

In this paper, the security requirements of user authentication were considered with the development of the 5G network and the increase of access equipments. We focused on the privacy protection in the biometric authentication and propose an authentication scheme based on soft biometric traits in the 5G cloud-fog hybrid environment. When the biometric authentication was performed, we used the key generated by the soft biometric traits to protect the user's biological characteristics. Because the soft biometric traits do not expose human's privacy information, this scheme can play a role in protecting the privacy of the users during transmission. We also formalized the proposed scheme by using Tamarin. The results show that our scheme is secure and can protect the biological characteristics of the users successfully during transmission in the authentication process. In the future, we will further consider how to ensure the efficiency and security of authentication in the scenario of group authentication, and consider using more soft biometrics in pratical application.

References

1. Ailisto, H., Vildjiounaite, E., Lindholm, M., Mäkelä, S.M., Peltola, J.: Soft biometrics-combining body weight and fat measurements with fingerprint biometrics. Pattern Recognit. Lett. **27**(5), 325–334 (2006)
2. Ali, M.M., Mahale, V.H., Yannawar, P., Gaikwad, A.: Overview of fingerprint recognition system. In: 2016 International Conference on Electrical, Electronics, and Optimization Techniques (ICEEOT), pp. 1334–1338. IEEE (2016)

3. Ali, Z., Hossain, M.S., Muhammad, G., Ullah, I., Abachi, H., Alamri, A.: Edge-centric multimodal authentication system using encrypted biometric templates. Futur. Gener. Comput. Syst. **85**, 76–87 (2018)
4. Babaeizadeh, M., Bakhtiari, M., Mohammed, A.M.: Authentication methods in cloud computing: a survey. Res. J. Appl. Sci. Eng. Technol. **9**(8), 655–664 (2015)
5. Basin, D., Cremers, C., Dreier, J., Sasse, R.: Symbolically analyzing security protocols using tamarin. ACM SIGLOG News **4**(4), 19–30 (2017). https://doi.org/10.1145/3157831.3157835
6. Belkhouja, T., Du, X., Mohamed, A., Al-Ali, A.K., Guizani, M.: Biometric-based authentication scheme for implantable medical devices during emergency situations. Futur. Gener. Comput. Syst. **98**, 109–119 (2019). https://doi.org/10.1016/j.future.2019.02.002, http://www.sciencedirect.com/science/article/pii/S0167739X18325792
7. Bertillon, A., McClaughry, R.W.: Signaletic Instructions Including the Theory and Practice of Anthropometrical Identification. Werner Company, Greenville (1896)
8. Bhatnagar, G., JonathanWu, Q.: A novel chaotic encryption framework for securing palmprint data. Procedia Comput. Sci. **10**, 442–449 (2012)
9. Bhatnagar, G., Wu, Q.: Enhancing the transmission security of biometric images using chaotic encryption. Multimed. Syst. **20**(2), 203–214 (2014)
10. Chen, C.K., Lin, C.L., Chiang, C.T., Lin, S.L.: Personalized information encryption using ECG signals with chaotic functions. Inf. Sci. **193**, 125–140 (2012)
11. Dantcheva, A., Velardo, C., D'angelo, A., Dugelay, J.L.: Bag of soft biometrics for person identification. Multimed. Tools Appl. **51**(2), 739–777 (2011)
12. Feng, L.: Speaker Recognition. Ph.D. thesis, September 2004
13. Fu, Y., Yan, Z., Li, H., Xin, X.L., Cao, J.: A secure SDN based multi-rans architecture for future 5G networks. Comput. Secur. **70**, 648–662 (2017)
14. Fu, Y., Yuan, X., Wang, K., Yan, Z., Li, H.: A security formal model for multiple channels communication. In: Proceedings of the Proceedings of Smart World Congress 2019 (2019)
15. Jain, A.K., Dass, S.C., Nandakumar, K.: Soft biometric traits for personal recognition systems. In: Zhang, D., Jain, A.K. (eds.) ICBA 2004. LNCS, vol. 3072, pp. 731–738. Springer, Heidelberg (2004). https://doi.org/10.1007/978-3-540-25948-0_99
16. Khan, M.K., Zhang, J., Alghathbar, K.: Challenge-response-based biometric image scrambling for secure personal identification. Futur. Gener. Comput. Syst. **27**(4), 411–418 (2011)
17. Kinnunen, T., Li, H.: An overview of text-independent speaker recognition: from features to supervectors. Speech Commun. **52**(1), 12–40 (2010)
18. Lamacchia, B., Lauter, K., Mityagin, A.: Stronger security of authenticated key exchange. IACR Cryptology ePrint Archive 2006, p. 73, January 2006
19. Lyle, J.R., Miller, P.E., Pundlik, S.J., Woodard, D.L.: Soft biometric classification using periocular region features. In: 2010 Fourth IEEE International Conference on Biometrics: Theory, Applications and Systems (BTAS), pp. 1–7, September 2010. https://doi.org/10.1109/BTAS.2010.5634537
20. Mehta, G., Dutta, M.K., Kim, P.S.: A secure encryption method for biometric templates based on chaotic theory. In: Gavrilova, M.L., Tan, C.J.K. (eds.) Transactions on Computational Science XXVII. LNCS, vol. 9570, pp. 120–140. Springer, Heidelberg (2016). https://doi.org/10.1007/978-3-662-50412-3_8
21. Niinuma, K., Park, U., Jain, A.K.: Soft biometric traits for continuous user authentication. IEEE Trans. Inf. Forensics Secur. **5**(4), 771–780 (2010)

22. Nixon, M.S.: A step beyond: advances in gait and 'soft' biometrics. Biom. Technol. Today **2016**(10), 9–11 (2016). https://doi.org/10.1016/S0969-4765(16)30158-8, http://www.sciencedirect.com/science/article/pii/S0969476516301588

23. Nixon, M.S., Correia, P.L., Nasrollahi, K., Moeslund, T.B., Hadid, A., Tistarelli, M.: On soft biometrics. Pattern Recognit. Lett. **68**, 218–230 (2015). https://doi.org/10.1016/j.patrec.2015.08.006, http://www.sciencedirect.com/science/article/pii/S0167865515002615, special Issue on Soft Biometrics

24. Ogbanufe, O., Kim, D.J.: Comparing fingerprint-based biometrics authentication versus traditional authentication methods for e-payment. Decis. Support Syst. **106**, 1–14 (2018). https://doi.org/10.1016/j.dss.2017.11.003, http://www.sciencedirect.com/science/article/pii/S0167923617302154

25. Padma, P., Srinivasan, S.: A survey on biometric based authentication in cloud computing. In: 2016 International Conference on Inventive Computation Technologies (ICICT), vol. 1, pp. 1–5 (2016). https://doi.org/10.1109/INVENTIVE.2016.7823273

26. Sabhanayagam, T., Venkatesan, V.P., Senthamaraikannan, K.: A comprehensive survey on various biometric systems. Int. J. Appl. Eng. Res. **13**(5), 2276–2297 (2018)

27. Schmidt, E.: Conversation with eric schmidt hosted by danny sullivan. In: Search Engine Strategies Conference (2006)

28. Shahzadi, R., et al.: Three tier fog networks: enabling IoT/5G for latency sensitive applications. China Commun. **16**(3), 1–11 (2019)

29. Sharma, V., Bansal, P.: A review on speaker recognition approaches and challenges. Int. J. Eng. Res. Technol. (IJERT) **2**(5), 1581–1588 (2013)

30. Singh, M., Singh, R., Ross, A.: A comprehensive overview of biometric fusion. Inf. Fusion **52**, 187–205 (2019). https://doi.org/10.1016/j.inffus.2018.12.003, http://www.sciencedirect.com/science/article/pii/S156625351830839X

31. Tome, P., Fierrez, J., Vera-Rodriguez, R., Nixon, M.S.: Soft biometrics and their application in person recognition at a distance. IEEE Trans. Inf. Forensics Secur. **9**(3), 464–475 (2014). https://doi.org/10.1109/TIFS.2014.2299975

32. Wayman, J.: Large-scale civilian biometric systems-issues and feasibility. In: Proceedings of Card Tech/Secur Tech ID, vol. 732 (1997)

33. Yang, L., Yang, G., Yin, Y., Xi, X.: Exploring soft biometric trait with finger vein recognition. Neurocomputing **135**, 218–228 (2014). https://doi.org/10.1016/j.neucom.2013.12.029, http://www.sciencedirect.com/science/article/pii/S0925231214000460

34. Yang, P., Zhang, N., Bi, Y., Yu, L., Shen, X.S.: Catalyzing cloud-fog interoperation in 5G wireless networks: an SDN approach. IEEE Network **31**(5), 14–20 (2017). https://doi.org/10.1109/MNET.2017.1600078

35. Yi, S., Li, C., Li, Q.: A survey of fog computing: concepts, applications and issues. In: Proceedings of the 2015 Workshop on Mobile Big Data, pp. 37–42 (2015)

36. Zhang, C., Zhu, L., Xu, C.: PTBI: an efficient privacy-preserving biometric identification based on perturbed term in the cloud. Inf. Sci. **409–410**, 56–67 (2017). https://doi.org/10.1016/j.ins.2017.05.006, http://www.sciencedirect.com/science/article/pii/S0020025516313639

37. Zhu, H., Wei, Q., Yang, X., Lu, R., Li, H.: Efficient and privacy-preserving online fingerprint authentication scheme over outsourced data. IEEE Trans. Cloud Comput. 1 (2018). https://doi.org/10.1109/TCC.2018.2866405

Obfuscation Padding Schemes that Minimize Rényi Min-Entropy for Privacy

Sebastian Simon, Cezara Petrui, Carlos Pinzón[✉], and Catuscia Palamidessi

Inria Saclay, France, Laboratoire d'Informatique de l'École Polytechnique (LIX), Palaiseau, France
carlos.pinzon@lix.polytechnique.fr

Abstract. Consider a set of users, each of which is choosing and downloading one file out of a central pool of public files, and an attacker that observes the download size for each user to identify the choice of each user. This paper studies the problem of padding the files to obfuscate the exact file sizes and minimize the expected accuracy of the attacker, without exceeding some given padding constraints. We derive the algorithm that finds the optimal padding scheme, prove its correctness, and compare it with an existing solution that uses a similar but different attack model. We also discuss how the two solutions are related in terms of private information leakage.

Keywords: obfuscation · privacy · padding · Rényi min-entropy

1 Introduction

Consider a set of users, each of which is choosing and downloading one file out of a central pool of public files, and an attacker that observes the download size for each user and is willing to identify the choice of each user. The files are public, but the choices are private. The objective is to pad the files with some small overhead to obfuscate the information gained by the attacker and reduce his chances of discovering the choices of the users. This paper studies the problem of minimizing the expected accuracy of the attacker by padding the files without exceeding some given padding constraints.

On one extreme, if the files are not padded at all, the attacker might easily map the observed download sizes with the original files; e.g., if there is just one file of size 10.32 MB and the attacker observes that the network traffic of some user corresponds to a file of size 10.32 MB, he will immediately know what file was chosen. This can be prevented by padding several files to common sizes to obfuscate the information gained by the attacker. On the other extreme, if all files are padded to a common size, this common size should be large enough to

S. Simon and C. Petrui—Authors contributed equally.

cover the largest file in the set, and, as a consequence, many small files will be padded excessively, increasing the bandwidth use. The ideal solution lies between these two extreme cases. For this reason, this paper considers the problem of maximizing privacy while respecting some flexible padding constraints, like, for example, that no file can increase its size more than 10%.

The attacker we consider makes just one attempt to re-identify the file, and to maximize his chances, he will of course guess a file that has the maximum posterior probability given the observed (obfuscated) size. This model of attack is known in literature as *one-try attack* [14], and it has been characterized in information-theoretic terms using *Rényi min-entropy*. More specifically, entropy in general represents the (lack of) information content of a discrete probability distribution, and Rényi min-entropy is a form of entropy that emphasizes the highest probability value. The prior and posterior entropies represent the probabilistic knowledge of the attacker before and after he observes the obfuscated size, respectively. In particular, Rényi posterior min-entropy is related to *hypothesis testing* and, as a measure, it closely corresponds to the *Bayes error*. The difference between the prior and posterior entropies represents how much the knowledge of the attacker (and hence his probability of success) increases thanks to the observation, and it is, therefore, a measure of the efficiency of the padding scheme. In literature this difference is known as Rényi min-entropy *leakage*.

The padding problem considered in this paper might also apply to equivalent scenarios in which an attacker exploits time side-channel information. For illustration, consider an intelligence service that is surveiling people entering and exiting a building. They can use the time each user took inside to infer the type of service he received, e.g., whether he was at the bank, shopping, or at the cinema in the mall. In this case, the users can waste some time inside the building on purpose to confuse the observer. Equivalently, a server can delay its responses in a planned manner to prevent an attacker from inferring the chosen type of request. More generally, an algorithm can sleep on purpose to prevent leaking information about the input, as exploited by timing attacks [13,15].

1.1 Contributions

- We propose two algorithms that derive the optimal padding schemes, one for the deterministic case, and one for the randomized case (PRP and POP, defined in Sect. 2).
- We prove the correctness of the algorithms and test the implementations against brute-force solutions using small synthetic datasets.
- Likewise, we compare our algorithms with an existing solution [11] that uses an attack model based on Shannon entropy, and discuss how the two approaches are related in terms of the type of private information leakage that each attacker represents.
- The code is publicly available at [10]. It includes not only the algorithms we propose, but also the reimplementation of the algorithms of [11] to support flexible padding constraints, multiple files having the same size, and sparse matrix representations.

1.2 Related Work

The model of attacker we use has been well investigated in the field of *Quantitative Information Flow* (QIF), which is a branch of security aimed at studying inference attacks, namely attackers that try to infer the value of the secret from related observations. The QIF theory actually formalizes a variety of models, each of them characterized by parameters that represent the capabilities and the goal of the attacker. For a detailed coverage of the topic we refer to [1].

This paper is strongly related with the work of Reed and Reiter [11], in which the authors consider the same problem with a different attack model, based on Shannon entropy, and more specifically, on measuring the leakage in terms of Shannon mutual information. Shannon mutual information is a well known notion that has been shown to be very useful in the several scientific fields. In security and privacy, however, it does not seem the right notion for modeling the attacker. Indeed, its operational interpretation corresponds to an attacker that can try to guess the exact secret by making an unbound number of attempts, and his objective is to minimize the expected number of attempts before he identifies it correctly. This seems a less natural model of attacker than those of QIF (and hence than the one we use, based on Rényi min-entropy), and it also sometimes leads to conclusions that are contrary to common sense. For a detailed discussion about this issue, refer to [14].

Reed and Reiter [11] propose three padding algorithms, called PrpSh, PopSh and PwoD (padding without a distribution), for finding padding schemes that minimize Shannon leakage under different bandwidth constraints. These algorithms do not support, however, multiple files having the same size nor flexible padding constraints as defined in this paper. We re-implemented their algorithms with these additional details before comparing them with our proposed solutions, and we explained in terms of attack models and information leakage the core difference between them.

In [4] they consider the BREACH/CRIME [7] security attack in which the attacker observes sizes and can also control a malicious script that runs in the browser of the victim. By exploiting the greedy mechanism of the Huffman encoder in the compression stage of the cookies, the attacker is able to use repeatedly the size information to discover the cookie secret and impersonate the victim. As they show, random gaussian padding can be used and is better than uniform padding to reduce the attacker's probability of success from 1.0 to 0.0026. Although this paper is more related with security than privacy, it shows how important padding can be to obfuscate information.

Lastly, one of the main conclusions in [16] is that the optimal way to reduce information obtained by an attacker that monitors traffic is to modify the traffic patterns so that they are confused with other patterns. We draw a similar conclusion formally in our problem (Proposition 1), proving that it is optimal to pad messages to reach the sizes other existing files.

2   Problem Formalization

The collection of public files is denoted as $E = \{e_1, e_2, \ldots, e_n\}$, where E is sorted non-decreasingly by the sizes $|e_i| \in \mathbb{N}$. For the sake of generality, we allow different files to have the same size, hence the set of file sizes $S \overset{\text{def}}{=} \{|e| \, | \, e \in E\}$ has $m \leq n$ unique elements, which we enumerate in increasing order as $S = \{s_1, s_2, \ldots, s_m\}$.

A *padding function* or padding scheme is a function $f : E \to \mathbb{N}$ respecting $f(e_i) \geq |e_i|$ that tells to what size each file should be padded. The padding constraints are expressed with the proposition $\forall i, \, f(e_i) \in [|e_i|, b_i]$, where each $[|e_i|, b_i] = \{|e_i|, |e_i| + 1, \ldots, b_i\}$ is an integer interval.

The sequence of users with their respective choices is modelled as a sequence of i.i.d. samples coming from the marginal distribution of the files. File e_i is chosen with frequency $p_i \in [0, 1]$, where $\sum_{i=1}^n p_i = 1$. We let X be a random variable satisfying $\mathbb{P}(X=e_i) \overset{\text{def}}{=} p_i$, thus, a sequence of users with choices can be represented as a sequence of i.i.d. choices following the distribution of X.

The attacker will predict, upon seeing a download of size $z \in \text{Im}(f)$ (where the image $\text{Im}(f) \overset{\text{def}}{=} \{z \in \mathbb{N} \mid \mathbb{P}(f(X)=z) > 0\}$ denotes the set of possible outputs of f), that the secret value of X is the file e_i that maximizes $\mathbb{P}(f(e_i)=z)$. To do this, he uses the public information he has access to and the information he can infer. The files and their sizes before padding are public, and he can determine the padding scheme by requesting each of the files himself, possibly multiple times in case of a randomized padding scheme. In addition, considering the worst-case scenario, we assume that he knows or has estimated the frequencies p_i with which files are chosen on average. With this information, the attacker can always find a file e_i that maximizes $\mathbb{P}(f(e_i)=z)$ for the observed z, and his expected probability of success is therefore

$$\sum_{z \in \text{Im}(f)} \max_{i \in [1..n]} \mathbb{P}(X = e_i \wedge f(X)=z) = \sum_{z \in \text{Im}(f)} \max_{i \in [1..n]} p_i \cdot \mathbb{P}(f(e_i) = z). \quad (2.1)$$

The objective is to find a padding function $f : E \to \mathbb{N}$ that minimizes the accuracy of the attacker while respecting the given padding constraints. In addition, two scenarios are considered separately: *per-object-padding* (POP) refers to the case when f is deterministic, hence the files are padded once and forever; *per-request-padding* (PRP) refers to the case when the padding is done on demand and f is probabilistic.

2.1   Presentation in Terms of Privacy Leakage

The objective of minimizing the attacker accuracy can equivalently be presented in terms of minimizing privacy leakage. There are several definitions for leakage $\mathbb{I}(|X|, f(X))$ of a padding function $f : E \to \mathbb{N}$. Particularly, Rényi min-entropy leakage [14], which we call *Rényi leakage* in this paper, is defined using Rényi min-entropy $\mathbb{H}_\infty$ as follows:

$$\mathbb{I}_\infty(f) \overset{\text{def}}{=} \mathbb{I}_\infty(|X|, f(X)) = \mathbb{H}_\infty(|X|) - \mathbb{H}_\infty(|X| \mid f(X)), \quad (2.2)$$

$$\mathbb{H}_\infty(|X|) = -\log_2 \max_{z \in \mathrm{Im}(f)} \mathbb{P}(|X|=z), \tag{2.3}$$

$$\mathbb{H}_\infty(|X| \mid f(X)) = -\log_2 \sum_{z \in \mathrm{Im}(f)} \max_{i \in [1..n]} (p_i \cdot \mathbb{P}(f(e_i) = z)). \tag{2.4}$$

The importance of Rényi leakage in more general contexts can be found in [9] and [14]. Basically, Rényi leakage is a special case ($\alpha = \infty$) of a family of leakages $\mathbb{I}_\alpha$ based on α-Rényi entropy $\mathbb{H}_\alpha$. Since Rényi-min entropy $\mathbb{H}_\infty(|X|)$ is constant in regard to the padding-scheme, minimizing Eq. (2.2) is equivalent to maximizing Eq. (2.4), which is in turn equivalent to minimizing Eq. (2.1). Therefore, Rényi leakage is in direct one-to-one correspondence with the probability of success of the attacker.

Another important case ($\alpha = 1$) is Shannon leakage, which is given by: $\mathbb{I}(|X|, f(X)) = \sum_{i,z} p_i \, \mathbb{P}(f(e_i)=z) \log_2 \frac{\mathbb{P}(f(e_i)=z)}{\mathbb{P}(f(X)=z)}$. With some effort, this leakage can also be interpreted in terms of an attacker that we call Shannon attacker. The Shannon attacker is assumed to have access to an oracle that answers queries of the type "is the file in *this set of files*?" for each user, and his objective is to find the right files using the minimal number of queries, as in a 20Q game. Although the oracle assumption makes the Shannon attacker unrealistic, defenses against him are useful against the Rényi attacker of this paper because, intuitively, the more queries the Shannon attacker needs, the harder it is to guess the correct file in a single try.

For this particular application, the direct pragmatic connection between Rényi leakage and a simple adversary success makes it more appealing than the Shannon attacker. The same argument is used in [3], whose privacy measure is closely related with ours. More generally in the privacy community, leakage functions are better described in terms of their associated attacker rather than their information theoretic properties [2,12].

2.2   Why Not Differential Privacy?

Differential privacy [5], is one of the most prevalent formalizations of privacy. For this particular problem, a padding scheme f satisfies ϵ-differential privacy if and only if for all input files $e_i, e_j \in E$ and all output sizes $z \in \mathrm{Im}(f)$, we have $\mathbb{P}(f(e_1) = z) \le \exp(\epsilon) \, \mathbb{P}(f(e_2) = z)$.

This notion of privacy represents an attacker whose success function is given by how much more likely one input file is *with respect to another one* for a given observation. However, this is excessively strong for the problem under consideration. Indeed, as Theorem 1 shows, differential privacy can only be achieved at the total detriment of bandwidth use.

Theorem 1. *For any $\epsilon > 0$, the padding scheme that satisfies ϵ-differential privacy and minimizes bandwidth is the one that pads all input files to the size of the largest one.*

Proof. Fix $\epsilon > 0$ and let $e_j \stackrel{\text{def}}{=} \arg\max_{e_i \in E} |e_i|$ be the largest file in E. For all sizes $z < |e_j|$, we have $\mathbb{P}(f(e_j) = z) = 0$ because e_j can not be padded to smaller sizes than $|e_j|$. Moreover, the differential privacy constraint forces every other file $e_i \neq e_j$ to satisfy $\mathbb{P}(f(e_i) = z) \leq \exp(\epsilon)\mathbb{P}(f(e_j) = z) = 0$ whenever $z < |e_j|$. In other words, all files must be padded to sizes at least as large as $|e_j|$, i.e. $\mathbb{P}(f(X) \geq |e_j|) = 1$. Among all the mappings f that have this property, the one that minimizes bandwidth is the one that pads all files exactly to the largest file size $|e_j|$, and it satisfies ϵ differential privacy trivially because it is a constant function.

Theorem 1 is the reason why we exclude differential privacy from the analysis and focus on the privacy notions discussed in the previous section. This theorem is a direct consequence of the inevitable fact that padding can only enlarge files and not reduce their sizes. Apart from putting in evidence the abusive overhead required by differential privacy, this theorem also shows that its parameter ϵ is irrelevant as a measure of privacy for the problem under consideration, making it inappropriate.

2.3 Simplification of the Output Set

We conclude this section by proving that optimal padding functions always map to sizes in S. This is a key-fact for the derivation of the algorithms and their proofs. Intuitively, if a set of files can be padded to a common certain size z, but can also be padded to $z - 1$, we can pad them to $z - 1$ and win some bandwidth without leaking any additional information. This forces the optimal padding functions to always pad to the sizes z for which it is not possible to pad to $z - 1$ without sacrificing privacy, which are precisely the sizes in S. The same holds true for padding schemes that minimize Shannon leakage, as shown in [11].

Proposition 1. *For any padding-scheme $f : E \to \mathbb{N}$, there exists a padding-scheme $f^* : E \to S$ such that $\mathbb{I}(f^*) \leq \mathbb{I}(f)$. Moreover, $\mathbb{P}(f^*(X) \leq f(X)) = 1$, hence f^* uses less padding (bandwidth) than f.*

Proof. Define f^* as the composition $f^* \stackrel{\text{def}}{=} g \circ f$, where $g(z) = \max\{s \in S : s \leq z\}$, that is, $f^*(X) = g(f(X))$. The function g is defined only for $z \geq \min S$ and f^* is well-defined because the padding constraints force $\mathbb{P}(f(X) \geq \min S) \leq \mathbb{P}(f(X) \geq |X|) = 1$. By definition, $g(z) \leq z$, thus $\mathbb{P}(f^*(X) \leq f(X)) = 1$. Let us now show, regarding privacy leakage, that $\mathbb{I}(f^*) \leq \mathbb{I}(f)$. Let I_{xs}^* denote $\mathbb{P}(X{=}x \wedge f^*(X){=}s)$ and I_{xz} denote $\mathbb{P}(X{=}x \wedge f(X){=}z)$. We will show that the accuracy of the attacker (Eq. 2.1) is smaller or equal for f^* than for f. This can be expressed as $\sum_s \max_x I_{xs}^* \leq \sum_s \sum_{z:g(z)=s} \max_x I_{xz}$. On the left and right-hand sides, we have summations on $s \in S$, so it suffices to prove that this inequality holds for each fixed s. At each $s \in S$, since $I_{xs}^* = \sum_{z:g(z)=s} I_{xz}$, the inequality becomes $\max_x \sum_{z:g(z)=s} I_{xz} \leq \sum_{z:g(z)=s} \max_x I_{xz}$, which is necessarily true. Indeed, letting $x^{(s)} \stackrel{\text{def}}{=} \arg\max_x \sum_{z:g(z)=s} I_{xz}$ for the left-hand side, we have for each z with $g(z) = s$ that $I_{x^{(s)}z} \leq \max_x I_{xz}$. $\square$

Proposition 1 can be seen as an instance of the Data Processing Inequality, which can be found as Theorem 8 of [6], or more generally for privacy contexts in [8].

Corollary 1. *A padding function that has minimal leakage must pad each file to the size of another file in the initial set.*

Having Corollary 1 in mind, the padding scheme f can be represented as an obfuscation channel matrix P where $p_{ij} = \mathbb{P}(f(e_i)=s_j)$, in which case, the problem can be specified as shown below, and the attacker accuracy becomes

$$\sum_j \max_{i\in[1..n]} p_i \cdot p_{ij}. \tag{2.5}$$

Problem input: (1) A set E of n files $\{e_i \,|\, i \in [1..n]\}$ with frequencies p_i, sorted sizes $|e_i|$ and set of unique sizes $S = \{s_1, ..., s_m\}$. (2) Padding constraints of the form $\forall i,\ s_{l_i} \leq f(e_i) \leq s_{r_i}$, parametrized with pairs of indices $l_i, r_i \in [1..m]$.

Desired output: A padding function $f : E \to S$ in the form of a channel matrix $p_{ij} = \mathbb{P}(f(e_i)=s_j)$ that minimizes Rényi leakage $\mathbb{I}_\infty(f)$ or equivalently Eq. (2.5). Depending on the problem variant, f must be deterministic (POP) or randomized (PRP).

3   Algorithms

In this section, we derive the algorithms `PopRe` and `PrpRe` that minimize the Rényi leakage (2.2) for the POP and PRP cases respectively. They contrast those for Shannon mutual information minimization found in the paper [11], denoted here as `PopSh` and `PrpSh`. The complexities of these algorithms are summarized in Table 1.

Table 1. Complexities, where $\bar{b} \stackrel{\text{def}}{=} (1/n) \sum_{i=1}^n r_i - l_i + 1$ is the matrix average band size. For practical reference, with reasonable padding constraints, if the files are diverse with a large and spread spectrum of sizes, one expects $\bar{b} \ll m \approx n$.

Algorithm	Minimizes	WC Runtime complexity	Memory
PopRe	Rényi leakage	$O(n^2 \bar{b})$	$n\bar{b}$
PrpRe, PrpReBa	Rényi leakage	$O(n \bar{b})$	$n\bar{b}$
PopSh	Shannon leakage	$O(n \bar{b})$	$n\bar{b}$
PrpSh	Shannon leakage	$O(\text{ITERS} \cdot n\, m)$	$n\, m$

Algorithm `PrpSh` is an approximation algorithm and has a runtime complexity that depends on the degree of accuracy imposed by the user and the limit number of iterations ITERS allowed. Also, the complexities of the dynamic programming algorithms correspond to the theoretical worst-case and might overestimate the actual implementations. For instance, although PopRe has two parameters varying in $[1..n]$, not all combinations need to be calculated in a top-down implementation.

3.1 Per-Object-Padding Scenario, PopRe

In this section we develop the algorithm that minimizes Rényi leakage in the POP variation, in which the matrix P is constrained to $p_{ij} \in \{0, 1\}$. Before describing the algorithm, we will prove Remark 1, which will be used as the main update of the entries of the channel-matrix.

Remark 1. Let f be a Rényi optimal padding-scheme and e_i be the file with the highest associated frequency p_i, and assume that $p_{ij} = 1$ for some $j \in [1..m]$. Then there exists a padding-scheme f^* with the same Rényi leakage such that $p_{kj} = 1$ for all $k \in [1..n]$ such that $j \in [l_k..r_k]$.

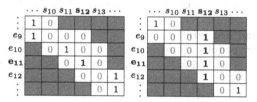

Fig. 1. Remark 1: if the file with maximal frequency is e_{11} and the left matrix (f) is optimal, the right one (f^*) must be as well.

Proof. We consider the padding-scheme f to be represented as the channel-matrix between the secrets and the observables. When we want to minimize (2.5) we sum over each column of the matrix P. In particular, on the column j we have $\max_{a \in [1..n]}(p_a \cdot p_{aj}) = p_i$ since p_i is the highest frequency among the frequencies of the files and $p_{ij} = 1$. Now, let us consider the padding-scheme f^* whose matrix P^*, consists on moving every 1 that we can to column j:

$$p_{ab}^* = \begin{cases} p_{ab} & \text{if } b \neq j \text{ and } a \in [1..n] \text{ such that } j \notin [l_a..r_a] \\ 1 & \text{if } b = j \text{ and } a \in [1..n] \text{ such that } j \in [l_a..r_a] \\ 0 & \text{otherwise} \end{cases}$$

On the column j of the matrix P^* we will still have $\max_{a \in [1..n]}(p_a \cdot p_{aj}^*) = p_i$ because the padding-scheme f^* preserves the maximum on column j. Moreover, on the rest of the columns, the maximum either decreases or stays the same since we created more entries $p_{ab}^* = 0$, which means that the product $p_a \cdot p_{ab}^* = 0$. However, we chose f to be the Rényi optimal padding-scheme and with the remarks above, f and f^* give the same leakage.   □

Figure 1 depicts an example of a sub-matrix of P as described in Remark 1. In the figure, we have exactly one entry equal to 1 in each line because the channel-matrix is stochastic, and we are in the POP case. Additionally, the quantity in (2.5) represents the sum of the maximum over columns where each 1 counts for the frequency of the file. Then, the update does not increase the (2.5) because the 1 with maximal frequency dominates its column, and moving all possible 1's above or below it does not increase Rényi leakage.

Algorithm 1. Per-object-padding pseudocode. This implementation uses recursion both for computation and reconstruction.

```
procedure RENYI POP                                        ▷ Main function
    MEMO ← {}                                              ▷ Empty map
    p_ij ← 0                                               ▷ A matrix p full of zeros
    renyi ← RECONSTRUCT(0, n)
    return (p, renyi)                          ▷ Output matrix p and its renyi leakage
end procedure
procedure RECONSTRUCT(a, b)
    (renyi, k, a*, b*) ← f(a, b)
    for j = a*..b* do p_jk ← 1 end for
    if a < a* then RECONSTRUCT(a, a*) end if
    if b* < b then RECONSTRUCT(b*, b) end if
    return renyi
end procedure
procedure f(a, b)
    if (a, b) ∈ MEMO then return MEMO[(a, b)] end if
    if a = b then return (0, ∞, a, b) end if
    best ← (∞, ∞, ∞, ∞)
    i_max ← arg max_{i=a..b} p_i
    for k = l_{i_max}..r_{i_max} do
        j_min, j_max ← range of files e_{j_min}..e_{j_max} that can be padded to size s_k
        a* ← max(a, j_min)
        b* ← min(b, j_max)
        renyi ← f(a, a*)[0] + p_{i_max} + f(b*, b)[0]   ▷ Index [0] is the renyi component
        this ← (renyi, k, a*, b*)
        best ← min(best, this)                  ▷ Lexicographic (compares first by renyi)
    end for
    (renyi, k, a*, b*) ← best                               ▷ Unpack tuple
    MEMO[(a, b)] ← (renyi, k, a*, b*)
    return (renyi, k, a*, b*)
end procedure
```

Using Remark 1 we can divide the padding problem into sub-problems that minimize (2.5) and leverage dynamic programming: $\forall a \leq b \in [1..n]$, we define

$$D[a][b] = \min_{P \text{ channel matrix}} \sum_{j \in [1..m]} \max_{i \in [a+1..b]} (p_i \cdot p_{ij}),$$

i.e. $D[a][b]$ gives the minimal leakage for the sub-problem that pads files from e_{a+1} to e_b, under the general constraints.

By convention, we consider $D[i][i] = 0$, which will be the base case. To write the recurrence formula, we need to take the file $e_{i_{max}}$ with maximum frequency $p_{i_{max}}, i_{max} \in [a+1, b]$. We go through every size index $k \in [1..m]$ such that $e_{i_{max}}$ can be padded to the size of s_k, and we update the channel-matrix according to Remark 1, i.e. add 1's on k-th column if we can (taking into consideration the padding constraints) and complete the lines that have a fixed 1 with 0's on the remaining entries. Then, we apply the recurrence on the rows which are not updated, i.e. from a to $a^* \overset{\text{def}}{=} \max(a, \max_{i \in [1..n]}\{i|r_i < k\})$, and, respectively, from $b^* \overset{\text{def}}{=} \min(k, b)$ to b. Hence,

$$D[a][b] = p_{i_{\max}} + \min_{k \in [l_{i_{\max}}..r_{i_{\max}}]} (D[a][a^*] + D[b^*][b])$$

After applying the dynamic algorithm program with the aforementioned recurrence, we get the minimization of (2.5) in $D[0][n]$, from which we can compute the minimal Rényi leakage. If we want to recover the channel-matrix itself, in $D[a][b]$ we pass on the index k for which the maximum happens, as an argument. In case of a tie, we choose the smallest index $k \in \{1, \ldots, n\}$ in order to reduce average padding. Hence, we know in each sub-interval $[a, b]$ what we pad everything to, so the information is enough to recover the channel matrix. A pseudocode summarizing all the logic is shown in Algorithm 1. A concrete optimized implementation can be found in [10].

In Fig. 2 we depict the channel-matrix of the files with sizes $S = \{1000, 1050, 1100,$ $1110, 1120, 1140\}$ and associated frequencies $\{22\%, 5\%, 23\%,$ $12\%, 18\%, 20\%\}$. As shown in the visual representation of the padding-scheme in the right, we observe that, for both of the existing padded sizes, there are

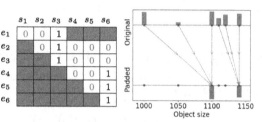

	s_1	s_2	s_3	s_4	s_5	s_6
e_1	0	0	1			
e_2		0	1	0	0	0
e_3			1	0	0	0
e_4				0	0	1
e_5					0	1
e_6						1

Fig. 2. PopRe on a dataset of 6 files.

multiple files that are padded to the same element, making them indistinguishable for an attacker. Moreover, the blue bars on the graph indicate the frequencies of the files, and the red bars, the maximum frequency among the frequencies of the files padded to each specific size. The red bars are effectively highlighting the terms of the sum (2.5).

3.2   Per-Request-Padding Scenario, PrpRe

In this section, we treat the case of Per-Request-Padding and provide an algorithm for finding the probabilistic channel-matrix P which minimizes the Rényi leakage. We will look at the joint distribution matrix I with entries $I_{ij} = p_i \cdot p_{ij}, \forall i \leq n, j \leq m$, for which $\sum_{j=1}^{m} I_{ij} = p_1$ for each $i \in [1..n]$.

We proceed by finding iteratively, for each of the m columns, starting from the last one, the Rényi optimal manner of setting the entries of I given the padding constraints. Furthermore, we define the *optimal distribution of p_i across the i-th row*, $1 \leq i \leq n$ to be the way we fill in the entries $p_{i1}, \ldots, p_{im}$ such as to obtain the minimum sum of the type (2.5) and preserve the relation $p_{i1} + \ldots + p_{im} = p_i$.

The proof of our algorithm requires us to consider sub-problems in which the sequence $(p_i)_{1 \leq i \leq n}$ is updated at each step of the algorithm, thus being different from the initial set of frequencies associated to each file. Hence, we rewrite the problem as a more general one in terms of a *budget* sequence $(b_i)_{1 \le i \le n}$ of length n (initialized as $(p_i)_{1 \le i \le n}$), which dictates the remaining value to be distributed across each row i, for $i \in [1..n]$. The general problem is "Given a non-negative budget sequence $(b_i)_{i=1}^k$ of length $k \in [1..n]$, find a solution matrix $I_{k \times m}$ that minimizes Eq. (2.5), under the padding constraints for rows $i \in [1..k]$, namely the set $\{[l_1, r_1], \ldots, [l_k, r_k]\}$ and $\sum_{j=1}^m I_{ij} = b_i$".

We will design the algorithm to solve the general problem recursively by returning the matrix I for the budget sequence $\{p_1, \ldots, p_n\}$ with n terms. The recurrence relationship can be described using the following observation that is used when creating the probabilistic channel-matrix for the padding-scheme f:

Remark 2. The solution $I_{k \times m}$ for a given $(b_i)_{i=1}^k$ that minimizes Rényi leakage satisfies the recurrence relationship

$$
I_{ij} = \begin{cases} b_i & \text{if } j = m \text{ and } i \in [1..k], |e_i| = s_m \\ b_i - b_i' & \text{if } j = m \text{ and } i \in [1..k-1], |e_i| \ne s_m, \\ & \qquad m \in [l_i..r_i] \\ I_{ij}' & \text{otherwise} \end{cases}
$$

where $I_{(k-t) \times (m-1)}'$ is the solution to the same minimization problem for the sequence $(b_i')_{i=1}^{k-t}$ of length $k - t$, $t =$ number of files from E which can be padded to s_m, such that for any $i \in [1..k-t]$, it is defined as:

$$
b_i' = \begin{cases} \max(b_i - b_{t_{\max}}, 0) & \text{if } m \in [l_i..r_i] \text{ and} \\ & \qquad b_{t_{\max}} = \max\{b_i | |e_i| = s_m\} \\ b_i & \text{otherwise} \end{cases}
$$

Proof. If there are no files among $\{e_1, \ldots, e_k\}$ which can be padded to s_m, we set $t = 0$ and solve the minimization problem for the same budget sequence and for the set of $m - 1$ sizes $\{s_1, \ldots, s_{m-1}\}$.

If there are files that can be padded to s_m, then due to the padding constraints, the element e_i can only be padded to s_m, so the entry I_{im} must necessarily be equal to b_i, for all i such that $|e_i| = s_m$. Let us denote by $T = \{k - t + 1, \ldots, k\}$ the set of indices satisfying $|e_i| = s_m, \forall i \in T$ and $b_{t_{\max}} = \max\{b_i | i \in T\}$. Clearly, for every $i \in T$, $I_{ij} = 0, \forall j \in \{1, \ldots, k-1\}$. On the m-th column of the matrix I, we have $\max_{i \in [1..k]} I_{im} \ge b_{t_{\max}}$.

In order to minimize the sum (2.5) and taking into consideration that the maximum entry on column m is at least $b_{t_{\max}}$, we aim to distribute for every i such that e_i can be padded to s_m and $|e_i| \ne s_m$, a quantity equal to $b_{t_{\max}}$ (or, if $b_i < b_{t_{\max}}$, then we distribute the whole b_i) on the entry I_{im}, so that we preserve the maximum on this last column to be $b_{t_{\max}}$. This way, we can assure that, among the other columns, we'll have to distribute a smaller fraction of b_i, which means that the maximum on each column between 1 and $m - 1$ will decrease, and so will (2.5).

The problem reduces to find the optimal sub-matrix $I_{(k-t) \times (m-1)}'$ to complete the first $k - t$ rows of I, and with the aforementioned remark, we can actually consider I' to be the solution given the updated sequence $(b_i')_{1 \leq i \leq k-t}$ which is defined, for every i such that file e_i that can be padded to s_m, as either 0, if $b_i \leq b_{t_{\max}}$, or as $b_i - b_{t_{\max}}$, if $b_i \geq b_{t_{\max}}$. When we reconstruct the matrix I, on the m-th column we will have the value $I'_{im} + b_{t_{\max}}$ or $I'_{im} + b_i$ (depending on whether b_i is smaller, respectively larger, than $b_{t_{\max}}$).

Now, let us show that, for the sub-matrix I', we have 0's on every entry of the m-th column. By definition, I' must be a Rényi optimal solution for the updated sequence of b_i''s. Using Proposition 1, there exists a Rényi optimal padding-scheme f' which maps $e_i, i \in [1..k-t] \rightarrow \{s_1, \ldots, s_{k-t}\}$, for any set of files $\{e_1, \ldots, e_{k-t}\}$ with the associated frequencies $\{b_1', \ldots, b_{k-t}'\}$. Consequently, for every $i \in [1..k-t], \mathbb{P}(f'(e_i) = s_m) = 0 \Rightarrow I'_{im} = 0.$ □

Algorithm 2. Per-request-padding pseudocode.

---

procedure RENYI PRP

    $\forall i, b_i \leftarrow p_i$ ▷ budget array

    $I \leftarrow$ Joint prob. matrix of zeros

    for j=m, m-1, ..., 1 **do**

        $t_{\max} = \arg\max_{\{i \, | \, |e_i| = s_j\}} b_i$

        if $b_{t_{\max}} > 0$ **then**

            $j_{\min}, j_{\max} \leftarrow$ range of files $e_{j_{\min}}..e_{j_{\max}}$ that can be padded to size s_j

            for $i = j_{\max}, j_{\max} - 1, ..., j_{\min}$ **do**

                $I[i, j] \leftarrow \min(b_{t_{\max}}, b_i)$

                $b_i = b_i - I[i, j]$

            end for

        end if

    end for

    $P \leftarrow$ channel matrix after dividing each row i of I by p_i

    return P

end procedure

Therefore, we have proved that the matrix I can be recursively expressed using the sub-matrices obtained when we update the budget sequence accordingly, at each step decreasing by 1 the number of columns and by at least 1 the number of rows of the matrix returned from the algorithm, until we reduce a problem to finding the Rényi optimal scheme for a budget sequence with a single element. Since we want to minimize (2.5) in the case of n files with frequencies $\{p_1, \ldots, p_n\}$ and the associated set of sizes $\{s_1, \ldots, s_m\}$, we proceed the induction on the number of rows and columns as described in Remark 2 and eventually fill in all the entries of the solution $I_{n \times m}$. The channel-matrix P is then computed as $p_{ij} = I_{ij}/p_i$, and this is the output of PrpRe.

This algorithm is presented in Algorithm 2 in the form of pseudocode, and it is implemented in [10] with some optimizations.

Bandwidth Minimization. Once `PrpRe` has found a channel matrix that minimizes Rényi leakage, it is still possible to use heuristics to search for other channel matrices with the same (minimal) leakage but with less bandwidth use. We call `PrpReBa` to be the algorithm that runs `PrpRe` and the bandwidth reduction heuristics afterwards.

Let the list C of maximums on each column after running `PrpRe`, i.e. $C = \{\max_{i \in [1..n]} I_{ij} | j \in [1..m]\}$, where $C_j = \max_{i \in [1..n]} I_{ij}$ for every $j \in [1..m]$. Define a *move* to be a change in the matrix I performed on two of the entries of the matrix at line i, for some $i \in [1..n]$ such that (I_{ia}, I_{ib}) becomes $(I_{ia} - \alpha, I_{ib} + \alpha)$ while keeping the entries of I positive, i.e. $\alpha \leq I_{ia}$.

Now, we will describe an *update* on the line i, which will consist of a series of *moves* and will return a new matrix I^*. We start with I^* to be the matrix I, but with 0's on the i-th line. Since the sum on row i is equal to p_i, we start with this quantity and go through the columns in order from $j = 1$ to $j = m$. For each column, we set:

$$I_{ij} = \begin{cases} C_j & \text{if } C_j + \sum_{k=1}^{j-1} I_{ik} \leq p_i \\ p_i - \sum_{k=1}^{j-1} I_{ik} & \text{otherwise} \end{cases}$$

4   Experiments and Comparison

Several experiments were carried out for three distinct purposes, namely, (1) to test the correctness of the implementations against brute-force algorithms for small sized problems, (2) to corroborate the direct link between Rényi leakage and the success rate of an attacker and (3) to compare the runtime, bandwidth and leakages of all the algorithms on a public dataset. The code of all the experiments is available in [10].

4.1   Brute-Force Tests for Correctness

To complement and corroborate the theory developed in this paper, all the algorithms were tested against brute-force implementations for small datasets (with at most 10 elements). More precisely, for each randomly generated test case of file sizes and frequencies, we explored (exhaustively) all the POP padding schemes satisfying the constraints, and chose among them, the ones that minimized Rényi leakage, Shannon leakage or bandwidth, with the purpose of comparing them with the solutions returned by our algorithms.

We ran ten thousand experiments (code available in [10]), all corroborating that: among all POP schemes, `PopRe` achieves minimal Rényi leakage, `PopSh` achieves minimal Shannon leakage, and `PrpRe` leaks at most the Rényi leakage of `PopRe`.

4.2 Attacker Test for Illustration

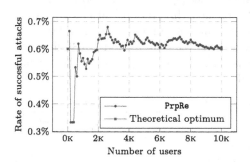

Fig. 3. Attacker's success convergence.

We simulated the attacker described in this paper by Eq. (2.1), who always guesses the original file with maximum probability given the priors and the padding scheme. Figure 3 shows that as the number of user increases, the success rate of the attacker against the padding proposed by `PrpRe` approaches the expected theoretical minimal possible success rate. This is a direct consequence of the law of large numbers as well as the equivalence between minimizing the expected success of the attacker (2.1) and the Rényi leakage, via Eq. (2.5).

4.3 Dataset Tests for Comparison

We used the dataset of NodeJS, proposed originally in [11]. This dataset consists of a list of 423,450 javascript packages provided by NPM for browser and nodeJS applications, each with its associated file size and access frequency, as of August 2021. Taking into account the large number of files and the availability of the access frequencies, we used the NodeJS dataset to benchmark the algorithms.

We used two versions of the NodeJS dataset: the *large* NodeJS dataset is the original dataset with 423,450 files, and the *small* consists of only the 1000 most frequently accessed files. The small NodeJS dataset allowed us to benchmark and compare the algorithms with large complexity, which timed-out on the large dataset. In all experiments, we parametrize the padding constraints with a single constant $c > 0$ that represents the constraint $|X| \leq f(X) \leq (1 + c) \cdot |X|$.

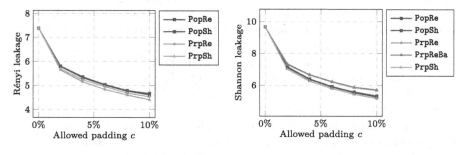

Fig. 4. Rényi and Shannon leakage on the small dataset.

Figure 4 depicts the variation of privacy leakage as a function of c on the small dataset. The trend is approximately equal in the large dataset, except that `PopRe` times out. The Rényi plot does not include `PrpReBa` to reduce redundancy, as it coincides with `PrpRe`. In the figure, we can appreciate the expected trend that larger c allows for more padding and less leakage of privacy, both in Rényi and Shannon definitions. It can also be verified that the algorithms tuned to minimize Rényi leakage, have a very small (but not minimal) Shannon leakage, and vice-versa. For instance, the differences between `PopRe` and `PopSh` in both leakages are inferior to 2%. This is a consequence of the information theoretical connection between the two types of leakage.

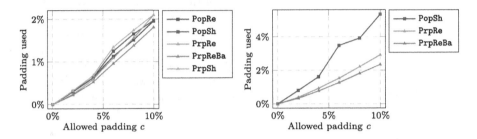

Fig. 5. Bandwidth increase on the small (left) and large (right) datasets.

The bandwidth increase generated by the padding of the files can be analyzed in Fig. 5. For reference, the average file size in the dataset, weighted by frequency is 52.5 KB, so 1% increase, means around 5.3 additional kilobytes. Several observations can be made out of Fig. 5. First, as anticipated, the larger the c, the larger the paddings on average. Second, the algorithms do not pad as much as they are allowed. Instead, when 10% is allowed, the optimal paddings lie at around 2% for the small dataset and 4% for the large dataset. For this particular example, the algorithms used more of the available padding on the large than in the small dataset, but we did not explore in depth in our experiments whether this pattern holds in general. Third, the improvements of `PrpReBa` over `PrpRe` can be corroborated, and estimated to approximately 20% less bandwidth use with the same Rényi leakage. Lastly, it appears empirically that the solutions that minimize Rényi leakage use less padding on average than those that minimize Shannon leakage.

Figure 6 depicts the runtime of the algorithms under analysis. We refer the reader to Table 1 for a richer analysis of the plots. The left plot does not have a clear tendency of longer executions for more relaxed padding constraints (higher c, thus also higher $\bar{b}$), meaning that for small datasets, all algorithms are suitable. In this regime, the runtime is not yet affected significantly by the growth of $\bar{b}$, possibly due to large constants that are masked by the complexity class and implementation details, especially for `PrpReBa`. Nevertheless, the difference between `PopRe` versus `PrpRe` and `PopSh` is already visible, and indeed, `PopRe` times out (several hours) for the large dataset. The right plot highlights the scalability of the algorithms. For all values of c plotted in this graph, the runtime for `PrpRe` is under 7 seconds, which makes it the fastest algorithm. `PrpReBa`

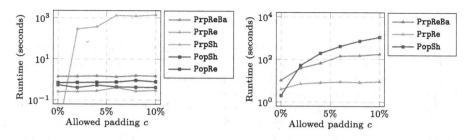

Fig. 6. Runtime plots on small (left) and large (right) datasets. The plots ignore the 7 additional seconds needed for JIT compilation.

peaks at $c = 10\%$ with around 3 minutes while `PopSh` needed 15 minutes. In this regime, the effect of increasing $\bar{b}$ via c on the runtime is clear.

5   Conclusion

We designed and proved the optimality of several algorithms (`PopRe`, `PrpRe`, `PrpReBa`) that minimize the expected success rate of an attacker. The algorithms were compared with existing solutions (`PopSh`, `PrpSh`) that consider a different attack model. The comparison was done both numerically via experiments and theoretically via privacy leakage.

Prioritizing scalability, we recommend using either `PrpRe` or `PrpReBa` for the PRP problem, as they are much faster and provide protection against a more reasonable attacker than the existing solutions (`PopSh`, `PrpSh`). Nevertheless, for the POP problem, we recommend any of either the existing solution `PopSh` or our algorithm `PopRe` that minimizes Rényi leakage, because even though our attack model is more realistic, the complexity of `PopSh` makes it more practical.

In general terms, the two attack models are correlated in the sense that the optimizing against one of them results in a strong, though not optimal, protection against the other one (with empirical differences of less than 2%). In more detail, however, the Rényi attacker is more realistic than the Shannon attacker, and the padding schemes that minimize Rényi leakage seem to use less bandwidth in practice, making our proposed algorithms even more appealing.

Acknowledgements. This work was supported by the European Research Council (ERC) project HYPATIA under the European Union's Horizon 2020 research and innovation programme. Grant agreement n. 835294.

References

1. Alvim, M.S., Chatzikokolakis, K., McIver, A., Morgan, C., Palamidessi, C., Smith, G.: The Science of Quantitative Information Flow. Information Security and Cryptography. Springer, Heidelberg (2020). https://doi.org/10.1007/978-3-319-96131-6
2. Alvim, M.S., Chatzikokolakis, K., Palamidessi, C., Smith, G.: Measuring information leakage using generalized gain functions. In: Proceedings of the 25th IEEE Computer Security Foundations Symposium (CSF), pp. 265–279 (2012). http://doi.ieeecomputersociety.org/10.1109/CSF.2012.26, http://hal.inria.fr/hal-00734044/en
3. Cherubin, G.: Bayes, not naïve: security bounds on website fingerprinting defenses. Proc. Priv. Enhanc. Technol. **2017**(4), 215–231 (2017). https://doi.org/10.1515/popets-2017-0046
4. Degabriele, J.P.: Hiding the lengths of encrypted messages via gaussian padding. In: Proceedings of the 2021 ACM SIGSAC Conference on Computer and Communications Security, pp. 1549–1565 (2021)
5. Dwork, C.: Differential privacy. In: Bugliesi, M., Preneel, B., Sassone, V., Wegener, I. (eds.) ICALP 2006. LNCS, vol. 4052, pp. 1–12. Springer, Heidelberg (2006). https://doi.org/10.1007/11787006_1
6. Espinoza, B., Smith, G.: Min-entropy leakage of channels in cascade. In: Barthe, G., Datta, A., Etalle, S. (eds.) FAST 2011. LNCS, vol. 7140, pp. 70–84. Springer, Heidelberg (2012). https://doi.org/10.1007/978-3-642-29420-4_5
7. Gluck, Y., Harris, N., Prado, A.: Breach: reviving the crime attack (2013). Dostupné také z http://css.csail.mit.edu/6 858 (2015)
8. M'rio, S.A., Chatzikokolakis, K., Palamidessi, C., Smith, G.: Measuring information leakage using generalized gain functions. In: 2012 IEEE 25th Computer Security Foundations Symposium, pp. 265–279. IEEE (2012)
9. Palamidessi, C., Romanelli, M.: Feature selection with Rényi min-entropy. In: Pancioni, L., Schwenker, F., Trentin, E. (eds.) ANNPR 2018. LNCS (LNAI), vol. 11081, pp. 226–239. Springer, Cham (2018). https://doi.org/10.1007/978-3-319-99978-4_18
10. Pinzón, C., Petrui, C., Simon, S.: Min-leakage-padding (2022). https://github.com/caph1993/min-leakage-padding. Accessed August 2022
11. Reed, A.C., Reiter, M.K.: Optimally hiding object sizes with constrained padding (2021). https://doi.org/10.48550/ARXIV.2108.01753, https://arxiv.org/abs/2108.01753
12. Romanelli, M.: Machine learning methods for privacy protection: leakage measurement and mechanisms design. Ph.D. thesis, Institut Polytechnique de Paris; Università degli studi (Sienne, Italie) (2020)
13. Schindler, W.: A timing attack against RSA with the Chinese remainder theorem. In: Koç, Ç.K., Paar, C. (eds.) CHES 2000. LNCS, vol. 1965, pp. 109–124. Springer, Heidelberg (2000). https://doi.org/10.1007/3-540-44499-8_8
14. Smith, G.: On the foundations of quantitative information flow. In: de Alfaro, L. (ed.) FoSSaCS 2009. LNCS, vol. 5504, pp. 288–302. Springer, Heidelberg (2009). https://doi.org/10.1007/978-3-642-00596-1_21
15. Song, D.: Timing analysis of keystrokes and SSH timing attacks. In: Proceedings of 10th USENIX Security Symposium (2001)
16. Wright, C.V., Coull, S.E., Monrose, F.: Traffic morphing: an efficient defense against statistical traffic analysis. In: NDSS, vol. 9. Citeseer (2009)

Cross-Border Data Security
from the Perspective of Risk Assessment

Na Wang[1,2], Gaofei Wu[2,3], Jingfeng Rong[2,5], Zheng Yan[3], Qiuling Yue[5], Jinglu Hu[6], and Yuqing Zhang[1,2,3,4,5(✉)]

[1] Guangzhou Research Institute, Xidian University, Guangzhou 510555, China
zhangyq@nipc.org.cn
[2] National Computer Network Intrusion Protection Center, University of Academy of Sciences, Beijing 101408, China
[3] School of Cyber Engineering, Xidian University, Xi'an 710126, China
[4] School of Computer Science and Technology, University of Chinese Academy of Sciences, Beijing 101408, China
[5] School of Cyberspace Security (School of Cryptography), Hainan University, Haikou 570100, China
[6] Graduate School of Information, Production and Systems, Waseda University, Shinjuku-ku 169-8050, Japan

Abstract. In the cross-border process of data, major issues such as national security and personal information security caused by complex processes and variable risk factors are gradually exposed. Based on the development status, this paper proposes a framework of cross-border data risk assessment model. The assessment framework not only considers the data protection capabilities of data controllers and data receivers, but also considers the impact of informed consent of data subjects on risk assessment results. The framework includes multiple evaluation modules such as data collection, data storage, etc., so that the framework can be updated and maintained at the module level in the future. This paper analyzes and extracts 18 important risk indicators in the six modules, as well as six potential risk events under cross-border data activities, to fully consider the possibility of potential risk accidents under each risk indicator. Finally, this paper analyzes the development needs of data cross-border risk assessment.

Keywords: Cross-border Data · Risk Assessment · Data Security · Data Classification and Grading

1 Introduction

The transformation of the traditional economy to digital economy has led to an exponential increase in the amount of data. The rapid development of cross-border e-commerce means the increasing demand of external communication. The speedy growth of high

This work was supported by the National Key Research and Development Program (2023QY1202), the National Natural Science Foundation of China (U1836210), the Key Research and Development Science and Technology of Hainan Province (GHYF2022010), and the Research Startup Foundation of Hainan University (RZ2100003335).

W. Meng et al. (Eds.): ISPEC 2023, LNCS 14341, pp. 91–104, 2023.
https://doi.org/10.1007/978-981-99-7032-2_6

technology not only makes cross-border data flow possible, but also makes it the new normalcy in the process of international communication nowadays. Therefore, the cross-border flow of data become a problem that more and more participating companies and countries must face gradually. In 2022, Didi was fined 8 billion yuan for illegally providing hundreds of millions of pieces of Chinese personal information to the United States, which seriously affected China's national security and users' privacy security. Cross-border data will inevitably involve the issue of data sovereignty with the increase of data security risk [1]. Therefore, the key problem of how to maximize the potential value of data in important areas while ensuring cross-border data security needs to be solved as soon as possible.

Contribution:

1) This article further improves the cross-border data security assessment framework.
2) Incorporate the influence and role of data subjects in cross-border data instances into the risk assessment framework model, fully guaranteeing the principle of informed consent of subjects.
3) Divide multiple risk factors to be evaluated within the data lifecycle into different evaluation modules, reducing the difficulty of maintaining and updating the evaluation framework.
4) This article analyzes and proposes several risk indicators and typical risk events that need to be considered in data cross-border risk assessment.

2   Cross-Border Data Status

Cross border data has not been clearly defined internationally. The Organization for Economic Co-operation and Development (OECD) defines cross-border data as the transmission of personal data of users in multiple countries or regions. The Convention of the European Parliament regards cross-border data flow as the cross-border flow of commercial or personal data through mobile networks after computer processing. On the opinion of the transnational corporations of the United Nations, cross-border data flow mainly refers to the operation of reading, accessing, processing, and using large amounts of data and other relevant information mainly stored in traditional media such as the Internet outside the country. Based on existing scientific research, China defines cross-border data as follows: network operators in China provide overseas institutions, organizations or individuals with personal data and important information collected during the operation process of companies or enterprises. There are two main types of understandings of cross-border data flow in academia and society:

- Data across physical borders.
- Overseas subjects remotely access and use native data through networks or other means [2].

Figure 1 shows the principle of cross-border data flow including two countries.

2.1   International Status

In terms of the principle of cross-border data, the EU mainly adopts a "whitelist" and "sufficient guarantee mechanism" to ensure the legal and safe cross-border transmission of data. Now the strictest data protection law in the world is the General Data Protection Regulation - GDPR passed by the EU in April 2016, which aims to protect personal identifiable information of data subjects resident in the EU [3]. In 2022, the EU issued "Data Act", which Supplements the regulation of cross-border flow of non-personal data based on GDPR, and further improves the cross-border data legal framework of EU.

European Union is deploying and improving the rule system for the cross-border flow of personal data, which has gradually drawn attention of other countries and international organizations as well [4]. In 2004, APEC established the APEC Cross-border Privacy Rules (hereinafter referred to as "CBPR system"). Members of the CBPR system can independently formulate rules for cross-border flow of personal data when the level of privacy protection meets the minimum requirements of APEC. The establishment of CBPR system not only guarantees the privacy of personal data, but also realizes the free flow of data across the Asia-Pacific region under certain conditions.

The United States in principle encourages the commercial use of personal data [5]. The United States pays more attention to the free flow of data and its economic benefits Compared with the EU's strict protection of personal data [6].

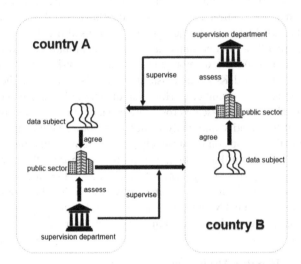

Fig. 1. Data cross-border flow process between two countries

2.2 Domestic Status

Personal information protection system of China is being perfected gradually. The "Cyber Security Law", "Data Security Law" and "Personal Information Protection Law" that have been promulgated all mention the principles and regulations of cross-border data. In addition, "Measures for the Security Evaluation of Personal Information and Important Data Outbound Security" (draft for comments) proposes to establish a two-level evaluation system which includes competent department assessment and network operator assessment, to expand the scope of data export and strengthen the risk management of cross-border data security.

Both domestic and foreign entities involved in the cross-border movement of personal data are required to conduct data security assessments besides the principle of consent. The "Cyber Security Law", "Measures for China Data Exit Assessment" and "Guidelines for Data Exit Security Assessment Application" and other related supporting regulations have initially established a basic framework for data outbound security assessment that combines self-assessment and regulatory agency assessments. Besides, the quantity and scope of personal data, the political and legal environment of the country, etc. are all important factors in the process of evaluating whether the risks arising from cross-border flows are controllable.

There is relatively little research on cross-border data security risks internationally. After the introduction of various data privacy protection frameworks and policies, foreign scholars in the field of internet technology mainly use machine learning, NLP, flow analysis and other technologies to develop automated compliance detection tools. Most of the research focuses on compliance analysis of privacy policies based on the GDPR standard [7–15]. Similarly, domestic research mainly focuses on content analysis and machine learning to achieve compliance analysis of privacy policies for applications and websites such as government affairs, healthcare, and e-commerce [16–24].

It is obvious that most domestic and abroad studies have not taken the potential cross-border risk of data as the research object. Li Jin et al. used the dichotomous network model of cross-border flow of important data to build a quantitative algorithm for the risk of data flow paths, used AUC indicators and K-kernel analysis to verify its robustness and effectiveness, and used K-means clustering analysis to classify the cross-border outgoing institutions of important data. However, the method of quantifying risk in this study is more suitable for large-scale cross-border data networks with multiple nodes, making it difficult to quantify and analyze the cross-border behavioral risks between few nodes systematically and comprehensively [25]. Moreover, this study only achieved classification and grading of data outgoing institutions, ignoring the important role of the data receiver in data cross-border activities. Therefore, this article will attempt to refine the risk assessment framework for cross-border data flow behavior based on the relevant indicators of data entry and exit institutions and explore suitable solutions for ensuring the security of cross-border data in subsequent international cooperation.

3   Data Cross-Border Risk Assessment

3.1   Introduction of Risk Assessment

Risk management is an essential measure in the process of maintaining information security. As one of the key procedures, security risk assessment has contracted the work of prediction, analysis, evaluation, and management of risk control. It has now become an important reference standard to measure whether data can leave the country. The European Data Protection Board (EDPB) has released the "Guidelines 07/2022 on Certification as a tool for transfers" [26], which elaborates on the roles of all parties involved in the certification process and specific certification standards used to demonstrate the existence of appropriate cross-border transmission safeguards. Due to the strictness of GDPR regulations in data protection principles, the certification process is also relatively complex. Therefore, we should set up the scope and procedure of security assessment according to the specific situation of China, to balance fairness and efficiency [27].

The taking of relevant measures such as information security risk management is necessary to ensure the integrity and security of data. Information security risk management includes a series of scientific means to identify the vulnerabilities of information system. The reasonable measures will be adopted to predict and manage the risk after analyzing the seriousness of risks, which can be beneficial to reduce the risk of undertaking the damage caused by the vulnerabilities for enterprises. Therefore, risk management can be generalized as a systematic process from risk discovery to risk control [28].

Figure 2 shows the information security risk management principles, frameworks, and processes under the ISO31000 standards [29, 30]. The principal part refers to the principles that enterprises or institutions need to follow in risk management. It also helps to provide guiding opinions at the framework level. In addition, the risk management framework needs to be adapted to the situation of organization and the needs of relevant stakeholders. After rigorous planning and design, the framework, policies, and decisions would be continuously improved based on the actual results of framework management and examination. The risk management process includes communication and negotiation with internal and external stakeholders, which takes place at all stages of risk management. During this process, it is necessary to clarify the internal and external situations as well as the relevant information of the risk management process. Secondly, the risk evaluation process should be carried out, which includes three operations: risk identification, risk analysis, and risk assessment. Finally, the risk treatment process should be followed. In addition, all aspects of the risk management process need to be tested and reviewed, and the results will also guide the improvement of the risk management process in the opposite direction.

Risk assessment plays a critical role in the process of information security management. Different from the ordinary business involving data collection and use by enterprises, cross-border data flow involves multiple parties including data subject (the owner of the data), cross-border initiator, and receiver [31]. Moreover, if the data is transferred across multiple countries, different policies and control measures will make the situation even worse and the risks associated with it will also increase significantly.

Therefore, cross-border risk assessment of data should be considered from two dimensions, before and after cross-border. The main scope of risk assessment before cross-border is the process of the initiator's collection and storage of massive data, which are like traditional data usage scenarios. Consequently, existing methods can also be used for assessments at this stage [32–37].

However, compared to the first stage of data being only used and stored locally, cross-border data will face relatively uncontrollable environmental, managerial, and technological risk factors in the new operational stage. Therefore, in the future, the risk assessment of cross-border data should be based on the comprehensive consideration of risk factors. It is necessary to formulate evaluation scheme, determine the evaluation index and select the appropriate method after considering the characteristics of the current cross-border data. What's more, the evaluation ought to be carried out from two stages of the initiator's local storage and the receiver's cross-border use.

3.2   Data Cross-Border Risk Assessment Framework

Wang Na et al. proposed to divide the data cross-border risk assessment into two stages [38]: domestic risk assessment and foreign cross-border process assessment with dual processes and multi cycles. The scheme provides continuous monitoring and management of cross-border data from the perspective of data controller and data receiver. However, the data subject is the largest privacy security stakeholder in the data cross-border process, whose attitude and right of absolute control over the data cannot be ignored. That's why we believe that the data subject should be included in the risk assessment. The following Fig. 3 is an overview of the risk assessment model.

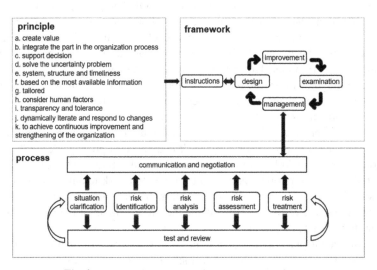

Fig. 2. Information security risk management factors

As shown in the Fig. 3, the top level is the national policies and regulations, which is the primary premise and principle to guide data operations, and each link of data cross-border behavior is constrained and controlled by it. Due to the different measures and attitudes adopted by the world's major economies, there are varying degrees of restrictions and requirements on data cross-border. For instance, The United States allows cross-border data to obtain more commercial benefits, the European Union allows the free flow of data within the EU, while Russia takes data localization measures to strictly restrict the outbound behavior of data [39]. Therefore, it is necessary to assess whether multiple countries meet the corresponding policy and legal requirements before data cross-border. Secondly, we divide the evaluation object into three parts: data subject, data controller and data receiver, to evaluate the cross-border data activities from different perspectives.

Nowadays, many countries or organizations in the world have reached the consensus of giving priority to the principle of informed consent of data subject, and they have the right to stop cross-border data and other operational processes at any time. That is, at any stage of cross-border data flow, when the data subject no longer agrees to use their

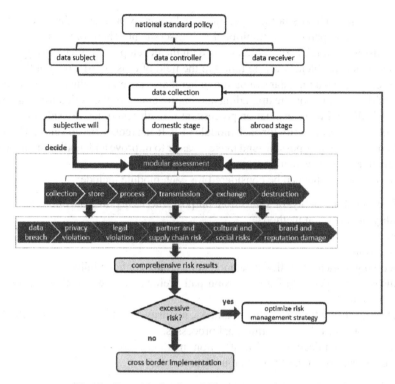

Fig. 3. Cross-border data risk assessment framework

personal data for cross-border purposes, the initiating party should immediately stop the cross-border behavior of the corresponding data. If the receiving party has already stored and used the data, the corresponding data should be immediately deleted from the storage medium, and the traces and impacts of such data usage should be minimized and eliminated as much as possible. Therefore, the main factor for the evaluation of data subject is their subjective will after measuring the advantages and disadvantages of cross-border behavior independently themselves. After collecting data, data processors need to provide avenues for data subject to detect or monitor personal data processing behavior. Whenever the subject's personal data needs to be processed, the data subject shall be notified by instant messaging such as pop-up windows, e-mail or SMS when providing business services for the data subject to seek its consent for data processing. In addition, when data subjects who do not agree to engage in cross-border data activities account for a certain percentage of the total data volume, all cross-border data activities should be forcibly stopped.

3.3 Modular Risk Assessment

The evaluation objects of cross-border data operators are divided into data controllers and data receivers. Based on the evaluation model in reference [38], this study will add modular evaluations to these two objects from both domestic and foreign scenarios.

Due to the variety of cross-border operations and complex processes, the potential risks are diversified compared with traditional risk assessment. Therefore, it is not enough to take existing factors into consideration. With the development of technology and the times, more new problems may be found in the field of cross-border data in the future. Therefore, we adopt a modular evaluation rather than an overall evaluation to reduce the impact of this situation on the upgrading and improvement of the evaluation framework and model. We divide the evaluation process into smaller modules, considering the risk factors of smaller granularity for each module [40]. It can reduce the correlation between each module as much as possible and make it easier to improve and modify them without major changes to the evaluation framework in the future.

The risk factors that can be considered for each module include:

- Collection: Rationality of collection purpose, necessity of collection scope, and legality of collection methods.
- Storage: storage duration, storage medium stability, integrity of storage access control mechanism.
- Processing: data availability, data authenticity, data confidentiality.
- Transmission: security of transmission path, reliability of encryption method, and data integrity.
- Exchange: ability to resist network attacks, maturity of data security technology, and completeness of relevant institutional processes.
- Destruction: applicability of destruction methods, compliance with destruction processes, and potential for malicious data recovery.

In addition, the risk modules need to be considered for cross-border data include the initial data collection, to the data storage and use before and after cross-border, as well as the transmission problems in the cross-border process, the selection and risk control of sharing media, the subsequent punishment, security issues, etc.

3.4 Cross-Border Data Risk Analysis

In the process of cross-border data transfer, various types of risk events may be encountered, which will have significant implications for the stakeholders involved in cross-border transactions.

- **Data breach** In the process of cross-border data transmission or storage, unauthorized access, hacker attacks, technical failures or human errors may lead to data breach. The expose of personal information, trade secrets or other sensitive data will cause significant damage to individuals and organizations.
- **Privacy violation** Cross-border data transfer may violate the privacy regulations of the target country or region, resulting in violation of personal privacy. This may involve unauthorized collection, use or disclosure of data that is detrimental to individual rights and privacy rights.
- **Legal violation** Cross-border data transfer may violate the data protection laws and privacy regulations of the target country or region, resulting in legal violation. This could trigger legal litigation, fines, or other legal consequences, causing legal risk and financial loss to the organization.

- **Partner and supply chain risk** There may be security breaches, compliance issues, or reputational risks in partners and supply chains involved in cross-border data transfers. This could lead to data access or misuse by third parties, which brings risks to data security and compliance.
- **Cultural and social risks** Differences in culture, values, and perceptions of data privacy and protection in different countries can lead to social and cultural risks. This may involve controversy, litigation, political pressure, or public opposition, adversely affecting the organization's reputation and business operations.
- **Brand and reputation damage** Data breaches, privacy breaches, or other security incidents can negatively impact an organization's or brand's reputation. With growing public concern over data protection and privacy, brand and reputation damage can lead to loss of customers, trust, and market share.

Determine the impact of the risk indicators to be investigated in each module on the potential risk events in the cross-border data above, then integrate the probability of each risk event, and summarize the cross-border data risk from multiple dimensions to obtain the overall cross-border data security assessment results. Based on the results, data controller and data receiver decide whether to optimize the risk management strategy. If the risk exceeds the expectation, they should carry out the risk assessment after the strategy optimization operation until all risk factors meet the cross-border requirements.

3.5 Summary

Even though the evaluation framework and model are similar, the evaluation objects of data controller and data receiver may be different because of the differences in data operations, needs and authorities of these two parties caused by the distinction of their roles in the processes. Therefore, it is necessary to comprehensively analyze the results of risk assessment after the investigation of both parties to determine whether they meet the security standards required for cross-border data, and then decide whether to conduct cross-border operations.

In addition, as time goes by, factors such as the policy considered in the assessment, or the way of processing data may change. Therefore, besides the initial risk assessment, it is necessary to continue tracking and monitoring after cross-border implementation and take corresponding measures at any time according to the risk status of both parties to better ensure data security.

4   Remaining Problems

Although China has tried to formulate and improve relevant systems and frameworks, there are still some problems to be solved.

4.1   Data Classification and Grading

China is trying to establish classification and grading systems for data in different fields [40], which can assist in building and perfecting the model of cross-border data risk assessment. Firstly, the data classification and grading results can be used as one of risk indicators for more granular evaluation; Secondly, on the premise of meeting the national policies, enterprises and organizations can flexibly adjust cross-border business needs and data cross-border security measures according to the evaluation results of the data classification and grading system and the corresponding cross-border restrictions, so as to ensure data security or maximize data value.

4.2 Risk Assessment Methods

The existing information security risk assessment methods can be roughly divided into three types: qualitative methods, and quantitative methods, and the other one is the combination of qualitative and quantitative methods.

Qualitative methods mainly rely on the experience and knowledge accumulation of evaluators to judge risks. The evaluation is more comprehensive, and the process is relatively simple. Different levels of evaluators may have different ways and angles to treat problems, which will greatly affect the evaluation result. Quantitative methods rely more on objective quantities and indicators to evaluate the impact and risk of information security. It also relies on professional mathematical algorithms to calculate and analyze in the evaluation process, to draw quantitative conclusion data. The advantage of quantitative methods is that they are more scientific and intuitive, but risk factors of complex things are difficult to accurately describe with simple modeling since errors and inaccurate probability will inevitably occur in the evaluation process [32, 41].

For risk assessment, there are three problems to be solved in future research: How to select appropriate methods to achieve an accurate and objective description of the facts? How to make it more consistent with the characteristics of the modular assessment model? How to formulate the potential risk criteria for each module and depict them with clear numerical values, to comprehensively analyze the results of risk assessment?

5   Suggestions on Cross-Border Data

5.1   Promote Data Classification and Grading

Establish a data classification management system as soon as possible after consulting with enterprises, society, experts, and other personnel, to take a more scientific and orderly management method for sensitive data related to national security. Additionally, speed up the construction of the systematic system of cross-border data flow through the establishment of special data supervision institutions, which is responsible for supervising and managing organizations involved in data collection and storage, and establishing specific audit mechanisms for enterprises performing cross-border data operations.

5.2   Improve Relevant Standards

At present, China has issued special laws on data security and personal information protection to regulate relevant data operations. These laws also clarify and explain the regulation of cross-border data flow. However, the specific methods and guidelines for risk assessment are still under negotiation. The improvement of these important standards can effectively help promote cross-border data activities. Enterprises can better evaluate and supervise the implementation of cross-border business according to relevant standards, to better manage and use data and ensure the stable development of cross-border data in the future.

5.3 Research and Develop Technology or Method

In recent years, with the continuous innovation of network architecture, it is necessary to explore new technologies to solve security problems. For data security, the new security technologies from the perspectives of secure storage, encrypted network, traffic monitoring, and authority control ought to be developed and improved. Furthermore, new Internet technologies such as Blockchain, artificial intelligence, and cloud computing can also be applied to cross-border data to continuously seek more reliable and convenient solutions for data security [42–47].

5.4 Actively Participate in Global Governance Framework

Cross-border data flow is the basis for supporting the development of global digital trade in the future, which has far-reaching influence in the whole field of trade. However, different international standards and management models hinder data cross-border to some extent. As a result, it is still necessary for countries to adopt interoperability mechanisms, actively participate in the exploration and establishment of international law enforcement cooperation mechanisms and accelerate the construction of future global digital trade rules and digital governance frameworks while improving their own legal systems [48–51].

6 Summary and Outlook

Data cross-border is an important area related to the future global economic and trade strategic layout. The national management system is still in its infancy. The rapid updating of science and technology requires more convenient cross-border exchanges. Under the framework of national strength, political and economic strategies and international diplomatic concepts and policies, our key research directions in the future will focus on the problem of how to protect cross-border data through technologies or management tools such as risk assessment, taking into account the development of national enterprises and data security to balance the contradiction between the free flow of cross-border data and the legitimate cross-border policy objectives. We believe that we will eventually find the most suitable solution to promote the sustainable development of cross-border data and provide a better platform for cross-border exchanges in various fields through continuous research and exploration.

References

1. Ran, C., He, M., Liu, X.: Research on governance and countermeasures of cross border data flow in china from the perspective of data sovereignty. Libr. Intell. (4), 1–14 (2021)

2. Lun, Y.: Practice and enlightenment of cross-border data flow in Australia. Inf. Secur. Commun. Confidentiality (05), 25–32 (2017)
3. Mazetova, E.: Data protection regulation and international arbitration: can there be harmonious coexistence (with the GDPR requirements concerning cross-border data transfer)? Legal Issues Digit. Age **2**(2), 21–48 (2021)
4. Zhao, W.: Regulation of cross-border flow of personal data. Master's degree thesis. Dalian Maritime University, Liaoning (2019)
5. Fan, S.: Personal data protection in cross-border data flow. Electron. Intellect. Prop. Rights (6), 85–97 (2020)
6. Jimenez-Gomez, B.S.: Cross-border data transfers between the EU and the US: a transatlantic dispute. Santa Clara J. Int. L. **19**, 1 (2021)
7. Rahat, T.A., Long, M., Tian, Y.: Is your policy compliant? A deep learning-based empirical study of privacy policies' compliance with GDPR. In: Proceedings of the 21st Workshop on Privacy in the Electronic Society (WPES 2022), pp. 89–102. Association for Computing Machinery, New York (2022). https://doi.org/10.1145/3559613.3563195
8. Story, P., Zimmeck, S., Ravichander, A., et al.: Natural language processing for mobile app privacy compliance. In: AAAI Spring Symposium on Privacy-Enhancing Artificial Intelligence and Language Technologies, p. 10 (2019)
9. Asif, M., Javed, Y., Hussain, M.: Automated analysis of Pakistani websites' compliance with GDPR and Pakistan data protection act. In: 2021 International Conference on Frontiers of Information Technology (FIT), pp. 234–239 (2021). https://doi.org/10.1109/FIT53504.2021. 00051
10. Liu, S., Zhao, B., Guo, R., Meng, G., Zhang, F., Zhang, M.: Have you been properly notified? Automatic compliance analysis of privacy policy text with GDPR Article 13. In Proceedings of the Web Conference 2021 (WWW 2021), pp. 2154–2164. Association for Computing Machinery, New York (2021). https://doi.org/10.1145/3442381.3450022
11. Libal, T.: Towards automated GDPR compliance checking. In: Heintz, F., Milano, M., O'Sullivan, B. (eds.) TAILOR 2020. LNCS, vol. 12641, pp. 3–19. Springer, Cham (2021). https://doi.org/10.1007/978-3-030-73959-1_1
12. Zimmeck, S., Story, P., Smullen, D., et al.: MAPS: scaling privacy compliance analysis to a million apps. Proc. Priv. Enhanc. Technol. **2019**(3), 66–86 (2019)
13. Andow, B., Mahmud, S.Y., Whitaker, J., et al.: Actions speak louder than words: {entity-sensitive} privacy policy and data flow analysis with {PoliCheck}. In: 29th USENIX Security Symposium (USENIX Security 2020), pp. 985–1002 (2020)
14. Guamán, D.S., Del Alamo, J.M., Caiza, J.C.: GDPR compliance assessment for cross-border personal data transfers in android apps. IEEE Access **9**, 15961–15982 (2021). https://doi.org/ 10.1109/ACCESS.2021.3053130
15. Guamán, D.S., Ferrer, X., del Alamo, J.M., et al.: Automating the GDPR compliance assessment for cross-border personal data transfers in android applications. arXiv preprint arXiv: 2103.07297 (2021)
16. Yuan, H., Zhang, S.: Content analysis of privacy policy of government APP under the environment of "internet plus+government services." Mod. Intell. **42**(3), 121–132 (2022). https:// doi.org/10.3969/j.issn.1008-0821.2022.03.014
17. Ma, C., Liu, Q.: Comparative study on the protection of personal health information between China and the United States: analysis of privacy policy based on 60 mainstream mobile medical APPs. Electron. Intellect. Prop. **1**, 27–36 (2021). https://doi.org/10.3969/j.issn.1004-9517.2021.01.004
18. Zhao, J., Yuan, Q., Chen, J.: Research on B2C network merchant privacy policy based on content analysis. Mod. Intell. **40**(4), 101–110 (2020). https://doi.org/10.3969/j.issn.1008-0821. 2020.04.012

19. Zhang, Y., Qiu, Y.: Research on the compliance of privacy policy of mobile reading APP in China under hard rules. Mod. Intell. **42**(1), 167–176 (2022). https://doi.org/10.3969/j.issn. 1008-0821.2022.01.016

20. Zhao, Y., Yan, Z., Shen, Q., et al.: Research on the compliance of privacy policy of medical health APP based on machine learning. Data Anal. Knowl. Discov. **6**(5), 112–126 (2022). https://doi.org/10.11925/infotech.2096-3467.2021.0897

21. Liang, D.: The normative path for the protection of personal information of E-commerce consumers: an empirical study based on the privacy policy of 6 categories and 12 home appliance business platforms. J. Dalian Univ. Technol. (Soc. Sci. Edn.) **43**(3), 102–112 (2022). https://doi.org/10.19525/j.issn1008-407x.2022.03.011

22. Wang, X.: Research on compliance of privacy policy in mobile social APP - content analysis based on 20 privacy policy texts. Netw. Secur. Technol. Appl. (1), 143–146 (2022). https://doi.org/10.3969/j.issn.1009-6833.2022.01.090

23. Zhu, Z., Lu, Y., Tang, Z., et al.: Application classification based on privacy policy terms and machine learning. Commun. Technol. **53**(11), 2749–2757 (2020). https://doi.org/10.3969/j. issn.1002-0802.2020.11.022

24. Xu, Q.: Research on compliance with privacy policy of mobile internet APP based on the personal information protection law. Wuhan University, Hubei (2022)

25. Li, J., Zhang, L., Li, J., Xing, X.: Classified control and influencing factors for risks management in institutions with cross-border data flow. J. Syst. Sci. Math. Sci. **42**(9), 2347–2366 (2022)

26. Kuner, C.: Protecting EU data outside EU borders under the GDPR. Common Mark. Law Rev. **60**(1), 77–106 (2023)

27. Du, S.: The enlightenment of EU legislation on cross-border flow of personal data to China. Master's degree thesis. Shandong University, Shandong (2018)

28. Li, S.: Research on information security risk assessment method based on improved neural network. China University of Mining and Technology (2018)

29. Iso, A.N.: AS_NZS ISO 31000:2009 risk management - principles and guidelines (2009)

30. Purdy, G.: ISO 31000:2009—setting a new standard for risk management. Risk Anal. **30**(6), 881–886 (2010)

31. Becker, R., Thorogood, A., Bovenberg, J., et al.: Applying GDPR roles and responsibilities to scientific data sharing. Int. Data Priv. Law **12**(3), 207–219 (2022)

32. Dang, D., Meng, Z.: Information security risk assessment based on support vector machine. J. Huazhong Univ. Sci. Technol. (Nat. Sci. Edn.) **38**(03), 46–49 (2010)

33. Tao, Z., Mu, D., Ren, S., Yao, L.: An information security risk assessment model based on risk matrix method. Comput. Eng. Appl. **46**(05), 93–95 (2010)

34. Xiao, L., Qi, Y., Li, Q.: Information security risk assessment based on AHP and fuzzy comprehensive evaluation. Comput. Eng. Appl. **45**(22), 82–85 + 89 (2009)

35. Zhao, D., Liu, H., Liu, C.: Information security risk assessment based on BP neural network. Comput. Eng. Appl. (01), 139–141 (2007)

36. Fu, Y., Wu, X., Yan, C.: Information security risk assessment method based on Bayesian network. J. Wuhan Univ. (Sci. Edn.) (05), 631–634 (2006)

37. Banton, M., Bowles, J., Silvina, A., et al.: On the benefits and security risks of a user-centric data sharing platform for healthcare provision. In: Adjunct Proceedings of the 29th ACM Conference on User Modeling, Adaptation and Personalization, pp. 351–356 (2021)

38. Na, W., Gaofei, W., Qiuling, Y., Jinglu, H., Zhang, Y.: Research on security assessment of cross border data flow. In: Cao, C., Zhang, Y., Hong, Y., Wang, D. (eds.) FCS 2021. CCIS, vol. 1558, pp. 327–341. Springer, Singapore (2022). https://doi.org/10.1007/978-981-19-0523-0_21

39. Na, W., Gu, M., Wu, G., et al.: The current situation, analysis, and prospects of cross border data flow. Inf. Secur. Res. **7**(6), 488–495 (2021)

40. Parretti, C., Pourabbas, E., Rolli, F., et al.: Robust privacy assessment in transnational health-care systems. In: IOP Conference Series: Materials Science and Engineering, vol. 1174, no. 1, p. 012015. IOP Publishing (2021)
41. Tan, C., Chen, H.: Research on information security risk assessment methods. Confidential Sci. Technol. (10), 40–43 (2017)
42. Singh, P., Masud, M., Hossain, M.S., et al.: Cross-domain secure data sharing using blockchain for industrial IoT. J. Parallel Distrib. Comput. **156**, 176–184 (2021)
43. Rahman, M.S., Al Omar, A., Bhuiyan, M.Z.A., et al.: Accountable cross-border data sharing using blockchain under relaxed trust assumption. IEEE Trans. Eng. Manage. **67**(4), 1476–1486 (2020)
44. Heider-Aviet, A., Ollik, D.R., Berlato, S., et al.: Blockchain based ran data sharing. In: 2021 IEEE International Conference on Smart Data Services (SMDS), pp. 152–161. IEEE (2021)
45. Spanakis, E.G., Sfakianakis, S., Bonomi, S., et al.: Emerging and established trends to support secure health information exchange. Front. Digit. Health **3**, 636082 (2021)
46. Guo, T.: Reflections on the regulation of cross border data flow in the digital economy era. World Sci. Technol. Res. Dev. 1 (2022)
47. Syroid, T.L., Kaganovska, T.Y., Shamraieva, V.M., et al.: The personal data protection mechanism in the European union. Int. J. Comput. Sci. Netw. Secur. **21**(5), 113–120 (2021)
48. Yang, X.: Regulatory approaches of cross-border data flow in the big data era: china's choice. J. Phys.: Conf. Ser. **1848**(1), 012026 (2021)
49. Zheng, G.: Trilemma and tripartition: the regulatory paradigms of cross-border personal data transfer in the EU, the US and China. Comput. Law Secur. Rev. **43**, 105610 (2021)
50. Casalini, F., González, J.L., Nemoto, T.: Mapping commonalities in regulatory approaches to cross-border data transfers (2021)
51. Ziyi, X.: International law protection of cross-border transmission of personal information based on cloud computing and big data. Mob. Inf. Sys. **2022** (2022)

IoT-REX: A Secure Remote-Control System for IoT Devices from Centralized Multi-designated Verifier Signatures

Yohei Watanabe[1,2(✉)], Naoto Yanai[2,3], and Junji Shikata[4]

[1] The University of Electro-Communications, Tokyo, Japan
watanabe@uec.ac.jp
[2] Japan Datacom Co., Ltd., Tokyo, Japan
yanai@ist.osaka-u.ac.jp
[3] Osaka University, Osaka, Japan
[4] Yokohama National University, Yokohama, Kanagawa, Japan
shikata-junji-rb@ynu.ac.jp

Abstract. IoT technology has been developing rapidly, while at the same time, notorious IoT malware such as Mirai is a severe and inherent threat. We believe it is essential to consider systems that enable us to remotely control infected devices in order to prevent or limit malicious behaviors of infected devices. In this paper, we design a promising candidate for such remote-control systems, called *IoT-REX (REmote-Control System for IoT devices)*. IoT-REX allows a systems manager to designate an arbitrary subset of all IoT devices in the system and every device can confirm whether or not the device itself was designated; if so, the device executes a command given from the systems manager. Towards realizing IoT-REX, we introduce a novel cryptographic primitive called *centralized multi-designated verifier signatures* (CMDVS). Although CMDVS works under a restricted condition compared to conventional MDVS, it is sufficient for realizing IoT-REX. We provide an efficient CMDVS construction from any approximate membership query structures and digital signatures, yielding compact communication sizes and efficient verification procedures for IoT-REX. We then discuss the feasibility of IoT-REX through cryptographic implementation of the CMDVS construction on a Raspberry Pi. Our promising results demonstrate that the CMDVS construction can compress communication size to about 30% compared to a trivial construction, and thus its resulting IoT-REX becomes three times faster than a trivial construction over typical low-power wide area networks with an IoT device.

Keywords: Broadcast authentication · Remote-control system · Multi-designated verifier signatures

1 Introduction

Internet-of-Things technologies have been spreading rapidly and enriching our lives. According to a Cisco report [1], tens of billions of IoT devices are expected

W. Meng et al. (Eds.): ISPEC 2023, LNCS 14341, pp. 105–122, 2023.
https://doi.org/10.1007/978-981-99-7032-2_7

to be deployed over the next few years. On the other hand, along with the rapid development of IoT technologies, we have to focus our efforts on cybersecurity, though there are several constraints on that in the context of IoT devices. For example, most IoT devices, unfortunately, do little to protect the data stored inside, most likely due to the development cost and restricted resources. This has a profound effect on the real world; for instance, a notorious IoT malware 'Mirai' infected many IoT devices, turning them into botnets. The botnets infected nearly 65,000 IoT devices in its first 20 h [3]. The widespread outbreak of Mirai had a considerable impact on the world. As described above, most IoT devices do not have sufficient resources to implement and deploy security functions for each specific security threat [6]. Hence, there seem to be no versatile solutions [5].

One possible approach is to design cryptographic schemes that can be used in cooperation with existing methods such as controlling [35,37,39] or surveillance [20,24,29] of individual devices. Cryptographic schemes can provide *provable security* that theoretically guarantees the security of a cryptographic protocol through mathematical proofs.

In this paper, we present a novel system based on cryptography, *IoT-REX* (REmote-Control System for IoT devices), which has an arbitrary subset of all IoT devices and executes any commands remotely and securely. The most likely scenario is to disable compromised IoT devices, e.g., those infected with malware. IoT-REX allows such devices to be brought to a halt as soon as possible. It is expected to, for example, stop and reboot malware-infected devices all at once, whereby a sender can communicate with many devices simultaneously with a single piece of data.

We note that the efficient design of IoT-REX is *non-trivial*. One might think IoT-REX can be realized with a standard digital signature; regarding an arbitrary subset of devices' identifiers as a single message and signing it. However, it is insufficient because the communication size is linear in the size of the subset. Since IoT devices are resource-constrained [15], their battery life is also limited. Even if the latency on a CPU is small enough, the communication should be used sparingly to avoid consuming energy too quickly as well [18]. Namely, we need to achieve the small communication size as well as the functionality to choose an arbitrary subset of receivers. As an advanced cryptographic approach, broadcast authentication [27] might be employed; it can broadcast a single piece of data to many receivers, i.e., IoT devices, with data authenticity for controlling them. However, existing broadcast authentication schemes [8,26,27,30,32,34] except for a recent work [37] cannot support the functionality that a sender chooses an arbitrary subset of receivers. Though the only exception [17], i.e., the broadcast authentication scheme that supports such functionality, may be applied to IoT-REX, it still has the major drawback of communication sizes since it just combines individual authenticators for all designated devices.

To this end, we propose a novel cryptographic scheme, centralized multi-designated verifier signatures (CMDVS), as a core primitive for IoT-REX. We define the security of CMDVS formally and then propose an efficient CMDVS construction from any approximate membership query (AMQ) structure and digital signatures, which yields an efficient design for IoT-REX. The proposed construction is provably secure. Note that we show CMDVS provides more efficient communication sizes than the two trivial approaches described in the previous paragraph.

We also discuss the feasibility of IoT-REX for IoT devices through the implementation of the proposed CMDVS construction with EdDSA [4] and vacuum filters [36], which is one of the efficient AMQ structures. We then demonstrate that the proposed CMDVS construction can compress communication size to about 30% compared to the trivial approach with standard digital signatures. (Hereafter, we call this approach *trivial construction*.) We also show that our scheme can also compress communication size to about 4% compared to the broadcast-authentication-based approach [37], which is simply called *broadcast authentication* hereafter. Our promising results also show that, by virtue of the compression of the communication size, IoT-REX is three times faster than the trivial construction and 25 times faster than the broadcast authentication over typical low-power wide area networks with a Raspberry Pi3 as an IoT device. We also evaluate the communication overheads. We have released our source code for reproducibility and subsequent work (https://github.com/naotoyanai/fiilter-signature_ABA).

To sum up, our primary goal is to design IoT-REX, and we make the following technical contributions:

- We propose CMDVS as a novel cryptographic primitive to instantiate IoT-REX. We formally define and prove the security of the proposed construction from digital signatures and AMQ structures.
- Through an implementation, we experimentally demonstrate that the proposed CMDVS construction can compress communication size to about 30% compared to the trivial construction and 4% compared to the broadcast authentication. We have released our code via GitHub.

2   IoT-REX: REmote-Control System for IoT Devices

2.1   System Setting

Suppose a large, simple system called IoT-REX (REmote-Control System for IoT devices) among a systems manager and many IoT devices such as sensors and surveillance cameras below.

IoT-REX: An Overview. There are a systems manager and a number of IoT devices. For some reason (e.g., based on data from outside sources such as device owner's request and information on vulnerable devices), the systems manager generates and broadcasts authenticated information in order to make only designated IoT devices execute a command cmd remotely and securely, while the devices themselves can detect a forgery of the authenticated information that aims to change the designated-device set and/or the command.

Expected Applications. We believe there are various applications of IoT-REX. For example, it enables one to put only designated devices to sleep, e.g., in order to extend their operational lives. At the same time, it prevents an adversary from forging the authenticated information on the 'sleep' command and which devices are designated. Besides, let us explain another important application: the IoT devices usually communicate with each other via the Internet, and could be infected with malware. As explained in the introduction, it seems difficult to completely eliminate the chance of devices being infected with malware, and IoT malware spreads rapidly between IoT devices once the initial infection occurs. Therefore, IoT-REX can bring infected devices to a halt as soon as possible in order to prevent or limit malicious behavior by said devices (e.g., DDoS attacks), rather than preventing the initial infection.

2.2 System Model

Based on the above discussion, we formally define IoT-REX as a protocol among the following entities: a device owner O, a systems manager SM, and IoT devices D. Let $\mathcal{I}$ be a set of possible identifiers in the system, and $\mathcal{I}_{\mathsf{Act}}$ be an identifier set of activated devices, i.e., IoT devices taking part in the system. We denote an identifier set of devices designated by SM so that they execute a command cmd by $\mathcal{I}_{\mathsf{Dsg}}$. We have $\mathcal{I}_{\mathsf{Dsg}} \subset \mathcal{I}_{\mathsf{Act}} \subset \mathcal{I}$.

System Overview. Suppose that the device owner O manages many IoT devices $\{\mathsf{D}_{\mathsf{id}}\}_{\mathsf{id} \in \mathcal{I}_{\mathsf{Act}}}$. Note that O can dynamically add and remove IoT devices. Let us explain the protocol overview as follows.

① O sends SM a request to have an arbitrary subset (i.e., $\mathcal{I}_{\mathsf{Dsg}}$) of all devices execute a command cmd.

② SM generates an authenticated command $\widehat{\mathsf{cmd}}$, which is an authenticated version of cmd and contains the information on the designated devices $\mathcal{I}_{\mathsf{Dsg}}$, and broadcasts it to *all* devices.

③ All IoT devices $\{\mathsf{D}_{\mathsf{id}}\}_{\mathsf{id} \in \mathcal{I}_{\mathsf{Act}}}$ (including non-designated ones) receive $\widehat{\mathsf{cmd}}$ and check its validity. If $\widehat{\mathsf{cmd}}$ is *not* valid, the devices reject it and terminate the process.

④ If an IoT device D_{id} confirms that the authenticated command $\widehat{\mathsf{cmd}}$ is valid and directed at the device, D_{id} executes cmd. Otherwise, i.e., if $\widehat{\mathsf{cmd}}$ is valid but does not designate D_{id}, the device does nothing and terminates the process.

2.3 Assumptions and Requirements

Adversarial Model and Assumptions. Suppose that the systems manager SM broadcasts an authenticated command $\widehat{\mathsf{cmd}}$ to all devices $\{\mathsf{D}_{\mathsf{id}}\}_{\mathsf{id} \in \mathcal{I}_{\mathsf{Act}}}$. We assume an adversary A can eavesdrop, insert, delay, and modify all the transmitted information. We also assume that A's main purpose is to maliciously modify authenticated commands so that some designated devices do not execute cmd and/or some non-designated devices execute cmd. More formally, we assume that A mainly aims to modify $\widehat{\mathsf{cmd}}$ in order to change a pair of $(\mathsf{cmd}, \mathcal{I}_{\mathsf{Dsg}})$ to a different pair $(\mathsf{cmd}', \mathcal{I}'_{\mathsf{Dsg}})$ in order to accomplish any of the goals below:

(a) At least one designated device D_{id} for $id \in \mathcal{I}_{Dsg}$ does not execute cmd as a regular process.
(b) At least one designated device D_{id} for $id \in \mathcal{I}_{Dsg}$ executes cmd' ($\neq$ cmd) as a regular process.
(c) At least one non-designated device D_{id} for $id \in \mathcal{I}'_{Dsg} \setminus \mathcal{I}_{Dsg}$ executes cmd', which might be the same as cmd, as a regular process.

Note that the above goals include that A tries to impersonate the systems manager SM and create new (forged) authenticated commands. However, we assume A is not capable of forging any CMDVS signature, which is a core element of authenticated commands $\widehat{cmd}$, according to Definition 1, which will be defined later.

For simplicity, we assume that all devices receive the same information; if authenticated commands are modified, all devices receive the modified ones. We also note that preventing attacks in the physical layer is out of the scope, i.e., jamming. It can be prevented by existing techniques such as the spread spectrum [22].

Requirements. Following the discussion in the introduction and our system goal, the secure system for remotely controlling IoT devices, IoT-REX, should possess the following four properties.

- *Completeness*: Only designated devices $\{D_{id}\}_{id \in \mathcal{I}_{Dsg}}$ execute a command cmd unless the corresponding authenticated command $\widehat{cmd}$ is externally modified. In other words, any non-designated device D_{id}, where $id \in \mathcal{I}_{Act} \setminus \mathcal{I}_{Dsg}$, never executes cmd as long as it receives $\widehat{cmd}$ as it is. The system might have allowable errors; a very small percentage of devices might not work as expected. This error seems likely in most large-scale applications.
- *Integrity*: If an authenticated command $\widehat{cmd}$ is externally modified, any device can detect it and reject $\widehat{cmd}$.
- *Scalablity*: The system allows a large number of IoT devices, e.g., up to a million. In particular, the size of authenticated commands should be small, i.e., it does not depend on the number of designated devices linearly. Ideally, it should be independent of the number of designated devices in the system.
- *Light weight*: The devices' resources might be poor. Thus, the verification process executed by the devices should be efficient enough that, ideally, even microcomputers such as an ARM Cortex-M3 can run the process.

The first two requirements—completeness and integrity—are the fundamental properties to have IoT-REX work well in practice. The last two requirements—scalability and light weight—are also important properties for IoT-REX since we focus on various IoT devices. including microcomputers. Indeed, a trivial system can be constructed by an arbitrary digital signature or MAC: SM just sends each designated IoT device a command cmd with its signature/MAC. This trivial construction requires the $\mathcal{O}(d \cdot \kappa)$ communication size, where d is the number of designated devices and κ is a security parameter, whereas its verification process is lightweight since it requires only a single signature/MAC verification.

Hence, achieving both scalability and lightweight is another important goal for IoT-REX.

3 Centralized Multi-designated Verifier Signatures

We introduce *centralized MDVS* (CMDVS), which is a core cryptographic primitive for IoT-REX. Unlike existing MDVS schemes [10,19], in CMDVS we consider a situation where there are only one signer and multiple verifiers. Note that CMDVS is not a special case of MDVS; there are multiple users, who are potential signers and/or verifiers, in MDVS.

Notations. For any natural numbers $a, b \in \mathbb{N}$ s.t. $a \leq b$, $\{a, \ldots, b\}$ is denoted by $[a, b]$. In particular, if $a = 1$, we denote $[b] := \{1, \ldots, b\}$. For any real numbers $a, b \in \mathbb{R}$ s.t. $a \leq b$, let $(a, b]$ be a half-open interval. Concatenation is denoted by $\|$. For a finite set $\mathcal{X}$, we denote by $|\mathcal{X}|$ the cardinality of $\mathcal{X}$. For any algorithm A, out $\leftarrow$ A(in) means that A takes in as input and outputs out. Throughout the paper, we denote by κ a security parameter and consider probabilistic polynomial-time algorithms (PPTAs). We say a function $\mathsf{negl}(\cdot)$ is negligible if for any polynomial $\mathsf{poly}(\cdot)$, there exists some constant $\kappa_0 \in \mathbb{N}$ such that $\mathsf{negl}(\kappa) < 1/\mathsf{poly}(\kappa)$ for all $\kappa \geq \kappa_0$. In security games, a flag flag, which indicates an adversary's winning condition, is initialized as zero.

3.1 Syntax

First of all, a signer runs Setup to get a public parameter pp and a signing key sk. The signer can run KeyGen with (pp, sk) to generate a verification key $\mathsf{vk_{id}}$ for any id $\in \mathcal{I}$. Let $\mathcal{V}$ be a verifier set, i.e., a set of identities whose key-pairs have been generated by KeyGen. To create a signature σ so that only a designated-verifier set $\mathcal{D}_V \subset \mathcal{V}$ accepts it, the signer executes Sign with sk, $\mathcal{D}_V$, and a message m. Each verifier can check the validity of (m, σ) by Vrfy with pp and $\mathsf{vk_{id}}$ if the verifier was designated by the signer, i.e., id $\in \mathcal{D}_V$. In other words, for any non-designated verifier id $\notin \mathcal{D}_V$, Vrfy with (pp, $\mathsf{vk_{id}}$) outputs $\perp$ even if the pair (m, σ) is a valid one.

CMDVS $\Pi =$ (Setup, KeyGen, Sign, Vrfy) for an identity set $\mathcal{I}$ is defined as follows.

- Setup(1^κ) $\rightarrow$ (pp, sk): a probabilistic algorithm for setup. It takes a security parameter 1^κ as input, and outputs a public parameter pp and a signing key sk. It initializes a verifier set $\mathcal{V}$.
- KeyGen(pp, sk, id) $\rightarrow$ $\mathsf{vk_{id}}$: an algorithm for verification-key generation. It takes pp, sk, an identity id $\in \mathcal{I}$ as input, and outputs a verification key $\mathsf{vk_{id}}$ for id. It also updates $\mathcal{V} := \mathcal{V} \cup \{\mathsf{id}\}$.
- Sign(sk, $\mathcal{D}_V$, m, len) $\rightarrow \sigma \,/\, \perp$: a signing algorithm. It takes sk, a designated-verifier set $\mathcal{D}_V \subset \mathcal{V}$, a message m $\in \mathcal{M}$, and the maximum length of a signature len as input, and outputs the signature σ for $\mathcal{D}_V$ or $\perp$, which indicates "failure of signature generation".

- Vrfy(pp, vk$_{id}$, m, σ) $\rightarrow \top$ / $\bot$: a deterministic algorithm for verification. It takes pp, vk$_{id}$, m and σ as input, and outputs $\top$ indicating "accept" or $\bot$ indicating "reject".

Experiment: $\mathsf{Exp}_{\Pi,A}^{\mathsf{UF}}(\kappa)$

1: $(\mathsf{pp}, \mathsf{sk}) \leftarrow \mathsf{Setup}(1^\kappa)$
2: $(\mathcal{D}_V^\star, m^\star, \sigma^\star) \leftarrow A^{O_{\mathsf{KG}}, O_s}(1^\kappa, \mathsf{pp})$
3: **if** $(\mathcal{D}_V^\star, m^\star) \notin \mathcal{Q}$ **then**
4:     **if** $\exists id^\star \in \mathcal{D}_V^\star$ s.t. $\mathsf{Vrfy}(\mathsf{pp}, \mathsf{vk}_{id^\star}, m^\star,$
         $\sigma^\star) \rightarrow \top$ **then**
5:         $\mathsf{flag} := 1$
6: **return** flag

Fig. 1. The unforgeability game for CMDVS.

Experiment: $\mathsf{Exp}_{\Pi,A}^{\mathsf{UF}}(\kappa)$

1: $(\mathsf{pp}, \mathsf{sk}) \leftarrow \mathsf{Setup}(1^\kappa)$
2: $(\mathcal{D}_V^\star, m^\star, \sigma^\star) \leftarrow A^{O_{\mathsf{KG}}, O_s}(1^\kappa, \mathsf{pp})$
3: **if** $(\mathcal{D}_V^\star, m^\star) \notin \mathcal{Q}$ **then**
4:     **if** $\exists id^\star \in \mathcal{D}_V^\star$ s.t. $\mathsf{Vrfy}(\mathsf{pp}, \mathsf{vk}_{id^\star}, m^\star,$
         $\sigma^\star) \rightarrow \top$ **then**
5:         $\mathsf{flag} := 1$
6: **return** flag

Fig. 2. The consistency game for CMDVS.

Remark 1 (On the Maximum Length len of Signatures). CMDVS allows a signer to specify the maximum length len when generating the corresponding signature, since we aim to design IoT-REX so that it is compatible with various environments, including wireless ones, which often restricts bandwidth. The length specification feature enables us to generate signatures so that they fit in the channel's bandwidth. Indeed, a trivial construction using digital signatures produces signatures whose length depends on the number of designated verifiers, whereas the proposed generic construction in Sect. 4 allows flexible parameter settings, i.e., a signer first fixes len and then chooses other parameters.

3.2 Correctness and Security

We introduce the correctness property and security notions for CMDVS.

Oracles. We consider the following oracles. Let List$_{\mathsf{VK}}$ and $\mathcal{Q}$ be an array and a set, respectively, and they are initialized as empty ones. For any id $\in \mathcal{I}$, a key-generation oracle $O_{\mathsf{KG}}(\mathsf{pp}, \mathsf{sk}, \cdot)$ runs $\mathsf{KeyGen}(\mathsf{pp}, \mathsf{sk}, id)$ to get vk$_{id}$. It adds id and vk$_{id}$ to $\mathcal{V}$ and List$_{\mathsf{VK}}$[id], respectively, and returns vk$_{id}$. For any $(\mathcal{D}_V, m,$ len$) \in 2^{\mathcal{V}} \times \mathcal{M} \times \mathbb{N}$, a signing oracle $O_s(\mathsf{sk}, \cdot)$ returns $\mathsf{Sign}(\mathsf{sk}, \mathcal{D}_V, m, \mathsf{len})$. It adds $(\mathcal{D}_V, m)$ to $\mathcal{Q}$ if $\mathsf{Sign}(\mathsf{sk}, \mathcal{D}_V, m, \mathsf{len}) \neq \bot$.

Correctness. The correctness property guarantees that each verifier correctly obtains the output of Vrfy algorithm unless signatures are maliciously modified. We give the formal definition in the full version [38].

Unforgeability. We define unforgeability as a standard security notion for CMDVS. Intuitively, unforgeability guarantees that no adversary can (maliciously) modify a signature for $\mathcal{D}_V^\star \subset \mathcal{V}$ so that at least one non-designated verifier id $\in \mathcal{V} \setminus \mathcal{D}_v^*$ accepts it. Specifically, we consider a security game, given in Fig. 1, against an adversary A, and let $\mathsf{Adv}_{\Pi,A}^{UF}(\kappa) := \Pr[\mathsf{Exp}_{\Pi,A}^{UF}(\kappa) = 1]$ be A's advantage in the game.

Definition 1 (Unforgeability). Let Π be a CMDVS scheme. Π is said to meet unforgeability if for any sufficiently large $\kappa \in \mathbb{N}$ and any PPTA A, it holds $\mathsf{Adv}_{\Pi,A}^{UF}(\kappa) < \mathsf{negl}(\kappa)$.

Consistency. We consider *consistency*, which was originally introduced by Damgård et al. [10] as a security notion for ordinary MDVS. Roughly speaking, consistency guarantees that if at least one designated verifier accepts a signature, then all others also do so. This notion is important in our setting, i.e., remote-control systems for IoT devices, for several possible reasons: for example, it seems difficult to collect the acknowledgment messages from all IoT devices; or, there might be only downstream communication from the systems manager to IoT devices. Therefore, it seems hard to check which designated verifiers accepted a signature (without being maliciously modified). Consistency allows the signer to just check a verification result of a specific designated verifier in order to confirm all verifiers accept the signature.[1]

Specifically, we consider a security game, given in Fig. 2, against an adversary A, and let $\mathsf{Adv}_{\Pi,A}^{Cons}(\kappa) := \Pr[\mathsf{Exp}_{\Pi,A}^{Cons}(\kappa) = 1]$ be A's advantage in the game.

Definition 2 (Consistency). Let Π be a CMDVS scheme. Π is said to meet consistency if for any sufficiently large $\kappa \in \mathbb{N}$ and any PPTA A, it holds $\mathsf{Adv}_{\Pi,A}^{Cons}(\kappa) < \mathsf{negl}(\kappa)$.

4   CMDVS Constructions

We can easily construct a CMDVS scheme $\Pi = (\mathsf{Setup}, \mathsf{KeyGen}, \mathsf{Sign}, \mathsf{Vrfy})$ from any digital signature scheme $\Pi_{DS} = (\mathsf{SigGen}, \mathsf{SigSign}, \mathsf{SigVer})$ by computing $\sigma_{DS} \leftarrow \mathsf{SigSign}(\mathsf{sigk}, \mathcal{D}_V \| m)$ and setting $\sigma := (\mathcal{D}_V, \sigma_{DS})$, where sigk is a signing key. Although this construction is quite simple, the signature size $|\sigma|$ is $|\mathcal{D}_V| \cdot \log_2 |\mathcal{I}| + |\sigma_{DS}|$. Namely, the maximum signature length len must always satisfy $\mathsf{len} \geq |\mathcal{D}_V| \cdot \log_2 |\mathcal{I}| + |\sigma_{DS}|$.

We show a CMDVS scheme from an AMQ structure and DS scheme. Compared to the trivial construction, we can succeed in drastically reducing the signature size by allowing a *small* false-positive probability, which can be made negligible with appropriate parameter settings. In particular, it can flexibly specify len s.t. $\mathsf{len} = o(|\mathcal{D}_V|)$ with adjustment for other parameters.

Approximate Membership Query (AMQ) Structures. For an arbitrary set $\mathcal{U} \subset \{0,1\}^*$, an AMQ data structure $\Pi_{AMQ} = (\mathsf{Gen}, \mathsf{Insert}, \mathsf{Lookup})$ over $\mathcal{U}$ is defined as follows.[2]

---

[1] We assume all verifiers (including non-designated ones) receive the same data regardless of whether it is modified.

[2] Although there are various AMQ structures supporting deletion operations, we do not consider them since we do not require deletion operations for our schemes.

- Gen($\mathcal{U}$, par) $\rightarrow$ (T, aux): it takes $\mathcal{U}$ and a parameter par as input, and outputs an initial structure T and auxiliary information aux. The parameter par varies depending on concrete AMQ structure constructions.
- Insert(T, x, aux) $\rightarrow$ T′: it takes a data structure T, an element $x \in \mathcal{U}$, auxiliary information aux as input, and outputs an updated structure T′.
- Lookup(T, x, aux) $\rightarrow$ true/false: it takes a data structure T, an element $x \in \mathcal{U}$, auxiliary information aux as input, and outputs true or false.

An AMQ structure meets the following completeness, while it allows false positives to make the structure size smaller and its probability can be bounded. Note that false negatives never occur.

Definition 3 (Completeness). For any par, any $(T_0, \text{aux}) \leftarrow \text{Gen}(\mathcal{U}, \text{par})$, any $\mathcal{S} = \{x_1, \ldots, x_{|\mathcal{S}|}\} \subset \mathcal{U}$, we define $\widehat{T} := T_{|\mathcal{S}|}$ as $T_i \leftarrow \text{Insert}(T_{i-1}, x_i, \text{aux})$ for $i \in [|\mathcal{S}|]$. Then, for all $x \in \mathcal{S}$, it holds $\Pr[\text{Lookup}(\widehat{T}, x, \text{aux}) = \text{true}] = 1$.

Definition 4 (Bounded False-Positive Probability). Let Π_{AMQ} be an AMQ structure over $\mathcal{U}$, and suppose that $\widehat{T}$ is generated as in Def. 3 and $n := |\mathcal{S}|$. Then, there exists $\mu_n \in (0, 1]$ such that it holds $\Pr[\text{Lookup}(\widehat{T}, x,$ aux$) = \text{true}] \leq \mu_n$ for any $x \in \mathcal{U} \setminus \mathcal{S}$, where the probability is over Gen and Insert.

AMQ structures mainly aim to compress the description length of $\mathcal{S}$ by allowing false positive errors. Therefore, the size of the structure $\widehat{T}$ should be smaller than the following trivial solutions: (1) encode each element of $\mathcal{S}$ and list them, i.e., $|\mathcal{S}| \cdot \log_2 |\mathcal{U}|$ bits; and (2) prepare an $|\mathcal{U}|$-bit string and set every i-th bit to one if and only if $x_i \in \mathcal{S}$. Namely, it should hold $|\widehat{T}| \leq \min\{|\mathcal{S}| \cdot \log_2 |\mathcal{U}|, |\mathcal{U}|\}$.

There are many instantiations of AMQ structures: the Bloom filter [7] and its variants [16,25], cuckoo filter [12], vacuum filter [36], etc. Although the Bloom filter has been theoretically well-analyzed due to its simple structure, recent constructions (e.g., [12,36]) are (experimentally) more efficient in terms of structure sizes.

Our Generic Construction. In the following, we suppose a function Assign : $\mathbb{N} \times \mathcal{I} \rightarrow 2^{\mathcal{U}}$ over $\mathcal{U}$. Roughly speaking, Assign is a function that uniquely assigns multiple elements in $\mathcal{U}$ to an arbitrary identity, and we assume that for any fixed $\ell \in \mathbb{N}$ and for any id, id′ $\in \mathcal{I}$, it holds Assign(ℓ, id) $\cap$ Assign(ℓ, id′) $= \emptyset$. Note that such a function can be realized in the following way: suppose $\mathcal{I} := \{0,1\}^\gamma, \mathcal{U} := \{0,1\}^{\gamma + \lfloor \log_2 \ell \rfloor + 1}$, and for any ℓ and any id $\in \mathcal{I}$, we define Assign(ℓ, id) $:= \{\beta_1 \| \text{id}, \beta_2 \| \text{id}, \ldots, \beta_\ell \| \text{id}\}$, where β_i is binary representation of $i \in [\ell]$. Our CMDVS scheme from an AMQ structure $\Pi_{\text{AMQ}} = (\text{Gen}, \text{Insert}, \text{Lookup})$ over $\mathcal{U} \subset \{0,1\}^*$ and a DS scheme $\Pi_{\text{DS}} = (\text{SigGen}, \text{SigSign}, \text{SigVer})$ as follows.

- Setup(1^κ): It arbitrarily chooses $\ell \in \mathbb{N}$, and it returns (pp, sk), where pp $:=$ (verk, ℓ) and sk $:=$ (sigk, ℓ).
- KeyGen(pp, sk, id): It returns vk$_{\text{id}} :=$ Assign(ℓ, id).

- $\mathsf{Sign}(\mathsf{sk}, \mathcal{D}_\mathsf{V}, \mathsf{m}, \mathsf{len})$: It derives an appropriate parameter par from $\mathcal{D}_\mathsf{V}$, m, and len. If par cannot be derived, it returns $\bot$. For every $\mathsf{id}_i \in \mathcal{D}_\mathsf{V}$, let $\mathcal{X}_i = \{x_{(i-1)\ell+1}, \ldots, x_{i\ell}\} := \mathsf{Assign}(\ell, \mathsf{id}_i)$.[3] It runs $(\mathsf{T}_0, \mathsf{aux}) \leftarrow \mathsf{Gen}(\mathcal{U}, \mathsf{par})$ and for every $i \in [\ell|\mathcal{D}_\mathsf{V}|]$, it computes $\mathsf{T}_i \leftarrow \mathsf{Insert}(\mathsf{T}_{i-1}, x_i, \mathsf{aux})$. It sets $\sigma := (\widehat{\mathsf{T}}, \mathsf{aux}, \sigma_{\mathrm{DS}})$, where $\widehat{\mathsf{T}} := \mathsf{T}_{\ell|\mathcal{D}_\mathsf{V}|}$ and $\sigma_{\mathrm{DS}} \leftarrow \mathsf{SigSign}(\mathsf{sigk}, \mathsf{m}\|\widehat{\mathsf{T}}\|\mathsf{aux})$. If $|\sigma| > \mathsf{len}$, it returns $\bot$; otherwise, it returns σ.
- $\mathsf{Vrfy}(\mathsf{pp}, \mathsf{vk}_{\mathsf{id}}, \mathsf{m}, \sigma)$: It runs $\mathsf{SigVer}(\mathsf{verk}, (\mathsf{m}\|\widehat{\mathsf{T}}\|\mathsf{aux}, \sigma_{\mathrm{DS}}))$. If the output is $\bot$, it returns $\bot$ and terminates. For every $x \in \mathcal{X}_{\mathsf{id}}$, it returns $\bot$ and terminates if $\mathsf{Lookup}(\widehat{\mathsf{T}}, x, \mathsf{aux})$ outputs $\mathtt{false}$. It returns $\top$ (if all Lookup outputs are $\mathtt{true}$).

The above construction meets the desirable properties below. Due to the page limitation, we give the proof in the full version [38].

Theorem 1. *If a DS scheme Π_{DS} meets UF-CMA security and an AMQ structure Π_{AMQ} meets completeness and bounded false-positive probability such that it holds $\mu_{\ell|\mathcal{D}_\mathsf{V}|} = 2^{-\mathcal{O}(\kappa)}$ for all possible $\ell \in \mathbb{N}$ and $\mathcal{D}_\mathsf{V} \subset \mathcal{V}$ in the above construction, the above CMDVS scheme Π meets correctness, unforgeability, and consistency.*

Instantiations. The above construction can be instantiated with any AMQ structures and digital signatures. After the seminal work of AMQ structures, i.e., the Bloom filter [7], there are various (heuristically) efficient AMQ structure constructions such as the cuckoo filter [12] and the vacuum filter [36]. In this paper, we will employ the vacuum filter as the underlying AMQ structure for implementations in Sect. 5. We also give the theoretical performance of the construction instantiated by the Bloom filter in the full version [38].

System Description. Due to space limitation, we give a concrete description of IoT-REX with the above CMDVS construction in the full version [38].

5   Experiments

In this section, we describe experimental evaluations of IoT-REX. Our primary motivation for the evaluations is to confirm how communication sizes can be reduced by virtue of an AMQ structure compared with the trivial construction and broadcast authentication [37], which supports the functionality that a sender chooses an arbitrary subset of receivers.[4] We implemented the proposed CMDVS constructions in the C++ language with EdDSA [4] and vacuum filters [36]. EdDSA is implemented in the libsodium[5] library version 1.0.18-stable and the vacuum filter is implemented in the Vacuum-Filter library.[6]

---

[3] Namely, $\bigcup_{i=1}^{|\mathcal{D}_\mathsf{V}|} \mathcal{X}_i = \{x_1, x_2, \ldots, x_{\ell|\mathcal{D}_\mathsf{V}|}\}$.

[4] Although the broadcast authentication in [37] is based on message authentication codes (MAC), we simply say signatures as MAC for the sake of convenience.

[5] https://libsodium.gitbook.io/doc/.

[6] https://github.com/wuwuz/Vacuum-Filter.

We first measure the communication size when the proposed CMDVS constructions are implemented on a laptop PC. Our code returns a bit length per designated device via the vacuum filter library and then we count up the total size for communication with the bit length. We also implemented the broadcast authentication [37] with the OpenSSL library version 1.1.1. The environment of the laptop PC is Ubuntu 18.04.5 LTS on the Windows Subsystem for Linux over Windows 11 and is with Intel Core i7-8565U and 16 GB memory. We assume that a device identifier is 64 bits and the bit length of commands for designated devices is 256 bits.

We then discuss the feasibility of IoT-REX by estimating the entire process on a Raspberry Pi over LoRa with its maximum transmission speed of 250 kilobits per second as a typical wireless network setting. On the system model of IoT-REX described in Sect. 2, the laptop PC corresponds to a systems manager SM, and the Raspberry Pi corresponds to an IoT device among the designated devices $\mathcal{I}_{\mathsf{Dsg}}$. Since a Raspberry Pi has become popular, we believe that the estimation gives us insight into IoT-REX in the real world.

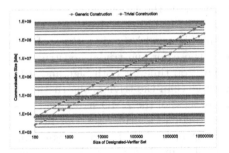

Fig. 3. Communication size versus size of designated-verifier set: The red line, denoted by Generic Construction, represents the proposed generic construction while the blue line, denoted by Trivial Construction, represents the trivial construction, respectively. (Color figure online)

Fig. 4. Computation time versus size of designated-verifier set for Sign: This figure is a box-and-whisker plot. Other setting is common with Fig. 3. The yellow line, denoted by Broadcast Authentication, represents the scheme in [37].

5.1 Results

Communication Size. The results of the communication size are shown in Fig. 3. According to the figure, the communication size for the generic construction becomes four times smaller than the trivial construction and 25 times smaller than the broadcast authentication, respectively. Such advantage of the communication size is obtained by an AMQ structure, i.e., the vacuum filter. The false-positive probability of the vacuum filter is about 0.01% in this measurement.

The bit length per designated device for the generic construction is about 20 bits and is almost stable for any number of the designated devices. It means that the communication size could be compressed by about 30% because the bit length per designated device for the trivial construction is 64 bits. Notably, the communication size could be compressed by about 4% compared to the broadcast authentication.

Computation Time. We also measure the computation time for the Sign and Vrfy algorithms. For the Sign algorithm, the generic construction and the trivial construction are two orders of magnitude faster than the broadcast authentication (see in Fig. 4). Indeed, the generic construction and the trivial construction generate only a single signature while the broadcast authentication needs to generate individual signatures in proportion to the number of devices. Consequently, the computation time could be drastically improved compared to the broadcast authentication.

We also compare the generic construction with the trivial construction in detail, and their results are shown in Fig. 5 and Fig. 6, respectively. According to the figures, the computation times for the Sign and Vrfy algorithms of the generic construction are almost identical to those for the trivial construction until 200,000 devices. Meanwhile, the computation time for both Sign and Vrfy algorithms of the generic construction is greater than the trivial construction.

The reason is that the Insert and Lookup process of the AMQ structure takes a long time in proportion to the size of a designated-verifier set $\mathcal{D}_V$. In contrast, the trivial construction needs only string operations for each algorithm, i.e., concatenation of $\mathcal{D}_V$ for Sign and search of id in $\mathcal{D}_V$ for Vrfy. We note that the computation time for the generic construction should be longer than that for the trivial construction, because the generic construction executes the Insert and Lookup processes as well as the generation of the EdDSA signatures, whereas the trivial construction generates only the EdDSA signatures. The above phenomenon is common with the broadcast authentication since it compute a single verification computation in the Vrfy algorithm.

It also indicates that the overheads caused by the AMQ structure can be represented in the differences between the generic construction and the trivial construction in Fig. 5 and Fig. 6. Specifically, the computation time for the Sign algorithm of the generic construction becomes about five times longer by using the AMQ structure than that of the trivial construction after 500,000 devices. We also note that the computation time for the Vrfy algorithm of the generic construction becomes a hundred times longer due to the use of the AMQ structure.

Entire Performance. Based on the results in the previous subsections, we discuss the feasibility of IoT-REX. The entire performance of IoT-REX over the LoRa network with the Raspberry Pi is estimated as shown in Fig. 7. This figure shows the entire performance of IoT-REX over the LoRa network, including the

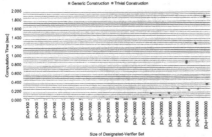
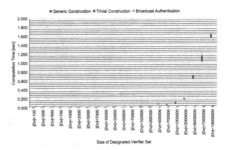

Fig. 5. Computation time versus size of designated-verifier set for Sign: This figure is a box-and-whisker plot. Other setting is common with Fig. 3.

Fig. 6. Computation time versus size of designated-verifier set for Vrfy: The setting is common with Fig. 5.

computation for the Sign and Vrfy algorithms, wherein a systems manager SM generates an authenticated command $\widehat{cmd}$ and each device id receives $\widehat{cmd}$. Here, the entire performance is then estimated over LoRa with its maximum transmission speed of 250 kilo-bits per second as described above.

According to the figure, the performance of IoT-REX based on the generic construction is three times faster than that based on the trivial construction. Compared to the broadcast authentication, it is 25 times faster than the broadcast authentication, and therefore two orders of magnitude faster. In particular, the elapsed time per device is about 0.08 milliseconds for the generic construction, about 0.26 milliseconds for the trivial construction, and about 2 milliseconds for the broadcast authentication, respectively. The performance improvement is obtained by virtue of compressing the communication size via the AMQ structures.

Since the performance improvement by the proposed construction is stable for any number of devices in $\mathcal{D}_V$, we can also estimate the number of IoT devices which can be controlled within a second. Notably, devices of more than 12,000 can be controlled by IoT-REX based on the proposed construction over LoRa, which is greater than 4,000 devices by the trivial construction and 400 devices by the broadcast authentication.

Communication Overheads on Low-Power Wide Area Networks. We discuss IoT-REX over low-power wide area networks other than LoRa as further applications. We know eMTC[7] with its maximum transmission speed of 1 megabits per second and SIGFOX[8] with its maximum transmission speed of 600 bits per second as specifications for low-power wide area networks.

---

[7] https://halberdbastion.com/technology/iot/iot-protocols/emtc-lte-cat-m1#:~:text=An%20eMTC%20Cat%2DM1%20network,any%20existing%20LTE%20channel%20width..

[8] https://www.sigfox.com/en/what-sigfox/technology.

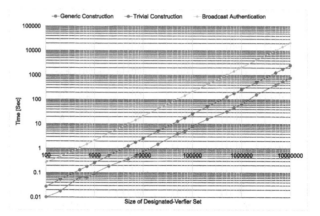

Fig. 7. Entire performance versus the size of the designated-verifier set. The setting is common with Fig. 3. This figure includes both the communication time and the computation time.

IoT-REX based on the generic construction is stably three times faster than the trivial construction and 25 times faster than the broadcast authentication over these networks by virtue of compressing the communication cost. For instance, in the case of SIGFOX, 12,000 devices are controlled within about 308 s by the generic construction, within about 1200 s by the trivial construction, and within 10240 s by the broadcast authentication. In the case of eMTC, 12,000 devices can be controlled within about 0.24 s by the generic construction, 0.64 s by the trivial construction, and 6.59 s by the broadcast authentication.

Overall, for a communication protocol with its maximum transmission speed of 50 mega-bits per second, IoT-REX based on the generic construction is faster than the trivial construction. For a communication protocol whose maximum transmission speed is 100 greater than mega-bits per second, IoT-REX based on the generic construction is still faster than the trivial construction as long as the number of IoT devices is fewer than 700,000. Moreover, it is also faster than the broadcast authentication over 5G with its maximum transmission speed of 10 gigabits per second by virtue of the use of a single signature.

6   Related Work

Cryptographic Protocols Based on AMQ Structures. Most of the cryptographic research related to AMQ structures (e.g., [11, 23]) focus on the Bloom filter [7] since unlike recent experimentally-efficient AMQ structures, it has been well analyzed in a theoretical sense. However, the previous works have completely different goals from ours. To the best of our knowledge, there is no research on cryptographic protocols based on AMQ structures in the context of secure remote control.

Message Authentication Protocols for Many Users. MDVS [19] is digital signatures in the multi-user setting. Each user has signing and verification keys, and any user can designate an arbitrary subset of other users and generate a signature so that only the designated users can check the validity of the signature. On the other hand, CMDVS is a restricted version of MDVS, and our CMDVS construction only requires AMQ structures and standard digital signatures, which are lightweight enough for IoT environments. For the efficiency reason, we only employed our CMDVS scheme for the experimental evaluations.

Broadcast authentication [8,26,27,30,32,34] aims to broadcast a single piece of data to many receivers with data authenticity. However, except for Watanabe et al.'s work [37], the existing works do not support the functionality that a sender chooses an arbitrary subset of receivers; data is always broadcast to all receivers. Watanabe et al. [37] introduced anonymous broadcast authentication (ABA), which supports such functionality and provable anonymity. Although ABA and CMDVS have similar functionality, they have a clear difference between them: due to the provable anonymity, the lower bound on the authenticator sizes of ABA is $\Omega(d \cdot \kappa)$, where d is the number of designated receivers and κ is the security parameter. Our CMDVS construction overcame the lower bound.

IoT Security. IoT security can be realized from the firmware level [9] to the application [31]. Although the conventional approach focuses on controlling the data flow [13,14], the cryptographic approach is discussed in recent years [2,18, 28]. To the best of our knowledge, the IoT security in recent years is based on two ways [33], machine learning [21,24] or trusted execution environments [35,39]. These approaches often utilize a central server to control resource-constrained IoT devices outside of them. In contrast, our approach is built-in for IoT devices because the Vrfy algorithm is embedded in them.

7 Concluding Remarks

In this paper, we proposed IoT-REX, a secure system aiming to control IoT devices remotely. IoT-REX enables us to not only bring infected IoT devices to a halt but also have any subset of all IoT devices execute arbitrary commands. To this end, we introduced a novel cryptographic primitive for IoT-REX, called centralized multi-designated verifier signatures (CMDVS). We also provided an efficient CMDVS construction, which yields compact communication sizes and fast verification procedures for IoT-REX. We further discussed the feasibility of IoT-REX by implementing the CMDVS construction with vacuum filters and its experimental evaluation with a Raspberry Pi. We have released our source to provide reproducibility and expect further subsequent work. According to the evaluation results, the CMDVS construction can compress communication size to about 30% for the trivial construction and 4% for the broadcast authentication; hence, it is expected to IoT-REX based on the CMDVS construction is three times faster than the trivial construction and 25 times faster than the broadcast authentication over typical low-power wide area networks even with an IoT device. Furthermore, we discussed that IoT-REX is feasible with respect to the communication overheads on low-power wide area networks. We thus conclude that IoT-REX based on the CMDVS construction is practical. We plan to conduct experiments of IoT-REX in the real world for further evaluation, including physics features.

Acknowledgment. This research was conducted under a contract of "Research and development on IoT malware removal/make it non-functional technologies for effective use of the radio spectrum" among "Research and Development for Expansion of Radio Wave Resources (JPJ000254)", which was supported by the Ministry of Internal Affairs and Communications, Japan.

Code Availability. Our source code is publicly available via GitHub (https://github.com/naotoyanai/fiilter-signature_ABA).

References

1. The internet of things reference model. Technical report, Cisco (2014)
2. Andersen, M.P., et al.: WAVE: a decentralized authorization framework with transitive delegation. In: USENIX Security 2019, pp. 1375–1392. USENIX Association (2019)
3. Antonakakis, M., et al.: Understanding the Mirai botnet. In: USENIX Security 2017, pp. 1093–1110. USENIX Association (2017)
4. Bernstein, D.J., Duif, N., Lange, T., Schwabe, P., Yang, B.: High-speed high-security signatures. J. Cryptogr. Eng. **2**(2), 77–89 (2012)
5. Bertino, E., Islam, N.: Botnets and internet of things security. Computer **50**(2), 76–79 (2017)
6. binti Mohamad Noor, M., Hassan, W.H.: Current research on internet of things (IoT) security: a survey. Comput. Netw. **148**, 283–294 (2019)
7. Bloom, B.H.: Space/time trade-offs in hash coding with allowable errors. Commun. ACM **13**(7), 422–426 (1970)
8. Chan, H., Perrig, A.: Round-efficient broadcast authentication protocols for fixed topology classes. In: IEEE S&P 2010, pp. 257–272 (2010)
9. Costin, A., Zaddach, J., Francillon, A., Balzarotti, D.: A large-scale analysis of the security of embedded firmwares. In: USENIX Security 2019, pp. 95–110. USENIX Association (2014)
10. Damgård, I., Haagh, H., Mercer, R., Nitulescu, A., Orlandi, C., Yakoubov, S.: Stronger security and constructions of multi-designated verifier signatures. In: Pass, R., Pietrzak, K. (eds.) TCC 2020. LNCS, vol. 12551, pp. 229–260. Springer, Cham (2020). https://doi.org/10.1007/978-3-030-64378-2_9
11. Derler, D., Jager, T., Slamanig, D., Striecks, C.: Bloom filter encryption and applications to efficient forward-secret 0-RTT key exchange. In: Nielsen, J.B., Rijmen, V. (eds.) EUROCRYPT 2018. LNCS, vol. 10822, pp. 425–455. Springer, Cham (2018). https://doi.org/10.1007/978-3-319-78372-7_14
12. Fan, B. Andersen, ,D.G., Kaminsky, M., Mitzenmacher, M.D.: Cuckoo filter: practically better than Bloom. In: CoNEXT 2014, pp. 75–88. ACM (2014)
13. Fan, J., He, Y., Tang, B., Li, Q., Sandhu, R.: Ruledger: ensuring execution integrity in trigger-action IoT platforms. In: IEEE INFOCOM 2021, pp. 1–10. IEEE (2021)

14. Fernandes, E., Paupore, J., Rahmati, A., Simionato, D., Conti, M., Prakash, A.: FlowFence: practical data protection for emerging IoT application frameworks. In: USENIX Security 2016, pp. 531–548. USENIX Association (2016)

15. Iftikhar, Z., et al.: Privacy preservation in resource-constrained IoT devices using blockchain-a survey. Electronics 10(14), 1–26 (2021)

16. Kirsch, A., Mitzenmacher, M.: Less hashing, same performance: building a better bloom filter. In: Azar, Y., Erlebach, T. (eds.) ESA 2006. LNCS, vol. 4168, pp. 456–467. Springer, Heidelberg (2006). https://doi.org/10.1007/11841036_42

17. Kobayashi, H., Watanabe, Y., Shikata, J.: Asymptotically tight lower bounds in anonymous broadcast encryption and authentication. In: Paterson, M.B. (ed.) IMACC 2021. LNCS, vol. 13129, pp. 105–128. Springer, Cham (2021). https://doi.org/10.1007/978-3-030-92641-0_6

18. Kumar, S., Hu, Y., Andersen, M.P., Popa, R.A., Culler, D.E.: JEDI: many-to-many end-to-end encryption and key delegation for IoT. In: USENIX Security 2019, pp. 1519–1536. USENIX Association (2019)

19. Laguillaumie, F., Vergnaud, D.: Multi-designated verifiers signatures. In: Lopez, J., Qing, S., Okamoto, E. (eds.) ICICS 2004. LNCS, vol. 3269, pp. 495–507. Springer, Heidelberg (2004). https://doi.org/10.1007/978-3-540-30191-2_38

20. Lei, X., Tu, G.-H. , Li, C.-Y., Xie, T., Zhang,M.: SecWIR: securing smart home IoT communications via Wi-Fi routers with embedded intelligence. In: MobiSys 2020, pp. 260–272. ACM (2020)

21. Mothukuri, V., Khare, P., Parizi, R.M., Pouriyeh, S., Dehghantanha, A., Srivastava, G.: Federated-learning-based anomaly detection for IoT security attacks. IEEE Internet Things J. 9(4), 2545–2554 (2022)

22. Mpitziopoulos, A., Gavalas, D., Pantziou, G., Konstantopoulos, C.: Defending wireless sensor networks from jamming attacks. In: 2007 IEEE 18th International Symposium on Personal, Indoor and Mobile Radio Communications, pp. 1–5. IEEE (2007)

23. Naor, M., Yogev, E.: Bloom filters in adversarial environments. In: Gennaro, R., Robshaw, M. (eds.) CRYPTO 2015. LNCS, vol. 9216, pp. 565–584. Springer, Heidelberg (2015). https://doi.org/10.1007/978-3-662-48000-7_28

24. Nguyen, T.D., Marchal, S., Miettinen, M., Fereidooni, H., Asokan, N., Sadeghi, A.-R.: DIoT: a federated self-learning anomaly detection system for IoT. In: IEEE ICDCS, pp. 756–767. IEEE (2019)

25. Pagh, A., Pagh, R., Rao, S.S.: An optimal Bloom filter replacement. In: ACM-SIAM Symposium on Discrete Algorithms, SODA 2005, pp. 823–829. SIAM (2005)

26. Perrig, A.: The BiBa one-time signature and broadcast authentication protocol. In: ACM CCS 2001, pp. 28–37. ACM (2001)

27. Perrig, A., Canetti, R., Tygar, J.D., Song, D.: Efficient authentication and signing of multicast streams over lossy channels. In: IEEE S&P 2000, pp. 56–73 (2000)

28. Rana, M., Mamun, Q., Islam, R.: Lightweight cryptography in IoT networks: a survey. Futur. Gener. Comput. Syst. 129, 77–89 (2022)

29. Raza, S., Wallgren, L., Voigt, T.: SVELTE: real-time intrusion detection in the internet of things. Ad Hoc Netw. 11(8), 2661–2674 (2013)

30. Rezazadeh Baee, M.A., Simpson, L., Boyen, X., Foo, E., Pieprzyk, J.: ALI: anonymous lightweight inter-vehicle broadcast authentication with encryption. IEEE Trans. Dependable Secure Comput. 1 (2022). (Early Access)

31. Ronen, E., Shamir, A., Weingarten, A.-O., O'Flynn, C.: IoT goes nuclear: creating a ZigBee chain reaction. In: IEEE S&P, pp. 195–212. IEEE (2017)

32. Safavi-Naini, R., Wang, H.: Broadcast authentication for group communication. Theoret. Comput. Sci. 269(1), 1–21 (2001)

33. Schiller, E., Aidoo, A., Fuhrer, J., Stahl, J., Ziörjen, M., Stiller, B.: Landscape of IoT security. Comput. Sci. Rev. **44**(100467), 1–18 (2022)
34. Shim, K.: BASIS: a practical multi-user broadcast authentication scheme in wireless sensor networks. IEEE Trans. Inf. Forensics Secur. **12**(7), 1545–1554 (2017)
35. Suzaki, K., Tsukamoto, A., Green, A., Mannan,M.: Reboot-oriented IoT: life cycle management in trusted execution environment for disposable IoT devices. In: ACSAC 2020, pp. 428–441. ACM (2020)
36. Wang, M., Zhou, M., Shi, S., Qian, C.: Vacuum filters: more space-efficient and faster replacement for Bloom and cuckoo filters. VLDB **13**(2), 197–210 (2019)
37. Watanabe, Y., Yanai, N., Shikata, J.: Anonymous broadcast authentication for securely remote-controlling IoT devices. In: Barolli, L., Woungang, I., Enokido, T. (eds.) AINA 2021. LNNS, vol. 226, pp. 679–690. Springer, Cham (2021). https://doi.org/10.1007/978-3-030-75075-6_56
38. Watanabe, Y., Yanai, N., Shikata, J.: IoT-REX: a secure remote-control system for IoT devices from centralized multi-designated verifier signatures (2022)
39. Xu, M., et al.: Dominance as a new trusted computing primitive for the internet of things. In: IEEE S&P, pp. 1415–1430. IEEE (2019)

CVAR-FL IoV Intrusion Detection Framework

Jia Zhao[1,2], Xinyu Rao[1,2(✉)], JiQiang Liu[1,2], Yue Guo[1,2], and BoKai Yang[1,2]

[1] Beijing Key Laboratory of Security and Privacy in Intelligent Transportation, Beijing Jiaotong University, Beijing 100044, China
{zhaojia,22125303,jqliu,22125178,19281025}@bjtu.edu.cn
[2] School of Computer and Information Technology, Beijing Jiaotong University, Beijing 100044, China

Abstract. With the popularization of internet of vehicles (IoV) applications, security issues are becoming increasingly prominent. IoV is vulnerable to various attacks, which may endanger users' privacy, functionality, property and even life. The security problems in IoV have the characteristics of dynamism, complexity and concealment. Therefore, IoV intrusion detection is a key technology to ensure network security. In this paper, we first analyze the existing intrusion detection schemes, and propose an IoV intrusion detection system based on CVAR-FL, which distributes the functions of intrusion detection system (IDS) to roadside units (RSU), and adopts the idea of ensemble learning, combining four deep learning (DL) models: cnn, vgg16, alexnet, resnet18, with federated learning (FL) algorithm, to provide more diversified detection model choices. In addition, we also propose to use an encryption strategy based on elliptic curve cryptography (ECC) based ciphertext-policy ABE (CP-ABE) to protect the data exchange between RSU and vehicles, thus improving the efficiency and confidentiality of network communication. Finally, we verify the effectiveness of the proposed scheme through experiments and conduct relevant analysis.

Keywords: IoV · Security issues · IDS · CP-ABE · Federated learning

1 Introduction

With the progress of smart networking and digitization, the architecture of smart connected vehicles will become more complex [18,22]. The internet of vehicles (IoV) uses IEEE 802.11p to form a network of vehicles and infrastructure that can handle vehicle data for various services [5,9]. Since the vehicle consists of multiple components, such as vehicle machines, internal gateways and controllers with different compilation environments, operating systems and transport protocols, existing network intrusion detection systems (IDSs) cannot fully prevent

Supported by organization the National Key R&D Program of China (2020YFB2103800).

and isolate threats against vehicles [10], such as the FusionRipper attacks that compromise multi-sensor fusion (MSF) algorithms mentioned in paper [19]. In-vehicle networks are also vulnerable and hackers can control the vehicle's main controller by attacking the controller area network (CAN) bus, leading to accidents, for example in paper [3,4,14] and other attacks against the CAN bus mentioned therein. Therefore, it is crucial to prevent cyber attacks on the IoV.

Intrusion detection systems (IDSs) can be used as a second line of defense after preventive protection mechanisms such as software integrity verification [13], enabling continuous event monitoring [15]. Machine learning techniques are playing an increasingly important role in reducing the problems associated with smart vehicles [23], thus driving changes in the development of intrusion detection for the connected vehicle. The controller area network (CAN) bus is a low fault-tolerant protocol used mainly for real-time communication between ECUs and in-vehicle networks [12], which is widely used in in-vehicle networks for its low cost, noise immunity, and fault tolerance, but sending highly real-time messages causes significant delays and is therefore not suitable for introducing heavy security mechanisms.

Limited Computational Resources. Nodes in the vehicular network may have limited computation and memory capacities. However, the training process of deep learning models, both in terms of data sampling and analysis, will consume a large number of node resources. Therefore, the performance overhead that the model imposes on the smart car needs to be considered.

Dynamicity. One of the major differences between the internet of things (IoT) and the IoV is the dynamic nature of vehicles, which means that the topology of the entire IoV is frequently changing and vehicle nodes have random access to the network [18], which will lead to objective conditions such as network quality and the amount of data received between RSUs in different regions having large variations. However, the detection performance of deep learning models is highly dependent on these values.

Privacy Data Leakage. Privacy data leakage can occur due to a large number of devices and communication protocols involved in the IoV system.

Our contributions are as follows:

- We propose the CVAR-FL IoV intrusion detection framework. Federated learning for model training only requires the transmission of local model gradients instead of the raw data, which can reduce the transmission bandwidth consumption in the IoV. We also integrate four deep learning (DL) models such as convolutional neural network (CNN), vgg16, alexnet, and resnet18 into the proposed FL intrusion detection framework as a way to provide more diverse choices to users.
- As mentioned in [11], data leakage is inevitable in the IoV, but the availability, mobility, computing power and real-time performance of the IoV system require a faster and lighter encryption protocol. Therefore, we propose to apply the CP-ABE algorithm for confidentiality protection in data transmission.

– Experiments are designed to investigate the feasibility of the proposed model. Simulation results show that the designed framework has significant potential in securing the IoV.

The rest of the paper is organized as follows. Section 2 reviews the related work. Section 3 describes the FL based IDS. Numerical results are provided to evaluate the proposed intrusion detection method in Sect. 4. Section 5 summarises our work and provides an outlook of future work on data-driven intrusion detection in intelligent connected vehicles.

2   Related Work

[2] presents an AI-based intrusion detection architecture that is deployed on a MEC server in an IoV network. It proposes two classification techniques: direct time-series-based classification and sequence image-based classification, and shows that CNNs achieve the best performance through experiments. [1] extends the model from [2] by comparing three classes of deep learning models for fine-grained vehicle classification. [25] proposes a ConvLSTM-based intrusion detection method for IVNs that leverages the periodicity of network message IDs. None of the above papers consider the privacy issues of data transmission in Telematics and the computational resource issues faced when the models are deployed. [26] presents an intelligent IDS using tree models, which is applicable not only to the CAN bus of self-driving cars, but also to the general vehicle network. [27] applies CNN with hyperparameter optimization, transfer learning, and ensemble learning for IoV. [24] presents a robust transformer-based intrusion detection system (RTIDS). Although all these schemes take into account the computational resource consumption of the model runtime to some extent, they still focus on the detection of malicious samples and do not discuss much about the risk of leakage in data transmission. [8] proposes a FL based IDS to provide a security solution for the IoV under a SDN architecture. The proposed IDS integrates trust indicators to help secure the IoV. [28] uses Federated LSTM to detect network intrusions in smart connected cars, and introduces the Telematics system model and CAN data framework. However, some scholars [7] point out that federal learning does not fully guarantee the security of private data.

3   CVAR-FL Framework

This paper presents a system architecture that is illustrated in Fig. 1. The system consists of vehicles, RSUs, and MEC (Multi-access Edge Computing) to form a three-tier architecture. The MEC provides computational support and is responsible for aggregating federated model updates and storing data. The RSU, as the core of the whole system, performs local model training, data collection and processing, and intrusion detection. When a vehicle enters the RSU's service area, it can request a detection service, and the RSU will collect the CAN data transmitted by the vehicle and use it to clean and train the model.

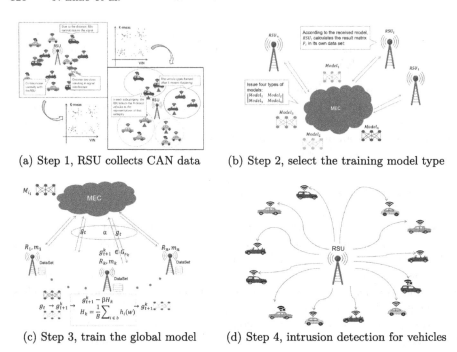

(a) Step 1, RSU collects CAN data   (b) Step 2, select the training model type

(c) Step 3, train the global model   (d) Step 4, intrusion detection for vehicles

Fig. 1. Schematic diagram of CVAR-FL framework

3.1   Data Transfer Between Vehicle and RSU

The first thing to consider when bringing FL into the IoV domain is the dynamic nature of vehicles. The movement of vehicles can cause the data quality collected by RSU to decline (transmission delay, message collision or interruption). The benefit of intrusion detection is for the detected vehicles rather than RSU, so we assume that the vehicles in the system are active participating members, and they will transmit vehicle identification number (VIN) and location information to RSU when their own conditions are ready. As shown in Fig. 1(a), RSU classifies the vehicles within the range according to VIN code by K-means clustering, assuming that they can be divided into N categories. RSU will select kN vehicles from these N categories as local data sources according to the Euclidean formula (each category selects $k \geq 1$ vehicles).

We want the data transmitted from the vehicle to the RSU to not be leaked to an attacker outside the system. Moreover, the vehicle itself is a constantly changing process, and too frequent encryption and decryption will increase system latency and decrease resource utilization. [6,17,21] and others have proposed the application of elliptic curve elliptic curve cryptography (ECC) to ciphertext-policy ABE (CP-ABE), where ECC can guarantee fine-grained access control to data or resources in less computation time and is suitable for resource-constrained IoT frameworks. The EPSAR-CP-ABE scheme proposed by [17] allows the user's access rights to be modified without changing their original key, making it ideal for vehicles in dynamic scenarios. Since it is an improvement on CP-ABE-CSSK, its encryption and decryption times are less than those of other CP-ABE schemes. For this reason, we will use the EPSAR-CP-ABE scheme for data encryption and decryption. The following is a brief description of the application process for the EPSAR-CP-ABE scheme:

Initialization. The vehicle will perform the key initialization phase, using a large prime number p to define an elliptic curve group $\mathcal{G} = \{p, E_p(a, b), P\}$, where P is the base point of the elliptic curve, E_p is an encryption-friendly elliptic curve, $4a^3 + 27b \neq 0$, and $a, b \in P$. Choose three random numbers α, k_1 and k_2 from the range of p to generate the global key $GSK = \{\alpha, k_1, k_2\}$. Define the number of attributes n in the system. Calculate $P_i = \alpha^i P, U_i = k_1 P_i, V_i = k_2 P_i, \forall i \in 1 \ldots n$. Define 4 hash functions as shown in Eq. 1, where σ is some large random number, M is the message to be encrypted, and $|x|$ denotes the length of the string x.

$$
\begin{aligned}
H_1, H_4 &: \{0,1\}^* \to Z_p^* \\
H_2 &: \{0,1\}^* \to \{0,1\}^\sigma \\
H_3 &: \{0,1\}^* \to \{0,1\}^{|M|}
\end{aligned}
\tag{1}
$$

This generates the global public key $GPK = \{\mathcal{G}, P_i, V_i, U_i, H_1, H_2, H_3, H_4\}$. Next, generate a private key for the RSU with ID number r. The RSU attribute set $\mathcal{A} = \{a_1, a_2, \ldots, a_n\}$ specifies the brand, model, hardware information, software equipment, etc. of the RSU. The vehicle can change the access policy according to $\mathcal{A}$ and provide fine-grained access permission for each RSU to prevent malicious RSU problems. Define the function $\lambda_i = (\alpha + H_4(i))^{(1-a_i)}, z(\alpha, \mathcal{A}) = \prod_{i=1}^{n} \lambda_i$. Generate two non-zero random numbers k_4 and k_5 for r, and use them in Eq. 2 to obtain u_1, u_2 and u_3. Then save λ_i for each vehicle.

$$
\begin{aligned}
u_1 &= k_4 + k_1 \cdot z(\alpha, \mathcal{A})(\mathrm{mod}\, p) \\
u_2 &= k_5 - k_2 \cdot z(\alpha, \mathcal{A})(\mathrm{mod}\, p) \\
u_3 &= k_4 k_2 + k_5 k_1 (\mathrm{mod}\, p)
\end{aligned}
\tag{2}
$$

Store $\{r, X_i = u_3 \cdot z(\alpha, \mathcal{A}), \mathcal{A}\}$ on the vehicle. The RSUr key is $k_r = \{u_1, u_2\}$.

Encryption. Before transmitting the data, the vehicle encrypts the plaintext M with the access policy $\mathcal{P} = \{b_1, b_2 \ldots b_n\}$. Choose a random number σ_m. The key derivation function $KDF()$ to calculate $r_m = H_1(\mathcal{P}, M, \sigma_m)$ and $k_m = KDF(r_m \mathcal{P})$. The encryption formula is as follows:

$$
\left\{
\begin{aligned}
z(\alpha, \mathcal{P}) &= \prod_{i=1}^{n}(\alpha + H_4(i))^{(1-b_i)} \\
P_{m,i} &= r_m P_i, i \in \{1, \cdots, n - |\mathcal{P}|\} \\
K_{1,m} &= r_m k_1 z(\alpha, \mathcal{P}) P \\
K_{2,m} &= r_m k_2 z(\alpha, \mathcal{P}) P \\
C_{\sigma_m} &= H_2(k_m) \oplus \sigma_m \\
C_m &= H_3(\sigma_m) \oplus M
\end{aligned}
\right.
\tag{3}
$$

Output cipher $C = \{\mathcal{P}, P_{m,i}, K_{1,m}, K_{2,m}, C_{\sigma_m}, C_m\}$ to RSU.

Decryption. The RSU receives the ciphertext and calculates $U = u_2 K_{1,m}$ and $V = u_1 K_{2,m}$. Return $\{U, V, r'\}$ to the vehicle that sent the ciphertext C. The vehicle uses Eq. 4 and the received U, V, r' to compute T, and sends T back to the RSU r'. Here, Z_i is the coefficient of x_i in $Z(x)$.

$$Z(\alpha, \mathcal{A}, \mathcal{P}) = \sum_{i=1}^{n-|\mathcal{P}|} (\alpha + H_4(i))^{(a_i - b_i)}$$

$$Q = \frac{U + V}{X_i} = \frac{r_m u_3 Z(\alpha) P}{X_i} \tag{4}$$

$$W = r_m Z(\alpha) P - r_m Z_0 P$$

$$T = \frac{1}{F_0}(Q - W)$$

The Eq. 6 is used to decrypt the RSU based on the received T. The RSU that satisfies the Eq. 5 matches the policy $\mathcal{P}$ for the property $\mathcal{A}$.

$$Q = r_m Z(\alpha) P$$
$$T = r_m P \tag{5}$$

The original message M is the same as message M' if $r'_m P = T$, otherwise, the process fails.

$$\sigma'_m = H_2(KDF(T)) \oplus C_{\sigma_m}$$
$$M' = C_m \oplus H_3(\sigma'_m) \tag{6}$$
$$r'_m = H_1(\mathcal{P}, M', \sigma'_m)$$

3.2 DL Model Selection for RSU

As IoT devices, RSUs have various types, and RSUs produced by different manufacturers have different software and hardware resources. Moreover, in the same period, the CAN data received by RSUs on the main roads of the city will be much more than those on the branches of towns and villages. Therefore, we need to provide more personalized models for RSUs in different places. As shown in Fig. 1(b), we adopt the idea of ensemble learning and integrate four pre-trained DL models (CNN, vgg16, resnet18, alexnet) in MEC. At the beginning of system startup, MEC will distribute these four models to selected α RSUs. Let the i-th RSU be R_i, then R_i will use four models to train on the local dataset, and return the updated gradient $g_k, k \in [1, 4]$ and F1 score $f_k, k \in [1, 4]$ to MEC after the model converges, where g_k and f_k correspond one by one, indicating the values obtained by training the k-th model. The formula for calculating F1 score is shown in Eq. 11. F'_i represents the temporary result matrix of R_i, then F'_i is shown in Eq. 7.

$$F'_i = \begin{bmatrix} f_1 \ g_1 \\ f_2 \ g_2 \\ f_3 \ g_3 \\ f_4 \ g_4 \end{bmatrix} \tag{7}$$

The specific four types of models will be selected according to resource dependency. We define a coefficient matrix θ, and set four resource-related parameters: maximum training time t, minimum loss value l, model size u, and CPU performance required for training c. For the four types of models CNN, vgg16, resnet18, and alexnet, the maximum training time t, model size u, and CPU performance required for training c are all different, while the minimum loss value l is the same. At the same time, define a scaling function $\mathcal{F}$, such that $\mathcal{F}(t), \mathcal{F}(l), \mathcal{F}(u), \mathcal{F}(c) \in (0, 1]$, since we hope that these four values are as small as possible, we can get Eq. 8:

$$\theta = \begin{bmatrix} \mathcal{F}(t_1)\mathcal{F}(l)\mathcal{F}(u_1)\mathcal{F}(c_1) \\ \mathcal{F}(t_2)\mathcal{F}(l)\mathcal{F}(u_2)\mathcal{F}(c_2) \\ \mathcal{F}(t_3)\mathcal{F}(l)\mathcal{F}(u_3)\mathcal{F}(c_3) \\ \mathcal{F}(t_4)\mathcal{F}(l)\mathcal{F}(u_4)\mathcal{F}(c_4) \end{bmatrix} = \begin{bmatrix} \theta_1 \\ \theta_2 \\ \theta_3 \\ \theta_4 \end{bmatrix} \tag{8}$$

Thus the final result matrix F_i is shown in Eq. 9.

$$F_i = \begin{bmatrix} f_1/\theta_1 \ g_1 \\ f_2/\theta_2 \ g_2 \\ f_3/\theta_3 \ g_3 \\ f_4/\theta_4 \ g_4 \end{bmatrix} \tag{9}$$

3.3 MEC Federal Learning

After MEC receives the result matrices from all RSUs, it will get the set $F = \{F_1, F_2, \ldots, F_n\}$. Next, MEC performs a matrix addition operation to obtain the cumulative score matrix F_{sum} of the F1 values of the four types of models and its corresponding gradient matrix G_{sum}, as shown in Eq. 10:

$$F_{sum} = [\sum_{i=1}^{n}(F_i \begin{bmatrix} 1 \\ 0 \end{bmatrix})]^\top = [F_{s_1} \ F_{s_2} \ F_{s_3} \ F_{s_4}] \ (i \in n)$$

$$G_{sum} = [G_{s_1} \ G_{s_2} \ G_{s_3} \ G_{s_4}]$$

$$= \begin{bmatrix} F_{1_{11}} & F_{1_{12}} & F_{1_{13}} & F_{1_{14}} \\ F_{2_{11}} & F_{2_{12}} & F_{2_{13}} & F_{2_{14}} \\ \vdots & \vdots & \vdots & \vdots \\ F_{n-1_{11}} & F_{n-1_{12}} & F_{n-1_{13}} & F_{n-1_{14}} \\ F_{n_{11}} & F_{n_{12}} & F_{n_{13}} & F_{n_{14}} \end{bmatrix} \tag{10}$$

Take the maximum value $F_{s_k} = MAX(F_{sum})$ in F_{sum} as the final model M_{select} in the FL system, and get the corresponding gradient $g_{select} = G_{s_k}$. As shown in Fig. 1(c), suppose in the t-th round, the global model on MEC is M_{i_t}, the set of RSUs participating in the update is $R = \{R_1, R_2, \ldots, R_n\}$, $R_k \in R$, the size of the corresponding data index set is m_k, and the total number of samples in the data sets of all participants is $m = \sum_{k=1}^{n} m_k$. On MEC, there is a proportion $\alpha \in (0, 1]$ of RSUs participating in FL, then the number of RSUs participating in the t-th round of iteration is $max(\alpha n, 1) \to m$. β is the learning rate, the loss function is $H_k = \frac{1}{B} \sum_{i \in b} h_i(w)$, where B is the training batch size, b is a data index in a batch in R_k, then the total loss function of FL is $H(w) = \sum_{k=1}^{m} \frac{m_k}{m} H_k(w, b)$. R_k uses the model gradient g_t issued by MEC to initialize the model on M_{select} as $g_t \to g_{t+1}^k$, then divides its own data set into several batches of size B, updates the local model parameters in each iteration as $g_{t+1}^k - \beta H_k \to g_{t+1}^k$, and then transmits the updated local model parameters $g_{t+1}^k \in G_{s_k}$ to MEC. MEC aggregates all the parameters as $g_{t+1} = \sum_{k=1}^{n} \frac{m_k}{m} g_{t+1}^k$, and then sends the result back to all RSUs participating in training. The whole system will repeat this process until g_{t+1} converges.

As shown Fig. 1(d), RSU will use the converged global model to perform intrusion detection on the vehicles within its service range. MEC will continuously monitor the global model that reaches the convergence state. Once it finds that the model detection performance is degraded due to reasons such as the change of CAN data collected by RSU due to vehicle movement, special RSU offline, etc., it will restart the entire FL process again.

4   Experimental Setup

4.1   Evaluation Index

Accuracy. We use the F1 score as a measure of accuracy for our classification model, as it combines both precision and recall in a single metric. The F1 score is defined by Eq. 11, where TP, FP, and FN are the abbreviations of true positives, false positives, and false negatives, respectively. The F1 score ranges from 0 to 1, with higher values indicating better performance.

$$F1 = \left(\frac{2 + FP/TP + FN/TP}{2}\right)^{-1} \tag{11}$$

System Time Consumed. The RSU performs the intrusion detection, while the vehicles within the RSU's coverage area are the targets of intrusion detection. Both the RSU and the MEC are static physical models, so the communication between them can support long and continuous transmission. As a dynamic model, the vehicle has to consider the time limit for data transmission with the RSU. Therefore, we assume that the vehicle being detected initiates the intrusion detection request to the RSU. The RSU will only run the model when it receives a request from a vehicle that meets the detection criteria. The delay T as Eq. 12 can be optimized in the system mainly consists of the data pre-processing time t_p and the model training time t_t.

$$T = t_p + t_t \tag{12}$$

Resource Consumption. We will evaluate the storage space and the memory required for model training to filter out the models that can fit the RSU.

4.2 Dataset Introduction

We use the Car-Hacking dataset for the experiments. This dataset contains DoS attacks, fuzzing attacks, and two spoofing attacks (driver spoofing and RPM instrumentation spoofing). It is based on real CAN intrusion traffic through the OBD-II port. It is a widely used dataset for detecting various types of vehicle internal attacks [16,20]. We simulated RSU's preprocessing of the local dataset on a window 11 machine, with an Intel Core i5-8300H CPU @ 2.30 GHz processor, 24.0 GB of memory, and operating system version 22000.2057. Due to the large size of the Car hacking dataset (902.01 MB), we only selected 5% of the data as the CAN data collected by two RSUs (818,440 data points). We analyzed this dataset, as shown in Fig. 2, and found that normal traffic accounted for 85.5% of the dataset, indicating a moderate degree of class imbalance. Figure 3 shows the distribution of the raw data for the nine features. The horizontal axis represents the feature values and the vertical axis represents the frequency. It can be seen that the feature "car id" has a significantly different value range from the other features. So we will do the operations described in the Sect. 4.3.

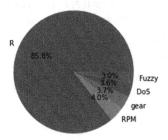

Fig. 2. Data type distribution

4.3 Data Preprocessing

Step 1, Data Under Sampling. We compare Random UnderSampler (RUS), Tomek Links (TL), One-Sided Selection (OSS), Condensed Nearest Neighbour (CNN), Edited Nearest Neighbours (ENN), All-KNN and other undersampling schemes with Near Miss (NM). The results are shown in Table 1, where we record the time and the number of samples for each scheme after the undersampling operation. We find that the condensed nearest neighbor and its variant (CNN and OSS) perform poorly on the car hacking dataset, while the nearest neighbor algorithms (ENN and All-KNN) and Tomek Links perform moderately on the car hacking dataset and do not solve the sample imbalance problem completely.

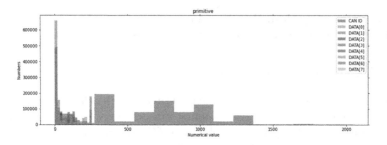

Fig. 3. Histogram of raw data distribution

Random Under Sampler (RUS) is a fast but simple method that randomly samples the majority class samples to reduce their proportion in the original data set. It is not suitable for hacking data sets that have a large imbalance between positive and negative samples. Therefore, we chose Near Miss as the optimal solution.

Table 1. Sampling scheme and its running result

	Original	RUS	NM	TL	OSS	CNN	ENN	Allknn
t_p(s)		5.2877	120.5872	729.3354	714.1104	3526.6085	802.8669	2211.7898
R	701832	24624	24624	701831	682795	60	701824	701824
DOS	29501	24624	24624	29501	1	1	29501	29501
RPM	32539	24624	24624	32539	0	1	32539	32539
Gear	29944	24624	24624	29944	1	1	29944	29944
Fuzzy	24624	24624	24624	24624	24624	24624	24624	24624

Step 2, Data Non-linear Transformation. Figure 4 shows the histograms of the data after Near Miss downsampling, two power transformations, and min-max normalization. It can be seen that the quantile transformer transforms the data into a strict Gaussian distribution, whereas the yeo-Johnson power transformation does not produce such a clear histogram.

Step 3, Generate Image. Since we use a CNN-based model, we need to convert the original text-like data into images. We follow the processing scheme from [27].

4.4   Model Evaluation

The FL model training was conducted on an Ubuntu 16.04.6 LTS with a disk size of 123G. The CPU device we used was Intel Xeon Processor E52609 v4 @1.70 GHz, with a cache size of 20,480 KB and 8 cpu cores. Considering that we simulated resource-constrained IoT devices, we did not use GPU. We implemented the model of the whole system using Pysyft, which is a Python library for secure and private deep learning. The pre-trained DL, except for CNN, were from the official pytorch website.

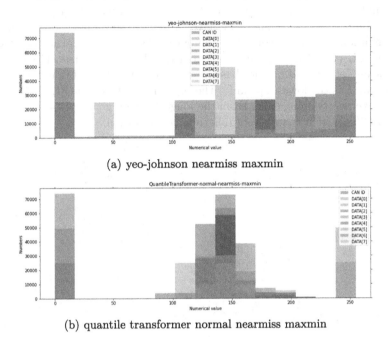

(a) yeo-johnson nearmiss maxmin

(b) quantile transformer normal nearmiss maxmin

Fig. 4. Two kinds of histograms after power transformation

We split the generated images into a training set and a test set with an 8:2 ratio. We define two participants and propose a CNN architecture as the baseline which consists of two convolutional layers, each followed by a pooling layer. The first convolutional layer uses average pooling, while the second one uses max pooling. This design aims to capture both local and global features of the input images. Figure 5 compares the training results of the yeo-Johnson power transformation and quantile transformer power transformation on the CNN baseline. The results show that the loss decreases faster and the optimal accuracy is reached sooner after the yeo-Johnson transformation than after the quantile transformer transformation. To evaluate the quality of the classification task, we drew confusion matrices for each classification. Its columns are the predicted categories and its rows are the actual categories. The diagonal values are the number/proportion of correct predictions and the off-diagonal elements are the fraction of incorrect predictions. We want to obtain a confusion matrix with high diagonal values, which would indicate that many classes were correctly predicted. Figure 6 shows the confusion matrix of the 4 FL models after classification. We can see that all the DL models except ResNet18 correctly classify most classes, and only some of the normal data are misclassified as attack types.

ResNet18 can correctly classify all normal classes, so we kept it in the hope that it would perform better in special scenarios. Figure 7 shows the ROC curves of the four types of FL models. We can see that the macro AUC values of CNN, vgg16, and alexnet models are all 1, and ResNet18 can reach 0.94. This indicates that the four types of FL models we have chosen are suitable for performing the daily intrusion detection work. We compared the model performance of CNN based on FL (FL-CNN, vgg16 based on FL (FL-VGG16), resnet18 based on FL (FL-ResNet18), and alexnet based on FL (FL-AlexNet). Table 2 shows that FL-AlexNet has the lowest epoch for the best model state, but FL-CNN has the shortest average training time. Even the longest training time, FL-VGG16, only takes 712.26 s, which is an acceptable time consumption.

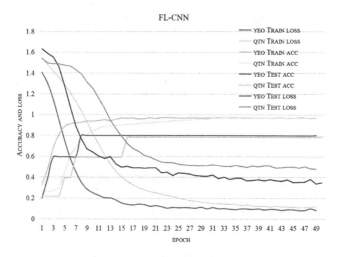

Fig. 5. The accuracy of the data processed by yeo-Johnson vs quantile transformer on CNN baseline

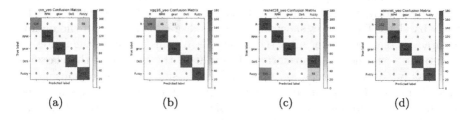

Fig. 6. Confusion matrix of 4 types of models

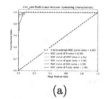 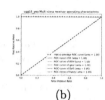 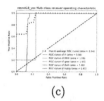 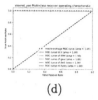

(a)   (b)   (c)   (d)

Fig. 7. ROC curve and AUC area of five types of models

Table 2. Four FL models

	FL-CNN	FL-VGG16	FL-ResNet18	FL-AlexNet
$t_t(s)$	82.242301	713.2586751	244.2694107	146.4923077
Best Epoch	9	3	34	5
Size(KB)	222	524,541	43,725	222,754
Accuracy	0.932878271	0.924914676	0.671217292	0.928327645
Accuracy P	0.949137931	0.939104478	0.568126491	0.946107841
Recall	0.932571429	0.924571429	0.663583815	0.928
F1 Score	0.930314369	0.920275282	0.604710494	0.925649556
Roc_auc R	0.991347403	1	0.864147727	1
Roc_auc RPM	1	1	1	1
Roc_auc Gear	1	1	1	1
Roc_auc Dos	1	1	1	1
Roc_auc Fuzzy	0.996782328	1	0.806792317	0.999885376

5   Conclusion

Smart vehicles are becoming more functional, but also more vulnerable to attacks. These attacks can cause privacy leakage, functional failure, property loss, and even life threat to users and enterprises. We have found that the security issues in the IoV are dynamic, complex, and covert. To address the dynamic nature, we propose to assign the IDS role to the static RSU, while the moving vehicles are the detected ones. We propose to apply the CP-ABE encryption strategy based on ECC to the data exchange between RSU and vehicles, which can ensure the efficiency and security of network communication. To address the complexity and stealthiness of IoV attacks, we propose integrated learning combined with FL techniques for intrusion detection. Next, we consider backdoor attacks, poisoning attacks, and negative participants in federation learning to improve the robustness of our proposed model.

References

1. Alladi, T., Kohli, V., Chamola, V., Yu, F.R.: A deep learning based misbehavior classification scheme for intrusion detection in cooperative intelligent transportation systems. Digit. Commun. Netw. (2022). https://doi.org/10.1016/j.dcan.2022.06.018, https://www.sciencedirect.com/science/article/pii/S2352864822001407
2. Alladi, T., Kohli, V., Chamola, V., Yu, F.R., Guizani, M.: Artificial intelligence (AI)-empowered intrusion detection architecture for the internet of vehicles. IEEE Wirel. Commun. **28**(3), 144–149 (2021)
3. Asmae, Z., Nabih, E.O.: Implementation of a bluetooth attack on controller area network (can). Indon. J. Electr. Eng. Comput. Sci. **21**, 321–327 (2021)
4. Buscemi, A., Turcanu, I., Castignani, G., Panchenko, A., Engel, T., Shin, K.G.: A survey on controller area network reverse engineering. IEEE Commun. Surv. Tutor. 1 (2023). https://doi.org/10.1109/COMST.2023.3264928
5. Cunha, F., et al.: Data communication in VANETs: protocols, applications and challenges. Ad Hoc Netw. **44**, 90–103 (2016). https://doi.org/10.1016/j.adhoc.2016.02.017, https://www.sciencedirect.com/science/article/pii/S1570870516300580
6. Das, S., Namasudra, S.: Multiauthority CP-ABE-based access control model for IoT-enabled healthcare infrastructure. IEEE Trans. Industr. Inf. **19**(1), 821–829 (2023). https://doi.org/10.1109/TII.2022.3167842
7. Geiping, J., Bauermeister, H., Dröge, H., Moeller, M.: Inverting gradients - how easy is it to break privacy in federated learning? In: Proceedings of the 34th International Conference on Neural Information Processing Systems, NIPS 2020. Curran Associates Inc., Red Hook (2020)
8. Hbaieb, A., Ayed, S., Chaari, L.: Federated learning based ids approach for the IoV. In: Proceedings of the 17th International Conference on Availability, Reliability and Security, ARES 2022. Association for Computing Machinery, New York (2022). https://doi.org/10.1145/3538969.3544422
9. Javaid, U., Aman, M.N., Sikdar, B.: A scalable protocol for driving trust management in internet of vehicles with blockchain. IEEE Internet Things J. **7**(12), 11815–11829 (2020)
10. Javed, A.R., Rehman, S.U., Khan, M.U., Alazab, M., Reddy, T.: CANintelliIDS: detecting in-vehicle intrusion attacks on a controller area network using CNN and attention-based GRU. IEEE Trans. Netw. Sci. Eng. **8**(2), 1456–1466 (2021). https://doi.org/10.1109/TNSE.2021.3059881
11. Karim, S.M., Habbal, A., Chaudhry, S.A., Irshad, A.: Architecture, protocols, and security in IoV: taxonomy, analysis, challenges, and solutions. Secur. Commun. Netw. (2022)
12. Khan, J., Lim, D.W., Kim, Y.S.: Intrusion detection system can-bus in-vehicle networks based on the statistical characteristics of attacks. Sensors **23**(7) (2023). https://doi.org/10.3390/s23073554, https://www.mdpi.com/1424-8220/23/7/3554
13. Oguma, H., Yoshioka, A., Nishikawa, M., Shigetomi, R., Otsuka, A., Imai, H.: New attestation based security architecture for in-vehicle communication. In: IEEE GLOBECOM 2008-2008 IEEE Global Telecommunications Conference, pp. 1–6. IEEE (2008)
14. Sagong, S.U., Ying, X., Clark, A., Bushnell, L., Poovendran, R.: Cloaking the clock: emulating clock skew in controller area networks. In: 2018 ACM/IEEE 9th International Conference on Cyber-Physical Systems (ICCPS), pp. 32–42 (2018). https://doi.org/10.1109/ICCPS.2018.00012

15. Scarfone, K., Mell, P., et al.: Guide to intrusion detection and prevention systems (IDPS). NIST Spec. Publ. **800**(2007), 94 (2007)
16. Seo, E., Song, H.M., Kim, H.K.: GIDS: GAN based intrusion detection system for in-vehicle network. In: 2018 16th Annual Conference on Privacy, Security and Trust (PST), pp. 1–6 (2018). https://doi.org/10.1109/PST.2018.8514157
17. Sethia, D., Sahu, R., Yadav, S., Kumar, R.: Attribute revocation in ECC-based CP-ABE scheme for lightweight resource-constrained devices. In: 2021 International Conference on Communication, Control and Information Sciences (ICCISc), vol. 1, pp. 1–6 (2021). https://doi.org/10.1109/ICCISc52257.2021.9485016
18. Sharma, N., Chauhan, N., Chand, N.: Security challenges in internet of vehicles (IoV) environment. In: 2018 First International Conference on Secure Cyber Computing and Communication (ICSCCC), pp. 203-chel (2018). Title = Architecture, protocols, and security in IoV: taxonomy, analysis, challenges, and solutions, author = Sulaiman M. Karim and Adib Habbal and Shehzad Ashraf Chaudhry and Azeem Irshad, journal = Security and Communication Networks, year = 2022
19. Shen, J., Won, J.Y., Chen, Z., Chen, Q.A.: Drift with devil: security of multi-sensor fusion based localization in high-level autonomous driving under GPS spoofing. In: Proceedings of the 29th USENIX Security Symposium (USENIX Security 2020). Boston, MA (2020)
20. Song, H.M., Woo, J., Kim, H.K.: In-vehicle network intrusion detection using deep convolutional neural network. Veh. Commun. **21**, 100198 (2020)
21. Sowjanya, K., Dasgupta, M., Ray, S.: A lightweight key management scheme for key-escrow-free ECC-based CP-ABE for IoT healthcare systems. J. Syst. Archit. **117**, 102108 (2021). https://doi.org/10.1016/j.sysarc.2021.102108, https://www.sciencedirect.com/science/article/pii/S1383762121000849
22. Sun, Y., et al.: Attacks and countermeasures in the internet of vehicles. Ann. Telecommun. **72**, 283–295 (2016). https://doi.org/10.1007/s12243-016-0551-6
23. Ullah, S., et al.: HDL-IDS: a hybrid deep learning architecture for intrusion detection in the internet of vehicles. Sensors **22**(4), 1340 (2022)
24. Wu, Z., Zhang, H., Wang, P., Sun, Z.: RTIDS: a robust transformer-based approach for intrusion detection system. IEEE Access **10**, 64375–64387 (2022). https://doi.org/10.1109/ACCESS.2022.3182333
25. Yang, J., Hu, J., Yu, T.: Federated AI-enabled in-vehicle network intrusion detection for internet of vehicles. Electronics **11**(22) (2022). https://doi.org/10.3390/electronics11223658, https://www.mdpi.com/2079-9292/11/22/3658
26. Yang, L., Moubayed, A., Hamieh, I., Shami, A.: Tree-based intelligent intrusion detection system in internet of vehicles. In: 2019 IEEE Global Communications Conference (GLOBECOM), pp. 1–6. IEEE (2019)
27. Yang, L., Shami, A.: A transfer learning and optimized CNN based intrusion detection system for internet of vehicles. arXiv preprint arXiv:2201.11812 (2022)
28. Yu, T., Hua, G., Wang, H., Yang, J., Hu, J.: Federated-LSTM based network intrusion detection method for intelligent connected vehicles. In: ICC 2022 - IEEE International Conference on Communications, pp. 4324–4329 (2022). https://doi.org/10.1109/ICC45855.2022.9838655

Transparent Security Method for Automating IoT Security Assessments

Rauli Kaksonen[1]([✉]) [ID], Kimmo Halunen[1,2] [ID], Marko Laakso[1], and Juha Röning[1] [ID]

[1] University of Oulu, Oulu, Finland
{rauli.kaksonen,kimmo.halunen,marko.laakso,juha.roning}@oulu.fi
[2] Department of Military Technology, National Defence University of Finland, Helsinki, Finland
https://www.oulu.fi, https://www.mpkk.fi

Abstract. People and businesses are dependent on the security of the Internet of Things (IoT). Vendor-independent security assessment and certification intends to provide an objective view of the security of an IoT product. Unfortunately, the assessment is often done for a single version and configuration of the product and usually does not yield data to reproduce the assessment. We present the *Transparent Security Method*, in which product security is described by a machine-readable *security statement*. A security statement can be verified using tools for automated assessment, which can be repeated for different product versions and configurations to cover the product life-cycle. As a case study, we create an entry-level security statement for a real IoT product and do the verification using common security tools. In the study, 12 out of 15 security claims are verified fully or partially by automation. A security statement can be used in certification or labeling to speed up security assessment, especially in re-certification. Tool-based verification discourages inflated security claims, as they can be scrutinized. Eventually, this should drive product security improvements, as products without security statements are less attractive.

Keywords: IoT · security · cybersecurity · certification · security tools

1 Introduction

For a long time, there has been a need for cybersecurity in Information Technology (IT) systems. The Internet of Things (IoT) increased the stakes as our society became dependent on widely deployed and heterogeneous systems with unknown security properties [27]. The need to improve the cybersecurity of IoT devices has been widely recognized [23,29]. Users need to know that the systems are secure to trust them. The lack of security in IoT will undermine the users' trust and hamper the adoption of new products.

This work is supported by the Finnish Scientific Advisory Board for Defence (MATINE/2500M-0152).

Security assessment techniques tend to be complex and must be performed by cybersecurity experts [23]. If the product meets the requirements, a certificate, label, or other indication of conformance is given. Major challenges with this approach are the high cost, delays to product launch, re-certification as products have to be updated, and overall scalability to cover the huge number of products in the market [23].

1.1 Security Certification

There are many IoT security certification and labeling schemes [9,19,22,23]. They are divided into *self-certifications* and *third-party certifications*. In self-certification the product vendor itself asserts conformance to the security requirements. Third-party certification is more expensive and adds delay, but provides an independent expert opinion about the security posture. Third-party approach is common in higher security assurance levels [14]. The assessment techniques and tools are usually not disclosed, it is only possible to check that the certificate or label is granted. There are no good means for a vendor to highlight that it has taken security mechanisms beyond the minimum requirements.

The updates required to maintain product security are problematic for security certification [14]. The product must be either re-certified or the certification must allow updates without being invalidated. The cryptographic key lengths and other parameters must be upgraded from time to time [9]. The continuous emergence of new attacks and vulnerabilities calls for automated monitoring, testing, and mitigation tools [9]. Indeed, various IoT testing frameworks have been proposed for automating security testing [5,6]. However, as Waraga et al. acknowledge *"Assessing the security of IoT devices is difficult due to the wide variety and functionality of IoT devices"*. The same issue is raised by Matheu et al. [23]. The use of proprietary functionality, even for common tasks like authentication, makes it difficult to assess IoT security with automation. Still, there is a large body of tools which could be used in security certification for verification and validation of implementation [21,26].

The Common Criteria for Information Technology Security Evaluation (CC) is a third-party certification scheme standardized as ISO/IEC 15408 [2]. Certification requires the definition of *Security Problem, Security Objectives* and selection of certified *Security Requirements*. A *Protection Profile* defines the security problem, objectives, and requirements by target types, such as firewalls. There are seven *evaluation assurance levels* (EAL) which determine the rigour of the evaluation. The evaluation in the lowest layer EAL 1 can be performed without vendor cooperation [2]. EAL 2 requires some vendor involvement but within normal *"good commercial practice"*. The higher assurance levels require heavier vendor involvement. Common criteria is a well-recognized security certification approach, but its cost and complexity seriously hinder its adoption for IoT [23].

Finland, Germany, and Singapore have national cybersecurity labels for consumer products with limited cross-certification [7,11,29]. An external evaluation is required to get the label in Finland and for higher levels in Singapore. The German label is based on a vendor self-certification. These labeling schemes are based on ETSI EN 303 645 set of baseline security requirements for consumer IoT devices [1]. An example of an industry-driven security label is the *ioXt* security certification scheme by the *ioXt* Alliance [17], which has its own set of requirements. It supports both self-certification and third-party certification.

The list of certified products is public in all aforementioned schemes, thus anyone can check if a product has been approved. Websites of Common Criteria, ioXt, and Finnish label contain per requirement verdict for the approved products. Singapore and Germany labels contain just the name and identification information for the products.

The requirements covered by most IoT security standards are for security design, interface security, authentication, data protection, and system updates [19]. The most common process requirements are vulnerability management, security requirements, and the use of security standards. The *ioXt* scheme has a security pledge with eight principles: no universal passwords, secured interfaces, proven cryptography, security by default, verified software, automated security updates, a vulnerability reporting program, and a security expiration date [17]. Vulnerabilities are frequently discovered in all parts of IoT systems: devices, backends, web front-ends, mobile applications, and operating systems [20]. Many of the vulnerabilities are quite mundane. For example, in 16 IoT device security studies, four discovered insecure communication protocols, three transfers of confidential data in plaintext, four unprotected firmware updates, and two vulnerabilities in respective mobile applications [5].

1.2 Manufacturer Usage Description

The security requirements for an IoT product could be used for operational security enhancement. *Manufacturer Usage Description* (MUD) is defined for devices to signal what kind of network access they require to function properly. [25]. Deviation from this could indicate a security compromise. The description is intended to be created by the vendor and stored on a file server for public access. So far, MUD has not been adopted widely in the industry.

Originally MUD was meant for network access control, but it has been proposed for various other purposes [16]. Gangurde proposed the use of information in MUD to perform pre-certification security tests for devices [15].

1.3 Research Contribution

The objective of this research is to develop an IoT security assessment which is lightweight, can be repeated without the involvement of security experts, and applies to the whole product life-cycle. The method uses an approach somewhat similar to MUD, but we implement a *Domain Specific Language* (DSL) for a more general description of system security-related properties. The method takes advantage of the existing security tools.

In Sect. 2 we introduce the *Transparent Security Method* and present a real-world case study in Sect. 3. In Sect. 4 we extend the method for better coverage. Finally, we discuss and present conclusions.

2   Transparent Security Method

A strategy to solve difficult problems is to divide them into sub-problems and solve those. The transparent security method divides security assessment into three parts: 1) the creation of a *security statement*, 2) verification of the statement, and 3) evaluation against security criteria. The familiar certification process can be applied: the product vendor creates the security statement, an independent reviewer verifies the statement, and the customer then uses the information in the security statement. However, also the customer can perform the verification, as it is tool-based and does not require deep cybersecurity expertise. The security statement may also be created by an independent security researcher. This may not be far-fetched as independent research is already published in various blogs, articles, etc. using ad-hoc formats.

2.1   Security Statement and Claims

A security statement is made up of security *claims* which describe the attack surface, security controls, and other security-relevant properties of the product. For the statement to be valid in different environments, the claims are about the product and exclude the environment. The claims are machine-readable and tool verifiable, as far as possible. The statement can be visualized or presented in a table for human understanding. Verification tools are selected and preconfigured as part of the security statement. The verification usually requires a running instance of the product. The verification supports the whole life-cycle of the product, as it can be repeated for different environments, configurations, and versions.

The security statement must be evaluated against customer security policies or standards like ETSI EN 303 645 [1]. Later we briefly discuss how to use the transparent security method in security certification. Statements can be viewed side-by-side to compare different products. Tenders could contain a requirement to provide a security statement, which is then used as a ranking criterion.

2.2   Entry-Level Security Claims

For entry-level security statement claims, we use the requirement categories commonly seen in IoT security standards: *Security design, Interface security, Authentication, Data protection, Updates* and *Vulnerability process* [19]. *Web security* is its own important category, as web interfaces are a hotspot of vulnerabilities [20]. *Mobile applications* are part of many IoT products. They are installed into user's mobile devices and bring their own security and privacy risks [8]. Table 1 shows the entry-level security statement claims and the type of tools applicable for their verification.

For a security assessment, we must know the system architecture. The first claims expect the network nodes, applications, services, and connections of the system to be defined. Best practices must be used to secure interfaces, including the web interfaces. The users and components using critical services must be

Table 1. Entry-level security claims, derived from established security requirements and common vulnerabilities, and the types of tools to automate the claim verification.

Category	Claim	Network scan	Traffic capture	HAR analysis	Protocol-specific	Internet searches	Internet scraping	SCA	Vulnerability data	App analysis
Security design	Network nodes are defined	x	x	-	-	-	-	-	-	-
	Network services are defined	x	x	x	-	x	-	-	-	-
	Network connections are defined	-	x	x	-	-	-	-	-	-
Interface security	Protocol best practices are used	-	-	-	x	-	-	-	-	-
Web security	Web best practices are used	-	-	x	x	x	-	-	-	-
Authentication	Services are authenticated	x	x	x	x	x	-	-	-	-
Data protection	Connections are encrypted	x	x	x	x	x	-	-	-	-
	Private data is defined	-	-	x	x	-	-	-	-	x
	Privacy policy is defined	-	-	-	-	-	x	-	-	-
Updates	Updates are secure and automatic	-	x	-	-	-	-	-	-	-
	SBOM is defined	-	-	-	-	-	-	x	-	-
	No vulnerabilities are known	-	-	-	-	-	-	x	x	-
Vulnerability process	Security policy is defined	-	-	-	-	-	x	-	-	-
	Release history is available	-	-	-	-	-	x	-	-	-
Mobile applications	Permissions are appropriate	-	-	-	-	-	-	-	-	x

properly authenticated. Data protection in transit requires strong encryption of connections, usually by standard protocols. European *General Data Protection Requirements* (GDPR) require disclosure of the collected private data, the purpose of the collection, where the data is stored, and how long the data is held [13]. Verification of private data claims is challenging, as private data should be encrypted. All software components should be automatically updated to mitigate exposed vulnerabilities. This requires an up-to-date *Software bill of materials* (SBOM) to know which vulnerabilities are relevant. Vendors must follow information about the vulnerabilities and provide mitigation. Product version release history provides information about actual update intervals if it is available. Mobile application permissions are often excessive, but they can be checked from the application meta-data [8].

2.3 Verification Tools

Automated claim verification should produce either *pass* or *fail* verdict or *inconclusive* if a verdict cannot be determined. Used tools should be well-known, high-quality, relevant, and freely available. A well-known tool is more likely to be effective and maintained. Many people can scrutinize the use of such a tool in a security statement. For automation, a claim should include the configuration for the tool and the code to check that the tool output matches the claim. Popular open-source security tools exist for traffic analysis, network scanning, web security, file analysis, host verification, binary analysis, and for other tasks [21].

Network hosts and services can be verified by using network scanning and traffic capture tools. Scanning is an active way to collect information, while capture requires the product to be exercised for it to use its network resources. Internet search engines provide information about remote services. Different protocol-specific tools can be used to check protocol versions and parameters, including tools to probe the security of web services. Verifying authentication functionality can be tricky, as only non-proprietary protocols can be checked by common tools. The use of encryption prevents checking which data is collected and transmitted. *HTTP archive* (HAR) is a format supported by many browsers to capture web session traffic for analysis despite the use of encrypted sessions [18]. Moreover, man-in-the-middle (MITM) tools could check whether the transport encryption is implemented properly.

Verifying an SBOM can be done using *Software Composition Analysis* (SCA) tools. Once components are known, they could be compared against vulnerability databases, such as National Vulnerability Database (NVD) [24]. A vendor which provides a readable version history would allow claims about the update frequency. Component vulnerability information and release history could be combined to calculate vendor response times for vulnerabilities.

While some tools can be run against mere powered-up devices, or even without them, complete verification requires the use of the product while the network traffic is captured. The verification time and complexity depend on the product, which may require environment setup or special instrumentation. It is possible to verify only a subset of the claims and run only some of the tools, if time is critical or not all features of the product are interesting.

3   Case Study

As a case study, we created a proof-of-concept security statement for *Ruuvi* Gateway and Tags IoT product [4]. The system is made up of Ruuvi Bluetooth Low-Energy (BLE) tags, which broadcast environmental data such as temperature and humidity. An optional Ruuvi Gateway collects the data and uploads it to a cloud service. The system can be controlled by a mobile phone application and web interface in the gateway and cloud.

```
system = Builder("Ruuvi Gateway & Tags")

gateway = system.device("Ruuvi Gateway").serve(EAPOL, ARP, ICMP)
setup_http = gateway / HTTP

tags = system.device("Ruuvi Tags")
ble_ad = system.broadcast(BLEAdvertisement(event_type=0x03))
tags >> ble_ad

user = system.any("User browser", node_type=USER)
user >> setup_http

mobile = system.mobile("Ruuvi app")

HTTP_rd = HTTP().redirect()
web_1 = system.backend("Home & Webshop").serve(SSH, TLS).dns("ruuvi.com")
web_2 = system.backend("Data UI").serve(SSH, HTTP, NTP, TLS).dns("station.ruuvi.com")
web_3 = system.backend("Analytics").serve(HTTP_rd, TLS).dns("gtm.ruuvi.com")
user >> web_1 / TLS
user >> web_2 / TLS
user >> web_3 / TLS

backend_1 = system.backend("Data backend").serve(TLS).dns("network.ruuvi.com")
backend_2 = system.device("Code repository").serve(HTTP_rd, TLS).dns("api.github.com")
gateway >> backend_1 / TLS
gateway >> backend_2 / TLS
mobile >> backend_1 / TLS
mobile >> backend_2 / TLS

any_host = system.any("Service")
gateway >> any_host / DHCP / DNS / NTP
```

Fig. 1. Ruuvi Gateway and Tags partial security statement DSL.

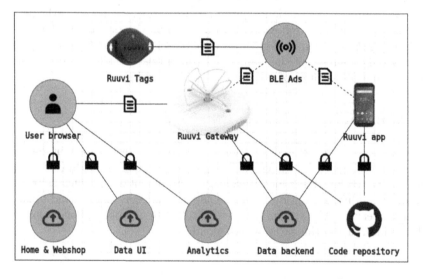

Fig. 2. Ruuvi security architecture rendered from the DSL description.

Figure 1 shows the partial system security statement in Python-based *domain specific language* (DSL) designed by us. The DSL starts with the definition of `system`. Next, local network nodes are defined as `gateway`, `tags`, `user`, and `mobile` for the Ruuvi Gateway, Ruuvi tags, User browser, and Mobile application, respectively. BLE advertisements, event type `0x03`, are modelled by conceptual node `ble_ad`. Relevant websites are `web_1` to `web_3` for Ruuvi home and Webshop, Data user interface, and Analytics pages, respectively. Remote backend servers are `backend_1` and `backend_2` for Data backend and Code repository hosted in the *Github* service[1]. Automated updates for Gateway are fetched from the Code repository. Ruuvi tag and application are updated outside of the security statement. Local nodes are identified by their hardware or IP addresses, configured separately for each environment. Remote servers are identified by DNS names. Infrastructure services DHCP, DNS, and NTP are captured into the conceptual `any_host` service. Services HTTP, TLS, SSH, and NTP are added to nodes. The special object `HTTP_rd` represents an HTTP service which only redirects plain HTTP requests into the corresponding HTTPS (TLS) service. The connections from nodes into services are added, e.g. `gateway >> backend_1 / TLS` stands for connection from Gateway to the Data backend TLS service.

Services ICMP, EAPOL, ARP, DHCP, DNS, and NTP are considered *administrative*. They are usually implemented by standard components. The remaining connections are application specific and likely more interesting for security assessment. Encrypted connections use TLS and SSH, but a few application plaintext connections are using plain HTTP or BLE. Figure 2 shows the security architecture diagram rendered from the DSL description. The diagram shows the network nodes and the connections between the services in the nodes. The lock icon marks the encrypted connections. Administrative connections are omitted for clarity.

Security claims were the ones shown in Table 1. We chose the used tools and implemented the verification automation. Then, we set up the product, ran the tools, and used the product while capturing network traffic. The output from the tools was automatically compared with the model created by DSL to verify the claims. Results are shown in Table 2, which gives the automation status and the used tools and methods for each claim. The table indicates how many of the possible automated checks were performed ("Yes") and how many were not done ("No"). From the 15 security claims, six could be fully and six partially verified by automation. Two claims could only be verified manually and no evidence was observed for one claim. Short descriptions and home pages for the tools are listed in Table 3.

---

[1] https://www.github.com.

Table 2. Ruuvi security statement claims, verification automation status, and used tools and methods.

Claim	Automatic verification?		
	Yes	No	Tools and methods
Network nodes are defined	10	0	*Nmap, Censys, Tcpdump*
Network services are defined	12	0	*Nmap, Censys, Tcpdump*
Network connections are defined	8	1	*Tcpdump*, HAR analysis, *HCIdump*
Protocol best practices are used	5	0	*Testssl.sh* for TLS
	2	0	*Ssh-audit* for SSH
Web best practices are used	5	1	*Censys, ZED proxy*, HAR analysis
Services are authenticated	0	4	Only manual review
Connections are encrypted	6	1	*Tcpdump*
Private data is defined	0	3	Only manual review
Privacy policy is defined	1	0	Web page scraping
Updates are secure and automatic	0	1	*Tcpdump*
SBOM is defined	1	2	*Black Duck*
No vulnerabilities are known	1	2	*Black Duck*
Security policy is defined	1	0	Web page scraping
Release history is available	3	0	*Gitlab* API request
Permissions are appropriate	1	1	*APKPure, Apktool*

Table 3. Tools used for Ruuvi security analysis

Name	Description	Home page
APKPure	APK repository	https://apkpure.com/
Apktool	APK analysis tool	https://ibotpeaches.github.io/Apktool/
Black Duck	SCA service (commercial)	https://protecode-sc.com/
Censys	Internet search service	https://search.censys.io
Github	Repository hosting service	https://github.com
HCIdump	Bluetooth Low Energy recorder	https://www.bluez.org
Nmap	Network scanner	https://nmap.org
Ssh-audit	SSH test tool	https://github.com/jtesta/ssh-audit
Testssl.sh	TLS test tool	https://testssl.sh
Tcpdump	Traffic recorder	https://www.tcpdump.org
ZED	Web security scanner	https://www.zaproxy.org/

Security design claims were verified by network scanning and capture by tools *Nmap, Tcpdump* and *HCIdump*. The *Censys* service provided information about remote hosts and services. HAR analysis provided information about browser sessions. In the end, the verification confirmed all network nodes and services, but one connection was not observed. No unexpected network nodes, services, or connections were encountered. Two out of nine connections, BLE advertisements and setup connection between browser and Gateway, are plaintext and the rest are encrypted by TLS. TLS and SSH best practices were checked using *Testssl.sh* and *ssh-audit* tools, respectively. Web services were checked by the *ZED* attack proxy. We did not implement verification of the authentication functionality.

We checked the availability of privacy and security policies by scraping the pages from the Internet. We did not analyze the page content, only that it remains available. This approach could be improved by checking that the content remains unmodified after a manual review. We could not automatically verify the collected private data, which probably cannot be done in most cases.

The remote and local nodes are all running software, but only Gateway software automatic updates are part of the described system. The update mechanism was not verified, as we did not observe the update connection during the capture. We had SBOM only for the Mobile app. For SCA we used the commercial Black Duck Binary Analyzer, as there are no obvious free tools available. Software releases are done through GitHub cloud service and the release histories are accessible. The Ruuvi Android application is available online through *APKPure* service and we analyzed it using *Apktool*.

4   Extending the Transparent Security Method

Earlier sections presented the entry-level set of claims and tools, but more should be added to improve coverage of the system security posture.

4.1   More Claims and Tools

The systems could be designed for more efficient security claim verification. The security community should innovate new tools for checking new types of claims. One gap is user and node authentication. Verifiable claims would require use of common protocols or components to implement the authentication, e.g. *ACE-OAuth* [28]. Vendors should use established technologies and common components. There seems to be little value in creating proprietary security functionality and vendors may lack the required expertise to make them robust. The adoption of standards, like *Matter*, is likely to help in this respect [10].

As web interfaces are hotspots of vulnerabilities in IoT, more security claims should be for web security [20]. A vendor could describe their web service, e.g. the using OpenAPI specification format, which would allow additional security checks [3]. The cookies used by the web service should be described and checked e.g. from HAR captures. This provides a check for one aspect of privacy, an area which is hard to probe. The entry-level claims only included the permissions of the mobile application, but the application packages contain a lot of other information, which can be used for security analysis [8].

IoT systems often take advantage of cloud services and IoT frameworks for functionality like authentication, data collection, and storage. The frameworks could allow security claims for the internals of the IoT system. These claims could be for the software components, configuration of services, encryption of sensitive files, permissions of critical processes, etc. [21].

The introduction of new claims and tools is encouraged in the transparent security method for openness, to keep up with the latest development, and allow demonstration of novel security features. Unfortunately, this may bring 1) claims which are not effectively checked by tools, 2) claims with little or no real value describing the security of the product, or 3) tools or tool configurations which do not assign proper verdicts. These can be exploited by vendors to look better without improving security. For example, there could be claims about supported IP-options without any clear impact on security. To avoid these problems, an evaluator can only take into account the claims she is familiar with. In the end, there likely is a need to come up with a recommended or official list of claims and their verification tool configurations.

Transparent security framework is a system which reads the security statement, fetches and runs the tools, and verifies the tool output. Security claims which are not validated, e.g. because of how the product is exercised or configured, are marked inconclusive. The framework does not need to be an actual security scanner. Its role is to take the security statement and verify that it is correct. When something unexpected is encountered, like an extra service port, the verification fails but there is no need to determine if this is a security vulnerability or not. The author of the security statement is expected to add the port to the model with appropriate claims or close the port if it is not required. This greatly simplifies the design of the framework and avoids subjective decisions about what constitutes a vulnerability or weakness and which is a secure feature.

Some security tools may give security warnings which contain *false positives* that clutter the verification output. In such a case, the vendor must have a chance to explain why a particular finding is not an issue. Again, it would be preferable that the tool is well known so that the explanations can be appropriately reviewed.

4.2   Security Certification

According to Cirne et al., an IoT security certification scheme should include a security assessment, privacy impact assessment, and product update policy [9]. A good scheme would reuse other relevant security standards and provide fast certification and compliance with regulations.

The transparent security method would contribute to the security assessment or even perform it completely if the used tools and techniques provide sufficient coverage. Re-certification is supported by automated verification. Transparent security method should speed up the initial certification when the security statement already exists. A security statement is a machine-readable way to convey information from the vendor to the certification lab effectively. As tool-based verification is fully traceable, it would support cases where regulation demands proof of compliance.

In the transparent security method, the vendor providing the security statement performs security self-certification. Independent verification of the security statement is a kind of third-party certification.

4.3   Other Uses

The verification tests could be used in the continuous integration/continuous delivery (CI/CD) of the software development process. The verification would be performed during product integration and system tests, and any violation would lead to build failure. This would make sure that all versions of the product meet the statement. A test driven development process could use a security statement to maximize the testability of the product security.

The information in the statements could be used operationally. An *intrusion detection system* (IDS) could observe the behaviour during operations and report if a device or service no longer follows its security statement. This might indicate a compromise of the system. A product could also be sandboxed so that only the specified connections, requests, etc. are allowed.

5 Discussion

We introduced the *Transparent Security Method* for lightweight security verification IoT products. In the method, a machine-readable *security statement* of a product is created to describe its security-related characteristics. The security statement is verified by tools. Manual work is replaced with measurements which are automated, repeatable, and traceable. New versions and different configurations can be verified by the vendor, customer, or third-party. The transparent security method could be used in security certification and labeling schemes. Transparency helps with the problem described by Emami-Naeini et al. *"Companies may be able to game the ratings to get all of the stars and, eventually, all products will have all stars, whether they deserve them or not"* [12]. When claims are based on verifiable data, and the process can be reproduced, the claims can be challenged and verification can be scrutinized. With a traditional security certificate, a vendor may have no motivation to improve security once conformance is achieved. Additional security claims allow them to demonstrate new security features.

Verification failures or excessive inconclusive verdicts may be difficult to interpret for non-experts performing verification. They may indicate a problem in the tools, changes in products, or a real security vulnerability. Most likely, a security expert is required to resolve such cases.

In the transparent security method, the vendors need to disclose details that they have not published before. Public security descriptions could be an incentive for vendors to improve security, e.g. have only a few exposed services in the products [12]. To gain traction, openness needs to give a competitive advantage or be required in tenders or by the regulator. An alternative would be independently created security statements created by reverse engineering. This could be community work similar to Wikipedia or open-source software. This would greatly enhance the usability of the results from independent research, as they would be available in a verifiable and machine-processable format. Of course, potential attackers can use security statements to understand the weak points of the systems. This seems to favor keeping the information secret. However, *security by obscurity* has been dismissed in the cybersecurity domain, as most actors cannot reliably design secure algorithms or protocols, thus it is better to use the publicly scrutinized ones.

If products are compared by their security claims, it creates a situation where the ones with more claims get a competitive advantage. Vendors would be pressured to add more claims, which ideally leads to security improvements. However, vendors could also come up with irrelevant or unverifiable claims or select tools and configurations which add no value. In the end, a recommended set of security claims and tools would be required. As verification depends on the quality of the tools, they must also be monitored and their development supported.

A verified security statement can be compared against used security policies or standards. A policy could state that all connections must be encrypted and services authenticated. Unfortunately, the comparison may not be so straightforward. The experience of the authors is that security requirements tend to defy automated verification. A verifiable claim can demonstrate conformity to a security requirement, but often it is impossible to show that the requirement is met in all circumstances. For example, an encrypted connection demonstrates secure handling of data, but not that data is stored and processed securely. A vendor has many ways to implement functionality and it is hard to write testable requirements which cover all possibilities. Going forward, new technologies and tools can make the transparent security method more comprehensive. Vendors need to shift away from proprietary functionality and use standard solutions which allow automated analysis of correctness and security. Cloud services direct IoT developers to use common backend services and frameworks, which could promote additional security claims and verification tools.

Cirne et al. list open research topics for IoT security certification [9]. The topics include the focus to the dynamic nature of IoT systems and not just the devices, schemes to better address the vulnerabilities unknown at the certification time, and customer-initiated certification. As transparent security method verification is lightweight, it can be repeated for different environments and customers. Periodic verification of the product with updated reference information, such as new vulnerabilities and key-length requirements, keeps security information fresh. Using the latest versions of used tools also gives new information.

Matheu et al. provide recommendations and potential ways forward for IoT certification [23]. They call for an efficient re-evaluation to cover the entire lifecycle. They suggest the use of machine-readable information in a secure and automated deployment of devices. As we described, such information can be also exploited on verifying product security requirements. Matheu et al. emphasize the role of the testing procedures in the efficiency of the certification - a problem the transparent security method aims to improve. They also call for cooperation between stakeholders, such as end users, manufacturers, and institutions [23]. We feel that a security statement is an efficient way to convey information and generate different illustrations of the security posture for different consumers.

A system cannot be assumed to be secure, just because it cannot be proven vulnerable. Claims of security which cannot be checked do not provide the basis for solid security certification. Finding all vulnerabilities in a complex product with many details unavailable is not feasible. As an attacker only needs to find a single vulnerability, the situation is dire. We should focus on asserting that a product is using strong and testable technologies and components. The vendors should support security assessment by providing the required information. With the transparent security method, we can scale up the analysis to match the volume of IoT products and take the initiative away from the attackers, who must still find vulnerabilities to be successful.

6   Conclusions

In this work, we introduced the Transparent Security Method, in which the security statement describes the security of a product in a tool-verifiable way. We derived entry-level security claims from security standards and common vulnerabilities, implemented a domain specific language to describe these claims, and successfully used common tools to automatically verify security claims in a case study of a real IoT product. The key advantages of the transparent security method compared to the mainstream assessment methods are the following.

- Codification of security-relevant information into security statement
- Coverage of all product versions, configurations and environments
- Independent tool-based verification of security statements
- Possibility to demonstrate new product security features
- Comparison of product security between different products

The key disadvantages are the following.

- Creation of security statements is additional work and requires information currently held back or not even collected
- Coverage is limited by the available tools and technologies
- Security is not represented by an easily digestible stamp or rating

Transparent security statements, whether made by vendors or security researchers, could be a boost for product security. Products could be scrutinized, compared and ranked by their security characteristics. Security labels and certifications could be based on verified security statements. Vendors would need to improve their security to keep up with the market.

References

1. Cyber Security for Consumer Internet of Things: Baseline Requirements v2.1.1. ETSI EN 303 645, ETSI (2020)
2. Common Criteria for Information Technology Security Evaluation, Parts 1–5. Standard (2022). https://www.commoncriteriaportal.org/
3. OpenAPI Specification (2023). https://swagger.io/resources/open-api/
4. Ruuvi home page (2023). https://ruuvi.com
5. Abu Waraga, O., Bettayeb, M., Nasir, Q., Abu Talib, M.: Design and implementation of automated IoT security testbed. Comput. Secur. 88, 101648 (2020)
6. Akhilesh, R., Bills, O., Chilamkurti, N., Mohammad Jabed, M.C.: Automated penetration testing framework for smart-home-based IoT devices. Future Internet 14(10), 276 (2022)

7. BSI, Germany: Baseline Requirements for consumer IoT devices (2023). https://www.bsi.bund.de/dok/ciot-standard

8. Chatzoglou, E., Kambourakis, G., Smiliotopoulos, C.: Let the cat out of the bag: popular android IoT apps under security scrutiny. Sensors **22**, 513 (2022)

9. Cirne, A., Sousa, P.R., Resende, J.S., Antunes, L.: IoT security certifications: challenges and potential approaches. Comput. Secur. **116**, 102669 (2022)

10. Connectivity Standards Alliance Inc: Matter Specification, Version 1.0. Standard (2022)

11. Cyber Security Agency of Singapore: Cybersecurity Labelling Scheme (2023). https://www.csa.gov.sg/our-programmes/certification-and-labelling-schemes/cybersecurity-labelling-scheme

12. Emami-Naeini, P., Dheenadhayalan, J., Agarwal, Y., Cranor, L.F.: An informative security and privacy "nutrition" label for internet of things devices. IEEE Secur. Priv. **20**(2), 31–39 (2022)

13. European Commission: Regulation (EU) 2016/679 of the European Parliament and of the Council of 27 April 2016 on the protection of natural persons with regard to the processing of personal data and on the free movement of such data, and repealing Directive 95/46/EC (General Data Protection Regulation) (2016)

14. European Cyber Security Organisation (ECSO): European Cyber Security Certification, A Meta-Scheme Approach v1.0. WG1 - Standardisation, certification, labelling and supply chain management, ESCO (2017)

15. Gangurde, C.: Automation of IoT pre-certification security testing environment based on the manufacturing usage description. Master thesis, Eindhoven University of Technology (2019)

16. Hernández-Ramos, J.L., et al.: Defining the behavior of IoT devices through the MUD standard: review, challenges, and research directions. IEEE Access **9**, 126265–126285 (2021)

17. ioXt Alliance: ioXT Internet of secure things (2023). https://www.ioxtalliance.org/

18. Jan Odvarko: HTTP Archive 1.2 Specification (2007). http://www.softwareishard.com/blog/har-12-spec/

19. Kaksonen, R., Halunen, K., Röning, J.: Common cybersecurity requirements in IoT standards, best practices, and guidelines. In: Proceedings of the 7th International Conference on Internet of Things, Big Data and Security - vol. 1: IoTBDS, pp. 149–156. INSTICC, SciTePress (2022)

20. Kaksonen, R., Halunen, K., Röning, J.: Vulnerabilities in IoT devices, backends, applications, and components. In: ICISSP - 9th International Conference on Information Systems Security and Privacy. INSTICC, SciTePress (2023)

21. Kaksonen, R., Järvenpää, T., Pajukangas, J., Mahalean, M., Röning, J.: 100 popular open-source Infosec tools. In: Jøsang, A., Futcher, L., Hagen, J. (eds.) SEC 2021. IAICT, vol. 625, pp. 181–195. Springer, Cham (2021). https://doi.org/10.1007/978-3-030-78120-0_12

22. Khurshid, A., Alsaaidi, R., Aslam, M., Raza, S.: EU cybersecurity act and IoT certification: landscape, perspective and a proposed template scheme. IEEE Access **10**, 129932–129948 (2022)

23. Matheu, S.N., Hernández-Ramos, J.L., Skarmeta, A.F., Baldini, G.: A survey of cybersecurity certification for the internet of things. ACM Comput. Surv. **53**(6), 1–36 (2020)

24. National Institute of Standards and Technology (NIST): National Vulnerability Database (2023). https://nvd.nist.gov/

25. Rekhter, Y., Li, T.: Manufacturer Usage Description Specification. RFC - Proposed Standard, RFC Editor (2019)

26. Rollo, J.: D1.2 List of tools and techniques applicable for high and medium assurance for efficient assurance. Report DS-01-731456 / D1.2 / V1.0, Project: Compositional security certification for medium to high-assurance COTS-based systems in environments with emerging threats (2017)
27. Schiller, E., Aidoo, A., Fuhrer, J., Stahl, J., Ziörjen, M., Stiller, B.: Landscape of IoT security. Comput. Sci. Rev. **44**, 100467 (2022)
28. Seitz, L., Selander, G., Wahlstroem, E., Erdtman, S., Tschofenig, H.: Authentication and Authorization for Constrained Environments Using the OAuth 2.0 Framework (ACE-OAuth). RFC - Proposed Standard, RFC Editor (2022)
29. Traficom, Finland: The Cybersecurity Label, National Cyber Security Center, Finnish Transport and Communications Agency (2023). https://tietoturvamerkki.fi/en/

DIDO: Data Provenance from Restricted TLS 1.3 Websites

Kwan Yin Chan[✉], Handong Cui, and Tsz Hon Yuen

The University of Hong Kong, Pok Fu Lam, Hong Kong
{kychan,hdcui,thyuen}@cs.hku.hk

Abstract. Public data can be authenticated by obtaining from a trustworthy website with TLS. Private data, such as user profile, are usually restricted from public access. If a user wants to authenticate his private data (e.g., address) provided by a restricted website (e.g., user profile page of a utility company website) to a verifier, he cannot simply give his username and password to the verifier. DECO (CCS 2020) provides a solution for liberating these data without introducing undesirable trust assumption, nor requiring server-side modification for TLS 1.2.

In this paper, we propose an optimized solution for TLS 1.3 websites. We tackle a number of open problems, including the support of X25519 key exchange in TLS 1.3, the design of round-optimal three-party key exchange, the architecture of two-party computation of TLS 1.3 key scheduling, and circuit design optimized for two-party computation. We test our implementation with real world website and show that our optimization is necessary to avoid timeout in TLS handshake.

Keywords: TLS 1.3 · two-party computation · decentralized oracle

1 Introduction

Fact-checking over public information can be done by verifying the data from a trustworthy website. By retrieving a news article from a trusted news website with TLS, one can ensure that the information comes from a legitimate source and it is not altered. However, it is hard to obtain the same security guarantee for data with restricted access. Suppose Alice wants to apply for a deposit account in an online bank (which does not have any physical branch) and she needs to provide an address proof. The picture or PDF of her utility bill may be digitally edited. It is not feasible to ask Alice to provide her username and password of her online utility account for validating her address. If Alice logins to her online utility account and then forwards the encrypted HTML page returned by the server to the bank, the bank will not accept this proof since TLS only provides authenticity and data integrity to the client only, but not towards any third party. The session key (derived from TLS handshake) used to authenticate the HTML page is known to Alice and hence she is able to modify the page.

In general, user's private data is often locked up by data owner. There is a strict demand for providing data provenance over such restricted information.

© The Author(s), under exclusive license to Springer Nature Singapore Pte Ltd. 2023
W. Meng et al. (Eds.): ISPEC 2023, LNCS 14341, pp. 154–169, 2023.
https://doi.org/10.1007/978-981-99-7032-2_10

A number of existing solutions have different limitations. Some rely on trusted hardware [14], but various attacks on hardware exist [11]. Some require changing the server setup, like installing TLS extension for server [12], or changing the application-layer logic [5,13] which are incompatible with existing TLS websites. To achieve a generic solution with backward compatibility, it is ideal to not modify anything from the server side nor any hardware requirement.

1.1 Decentralized Oracles for TLS

TLSNotary [1] proposed an architecture allowing prover to provide irrefutable evidence to a third party (the verifier) that certain web traffic occurred between himself and a server. It is designed for the depreciated TLS 1.0 and 1.1, by using two-party computation (2PC) with RSA key exchange.

Zhang *et al.* [15] formalized the notion of *decentralized oracle*, which provide *authenticity* and *privacy assurances* to Internet data from any website running standard TLS. They proposed a decentralized oracle protocol DECO, which used TLSNotary's high-level architecture with the adoption of TLS 1.2 for data authenticity, and also provided privacy protection for the decrypted traffic with the use of zero-knowledge proof. Firstly, DECO used a three-party handshake for Elliptic-Curve Diffie-Hellman Ephemeral (ECDHE) using the curve secp256r1. The prover and the verifier compute additive shares of the ECDHE session key k (by a protocol called ECtF). Then, they derive secret-shared session keys (master secret, encryption keys, mac keys) by securely evaluating the HMAC-SHA256 function by using 2PC. The prover prepares an encrypted request to the server. Finally, the prover receives an encrypted response from the server and commits it to the verifier. The verifier returns his share of the server mac key. The prover decrypts to obtain the response R and a tag τ'. The tag τ' is verified with the reconstructed server mac key. Finally, the prover uses a zero-knowledge proof SNARK [2] to show that the response R is correctly decrypted and verified by τ', and it satisfies some relation. The prover can reveal partial information of R.

1.2 Motivation: Compatibility with TLS 1.3

TLS 1.2 was standardized in 2008. Many of the major vulnerabilities in TLS 1.2 is caused by the use of older cryptographic algorithms that were still supported. TLS 1.3 was published in 2018. It drops support for these vulnerable crypto-graphic algorithms, simplifies the selection of cipher suites, and is faster than TLS 1.2. According to a recent survey[1], TLS 1.3 becomes the preferred TLS protocol for 63% of the top one million web servers on the Internet in 2021.

During the TLS handshake stage, the hello messages and the key shares are sent in plaintext, while the finish messages (including the HMAC value) are encrypted by the derived keys (as shown in Fig. 1). Most servers have a specific timeout value on the *TLS handshake timeout*. The default value is usually around

---

[1] www.f5.com/labs/articles/threat-intelligence/the-2021-tls-telemetry-report.

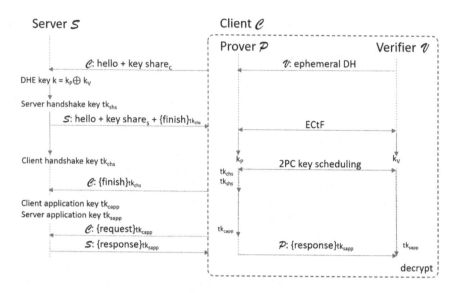

Fig. 1. Modified system architecture for TLS 1.3. The symbol $\{m\}_k$ stands for the symmetric key authenticated encryption of m using the key k.

10–15 s[2] It is challenging to finish the 2PC within the time limit, due to the complexity of the key derivation.

There are some changes in TLS 1.3 that makes it difficult to build a decentralized oracle for TLS 1.3, namely the changes in TLS 1.3 key scheduling and the X25519 key exchange protocols.

TLS 1.3 Key Scheduling. In TLS 1.2, the DHE key is taken as the input key of the HMAC-SHA256 function to derive a master secret. The master secret is then used to compute HMAC and to derive all other keys. Hence, a total of four 2PC-HMAC is needed. In DECO, a 2PC-HMAC is computed by one invocation of 2PC-SHA256 and it takes around 2.5 s for the WAN setting [15]. Hence, the 2PC-HMAC part already uses 10 s in the TLS 1.2 handshake.

In TLS 1.3, the key scheduling is much more complicated (as shown in Fig. 3) than the TLS 1.2 version. Starting from the DHE key, it requires five HMAC-SHA256 (used in HKDF.Extract and HKDF.Expand) to generate the handshake keys tk_{chs} and tk_{shs}, and an extra six HMAC-SHA256 to generate the application encryption keys tk_{capp} and tk_{sapp}. Hence, the 2PC of the TLS 1.3 key scheduling is much more complicated and time consuming.

X25519 Key Exchange. TLS 1.2 supports a number of elliptic curves for ECDHE. TLS 1.3 simplified that to five curves, in which X25519 and X448 (ECDHE over Curve25519 and Curve448) are newly added to the standard. It is

---

[2] E.g., https://www.ibm.com/docs/en/zos/2.5.0?topic=considerations-handshake-ti mer.

not easy to integrate DECO with these new curves for two reasons: the difference in the elliptic curve equation, the API defined in the RFC 7748 standard.

1.3 Our Contributions

In this work, we construct a practical decentralized oracle for TLS 1.3. In particular, we work on improving the three-party handshake protocol, and design our own 2PC key scheduling for TLS 1.3.

For three-party handshake using ECDHE, we first modify the ECtF protocol to support the Curve25519 and Curve448. The original ECtF protocol in DECO has 8 rounds of communication between the prover and the verifier. The total round-trip time of ECtF (4×67 ms $= 268$ ms in [15]) already contributes to 9.4% of the online running time of the handshake in DECO. We propose a round-optimal ECtF protocol to reduce the total round complexity from 8 to 3. We achieve this by designing our dedicated multiplicative-to-additive (MtA) protocol[3], instead of using the existing MtA protocol as in DECO [15], as shown in Sect. 3.1.

During our implementation, we solved the API problem for running the ECtF protocol with X25519. In particular, we make use of the API for EdDSA in TLS 1.3. We observe that the twisted Edward curve for Ed25519 is equivalent to the Curve25519. Hence, we need to do a coordinate conversion and use the elliptic curve arithmetic API provided in the Ed25519 library. Some other API techniques can be found in Sect. 3.2.

In TLS 1.3, the two-party computation on key scheduling becomes the bottleneck of the entire protocol. In [15], it is estimated that the 2PC circuit involves roughly 30 invocations of SHA256 (around 75.6 s using the running time over WAN in [15]). In this paper, we investigate how to efficiently design two different types of 2PC-HMAC: shared message and shared key ([15] only works on 2PC-HMAC with shared message for TLS 1.2). We also design our own optimized 2PC for modular addition over the finite field of Curve25519. We saved around 50% of AND gates as compared to the traditional method. Details can be found in Sect. 4.

We relax the *privacy* requirement from DECO, so that we only consider the privacy of the prover's input only. As a result, a number of invocations to 2PC-HMAC and 2PC-AES are saved.

Finally, we apply our techniques and build our solution for decentralized oracles over TLS 1.3 as Decentralized IDentification Oracles (DIDO). We demonstrate that DIDO can access restricted information from some utility webpages within 10 s.

2 Data Provenance with TLS 1.3

DECO [15] allows users to prove that a piece of data accessed via TLS came from a particular TLS 1.2 website. However, a straightforward implementation

---

[3] Alice (holding a secret α) and Bob (holding a secret β) can obtain shares x and y respectively such that $\alpha\beta = x + y$.

Input. The prover $\mathcal{P}$ takes θ_s as a private input. The verifier $\mathcal{V}$ holds a query template Query. The server $\mathcal{S}$ has no input.

Functionality $\mathcal{F}$.

– At any time of the session, for a message (sid, receiver, m) in which receiver $\in \{\mathcal{P}, \mathcal{V}, \mathcal{S}\}$ is received from $\mathcal{A}$, forward (sid, m) to receiver and forward any responses to $\mathcal{A}$.

– Upon receiving (sid, Query) as input from $\mathcal{V}$, send (sid, Query) to $\mathcal{P}$. Wait for $\mathcal{P}$ reply with message "ok" and θ_s.

– Send (sid, Q) to $\mathcal{S}$ and record its response (sid, R), where $Q = $ Query(θ_s). Send (sid, $|Q|, |R|$) to $\mathcal{A}$.

– Send (sid, Q) to $\mathcal{P}$ and (sid, $R, \mathcal{S}$) to $\mathcal{V}$.

Fig. 2. The functionality $\mathcal{F}$ of decentralized oracles.

of [15] in TLS 1.3 cannot access a real-world TLS 1.3 website before time-out. In this paper, we propose optimization for supporting the real-world TLS 1.3 website with the base of DECO framework.

DECO [15] also supports (optionally) proving statements about the TLS-encrypted data in zero-knowledge. The similar technique can also be applied to our scheme. We will not further discuss the selective opening since it is out of the scope of the paper. We consider the simple case that the verifier obtains the entire message sent from the server. As a result, we modify the system requirements and security definitions of decentralized oracles in [15] for this relaxed definition.

2.1   Notations and Definitions

We denote by $\mathcal{P}$ the prover, $\mathcal{V}$ the verifier and $\mathcal{S}$ the TLS server. We use the ideal protocol execution [3] and model the essential properties (with relaxed privacy) using a functionality $\mathcal{F}$. Messages are tagged with a unique session identifier sid to separate parallel execution of $\mathcal{F}$.

$\mathcal{F}$ takes θ_s for $\mathcal{P}$ as private input, and take a query template Query for $\mathcal{V}$ as input. For example, $\theta_s = $ (username, password) is the private input of $\mathcal{P}$, and $Q = $ Query(θ_s) is the HTTPS request sent to the gas company user account webpage using the username and password in θ_s. Denote the honest response from the server by $\mathcal{S}(Q)$. We also define the decentralizaed oracles as the protocol that does not require any server-side collaboration.

Definition 1. *A decentralized oracle protocol for TLS is a three party protocol* $\mathsf{P} = (\mathsf{P}_\mathcal{S}, \mathsf{P}_\mathcal{P}, \mathsf{P}_\mathcal{V})$ *such that* P *realizes $\mathcal{F}$ and $\mathsf{P}_\mathcal{S}$ is the standard TLS with an application-layer protocol.*

Adversarial Model. We consider a static network adversary $\mathcal{A}$. There are two possible models for corrupting $\mathcal{P}$ or $\mathcal{V}$. (i) **Semi-honest:** $\mathcal{P}$ or $\mathcal{V}$ may reveal their states to $\mathcal{A}$, but it still follows the protocol. and (ii) **Malicious:** $\mathcal{P}$ or $\mathcal{V}$ may deviate arbitrarily from the protocol and reveal their states to $\mathcal{A}$.

Security Properties. The security holds when either $\mathcal{P}$ or $\mathcal{V}$ is corrupted. Similar to DECO, there are three security guarantees for the functionality $\mathcal{F}$ for malicious adversary: prover-integrity, verifier-integrity and privacy.

Due to the performance issue (to be discussed in the next section), we can only use building blocks secure against semi-honest adversary in our implementation. The final implementation is secure against semi-honest adversary. In this setting, prover-integrity and verifier-integrity are guaranteed by the semi-honest adversary. Hence we only need **privacy**: an adversarial $\mathcal{V}$ only learns public information (Query, $\mathcal{S}$) and obtains R.

2.2 Estimating the Performance of DECO with TLS 1.3

DECO [15] mainly implemented building blocks for TLS 1.2 and obtained some online and offline running time in the WAN setting. The source code of DECO is not publicly available. We perform a rough estimation on implementing DECO with TLS 1.3 and see if it will trigger a timeout.

Running Time of ECtF. [15] only provided the running time of 2.85 s (online) and 10.29 s (offline) for running the three-party handshake, which mainly consists of an iteration of ECtF and also a 2PC-SHA256 for deriving the master secret. The running time of the 2PC-SHA256 is similar to the running time of 2PC-HMAC in [15], which is about 2.52 s (online) and 3.19 s (offline). It implies that the running time of ECtF is about 0.33 s (online) and 7.1 s (offline).

Running Time of TLS 1.3 Key Scheduling. As estimated in [15], the 2PC circuit for TLS 1.3 key scheduling roughly takes 30 invocations of 2PC-SHA256. It takes 75.6 s (online) and 95.7 s (offline).

Running Time of Query Execution. As shown in [15], the running time of 2PC-AES-GCM for 256 bytes data is 1.21 s (online) and 12.01 s (offline).

We can see the estimated running time in the WAN setting is 77.14 s (online) and 114.81 s (offline), even without doing any selective opening in [15]. It is very likely that it will trigger a timeout and hence it is not practical.

2.3 Overview of Our Design

There is a huge gap between the estimated running time of 77.14 s and our target running time of 10 s before TLS timeout. The most significant part (98%) of the running time comes from the large number of 2PC-SHA256 in TLS 1.3 key-scheduling.

TLS 1.3 key scheduling is illustrated in Fig. 2 of [7]. In our Fig. 3, we extend it by including the final session keys used for encrypting the application traffic (tk_{capp} for client's key and tk_{sapp} for server's key), which are derived from CATS and SATS. Assume that we do not have pre-shared key (PSK) for the initial connection. We can treat the keys derived only from PSK as constant. Hence we can simplify the key scheduling by considering the key dES as a constant number. The other input DHE is the output of the ECtF protocol, which is shared

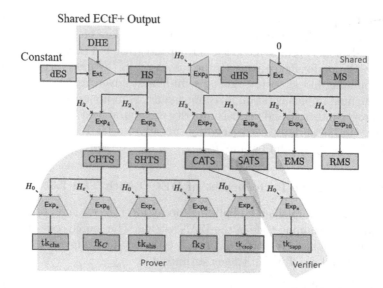

Fig. 3. Design for 2PC key scheduling for TLS 1.3 (without selective opening).

by the prover and the verifier. As estimated in DECO [15], each 2PC computation of HKDF.Extract and HKDF.Expand requires two or three invocations of 2PC-SHA256 (depending on which input is shared, refer to Sect. 4.1 and 4.2 for details). Since there are 15 invocations of HKDF.Extract and HKDF.Expand, it sums up to at least 44 invocations of 2PC-SHA256.

Design Without Selective Opening. Assume that selective opening is *not* needed in the application. Recall that the server's application key tk_{sapp} is used to decrypt and to authenticate the data sent from the server. Hence, it should not be fully revealed to the prover during key scheduling. In order to reduce the number of 2PC computation, we set tk_{sapp} and SATS to be completely revealed to the verifier.

Since the client's application key tk_{capp} is used to encrypt some secret information of the prover (e.g., password or cookie file), tk_{capp} and CATS should not be known to the verifier. It implies that the key MS should be shared between the prover and the verifier. The overall design for the 2PC key scheduling is shown in Fig. 3. This design has three improvements in terms of running time when selective opening is not needed: (1) Reduce the invocations of 2PC-SHA256 in key scheduling; (2) Remove the 2PC-AES-GCM for query execution. The verifier can decrypt the HTML page completely by himself; (3) Save the running time for selective opening. Based on our key scheduling design and the TLS 1.3 protocol, our overall system architecture is modified, as shown in Fig. 1.

3   Three-Party ECDHE Handshake

In DECO [15], the prover and the verifier jointly act as the client and interact with the server. Their three-party handshake (3P-HS) involves a ECDHE key exchange, the ClientHello and ServerHello messages in TLS 1.2, and the key derivation function. In this paper, we will separate them and analyse each protocol individually. The three-party ECDHE (3P-DH) runs as follows.

(1) The verifier picks a random x_v and sends x_vG to the prover. The verifier computes a zero-knowledge proof π_v of x_v with respect to x_vG.

(2) If π_v is valid, the prover picks a random x_p, sends $x_pG + x_vG = (x_p + x_v)G$ to the server as the *client key share* following the TLS 1.3 ECDHE protocol.

(3) The server replies with the *server key share* yG. The prover forwards it to the verifier. The prover also sends to the verifier x_pG and a zero-knowledge proof π_p of x_p with respect to x_pG. The prover computes x_pyG and the verifier computes x_vyG if π_p passes the verification.

(4) The prover and the verifier have to perform a two-party computation for the generated session key, i.e., sharing the x-coordinate of $(x_p + x_v)yG = x_pyG + x_vyG$. It is called ECtF: converting shares in $EC(\mathbf{F}_p)$ to shares in $\mathbf{F}_p$.

DECO [15] used the secret-sharing-based Multiplicative-to-Additive (MtA) protocols in [8] to construct ECtF. There are two main issues. Firstly, ECtF is expensive in terms of round complexity. It has 8 rounds of communication, which includes 6 rounds for using the 3 MtA protocols in ECtF. The online running time of DECO's handshake protocol in the LAN and WAN is 368.5ms and 2850ms respectively [15]. There is a round-trip time of 67ms between two nodes in their WAN setting. In other words, the 8 rounds of communication in ECtF already used 9.4% (268ms) of the running time. The second issue is that DECO only considers ECDHE on the elliptic curve of the form $Y^2 = X^3 + a_1X + a_0$ mod p (e.g., secp256r1, secp384r1 and secp521r1 in TLS 1.3). Their ECtF does not support the Montgomery curve of the form $Y^2 = X^3 + a_2X^2 + a_1X$ mod p (e.g., Curve25519 and Curve448 in TLS 1.3), which is also widely used in practice.

3.1   Round-Optimal ECtF+ Protocol for All TLS 1.3 Curves

In this paper, we propose an improved version of the ECtF protocol. Instead of using the MtA protocols in [8] in a black-box manner, we design our two-party computation protocol from scratch and construct a round-optimal ECtF+ protocol. It only has 3 rounds of communication. In addition, it supports *all* elliptic curves in the TLS 1.3 standard.

Point Addition on Elliptic Curve. Consider an elliptic curve of the general form: $v^2 = u^3 + a_2 \cdot u^2 + a_1 \cdot u + a_0$ mod p. Consider that the prover P and the verifier V have ECC points $P_1 = (u_1, v_1)$ and $P_2 = (u_2, v_2)$ respectively. They want to jointly compute $K = P_1 + P_2$ and they get k_1 and k_2 such that $k_1 + k_2 = u_k$ mod p and $K = (u_k, v_k)$. Recall that by the elliptic curve computation, we have $u_k = \lambda^2 - a_2 - u_1 - u_2$, where $\lambda = (v_2 - v_1)/(u_2 - u_1)$.

Our Scheme. The intuition of our ECtF+ protocol is to run two specially designed MtA protocols in parallel. Suppose the prover P chooses random r_1 and the verifier V chooses random r_2. P and V run the MtA for $\delta = (r_1 + r_2)(u_1 - u_2)$

[**Offline**] Suppose that $(\mathsf{KGen}, \mathsf{Enc}, \mathsf{Dec})$ is an additive homomorphic encryption scheme. The prover P runs $(\mathsf{sk}, \mathsf{pk}) \leftarrow \mathsf{KGen}()$ and sends pk to the verifier V.
[**Online**] P and V has a private input (u_1, v_1, sk) and (u_2, v_2) respectively.

1. P picks a random $r_1 \in \mathbb{Z}_p$ and computes:
   $C_u := \mathsf{Enc}_{\mathsf{pk}}(u_1), \quad C_v := \mathsf{Enc}_{\mathsf{pk}}(v_1), \quad C_r := \mathsf{Enc}_{\mathsf{pk}}(r_1), \quad C_{rv} := \mathsf{Enc}_{\mathsf{pk}}(r_1 v_1).$
   P sends (C_u, C_v, C_r, C_{rv}) to V.

2. V picks some random $r_2, \beta_2, \gamma_2, \alpha_2 \in_R \mathbb{Z}_p$ and computes:
   - $C_\beta = C_u^{r_2} \cdot C_r^{-u_2} \cdot \mathsf{Enc}_{\mathsf{pk}}(-\beta_2) \; = \mathsf{Enc}_{\mathsf{pk}}(u_1 r_2 - u_2 r_1 - \beta_2),$
   - $C_\gamma = C_v^{r_2} \cdot C_r^{-v_2} \cdot \mathsf{Enc}_{\mathsf{pk}}(-\gamma_2) \; = \mathsf{Enc}_{\mathsf{pk}}(v_1 r_2 - v_2 r_1 - \gamma_2),$
   - $\delta_2 = \beta_2 - r_2 u_2 \mod p,$
   - $\omega_2 = \gamma_2 - r_2 v_2 \mod p,$
   - $C_\alpha = (C_\gamma \cdot C_{rv})^{\omega_2} \cdot \mathsf{Enc}_{\mathsf{pk}}(-\alpha_2) \; = \mathsf{Enc}_{\mathsf{pk}}((\gamma_1 + r_1 v_1)\omega_2 - \alpha_2).$
   V sends $(C_\beta, C_\gamma, \delta_2, C_\alpha)$ to P.

3. P runs $\beta_1 := \mathsf{Dec}_{\mathsf{sk}}(C_\beta)$, such that $\beta_1 + \beta_2 = u_1 r_2 - u_2 r_1$. P first sends $\delta_1 := \beta_1 + r_1 u_1 \mod p$ to V.
   P locally runs $\gamma_1 := \mathsf{Dec}_{\mathsf{sk}}(C_\gamma)$, such that $\gamma_1 + \gamma_2 = v_1 r_2 - v_2 r_1$. P computes:
   - $\delta = \delta_1 + \delta_2 = u_1 r_2 - u_2 r_1 + r_1 u_1 - r_2 u_2 = (r_1 + r_2)(u_1 - u_2) \mod p,$
   - $\omega_1 = \gamma_1 + r_1 v_1 \mod p,$
   - $\alpha_1 = \mathsf{Dec}_{\mathsf{sk}}(C_\alpha) = (\gamma_1 + r_1 v_1)\omega_2 - \alpha_2,$
   - $s_1 = (\omega_1^2 + 2\alpha_1)\delta^{-2} - a_2 - u_1 \mod p.$
   P outputs s_1.

4. V computes $\delta := \delta_1 + \delta_2 \mod p$, $s_2 := (\omega_2^2 + 2\alpha_2)\delta^{-2} - u_2 \mod p$. V outputs s_2.

Fig. 4. The protocol ECtF+.

and $\omega = (r_1 + r_2)(v_1 - v_2)$ in parallel. Hence they obtain $\lambda = \omega/\delta$ and calculate $u_k = \lambda^2 - a_2 - u_1 - u_2$ accordingly. Fig 4 gives the ECtF+ protocol. It is easy to check that s_1, s_2 are additive shares of u_k, namely, $s_1 + s_2 = u_k$. We will present the security of ECtF+ in our full version [6].

ECtF+ Implementation. We implement DECO's ECtF and our ECtF+ in both the LAN and the WAN settings. We test the schemes by using both the Paillier encryption and the CL encryption [4] under the curve secp256r1 and Curve25519. The round-trip time in the WAN setting is 58 ms. Since the Paillier version is 10 times faster than the CL version in LAN, we only proceed to the Paillier version in WAN and show the results in Table 1. For the experimental details, please refer to the full version of this paper [6].

Our ECtF+ outperforms DECO's ECtF in three ways. Firstly, our ECtF+ is around 7.9% faster than DECO's ECtF in the LAN setting, as shown in Table 1. Secondly, our scheme has only 3 rounds of communication while [15] has 8 rounds. Our ECtF+ is around 13.1% faster than DECO's ECtF in the WAN setting. Thirdly, our ECtF+ supports the efficient operation over Curve25519. We will use X25519 for the TLS handshake protocol for the rest of the paper.

3.2 Three-Party Handshake with X25519

In TLS 1.3 ECDHE, the elliptic curve points are sent differently for different curves. For the curves secp256r1, secp384r1, and secp521r1, the binary repre-

Table 1. Online running time of ECtF(+) on different elliptic curves in Paillier and CL encryption with the LAN, and Paillier encryption with the WAN.

Curves	Paillier (LAN)		CL [4] (LAN)		Paillier (WAN)	
	ECtF [15]	Our ECtF+	ECtF [15]	Our ECtF+	ECtF [15]	Our ECtF+
secp256r1	0.350 s	0.308 s	3.012 s	2.544 s	0.423 s	0.386 s
Curve25519	× (0.363 s)	0.317 s	× (2.971 s)	2.660 s	× (0.428 s)	0.386 s

sentation of the entire (x, y)-coordinate is sent. However, only the u-coordinate on the Montgomery curve is sent for X25519 and X448 as shown in RFC 7748. In TLS libraries that support X25519 and X448, the API usually outputs the u-coordinate for ECDHE computation only. It is not compatible with the ECtF protocol, since we need the (u, v)-coordinates of $x_p yG$ and $x_v yG$ for the prover and the verifier respectively as the input to ECtF.

In the X25519 standard in RFC 7748, a function $X25519(k, u)$ is defined, where k is a 32 bytes string and u is a u-coordinate. The function first decodes k as an integer scalar, sets the three least significant bits of the first byte and the most significant bit of the last to zero, sets the second most significant bit of the last byte to 1 and, finally, decodes as little-endian. The scalar multiplication can be computed by the decoded number and u, using the Montgomery formula (a pseudocode is given in RFC 7748). If Alice and Bob choose random strings k_a and k_b respectively, and u_* is the base point of Curve25519, their session key is $X25519(k_a, X25519(k_b, u_*)) = X25519(k_b, X25519(k_a, u_*))$. The case of X448 is almost the same and we omit it for simplicity.

The integration of the three-party handshake (3P-HS) protocol in [15] with X25519 is not straightforward since: **(1)** The function $X25519(\cdot, \cdot)$ only returns the u-coordinate. With only the u-coordinate, the prover cannot calculate point addition in Step 2 of 3P-HS, and also cannot run the ECtF protocol in Step 4. The (u, v)-coordinate is needed. **(2)** There is a lack of Curve25519 point addition API for Step 2 of 3P-HS. The only compulsory API is $X25519(\cdot, \cdot)$ as defined in RFC 7748. Many TLS libraries do not provide Curve25519 point addition API. **(3)** The scalar k is masked before use. In order to support X25519 and X448, one needs to find a TLS library without the above obstacles, or develop his own library (which is time consuming and error-prone). Instead, we propose alternative approaches to address the above three problems: The first problem can be solved by using Tonelli-Shanks algorithm. The second problem can be solved by using APIs of EdDSA signatures (Ed25519 and Ed448) and equation conversions between Montgomery and twisted Edwards curves. For the third problem, ECtF protocol could output the shares of the u-coordinate of $(x_p + x_v)yG$ or $(x_p - x_v)yG$. It is the same as the session key computed by the server with 50% probability. To avoid this ambivalence, we use a special technique which is discussed in details in our full version [6].

4 Design for 2PC Key Scheduling

In this section, we discuss how to implement the 2PC key scheduling in Fig. 1.

2PC Key Scheduling for TLS 1.3. Recall that after running ECtF+, the prover and the verifier have the additive shares of the ECDHE session key DHE. The goal of our key scheduling is to ensure that the prover cannot obtain the server application traffic secret SATS, which is used to authenticate the information returned by the server. On the other hand, we also do not want the verifier to obtain the client application traffic secret CATS, since it is used to encrypt the information sent from the prover. As a result, we need to set MS as the shared secret between the prover and the verifier according to Fig. 1. It further implies that dHS and HS are both shared secrets. For the generated session keys, it is safe to give the client handshake key tk_{chs} and the server handshake key tk_{shs} to the prover. Hence, 2PC computation is required for the purple box in Fig. 1.

In order to complete the 2PC key scheduling with shared ECDHE session key DHE as input, we need to implement 2PC for the functions HKDF.Extract and HKDF.Expand. In TLS 1.3, we have: HKDF.Extract$(salt, k) =$ HMAC$(salt, k)$, HKDF.Expand$(k, \texttt{Label}_j || H_i) =$ HMAC$(k, \texttt{Label}_j || H_i)$.

The definition of the constant $\texttt{Label}_j$ and H_i can be found in [7]. Recall the definition of HMAC function for a key K and a message M (when $|K|$ matches the key length of the hash function H): HMAC$(K, M) = H((K \oplus opad) || H((K \oplus ipad) || M))$, where $opad$ is 512 bits of repeated bytes 0x5c, $ipad$ is 512 bits of repeated bytes 0x36. From Fig. 1, we need to use both 2PC-HMAC for shared message M and 2PC-HMAC for shared key K.

4.1 2PC-HMAC for Shared Message

We only need to use 2PC-HMAC for shared message once, where the message $M = $ DHE is shared by the prover and the verifier and the key $K = $ dES is a constant. We use SHA-256 as the hash function H in our implementation, which is supported by TLS 1.3. If we break down HMAC by the SHA-256 compression function SHA256$(\cdot, \cdot)$, the computation of HMAC(dES, DHE) is as follows.

(1) Compute the chaining state $cs_1 = $ SHA256$(IV, $ dES $\oplus ipad)$, where IV is the initialization vector for SHA-256.
(2) Compute the chaining state $cs_2 = $ SHA256$(IV, $ dES $\oplus opad)$.
(3) Compute the 256 bit padding pad^4. Compute $h_1 = $ SHA256$(cs_1, $ DHE$||pad)$.
(4) Output HS $= $ SHA256$(cs_2, h_1 || pad)$.

Since dES is a constant (when there is no pre-shared key), we can precompute cs_1 and cs_2. Recall that the prover has a share u_p and the verifier has a share u_v such that $u_p + u_v = $ DHE mod p. To compute 2PC-HMAC(dES, DHE), we need to run as follows.

(1) The prover and the verifier run a 2PC-Modular-Addition with private input u_p and u_v respectively. They will obtain a XOR share of DHE.

---

[4] In HMAC's padding rules, it follows $1|| < 191$ bits of $0 > || < 64$-bit $768_2 >$.

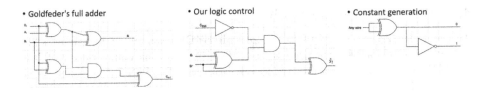

Fig. 5. Our circuit design.

(2) The prover and the verifier run a 2PC-SHA256(cs_1, DHE$\|pad$) with the XOR shares of DHE as input. They will obtain a XOR share of h_1.

(3) The prover and the verifier run a 2PC-SHA256(cs_2, $h_1\|pad$) with the XOR shares of h_1 as input. They will obtain a XOR share of HS.

We use the efficient implementation of 2PC-SHA256 in the emp-sh2pc library[5], which uses garbled circuits and oblivious transfer. Hence, we only need to design an efficient 2PC-Modular-Addition protocol.

2PC-Modular-Addition. There are a number of circuits designed for 2PC addition of 64 bits. To the best of the authors' knowledge, there are no modular addition circuits available for the 2PC library emp we used. Hence we design our own modular addition circuit for 2PC.

Adder. Our 2PC-Modular-Addition circuit design for Curve25519: (1) We first build a 255 bits ripple adder circuit with 254 Goldfeder's full adder [9] and 1 half adder in the least significant bit; (2) If the final carry bit c_{255} is 1, add 19 to the 255-bit output, since $X = X - (2^{255} - 19)$ mod $2^{255} - 19$. Else, simply output X. To implement the second step, we need a circuit to generate the constant term 19 and the logic gates for "if-else". We observe that b XOR $b = 0$ for any $b = 0/1$. Hence constant 0 can be generated by one XOR gate. The constant 1 can be obtained by applying an INV gate to 0. Finally we obtain 19_2 (Fig. 5).

Logic control. The "if-else" logic can be implemented as follows. Assume that s_i is the i-th bit of a 255 bit number S, and s_i^* is the i-th bit of a 255 bit number $S + 19$. The traditional "if-else" logic can be implemented by: $\hat{s}_i = (c_{255}$ AND $s_i^*)$ XOR $((\text{INV } c_{255})$ AND $s_i)$. This circuit runs for 255 times and the final output is $(\hat{s}_{255}, \ldots, \hat{s}_1)$. However, this "if-else" logic circuit is not optimized for 2PC with the use of two AND gates. We give a new design by using one AND gate, one INV gate and two XOR gates, as shown in Fig. 5.

Result. As compared with the traditional approach (simple full adder, half adder and logic control) in Table 3, our current approach saves about half of the AND gates. As a result, the efficiency of our 2PC-Modular-Addition can be improved by about 50%, by using the *free XOR* technique in 2PC [10].

Remark that our circuit determines the modulus $2^{255} - 19$ with only the carry c_{255}. With this operation, it leaves $2^{255} - 18$ to $2^{255} - 1$ which we treat them as the case *no need to take mod*. This leads to a negligible probability of error.

---

[5] https://github.com/emp-toolkit/emp-sh2pc.

4.2 2PC-HMAC for Shared Key

To compute $MS = HMAC(dHS, 0)$, and all $HKDF.Expand(\cdot, \cdot)$ functions with shared keys HS or MS, we need to use 2PC-HMAC. The computation of the 2PC-HMAC(K, M) function is as follows. Note that for TLS 1.3, message M is less than 64 bytes.

(1) Compute the shared chaining state $cs_1 = 2PC\text{--}SHA256(IV, K \oplus ipad)$.
(2) Compute the shared chaining state $cs_2 = 2PC\text{--}SHA256(IV, K \oplus opad)$.
(3) Compute the padding pad_1 and $h_1 = 2PC\text{--}SHA256(cs_1, M\|pad_1)$.
(4) Compute the padding pad_2. Output $HS = 2PC\text{--}SHA256(cs_2, h_1\|pad_2)$.

Alternatively, one can output the entire cs_1 to the prover and he computes h_1 on his own in step 3. The value h_1 is treated as a public input in step 4. This modification reduces the number of 2PC–SHA256 from four to three. However, it requires the library to provide an interface to modify the internal chaining state of SHA-256 to cs_1. We do not use this method in our implementation due to the complexity in engineering work.

5 Decentralized Identification Oracles (DIDO)

In this section, we integrate our techniques above and construct a decentralized oracle for TLS 1.3. We call our scheme as Decentralized IDentification Oracles

---

$P_{\mathcal{S}}$: Follow the standard TLS 1.3 protocol using ECDHE for key exchange.

$P_{\mathcal{P}}$ and $P_{\mathcal{V}}$:

- $\mathcal{P}$ receives (sid, Query) from $\mathcal{V}$, where Query is the template of query.
- $\mathcal{P}$ starts the handshake if it chooses to proceed after examining the Query.
- (3P-DH) $\mathcal{P}, \mathcal{V}$ execute the three-party ECDHE protocol with $\mathcal{S}$. After Step 1-2, $\mathcal{P}$ sends the client hello message and key share (sid, m_{chs}) to $\mathcal{S}$. $\mathcal{S}$ replies with the server hello message, key share and an encrypted finish message (sid, m_{shs}). By using the server key share, $\mathcal{P}, \mathcal{V}$ execute Step 3-4 of the three-party ECDHE protocol. $\mathcal{P}$ obtains a share of the ECDHE key $k_{\mathcal{P}}^{DHE}$ and $\mathcal{V}$ obtains another share $k_{\mathcal{V}}^{DHE}$, such that $k_{\mathcal{P}}^{DHE} + k_{\mathcal{V}}^{DHE} = k^{DHE}$, which is the ECDHE key obtained by $\mathcal{S}$.
- (Key Scheduling) $\mathcal{P}, \mathcal{V}$ execute the 2PC Key Scheduling with private input $k_{\mathcal{P}}^{DHE}$ and $k_{\mathcal{V}}^{DHE}$ respectively. $\mathcal{P}$ obtains the TLS 1.3 secrets CHTS, SHTS and CATS. $\mathcal{V}$ obtains the secret SATS. $\mathcal{P}$ uses SHTS to decrypt and to validate the server finish message in m_{shs}.
- (Query) $\mathcal{P}$ sends the client handshake finish message (sid, m_{cfin}) to $\mathcal{S}$ using keys derived from CHTS. $\mathcal{P}$ prepares the query Query(θ_s) and encrypts it to client application message m_{capp} using keys derived from CATS. $\mathcal{P}$ sends (sid, m_{capp}) to $\mathcal{S}$. $\mathcal{S}$ replies with the response (sid, m_{sapp}) to $\mathcal{P}$.
- (Open) After receiving a response (sid, m_{sapp}) from $\mathcal{S}$, $\mathcal{P}$ forwards it to $\mathcal{V}$. $\mathcal{V}$ then decrypts m_{sapp} using keys derived from SATS and outputs the decrypted response.

Fig. 6. The protocol P_{DIDO}.

Table 2. Running time of our DIDO implementation on different websites.

	$\mathcal{P}$ and $\mathcal{V}$ in LAN	$\mathcal{P}$ and $\mathcal{V}$ in WAN
www.google.com	4.266 s	7.848 s
www.youtube.com	6.384 s	27.233 s
github.com	4.717 s	12.594 s
www.microsoft.com	4.984 s	6.275 s
yahoo.com	4.468 s	6.650 s
wikipedia.org	4.338 s	6.447 s
easychair.org	5.665 s	6.928 s

Table 3. Number of gates for a modular addition circuit for Curve25519.

	# AND	# XOR	# INV
Traditional	1528	1783	2
This paper	765	2546	2

Table 4. Running time of DIDO on different utility companies.

	$\mathcal{P}$ and $\mathcal{V}$ in LAN	$\mathcal{P}$ and $\mathcal{V}$ in WAN
Gas company	4.003 s	6.770 s
Electricity company	6.303 s	8.456 s

(DIDO), as our application is mainly for identification purpose. We define the DIDO protocol in Fig. 6. For security claim, it follows a modification of Theorem 4.1 in DECO [15] that P$_{\text{DIDO}}$ UC-securely realizes $\mathcal{F}$ in the $\mathcal{F}_{\text{2PC}}$ world, against a static semi-honest adversary, assuming the discrete logarithm problem is hard in the ECDHE group used, the zero-knowledge proof used is secure and the compression function f of SHA-256 is a random oracle.

In [15], the authors give a real example of using stock price API with DECO. By assessing the stock price API, a JSON output for a stock will be returned. In this paper, we consider a normal HTML webpage which provides some authenticated user information (the information is usually validated offline by a trustworthy webpage owner). In [15], it is mentioned that a university has the name and the date of birth for a student, but the university does not provides an open API for accessing this information. However, such an open API may not be always available. In this paper, we consider using the login account information of an utility company (e.g., electricity or gas) as the address proof, for applying some online financial services (e.g., virtual bank account, credit card or loans). As an example, we first demonstrate that our DIDO implementation can open a popular TLS 1.3 website, then can serve as the address proof for user in some utility websites.

Some Popular TLS 1.3 Websites. We test DIDO on some popular websites supporting TLS 1.3. DIDO can successfully access them and the verifier is able to decrypt the payloads accordingly. We show the results in Table 2. It can be seen that there are some web pages with longer running time, and may have a big difference between LAN and WAN. The running time discrepancy is affected by the length of the content of the web page, and the response time of the server.

Address Proof. In a webpage of a utility company (e.g., electricity or gas), a user can login his account by using username and password and acquire his current address. It is common for a web server to send a cookie file after entering the username and password. By using cookie file, the client browser can open the webpage with personal information. We present the details of the test of

DIDO using a real gas and electricity company's webpage in our full version [6]. We use the same setting in Sect. 3.1 for testing the performance of our DIDO implementation in both the LAN and the WAN settings. The running time is shown in Table 4. We can see that the verifier V can receive the HTML page from the server within 10 s.

6   Conclusion

So far, we proposed DIDO for a decentralized oracle with TLS 1.3. We provided support to X25519, proposed a 2PC key scheduling, and optimized its circuits.

References

1. Tlsnotary - a mechanism for independently audited https sessions. White paper (2014). https://tlsnotary.org/TLSNotary.pdf
2. Ben-Sasson, E., Chiesa, A., Tromer, E., Virza, M.: Succinct non-interactive zero knowledge for a von Neumann architecture. In: Fu, K., Jung, J. (eds.) USENIX 2014, pp. 781–796. USENIX Association (2014)
3. Canetti, R.: Universally composable security: a new paradigm for cryptographic protocols. In: FOCS 2001, pp. 136–145. IEEE Computer Society (2001)
4. Castagnos, G., Laguillaumie, F.: Linearly homomorphic encryption from DDH. In: Nyberg, K. (ed.) CT-RSA 2015. LNCS, vol. 9048, pp. 487–505. Springer, Cham (2015). https://doi.org/10.1007/978-3-319-16715-2_26
5. Cavage, M., Sporny, M.: Signing http messages (2019). https://tools.ietf.org/id/draft-cavage-http-signatures-12.html
6. Chan, K.Y., Cui, H., Yuen, T.H.: DIDO: data provenance from restricted TLS 1.3 websites. Cryptology ePrint Archive, Paper 2023/1056 (2023). https://eprint.iacr.org/2023/1056
7. Dowling, B., Fischlin, M., Günther, F., Stebila, D.: A cryptographic analysis of the TLS 1.3 handshake protocol. J. Cryptol. **34**(4), 37 (2021)
8. Gennaro, R., Goldfeder, S.: Fast multiparty threshold ECDSA with fast trustless setup. In: Lie, D., Mannan, M., Backes, M., Wang, X. (eds.) CCS 2018, pp. 1179–1194. ACM (2018)
9. Goldfeder, S.: A Boolean circuit for SHA-256. http://stevengoldfeder.com/projects/circuits/sha2circuit.html
10. Kolesnikov, V., Schneider, T.: Improved garbled circuit: free XOR gates and applications. In: Aceto, L., Damgård, I., Goldberg, L.A., Halldórsson, M.M., Ingólfsdóttir, A., Walukiewicz, I. (eds.) ICALP 2008. LNCS, vol. 5126, pp. 486–498. Springer, Heidelberg (2008). https://doi.org/10.1007/978-3-540-70583-3_40
11. Nilsson, A., Bideh, P.N., Brorsson, J.: A survey of published attacks on intel SGX. CoRR abs/2006.13598 (2020). https://arxiv.org/abs/2006.13598
12. Ritzdorf, H., Wüst, K., Gervais, A., Felley, G., Capkun, S.: TLS-N: non-repudiation over TLS enablign ubiquitous content signing. In: NDSS 2018. The Internet Society (2018)
13. Yasskin, J.: Signed http exchanges. Internet-Draft: draft-Yasskin-http-origin-signed-responses-latest (2022)

14. Zhang, F., Cecchetti, E., Croman, K., Juels, A., Shi, E.: Town crier: an authenticated data feed for smart contracts. In: Weippl, E.R., Katzenbeisser, S., Kruegel, C., Myers, A.C., Halevi, S. (eds.) CCS 2016, pp. 270–282. ACM (2016)
15. Zhang, F., Maram, D., Malvai, H., Goldfeder, S., Juels, A.: DECO: liberating web data using decentralized oracles for TLS. In: Ligatti, J., Ou, X., Katz, J., Vigna, G. (eds.) CCS 2020, pp. 1919–1938. ACM (2020)

QR-SACP: Quantitative Risk-Based Situational Awareness Calculation and Projection Through Threat Information Sharing

Mahdieh Safarzadehvahed[1(✉)], Farzaneh Abazari[2], and Fateme Shabani[3]

[1] Queen's University, Kingston, Canada
`22ms70@queensu.ca`
[2] Former postdoctoral fellow at University of Saskatchewan, Saskatoon, SK, Canada
`faa851@usask.ca`
[3] Tarbiat Modares University, Tehran, Iran
`fateme.shabani@modares.ac.ir`

Abstract. When a threat is observed, one of the most important challenges is to choose the most appropriate and adequate timely decisions in response to the current and near future situation in order to have the least consequences and costs. Making the appropriate and sufficient decisions requires knowing what situations the threat has engendered or may engender. In this paper, we propose a quantitative risk-based method called QR-SACP to calculate and project situational awareness in a network based on threat information sharing. In this method, we investigate a threat from different aspects and evaluate the threat's effects through dependency weight among the network's services. We calculate the definite effect of a threat on a service and the cascading propagation of the threat's definite effect on other dependent services to that service. In addition, we project the probability of a threat propagation or recurrence of the threat in other network services in three ways: procedurally, through network connections and similar infrastructure or services. Experimental results demonstrate that the QR-SACP method can calculate and project definite and probable threats' effects across the entire network and reveal more details about the threat's current and near future situations.

Keywords: Situational Awareness · SA Quantitative Calculation · Risk-based SA · Security Situation Assessment

1 Introduction

When a threat is observed, one of the most important challenges is to choose the most appropriate and adequate timely decisions, so-called decision-making in response to the situation that the threat has caused or may cause in the future. Decision-making in response to the threat has different consequences

© The Author(s), under exclusive license to Springer Nature Singapore Pte Ltd. 2023
W. Meng et al. (Eds.): ISPEC 2023, LNCS 14341, pp. 170–193, 2023.
https://doi.org/10.1007/978-981-99-7032-2_11

and costs. What decision to make and when to deal with it in the threat cycle directly impacts the cost and the damage it may cause. Making the appropriate and adequate decision requires knowing what the threat is, what impacts it has, and what situation the threat has engendered or may engender. One of the concepts that can help is situational awareness (SA). In the field of SA, various studies [2,3,11,14,20,22,24,26–28] have been done on different parts of SA, including definition, architecture, modeling, uncertainty and risk management, projection and calculation. Despite having the current and the future situations that a threat has posed or may pose, there is still no proper answer about which threat should be investigated first, how SA should be quantified and how probable near future threats' effects should be considered in calculating and projecting the SA.

In this paper, we present a novel algorithm for calculating and projecting SA that by knowing the past and receiving a threat, calculates the SA to depict the present and projects the consequences of the threat to predict the future through a risk-based approach. The obtained quantitative SA values can be used to select a high-priority threat to investigate.

One of the most important factors for decision-making is to get an accurate and comprehensive view of the current situation of the entire network due to a threat. We present an algorithm that perceives and calculates the impacts of a threat across the entire network using threat information sharing, organizational historical information about threats and international threats databases. It is also necessary to achieve a comprehensive and integrated view of the network under attack and its connected networks to make a comprehensive decision. This requires understanding what has happened or will happen due to the threat. To achieve this goal, we investigate the threat from different dimensions and calculate and project its impacts. Making inappropriate and insufficient decisions can lead to the continuation of the threat and its impacts. For this reason, it is necessary to project the near future situation in addition to understanding the current situation that arises when the threat occurs. In contrast to earlier algorithms and methods, we project a risk-based near future situation with more details in the proposed algorithm.

The number of threats in a network is very high [4]. Hence, we need a way to select a threat with more priority. Most studies display SA qualitatively cold-coded. In this case, a large number of threats will be categorized into one color group. Therefore, we cannot choose a threat with a higher priority among them to investigate. In addition, two threats may have the same color but possess different properties. As a result, providing a color is not enough to select high-priority threats. Hence, we calculate and display the SA quantitatively by considering more details. Our main contributions are as follows. (1) We propose an algorithm that investigates each threat from different dimensions and uses service dependency among network's services to calculate the definite effect of the threat on the service and the cascading propagation of the threat's definite effect to other dependent services with more details. (2) We propose an algorithm for projecting the probable impacts of the threat on the network and predicting a risk-based near future network situation. The algorithm projects the probability of propagation or recurrence of the threat in other dependant network services. (3) We propose a method to map a network's situational awareness to a four elements vector. Each part of it reveals different, various, definite and probable effects of a threat on the network. These four parts provide a comprehensive view of the network's situational awareness.

The remainder of the paper is as follows. In Sect. 2, we review some related works and discuss their limitations in calculating and projecting SA. In Sect. 3, we present assumptions and concepts to calculate SA and model a network and a threat. In Sect. 4, we propose QR-SACP, a novel technique that uses service dependencies and probability of propagation or recurrence of the threat to calculate and project SA, and then we evaluate the effectiveness of QR-SACP by using various threats in Sect. 5. Finally, we draw conclusions in Sect. 6.

2   Related Work

Some studies [1,2,11,14] have done a comprehensive literature review that provide information about different aspects of situational awareness, including SA models, frameworks, architecture and uncertainty management and attack prediction. Since this paper presents a method to calculate and project SA quantitatively, related works have been selected in such a way that they have been done in the field of SA calculation and projection.

Zhang et al. [28] present a network SA model based on threat intelligence to conduct situational perception and discover internal threats. They collect situation elements of network asset status, risk status, and log warnings. However, they do not specify what details and parameters these inputs contain. They filter and clean collected data and correlate them with external threat intelligence to find internal threats. They use game theory to quantify the current network security situation of the system and evaluate the network security status. They also use Nash equilibrium to predict attacks behavior. One of the most important parts of this model is to calculate the situational awareness based on attacker and defender strategies, but they do not introduce these strategies. In this study, situational awareness is equivalent to the difference between an attacker and defender utility. However, this approach does not provide how the attacker and defender utility is calculated, and they discard dependency among systems in a network.

Alavizadeh et al. [3] introduce a framework to select a response strategy in order to defend against possible attacks. They consider two defense strategies: Virtual Machine Live Migration (VM-LM) and Patching. To choose a defense strategy, they calculate risk values. For this purpose, they propose three security metrics: 1) risk of exploiting a VM, 2) security Return on the Attack (RoA) and 3) Mean of Attack Path Length (MAPL). They select the defense strategy based on the risk of exploiting a VM security metric. They suppose SA calculation is equivalent to risk calculation by considering vulnerabilities. They ignore attacks' and incidents' effects on VMs to select the defense strategy. The risk of spreading a threat is not only due to a vulnerability on the victim system or network, but it can also be due to obtained privileges that an attacker gains. After gaining privilege, an attacker no longer needs to exploit a vulnerability to access another system because he can continue his objectives by performing authorized actions with the obtained privileges. Moreover, the value of assets is not considered in the calculation of situational awareness.

Rongrong et al. [23] propose a framework to evaluate a network security situation through three dimensions: threat, vulnerability and stability. They calculate the average value for each dimension and merge these three dimensions' results to measure the overall network security situation. They consider the successful probability of attacks and their severity to assess threats. To evaluate network vulnerability situation, they consider vulnerability vendor name, product name, type, severity and the duration between the data a vulnerability is disclosed and a patch is released for it. They consider TCP, UDP and ICMP input and output traffic to assess stability. They do not consider dependencies among systems or services in threat assessment. Therefore, they cannot calculate an attack propagation impact. Furthermore, the average of items is calculated instead of adding the calculated value for each item in each dimension with the other items in that dimension.

Kou et al. [16] present a method to evaluate a network security situation based on attack intention. The method recognizes the attack intention and attack stages, calculates the network SA and predicts the next attack stage based on achieved attack stages. This method determines attack paths, then calculates the SA for each path by multiplying the probability of the attack stage with the destructiveness of the attack and the weight of the node in which the attack occurred. Finally, it sums the SA of each attack path together to obtain the SA of the whole network. The research method of this paper depends on the known attack patterns. Therefore, it cannot calculate the network SA for unknown attacks. They do not consider systems' defense measures in the network to calculate SA. In addition, they have considered the existence of a vulnerability as the only reason for spreading the threat while the procedural relationship and the existence of similar assets can cause threat recurrence.

Zhang et al. [27] present a framework for assessing network security situational awareness in cloud computing through stochastic games. They predict the attack behavior using a fuzzy optimization method and Nash equilibrium [18]. This method has been provided for use in the cloud computing environment. In addition, to determine situational awareness, this method considers threatening failure on a host and does not consider its propagation in the network due to the dependency among hosts and services they provide. It also does not consider the possibility of spreading threats in the network.

Xiao-Lu et al. [12] propose a model and methodology to assess big data security situation. This model includes an index system and a fuzzy comprehensive evaluation algorithm to assess big data security situations. They consider two index levels. The first index level reflects the big data security situation from four dimensions, including the damage degree of harmful procedures, the damage degree of information destruction, the degree of menace and the damage degree of attacks. The second index level is designed according to the first level but with finer granularity. They use the fuzzy comprehensive evaluation algorithm to assess big data security situations. First, they identify big data security important features. Then they establish measurable index factor sets. In the third step, they establish a measurement level. After that, they establish a fuzzy relation matrix. In the fifth step, they determine the weight vector of the index. Next, they calculate big data security situations comprehensive evaluation. In this article, a general calculation method is presented and no parameters are mentioned.

Marcus et al. [21] propose measuring system-level security through a security metrics framework based on metrics of system vulnerabilities, defense mechanisms, threat severity and situations. To investigate the relationships among these four sub-metrics, they propose a hierarchical ontology with four sub-ontologies corresponding to the four sub-metrics. They calculate a network SA at time t as a function of $V(t)$, $D(t)$ and $A(t)$ which are a function of vulnerabilities, defenses and attacks at time t, respectively.

3   Assumptions and Modeling

The proposed situational awareness computational model has been presented to use in a threat information network like IT-ISAC [13], the largest available network in each country. There may be restrictions on information sharing, in which case this model cannot be used in these networks. Due to the inclusion of all the components utilized in our proposed model, such as services and their interdependencies within various networks, this model is applicable to any network as well. In the following, wherever we mention the network, we mean the IT-ISAC network. Since in such a network, each service may be provided by more than one organization, such as the Internet service that is provided by several ISPs, for better understanding and readability, here we display each service as a service-organization.

In this paper, we want to calculate SA quantitatively. Endsley [10] defined SA as "the perception of the elements in the environment within a volume of time and space, the comprehension of their meaning and the projection of their status in the near future." Hence, to calculate SA, we should understand the impacts of a threat on a network and the projection of risks that the threat may pose in the near future on the network taking into account the historical information of the monitoring network, international threats databases include NVD [19], CVE [6] and CAPEC [17] and monitoring devices.

To calculate SA, data must be collected from a set of monitoring devices and analyzes must be performed. In this paper, we focus on how SA is calculated. Our purpose is to monitor the situation of critical services although all services can be monitored, and we suppose the network's assets are critical services that from now on, we call them services.

3.1   Modeling Network

Let $\mathcal{N}$ be a network of different organizations that provides services to users as shown in Fig. 1. We represent each provided service S_i by organization O_j by $S_i - O_j$ and call it service-organization $S_i - O_j$. Each organization can provide more than one service, and some organizations may rely on services provided by other organizations to offer some of their services. For example, the organization that provides the SIM card sales service is dependent on the person profile inquiry service from the Civil Registration Organization. We model network $\mathcal{N}$ by a weighted directed graph whose nodes represent the service-organizations in the network, whose directed edges represent the dependency relationships between them and the weight of each directed edge represents the value of the dependency relationship. Formally, a service dependency graph is a pair $\mathcal{G} = (S, D)$, where $S \subseteq \mathcal{S}$ is a finite set of nodes or service-organizations and $D \subseteq S \times S$ is a finite set of directed edges between the nodes of the graph. In this study, we represent each service by a 9-tuple $(Sid, Oid, Crit, P_e, \{Destsrv, W\}, Confdemand, Integdemand, Avldemand)$ in which Sid and Oid are the identifiers of the service and the organization which provides the service, respectively. Also, $Crit$ is the criticality of the service in the network, $Destsrv$ is the service which depends on the service Sid, P_e reflects the service's security controls to protect it against the threats, W is the weight of dependency between Sid and $Destsrv$, $Confdemand, Integdemand$ and $Avldemand$ are the required value for Confidentiality, Integrity and Availability of service Sid that the service should have to be secure, respectively. More formally, for any given service s, we write $Sid(s), Oid(s), Crit(s), Destsrv(s), P_e(s), W(s), Confdemand(s), Integdemand(s), Avldemand(s)$ to denote its associated id, organization, destination service, defensive probability, dependency weight and demanded Confidentiality, Integrity and Availability, respectively. We also represent each organization by a 6-tuple $(Oid, Crit, P_e, Confdemand, Integdemand, Avldemand)$ in which Oid is the identifier of the organization, $Crit$ is the criticality of the organization, P_e reflects the organization's security controls to protect it against the threats, $Confdemand, Integdemand, Avldemand$ are the required value for Confidentiality, Integrity and Availability of organization that the organization should have to be secure, respectively. More formally, for any given organization o, we write $Oid(o), Crit(o), P_e(o), Confdemand(o), Integdemand(o),$

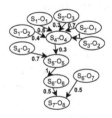

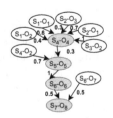

Fig. 1. A Typical Network includes some service-organizations

Fig. 2. A threat effects on services using the cascade propagation

Avldemand(*o*) to denote its associated identifier, criticality, defensive probability and demanded Confidentiality, Integrity and Availability, respectively. Regarding determining the criticality of the service, the organization and the weight of dependency relationship between the services, the opinions of the organization and the legislator were collected. The final values was calculated using Crown Jewels Analysis (CJA) [15]. It is a technique to assess asset values based on their dependencies and importance. According to this model, each organization uses a set of assets to provide critical services. Each critical service belongs to an organization or organizations, and critical services may be interdependent.

Example 1. In Fig. 1, when the weight of dependency relationship between $S_6 - O_6$ and $S_7 - O_8$ is 0.5 means service S_7 of organization O_8 to provide its service is fifty percent dependent on service S_6 of organization O_6.

3.2   Modeling Threat

Various threats target networks [7]. This diversity can be examined in terms of a threat's type, severity, complexity and effects that the threat has on a network. NIST defines a threat as follows [8]: "A cyber threat is any circumstance or event with the potential to adversely impact organizational operations (including mission, functions, image, or reputation), organizational assets, individuals, other organizations, or the Nation through an information system via unauthorized access, destruction, disclosure, modification of information, and/or denial of service." We divide each threat into the following three categories based on the above definition and the effects that threat has and the probable consequences that come with it:

- A vulnerability is a threat that does not currently affect the network, but if it exists in an asset, it may have consequences in the future
- An attack is a threat that may have impacts on the network and may have consequences in the future
- An incident is a threat that has definite effects and may have consequences in the future.

Let's consider a scenario where there is a Windows 7 operating system installed on a host, which possesses Eternal Blue (MS17-010) vulnerability. At this point, the system is considered vulnerable. If an attacker takes advantage of the vulnerability by utilizing an exploit code, the system becomes the target of an attack. The success of this attack may vary, granting the attacker access to the system or not. In the event of a successful attack, the attacker gains the ability to delete sensitive data from the system, resulting in the incident of loss of sensitive data.

We can investigate each threat from four dimensions, each threat 1) has some properties, 2) has some impacts, 3) occurs in an infrastructure and configuration and 4) can propagate through the network and infect other connected systems and networks. Hence, we should consider the mentioned dimensions to calculate and project SA. We introduced threat types earlier, and now we define four dimensions of a threat in the following.

Threat Properties. Each threat has some properties which is defined by them. In this study, we represent each threat by a 10-tuple $(Tid, Type, Vulid,$ $Atkid, P_A, AConfimp, AIntgimp, AAvlimp, Sid, CPEid)$ in which Tid, $Vulid$, $Atkid$, Sid and $CPEid$ are the identifiers of the reported threat, vulnerability in CVE [6], attack in CAPEC [17], service and asset on which threat is observed, respectively. Also, Type is the type of the threat which can be vulnerability, attack or incident, P_A is the probability of successful occurrence of the threat, $AConfimp$, $AIntgimp$ and $AAvlimp$ are the announced impacts by the organization which threat has had on the service certainly, respectively. More formally, for any given threat t, we write $Tid(t), Type(t)$, $Vulid(t)$, $Atkid(t)$, $P_A(t)$, $AConfimp(t)$, $AIntgimp(t)$, $AAvlimp(t)$, $Sid(t)$, $CPEid(t)$ to denote its associated Identifier, Type, Vulnerability, Attack, successful occurrence probability, definite Confidentiality, Integrity and Availability impact, service and asset, respectively. We extract these properties from CVE [6], NVD [19] and CAPEC [17].

Threat Occurrence Infrastructure and Configuration. Each threat can occur in a service in an organization, but services can be equipped with security controls, for example, preventive security tools, secure configurations, best practices and the like. Hence, the threat may not occur successfully because of security controls. As a result, security controls should be considered besides threat properties to calculate SA. For instance, when a threat targets port 80, but it is reported closed in security controls, the threat is unsuccessful. Therefore, we should take threat occurrence infrastructure into account in the SA calculation. As mentioned in Sect. 3.1 we use P_e parameter to show each service or organization defensive probability against threats that reflects security controls that there are on them to protect them.

Threat Impacts. Although each threat has its own effects, it may have different effects in practice. For each threat, we can have two types of impacts:

- The potential impact, once a threat is observed in a service, it may have some impacts on the service's Confidentiality, Integrity and Availability. The impacts that each threat has on a service potentially in case of the successful vulnerability exploitation is called the "Adjusted Impact" that we represent it by $CIAI$. We calculate Adjusted Impact by using Eq. 1 from the paper [9], but we did not consider the criticality. We obtain $Confimp(t)$, $Intgimp(t)$, $Avlimp(t)$ values from $Vulid(t)$ specifications using CVE [6], NVD [19].
- The affected impact, each threat may not have all of its impacts on a service because of applying security controls. We name impacts that each threat certainly has on a service the "Affected Impact" and represent it by $CIAAI$ for threat t. We represent these impacts for threat t by $AConfimp(t)$, $AIntgimp(t)$ and $AAvlimp(t)$ which are announced by the victim organization as mentioned earlier. We calculate the Affected Impact through Eq. 1 by replacing $Confimp(t)$, $Intgimp(t)$, $Avlimp(t)$ values by $AConfimp(t)$, $AIntgimp(t)$ and $AAvlimp(t)$.

$$CIAI(t) = min(10, 10.41 \times (1 - (1 - Confimp(t)) \times (1 - Intgimp(t)) \times (1 - Avlimp(t))))$$
$$(1)$$

Threat Propagation. When a threat occurs in an isolated service-organization, it has a different SA than in a service-organization that has connections to other service-organizations. Service-organizations may have similarities in infrastructure or have communications together which may lead to the propagation and repetition of a threat from one service-organization to other service-organizations associated with it. Therefore, the threat can also propagate to other service-organizations and affect them. Each threat may propagate in a network through three following methods:

Threat Propagation Procedurally. Organizations in a network may exchange information together procedurally. This means they send data and information to each other via email, automation systems, sending USB flash drives and so on. If a threat occurs in an organization, the organization may transfer the threat to other organizations with which it communicates.

Threat Propagation Through Network Connections An organization in a network may connect to other organizations through network connections and provide services to them or benefit from their services. When a threat occurs in an organization, the threat may be transmitted from that organization to organizations connected with it through the network. In addition, an attacker may infiltrate an organization then infiltrate other organizations by exploiting the first organization's connections with them.

Recurrence of a Threat in Other Organizations Due to Similar Infrastructure or Services. Each organization has a specific infrastructure, including hardware and software, or provides some services. If a threat occurs on hardware, software or a service in an organization, this threat may occur in other organizations with similar infrastructure or services.

4 Quantitative Risk-Based Situational Awareness Calculation and Projection

We define two types of SA for a network:

- Network's SA for a threat as $SA(t_i)$
- Network's SA for all threats as $SA(Network)$

We explain how to calculate $SA(t_i)$, the network's SA for a threat, in the following and how to calculate the network's SA for all threats in Sect. 4.2. When a threat occurs, it may cause definite effects at present or probable effects in the near future. Hence, $SA(t_i)$ consists of the definite effects of the threat t_i

and projection of its probable effects in the near future on the network. The definite effect is divided into two parts: Instant definite effect which refers to the effect that a threat has definitely on a service, and gradual definite effect which is the propagation of the threat's definite effect on the service-organizations depending on that service. As mentioned earlier in Sect. 3.2 threats can propagate on other service-organizations because of similarities in infrastructure or the existence of procedural communications or network connections among the service-organizations. We call risks that may occur as a result of propagation a threat through these three categories the probable effects. Therefore, we divide the probable effects into the following three categories:

- Risks of threat propagation procedurally
- Risks of threat propagation through network connections
- Risks of recurrence of a threat in other organizations due to similar infrastructure or services

Hence, we calculate and project the threat's SA according to the Fig. 3.

4.1   Definite Effect Calculation

When a threat of type of attack or incident occurs on a service-organization, the threat may have some definite effects on it. Suppose the other service-organizations in the network depend on and receive a service from that service-organization. In that case, if the threat is an incident, these service-organizations are definitely affected by the threat. Other service-organizations that depend on the second service-organizations and the like are definitely affected by the threat, too. In this way, this definite effect can be disseminated as a cascade in the network which we call it cascade propagation.

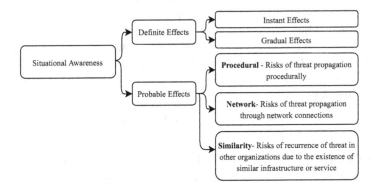

Fig. 3. Situational Awareness's detailed components

Definition 1 (Cascade Propagation). *Propagation of threat's definite effect on other service-organizations because of dependencies among them is cascade propagation.*

Example 2. If in Fig. 1 threat t_i occurs on the service-organization $S_4 - O_4$, the service S_4 will be affected in proportion to the threat effects which we name it instant definite effect. But due to the cascade propagation, the service-organizations $S_5 - O_5$ may also be affected, and again the service-organization $S_6 - O_6$, which depends on the service $S_5 - O_5$ may also be affected which we call it gradual definite effect.

As a result of Example 2, the definite effect of a threat affects the service-organization in which the threat occurs and the network to which the service-organization belongs as shown by red color in Fig. 2. The basic formula is used to calculate the definite effect of a threat on a service is Eq. 2:

$$Threat\ Effects = Service\ value \times Definitive\ consequences\ of\ the\ threat \quad (2)$$

We present Eqs. 3, 4 to calculate the instant and gradual definite effect of a threat from the Eq. 2.

$$Definite\ Effect(t_i) = W_{(S_j-O_u)(S_j-O_u)} * Crit(S_j-O_u) * CIAAI_j + Imp(S_j-O_u) \quad (3)$$

$$Imp(S_f - O_h) = \sum_{k \in K} AW_{(S_f-O_h)(S_k-O_l)} * Crit(S_k - O_l) * CIAD_k + Imp(S_k - O_l) \quad (4)$$

Suppose the threat t_i occurs on the service-organization $S_j - O_u$. K is a set which contains the dependent services to $S_j - O_u$. In Eq. 3, for attacks we use $CIAI_j$, the "Adjusted Impact" instead of $CIAAI_j$. In Eq. 4, as we do not have the $CIAAI_k$ value, we use $CIAD_k$ which is CIA demand.

- $W_{(S_j-O_u)(S_j-O_u)}$ is the dependency weight of an service-organization with itself and is always equal to one.
- $Imp(S_j - O_u)$ is the amount of damage caused by cascading propagation and equal to the gradual definite effect of the threat on dependent service-organizations which is calculated recursively.
- $AW_{(S_f-O_h)(S_k-O_l)}$ is the affected dependency weight between $(S_f - O_h)$ and other $(S_k - O_l)$ dependent services. If the threat occurs on $(S_f - O_h)$, $AW_{(S_f-O_h)(S_k-O_l)}$ is equal to $W_{(S_f-O_h)(S_k-O_l)}$ otherwise it is calculated through using Eq. 5.

$$AW_{(S_f-O_h)(S_k-O_l)} = [W_{(S_f-O_h)(S_k-O_l)} \times \sum_{b \in B} \prod_{a \in A} W_{(S_y-O_i)(S_f-O_h)}] \quad (5)$$
$$until\ W_{(S_y-O_i)} = W_{(S_j-O_u)}$$

B is a set which contains the number of paths between $(S_f - O_h)$ and $(S_j - O_u)$, the first service-organization that the threat has been occurred on it. A is a set of edges that are in the path between $(S_f - O_h)$ and $(S_j - O_u)$. To calculate definite effects, we propose an algorithm which Algorithm 1 shows the pseudo-code in detail. We calculate gradual definite effects after creating the definite effect graph $\mathcal{DE} = (V, A)$. By starting from a threatened service, our goal is to find all affected services and calculate instant and gradual definite effects using the Eqs. 3, 4 and 5.

Algorithm 1. Definite Effect Calculation and Graph Construction

Input:
A service-organization dependency graph $\mathcal{G} = (S, D)$
Type(t), Confimp(t), Intgimp(t), Avlimp(t)
Sid(s), Oid(o)

Output:
Definite Effect Graph $\mathcal{DE} = (V, A)$
Definite_Effect

1: Mark all edges in $D(\mathcal{G})$ as unvisited
2: Set $V(\mathcal{DE})$ and $A(\mathcal{DE})$ to the empty
3: **if** threat type is equal to Incident or Attack **then**
4:    Calculate definite effect for the first service Sid(s)
5: **end if**
6: **if** threat type is equal to Incident **then**
7:    Set visited edges to the empty list and call it VE
8:    Add $sid(s)$ to an empty queue $\mathcal{Q}$
9:    **while** $\mathcal{Q}$ is not empty **do**
10:       Remove the first element of $\mathcal{Q}$ and call it r
11:       Add r to $V(\mathcal{DE})$
12:       Let $\Gamma(r)$ be the neighbor set of r in $\mathcal{D}$
13:       **for** each node $z \in \Gamma(r)$ **do**
14:          Let e be the edge $(r, z) \in D(\mathcal{G})$
15:          **for** each entry in VE **do**
16:             **if** e is unvisited **then**
17:                Add z to the end of $\mathcal{Q}$
18:                Add e to VE
19:                Draw an edge from r to z in $\mathcal{DE}$
20:             **end if**
21:          **end for**
22:       **end for**
23:    **end while**
24:    Calculate definite effect using Equations 3, 4, 5 and add it to the first service's definite effect
25:    return definite effect
26: **end if**
27: return first service's definite effect

4.2 Probable Effect

As shown in Fig. 3, the probable effect is divided into three categories. We defined these three categories in Sect. 3.2. In the following, these three categories and how we calculate them are presented. we use Eq. 6 from [5] to calculate these probable effects as the base equation and generate Eqs. 7,8 and 9.

Probable Effect of a Threat $= Impact \times Possibility\ of\ Propagation \times Service\ Value$

$$(6)$$

Risks of Threat Propagation Procedurally. This category measures the risks that may be posed by the spread of a threat by an organization to other procedurally connected organizations in the network by observing a threat of type of attack or incident. We call this part of SA, Procedural Effect and calculate it through using Eq. 7.

$$Procedural\ Effect(t_i) = P_A \sum_{k=1}^{n} ((1 - P_{E_k}) \times P_{proc} \times Crit(O_k) * CIAI_k) \quad (7)$$

P_{proc} is the procedural probability propagation between organizations. To calculate procedural effects, we propose an algorithm which Algorithm 2 shows the pseudo-code in detail. By starting from a service on which a threat has occurred, our goal is to find all affected organizations and calculate procedural effects using the Eq. 7.

Algorithm 2. Procedural Effect Calculation and Graph Construction

---

Input:
 Type(t), Confimp(t), Intgimp(t), Avlimp(t)
 $P_A(t)$, Sid(s), Oid(o)
Output:
 Procedural Effect Graph $\mathcal{PE} = (V, A)$
 Procedural_Effect

1: Set $V(\mathcal{PE})$ and $A(\mathcal{PE})$ to the empty
2: **if** threat type is equal to Incident or Attack **then**
3: Add o to $V(\mathcal{PE})$
4: Add organizations that has procedural relationship to the Oid(o) to a list and call it PRL
5: **for** each node $y \in PRL$ **do**
6:   Draw an edge from o to y in PE
7:   Calculate the procedural effect (o, y) using Equation 7 and add it to procedural effect
8: **end for**
9: return procedural effect
10: **end if**

Risks of Threat Propagation Through Network Connections. This category projects the risks of spreading the threat through network connections with other organizations by observing a threat of type of attack or incident. We name this part of SA Network Effect and calculate it through Eq. 8.

$$Network\ Effect(t_i) = P_A \sum_{k=1}^{r} ((1 - P_{E_k}) \times P_{net_{jk}} \times Crit(O_k) * CIAI_k) \quad (8)$$

$P_{net_{jk}}$ is the probability of spreading the threat through the network connection between two organizations O_j and O_k. To calculate this probability, we consider the privileges that an attacker obtains through the threat because she/he can extend her/his threat to other connected organizations through the network based on the obtained privileges. To determine these probabilities, we use Snort's [25] attack classifications as shown in Table 3.

Risks of Recurrence of a Threat in Other Organizations Due to Similar Infrastructure or Service. In this category, risks of recurrence of a threat in other organizations due to similar infrastructure or services are projected by observing all kinds of threats. For example, when a threat occurs on Windows 7 in an organization, this category examines what organizations have Windows 7, how likely they are threatened, how malicious the threat may be, if it occurs, and calculates the extent of its future damage. We name this part of SA Infrastructural Effect and calculate it through using Eq. 9.

$$Infrastructural\ Effect(t_i) = P_A \sum_{k=1}^{q} ((1 - P_{E_y}) \times Crit(O_y) \times CIAI_y)$$
(9)

Since algorithms of risks of threat propagation through network connections and similar infrastructure or service are similar to Algorithm 2, we do not mention them. Since these four amounts represent $SA(t_i)$ from different dimensions, Network's SA for a threat $SA(t_i)$ is represented as the following four elements vector:

$$SA(t_i) = [Definite\ Effect, Procedural\ Effect, Network\ Effect, Infrastructural\ Effect]$$
(10)

We obtain diverse information from each part of this vector.

Network's SA. We presented the method of calculating and projecting the network's SA for a threat $SA(t_i)$ in the form of a four elements vector so far. To obtain the network's SA for all threats, we add each part of the four elements vector for each reported threat together. The final vector is also a four elements vector. Equation 11, shows how to calculate a network's SA.

$$SA(Network) = SA(Network) + SA(t_i)$$
(11)

SA Reduction. Over time the observed threats' effects should be reduced by doing and making the necessary actions and decisions. For this purpose, by receiving feedback from the organization that has reported the threat t_i, the amount of $SA(t_i)$ is reduced from the SA(Network) through Eq. 12.

$$SA(Network) = SA(Network) - SA(t_i)$$
(12)

5   Evaluation

In this section, we evaluate the effectiveness of QR-SACP for calculating and projecting situational awareness.

5.1   Evaluation Lab

Threats data that have been used during the evaluation are real. We used Information and Communication Technologies-Information Sharing and Analysis Center (ICT-ISAC) threat data to evaluate QR-SACP. ICT-ISAC is a network similar to IT-ISAC. ICT-ISAC receives threat data from ICT member organizations and shares them with other ICT member organizations to increase the security of ICT sector. Among the services that send threat information to ICT-ISAC are Internet Service providers, VoIP service providers, telecommunications infrastructure and hosting service providers. Since the values used for service, organization, and threat specifications and how to extract them are essential in our evaluation, and whether the service name is ISP or S_{11} does not make a difference in evaluating the effectiveness of the proposed algorithms, we used aliases to anonymize services, organizations, and threats name to preserve their privacy.

The evaluation network and dependencies among services of organizations has been shown in Fig. 4. In this evaluation, threat data belong to 30 critical services from 12 ICT-ISAC member organizations. Tables 2, 3, 4, 5 and 6 shows organization information, service information, probability of threat propagation procedurally, probability of threat propagation through network and summary of threats and the obtained results, respectively. The tables are presented in Appendix A.

Questionnaires were presented to the organizations to receive their assets CPE_{id} and the values of service and organization CIA Demand, P_e, P_{proc} and P_{net}. The legislator finalized the received values based on the importance of the services and organizations in the ICT sector. The criticality of service and organization in this model should be determined. There are different methods to define it that we left the initial determination of this value to the legislator. The composition of the legislator, which falls outside the scope of this article, is contingent upon the laws specific to each country. CIA demand for each service or organization is a combination of $(Confdemand, Integdemand, Avldemand)$. Threat CIA has been collected from [19].

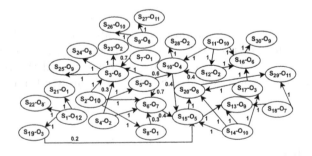

Fig. 4. The Evaluation Network

5.2 Evaluation Results

We received 25 threats during the 30-day evaluation period through threat information sharing shown in Table 6. Ten of these threats are vulnerabilities, nine are attacks and six are incidents. We calculated and projected the network SA for the mentioned threats using the presented algorithms which have been shown in Figs. 5, 6, 7, 8 and 9. The four elements vector of SA was calculated and projected for each threat and all threats in the network. In columns 9 to 12 of Table 6, the first value shows network's SA for each threat, and the second value is the sum of the values for all threats up to that threat and shows network's SA for all threats. Figures 5, 6 show $SA(t_i)$, the four values of the network's SA for each threat. By looking at them, we understand the definite effect that each threat has left on the network, the probability that the threat may propagate in other organizations procedurally, the probability that the threat may propagate in other organizations through network connections and the probability that the threat occurs again in other organizations because of the similarity of infrastructure or services. In this way, we can understand how each threat can spread in the network and exert its destructive effects. It is also possible to compare the intensity of threats in each category. For example, t_{21} cannot spread through the network, but t_7 can. The definite effect of t_2 is greater than other threats, t_{23} has the highest probability of spreading procedurally and t_{11}, t_{21} and t_{23} have the highest probability of spreading due to similar infrastructure or service. t_7 has the highest probability of spreading through the network. In addition, to deal with the t_2 we know we should pay attention to its dependent services in comparison to t_{11} that we should pay attention to its dependent organizations which have procedural relationship with it. Figures 7 and 8 show the four values of network's SA for all threats in the network. Due to the large difference between the value definite effect and three other values, we presented their values separately in two graphs for a better display.

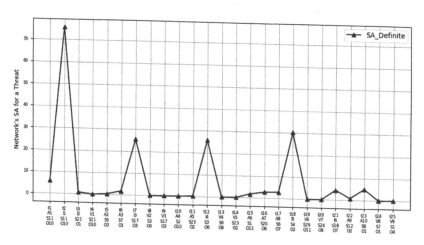

Fig. 5. Definite effect for each threat in the evaluation network

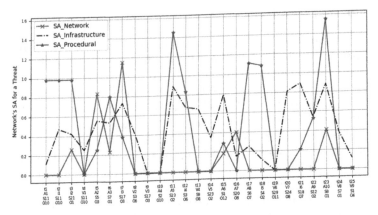

Fig. 6. Network, procedural and infrastructural effects for each threat in the evaluation network

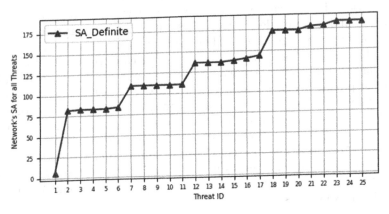

Fig. 7. Definite effects for all threats in the evaluation network

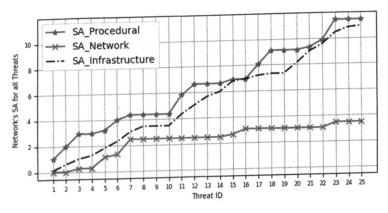

Fig. 8. Network, procedural and infrastructural effects for all threats in the evaluation network

5.3   Discussion

The Advantage of Quantifying SA Compared to Representing it in Colors. In the case of qualitative demonstration of SA using colors, threats t_7, t_{12}, and t_{18} are displayed in yellow and are seen as equally important. However, in the case where we have quantified the SA, just by looking at the Figs. 5 and 6 we can easily understand that the threat t_{18} can cause the most damage and needs to be investigated more quickly.

Demonstration of a Threat's Effects by Four Elements. By separating the effects of each threat based on its destruction and expansion in the network into four elements, it is possible to make decisions and provide more effective action for each threat. For example, regarding t_5 and t_7, we can see from the Fig. 6 that they can have the highest amount of threats through the network. In the case of t_{11}, it can cause the greatest amount of destruction through similar infrastructure. t_{23} can leave the greatest amount of destruction procedurally. In this way, we can take more effective measures to deal with them.

Calculation of Instant and Gradual Definite Effects. Figure 9 displays the definite effect for each threat in the network in the form of three plots, including instant, gradual and the sum of two previous values so called the aggregate value. Dividing the results into two categories, instant and gradual, is very effective in carrying out actions and prioritizing them. The aggregate value helps to choose the threat with high priority. High instant value tells us that more attention should be paid to the service of the organization in which the threat occurred and high gradual value says that many services are dependent on this source service and they should be considered. Accordingly, if we want to

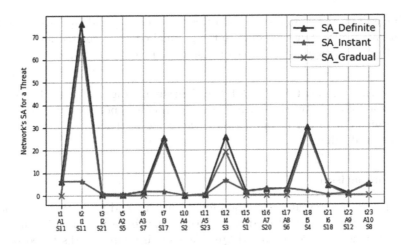

Fig. 9. Instant, gradual and aggregated definite effects in the evaluation network

Table 1. Comparison between input data and results of QR-SACP and other related work

Method	QR-SACP	Alavizadeh et al. [3]	Marcus et al. [21]	Kou et al. [16]	Rongrong et al. [23]	Zhang et al. [28]
Input Data						
Asset Criticality	✓	✗	✗	✓	✗	✗
Security Controls	✓	✓	✓	✗	✗	✗
P_{net}	✓	✗	✗	✗	✗	✗
P_{proc}	✓	✗	✗	✗	✗	✗
Infrastructure Similarity	✓	✗	✗	✗	✗	✗
P_A	✓	✓	✓	✓	✓	✓
Threat Properties	✓	✓	✓	✓	✓	✓
Threat Type	V,A,I	V	V	V	V,A	V,A
Service Dependency	✓	✗	✗	✗	✗	✗
Results						
Instant Effect	✓	✓	✓	✗	✗	✗
Gradual Effect	✓	✗	✗	✗	✗	✗
Definite Effect	✓	✗	✗	✓	✓	✓
Prop using Network	✓	✓	✗	✓	✓	✗
Prop Procedurally	✓	✗	✗	✗	✗	✗
Similar Infrastructure	✓	✗	✗	✗	✗	✗

decide based on the instant effect of a threat, threats t_2 and t_{12} have the same level of importance, but according to the gradual effect calculated for them, we realize that t_2 has a greater degree of destruction compared to t_{12}.

Display the General Status of the Network. Figures 7 and 8 show the overall state of the network after receiving 25 threats. Upon receiving the report of neutralizing a threat in the network, the value of that threat is subtracted from the total value.

5.4   Comparison

In this paper, we presented a method for calculating and projecting SA. Therefore, for comparison, we selected related works that have also provided methods for quantifying SA. We compared QR-SACP with related works based on the input data and the generated result. The results have been shown in Table 1.

Considering assets value and the dependency between assets are very important factors in calculating SA but as it has been shown in Table 1, most of the methods have not considered it. Spreading the threat in the network through different methods, including network, procedurally and similar infrastructure is very important, but most methods have focused on the instant impacts of the threat. The calculation method in [3] considers SA calculation equal to risk calculation by considering just vulnerabilities. Therefore, it cannot calculate and project attacks' and incidents' effects. In addition, [3] does not consider dependencies among services in the network. Therefore, it cannot pay attention to cascade propagation in decision-making. For example, [3] selects threat number t_1 to investigate first and ignores threats number t_2 and t_{12} that we should give them more priority. Also, [21,23,28] and [16] do not consider the possibility of spreading threats in the network procedurally, through a network connection and the similarity among services and infrastructures to project threats effect. In addition, they do not consider dependency among systems in a network. They can calculate values like the values green diagram in Fig. 9 for incidents or attacks, but it cannot predict that threats t_2, t_{18}, and t_{12} will have further destructive effects in the network in the near future. Furthermore, [23] calculates the average of SAs as the network's SA and does not consider the summation of SAs. Hence, we cannot have an integrated perspective from the network situation in this method like what we have in Fig. 8. What [16] calculates is equal to the summation values definite effects and network effects of QR-SACP. Therefore, it cannot calculate threats' procedural and infrastructural effects. In addition, because [16] sums the two values definite effects and network effects together, it cannot determine whether the threat has been happened or may happen in the future.

6   Conclusion and Future Works

In this paper, we proposed QR-SACP, a novel technique that investigates a threat from different aspects through using diverse resources to calculate and project a network's SA for each and all threats. In this technique, a SA's four elements vector is calculated and projected by receiving a threat through threat information sharing, in proportion to the type of threat. We investigate the threat from different dimensions and extract information, including the threat's properties, infrastructure and configuration on which the threat occurs, impacts that the threat has and ways the threat can propagate across the network and contaminate other services and organizations. If the threat is an incident or attack, all parts of the SA's vector are calculated otherwise in case the threat is a vulnerability only the fourth part of the SA's vector is calculated. We calculate the instant definite effect of the threat on a service. If the threat is an incident, it may have definite effects on the service, such as service interruptions and breakdowns, loss

Table 2. Service Information

Service	O_{id}	Criticality	CIA Demand	P_e
S_1	O_{12}	0.8	(0.6, 0.2, 0.9)	0.8
S_2	O_{10}	0.9	(0.1, 0.2, 0.9)	0.1
S_3	O_6	0.7	(0.9, 0.6, 0.8)	0.4
S_4	O_2	0.6	(0.4, 0.1, 0.7)	0.3
S_5	O_3	0.3	(0.2, 0.1, 0.7)	0.3
S_6	O_7	0.6	(0.5, 0.5, 0.7)	0.7
S_7	O_1	0.5	(0.4, 0.3, 0.7)	0.4
S_8	O_1	0.6	(0.9, 0.2, 0.7)	0.4
S_9	O_8	0.3	(0.3, 0.6, 0.8)	0.2
S_{10}	O_4	0.5	(0.4, 0.5, 0.7)	0.3
S_{11}	O_{10}	0.8	(0.2, 0.1, 1)	0.9
S_{12}	O_2	0.5	(0.2, 0.3, 0.6)	0.5
S_{13}	O_9	0.4	(0.2, 0.3, 0.7)	0.4
S_{14}	O_{10}	0.8	(0.2, 0.3, 1)	0.6
S_{15}	O_5	0.7	(0.2, 0.6, 0.8)	0.5
S_{16}	O_6	0.1	(0.6, 0.4, 0.7)	0.3
S_{17}	O_3	0.3	(0.3, 0.1, 0.7)	0.2
S_{18}	O_7	0.1	(0.5, 0.2, 0.6)	0.3
S_{19}	O_3	0.5	(0.2, 0.2, 0.6)	0.6
S_{20}	O_8	0.6	(0.8, 0.6, 0.2)	0.5
S_{21}	O_1	0.2	(0.3, 0.5, 0.8)	0.3
S_{22}	O_8	0.4	(0.4, 0.8, 0.3)	0.3
S_{23}	O_2	0.1	(0.2, 0.1, 0.3)	0.2
S_{24}	O_8	0.3	(0.2, 0.4, 0.5)	0.1
S_{25}	O_9	0.3	(0.3, 0.6, 0.3)	0.4
S_{26}	O_4	0.1	(0.2, 0.3, 0.6)	0.1
S_{27}	O_{11}	0.2	(0.3, 0.5, 0.2)	0.3
S_{28}	O_2	0.4	(0.3, 0.6, 0.2)	0.2
S_{29}	O_{11}	0.2	(0.1, 0.1, 0.1)	0.3
S_{30}	O_9	0.2	(0.4, 0.2, 0.1)	0.5

Table 3. Network Probability Propagation

Classification	Prob.
Successful-admin	1
Trojan-activity	1
Shellcode-detect	1
Web-application-attack	0.9
Unauthorized access to data	0.9
Successful-user	0.85
Successful-recon-largescale	0.7
Denial-of-service	0.5
Attempted-admin	0.4
Attempted-user	0.3
Default-login-attempt	0.3
Suspicious-filename-detect	0.3
Suspicious-login	0.3
Scan	0.2
Other	0.1

of data confidentiality, and so on. Since other services in the network may depend on the threatened service, the threat may affect these dependent services, too. Therefore, we calculate the propagation of the threat's definite effects across the network and name it gradual definite effect. To calculate gradual definite effect, we consider service dependencies in the network and model them by a weighted directed graph called a service dependency graph. Furthermore, by calculating procedural effects, network effects and infrastructural effects, we project probability of propagation or recurrence of the threat in other network's services and organizations through three categories, namely threat propagation procedurally, threat propagation through network connections, recurrence of a threat in other organizations due to similar infrastructure or services. The experimental results demonstrate QR-SACP method can calculate and project definite and probable threat's effects across the entire network effectively and reveals more details from the threat's current and near future situation to make timely decisions and reduce threat's costs and consequences.

A   Appendix A

The following tables show services, organizations properties, network and procedural probabilities and summary of threats that have been used in evaluation. In Sect. 3, the terms used in the tables have been introduced in detail.

Table 4. Organization Information

Oid	Criticality	CIA Demand	P_e
O_1	0.5	(0.5, 0.5, 0.8)	0.4
O_2	0.4	(0.2, 0.2, 0.7)	0.2
O_3	0.6	(0.4, 0.1, 0.9)	0.5
O_4	0.7	(0.8, 0.3, 0.7)	0.5
O_5	0.5	(0.5, 0.9, 0.8)	0.3
O_6	0.6	(0.7, 0.5, 0.7)	0.6
O_7	0.5	(0.7, 0.4, 0.7)	0.6
O_8	0.3	(0.6, 0.8, 0.6)	0.4
O_9	0.2	(0.2, 0.2, 0.7)	0.2
O_{10}	0.9	(0.4, 0.4, 0.9)	0.8
O_{11}	0.3	(0.2, 0.5, 0.8)	0.3
O_{12}	0.8	(0.4, 0.3, 0.9)	0.9

Table 5. Procedural Probability Propagation

Oid	Oid, Probability
O_1	$\{O_2,0.2\}$, $\{O_6,0.3\}$, $\{O_{10},0.5\}$
O_2	$\{O_1,0.1\}$, $\{O_5,0.4\}$, $\{O_{11},0.3\}$
O_3	$\{O_7,0.3\}$
O_4	-
O_5	$\{O_2,0.4\}$
O_6	$\{O_1,0.4\}$
O_7	$\{O_3,0.6\}$
O_8	-
O_9	-
O_{10}	$\{O_1,0.4\}$
O_{11}	$\{O_2,0.4\}$
O_{12}	$\{O_8,0.5\}$

Table 6. Summary of Threats and Results

#	Threat Type	Service	O_{id}	Threat CIA	P_e	P_{net}	CPE_{id}	Def. Eff.	Proc. Eff.	Net. Eff.	Infra. Eff.
t_1	Atk	S_{11}	O_{10}	(C, C, C)	1	–	748	6.03,6.03	0.98,0.98	0,0	0.11,0.11
t_2	Inc	S_{11}	O_{10}	(C, C, C)	1	–	602	75.63,81.66	0.98,1.96	0,0	0.47,0.58
t_3	Inc	S_{21}	O_1	(C, N, P)	0.95	0.3	70	0.77,82.42	0.98,2.94	0.26,0.26	0.42,1.0
t_4	Vul	S_{11}	O_{10}	(P, P, C)	0.85	–	104	0,82.42	0,2.94	0,0.26	0.25,1.25
t_5	Atk	S_5	O_3	(P, C, N)	1	0.3,0.4	56	0.36,82.78	0.25,3.19	0.83,1.08	0.55,1.8
t_6	Atk	S_7	O_1	(P, P, P)	0.9	0.3	15	1.77,84.55	0.8,3.99	0.23,1.31	0.53,2.33
t_7	Inc	S_{17}	O_3	(P, C, C)	0.9	0.3,0.4	135	25.47,110.02	0.38,4.37	1.15,2.46	0.73, 3.06
t_8	Vul	S_3	O_6	(C, C, C)	0.85	–	729	0,110.02	0,4.37	0,2.46	0.4,3.46
t_9	Vul	S_{17}	O_3	(N, N, N)	1	–	523	0,110.02	0,4.37	0,2.46	0,3.46
t_{10}	Atk	S_2	O_{10}	(N, N, N)	0.95	–	916	0,110.02	0,4.37	0,2.46	0,3.46
t_{11}	Atk	S_{23}	O_2	(C, C, P)	0.85	–	351	0.26,110.28	1.45,5.82	0,2.46	0.89,4.35
t_{12}	Inc	S_3	O_6	(C, C, C)	0.85	–	126	25.72,136.01	0.83,6.65	0,2.46	0.67,5.02
t_{13}	Vul	S_9	O_8	(P, P, P)	0.9	–	281	0,136.01	0,6.65	0,2.46	0.65,5.67
t_{14}	Vul	S_{23}	O_2	(P, C, N)	0.9	–	104	0,136.01	0,6.65	0,2.46	0.35,6.02
t_{15}	Atk	S_1	O_{12}	(P, P, N)	0.9	0.5	248	1.75,137.76	0.29,6.94	0.18,2.65	0.79,6.81
t_{16}	Atk	S_{20}	O_8	(P, P, C)	1	0.2	34	2.71,140.47	0,6.94	0.4,3.05	0.15,6.96
t_{17}	Atk	S_6	O_7	(N, N, C)	1	–	166	2.88,143.35	1.11,8.05	0,3.05	0.25,7.21
t_{18}	Inc	S_4	O_2	(P, P, P)	1	–	439	30.16,173.51	1.08,9.13	0,3.05	0.11,7.32
t_{19}	Vul	S_{29}	O_{11}	(N, N, N)	1	–	135	0,173.51	0,9.13	0,3.05	0,7.32
t_{20}	Vul	S_{24}	O_8	(P, P, P)	0.95	–	869	0,173.51	0,9.13	0,3.05	0.81,8.13
t_{21}	Inc	S_{18}	O_7	(P, P, N)	0.85	–	6	4.46,177.97	0.21,9.34	0,3.05	0.89,9.02
t_{22}	Atk	S_{12}	O_2	(N, N, P)	1	–	446	0.85,178.82	0.53,9.87	0,3.05	0.54,9.56
t_{23}	Atk	S_8	O_1	(C, C, C)	0.9	0.3	281	5.06,183.88	1.55,11.42	0.41,3.46	0.88,10.44
t_{24}	Vul	S_7	O_1	(C, C, P)	0.95	–	149	0,183.88	0,11.42	0,3.46	0.38,10.82
t_{25}	Vul	S_{10}	O_4	(C, C, C)	0.95	–	255	0,183.88	0,11.42	0,3.46	0.11,10.93

References

1. Ahmad, A., Maynard, S.B., Desouza, K.C., Kotsias, J., Whitty, M.T., Baskerville, R.L.: How can organizations develop situation awareness for incident response: a case study of management practice. Comput. Secur. **101**, 102122 (2021)
2. Alavizadeh, H., et al.: A survey on threat situation awareness systems: framework, techniques, and insights. arXiv preprint arXiv:2110.15747 (2021)
3. Alavizadeh, H., Alavizadeh, H., Jang-Jaccard, J.: Cyber situation awareness monitoring and proactive response for enterprises on the cloud. In: 2020 IEEE 19th International Conference on Trust, Security and Privacy in Computing and Communications (TrustCom), pp. 1276–1284. IEEE (2020)
4. blackbery: Global threat intelligence report (2023). https://www.blackberry.com/us/en/pdfviewer?file=/content/dam/bbcomv4/blackberry-com/en/solutions/threat-intelligence/2023/threat-intelligence-report-april/blackberry-global-threat-intelligence-report-apr23.pdf
5. Boehm, B.: Software risk management. In: Ghezzi, C., McDermid, J.A. (eds.) ESEC 1989. LNCS, vol. 387, pp. 1–19. Springer, Heidelberg (1989). https://doi.org/10.1007/3-540-51635-2_29
6. ccvedetails: (2023). https://www.cvedetails.com/

7. deepwatch: 2023 annual threat intelligence report (2023). https://www.deepwatch.com/2023-deepwatch-ati-threat-report/?utm_campaign=Threat%20Intel

8. computer security division, N.: Guide for conducting risk assessments (2012). https://doi.org/10.6028/NIST.SP.800-30r1

9. Doynikova, E., Kotenko, I.: CVSS-based probabilistic risk assessment for cyber situational awareness and countermeasure selection. In: 2017 25th Euromicro International Conference on Parallel, Distributed and Network-based Processing (PDP), pp. 346–353. IEEE (2017)

10. Endsley, M.R.: Design and evaluation for situation awareness enhancement. In: Proceedings of the Human Factors Society Annual Meeting, vol. 32, pp. 97–101. Sage Publications Sage CA: Los Angeles, CA (1988)

11. Franke, U., Brynielsson, J.: Cyber situational awareness-a systematic review of the literature. Comput. Secur. **46**, 18–31 (2014)

12. Han, X.L., Liu, Y., Zhang, Z.J., Lü, X., Li, Y.: Research on model and methodology of big data security situation assessment based on fuzzy set. J. Comput. **29**(3), 156–164 (2018)

13. IT-ISAC: www.it-isac.org (2023). https://www.it-isac.org

14. Jajodia, S., Liu, P., Swarup, V., Wang, C.: Cyber Situational Awareness. Springer, Cham (2009)

15. Jim, W., Morrissey, S., Bodeau, D., Powers, S. C.: The risk-to-mission assessment process (RiskMAP): a sensitivity analysis and an extension to treat confidentiality issues (2009). https://www.mitre.org/sites/default/files/pdf/09_2994.pdf

16. Kou, G., Wang, S., Tang, G.: Research on key technologies of network security situational awareness for attack tracking prediction. Chin. J. Electron. **28**(1), 162–171 (2019)

17. mitre.org: capec.mitre.org (2023). https://capec.mitre.org

18. Nash, J.: Non-cooperative games. Ann. Math. **54**(2), 286–295 (1951)

19. NVD: nvd.nist.gov (2023). https://nvd.nist.gov

20. Pahi, T., Leitner, M., Skopik, F.: Analysis and assessment of situational awareness models for national cyber security centers. In: International Conference on Information Systems Security and Privacy, vol. 2, pp. 334–345. SCITEPRESS (2017)

21. Pendleton, M., Garcia-Lebron, R., Cho, J.H., Xu, S.: A survey on systems security metrics. ACM Comput. Surv. (CSUR) **49**(4), 1–35 (2016)

22. Pöyhönen, J., Rajamäki, J., Ruoslahti, H., Lehto, M.: Cyber situational awareness in critical infrastructure protection. Ann. Disaster Risk Sci. ADRS **3**(1) (2020)

23. Rongrong, X., Xiaochun, Y., Zhiyu, H.: Framework for risk assessment in cyber situational awareness. IET Inf. Secur. **13**(2), 149–156 (2019)

24. Skopik, F., Ma, Z., Smith, P., Bleier, T.: Designing a cyber attack information system for national situational awareness. In: Aschenbruck, N., Martini, P., Meier, M., Tölle, J. (eds.) Future Security 2012. CCIS, vol. 318, pp. 277–288. Springer, Heidelberg (2012). https://doi.org/10.1007/978-3-642-33161-9_42

25. Snort: manual-snort-org.s3-website-us-east-1 (2023). http://manual-snort-org.s3-website-us-east-1.amazonaws.com/node31.html

26. Solutions, M.C.: An overview of MITRE cyber situational awareness solutions

27. Zhang, H., Yi, Y., Wang, J., Cao, N., Duan, Q., et al.: Network security situation awareness framework based on threat intelligence. CMC: Comput. Mater. Continua **56**(3), 381–399 (2018)

28. Zhang, H., Yin, Y., Zhao, D., Liu, B., Gao, H.: Network security situational awareness model based on threat intelligence. In: Xiong, J., Wu, S., Peng, C., Tian, Y. (eds.) Mobile Multimedia Communications. LNICST, pp. 526–536. Springer, Cham (2021). https://doi.org/10.1007/978-3-030-89814-4_38

Dynamic Trust Boundary Identification for the Secure Communications of the Entities via 6G

Rabeya Basri[1]([⊠])[ID], Gour Karmakar[1]([⊠])[ID], Joarder Kamruzzaman[1][ID],
S. H. Shah Newaz[2][ID], Linh Nguyen[1][ID], and Muhammad Usman[1][ID]

[1] Institute of Innovation, Science and Sustainability, Federation University Australia,
Ballarat, Australia
rbasri@students.federation.edu.au,
{gour.karmakar,joarder.kamruzzaman,l.nguyen,m.usman}@federation.edu.au
[2] School of Computing and Informatics, Universiti Teknologi Brunei,
Bandar Seri Begawan, Brunei
shah.newaz@utb.edu.bn

Abstract. 6G is more likely prone to a range of known and unknown cyber-attacks because of its highly distributive nature. Current literature and research prove that a trust boundary can be used as a security door (e.g., gateway/firewall) to validate entities and applications attempting to access 6G networks. Trust boundaries allow these entities to connect or work with entities of other trust boundaries via 6G by dynamically monitoring their interactions, behaviors, and data transmissions. The importance of trust boundaries in security protection mechanisms demands a dynamic multi-trust boundary identification. There exists an automatic trust boundary identification for IoT data. However, it is a binary trust boundary classification and the dataset used in the approach is not suitable for dynamic trust boundary identification. Motivated by these facts, to provide automatic security protection for entities in 6G, in this paper, we propose a mechanism to identify dynamic and multiple trust boundaries based on trust values and geographical location coordinates of 6G communication entities. Our proposed mechanism uses unsupervised clustering and splitting and merging techniques. The experimental results show that entities can dynamically change their boundary location if their trust values and locations change over time. We also analyze the trust boundary identification accuracy in terms of our defined two performance metrics, i.e., trust consistency and the degree of gateway coverage. The proposed scheme allows us to distinguish between entities and control their access to the 6G network based on their trust levels to ensure secure and resilient communication.

Keywords: 6G · Security · Trust boundary · Unsupervised clustering · Splitting and Merging

1 Introduction

6G is expected to provide a high-speed data rate of up to 1 Tbps and low latency (10–100 µs) in wireless communication [8]. This enables 6G to support

© The Author(s), under exclusive license to Springer Nature Singapore Pte Ltd. 2023
W. Meng et al. (Eds.): ISPEC 2023, LNCS 14341, pp. 194–208, 2023.
https://doi.org/10.1007/978-981-99-7032-2_12

many smart applications, technologies, and services, such as extended reality, autonomous vehicles, THz communication, VLC (Visible Light Communication), and quantum communication which cannot be provided by 5G. The architecture and design of 6G is still under study. Most of the information is still around use cases. Therefore, we have considered a potential 6G infrastructure [11] that will provide ubiquitous connectivity in space, air, ground, and ocean by utilizing the Internet, satellites, and underground cables, presented in Fig. 1.

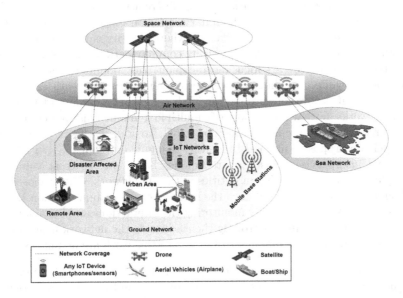

Fig. 1. A potential 6G infrastructure with massive communication coverage in space, air, ground, and sea networks.

6G will connect customer networks (LAN, WAN, and IoT networks) and entities to ensure complete distributed communications with cloud core networks and edge servers. In this paper, entities specifically refer to any object, device, application, or network. Hence, the number of IoT devices in 6G will be ten times greater than IoT devices in 5G which will pose remarkable security risks and potential threats [17]. It is expected that known and unknown entities will communicate via 6G. Moreover, in 6G, entities will share a large amount of data during communication which might open doors for many known and unknown attacks, e.g., Distributed Denial of Service (DDoS) and Man-in-the-Middle (MITM) attacks [12]. Besides, network softwarization vulnerabilities disrupt the dynamicity and automation of 6G, as certain security measures that rely on encryption technology are not ideal for quantum computing in 6G. Because of the requirement of key distribution, encryption cannot be applied to unknown entities. Therefore, ensuring protection against cyber attacks in 6G to overcome potential security challenges to maintain accountability, integrity, confidentiality, and authenticity of data clearly indicates the demand for dynamic security protection using multiple trust boundaries identification.

While perceiving the importance of security for national critical communication infrastructures (smart grid, healthcare, etc.), roaming attacks, and cyber resiliency, trust boundary appears to be an essential vehicle for providing security protection in communication networks. For the security aspect, the trust boundary can be defined as a security safeguard that controls the access of all types of entities that are trying to enter a network based on their current trust levels. Inside a trust boundary, all entities of a network occupy almost similar trust levels. On the contrary, entities having different trust levels are categorized under different boundaries. This boundary isolation ensures dynamic security protection in distributed networks like 6G, where security is the utmost concern to handle a large number of entities during communication and data exchange.

Currently, researchers are focusing to exploit trust boundaries for managing security levels while providing services to different networks, entities, and systems. Current literature shows an automatic binary trust boundary identification for IoT networks [6] that fails to identify multiple dynamic trust boundaries that are required for better security protection in 6G. To address this research gap, in this paper, we propose a method to identify dynamic and multiple trust boundaries using unsupervised clustering techniques based on the trust values and geographical locations of different entities in the 6G network. Our proposed approach creates a pathway to enhance the security of 6G communication through trust boundaries by dynamically monitoring the interactions and behaviors of all heterogeneous entities and controlling their access to the network using security protection gateways. Our main contributions to this work are as follows:

- A mechanism to dynamically identify trust boundaries for 6G communication using unsupervised clustering and splitting and merging approaches is introduced.
- The experimental results generated using a sample 6G network show that the proposed mechanism enables entities to change their boundary location automatically if their trust values and locations are changed over time.
- The trust boundary identification accuracy is analyzed using our defined two performance metrics, i.e., trust Consistency and the degree of gateway coverage.
- The dynamic trust boundary identification provides insights on how to automate security services to protect systems, entities, and networks used in wireless communication networks.

2   Related Works

Trust boundaries are essential for providing segmented protection by isolating hardware and software components of a network and ensuring secure zone-to-zone communication. Providing security levels by utilizing trust differs from system to system, which may lead to different possible trust boundary identification mechanisms for different networks. Current literature shows that trust boundaries in IoT, IIoT, and beyond 5G or 6G can be identified based on three approaches, i.e., an intuitive process where trust boundaries are set intuitively [2,5,7,14], a learning-based process that uses machine learning algorithms with clustering techniques [6,9], and threat modeling related to various security threats, such as IoT botnets, DNS threats, ransomware, and unauthorized access to physical properties. Threat analysis tools, such as Microsoft's STRIDE, DREAD [3,4] and PASTA [15,16], are used for secure application design, security risk rating, and determining the impact of security risks on both IoT and IIoT applications.

A static security protection theory using intuitive trust boundaries in 6G for the customer networks is presented in [7]. Here, edge nodes are used as corporate firewalls. The serving edge node communicates with the destination edge node via the federated public service domain using trust boundaries. Utilizing the chain of trust boundaries, destination edge nodes either allow (e.g., limit flow rate) or reject end-to-end communication initiated by the serving node. Thus, it protects the entire communication against cyber-attacks by ensuring an equal trust level for each entity within the customer network. However, the study needs to be tested against other applications and entities in 6G.

In addition, [6] classified 76 IoT nodes as trustworthy and untrustworthy using the K-means clustering algorithm considering five features of trusts. They used the support vector machine classifier to identify the threshold level for each feature to separate trustworthy and untrustworthy interactions through a decision boundary. This method simply considers an automatic binary trust boundary identification based on static trust values that are not dynamically updated. To detect changes in the node behavior over time to ensure better security for practical implementation, continuous trust values of each entity need to be considered that are updated from time to time.

Motivation for Dynamic Trust Boundary Identification. Dynamic trust boundaries allow 6G networks to better isolate sensitive data, making it more difficult for malicious actors to access and exploit. Besides, a dynamic trust boundary ensures secure data exchange between different entities in the communication network, such as nodes, mobile devices, and base stations by controlling their access to sensitive data and restricting their interactions based on their trust levels. This prevents malicious actors from intercepting or altering data in transit through continuous monitoring and thus protects the network from various known and unknown attacks, such as MITM and DDoS attacks.

An automatic binary trust boundary identification model is presented in [6]. The main loopholes of this model are: (a) nodes are classified as trusted or untrusted (binary trust classification) and (b) data used in this model is not suitable for dynamic trust boundary identification. Other existing approaches identifying trust boundaries using intuitive process [14] or threat analysis [16] are static. But, security threats can emerge at any time and bypass existing protections. As a result, the identification of trust boundaries is required in an ad-hoc and automatic manner. Entities involved in 6G communication need to be dynamically re-categorized into different trust levels for identifying trust boundaries at a particular time instant.

3   Proposed Dynamic Trust Boundary Identification Mechanism

Dynamic trust boundary identification plays a pivotal role in the realm of 6G networks, entailing the constant monitoring and delineation of boundaries amidst varying levels of trust. This critical process is indispensable for safeguarding sensitive data and regulating access to entities, shielding them from potential cyber threats, while simultaneously identifying and mitigating any security risks that may arise. Given the nascent stage of 6G networks, a concrete methodology for dynamic trust boundary identification is yet to be established. Furthermore, it is imperative to configure Security Protection Gateways (SPGs) with indispensable security policies to shield entities within trust boundaries against cyber threats. These gateways assume control over incoming traffic, exercising discretion to permit or deny access based on the trustworthiness of the requesting entity and the corresponding trust boundary. Consequently, this meticulous filtering guarantees that exclusively trusted entities can interact with entities residing within another trust boundary, effectively fortifying the networks against an array of cyber-attacks.

Our proposed method for dynamic trust boundary identification revolves around the concept that entities within a trust boundary exhibit a similar range of trust values and are located in close proximity to each other within the communication range offered by the 6G four-tier (ground-air-space-sea) architecture. The spatial proximity of these entities heightens the likelihood of successful communication with their respective gateways. To achieve this, continuous monitoring of entity behavior and their interactions become imperative. Any alterations in trust levels or entity locations over time prompt a dynamic adjustment of their corresponding boundary locations, ensuring entities are appropriately allocated to distinct boundaries. Otherwise, they will reside in the same boundary. Consequently, alongside trust values, the geo-location of entities can be taken into account as a determining factor for categorizing them into discrete boundaries.

3.1   Features for Dynamic Trust Boundary Calculation

To identify trust boundaries in an ad-hoc manner, we can use trust values, geo-locations, the communication range of entities, and 6G communication channel characteristics. However, in this paper, we specifically choose trust values, geo-locations, and the communication range of the entities for dynamic trust boundary identification. Including trust values, as alluded to before, the reason for choosing the geo-location is that it would be more likely that entities in close proximity will be able to communicate with their relevant security gateways. If there are any changes in the trust and location values over time, entities will change their boundary locations accordingly. This dynamic re-categorization into trust boundaries enables security segmentation between low and high-trusted entities.

3.2   Dynamic Trust Boundary Identification Techniques

Since the number of trust boundaries is not known in advance, one of the possible solutions for dynamic trust boundary identification is to use an unsupervised clustering technique to classify entities in different clusters, so that clusters can be organized by exploiting aspects of trust boundary attributes only. Unsupervised clustering is useful for network traffic analysis because of providing enhanced algorithms for grouping data and investigating frequent changes in data as well as reducing the dimensions of data for optimum results. Therefore, in this work, we use two unsupervised clustering algorithms, i.e., k-means with Elbow method [10] and self-organizing map (SOM) [13], to prove our concept by generating multiple clusters of entities. Both clustering techniques can efficiently allocate entities into the same clusters that have similar trust values and are closely located to each other within the 3-dimensional space with each cluster representing a trust boundary.

Our proposed method for identifying dynamic and multiple trust boundaries using the k-means clustering technique comprises two steps, i.e., clustering data intuitively into 'k' number of clusters and finding the optimum number of clusters using the Elbow method and re-clustering. However, unlike k-means, the SOM automatically selects the optimum number of clusters. The SOM automatically creates a map for clustering the data points using a set of neurons, where each neuron represents a cluster of similar data points. The SOM updates neuron weights iteratively until convergence and thus reduces the number of clusters [13].

3.3   Splitting and Merging Trust Boundary Considering Communication Coverage

SPGs associated with trust boundaries (refer to Fig. 2) typically use a variety of communication interfaces to cover different entities nationally or globally. The national communication range refers to the extent to which communication can occur anywhere in a particular country. On the other hand, the global communication range refers to the ability to communicate across the entire world, regardless of geographical boundaries. The specific interfaces used vary depending on the configuration of gateways and the types of entities communicating with them. Common communication interfaces along with their possible communication ranges and relevant devices that can be used to connect with SPGs are as follows:

- WiFi (100 m): Sensors, smartphones, and other smart devices
- Cellular networks (national with LTE's maximum coverage 40 km) (4G LTE/5G/6G): Base stations, drones, UAVs, ships, and smartphones
- Bluetooth (10 m): Short-range communication between devices like smartphones and sensors
- Satellite (global 36,000 km): Remote devices (where traditional communication infrastructure is not available) like ships in the sea and base stations

– Internet (global): TCP/IP networking enabled devices

Dynamic trust boundary identification using the clustering approaches that consider trust values and geo-locations of entities cannot ensure that the entities of a particular trust boundary are within the coverage range of its SPGs and the consistency of its entities' trust values is fully optimized. To ensure SPGs communication covers and optimizes the intra-boundary trust consistency, splitting and merging of the initial trust boundaries produced by clustering approaches is required. The algorithm of the splitting and merging technique is presented below (refer to Algorithm 1).

Algorithm 1. Splitting and merging algorithm for dynamic trust boundary identification

---

1: Input:
2: $E_{ij} = j^{th}$ entity belongs to i^{th} trust boundary
3: $B_i = i^{th}$ trust boundary
4: $SPG_i =$ security protection gateways for i^{th} trust boundary
5: $N =$ Number of trust boundary
6: $\eta_i =$ Number of entities in i^{th} trust boundary
7: Output:
8: Refined trust boundaries B
9: **for** $i = 1\ N$ **do**
10:     **for** $j = 1\ \eta_i$ **do**
11:         **if** E_{ij} is an outlier of B_i's entities' trust values or not under SPG_i's coverage **then**
12:             Remove E_{ij} from B_i
13:             Set k = 0
14:             Find a trust boundary B_k in such a way that ensures
15:             E_{ij} can communicate with SPG_i and optimize trust consistency
16:         **end if**
17:         **if** $k > 0$ **then**
18:             Merge E_{ij} with B_k
19:         **else**
20:             Create a new trust boundary that comprises E_{ij}
21:         **end if**
22:     **end for**
23: **end for**

By continuously monitoring and adjusting trust boundaries in real-time, the splitting and merging algorithm ensures that the 6G network remains secure and private as it is expected to be much larger than the previous generations of wireless communication. Regarding this, the algorithm needs to consider the communication range of the gateway with entities in the network to ensure seamless communication flow between different entities allocated in different trust boundaries. If the algorithm merges or splits entities without considering their communication range with the gateway, it could lead to communication failures, dropped connections, and thus reducing the network performance.

4   Experimental Simulation and Results

Based on the infrastructure shown in Fig. 1, our proposed mechanism for dynamic trust boundary identification is evaluated using a simplified 6G architecture. For simulations, a conceptual infrastructure of trust boundary protection mechanism for the 6G network is shown in Fig. 2. Trust boundaries comprising seven entities (i.e., drone, airplane, satellite, mobile base station, smartphone, ship, and static sensor) are presented using red dotted rectangles. Trust boundaries are used to protect 6G networks using SPGs by acting as a barrier between two different networks or entities of the same or different networks. Based on the security protection context, SPGs are allocated a particular zone of a trust boundary to control incoming traffic and the access of entities of a trust boundary to a network or an entity of another trust boundary. Along with access control managed by SPGs, all data have to pass through the SPGs prior to being routed for communication.

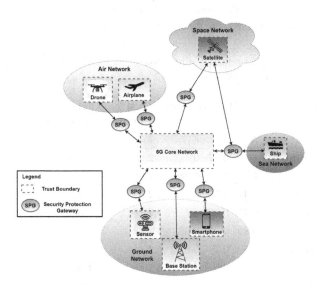

Fig. 2. A conceptual 6G infrastructure comprising trust boundaries used for simulation.

Trust boundary provides dynamic security protection for untrusted entities in 6G by following the Continuous Adaptive Risk and Trust Assessment (CARTA) principle [1]. Trust boundaries use policies to control incoming data, access control, and multi-factor authentication (MFA) through continuous risk monitoring and trust assessment to dynamically allocate entities into different trust boundaries depending on the observed risk and trust levels. The SPGs can detect any malicious activities or attacks by monitoring the behavior of nodes, data reliability, and traffic patterns. For example, if there is a sudden surge of traffic from a particular source (that is known to be associated with DDoS attacks), the SPGs could detect this and block the source. Additionally, the SPGs can use strong encryption and MFA-based authentication to identify and prevent MITM attacks. By monitoring the source and destination IP addresses, ports, data reliability, and other characteristics of incoming traffic, the SPGs can also detect and block other attacks.

4.1   Data Preparation

For dynamic trust boundary identification, as per our feature selection discussed in Sect. 3.1, we have considered the coordinates of seven entities (see Fig. 2) in a 3-dimensional space (X, Y, and Z) and their trust values (T) at different times as shown in Table 1. Trust values are intuitively assigned to each entity based on its behavior and data reliability. Therefore, the trust value of an entity will decrease significantly if it is compromised by an attack. Examples of such attacks include but are not limited to, packet drop, DDoS and MITM attacks launched by misbehaving nodes, and data poisoning and false data injection attacks. Besides, the geo-location data is used in dynamic trust boundaries to ensure entities having similar trust values are in close proximity increasing the likelihood of being in their security-specific gateway coverage.

Table 1. Intuitional trust boundary allocation to each entity using simulated location and trust data at morning 8.00 am.

Entity	Location of Entity			Trust Value	Trust Boundary Allocation
	X	Y	Z	T	TB
Base Station	1	0.97	0	2.95	TB 1
Satellite	1	1	0.98	2.89	TB 2
Static Sensor	0.47	0.56	0	2.5	TB 3
Drone	0.75	0.79	0.7	2.25	TB 4
Airplane	0.89	0.95	0.99	2.22	TB 5
Smartphone	0.5	0.7	0.82	2	TB 6
Ship	0.53	0.6	0.58	1.75	TB 7

For experiments, we have simulated 343 data samples that are estimated to be recorded within a 24-h time window starting at 8.00 am with 30-min time intervals. Initially, we have allocated each entity to 7 different trust boundaries intuitively to observe the changes in the boundary location after clustering. Each trust boundary has a distinct range of trust values. Entities having the highest trust values are allocated to Trust Boundary 1 (TB1) and the entities with the lowest trust values are allocated to TB7 accordingly (refer to Table 1). The first 7 data samples are not used for clustering. The remaining 336 data samples are divided into 3 equal sections, where each section contains 112 data samples. These 112 data samples are estimated to be collected over the course of 8 h, i.e., from 8.30 am to 4.00 pm, after 4:00 pm to 12:00 pm, and after 12:00 pm to 8:00 am to track changes in trust values and locations over time.

4.2 Metrics for Assessing the Accuracy of Trust Boundary Identification

For performance evaluation of the trust boundary identification, we define two metrics, i.e., trust consistency and the degree of gateway coverage.

i **Trust Consistency:** It indicates the consistency of entities' trust values within the trust boundary. It is chosen as a metric to represent the trust boundary identification accuracy because the higher the trust consistency is, the higher the trust values similarity will be, thus better the conformance will be with the trust boundary definition. The higher the trust values similarity is, the better chance of equipping fine grain security protection level will be. We can evaluate the trust consistency through the Standard Deviation (SD) of entities' trust values of a particular trust boundary. The lower the SD is, the higher the trust consistency is.

ii **Degree of Gateway's Coverage:** This metric represents the percentage of a trust boundary's entities that are within the communication range of their relevant SPG(s). The higher the coverage is, the higher the trust boundary identification accuracy will be.

4.3 Simulation Results and Discussions

We performed the clustering separately 3 times for 3 sets of data for both k-Means and SOM clustering. In the K-Means clustering, we initially set the cluster number equal to 7 intuitively. After that, we used the Elbow method to identify the optimum number of clusters automatically. With the Elbow method, we obtained 5 optimum clusters for the first set of data and 3 optimum clusters for the second and third sets of data. Figure 3 displays the Elbow graph indicating the optimal number of clusters. The differences between cluster formation before and after using the Elbow method are illustrated in Fig. 4. Similarly, we applied SOM clustering to verify the performance of our proposed mechanism for trust boundary identification. Unlike the K-means, the SOM provided three clusters for each data set.

After clustering, we monitored the changes in the entity's trust boundary location every 8 h. We plotted the results using the last data values of each entity taken at 4.00 pm, 12.00 am, and 8.00 am, respectively, for both k-means and SOM clustering, as illustrated in Fig. 5, 6, 7, where each cluster represents trust boundaries and trust values, represented by 'T'. We can see that there is a slight difference in trust boundary identification for the first data set, where the k-means identified four trust boundaries (trust boundaries 1, 2, 4, and 5) and the SOM identified three trust boundaries (trust boundaries 1, 2, and 3) for the first data set (refer to Fig. 5). The reason for this is, the SOM organized the data points into a total of three trust boundaries for all data sets by assigning them to the same trust boundary having the closest trust values and the nearest locations at 4.00 pm, 12.00 am, and 8.00 am, respectively. However, both k-means and SOM identified two trust boundaries (trust boundaries 1 and 2) having the

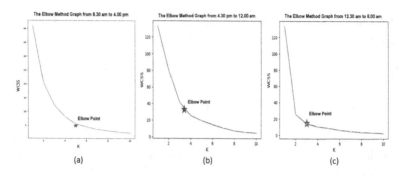

Fig. 3. Elbow Method Graph for Finding Optimum Number of Clusters: (a) 5 Clusters for data captured from 8.30 am to 4.00 pm (1st data set), (b) 3 Clusters for data captured from after 4:00 pm to 12:00 pm (2nd data set), and (c) 3 Clusters for data captured from after 12:00 pm to 8:00 am (3rd data set).

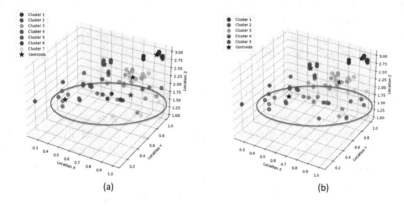

Fig. 4. Distribution of data points taken from 8:30 am to 4:00 pm, including locations and trust values of all entities, was organized into (a) 7 clusters without the elbow method and (b) 5 clusters with the elbow method.

same entities for the second data set (refer to Fig. 6), where trust boundary 1 contains the base station and satellite, while trust boundary 2 comprises drone, airplane, ship, smartphone, and static sensor. Similarly, for the third data set, Fig. 7 shows both k-means and SOM produced three trust boundaries having the same entities.

For the second set of data, no entities are allocated to trust boundary 3 in the SOM, particularly at 12.00 am. On the contrary, in k-means, no entities are allocated in trust boundary 3 for the first and second sets of data particularly at 4.00 pm and 12.00 am. However, within the time frame from 8.30 am to 12.00 am, entities can be allocated to trust boundary 3 depending on their trust and location values. For three different data sets generated in the three time windows, the different number of trust boundaries identified by k-means and SOM is because the trust values and locations have been changed over time.

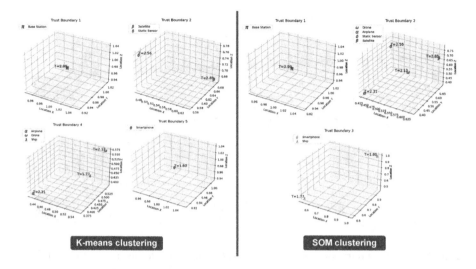

Fig. 5. Trust boundary location of entities at 4.00 pm after k-means and SOM clustering.

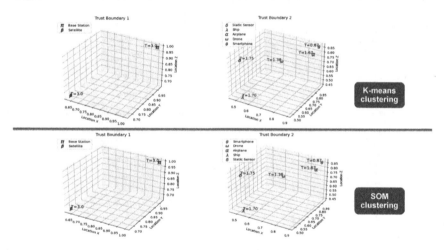

Fig. 6. Trust boundary location of entities at 12.00 am after k-means and SOM clustering.

This phenomenon indicates that our proposed mechanism is able to identify the trust boundaries dynamically.

From Fig. 5, 6, 7, it can be seen that the base station has a consistent range of highest trust values, thus it always belongs to trust boundary 1 for both k-means and SOM. However, the static IoT sensor has different trust values, thus it is allocated to different trust boundaries over time when these values are changed. Though the static sensors are usually fixed in locations to capture data, their trust values can be altered (refer to Fig. 7).

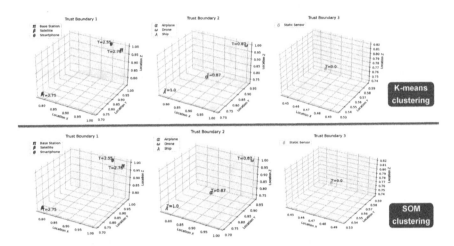

Fig. 7. Trust boundary location of entities at 8.00 am after k-means and SOM clustering.

Table 2. Overall results by proposed dynamic trust boundary (TB) identification.

Clustering Algorithm	4.00 pm				12.00 am				8.00 am			
	Entity	TB	Trust Range of TB	SD	Entity	TB	Trust Range of TB	SD	Entity	TB	Trust Range of TB	SD
K-means Clustering	Base Station	TB 1	2.9-3.0	N/A	Base Station	TB 1	2.0-3.0	0	Base Station	TB 1	2.0-3.0	0.13
	Satellite	TB 2	2.55-2.89	0.23	Satellite				Satellite			
	Static Sensor				Static Sensor				Smartphone			
		TB 3	2.4-2.54	N/A	Ship							
	Airplane	TB 4	1.75-2.39	0.27	Airplane	TB 2	0.7-1.99	0.37	Airplane	TB 2	0.7-1.99	0.07
	Drone				Drone				Drone			
	Ship				Smartphone				Ship			
	Smartphone	TB 5	1.0-1.74	N/A		TB 3	0.0-0.69	N/A	Static Sensor	TB 3	0.0-0.69	N/A
SOM Clustering	Base Station	TB 1	2.9-3.0	N/A	Base Station	TB 1	2.0-3.0	0	Satellite	TB 1	2.0-3.0	0.13
					Satellite				Base Station			
									Smartphone			
	Drone	TB 2	2.0-2.89	0.33	Smartphone	TB 2	0.7-1.99	0.37	Airplane	TB 2	0.7-1.99	0.07
	Airplane				Drone				Drone			
	Static Sensor				Airplane				Ship			
	Satellite				Ship							
					Static Sensor							
	Smartphone	TB 3	1.0-1.99	0.12		TB 3	0.0-0.69	N/A	Static Sensor	TB 3	0.0-0.69	N/A
	Ship											

Table 2 shows the entity's boundary location after every 8 h, such as at 4.00 pm, 12.00 am, and 8.00 am including the trust range and corresponding SD values reflecting the trust consistency of each trust boundary (TB). As we can see for the first and second sets of data, SD values are either very high (0.37 for TB2 in the second data set) or very low (0 for TB1 in the second data set) produced by k-means and SOM. On the contrary, for the third data set, we got consistently low SD values of 0.07 and 0.13 for TB2 and TB1 respectively for both k-means and SOM. Note that the SD value for TB3 is represented as N/A, as only one entity (static sensor) belongs to it. However, for the first data set, we got low SD values of 0.23 for TB2 in k-means compared to SOM which is 0.33. This is because, k-means allocated satellite and static sensor in TB2 and drone, airplane, and ship in TB4, whereas the SOM allocated all these five entities into TB2.

As defined in Sect. 3.3, we know that satellite and static sensor can communicate with their corresponding SPGs through satellite and WiFi transport connections, respectively. On the other hand, drone, airplane, and ship can use cellular transport connections to communicate with SPGs. However, the SOM allocated all of them into TB2, where the trust values of entities inside TB2 are 0.87 (smartphone), 1.38 (drone), 1.67 (Airplane), 1.70 (ship), and 1.75 (static sensor). Here, the splitting and merging algorithm detected the trust value of smartphone as an outlier. Therefore, this algorithm found a suitable trust boundary TB3, in which the smartphone can reside for optimizing trust consistency. After splitting, the SD value of TB2 and TB3 are 0.17 (less than 0.37 indicating optimized trust consistency) and N/A respectively. This is an example of how the splitting and merging algorithm split TB2 into TB2 and TB3.

5   Conclusion

As mentioned before, 6G is vulnerable to diverse security attacks, so security is the utmost concern in 6G. For this, a dynamic trust boundary can be used as a safeguard to protect network entities or devices from being hacked or compromised. Security protection gateways can be placed at each entry point between the entities inside a trust boundary and the 6G core network for access control and protecting sensitive data. In this work, multiple trust boundaries are identified dynamically using unsupervised clustering techniques and splitting and merging trust boundaries. Our results show that entities having similar trust values and the same transport connections with gateways are placed in the same trust boundary. This demonstrates that trust boundaries control the access of the entities communicating in a 6G network by automatically updating their boundary locations if their trust values and locations are changed over time. Dynamic trust boundaries appear to be a potential vehicle to protect national critical infrastructures (e.g., smart grid, smart health, and smart vehicle) from random cyber attacks and provide automatic security protection for entities communicating via 6G. Further, we will evaluate our proposed dynamic trust boundary identification considering more and different entities communicating through 6G.

References

1. Continuous adaptive risk and trust assessment (carta). https://www.ssh.com/academy/iam/carta. Accessed 22 Mar 2023
2. Barbosa, M., et al.: SAFETHINGS: data security by design in the IoT. In: 2017 13th European Dependable Computing Conference (EDCC), pp. 117–120. IEEE (2017)
3. Borgaonkar, R., Anne Tøndel, I., Zenebe Degefa, M., Gilje Jaatun, M.: Improving smart grid security through 5G enabled IoT and edge computing. Concurrency Comput. Pract. Experience **33**(18), e6466 (2021)

4. Fernandes, A.M., Pai, A., Colaco, L.M.M.: Secure SDLC for IoT based health monitor. In: 2018 Second International Conference on Electronics, Communication and Aerospace Technology (ICECA), pp. 1236–1241. IEEE (2018)
5. Hassan, M.M., Huda, S., Sharmeen, S., Abawajy, J., Fortino, G.: An adaptive trust boundary protection for IIoT networks using deep-learning feature-extraction-based semisupervised model. IEEE Trans. Industr. Inf. **17**(4), 2860–2870 (2020)
6. Jayasinghe, U., Lee, G.M., Um, T.W., Shi, Q.: Machine learning based trust computational model for IoT services. IEEE Trans. Sustain. Comput. **4**(1), 39–52 (2018)
7. Kantola, R.: 6G network needs to support embedded trust. In: Proceedings of the 14th International Conference on Availability, Reliability and Security, pp. 1–5 (2019)
8. Khan, L.U., Yaqoob, I., Imran, M., Han, Z., Hong, C.S.: 6G wireless systems: a vision, architectural elements, and future directions. IEEE Access **8**, 147029–147044 (2020)
9. Khan, M.A., Alghamdi, N.S.: A neutrosophic WPM-based machine learning model for device trust in industrial internet of things. J. Ambient Intell. Humanized Comput. **14**, 1–15 (2021)
10. Marutho, D., Handaka, S.H., Wijaya, E., et al.: The determination of cluster number at k-mean using elbow method and purity evaluation on headline news. In: 2018 International Seminar on Application for Technology of Information and Communication, pp. 533–538. IEEE (2018)
11. Nguyen, D.C., et al.: 6G internet of things: a comprehensive survey. IEEE Internet Things J. **9**(1), 359–383 (2021)
12. Nguyen, V.L., Lin, P.C., Cheng, B.C., Hwang, R.H., Lin, Y.D.: Security and privacy for 6G: a survey on prospective technologies and challenges. IEEE Commun. Surv. Tutorials **23**(4), 2384–2428 (2021)
13. Qu, X., et al.: A survey on the development of self-organizing maps for unsupervised intrusion detection. Mob. Netw. Appl. **26**, 808–829 (2021)
14. Riel, A., Kreiner, C., Macher, G., Messnarz, R.: Integrated design for tackling safety and security challenges of smart products and digital manufacturing. CIRP Ann. **66**(1), 177–180 (2017)
15. Tedeschi, S., Emmanouilidis, C., Mehnen, J., Roy, R.: A design approach to IoT endpoint security for production machinery monitoring. Sensors **19**(10), 2355 (2019)
16. Wolf, A., Simopoulos, D., D'Avino, L., Schwaiger, P.: The pasta threat model implementation in the IoT development life cycle. INFORMATIK 2020 (2021)
17. Ylianttila, M., et al.: 6G white paper: research challenges for trust, security and privacy. arXiv preprint arXiv:2004.11665 (2020)

RTR-Shield: Early Detection of Ransomware Using Registry and Trap Files

P. Mohan Anand$^{(\boxtimes)}$, P. V. Sai Charan, Hrushikesh Chunduri,
and Sandeep K Shukla

Department of Computer Science and Engineering, Indian Institute of Technology,
Kanpur, Kanpur, India
{pmohan,pvcharan,hrushicnv,sandeeps}@cse.iitk.ac.in

Abstract. The pre-encryption behaviour of ransomware refers to the period before the ransomware begins to encrypt the files, where it performs activities to conceal its presence or gather sensitive information of the victim system. For any detection model, it is crucial to restrain ransomware activity before it causes significant damage or spreads further throughout the system. In this regard, we propose **RTR-Shield** a novel rule based tool to detect and block crypto ransomware activity in its early stage of execution. The tool primarily relies on two monitoring blocks: Registry Activity Monitoring Block (RAMB) and File Trap Monitoring Block (FTMB). RAMB is derived based on forensic analysis of registry modifications performed by 27 recent ransomware families within the first 10 s of payload execution. We also reveal the common keys and values that a ransomware modifies in its pre-encryption phase. FTMB is constructed based on the study of different directories that the ransomware initially access and deploy trap files at strategic locations. In our evaluation, RTR-Shield demonstrates its efficacy in detecting and blocking ransomware activity during the initial stages of encryption, even for previously unseen ransomware variants.

Keywords: Windows Registry · Crypto-Ransomware · Pre-encryption · Early detection · Trap Files

1 Introduction

Crypto ransomware, a form of malware, encrypts files on a victim's system or network, rendering them inaccessible until a ransom is paid to the attackers. Over the past few years, the prevalence and sophistication of crypto ransomware attacks have significantly increased, with attackers employing various strategies to infiltrate systems while evading detection. In most cases, ransomware does not immediately encrypt the files in the victims system, rather it typically engages in pre-encryption activities, such as establishing persistence and gathering sensitive information from the victim. These activities are essential for the efficient execution of the encryption process. The pre-encryption behavior of crypto ransomware include:

W. Meng et al. (Eds.): ISPEC 2023, LNCS 14341, pp. 209–229, 2023.
https://doi.org/10.1007/978-981-99-7032-2_13

- **Information gathering**: Ransomware collects the victim's system information to determine the best way to carry out the attack, such as operating system version, file system structure, installed software and network configuration, etc.
- **Persistence**: Ransomware create registry keys or scheduled tasks to ensure it continues running even after a system reboot.
- **Disabling security measures**: Ransomware attempt to disable antivirus or other security software to avoid detection.
- **Obfuscating its activity**: Ransomware use various techniques to hide its presence, such as renaming its files, using encryption to hide its communication, or masquerading as legitimate software.

Ransomware carries out encryption when some or all of the activities mentioned above are performed on the targeted system and demands payment from the victim in exchange for the decryption key. During the pre-encryption phase, ransomware adds, updates, or deletes various keys and values to achieve persistence, gather information, or hide its presence. In this regard, the Windows registry can be an important source for investigation as it contains information about recently used programs or files, user account names and passwords, and network share connections, etc. [13]. The registry information can also be used to piece together a user activity timeline or identify potential sources of data theft, malware activity. The granular information obtained by conducting registry analysis aids in developing robust rules for detecting ransomware activity in real-time.

However, detecting ransomware solely based on registry-level modifications poses a challenge, as ransomware often scans for files to encrypt while simultaneously engaging in activities like shadow copy deletion or employing other persistence-maintaining techniques. To overcome this limitation, we also considered trap files alongside registry modifications. Trap files are special files placed on a system with the intention of detecting or preventing unauthorized access or activity. These files are meticulously crafted to resemble and behave like legitimate files that ransomware typically targets.

Therefore, it is essential to simultaneously monitor registry activity and trap files for effective detection of crypto ransomware in its early stages. The major contributions of this work include:

1. We propose RTR-Shield, a tool designed to detect crypto ransomware activity and prevent its execution in real-time by continuously monitoring registry modifications and trap files.
2. We highlight common patterns observed in the registry modifications by analysing 27 ransomware families in their pre-encryption stage.
3. We underline our strategic approach to deploy trap files that are commonly targeted by multiple ransomware families.

The remainder of the paper is organized as follows: Section-2 describes the proposed tool architecture, detailing multiple functional blocks and their importance in the early detection of ransomware. Section-3 covers the topic of registry analysis and pattern identification for multiple ransomware families. Section-4 describes the evaluation of RTR-Shield. Section-5 discusses related work on various methods of ransomware detection. Finally, in Sect.6, we summarize our findings and provide an overview of future research directions.

2   RTR-Shield - Design Overview

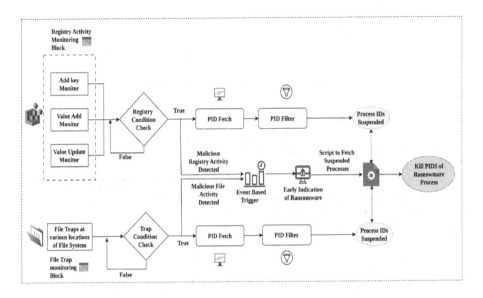

Fig. 1. RTR-Shield - Design Overview

We introduce RTR-Shield as a robust tool specifically developed to detect ransomware during its initial stages of attack. The core functionality of RTR-Shield relies on two essential components depicted in Fig. 1: the Registry Activity Monitoring Block (RAMB) and the File Trap Monitoring Block (FTMB). These blocks play a crucial role in monitoring and analyzing registry activities as well as file access behavior, enabling the early detection of ransomware incidents. The functionalities of these blocks are explained below:

1) Registry Activity Monitoring Block (RAMB): This block is responsible for monitoring unusual registry modification patterns. This is achieved by monitoring key additions, value additions, and value updates of various registry hives. Key addition involves the creation of new registry keys to effectively organize data, while value addition associates specific data with corresponding keys, enabling the precise storage of pertinent information. Additionally, value update operations allow for the modification of existing values, facilitating crucial configuration changes or timely updates. It is worth noting that these operations are commonly performed during software installation, system configuration, or when ransomware aims to manipulate the registry to achieve its goals.

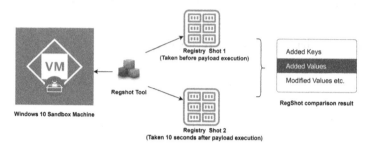

Fig. 2. Registry data extraction process

Registry Data Extraction Process:

In our work, we analyze ransomware samples from 27 prevalent families, including Revil, LockBit, Mangniber, Babuk, and Conti, among others. We perform dynamic analysis of ransomware samples in a sandbox environment using a Microsoft Windows 10 operating system with 8 GB of RAM and 256 GB disk space. We configured the network of the sandbox machine to host-only mode to restrict the ransomware's activity to the sandbox environment. Once the sandbox is set up, we installed "RegShot" tool on the Windows 10 sandbox machine. RegShot is a free and open-source registry comparison utility designed for the Windows operating

Table 1. List of registry hive categories commonly targeted by ransomware

S.No	Registry Category
1	Volume Shadow Copy Service (VSS)
2	Run Key
3	AppCompatFlags
4	Windows Script Host (WSH)
5	Restart Manager
6	RecentDocs
7	Class & Icon
8	Boot Configuration Data (BCD)
9	Background Activity Moderator (BAM)
10	Shell Bags
11	GlobalAssocChangedCounter
12	InstalledWin32AppsRevision

system, which captures a snapshot of the Windows registry containing information about installed programs, system settings, and user profiles. Also, it compares two registry snapshots taken at different times to detect any changes made to the registry during that period. This functionality of the tool is useful for analyzing changes made by ransomware, troubleshooting or monitoring system changes made by software installations, updates, or configuration changes [10].

Before executing each ransomware executable, we took a snapshot of the registry to store the state before the ransomware exhibits its behavior. Following the execution of the ransomware sample, we introduced a 10-second delay before capturing a second snapshot to observe its pre-encryption activities. Typically, most ransomware takes 8 to 10 s to start file encryption [17], so we choose a delay time of 10 s to capture the pre-encryption behavior of the ransomware effectively. Using RegShot, we obtained the list of changes made in the registry, including added keys, values, and modified values, for each ransomware executable as shown in Fig. 2. The changes made to the registry provides valuable insight into ransomware behavior and helps us build rules to stop ransomware activity at the earliest. Based on our comprehensive analysis, we discovered specific registry hives that are frequently targeted by multiple variants of ransomware for registry modifications as shown in Table 1. In Sect. 3, we present detailed registry modifications, including key additions, value additions, and value updates, for each registry hive category shown in Table 1, along with their correlation to ransomware activity.

Subcomponents of RAMB: RAMB utilize individual monitoring blocks dedicated to continuously monitor the registry for any abnormal modifications at intervals of 500 ms.

- *Key Addition Monitor*: This monitoring block constantly checks for the addition of new keys under various hive categories (refer Table 1), such as VSS, WSH, Restart Manager, Class & Icon, and BCD.
- *Value Addition Monitor*: This monitoring block continuously checks for the inclusion of new values under different hive categories, including Run, AppCompatFlags, WSH, Restart Manager, Class & Icon, BCD, and BAM.
- *Value Update Monitor*: This monitoring block continuously checks for value updates in keys belonging to categories such as RecentDocs, BAM, Shell Bags, and InstalledWin32AppRevision.

Each of these registry monitoring blocks constantly checks the registry for modifications, and once a change is made, the monitor will return "TRUE" as output. For example, if a new VSS key, such as "ASR Writer", is added to the registry path of "HKLM\SYSTEM\ControlSet001\Services\VSS\Diag", then the *Key Addition Monitor* will return TRUE. Similarly, when a new value is added or a value is updated, the *Value Addition Monitor* or the *Value Update Monitor* will return TRUE, respectively.

Operation of RAMB: After all three registry monitors return TRUE, an alert is raised for the unusual registry modifications. Following the alert, we identify all the running processes by their PID (Process IDs) and filter them by their creation time. We only consider processes that were created within the last 10 s, as this time frame corresponds to the average pre-encryption duration of ransomware, which typically ranges from 8 to 10 s. Subsequently, the respective processes obtained through the PID filter are transitioned into a *suspended state*, indicating a potential ransomware incident. Based on our analysis, the RAMB module takes an average of 5.83 s to raise the alert based on the ransomware samples considered in the experiment.

It is noteworthy that there is no registry category (refer Table 1), such as VSS or BCD, that is common to all three registry monitors. This configuration ensures that no benign application is falsely identified as an abnormal registry modification. For instance, when an application is installed, it may add a class to the registry to store its specific configurations and preferences. This installation may also involve adding new keys, new values, and value updates. However, our tool is specifically designed not to flag such updates as malicious.

2) File Trap Monitoring Block (FTMB):

While the registry access pattern may indicate a potential ransomware attack, we need to confirm it before issuing an alert. Moreover, some ransomware variants, such as Magniber, BlackMatter, and others, simultaneously scan for files to encrypt while deleting shadow copies or performing other techniques to maintain persistence. In such cases, waiting for registry-level changes to be detected may impede the early detection of ransomware. Therefore, we explore the use of trap files to identify any suspicious attempts to read or write access our files. The inclusion of trap files in ransomware detection serves the purpose of identifying unusual processes that attempt to read or write files that are not commonly accessed by legitimate programs. When ransomware attempts to encrypt a trap file, it triggers an alert or alarm, allowing security teams to take immediate action to prevent further damage. The use of trap files can be an effective way to detect and respond to ransomware attacks in real time.

Strategy for Positioning Trap Files: To achieve early detection of ransomware activity, trap files are placed in strategic locations on system. However, it is crucial to identify the file access pattern used by multiple ransomware families for encryption. To better understand this pattern, we analyzed the same 27 families of ransomware. Our objective is to identify files and directories that are initially targeted during the encryption process. The insights obtained from the analysis are mentioned below:

- The majority of ransomware families, such as REvil, Cerber, and Babuk, employ Depth-First Traversal in alphabetical order for encrypting files. However, only a few families, like Jigsaw and AvosLocker, utilize the Wide-Search Traversal, also known as Breadth-First Traversal, for file encryption.
- Families such as AvosLocker and GlobeImposter target "C:/Users/Public/*" first, before moving on to other directories.
- Sample belong to Cerber family start with the Desktop files and folders before traversing other parts of the disk.
- Few ransomware families also consider filenames or folder names containing numerics as an order of preference for performing encryption.
- Certain ransomware families, such as BlackMatter and Magniber, refrain from encrypting PowerShell script files as part of their encryption process. However, contrasting this behavior, families like LockBit deliberately focus on encrypting PowerShell script files in addition to other file types.

Based on the identified behavior of ransomware, we have strategically placed multiple trap files at various locations in the file system and ensured that each file is assigned an appropriate name. In the rare case of ransomware employing reverse alphabetical order of encryption, i.e., encrypting file names starting with 'Z' before those starting with 'A', we also placed multiple trap files accordingly. To ensure sufficient variability, we selected files ranging in size from very small (in KB) to very large (in GB) as traps to entice the ransomware. We illustrate

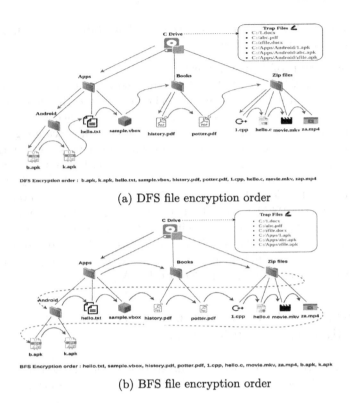

(a) DFS file encryption order

(b) BFS file encryption order

Fig. 3. Systematic trap file placement scenario

the order of encryption employed by various ransomware strains using both depth-first traversal and breadth-first traversal algorithms, as shown in Fig. 3. In Fig. 3a and 3b, we strategically position trap files in a manner that incorporates file size, alphabetic ordering, numeric naming convention, and reverse alphabetic ordering.

Operation of FTMB: This module generates a TRUE output if at least two trap files are accessed or modified within a time frame of less than one second. This constraint is implemented to minimize false positives, which encompass scenarios where a trap file is inadvertently accessed by a user. In such instances, no alert should be triggered to avoid unnecessary suspicion regarding the normal file access activity.

After FTMB returns TRUE, an alert is raised to indicate suspicious file access activity. Based on our analysis, the FTMB module takes an average of 7.74 s to raise the alert based on the ransomware samples considered in the experiment. Subsequently, we identify all running processes using their respective process IDs (PIDs) and filter them based on their creation time. We only consider processes that were created within the past 3 s, as this time frame aligns with the onset of file encryption activity. Finally, we move corresponding processes, which are obtained from the PID filter, to *suspended state*. This state serves as an indication of a potential ransomware incident.

3)Early detection of Ransomware:

While the RAMB and FTMB blocks may individually raise suspicions of potential ransomware incidents, it is crucial to validate the detection before issuing an alert. For instance, certain ransomware families like Magniber, Black-Matter, and others engage in simultaneous activities such as scanning for files to encrypt and deleting shadow copies or employing other persistence techniques. In such scenarios, the FTMB block may return a TRUE result first. Similarly, for different ransomware families, the RAMB block may return a TRUE result prior to the FTMB block. In our approach, we confirm a ransomware incident only when both the RAMB and FTMB blocks return TRUE within a 5-second timeframe. Once the ransomware activity is detected, we retrieve the suspended process IDs from both blocks (RAMB & FTMB) and *kill* the corresponding process IDs to halt the ransomware activity on the victim's machine. The algorithm for RTR-Shield tool is presented in **Appendix-A**

3   Correlation Between Ransomware Activity and Registry Modifications

As discussed in Sect. 2, the following sub-sections explains the list of identified registry hive categories and their significance in relation to ransomware execution.

3.1   Volume Shadow Copy Service (VSS)

Keys Added:

- HKLM\SYSTEM\ControlSet001\Services\VSS\Diag\ASR Writer
- HKLM\SYSTEM\ControlSet001\Services\VSS\Diag\COM+ REGDB Writer
- HKLM\SYSTEM\ControlSet001\Services\VSS\Diag\Registry Writer
- HKLM\SYSTEM\ControlSet001\Services\VSS\Diag\Shadow Copy Optimization Writer
- HKLM\SYSTEM\ControlSet001\Services\VSS\Diag\SwProvider_{new service provider ID}

Usage:
The registry keys shown above belong to the Volume Shadow Copy Service (VSS) diagnostics component of windows, which is used to diagnose and troubleshoot issues related to the VSS service. The VSS service is an important component of Windows that allows for backup and restore operations.

Assertion:
Ransomware modifies these registry keys to disrupt VSS functionality and prevent the recovery of encrypted files. For example, ransomware delete or disable the VSS service, delete VSS shadow copies, or modify VSS settings to prevent backups from being created.

3.2   Run Key

Values Added:

— HKCU\Software\Microsoft\Windows\CurrentVersion\Run\new value: "path of the executable" [OR]

— HKLM\SOFTWARE\Microsoft\Windows\CurrentVersion\Run\new value: "path of the executable"

Usage:

The "Run" key is used to configure programs to run automatically when the system starts up. There are two "Run" keys in the registry: one is located under the HKCU (HKEY_CURRENT_USER) hive, which represents the currently logged-on user, and the other is located under the HKLM (HKEY_LOCAL_MACHINE) hive, which represents the local machine. When a program is added to one of the "Run" keys, the full path to the executable file is stored as a value under the key. When Windows starts up, it reads these values and launches the corresponding programs. This feature can be useful for configuring programs that need to run continuously in the background, such as antivirus software or system utilities.

Assertion:

Ransomware achieves persistence using the "Run" key to ensure that it remains active even after a system reboot. Ransomware can add a new entry to this key, ensuring it runs automatically when the computer is restarted.

3.3   AppCompatFlags

Values Added:

— HKCU\Software\Microsoft\Windows NT\CurrentVersion \AppCompatFlags\Compatibility Assistant

\Store\path of a new executable: Hex Value

Usage:

The key "AppCompatFlags\Compatibility Assistant\Store" contains registry entries of type REG_BINARY that store binary data. The values for this key are created during the initial execution of a program and are updated with subsequent executions [18]. The value name corresponds to the full path of the executed program, providing valuable information for incident responders.

Assertion:

The "AppCompatFlags\Compatibility" registry key can be leveraged by malware to execute in compatibility mode, bypassing certain security features and restrictions on newer versions of Windows. Malware can modify this registry key to ensure that it runs in a certain compatibility mode and avoid detection by security software.

3.4   Windows Script Host (WSH)

```
Keys Added:

  — HKCU\Software\Microsoft\Windows Script
  — HKCU\Software\Microsoft\Windows Script\Settings
  — HKCU\Software\Microsoft\Windows Script\Settings\Telemetry
  — HKCU\Software\Microsoft\Windows Script\Settings\Telemetry\regsvr32.exe

Values Added:

  — HKCU\Software\Microsoft\Windows Script\Settings\Telemetry\regsvr32.exe\JScriptSetScript
    StateStarted: Hex Value
```

Usage:

The registry key "HKCU\Software\Microsoft\Windows Script\Settings" contains settings related to Windows Script Host (WSH), a scripting engine that allows users to automate tasks, run scripts, and perform other system management tasks using scripts written in languages such as VBScript and JScript. The key "HKCU\Software\Microsoft\Windows Script\Settings\Telemetry\regsvr32.exe" specifically tracks the usage of the *regsvr32.exe* - a Windows command-line utility used to register and unregister Dynamic Link Libraries (DLLs) and ActiveX Controls in the Windows Registry. It is commonly used by developers and system administrators to install and register DLLs and ActiveX Controls on a Windows system.

Assertion:

However, *regsvr32.exe* can also be used by attackers to execute malicious code on a victim's system. Attackers can use this utility to register a malicious DLL file on a victim's system, which can then be used to perform various malicious activities such as stealing sensitive information or downloading additional malware. As *regsvr32.exe* is a legitimate system utility, it can be difficult for security tools to detect when it is being used maliciously.

3.5   RestartManager

```
Keys Added:

  — HKCU\Software\Microsoft\RestartManager
  — HKCU\Software\Microsoft\RestartManager\Session0000

Values Added:

  — HKCU\Software\Microsoft\RestartManager\Session0000\Owner: Hexadecimal Value
  — HKCU\Software\Microsoft\RestartManager\Session0000\SessionHash: Hexadecimal Value
  — HKCU\Software\Microsoft\RestartManager\Session0000\Sequence: Hexadecimal Value
```

Usage:
One way to stop ransomware from encrypting your files is to prevent it from accessing them while they are in use by other programs. Windows has a built-in feature called the Restart Manager that can help with this. For example, if you have a Word document open in Microsoft Word and you try to run ransomware that targets that document, the Windows operating system will block the ransomware from accessing it since it is currently in use by another program. This is because the operating system sees that the file is already open and assumes that the user is still working on it.

Assertion:
The Restart Manager can be utilized to terminate the program that holds an open file, enabling ransomware to access and encrypt the file. This behavior is observed in the REvil ransomware, where files are encrypted without shared access (dwShareMode set to 0) [11]. By leveraging the Restart Manager, the ransomware activates the closure of the program holding the file, facilitating uninterrupted progress of the encryption process.

3.6   RecentDocs

> Values Updated:
>
> — HKCU\Software\Microsoft\Windows\CurrentVersion\Explorer\RecentDocs\MRUListEx

Usage:
The list of files that have recently been accessed directly from Windows Explorer is saved in the RecentDocs registry. This entry corresponds to %USERPRO-FILE%Recent (My Recent Documents) and stores just the filename in binary form from recently opened local or network files.

Assertion:
The "MRUListEx" subkey is used to keep track of the files that the user has recently opened in Windows Explorer. When a file is run using the Run command, it leaves a trail in the RecentDocs registry. Ransomware frequently modifies this key in order to conceal evidence of its operations on the system.

3.7   Adding a New Class Key and Icon

> Keys Added:
>
> — HKLM\SOFTWARE\Classes.lockbit
> — HKLM\SOFTWARE\Classes.lockbit\DefaultIcon
>
> Values Added:
>
> — HKLM\SOFTWARE\Classes.lockbit\DefaultIcon:43 3A 5C 77 69 6E 64 6F 77 73 5C 53 79 73 57 6F 77
>
> 36 34 5C 44 32 32 30 45 34 2E 69 63 6F

Usage:
The "SOFTWARE" subkey is one of the five main root keys in the windows registry. It contains information about software and application settings installed on the system. The "Classes" subkey within "SOFTWARE" contains information about file type associations and related information for different applications installed on the system. The presence of the '.lockbit' extension in the "Classes" subkey indicate that the LockBit ransomware has modified the registry to associate the '.lockbit' extension with its encryption routine.

Assertion:
"HKLM\SOFTWARE\Classes.lockbit\DefaultIcon" and the associated value is a hexadecimal string that represents the path to the default icon for files with the '.lockbit' extension. In this case, the hexadecimal string decodes to the following file path: "C:\windows\SysWow64\D220E4.ico" The value specifies the icon that will be displayed for files encrypted by LockBit ransomware with the '.lockbit' extension.

3.8   Boot Configuration Data (BCD)

```
Keys Added:

 —  HKLM\BCD00000000\Objects41216029-4a7f-11e9-9f82-d8ba40b6d8da\Elements\250000e0

Values Added:

 —  HKLM\BCD00000000\Objects41216029-4a7f-11e9-9f82-d8ba40b6d8da\Elements\250000e0\Element: 01
```

Usage:
The registry key shown here is associated with the Boot Configuration Data (BCD) in the Windows registry. It plays a crucial role in storing configuration settings for the operating system's boot process. Specifically, the key contains information about the elements required for booting the system, such as device drivers and system components.

Assertion:
Based on the registry updates shown above, the possible assertions that we can make to this subkey include:

- Adding, modifying, or deleting entries within the BCD store that are essential for booting the system, such as the boot manager or boot loader etc.
- Creating additional subkeys or values within "HKLM\BCD00000000" that perform malicious actions, such as launching the ransomware on boot [22].

3.9   Background Activity Moderator (BAM)

Values Added:

- HKLM\SYSTEM\ControlSet001\Services\bam\State\UserSettings\UserID\Device\HarddiskVolume1\
  Windows\System32\msiexec.exe: Hex Value

-

  HKLM\SYSTEM\ControlSet001\Services\bam\State\UserSettings\UserID\\Device\HarddiskVolume1\
  Windows\System32\vssadmin.exe: Hex Value

Values Updated:

- HKLM\SYSTEM\ControlSet001\Services\bam\State\UserSettings\UserID\SequenceNumber: New
  Value

Usage:
BAM (Background Activity Moderator) is a Windows service that monitors and regulates background apps that are running on a system. This service is exclusive to Windows 10 operating system. It keeps track of background program activity by logging in the registry key: "HKLM\SYSTEM\ControlSet001\Services\bam\State". The value for this key contains the complete path of the executable file that was executed on the system and the date & time of its last execution.

Assertion:
Ransomware try to avoid detection by executing their software in the background. This enables the ransomware to run without the user's awareness and to avoid being detected by antivirus or other protection tools. By changing the BAM registry, attackers can conceal their malicious activities and so avoid detection.

3.10   Shell Bags

Values Updated:

- HKCU\Software\Microsoft\Windows\Shell\Bags\1\Desktop\IconLayouts: New Value

Usage:
Shellbags are a set of registry keys that store pertinent information about a user's presently viewed folder, encompassing details such as size, position, and icon. Essentially, the registry keeps a record of all directory traversal data. These shellbags offer valuable timestamps, contextual information, and evidence of directory access and resource interaction, potentially shedding light on the existence of past evidence.

Assertion:
Shell bags can prove useful in detecting ransomware activity as they monitor the folder views and settings within a user's file system, which are often manipulated by ransomware to locate and encrypt critical files. By scrutinizing the shell bags, one can identify alterations to folder views, settings, file locations, and timestamps, providing potential indicators of ransomware presence and activity on the system.

Other Important Keys. Apart from the registry keys mentioned above, there are few more places where ransomware traces may be found. It contains the registry keys:

- "HKCU\Software\Microsoft\Windows\CurrentVersion\Explorer\ComDlg32\OpenSaveMRU"- Here most-recently-used is abbreviated as MRU. This key keeps a list of files that have recently been opened or saved using Windows Explorer-style dialog boxes (Open/Save dialog box) [12].
- Similarly,
  the registry key "HKLM\SOFTWARE\Microsoft\Windows\CurrentVersion\Explorer\GlobalAssocChangedCounter" is used by Windows to keep track of changes made to file associations. Whenever a change is made to a file type association, such as changing which program is used to open a particular file type, the value of this key is incremented.
- Furthermore, ransomware modifies the value of the registry key "HKCU\Software\Microsoft\Windows\CurrentVersion\Search\InstalledWin32Apps-Revision", which the Windows operating system uses to keep track of the revision number of installed Win32 apps. Win32 apps are traditional Windows desktop applications that are installed on the system. Some ransomware families modify the revision number to make the executable appear as if it is a legitimate Win32 app, or to prevent the Windows Search service from indexing its files and detecting its malicious activity.

Overall, the updates to the registry made by various ransomware families are shown in **Appendix-B**.

4   Evaluation of RTR-Shield

We conducted an evaluation of our tool based on four different criteria:

- *Ability to detect newer variants of Ransomware*: Although our tool successfully detected samples from the 27 analyzed ransomware families, we aimed to evaluate its efficacy on newer, unanalyzed ransomware families. To achieve this, we tested the tool using four samples from ransomware families, namely Phobos, GrandCrab, PlutoCrypt, and Dharma. During the evaluation on a sandbox machine, our tool effectively detected and halted the ransomware activity in all instances.

- *Benign application scenario*: We also tested our tool on various benign applications such as Antivirus (Avast), File encryption (VeraCrypt), File Archiver (WinRar), and other generic applications such as browsers and media players. In all scenarios, our tool did not produce false flags indicating a ransomware incident.
- *Dependency on 3rd party tools or libraries*: Our tool is built on PowerShell scripting and does not require any 3rd party tools or libraries, making it safe from malfunctions.
- *Load on the system*: Our tool consumed an average of 70 to 80 MB of memory and 6.5% of CPU resources for continuously monitoring the system for ransomware activity. We achieved this by constantly observing changes to the registry every 500 ms. Although higher sleep interval can reduce resource usage, it may affect early detection of ransomware.

The Comparison of Related Works, along with the key takeaways, is presented in Table 2.

Table 2. Comparison of Related Works

Method Name	File Traps	Registry Activity	Takeaways
R-Locker [19]	✓	✗	Certain ransomware families, like Cerber, bypass this method by considering the size of trap files.
R-Sentry [20]	✓	✗	The random encryption order poses a challenge for R-Sentry in the early detection of ransomware.
R-Trap [21]	✓	✗	No emphasis is given to the pre-encryption behavior of ransomware.
EldeRan [5]	✗	✓	Not suitable for the early detection of ransomware.
RTR-Shield	✓	✓	Early detection of ransomware activity is achieved by emphasizing pre-encryption behavior

5   Related Works

The existing body of research on ransomware is largely focused on detecting ransomware executables by monitoring API calls and network features [5–9]. In these works, authors perform dynamic analysis of ransomware samples and extract API calls and network-based features to develop classifiers for detecting the ransomware. However, many modern ransomware strains are designed to avoid making suspicious API calls that could trigger detection by security software. Instead, they may use low-level system functions to bypass security measures and encrypt files without being detected.

Hardware Performance Counter (HPC) based analysis is another method that has recently gained popularity for detecting ransomware activity. HPCs are a collection of special-purpose registers that are incorporated into modern microprocessors to monitor system performance under various conditions. In this approach, the load imposed by ransomware processes on the system is analyzed using HPC registers to build machine learning models for detecting ransomware activity. However, most HPC-based methods place little emphasis on ransomware's pre-encryption behavior in their proposed approaches [14–16].

In registry based analysis, Asghar et al. proposed RAMD [1], a unique technique that employs an ensemble classifier consisting of several one-class classifiers to identify known and unknown malware that exploits registry keys and values for malicious purposes. RAMD creates a model of benign application registry behavior and then use this model to identify malware by looking for unusual registry modifications.

In another work, Frank et al. [2] proposed a host-based intrusion detection system (IDS) for the windows operating system. This IDS is built on an algorithm that identifies malicious activities on a host machine by checking for unusual modifications to the windows registry. The key objective this research is to first build a model of regular registry activity on a windows host and then use this model to identify abnormal registry modifications during runtime. Here, authors verified that the proposed IDS detects virus programs, data-stealing malware, and password cracking tools based on registry activity.

Monika et al. [3] highlighted the changes made by the ransomware on the registry, including creating new keys and modifying existing key values to carry out its activity. Similarly, in another work [4], the authors highlighted the inclusion of *Run* and *RunOnce* keys by the ransomware during its execution. The inclusion of *Run* and *RunOnce* registry keys serves as a means to establish persistence and enable the automatic execution of a program upon user login. Also, Daniele Sgandurra et al. emphasized the significance of registry key operations in ransomware detection [5]. According to this research, registry keys and API stats are the two most important sets of information for building an effective classifier for identifying ransomware activity. However, this work did not mention the significant registry key modifications made during ransomware execution. Majority of registry-based approaches do not emphasize the pre-encryption behavior of ransomware [1–5].

Jose et al. proposed R-Locker, a file-based detection approach utilizing a honey file technique that employs multiple symbolic links on a single trap file to thwart ransomware activity [19]. However, certain ransomware families, such as Cerber, bypass this method by considering the size of trap files, leading to the exclusion of honeyfiles (symbolic links) deployed by R-Locker from the encryption process. In another work, Shina et al. implemented a method to place numerous traps throughout the system spanning various directories [20]. However, their proposed method is ineffective in early detection of ransomware if the encryption process follows a random order. Similarly, Gaddisa et al. introduced RTrap, a solution that dynamically selects trap files from legitimate user files using a data-driven machine learning approach [21]. This adaptive selection process considers directory file attributes and leverages existing user files to create new trap files for ceasing ransomware attacks.

Although adaptive methods for placing trap files aid in the early detection of ransomware, it is crucial to comprehend the pre-encryption behavior of ransomware in order to minimize file loss. The registry serves as a valuable source of information concerning pre-encryption activities, and integrating this information with trap files contributes to the development of robust ransomware detection engines.

6   Conclusion and Future Work

Our research focuses on investigating the pre-encryption activity of ransomware, which involves using the Windows Registry to identify the persistence, information gathering, and antivirus evasion strategies employed by ransomware during its operations. Our work reveals that the pre-encryption phase of ransomware typically involves several common traits, such as deleting shadow copies, modifying Boot Configuration Data (BCD), and Run key operations etc. In addition, we have identified a list of directories or paths that multiple ransomware families target in order to carry out file encryption activity. We use the trap files method to confirm the ransomware incident at the earliest, alongside the registry updates. Multiple older and recent ransomware variants have been observed performing similar actions to achieve persistence, file discovery, or privilege escalation. These actions are inherently reflected in the registry and are commonly associated with file access patterns. The persistence of these traces presents a challenge for attackers, as evading detection becomes difficult unless new methods of persistence or file discovery are employed. Based on our findings, we propose RTR-Shield - a rule based tool that is capable of detecting crypto ransomware in real-time. As part of future work, we plan to further enhance our tool by conducting tests on newer versions of the Windows operating system, specifically Windows 11, to identify the specific registry modifications required for effective detection and prevention of ransomware. Additionally, we aim to enhance the tool's capabilities by considering emerging ransomware variants that demonstrate high encryption rates and employ techniques like intermittent encryption.

A   Algorithm for RTR-Shield

Algorithm 1. RTR-Shield Algorithm

1: **function** RAMB
2:    $key\_addition\_monitor \leftarrow$ CREATE_MONITOR("key_addition")
3:    $value\_addition\_monitor \leftarrow$ CREATE_MONITOR("value_addition")
4:    $value\_update\_monitor \leftarrow$ CREATE_MONITOR("value_update")
5:    **while true do**
6:        **if** ($key\_addition\_monitor.detect() \wedge value\_addition\_monitor.detect() \wedge$ $value\_update\_monitor.detect()$) **then**
7:            $process\_list \leftarrow$ GET_RUNNING_PROCESSES
8:            $filtered\_list \leftarrow$ FILTER_PROCESSES(process_list)
9:            SUSPEND_PROCESSES(filtered_list)
10:           RAISE_ALERT("Suspicious registry activity detected")
11:           $RAMB\_time \leftarrow$ CURRENT_TIME
12:       **end if**
13:   **end while**
14: **end function**
15: **function** FTMB
16:   $trap\_monitor \leftarrow$ CREATE_MONITOR("trap_files")
17:   **while true do**
18:       **if** $trap\_monitor.detect()$ **then**
19:           $process\_list \leftarrow$ GET_RUNNING_PROCESSES
20:           $filtered\_list \leftarrow$ FILTER_PROCESSES(process_list)
21:           SUSPEND_PROCESSES(filtered_list)
22:           RAISE_ALERT("Suspicious file access activity detected")
23:           $FTMB\_time \leftarrow$ CURRENT_TIME
24:       **end if**
25:   **end while**
26: **end function**
27: **function** DETECT_RANSOMWARE
28:   **while true do**
29:       **if** RAMB **and** FTMB **then**
30:           **if** ($Time\_Difference(RAMB\_time, FTMB\_time) \leq 5s$) **then**
31:               $process\_list \leftarrow$ GET_SUSPENDED_PROCESSES
32:               KILL_PROCESSES(process_list)
33:               RAISE_ALERT("Ransomware detected and stopped")
34:           **end if**
35:       **end if**
36:   **end while**
37: **end function**
38: RAMB()
39: FTMB()
40: DETECT_RANSOMWARE()

B   Summary of Modifications Made to the Registry by Various Ransomware Families

Ransomware Family	VSS	RunKey	AppCompatFlags	Windows Script Host	RestartManager	RecentDocs
AtomSilo	✓	✗	✓	✗	✗	✓
AvosLocker	✓	✗	✓	✗	✓	✓
BlackMatter	✓	✗	✓	✗	✗	✓
Blackout	✓	✓	✓	✗	✗	✓
Bubuk	✓	✗	✓	✗	✗	✓
CBAP	✓	✗	✓	✗	✗	✓
Cerber	✓	✗	✓	✗	✗	✓
Conti	✓	✗	✓	✗	✗	✓
Cuba	✓	✗	✓	✗	✗	✓
Demonware	✓	✗	✓	✗	✗	✓
GlobeImposter	✓	✓	✓	✗	✗	✓
HelloXD	✓	✗	✓	✗	✗	✓
Hive	✓	✗	✓	✗	✗	✓
Intercobros	✓	✗	✓	✗	✗	✓
Jigsaw	✓	✗	✓	✗	✗	✓
Karma	✓	✗	✓	✗	✗	✓
Lockbit	✓	✓	✓	✗	✗	✓
Lorenz	✓	✗	✓	✓	✗	✓
Magniber	✓	✗	✗	✓	✓	✓
Makop	✓	✓	✓	✗	✗	✓
Mespinoza	✓	✗	✓	✗	✗	✓
MountLocker	✓	✗	✓	✗	✗	✓
Revil	✓	✓	✓	✗	✓	✓
Surtr	✓	✓	✓	✗	✗	✓
Vovabol	✓	✓	✓	✗	✗	✓
Zeppelin	✓	✓	✓	✗	✗	✓
Zeznzo	✓	✗	✓	✗	✗	✓

Ransomware Family	Class and Icon	BCD	BAM	ShellBags	GlobalAssocChangedCounter	InstalledWin32AppsRevision
AtomSilo	✗	✗	✓	✓	✗	✗
AvosLocker	✗	✗	✓	✓	✗	✓
BlackMatter	✗	✗	✓	✓	✗	✓
Blackout	✗	✗	✓	✓	✗	✗
Bubuk	✗	✗	✓	✓	✗	✓
CBAP	✗	✗	✓	✓	✗	✓
Cerber	✗	✗	✓	✓	✗	✓
Conti	✗	✗	✓	✓	✗	✓
Cuba	✗	✗	✓	✓	✗	✗
Demonware	✗	✗	✓	✓	✗	✓
GlobeImposter	✗	✗	✓	✓	✗	✓
HelloXD	✗	✗	✓	✓	✗	✗
Hive	✗	✗	✓	✓	✗	✗
Intercobros	✗	✗	✓	✓	✗	✓
Jigsaw	✗	✗	✓	✓	✗	✓
Karma	✗	✗	✓	✓	✗	✓
Lockbit	✓	✓	✓	✓	✓	✓
Lorenz	✗	✗	✓	✓	✗	✓
Magniber	✗	✗	✓	✓	✗	✓
Makop	✗	✗	✓	✓	✗	✗
Mespinoza	✗	✗	✓	✓	✗	✓
MountLocker	✓	✗	✓	✓	✗	✓
Revil	✗	✗	✓	✓	✗	✓
Surtr	✗	✓	✓	✓	✗	✗
Vovabol	✗	✗	✓	✓	✗	✗
Zeppelin	✗	✗	✓	✓	✗	✗
Zeznzo	✗	✗	✓	✓	✗	✗

References

1. Tajoddin, A., Abadi, M.: RAMD: registry-based anomaly malware detection using one-class ensemble classifiers. Appl. Intell. **15**(49), 2641–58 (2019)
2. Apap, F., Honig, A., Hershkop, S., Eskin, E., Stolfo, S.: Detecting malicious software by monitoring anomalous windows registry accesses. In: Wespi, A., Vigna, G., Deri, L. (eds.) RAID 2002. LNCS, vol. 2516, pp. 36–53. Springer, Heidelberg (2002). https://doi.org/10.1007/3-540-36084-0_3
3. Zavarsky, P., Lindskog, D.: Experimental analysis of ransomware on windows and android platforms: evolution and characterization. Procedia Comput. Sci. **1**(94), 465–72 (2016)
4. Chayal, N.M., Saxena, A., Khan, R.: A review on spreading and forensics analysis of windows-based ransomware. Ann. Data Sci. **8**, 1–22 (2022)
5. Sgandurra, D., Muñoz-González, L., Mohsen, R., Lupu, E.C.: Automated dynamic analysis of ransomware: Benefits, limitations and use for detection. arXiv preprint arXiv:1609.03020 (2016)
6. Chen, Z.G., Kang, H.S., Yin, S.N., Kim, S.R.: Automatic ransomware detection and analysis based on dynamic API calls flow graph. In: Proceedings of the International Conference on Research in Adaptive and Convergent Systems, pp. 196–201 (2017)
7. Vinayakumar, R., Soman, K.P., Velan, K.S., Ganorkar, S.: Evaluating shallow and deep networks for ransomware detection and classification. In: 2017 International Conference on Advances in Computing, Communications and Informatics (ICACCI), pp. 259–265 (2017)
8. Kok, S.H., Abdullah, A., Jhanjhi, N.Z., Supramaniam, M.: Prevention of crypto-ransomware using a pre-encryption detection algorithm. Computers. **8**(4), 79 (2019)
9. Anand, P.M., Charan, P.S., Shukla, S.K.: A comprehensive API call analysis for detecting Windows-based ransomware. In: 2022 IEEE International Conference on Cyber Security and Resilience (CSR), pp. 337–344 (2022)
10. RegShot Tool [online] https://github.com/Seabreg/Regshot
11. Intel blog on Revil Ransomware [online] https://intel471.com/blog/changes-in-revil-ransomware-version-2-2
12. Windows Registry Forensic Analysis - by AndreaFortuna [online] https://andreafortuna.org/2017/10/18/windows-registry-in-forensic-analysis/
13. Carvey, H.: Windows registry forensics: advanced digital forensic analysis of the windows registry. Elsevier (2011)
14. Ganfure, G.O., et al.: Deepware: imaging performance counters with deep learning to detect ransomware. IEEE Trans. Comput. **72**(3), 600–613 (2022)
15. Pundir, N., Tehranipoor, M., Rahman, F.: RanStop: a hardware-assisted runtime crypto-ransomware detection technique. arXiv preprint arXiv:2011.12248 (2020)
16. Manaar, A., et al.: Rapper: Ransomware prevention via performance counters. arXiv preprint arXiv:2004.01712 (2020)
17. Putrevu, M.A., Putrevu, V.S.C., Shukla, S.K.: early detection of ransomware activity based on hardware performance counters. In: Proceedings of the 2023 Australasian Computer Science Week, pp. 10–17 (2023)
18. Eşref, A.: Incident response-detection and analysis on recent versions of microsoft Windows. MS thesis. Fen Bilimleri Enstitüsü
19. Gómez-Hernández, J.A., Sánchez-Fernández, R., García-Teodoro, P.: Inhibiting crypto-ransomware on windows platforms through a honeyfile-based approach with R-Locker. IET Inf. Secur. **16**(1), 64–74 (2022)

20. Sheen, S., Asmitha, K.A., Venkatesan, S.: R-sentry: deception based ransomware detection using file access patterns. Comput. Electr. Eng. **103**, 108346 (2022)
21. Ganfure, G.O., et al.: RTrap: trapping and containing ransomware with machine learning. IEEE Trans. Inf. Forensics Secur. **18**, 1433–1448 (2023)
22. Charan, P.S., et al.: DOTMUG: a threat model for target specific APT attacks-misusing google teachable machine. In: 2022 10th International Symposium on Digital Forensics and Security (ISDFS). IEEE (2022)

MalXCap: A Method for Malware Capability Extraction

Bikash Saha[✉][iD], Nanda Rani[iD], and Sandeep Kumar Shukla[iD]

Indian Institute of Technology Kanpur, Kanpur, India
bikashs@iitk.ac.in, {nandarani,sandeeps}@cse.iitk.ac.in

Abstract. In the present cyber landscape, the sophistication level of malware attacks is rising steadily. Advanced Persistent Threats (APT) and other sophisticated attacks employ complex and intelligent malware. Such malware integrates numerous malignant capabilities into a single complex form of malware, known as multipurpose malware. As attacks get more complicated, it is increasingly important to be aware of what the detected malware can do and comprehend the complete range of functionalities. Traditional malware analysis focuses on malware detection and family classification. The family classification provides insights about the dominant capability rather than the full range of capabilities present in the malware, which is insufficient. Hence, we propose MalXCap to extract multiple functionalities (named malware capabilities) hidden within a single malware sample. MalXCap employs dynamic analysis and captures malware capabilities by identifying patterns of API call sequences to achieve the goal. In the current workflow, there is no publicly available malware capability dataset. Therefore, we analyze $8k$ malware samples collected from the public domain, identify 12 different capabilities, and prepare a dataset. We use this dataset to train MalXCap and learn the patterns of API sequences to detect different malignant capabilities. MalXCap demonstrates its efficiency by achieving 97.02% accuracy score and 0.0025 hamming loss. Analyzing the capabilities of malware enables security professionals to understand the advanced techniques used in malware, summarize the attack, and develop better countermeasures.

Keywords: Malware Analysis · Malware Capability Extraction · Multi-label Classification

1 Introduction

Malware's complexity and sophistication level are a growing threat to any organization. Cybercriminals with advanced technical skills and in-depth knowledge of computer systems typically develop advanced malware. Such malwares are highly sophisticated, sneaky, and capable of performing multiple functions [7,16]. One of the key characteristics of sophisticated malware is its ability to perform various tasks within the same executable, often called "multipurpose malware"

© The Author(s), under exclusive license to Springer Nature Singapore Pte Ltd. 2023
W. Meng et al. (Eds.): ISPEC 2023, LNCS 14341, pp. 230–249, 2023.
https://doi.org/10.1007/978-981-99-7032-2_14

[7,10,21]. These malwares are dangerous because they give attackers great flexibility to carry out a range of malicious activities and increase their chance of achieving their objectives. Piccussecurity[1] released the Red Report 2023 [9] early this year, which is an extensive study and in-depth examination of over 550,000 real-world malware samples. The firm warns of the emergence of multipurpose malware, also named it as "Swiss Army knife malware", capable of performing hazardous actions across the cyber-kill chain and eluding security measures. APT groups usually deploy sophisticated malware attacks [6]. These groups typically have highly skilled malware developer teams to develop new strains of sophisticated multipurpose malware for their attack campaign.

Multipurpose malware comes with multiple code and functionalities layers, making it harder to uncover its motivation and identify complete behaviour [7,31]. For example, complex malware from advanced ransomware may contain data exfiltration and encryption functionalities. At the same time, it can have key-logging ability to capture user's credentials and send them to the attacker for persistence [16,19]. We use malware functionalities and capabilities interchangeably in this paper because the functionalities represent what a malware can do if executed in the environment. Performing family classification uncover limited malignant capabilities and doesn't give insights into other hidden malignant capabilities. The present approach for identifying malware's complete behaviour requires multiple iterations of manual analysis and domain expertise. Therefore, we need an automatic mechanism to identify multiple malignant functionalities hidden in one complex piece of malware. To address this issue, we present MalXCap.

MalXCap is a novel proof of concept multi-label classification model that can uncover many capabilities planted within a single piece of malware. Inspired by various state-of-the-art malware analysis methodologies that show the importance of API sequences in identifying malware behaviour, MalXCap uses API sequence as input feature [12,13,23,27,29,30,34,37]. To identify multiple malignant capabilities present in single malware, MalXCap uses multi-label classification method on API call sequences called by malware during their execution. We evaluate MalXCap by performing various experiments to benchmark its performance. We employ two types of feature engineering methods: TF-IDF (Term Frequency and Inverse Document Frequency) and N-gram to convert API call sequences into vector form to feed it to the classification model and five different multi-label classification methods to identify malignant capabilities. In total we perform 15 in-depth experiments (each possible set of chosen feature and classification model) to identify the best combination for MalXCap. We obtain the best-performing set as tri-gram based input features with a neural network-based classification model and achieve the best performance as 97.02% accuracy along with 0.0025 hamming loss. The key contributions of proposed work are as following:

---

[1] A pioneer security firm. https://www.picussecurity.com.

- We identify a novel problem, i.e., extraction of malignant capabilities from malwares, which requires significant attention in the security community for better defense and prevention measures.
- We build a dataset consisting of 12 unique malignant capabilities over $8k$ malware samples for malware capability detection. Our security expert team manually prepares ground truth by labeling samples after performing extensive malware behaviour analysis.
- We present a tool named MalXCap to automatically identify the malignant capabilities of malware by identifying patterns in API sequences.
- We perform 15 extensive experiments with MalXCap on several feature and model set combinations to perform multi-label classification and compare the results of each feature-model combination set to obtain the best combination.
- We evaluate performance of MalXCap on real-world malware samples to demonstrate it's efficiency by comparing result with security firm's analysis.

1.1   Potential Application

MalXCap is capable to aid incident response teams in analyzing complex malware to identify its full capabilities. It is useful in many potential cybersecurity applications, which we discuss below:

- **Developing Effective Countermeasures:** Understanding malware capabilities can help to develop effective countermeasures to prevent and mitigate the effect of malware infections. For example, if malware is capable to exploit a specific vulnerability, analysts can prioritize such vulnerability and take countermeasures by developing the patches.
- **Enhancing Incident Response:** Understanding malware's capabilities can improve incident response. Security teams can prioritize and invest their efforts in mitigating the most severe threats first. In addition, knowing the capabilities of malware aids security teams in attack summarization by identifying the attacker's intent, the type of malware used, and its impact, which helps in understanding the scope and severity of the attack.
- **Improving Threat Intelligence:** Malware capability analysis can contribute to threat intelligence by revealing the tactics, techniques, and procedures (TTPs) used by attackers. Threat intelligence sharing can help identify and prevent upcoming threats.
- **Strengthening Cybersecurity Posture:** Organizations strengthen their cybersecurity posture by upgrading security controls, such as firewalls, intrusion detection and prevention systems, and endpoint protection solutions, based on malware capability analysis.
- **Attack Trend Analysis:** Security teams spot trends in malware development by looking at the malware's capabilities discovered over time. This knowledge enables analysts to predict future attacks and develop proactive security measures to prevent them.

The overall structure of this paper is as follows. Section 2 presents related work on extracting malware capabilities. Section 3 explains MalXCap methodology, feature engineering methods, and model implementation. Section 4 describes experimental setup, evaluation matrix, and dataset preparation. Section 5 explains experiment details, results, and observations. Section 6 presents experiment analysis performed on real-world malware samples to demonstrate the efficiency of MalXCap. Section 7 concludes this research and discusses possible future work.

2   Related Work

Traditional malware family classification methods assign malware family based on only dominating functionality and don't consider other associated malware functionalities [2,14,24,36]. The detection of multiple capabilities associated with a single malware receives limited attention. Qui et al. [3] propose A3CM to automatically annotate the capabilities of Android malware for the very first time. Further, in another paper [1], they extend their discussion on malware capability annotation with multi-view feature intelligence to learn the representation of malware samples and identify target capabilities. However, their methods are only related to security-privacy-related malware capabilities and are limited to Android malware. Further, Alrawi et al. [4] propose Forecast, which predicts malware capabilities using memory images. This work requires complex memory image analysis and is limited to only seven types of capabilities. Recently, Mandiant[2] announced the CAPA tool [8], which can detect malware capabilities based on signature matching of different capabilities identified statically. This tool limits its detection capability with the scope of defined rules and generalizability is limited. Also, this tool does not work on packed/encrypted malware.

The current literature lacks automated malware capability extraction methods that can extract multiple capabilities from malware. In addition, current literature tools are limited to Android malware, require extensive manual analysis, are based on rules, and cannot analyse packed malware. Therefore, we propose MalXCap, an automated tool that does not deal with complex analysis and generalize by adopting advanced machine learning to identify patterns of API sequence execution and spot several malignant capabilities present in the malware samples. As MalXCap is based on dynamic analysis features, it works well even for packed malware.

3   Proposed Methodology

In this research work we propose MalXCap, a proof of concept to identify malignant capabilities hidden in malware samples. We discuss development process of MalXCap in this sections.

3.1   MalXCap

The MalXcap development process consists of three phases: Malware execution, Feature transformation, and Training the model. The steps used to perform each stage are shown in Fig. 1. In the malware execution phase, we set up a sandbox

---

[2] A pioneer security firm. https://www.mandiant.com.

environment for running the malware sample. We create a virtual network and employ Cuckoo to set up the sandbox environment. Next, we execute collected malware samples in the sandbox environment and gather the cuckoo analysis reports. In the feature transformation phase, we extract API sequences called during malware execution from the sandbox analysis report and transform the API sequence into an input feature vector using TF-IDF and n-gram methods. For the model training phase, we divide the dataset into the 70:30 ratio as training and testing samples, respectively. MalXCap feeds the feature vector to the machine learning model for training in the next step. MalXCap applies multi-label classification on the feature vector to identify multiple labels for each sample. The reason for using multi-label is that complex malware may have more than one capability. Therefore, the expectation from the model is to extract multiple labels i.e., capabilities for each malware sample. Once MalXCap trains the model, we use test set samples to evaluate the model's performance. Based on the API sequence present in the test sample, the trained model provides a list of malignant capabilities for each test sample shown in Fig. 1.

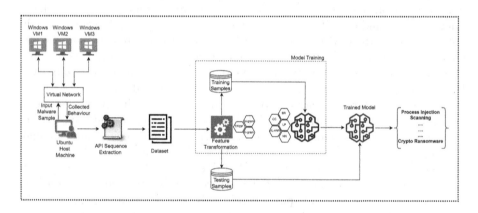

Fig. 1. MalXCap Architecture

Let's say, m_i denotes i^{th} malware sample and $L \in \{l_1, l_2, ..., l_n\}$ denotes a set of target labels for n number of capabilities. Then, for multi-label capability extraction problem is represented as,

$$m_i \rightarrow \{c : c \subseteq L\} \tag{1}$$

For any given data sample m_i, MalXCap predicts the set of capabilities (target labels) c as output of the model. This target output label set c ranges over 2^L (power set of L).

3.2   Feature Engineering

Once we extract the API sequence of malware samples (shown in Fig. 1), we transform API call sequences into vector form and feed them to the model for training. We use two different feature transformation methods: TF-IDF (Term Frequency and Inverse Document Frequency) [11] and N-gram [15] method, to perform feature engineering.

TF-IDF: TF-IDF combines Term Frequency (TF) and Inverse Document Frequency (IDF). It provides a score representing each term's importance within the given document. For the MalXCap case, a document implies a sequence of API calls of the malware, and the term implies an individual API call. Term Frequency refers to the number of times a specific API call appeared in an API call sequence. This parameter gives a high value to predominant API calls in the sequence. Inverse Document Frequency (IDF) calculates the rarity or uniqueness of a term throughout a set of documents. The main objective of applying TF-IDF on the API sequence is to feed the information related to the key API calls to the model which support the model to identify malignant capabilities. We calculate TF and IDF using below formula:

$$tf_{i,j} = \frac{\text{Number of occurence of API call } i \text{ in sequence j}}{\text{Total number of API calls present in sequence j}} \tag{2}$$

$$idf_i = log(\frac{n}{df_i}) \tag{3}$$

Here df_i is the number of API sequences containing i^{th} API call, and n is the total number of API sequences present. Finally, the term TF-IDF is calculated by multiplying both TF and IDF. The formula for TF-IDF is given below:

$$w_{i,j} = TF_{i,j} * IDF_i \tag{4}$$

Here $w_{i,j}$ is the TF-IDF score for i^{th} API call in j^{th} API sequence. This TF-IDF score reflects the importance of the ith term (API call) within the jth document (API sequence) relative to its importance in the entire collection of documents. We compute the score resulting in TF-IDF vectors comprising scores for each API call for each API sequence.

N-Gram: We employ bi-gram and tri-gram feature engineering techniques. We create all possible bi-gram and tri-gram API sequence sets and prepare two different datasets for both n-gram methods. Let $M \in \{m_1, m_2, ..., m_k\}$ where M is set of k number of malware samples. Then $m_i \in \{a_1, a_2, ..., a_j\}$ denotes the API sequence executed by i^{th} malware. We break this sequence and prepare mini-sequence of length 2 for bi-gram and length 3 for tri-gram. For any given malware API sequence, m_i, input feature for bi-gram and tri-gram gets transform into $\{a_1a_2, a_2a_3, a_3a_4, ..., a_{j-1}a_j\}$ and $\{a_1a_2a_3, a_2a_3a_4, a_3a_4a_5......, a_{j-2}a_{j-1}a_j\}$ respectively. Following this approach we transform whole input API sequence into bi-gram and tri-gram sequence. We obtain 804 unique bi-gram sequences and 3057 unique tri-gram sequences for our dataset. We utilize one hot encoding for input features and prepare the dataset. Similarly we prepare the tri-gram dataset as well.

Finally, we prepare three datasets based on input feature: TF-IDF, bi-gram, and tri-gram. We assess the efficacy of classification models based on the contribution of each feature set categories. Implementing three distinct feature sets aim to compare and determine which type of feature set is likely to achieve the best result and perform reasoning behind the better performance.

3.3   Model Implementation

Complex malware contains multiple capabilities, so the MalXCap prefers multi-label classification over multi-class classification [32]. Two broad categories of multi-label classification methods are available: a) Problem Transformation Method and b) Algorithm Adaptation Method [5,17]. The problem transformation methods perform single-label classification on multi-label classification problems by transforming the multi-label dataset into a single-label dataset. In the algorithm adaptation method, we utilize existing single-label classification algorithms to adapt and handle the multi-label classification problem. We usually change the cost function or apply different decision functions to achieve this. We consider both types of algorithms to identify the best model for MalXCap.

We employ the Binary Relevance (BR), Classifier Chain (CC), and Label Powerset (LP) model for problem transformation. In binary relevance approach, each class in the multi-label problem is treated as an independent binary classification problem. In this approach, each classifier makes an independent prediction, and the final multi-label output is obtained by combining the predictions of all classifiers. The classifier chain approach considers the interdependency between labels. In this approach, the binary classifiers are ordered in a chain, and each classifier's output is considered to perform prediction for all preceding classifiers in the chain. The label powerset method converts multi-label problems into multi-class problems. It creates a unique combination of labels for each data instance and considers this as a single class. Then, a single-label classifier is trained to classify within newly created label combinations. The trained

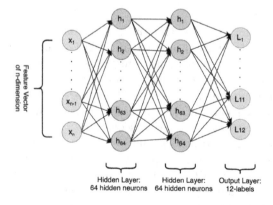

Fig. 2. Multi-Label classification based on Neural Network

classifier predicts the most probable label combination and maps it to the original multi-label problem. A detailed explanation of these models is present in the Appendix.

For the adaption algorithms method, we use ML-kNN (Multi-Label K-Nearest Neighbor) [20] and neural network model. The ML-kNN algorithm identifies k-nearest neighbors for each new instance based on a distance metric in the feature space. It calculates the probabilities for each label by considering the label sets of the k nearest neighbors. The probabilities are weighted based on the similarity of the neighbors to the new instance. The algorithm assigns the labels with the highest probabilities as the predicted labels for the new instance. In the case of multi-label, the number of labels is determined based on a threshold value. The detailed working of ML-kNN is present in the Appendix. For neural network model, we employ a deep neural network consisting of a 2-hidden layer as shown in Fig. 2. The hidden layer consists of 64 neurons and uses ReLU as an activation function. We compile the model using adam optimizer and binary cross-entropy loss function. We set 12 neurons at the output layer (each neuron for each capability label), and the binary decision (0 or 1) of each output layer decides whether corresponding capability (label) is present in the sample or not. The choice of binary cross-entropy loss function is particularly suitable as it aligns with the multi-label classification task, where each output neuron makes a binary decision for each label [38].

We implement total five different multi-label classification models. The key idea of using several different models, ranging from Machine Learning (ML) to Deep Learning (DL), is to evaluate the performance of models on various performance metrics such as accuracy, precision, recall, f1-score, and hamming loss.

4 Experimental Setup

4.1 Dataset

We collect $8k$ Windows malware samples from two research papers [26,34]. Each malware contains multiple labels, Fig. 3 shows the distribution of the number of malware containing capability labels. Scanning capability seems to be most common in the majority of the malware. We execute all malware samples on a Windows machine in a cuckoo sandbox environment and generate analysis reports. We extract the API sequence of each sample from the sandbox report based on the timestamp of API calls.

Our security expert team manually prepare ground truth for the dataset samples and assign 12 labels: Process Injection (PI), Anti-Debugging (AD), Scanning (Sc), Discover Running Processes (DRP), Crypto Ransomware (CR), Evasion (Ev), Capturing Input (CI), Alter Configuration (AC), Installed Software Exploration (ISE), Registry Modification (RM), Service Impairment (SI), and Spying (Sp). Each capability labels are self-explanatory, and also we explain each capability in Table 1.

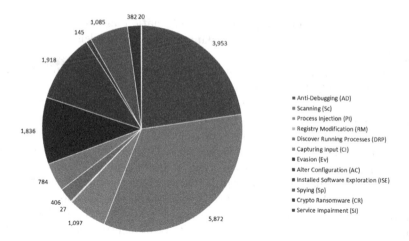

Fig. 3. Label statistics in Dataset

Our dataset contains 154 unique capability set combinations from all 12 capability labels. Because of space constraints, we present a glimpse of data distribution over capability set combinations in Fig. 4. The overlapped regions in the venn diagram represent the combination of malware capabilities labels, and the number within overlapped regions represents the number of malware samples belonging to combinations of malware capabilities.

Our team use a mixture of automated and manual procedures to label the ground truth of the dataset. In the first method, we automatically label samples based on their family behaviour. For example, a sample belonging to the ransomware family must have at least scanning and encryption capabilities. Again, if a sample belongs to a trojan, it must have at least evasion capability. Similarly, a keylogger should have at least input capture and exfiltration capabilities. Further, to find uncommon capabilities for the complex malwares, we manually investigate and synchronize network communications, system calls, and file system operations to identify the sequence of actions performed by the executable and pin down hidden capabilities for all samples.

4.2   System Setup

We perform experiments on an Inter(R) Core(TM) i7-9700 CPU @ 3.00 GHz × 8 with 64-bit Ubuntu 18.04.6LTS operating system(OS) having 32 GB of RAM and 2 TB of disk space. We use Ubuntu as the host OS and install VirtualBox 5.2.42 on the host machine. We configured three Windows 7 as a virtual machines, where each machine has 2 GB of RAM and 40 GB of disk space. We install the latest version of Cuckoo on the host and Cuckoo agent on the virtual machines. We use Windows virtual machine to run the malware samples and ship malware activity report on the host Ubuntu OS using Cuckoo agent installed on the system.

Table 1. Capability Description

Capability Name	Description
Process Injection (PI)	Malware try to inject their own code into a legitimate process running on a system and execute the injected code with the same privilege that the legitimate process is running
Anti-Debugging (AD)	The ability to detect and prevent malware execution in a debugging environment. In this technique, the attacker looks for the presence of a debugger and interrupts its activity
Scanning (Sc)	The ability to scan a system, services, software applications, or network to look for vulnerabilities present in the system to gain unauthorized access or perform malicious activities
Discover Running Process (DRP)	The ability to identify running processes on a compromised system. This step is useful to determine the potential target process to manipulate or terminate the process
Crypto Ransomware (CR)	The ability to encrypt files and folders to demand a huge ransom in exchange for a decryption key or password
Evasion (Ev)	Attackers use various mechanisms like polymorphism or encryption in their code while developing the malware to avoid detection by security software and other detection mechanisms
Capturing Input (CI)	The ability to capture user inputs such as keystrokes, mouse clicks, etc. Using such capability, malware can capture the victim's username, password, credit card number, and other sensitive information
Alter Configuration (AC)	The ability to modify system settings, configurations, or other critical settings within an operating system or software
Installed Software Exploration (ISE)	The ability to identify and gather information about installed software and the hardware and network settings present in the infected system
Registry Modification (RM)	The ability to add, delete, and modify settings in the Windows registry. Using this capability, attackers can increase their control over the infected system, making it more difficult for security analysts to detect and remove the malware
Service Impairment (SI)	The ability of malware to impair or disable essential services on an infected system. By doing this, the attacker can decrease system stability, security and impeding remediation
Spying (Sp)	The ability of malware to monitor and collect information about the activities of the user or infected system, without consent of the user

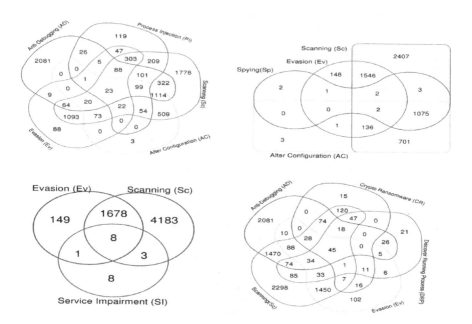

Fig. 4. Capability Label Overlapping in the Dataset

4.3   Evaluation Metrices

We follow the methods described in Sect. 3.2, and prepare all three categories of input feature vectors to develop five classification models for training and testing, as described in Sect. 3.3. We conduct 15 experiments for each possible combination of all five models and three feature sets. We aim to identify the best-performing input feature vector and model set. To choose best model, We evaluate model's performance based on the following evaluation metrics:

- **Accuracy:** Accuracy metric measures the degree of correctness in the test sample. For multi-label case, we consider a test sample as correctly predicted if all predicted labels match all true labels. For example, if true labels of a sample contain {a,b,c} and the predicted label for the same sample contains {a,c}, then we consider it as a wrong prediction, or if the predicted label for the same sample contains {a,b,c} then we considerate as a correct prediction. We use the below formula to calculate accuracy:

$$Accuracy = \frac{Number\ of\ correct\ predictions}{Total\ number\ of\ predictions} \times 100\% \tag{5}$$

- **Hamming Loss:** In the above accuracy example, we can see that even though, in the first case, the classifier correctly predicts labels a and c, that was still not considered accurate because the classifier incorrectly classified the entire label set. In such cases, accuracy may not be the only parameter determining the model's performance [5,17]. Therefore, we consider hamming loss along with accuracy to evaluate the best performance of the model. Hamming loss is a measure of the error rate in multi-label classification. It determines the ratio of incorrectly classified labels to all labels. We calculate hamming loss using the below formula:

$$\text{Hamming Loss} = \frac{\sum_{i=1}^{i=n}[y(i) \oplus \hat{y}(i)]}{n} \qquad (6)$$

Where n is the total number of instances, $y(i)$ is the true label vector for i^th instance, represented as a binary vector, $\hat{y}(i)$ is the predicted label vector for i^th instance, represented as a binary vector and $\oplus$ represents the element-wise exclusive OR (XOR) operator.

- **Precision:** It measures the accuracy of the positive predictions made by the model for each label individually. For multi-label classification and to deal with the problem mentioned in the accuracy formula, we calculate micro precision as follows [39]:

$$P_{micro} = \frac{\sum_L TP_L}{\sum_L TP_L + \sum_L FP_L} \qquad (7)$$

Here, L represents the classification label, TP_L is true positive of label L, and FP_L is false positive of label L.

- **Recall:** It measures the model's ability to identify all positive instances for each label correctly. Similar to precision, we calculate micro recall as [39]:

$$R_{micro} = \frac{\sum_L TP_L}{\sum_L TP_L + \sum_L FN_L} \qquad (8)$$

Here, FN_L is false negative of label L.

- **F1-score:** It provides a single metric to assess the model's performance in terms of both precision and recall for each label. We calculate micro F1 score as [39]:

$$F1_{micro} = 2 \times \frac{P_{micro} \times R_{micro}}{P_{micro} + R_{micro}} \qquad (9)$$

The metrics mentioned above provide insights into the performance of the multi-label classification model, accounting for the complexities of handling multiple labels per instance.

5   Experiment and Observation

We collect $8k$ malware samples and execute them into an isolated cuckoo sandbox environment. We analyze the sandbox reports and manually prepare the dataset consisting of 12 capabilities. We utilize three feature selection methods (TF-IDF, Bi-gram, and Tri-gram) and prepare our dataset to train on five models. We utilize the Gaussian naive Bayes for BR, CC, and LP classifier. The ML-kNN model combines the concept of kNN with $k = 20$ and Bayesian probability. After that, we implement a neural network-based multi-label classifier (architecture shown in Fig. 2).

In total, we conduct 15 experiments on prepared dataset. We divide 70:30 as train and test samples and calculate model performance on test set in terms of all discussed performance metrics. Table 2 presents the performance of each of the five models based on the TF-IDF feature vector. We aim to find a model that achieves high accuracy, f1-score, and low hamming loss. As we can see, the neural network outperforms all four models in terms of high accuracy with 95.64% and low hamming loss with 0.0054 for the TF-IDF feature set.

Table 2. Model performance on TF-IDF input Feature vector

Model	Accuracy (%)	P_{micro}	R_{micro}	$F1_{micro}$	Hamming Loss
Binary Relevance	46.91	0.49	0.96	0.57	0.1070
Classifier Chains	91.67	0.91	0.75	0.80	0.0100
Label Powerset	89.81	0.90	0.73	0.79	0.0147
Adapted Algorithm	90.15	0.96	0.82	0.86	0.0130
Neural Network	**95.64**	**0.99**	**0.96**	**0.97**	**0.0054**

Table 3 lists the model's performance for the bi-gram feature set. We observe that the neural network achieves the highest accuracy, best recall and low hamming loss whereas classifier chain and label powerset achieves best precision. We compare the efficacy of bi-gram-based models with TF-IDF-based models. We observe that the bi-gram-based model performs better than the TF-IDF-based model. The reason is that TF-IDF prepares feature vectors based on the importance of key APIs and ignores API patterns and context. But, The bi-gram feature engineering method adds patterns and contextual information as an API sequence.

Table 3. Model performance on Bi-gram input Feature vector

Model	Accuracy(%)	P_{micro}	R_{micro}	$F1_{micro}$	Hamming Loss
Binary Relevance	38.71	0.46	0.94	0.53	0.1526
Classifier Chains	94.43	**0.99**	0.90	0.94	0.0068
Label Powerset	92.70	**0.99**	0.88	0.93	0.0094
Adapted Algorithm	90.77	0.89	0.85	0.87	0.0120
Neural Network	**95.91**	0.98	**0.96**	**0.97**	**0.0055**

Table 4 presents the performance of models based on the tri-gram feature set. Like previous results, the neural network outperforms the other four models in terms of highest accuracy, best precision as well as low hamming loss and Binary relevence has the best recall score. We observe that the deep learning-based model, i.e., the neural network achieves the best performance in terms of accuracy, F1-score and hamming loss for all three input feature sets, demonstrating the supremacy of deep learning over machine learning for this case. Comparing results of tri-gram and bi-gram, we observe the better performance in tri-gram than bi-gram, indicating that tri-gram features capture more contextual information than bi-gram API sequences. The better performance of the tri-gram also demonstrates that the classifier can identify malware's capabilities based on the API sequence that malware executes.

Table 4. Model performance on Tri-gram input Feature vector

Model	Accuracy(%)	P_{micro}	R_{micro}	$F1_{micro}$	Hamming Loss
Binary Relevance	50.63	0.51	**0.99**	0.58	0.1097
Classifier Chains	95.78	0.99	0.92	0.94	0.0054
Label Powerset	96.63	1.00	0.95	0.97	0.0049
Adapted Algorithm	92.10	0.98	0.94	0.93	0.0112
Neural Network	**97.02**	**1.0**	0.98	**0.99**	**0.0025**

In addition, our experiment also demonstrate that how correlations between target labels helps to enhance the model efficacy. As we can see for all result Table 2, 3, 4, the performance of the classifier chain (CC) model enhance the performance over binary relevance. These results indicate that correlations between target labels exist, such as scanning and crypto-ransomware capabilities are correlated in ransomware, scanning and process discovery capabilities are correlated in trojans, and altering the configuration and registry modifications are correlated in backdoors. Even though there are some online sandbox environment that return a mapping of MITRE ATT&CK results [40], we can not find any standard document that explains how mapping is being done. Also, we consider capability such as Spying(Sp), which is not present in MITRE ATT&CK matrix. After comparing the outcomes of all 15 experiments, we conclude that the tri-gram dataset-trained on neural network outperforms the other 14 experiments. Therefore, we deploy MalXCap using a tri-gram feature vector and neural network model. We also evaluate the time taken by MalXCap to identify capabilities in malware samples. We observed that it takes 0.147 seconds to transform features from the API sequence and make predictions for a single sample. It demonstrates that MalXCap can speed up the analysis and minimize the manual effort of incident response team.

6   Real World Examples

In the real world, security firms publish malware analysis reports for the benefit of the security community, which describe malware's activity and functionality. We leverage such analysis reports to compare MalXCap results with real-world samples. This real-world experiment aims to verify MalXCap extraction capability by comparing results with the security community's analysis. Finding malware samples and their corresponding analysis reports in the public domain is challenging. We obtain recent advanced ransomware sample from MalwareBazaar[3] belongs to 4 different strains: H0lyGh0st[4], MedusaLocker[5], GpCode[6], and LockBit[7] and their analysis report published in security community [18,22,25,28,33,35]. We extract capabilities from these samples using the best performing combination of MalXCap, i.e., tri-gram feature transformation method (present in Sect. 3.2) and deep neural network model (present in Sect. 3.3). We prepare a list of capabilities (explained in natural language) for collected ransomware samples from their corresponding analysis reports as a ground truth. The extraction result is present in Table 5. MalXCap is able to identify 15 out of 17 ground truth labels correctly and misses only two capabilities (scanning for GpCode and registry modification for MedusaLocker). MalX-Cap extracts most of the ground truth capability present in the samples and demonstrates its ability to identify multiple malignant capabilities present within a single malware sample.

Table 5. Result of real-world ransomware samples. The ✓ represents predicted capability by MalxCap and ▓ represent ground truth collected from security firm's analysis reports.

Name	Capability											
	PI	AD	Sc	AC	ISE	RM	SI	DRP	CR	Ev	CI	Sp
H0lyGh0st		✓	✓						✓			
LockBit	✓	✓	✓					✓	✓	✓		
GpCode									✓	✓		
MedusaLocker			✓					✓	✓	✓		

7   Conclusion

In this paper, we investigate the feasibility of identifying malicious capabilities in malware using API call sequences. We present malware capability dataset consisting of $8k$ samples. We conduct 15 in-depth experiments using three feature engineering techniques and five multi-label classification models. The tri-gram feature engineering method with a neural network classification model gives the best results. MalXCap presents a proof of concept to develop a malware capability detection model using API call sequences. Our experiment demonstrates how

---

[3] MalwareBazaarhttps://bazaar.abuse.ch.

[4] H0lyGh0st: f8fc2445a9814ca8cf48a979bff7f182d6538f4d1ff438cf259268e8b4b76f86.

[5] Medusa: 26af2222204fca27c0fdabf9eefbfdb638a8a9322b297119f85cce3c708090f0.

[6] GpCode: e9ffda70e3ab71ee9d165abec8f2c7c52a139b71666f209d2eaf0c704569d3b1.

[7] LockBit: 2ecf1fe02d8fb099b68e4d9bceeeadbe5fc8347f5a76d52f35ed48b516963735.

introducing contextual information in feature vector helps to enhance the model performance. This experiment also shows the supremacy of the deep learning model over the machine learning model in terms of performance. In addition, our experiment illustrates how we can utilize the correlations between target labels to improve model efficacy. Further, we demonstrate the effectiveness of MalXCap on real-world advanced malware samples. In the real-world experiment, MalX-Cap shows that complex ransomware consists of multiple functionalities along with scanning and crypto capabilities. We develop MalXCap for 12 capabilities as an initial proof of concept, but given more diverse malignant functionality samples and huge manual analysis, it can increase to more number of capabilities. In the future, we expect to extend the capability list with more diverse malignant functionality and develop a model to identify the same. Our research investigates the necessity of detecting malware's capabilities and illustrates the potential application and use cases of the malware capability detection model in the cyberspace. In a nutshell, this research work has the potential to provide a new research dimension in the field of malware analysis and has the strength to serve as a foundation for several future studies on the malignant capability detection from malwares.

Acknowledgement. We thank to the C3i (Cyber Security and Cyber Security for Cyber-Physical Systems) Innovation Hub at IIT Kanpur for partially funding this research project. A special thanks to Mr. Vikas Maurya for his insightful feedback.

Appendix

Binary Relevance (BR). Binary Relevance is a popular and straightforward problem transformation method. In this method we chose 12 different gaussian naive bayes based single-label binary classifiers to predict 12 capabilities.

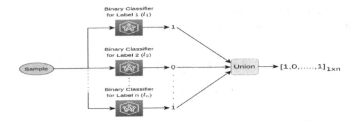

Fig. 5. Multi-Label classification based on Binary-Relevance

As illustrated in Fig. 5, each classifier produce output as 0/1 for each malware capability. We take the union of all outputs predicted by every classifier and consider them multi-label outputs for the given sample. This model's effectiveness suffers if the dataset's target labels are dependent or correlated with each other.

Classifier Chain (CC). This method solves the limitation of Binary Relevance by addressing the label correlation problem by using a chain of binary classifiers with same length as the number of target labels. As shown in Fig. 6, m_i represents a data sample which C_1 uses as input (step 1) and predicts output as l_1 (step 2), where $l_1 \in \{0, 1\}$. Further, C_2 uses m_i and l_1 combined as input (step 3) and produces output as l_2 (step 4), where $l_2 \in \{0, 1\}$. Similarly, this chain goes on till C_n, and we compute the union of each C_x, where $1 \leq x \leq n$, and produce a multi-label output of $1 \times n$ dimensions. Following this approach, the CC method solves the label correlation problem present in the binary Relevance method.

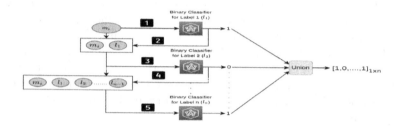

Fig. 6. Multi-Label classification based on Classifier-Chain

Label Powerset (LP). This method addresses the issue of simultaneously assigning multiple labels to an instance. This method considers all possible label combinations for every instance in the dataset. As shown in the Table 6, If a data sample associates with two target labels, L_1 and L_3, it obtains a new target label as $L_{1,3}$ in the dataset and repeat this for all data samples to transformed the dataset into single-label dataset. In the worst-case scenario, the LP method generates $2^{|L|}$ number of new single-label target classes for L multi-label target classes. Thus, this method's computational complexity poses a problem and it grows exponentially with the number of target classes.

Table 6. Label Powerset Transformation

Features	Labels		
	l_1	l_2	l_3
m_1	1	0	1
m_2	0	0	1
m_3	1	1	0

$\xrightarrow{2^3 \text{possible} \atop \text{labet sets}}$

l_1	l_2	l_3	Labels
0	0	0	-
0	0	1	l_3
0	1	0	l_2
0	1	1	$l_{2,3}$
1	0	0	l_1
1	0	1	$l_{1,3}$
1	1	0	$l_{1,2}$
1	1	1	$l_{1,2,3}$

$\xrightarrow{Transformed \atop Labels}$

Features	Labels
m_1	$l_{1,3}$
m_2	l_3
m_3	$l_{1,2}$

Multi-label k Nearest Neighbors (ML-KNN). ML-kNN is a lazy learning approach and combines the concepts of KNN and Bayesian probability to make predictions for multi-label classification. It consists of two phases: training phase and prediction phase. In the training phase, the first step is to preprocess the data. Let N denote training instances and L denote total target labels. Each training instance i is denoted by a feature vector X_i of dimension D (where D depends on the type of feature transformation method), and its label vector Y_i is a binary vector of length L, indicating the presence or absence of each label. After that, For each class j, we estimate the prior probability $P(Y_j)$ and the conditional probabilities $P(X|Y_j)$ for each feature given the class using maximum likelihood estimation. We follow formula as given below:

$$P(Y_j) = \frac{\text{Number of instances with label } Y_j}{N} \tag{10}$$

$$P(X_k|Y_j) = \frac{\text{Number of samples with label } Y_j \text{ and feature value } X_k}{\text{Number of samples with label } Y_j} \tag{11}$$

where $P(Y_j)$ represent prior probability and $P(X_k|Y_j)$ represent conditional probabilities. After that, we store the transformed training instances and their corresponding label vectors. In next prediction phase, we convert the test instance into the same format as the training instances. Let X_{test} denote the feature vector of test instance. We use euclidean distance as distance metric to find K training instances that are most similar to X_{test} test instance based on the feature values. Let N_k denote the indices of nearest neighbors. Now, for each label j, we calculate the conditional probabilities $P(Y_j|X_{test})$ using Bayes' theorem:

$$P(Y_j|X_{test}) = \frac{P(Y_j) * \prod_k P(X_k|Y_j)}{Z} \tag{12}$$

where X_k represents the feature values of kth nearest neighbor, and Z represent a normalization constant. The product $\prod$ is taken over all K nearest neighbors.

Further, we select the top labels with the highest probabilities $P(Y_j|X_{test})$ as the predicted labels for the given test instance. By considering the label probabilities and feature similarities, ML-kNN finds the K nearest neighbors and assigns labels based on their votes.

References

1. Qiu, J., et al.: Cyber code intelligence for Android malware detection. IEEE Trans. Cybern. **53**(1), 617–627 (2022)
2. Ahmadi, M., Ulyanov, D., Semenov, S., Trofimov, M., Giacinto, G.: Novel feature extraction, selection and fusion for effective malware family classification. In: Proceedings of the Sixth ACM Conference on Data and Application Security and Privacy, pp. 183–194 (2016)
3. Qiu, J., et al.: A3CM: automatic capability annotation for Android malware. IEEE Access **7**, 147156–147168 (2019). https://doi.org/10.1109/ACCESS.2019.2946392
4. Alrawi, O., et al.: Forecasting malware capabilities from cyber attack memory images. In: USENIX Security Symposium, pp. 3523–3540 (2021)

5. de Carvalho, A.C.P.L.F., Freitas, A.A.: A tutorial on multi-label classification techniques. In: Abraham, A., Hassanien, A.E., Snáašel, V. (eds.) Foundations of Computational Intelligence Volume 5. SCI, vol. 205, pp. 177–195. Springer, Heidelberg (2009). https://doi.org/10.1007/978-3-642-01536-6_8

6. Han, W., Xue, J., Wang, Y., Zhang, F., Gao, X.: APTMalInsight: identify and cognize APT malware based on system call information and ontology knowledge framework. Inf. Sci. **546**, 633–664 (2021)

7. von der Assen, J., et al.: A lightweight moving target defense framework for multipurpose malware affecting IoT devices. arXiv preprint arXiv:2210.07719 (2022)

8. CAPA, Mandiant. https://github.com/mandiant/capa. Accessed 29 Apr 2023

9. New Picus Red Report warns of "Swiss Army knife" malware. https://www.picussecurity.com/press-release/red-report-2023-warns-of-swiss-army-knife-malware

10. Multipurpose malware: Sometimes Trojans come in threes. https://www.kaspersky.co.in/blog/multipurpose-malware-sometimes-trojans-come-in-threes/6059/

11. Joachims, T.: A Probabilistic Analysis of the Rocchio Algorithm with TFIDF for Text Categorization. Carnegie-Mellon University Pittsburgh PA, Department of Computer Science (1996)

12. Kumar, N., Mukhopadhyay, S., Gupta, M., Handa, A., Shukla, S.K.: Malware classification using early stage behavioural analysis. In: 2019 14th Asia Joint Conference on Information Security (AsiaJCIS), Kobe, Japan, pp. 16–23 (2019). https://doi.org/10.1109/AsiaJCIS.2019.00-10

13. Han, W., Xue, J., Wang, Y., Liu, Z., Kong, Z.: MalInsight: a systematic profiling based malware detection framework. J. Netw. Comput. Appl. **125**, 236–250 (2019)

14. Gibert, D., Mateu, C., Planes, J.: The rise of machine learning for detection and classification of malware: research developments, trends and challenges. J. Netw. Comput. Appl. **153**, 102526 (2020)

15. Kondrak, G.: N-gram similarity and distance. In: Consens, M., Navarro, G. (eds.) SPIRE 2005. LNCS, vol. 3772, pp. 115–126. Springer, Heidelberg (2005). https://doi.org/10.1007/11575832_13

16. Multi-Purpose Ransomware Fuels DDoS Attacks. https://www.securityweek.com/multi-purpose-ransomware-fuels-ddos-attacks/

17. Zhang, M.-L., Zhou, Z.-H.: A review on multi-label learning algorithms. IEEE Trans. Knowl. Data Eng. **26**(8), 1819–1837 (2014). https://doi.org/10.1109/TKDE.2013.39

18. CISA Alert AA23-040A: Maui and HolyGhost Ransomware Target Critical Infrastructure. https://www.picussecurity.com/resource/blog/cisa-alert-aa23-040a-maui-and-holyghost-ransomware-target-critical-infrastructure

19. TrickBot: Not Your Average Hat Trick - A Malware with Multiple Hats. https://www.cisecurity.org/insights/blog/trickbot-not-your-average-hat-trick-a-malware-with-multiple-hats. Accessed 02 May 2023

20. Zhang, M.L., Zhou, Z.H.: ML-KNN: a lazy learning approach to multi-label learning. Pattern Recogn. **40**(7), 2038–2048 (2007)

21. Drew, J., Moore, T., Hahsler, M.: Polymorphic malware detection using sequence classification methods. In: 2016 IEEE Security and Privacy Workshops (SPW), pp. 81–87. IEEE (2016)

22. GlobeImposter Ransomware Being Distributed with MedusaLocker via RDP. https://asec.ahnlab.com/en/48940/

23. Li, C., Lv, Q., Li, N., Wang, Y., Sun, D., Qiao, Y.: A novel deep framework for dynamic malware detection based on API sequence intrinsic features. Comput. Secur. **116**, 102686 (2022)

24. Agarkar, S., Ghosh, S.: Malware detection & classification using machine learning. In: 2020 IEEE International Symposium on Sustainable Energy, Signal Processing and Cyber Security (iSSSC), pp. 1–6. IEEE (2020)
25. North Korean threat actor targets small and midsize businesses with H0lyGh0st ransomware. https://www.microsoft.com/en-us/security/blog/2022/07/14/north-korean-threat-actor-targets-small-and-midsize-businesses-with-h0lygh0st-ransomware/
26. Rani, N., Mishra, A., Kumar, R., Ghosh, S., Shukla, S.K., Bagade, P.: A generalized unknown malware classification. In: Li, F., Liang, K., Lin, Z., Katsikas, S.K. (eds.) SecureComm 2022. LNICST, vol. 462, pp. 793–806. Springer, Cham (2023). https://doi.org/10.1007/978-3-031-25538-0_41
27. Rani, N., Dhavale, S.V.: Leveraging machine learning for ransomware detection. arXiv preprint arXiv:2206.01919 (2022)
28. Malware Analysis - ransomware - b14c45c1792038fd69b5c75e604242a3. https://www.redpacketsecurity.com/malware-analysis-ransomware-b14c45c1792038fd69b5c75e604242a3/
29. Xu, Z., Fang, X., Yang, G.: MalBERT: a novel pre-training method for malware detection. Comput. Secur. **111**, 102458 (2021)
30. Rani, N., Dhavale, S.V., Singh, A., Mehra, A.: A survey on machine learning-based ransomware detection. In: Giri, D., Raymond Choo, K.K., Ponnusamy, S., Meng, W., Akleylek, S., Prasad Maity, S. (eds.) ICMC 2021. AISC, vol. 1412, pp. 171–186. Springer, Singapore (2022). https://doi.org/10.1007/978-981-16-6890-6_13
31. Deng, X., Mirkovic, J.: Malware behavior through network trace analysis. In: Ghita, B., Shiaeles, S. (eds.) INC 2020. LNNS, vol. 180, pp. 3–18. Springer, Cham (2021). https://doi.org/10.1007/978-3-030-64758-2_1
32. Ghamrawi, N., McCallum, A.: Collective multi-label classification. In: Proceedings of the 14th ACM International Conference on Information and Knowledge Management, pp. 195–200 (2005)
33. Rewterz Threat Alert - Lockbit Ransomware - Active IOCs. https://www.rewterz.com/rewterz-news/rewterz-threat-alert-lockbit-ransomware-active-iocs-13/
34. Singh, A., Handa, A., Kumar, N., Shukla, S.K.: Malware classification using image representation. In: Dolev, S., Hendler, D., Lodha, S., Yung, M. (eds.) CSCML 2019. LNCS, vol. 11527, pp. 75–92. Springer, Cham (2019). https://doi.org/10.1007/978-3-030-20951-3_6
35. North Korean H0lyGh0st Ransomware Has Ties to Global Geopolitics. https://blogs.blackberry.com/en/2022/08/h0lygh0st-ransomware
36. Abusnaina, A., et al.: DL-FHMC: deep learning-based fine-grained hierarchical learning approach for robust malware classification. IEEE Trans. Dependable Secure Comput. **19**(5), 3432–3447 (2021)
37. Amer, E., Zelinka, I.: A dynamic Windows malware detection and prediction method based on contextual understanding of API call sequence. Comput. Secur. **92**, 101760 (2020)
38. Ahmed, I., Xu, W., Annavajjala, R., Yoo, W.-S.: Joint demodulation and decoding with multi-label classification using deep neural networks (2021)
39. Opitz, J., Burst, S.: Macro F1 and Macro F1. arXiv preprint arXiv:1911.03347 (2019)
40. Fujii, S., Yamagishi, R., Yamauchi, T.: Survey and analysis on ATT&CK mapping function of online sandbox for understanding and efficient using. J. Inf. Process. **30**, 807–821 (2022). Released on J-STAGE 15 December 2022, Online ISSN 1882-6652. https://doi.org/10.2197/ipsjjip.30.807

Multimodal Software Defect Severity Prediction Based on Sentiment Probability

Ying Li[1,2], Yuhao Lin[1,3], Yongchao Zhong[1,3], Qiuling Yue[3], Jinglu Hu[4],
Wenjie Wang[1], Huiyang Shi[1], and Yuqing Zhang[1,2,3,5(✉)]

[1] National Computer Network Intrusion Protection Center
(University of Academy of Sciences), Beijing 101408, China
zhangyq@nipc.org.cn
[2] Zhongguancun Laboratory, Beijing 100194, China
[3] School of Cyberspace Security (School of cryptography), Hainan University,
Haikou 570100, China
[4] Graduate School of Information, Production and Systems, Waseda University,
Shinjuku-ku 169-8050, Japan
[5] School of Cyber Engineering, Xidian University, Xi'an 710126, China

Abstract. Software systems generate a large number of software bugs during their life cycle, and timely detection and repair of these bugs is a key issue in improving software quality and maintaining software security. Therefore, this paper proposes a severity prediction on affective probabilistic multimodel software bugs. First, this paper uses RoBERTa as a sentiment analysis model and proposes a model training method for defective knowledge enhancement. We use Stack Overflow to construct a manually annotated sentiment probability dataset. Evaluating consistency between sentiment annotators by calculating Fleiss' kappa values. Next, the difference in the impact of defects of different severity on users is reflected by the probability of sentiment. Using sentiment traits for the next stage of prediction. Finally, these include robust data processing of heterogeneous bug data, a complementary integrated learning framework that incorporates large linguistic and traditional tabular models, and a powerful model integration strategy based on a novel combination of multi-layer stacking and cyclic k-fold integrated bagging. Our comprehensive empirical assessment shows that SPM is more accurate and reliable than the popular defect severity prediction methods.

Keywords: software security · bug severity prediction · sentiment annotation · multimodality · integrated learning

This work was supported by the National Key Research and Development Program (2023QY1202), the National Natural Science Foundation of China (U1836210), the Key Research and Development Science and Technology of Hainan Province (GHYF2022010), and the Research Startup Foundation of Hainan University (RZ2100003335).

W. Meng et al. (Eds.): ISPEC 2023, LNCS 14341, pp. 250–265, 2023.
https://doi.org/10.1007/978-981-99-7032-2_15

1   Introduction

Software bugs are an essential indicator for evaluating software quality. It is mainly used to reflect the level of software quality. This also determines to some extent the difficulty of maintaining the software. Specifically, most research focus on improving the quality of bug reports for reporters. Most research focus on automating the classification and repair of bug reports for developers. Therefore, this paper examines the automation of bug reports from the developer's perspective.

In recent years, many efforts made by domestic and international researchers to develop automated techniques for software defect severity prediction. Sharmin et al. [1] use a combination of correlation coefficients, Pareto optimality theory and independence chi-square tests to refine descriptive information in defect reports. They use support vector machines and decision trees for defect severity prediction. Yang et al. [2] then capture the correlation between the emotional expressions of user-reported bugs and severity based on a sentiment dictionary. They use a support vector machine classifier for severity prediction, illustrating that bugs of different severity levels have different emotional impacts on software users. To reduce the dimensionality of defective text features Liu et al. [3] introduce a ranking-based strategy to improve existing feature selection algorithms and proposed an integrated feature selection algorithm combined with existing feature selection algorithms.

Although these studies contribute accordingly to some extent, they still have certain limitations. For example, they only address a single defect tracking system and are not universally applicable. We improve on the limitations of existing bug severity prediction studies. In summary, the contributions of this paper are as follows.

- A large-scale linguistic pre-training model is introduced to replace the previously studied text feature extraction and generic sentiment dictionary approaches. Use bug knowledge expansion methods to enhance the model's ability to characterise defective text. Add defective sentiment datasets for sentiment training and testing to complete reliable automated defective text sentiment annotation tasks.
- A comprehensive learning framework can learn different representations of different types of defective features for training models. This means that integrated learning frameworks containing large language models can train the fusion of multi-modal data.
- The performance of the proposed SPM method is systematically compared with the current defect severity prediction baseline. The F-measure, Precision and Recall assessment indicators yield the final assessment results. The results show that SPM is more accurate and reliable.

The remainder of this paper is structured as follows. In Sect. 2, presents some related works on Software bugs and natural language processing. In Sect. 3, describes our approach in detail. In Sect. 4, presents our results and the findings for the research question. In Sect. 5, discusses potential avenues for future works. In Sect. 6, summarizes and prospects the above works.

2   Related Work

2.1   Software Bugs

In software engineering, a software bug is any flaw or error in a software system that causes its behaviour to deviate from the expected or specified behaviour [4]. Software Bug Tracking System (BTS) can help the team effectively record and track these bugs, timely identify and fix problems, and improve the quality and stability of the software. A software bug tracking system, also known as a bug management database, is a tool used to record, manage, and track the entire life cycle of software defects [5].

Standard bug tracking systems include JIRA, Bugzilla, Mantis, etc. [6] These systems are usually web-based and can run on different platforms, providing a series of API interfaces to facilitate integration with other systems. [7] The definitions of defect severity for three popular BTS are described below and compared in Table 1.

Bugzilla. Bug severity indicates the severity of issues in Bugzilla ranging from blocking ("application unavailable") to trivial ("minor cosmetic issues") [8]. In addition, this field can be used to indicate whether the error is a feature enhancement request. Priority, however, defines how urgent a bug needs to fix. In Bugzilla, the combination of priority and severity defines the importance of the bug.

Jira. In Jira, bug severity is called priority and indicates the importance of a bug compared to other bugs from blocking ("highest priority") to minor ("low priority"). [9]

Issue Tracker. In Google Issue Tracker, Bug Severity, also known as Priority [10], indicates the priority of a bug compared to other bugs from P0 ("Needs immediate fix") to P4 ("Eventually needs immediate fix").

As can be seen, despite the importance of the severity of bug reports, different BTSs have their own set of severity evaluation systems, and there are even significant differences between different items within the same BTS. This makes the study of automated bug severity assessment very difficult, as no scheme can universally and objectively evaluate bug severity.

2.2   Natural Language Processing

The primary technique involved in the severity analysis of defects is natural language processing, and text pre-processing is the first key step in natural language processing. Effective text pre-processing is therefore crucial to the success of defect severity prediction. Text representation methods have broadly evolved through the following stages. **The Bag-of-Words (BoW)** model is to convert

Table 1. A Comparison of the Mozilla and RedHat Projects' Bug Severity Assessment Guidelines.

database	Severity	Description
Bugzilla	Blocker	A serious bug that caused the software to crash and not run
	Critical	seriously affects the functionality of the software the program has not yet completely crashed
	Major	a significant impact on the usability or performance of the software
	Normal	Bugs that have a moderate impact on the usability or performance of the software
	Minor	Errors that have a minor impact on the usability or performance of the software
Jira	Blocker	Software does not work
	Critical	Interference with software functionality and no solution
	Major	Errors that have a significant impact on availability or performance
	Minor	Non-critical functional issues and solutions exist
	Trivial	Secondary issues, such as cosmetic issues have little or no impact on the user
Issue Tracker	P0	Critical errors that require immediate attention and resolution. These errors can render the software completely unusable, or lead to serious data loss or corruption
	P1	High priority errors that have a significant impact on the functionality or performance of the software
	P2	Medium priority errors that have some impact on the functionality or performance of the software
	P3	Low priority errors that have a minor impact on the functionality or performance of the software

words into a unique thermal encoding vector, regardless of grammar and word order, and the vector size is the corpus lexicon size [11] **The TF-IDF model** measures the importance of a word to a collection of documents [12]. Its core idea is that if a word occurs more frequently in one document and less frequently in other documents, then the more significant the discriminatory power of the word for that document, the higher its importance. **Basic word embedding** represents words as high-dimensional vectors in a continuous space. The most popular current approach is the Word2vec algorithm, which assumes that the meaning of a word can be inferred from the context in which it occurs [13]. **The text embedding** uses words or phrases of different granularity as model inputs, and the N-Gram vectors of the sentences are transformed into Hidden vectors by a pre-training and overlay averaging method of word embedding to send them to the downstream task network layer [14]. **Ambiguous embedding** bases on a word embedding model with different contexts. This model can embed the same word into different spatial representations according to different contexts [15], thus better solving the problem of multiple semantics of words. **Large-scale pre-trained text representation methods** base on pre-trained models of large-scale corpora [16]. The language models learnt on these corpora enable word vector representations with rich semantic information to be obtained and can share the learned knowledge between different tasks.

3   Emotion Annotation Model Based on Knowledge Enhancement

3.1   Domain Enhancement

Most large-scale general-purpose corpus-based training relies on natural language processing pre-training models. The sentiment analysis model used in this paper is RoBERTa, which is an improved and optimised version of the BERT model that improves its performance by pre-training on a larger corpus. Also, this paper proposes a model training method for defective knowledge enhancement. Specifically, we collected 50,000 defective text data from BTS and Stack Overflow to build a label-free corpus of defects and continuously pre-trained RoBERTa. In addition, we collected a biotechnology corpus and a news corpus for experimental comparison, and Table 2 shows the details of the corpus structure in different knowledge contexts.

Also, to demonstrate the method's feasibility, we conducted a similarity analysis between the pre-trained corpus of RoBERTa and the software defect corpus, the news corpus and the biotechnology corpus. We counted the top 2000 high-frequency words from the different corpora, and Fig. 1 quantifies the analysis results. The figure shows that RoBERTa has a high overlap with the pre-trained corpus and the news corpus, but a low overlap with the software-defective corpus. The analysis shows the degree of gain expected from the adapting RoBERTa to different domains: the more significant the variability of the domains, the greater the potential for knowledge enhancement.

Table 2. Corpus Structure for Different Knowledge Domains.

Type of knowledge	Pre-training dataset	Token	Size
Biotechnology	Full-text papers from S2ORC	6.17B	20 GB
News	Articles from realnews	2.99B	15 GB
Software bugs	Bug description from BTS and Stack Overflow	3.63B	19 GB

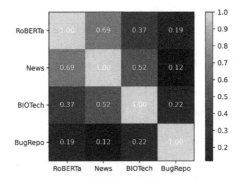

Fig. 1. Similarity Analysis of Different Corpuses.

3.2 Emotional Probability Labeling

The ultimate goal of conventional sentiment analysis is to assign a sentiment polarity label to text to achieve a text classification effect. However, sentiment in bug reports tends to be on the negative side. Differentiating the severity of different bugs in the form of sentiment polarity labels may instead lead to noise problems and affect the accuracy of the model.

Therefore, this paper after knowledge enhancement the high-quality sentiment dataset allows the model to further improve its sentiment analysis capabilities. In contrast to the lexicon-based approach, we consider using the confidence level of the RoBERTa model output to quantify the depth of each type of sentiment in the text to achieve fine-grained sentiment analysis. Specifically, we take the model output and run it through a Softmax layer to calculate the confidence level, or sentiment probability, of the output belonging to the corresponding sentiment. The newly generated augmented defect dataset will be used as a training set test set for the next stage of bug severity prediction.

4 Multimodel Defect Severity Prediction Based on Integrated Learning

The main content of a bug report is usually contained in the subject matter of the bug and in the descriptive text. This paper transforms the text classification task of bugs into a multimodal table classification task. Figure 2 illustrates some bug multimodal tabular data. Also, this paper proposes a complementary model fusion method. The method is able to integrate various models into the same dimension (from traditional machine learning to specified neural network models) and train them in a hierarchical manner to ensure that the bug data can be successfully transformed into high quality prediction results. Throughout the process, we mitigate the problem of model over-fitting by partitioning the dataset in various ways and carefully tracking Out-Of-Fold (OOF) predictions. We then describe each component of the method in detail and discuss how they are implemented.

summary	product	component	severity	comment_count	description	positive	netural	negtive
CVE-2001-0414 ntpd security hole	Security Response	vulnerability	medium	17.0	From Bugzilla Helper: User-Agent: Mozilla/5.0 ...	0.37235	0.30421	0.32344
CAN-2003-0543/0544 OpenSSL ASN.1 protocol crashes	Security Response	vulnerability	medium	3.0	Notified via NISCC on Sep12, NISCC 006489 CAN...	0.30527	0.42057	0.27416
CVE-2003-0618 leaks file existance information	Security Response	vulnerability	low	6.0	CAN-2003-0618 was reported 2003Jul29 to Debian...	0.22238	0.72567	0.05195
CAN-2004-0421 libpng can access out of bounds ...	Security Response	vulnerability	medium	3.0	From: Steve G <linux_4ever@yahoo com> In the ...	0.35765	0.37654	0.26581
CVE-2004-0967 temporary file vulnerabilities i...	Security Response	vulnerability	low	1.0	On September 10th 2004, Trustix shared some te...	0.12173	0.74135	0.13692

☐ Category   ☐ Value   ☐ Text

Fig. 2. Example of Multimodal Tabular Data for Software Defects.

4.1   Model Selection Phase

At this stage we follow the principle that models with reliable performance (e.g. random forests) are trained before more expensive or less reliable models (e.g. k-neighbourhoods). This is essential to improve the training and prediction efficiency of the model. In this study, we consider the RoBERTa language model as well as the classical tabular model.

Data Pre-processing Stage. This stage is divided into two aspects: model-independent pre-processing and model-specified pre-processing. We identify the type features listed in Table 3 and process them individually to convert them into a format that can be read by the machine learning model. In particular, the category column is mapped to monotonically increasing discrete values in the regular pre-processing. The numeric columns, on the other hand, are not altered in any way, but are simply identified as floating-point or integer types. The resulting text, numbers and categorical features are then passed to the specific model for further model-specified embedding operations.

Table 3. Type of Data Pre-processing.

bug database	Example
Number	1.0, -1, 333
Text	Cleans up shell checking after do_QueryReferent(weakShell) calls
Category	High, Low, Urgent

Fig. 3. Example of Multimodal Tabular Data for Software Defects.

Data Embedding. Although the language model of the Transformer architecture has strong textual representation capabilities, it has limited ability to
handle tabular data [17]. We have adopted a tabular data embedding approach
as shown in Fig. 3, with separate neural operations for each data type and aggregation only near the output layer. This design extracts higher-level numerical
representations from each modality.

Language Model Integration. Because the decision boundaries learned by
the neural network differ in geometry from the axis alignment of the tree-based
tabular model, they provide valuable diversity in combination with the tree.
To ensure prediction accuracy, various strategies were used to integrate the
RoBERTa model to fuse learning on multimodel inputs simultaneously.

This study uses stacking to combine the models, rather than simply aggregating the model outputs linearly. This trains an additional machine learning
model or models to learn the best model aggregation strategy, which we call a
metamodel. The input to the metamodel is a stitching together of the prediction
vectors from the outputs of all the basic models (including the language model).
We use multiple types of tabular models as stacking models. Figure 4 illustrates
the integration architecture of the stacking approach.

Integration Optimization. In this paper, we introduce an improved approach
to stacking integration, namely multi-layer stacking. specifically, we aggregate
the predictions output from multiple base models into new feature values that
are used as input to the next layer of models. The next layer consists of multiple
metamodels. These metamodels then continue to feed into another layer as the
output of the base model, as shown in Fig. 5. In addition, we also borrow the
idea of skip connection from deep learning: the metamodel takes as input not
only the predictive features of the previous layer's model, but also the original
data features themselves.

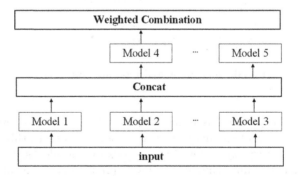

Fig. 4. Ensemble Learning Architecture of Stacking.

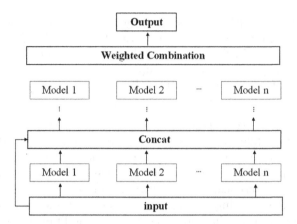

Fig. 5. Multi-layer Stacking Architecture.

Figure 6 illustrates the principle of cyclic k-fold integrated bagging. Specifically, we split the original dataset into k subsets, where k-1 subsets are used to train a model, which is then evaluated using the validation set. This process is repeated r times, each time using a different random split, resulting in k*r models.

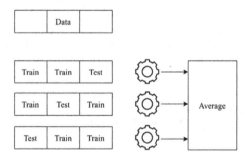

Fig. 6. Repeated k-fold Ensemble Bagging.

Ultimately, the predictions from these models are averaged and output as predictions for the whole model to the higher-level model. In this process, each model is required to produce OOF predictions on the blocks it is not trained on, so that each training sample gets OOF predictions from all models, and the output of the model is an average of all OOF predictions. The problem of OOF overfitting of the low-level model being amplified layer by layer was effectively addressed after circular bagging. In summary, with the addition of multi-layer stacking and cyclic K-fold bagging, the integrated learning model is further enhanced regarding defect severity prediction.

Table 4. RoBERTa Pre-training Hyperparameters Setting.

Hyperparameters	Value
Epochs	10
Patience	4
Batch size	64
Learning rate	2e-1
Dropout	0.2
Feedforward layer	1
Feedforward nonlinearity	Tanh
Classification layer	1

5   Evaluation

5.1   Experimental Assessment of Knowledge Enhancement

As a baseline for this study, we utilized the pre-trained RoBERTa base model and fine-tuned its parameters for sentiment classification on defective text. Additionally, we conducted comparative experiments on news corpora, biotechnology corpora, and defect corpora. Each corpus consisted of 50,000 randomly selected unlabeled data samples, and we trained the RoBERTa model on each corpus for 10,000 iterations. This training process was equivalent to training each knowledge background dataset once on a Tesla V100. The retraining resulted in three distinct knowledge-enhanced language models with different knowledge backgrounds. The detailed hyperparameter settings are provided in Table 4.

To visually illustrate the changes in masked language model (MLM) loss for the different knowledge background models before and after knowledge enhancement, we applied smoothing to the loss variation. We observed that all models experienced a reduction in MLM loss after retraining. Moreover, compared to the pre-enhancement models, the loss values of the pre-trained models in the biotechnology and software defect domains were significantly lower, as depicted in Figs. 7 and 9. However, as shown in Fig. 8, the pre-trained model in the news domain did not exhibit a widened gap but instead remained close to its state

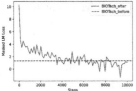  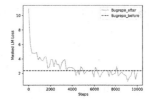

Fig. 7. Loss of BIOTech Corpus Re-pretraining. **Fig. 8.** Loss of News Corpus Re-pretraining. **Fig. 9.** Loss of Burgrepo Corpus Re-pretraining.

before knowledge enhancement. This finding indicates that the magnitude of knowledge domain differences influences the representation learning capability of the language model for specific knowledge background texts.

In each knowledge background, we performed fine-tuning training on the model for different types of text classification tasks and evaluated the final model's classification performance. As shown in Table 5, we randomly selected annotated texts from the news corpus, biotechnology corpus, and defect corpus based on the hierarchical classification labels for training, validation, and testing sets.

The test results, as shown in the "Knowledge Enhancement" column of Table 6, indicate that knowledge enhancement significantly improved the performance of RoBERTa across all knowledge backgrounds. While knowledge enhancement did not improve the performance of news text classification, we observed consistent improvements in RoBERTa's performance for the biotechnology and defect domains. This suggests that the effect of knowledge enhancement becomes more pronounced when the target domain is farther from RoBERTa's source domain.

Table 5. Structure of Datasets for Different Classification Tasks.

Type	Mission	Label	Categories Number	Training set	Validation set	Test set
BIOTech	ChemProt	Relationship	13	5169	517	776
BugRepo	Mozilla	Severity	4	6709	875	801
News	AGNEWS	Topic	4	5978	810	693

Furthermore, we conducted cross-comparative experiments on the knowledge-enhanced models with different knowledge backgrounds by transferring the language models to tasks unrelated to their pre-training knowledge. This aligns with our hypothesis that the performance improvement over the original RoBERTa model could be attributed solely to exposure to more data, irrespective of the knowledge background. In this setup, we used the biotechnology language model for the news task, the news language model for the defect task, and the defect language model for the biotechnology task. We guided these choices based on the vocabulary overlap statistics shown in Fig. 5.

Table 6. Comparing the Adaptation of RoBERTa to Relevant and Irrelevant Knowledge.

Type	Mission	RoBERTa	Related enhancements	No enhancement
BIOTech	ChemProt	0.819	0.847	0.794
BugRepo	Mozilla	0.603	0.755	0.589
News	AGNEWS	0.936	0.928	0.926

The results of these experiments are presented in the last column of Table 6. Therefore, the knowledge-enhanced pre-training specifically tailored to defect knowledge indeed contributes to the model's understanding of defect severity prediction tasks.

5.2 Emotional Analysis Assessment

To capture the deep-level user sentiment in defect severity prediction, this study quantified the sentiment polarity of bug text. Therefore, we utilized three different types of sentiment features: general sentiment lexicon, sentiment polarity, and sentiment probabilities to evaluate the impact of sentiment probabilities on bug severity prediction.

We employed the classic word embedding model Word2Vec and the pre-trained model RoBERTa to represent defect text. The bug dataset is preprocessed to remove file paths, URLs, email addresses, and code snippets, resulting in over 612,201,78 tokens. Subsequently, we split the defect dataset into a training set (70%) and a test set (30%) and performed stratified sampling to find the optimal vector representation for each word in our models. The vector representation of each text was calculated by taking the weighted average of all word vectors in the text.

For bug severity prediction, we uniformly used Support Vector Machine (SVM) to calculate the defect text vectors output result, i.e., severity level. This avoids interference from the native classifier of RoBERTa. For sentiment annotation based on the general lexicon, we directly annotated the defect dataset using the widely used SentiStrength sentiment analysis tool in current research. It employs a set of rules and a general lexicon to analyze sentiment polarity in the text and provide corresponding sentiment scores. We followed the automated annotation method used in this study.

From the experimental results, we observe that the method based on sentiment probabilities indeed improves the performance of defect severity prediction to some extent compared to the baseline method that uses sentiment lexicons (average precision improved by 1.68%, average recall improved by 3.27%, and average F-measure improved by 2.47%). This aligns with our expectations and demonstrates that the sentiment probability feature of defect text helps to differentiate subtle emotional differences in defects of different severity, thus improving the model's predictive performance for defect severity.

5.3 Bug Severity Prediction Models: Comparison with State-of-the-art Baseline Methods

The proposed method, SPM, will be compared with the baselines used in previous defect report severity prediction studies. Based on the survey of the research landscape conducted in this study, it is found that 90% of the studies only consider the description and summary information of defects. Therefore, we compare the latest research proposals on defect severity prediction from the past three years. In addition to traditional machine learning algorithms, deep neural networks such as LSTM, CNN, and Transformer is used in recent research. Hence, we include LSTM, CNN, and Transformer as additional experimental baselines. Lastly, to validate whether the integration of language models can improve prediction performance, we also considered an ensemble learning framework without the language model RoBERTa. Previous research has demonstrated that ensemble learning can enhance defect severity prediction performance.

For some machine learning algorithms and general ensemble learning models, we use the RoBERTa model to represent text embeddings to ensure a fair comparison with our proposed method, SPM. However, we use their default embeddings for LSTM, CNN, and Transformer to represent the texts.

We considered two factors for the multimodal defect table dataset: the time order of defect submissions and the category proportion of severity labels. We used 70% of the table data as the training set, 20% as the test set, and 10% as the validation set. This dataset-splitting method allows us to predict the severity of new defect reports using historical defect reports, reflecting real-world application scenarios and avoiding data imbalance issues. To evaluate the performance of these algorithms at the system level, 10-fold cross-validation was applied, and the average values of F-measure, precision, and recall were used as evaluation metrics.

The comparison results of our proposed method and the baselines on the training set are shown in Table 7. From this table, we can observe that the SPM method achieves better performance than all the baselines, with F-measure, precision, and recall reaching 92.78%, 93.95%, and 91.64% respectively. Compared to the baselines, the proposed SPM method improves the F-measure, precision, and recall on average by 14.86%, 15.73%, and 13.48% respectively. Furthermore, compared to the SPM method without the language model RoBERTa, there are improvements of 5.26%, 4.21%, and 6.23% in F-measure, precision, and recall respectively, demonstrating that the language model contributes to the performance enhancement of the ensemble framework for severity prediction.

6   Discussion

In order to further improve the performance of the bug severity prediction model and make it more relevant to practical application scenarios, the research in this paper will continue. Although the SPM method proposed in this study achieve better results, there may be room for improvement in different datasets and application scenarios. Future attempts can be made to expand the size and diversity of the dataset. This study used historical data from three bug-tracking repositories, which only covered a portion of software development projects. Adding more bug-tracking repositories and data from software development projects could be considered in the future to understand better the bug characteristics and severity distribution of different software projects. In addition, this study proposes an integrated learning approach that includes language models, but does not consider the excessive consumption of computational resources and

Table 7. Performance of SPM Methods versus Advanced Methods for Severity Prediction.

Type	Mission	RoBERTa	Related enhancements	No enhancement
Methods	Literature	F-measure(%)	Precision(%)	Recall(%)
SPM	-	92.78	93.95	91.64
SPM(without RoBERTa)	-	87.52	89.74	85.41
CNN/LSTM	Kim,2022	87.62	90.31 85.08	
LightGBM	Dao,2022	81.39	80.84	83.25
Word2vec/GPT2	Kamal,2022	89.77	90.43	89.12
Bert/SVM	Kumar,2021	87.09	88.16	86.05
Bert/AdaBoost	Kumar,2021	90.03	89.74	90.32
Sentiment Score/MLP	Baarah,2021	81.92	77.73	86.59
BoW/CNN	Rathnayake,2021	80.43	78.92	79.67
TextRank/FastText	Jia,2021	73.18	75.87	70.67
Entropy/KNN	Kumari,2020	56.53	60.23	58.55
Word2vec/LR	Tan,2020	66.22	69.73	63.05
TF-IDF/KNN	Sabor,2020	73.97	72.13	75.91
XGBoost/SVM	Mondreti,2020	75.66	70.50	81.63
Doc2Vec/MLP	Arokiam,2020	69.14	72.30	66.24

inefficiency of large language models. The architecture of integrated learning can be explored in the future to optimise it, for example, by using model distillation techniques to reduce the hyperparameter size of learning and by reducing the number of reuses of language models during model stacking to improve the prediction efficiency of the models and reduce resource consumption. We will also investigate the availability of defective code, consider graph neural network-based models to extract code features of defects and explore their intrinsic relationship with severity for future diversified severity assessment efforts.

7   Conclusion

Software defect severity prediction is a hot area for solving the problems of timeliness and maintenance costs of fixing software defects. As defect severity assessment performe in an automated manner, limited maintenance resources can be rationally allocated. This paper focuses on two factors that affect the performance of defect severity prediction models: sentiment analysis and multimodal training, using complete defect reports as the database for prediction.

These two aspects analyse in detail and new algorithms propose based on existing research. The main contributions of this paper are as follows.

The concept of defect knowledge enhancement is first proposed to improve the language model's ability to characterise defective texts. The sentiment information in the defect description text is further quantified based on the enhanced language model. The differences in the impact of defects of different severity on users are reflected through sentiment probabilities and ultimately used as enhanced features in the defect dataset to assist in the next stage of defect severity prediction. Design choices are then presented for supervised learning using multimodal defect datasets containing textual, numerical and category features. The structure of the multimodal dataset is optimised based on empirical analysis of the impact of defect report attributes on severity, enabling efficient use of defect reports. Finally, this paper proposes an SPM approach for defect severity prediction, whose key aspects include robust data processing of heterogeneous defect data, a complementary integrated learning framework fusing large linguistic and traditional tabular models, and a powerful model integration strategy based on a novel combination of multilayer stacking and cyclic k-fold integrated bagging. Our comprehensive empirical evaluation shows that SPM is more accurate and reliable than popular defect severity prediction methods.

References

1. Sharmin, S., Aktar, F., Ali, A.A., et al.: BFSP: a feature selection method for bug severity classification. In: 2017 IEEE Region 10 Humanitarian Technology Conference (R10-HTC). IEEE (2017)
2. Yang, G., Zhang, T., Lee, B.: An emotion similarity based severity prediction of software bugs: a case study of open source projects. IEICE Trans. Inf. Syst. **101**(8), 2015–2026 (2018)
3. Liu, W., Wang, S., Chen, X., et al.: Predicting the severity of bug reports based on feature selection. Int. J. Softw. Eng. Knowl. Eng. **28**(04), 537–558 (2018)
4. Li, D.: Research on the relationship between software defect severity and repair complexity. Huazhong Normal University (2020)
5. Liu, W.J.: Research on software defect report severity prediction. Dalian University of Technology (2020)
6. Jiang, H., Nazar, N., Zhang, J., et al.: PRST: a pagerank-based summarization technique for summarizing bug report with duplicates. Int. J. Softw. Eng. Knowl. Eng. **27**(06), 869–896 (2017)
7. Bo, Z., Neamtiu, I., Gupta, R.: Experience report: how do bug characteristics differ across severity classes: a multi-platform study. In: IEEE International Symposium on Software Reliability Engineering. IEEE (2016)
8. Wu, X., Zheng, W., Chen, X., et al.: CVE-assisted large-scale security bug report dataset construction method. J. Syst. Softw. **27**(06), 869–896 (2019)
9. Gomes, L.A.F., da Silva, T.R., Côrtes, M.L.: Bug report severity level prediction in open source software: a survey and research opportunities. Inf. Softw. Technol. **115**, 58–78 (2019)
10. Kukka, A., Mohana, R., Kumar, Y.: Does bug report summarization help in enhancing the accuracy of bug severity classification? Procedia Comput. Sci. **167**, 1345–1353 (2020)

11. Juluru, K., Shih, H.H., Keshava Murthy, K.N., et al.: Bag-of-words technique in natural language processing: a primer for radiologists. Radiographics **41**(5), 1420–1426 (2021)

12. Mikolov, T., Chen, K., Corrado, G., et al.: Efficient estimation of word representations in vector space. arXiv preprint arXiv:1301.3781 (2013)

13. Huang, X., Khetan, A., Cvitkovic, M., et al.: Tabtransformer: tabular data modeling using contextual embeddings. arXiv preprint arXiv:2012.06678 (2020)

14. Joulin, A., Grave, E., Bojanowski, P., et al.: Bag of tricks for efficient text classification. arXiv preprint arXiv:1607.01759 (2016)

15. Peters, M.E., Neumann, M., Iyyer, M., et al.: Deep contextualized word representations. arXiv preprint arXiv:1802.05365 (2018)

16. Devlin, J., Chang, M.W., Lee, K., et al.: Bert: pre-training of deep bidirectional transformers for language understanding. arXiv preprint arXiv:1810.04805 (2018)

17. Zhang, J., Wang, X., Zhang, H., et al.: A novel neural source code representation based on abstract syntax tree. In: 41st International Conference on Software Engineering (2019)

Recovering Multi-prime RSA Keys with Erasures and Errors

Guanghui Liu[1], Yuejun Liu[1(✉)], Yongbin Zhou[1,2,3], and Yiwen Gao[1]

[1] School of Cyber Science and Engineering, Nanjing University of Science and Technology, Nanjing, China
{ceaser,liuyuejun,zhouyongbin,gaoyiwen}@njust.edu.cn
[2] Institute of Information Engineering, Chinese Academy of Sciences, Beijing, China
[3] School of Cyber Security, University of Chinese Academy of Science, Beijing, China

Abstract. Since Heninger and Shacham first proposed a key recovery algorithm from random partial RSA private key bits obtained from cold boot attacks, the algorithm has been further investigated in many studies. However, the noisy leakage models assumed in the existing work all fall short of reality, and the studies are all based on CRT-RSA only. In this study, we target Multi-Prime RSA, which is supported by PKCS#1 v2.1 and allows faster decryption than CRT-RSA, and give the theoretical bound of the key recovery algorithm under the Binary Erasure Symmetric Error model. We also propose a more realistic Binary Erasure Asymmetric Error model, under which we give the theoretical bound of the key recovery algorithm as well. Finally, the theoretical bounds of the algorithm are explained in the context of information theory.

Keywords: Multi-Prime RSA · Cold Boot Attacks · Statistic Analysis

1 Introduction

RSA [13] is an asymmetric cryptosystem widely used in applications such as digital signatures, secure communications, and key exchange protocols. CRT-RSA is the most widely deployed variant of RSA that accelerates the decryption phase [12] via the Chinese Residue Theorem. In contrast, Multi-Prime RSA [1] uses multiple prime factors in the common modulus to provide faster decryption and signing, especially on multi-processor platforms. Under CRT, Multi-Prime RSA can also achieve faster decryption and signing speed using parallel modulo power operations. Its private key consists of decryption exponent d, different prime factors $\{r_1, r_2, \cdots, r_u\}$ of modulo N, and CRT factors $\{d_1, d_2, r_2^{-1}, < d_3, t_3 >, \cdots, < d_u, t_u >\}$ for acceleration.

Cold boot attacks [3] is a threatening physical attack that allows an attacker to obtain some of the random bits of an RSA private key and use them to obtain the correct private key. Since the leaked data is not necessarily complete and correct, there are cases such as bit erasure or error. In order to reconstruct the complete and correct private key, many algorithms [4,5,7–9,11,17] have been proposed to apply to different leakage scenarios. However, the main body of research on these algorithms is CRT-RSA, and there is a lack of research on

Multi-Prime RSA, an encryption method that may be more widely used in the future, in the context of corresponding leakage scenarios.

Related Work. Heninger and Shacham [5] first proposed an algorithm to recover the complete private key using random partial bits of the private key obtained from a cold boot attack in CRYPTO 2009. They reconstructed the private key by expanding it from low to high bits and combining the leaked bits for pruning. The conclusion shows that their attack algorithm requires at least 0.27 random bits of the private key to work properly. Henecka et al. [4] then apply Heniger et al.'s algorithm to a new cold boot attacks leakage scenario, where their work assumes that the adversary obtains the complete but partially erroneous bits of the RSA private key, and after statistical analysis, the conclusion shows that this expansion-pruning approach can work provided that the errored probability is less than 0.23. Paterson et al. [11] further considers the case where the errored probability of bits 0 and 1 is asymmetric and considers the extreme case of one-sided error (Z-channel). While Kunihiro et al. [9] combine bit error and random bit erasure to give recoverable bounds on the expansion-pruning algorithm for the new leakage scenario. On the other hand, Kunihiro and Honda [8] optimised the algorithm in terms of data sources, arguing that DRAM potential information (simulated data) after cold boot processing contains more information that can be used to improve the recoverability bound of the algorithm. The algorithm of Kunihiro and Takahashi [10] requires less stringent information about the noise required in the leakage scenario [8], and the private key recovery algorithm could work even when the variance of the noise in the noisy private key is unknown.

Motivation. The fact that Multi-Prime RSA is faster to decrypt than CRT-RSA, and is supported by the pkcs#1 standard, means that security analysis of Multi-Prime RSA is necessary. Although there is some previous work analyzing RSA variants [14,15], few studies have extended to cold boot attacks.

The only paper on security analysis for Multi-Prime RSA under cold boot attacks was presented by Terada and Villena [16] at ISC 2013, and their work applies to the key erasure-only model. Our study will extend the noisy leakage model on which their research is based. The study by Halderman et al. [3] shows that error bit situation exists in cold boot attacks. Moreover, the error bit is asymmetric, due to the physical characteristics of DRAM that the probability of a 0-bit in a low voltage state flipping to a 1-bit in a high voltage state (denoted as $\alpha := Pr[0 \to 1]$) is much lower than the probability of a 1-bit in a high voltage state flipping to a 0-bit in a low voltage state (denoted as $\beta := Pr[1 \to 0]$). And the work of [11] also indicates that introducing the consideration of asymmetric error can make the key recovery algorithm better to handle the case of real cold boot attacks.

Therefore, we study the key recovery algorithm for Multi-Prime RSA in the noisy leakage model with erasures and errors.

Contributions. Our study presents key recovery algorithms for Multi-Prime RSA under two noisy leakage models and explains the algorithms' theoretical bounds from an information theoretical viewpoint. The first noisy leakage model is the Binary Erasure Symmetric Error model which was considered the closest to the actual cold boot attack in previous study [9], and the second is the Binary Erasure Asymmetric Error model which considers the asymmetric error case.

The recovery algorithm in this paper does not need to use the full private key parameters. In particular, for a Multi-Prime RSA with private key $sk = \{d, r_1, r_2, d_1, d_2, r_2^{-1}, < r_3, d_3, t_3 >, \ldots, < r_u, d_u, t_u >\}$, our algorithm only needs to obtain the noisy sequence of all prime factors $\{r_1, r_2, \cdots, r_u\}$ to complete the decomposition of the modulus N, and hence d can be easily obtained, and it will be our future work to optimize our algorithm using the CRT factors $\{d_1, d_2, r_2^{-1}, < d_3, t_3 >, \cdots, < d_u, t_u >\}$ in the private key parameters.

We use δ to denote the erasure rate of the noisy leakage model and ϵ to denote the error rate. Under the Binary Erasure Symmetric Error model, the recovery algorithm can run in polynomial time as long as it satisfies:

$$(1 - \delta) \left(1 - H\left(\frac{\epsilon}{(1 - \delta)}\right)\right) \geq 1 - \frac{1}{u}$$

where $H(x)$ is the binary entropy defined by $H(x) = -x log_2(x) - (1-x) log_2(1-x)$. And in the case of asymmetric error, the probability of flipping 0 bits to 1 bit is denoted by α, and the probability of flipping 1 bit to 0 bits is denoted by β. Then the polynomial time theoretical bound of the algorithm is:

$$(1 - \delta) \left(H\left(\frac{1}{2} + \frac{\beta - \alpha}{2(1 - \delta)}\right) - \frac{H\left(\frac{\alpha}{1-\delta}\right)}{2} - \frac{H\left(\frac{\beta}{1-\delta}\right)}{2} \right) \geq 1 - \frac{1}{u}$$

The theoretical bound in this paper is given by Shannon's Noisy-Channel Coding Theorem, which means that we will use the channel capacity to explain the above theoretical bounds of the key recovery algorithm.

Organizations. The rest of this study is organized as follows: In Sect. 2, we introduce several noisy leakage models that appear in cold boot attacks. In Sect. 3, we introduce our key recovery algorithm under a realistic leakage scenario and provide providing theoretical bound. In Sect. 4, we discuss the implementation and performance of the attack algorithm. Finally, conclusions are given in Sect. 5.

2 Preliminaries

In the description of the leakage model in this paper, δ denotes the erasure rate of each bit in the RSA private key, and ϵ denotes the error rate of each bit. To clarify the difference of error rate between 0-bit and 1-bit in the asymmetric error leakage model, we use α to denote the probability of 0 bits being flipped to 1 bits and β to denote the probability of 1 bits being flipped to 0 bits.

The next part of this section outlines the tree attack algorithm, a method for recovering RSA private keys by constructing partial candidate solution trees. We first present the recovery algorithm for CRT-RSA, then describe how Terada and Villena apply this recovery algorithm to Multi-Prime RSA, and finally present the limitations of Terada and Villena's approach under a more realistic noisy leakage model.

Before we get started, we would like to give a brief introduction to the two research topics mentioned in this paper, CRT-RSA and Multi-Prime RSA. CRT-RSA is a variation of the RSA algorithm whose core idea is to reduce computation by splitting the modulo power operation into several smaller modulo operations. Since each small modulo operation is independent, they can be computed simultaneously, taking full advantage of multi-core processors and improving efficiency. However, the CRT factors (d_p and d_q) added to the private key parameters to use CRT also increase the redundancy of the private key parameters, which is an important reason why the recovery algorithm can work. Multi-Prime RSA, on the other hand, reduces the number of modulo power operations by increasing the number of prime factors of modulo N, and has better efficiency than CRT-RSA with further acceleration of CRT, which is also the reason why we take it as the main research object.

To better understand the content of the algorithm, we would like to introduce the Multivariate Hensel's Lemma, which will be used in the expansion phase of the tree-based recovery algorithm.

Lemma 1 (Multivariate Hensel's Lemma). *A root* $r = (r_1, r_2, \cdots, r_n)$ *of the polynomial* $f(x_1, x_2, \cdots, x_n) \mod \pi^i$ *can be lifted to a root* $r + b \mod \pi^{i+1}$ *if* $b = (b_1\pi^i, b_2\pi^i, \cdots, b_n\pi^i)$, $0 \le b_j \le \pi - 1$ *is a solution to the equation*

$$f(r + b) \equiv f(r) + \sum_j b_j \pi^i f_{x_j}(r) \equiv 0 \ (\mod \pi^{i+1})$$

(Here, f_{x_j} is the partial derivative of f with respect to x_j).

2.1 Noisy Leakage Models

We formalize the noisy model discussed in this paper with ϵ and δ being real numbers satisfying $0 \le \epsilon < 1/2$, $0 \le \delta < 1$ and $0 \le \epsilon + \delta < 1$. The noisy sequence of private keys obtained by cold boot attacks has the following property: each bit in the sequence of private key bits is either erased with probability δ, errored with probability ϵ or kept constant with probability $1 - \delta - \epsilon$. We call this noisy model the Binary Erasure Symmetric Error (BESE) model. When $\epsilon = 0$ (but $\delta > 0$), this noisy model is called the Binary Erasure (BE) model. When $\delta = 0$ (but $\epsilon > 0$), this noisy model is called the Binary Symmetric Error (BSE) model.

Furthermore, we also consider the asymmetry error probabilities in our work, which we call the Binary Erasure Asymmetric Error (BEAE) model. In this noisy leakage model, each 0-bit (1-bit) in the original key is erased with probability δ, errored with probability α (β), or remains unchanged with probability $1 - \delta - \alpha - \beta$. With $\delta = 0$ ($\alpha \neq \beta$), this model is called the Binary Asymmetric Error (BAE) model. Although the error rate α or β is generally not zero, and more often $\beta \gg \alpha > 0$ [3], we consider the case $\alpha = 0$ (but $\beta \neq 0$) for the sake of completeness, which is also referred to as the Z-channel model with erasure.

The work of [16] is based on the BE model. The existing literature on CRT-RSA includes studies based on the BE model [5], the BSE model [4], the BAE model [11,17], and the BESE model [7,9]. In all these studies, the researchers used tree-based recovery algorithm to recover keys.

2.2 Recovering CRT-RSA Key Using Tree-Based Recovery Algorithm

Here we review the tree-based recovery algorithm for CRT-RSA. First we describe the key setting for CRT-RSA under the PKCS#1 standard. Under this standard, the public key $pk = \{N, e\}$, where N is the modulus and e is the encryption exponent. The private key $sk = \{p, q, d, d_p, d_q, q^{-1} \mod p\}$, where p and q are two prime factors of modulus N, d is the private key exponent, and d_p is d reduced modulo $p - 1$, similar for d_q, which we will refer to as the CRT factors. In particular, $q^{-1} \mod p$ is the inverse of q modulo p.

The private key in CRT-RSA satisfies the following relationships and equations:

$$N = p \cdot q$$
$$ed \equiv 1 \mod (p-1)(q-1)$$
$$ed_p \equiv 1 \mod (p-1)$$
$$ed_q \equiv 1 \mod (q-1)$$

To simplify the analysis, we introduce three integer variables k, k_p, k_q and express the above equation as:

$$N = p \cdot q$$
$$ed = k \cdot (p-1) \cdot (q-1) + 1$$
$$ed_p = k_p \cdot (p-1) + 1 \tag{1}$$
$$ed_q = k_q \cdot (q-1) + 1$$

In practice, e is often assumed to be $2^{16} + 1$, in which case the values of k, k_p, k_q are assumed to be known.

In the previous work, sk is used to denote the correct private key for CRT-RSA, $\overline{sk}$ denotes the private key observation under the noisy leakage model, and m denotes the number of private key elements involved. For example, if $sk = (p, q, d, d_p, d_q)$, then $m = 5$ and if $sk = (p, q)$, then $m = 2$.

The tree-based recovery algorithm is presented below as an example with $sk = (p, q, d, d_p, d_q)$. We denote by $\tau(X)$ the maximum exponent of an integer X such that $2^{\tau(X)} | X$. Denote by $x[i]$ the i-th bit of an n-bit binary sequence $x \in \{0, 1\}^n$, with the lowest bit being the 0-th bit. We define $slice(i)$ as follows:

$$slice(i) := (p[i], q[i], d[i + \tau(k)], d_p[i + \tau(k_p)], d_q[i + \tau(k_q)])$$

Suppose we have obtained the candidate partial solution $sk' = (p', q', d', d'_p, d'_q)$ by computing from $slice(0)$ to $slice(i - 1)$. For CRT-RSA, we perform Hensel lifting on Eq. (1) and propose the following identities:

$$p[i] + q[i] = (N - p'q')[i] \quad \mod 2 \tag{2}$$
$$d[i + \tau(k)] + p[i] + q[i] = (k(N + 1) + 1 - k(p' + q') - ed')[i + \tau(k)] \quad \mod 2 \tag{3}$$
$$d_p[i + \tau(k_p)] + p[i] = (k_p[p' - 1] + 1 - ed'_p)[i + \tau(k_p)] \quad \mod 2 \tag{4}$$
$$d_q[i + \tau(k_q)] + q[i] = (k_q[q' - 1] + 1 - ed'_q)[i + \tau(k_q)] \quad \mod 2 \tag{5}$$

We can easily see that $p[i]$, $q[i]$, $d[i + \tau(k)]$, $d_p[i + \tau(kp)]$, and $d_q[i + \tau(kq)]$ are not independent and the degree of freedom is 1 [6].

With the above background knowledge, we next introduce the four phases of the tree-based recovery algorithm.

Initialization Phase. Initialize the value of $slice(0)$. Since p, q are large prime numbers, we can easily obtain $slice(0) = (1, 1, d[\tau(k)], d_p[\tau(k_p)], d_q[\tau(k_q)])$.

Expansion Phase. Based on the information from $slice(0)$ to $slice(i - 1)$ that has been reconstructed in the partial candidate solutions, obtain the possible values of $slice(i)$ by Lemma 1 (Multivariate Hensel's Lemma) and combine them with Eq. (2–5). Incorporate the newly generated partial candidate solution into the candidate solution set.

Pruning Phase. Discard some of the candidate solutions that do not meet the requirements according to the score criteria.

Final Phase. Verify the final retained candidate solution by the public key (N, e), and the candidate solution satisfying $N = p'q'$ is the correct solution.

The work of [5] et al. has been done by designing scoring criteria and modifying the expansion and pruning phases so that the running time of the tree-based algorithm is polynomial in n when the correct solution is maximally preserved.

2.3 Terada-Villena Method [16]

This subsection focuses on how Terada and Villena apply the tree-based recovery algorithm to Multi-Prime RSA.

First, we briefly describe the public and private key structure of Multi-Prime RSA under the PKCS#1 v2.1 standard, which does not differ much from CRT-RSA in terms of key setting; their public keys are both composed of $\{N, e\}$. However, in Multi-Prime RSA, the private key $sk = \{d, r_1, r_2, d_1, d_2, r_2^{-1}, < r_3, d_3, t_3 >, \ldots, < r_u, d_u, t_u >\}$, where $\{r_1, r_2, \cdots, r_u\}$ is the u prime factor of modulo N of close length, d_i is the decryption exponent d modulo r_i, satisfying:

$$N = \prod_{i=1}^{u} r_i, \qquad e \cdot d \equiv 1 \mod \prod_{i=1}^{u}(r_i - 1)$$

and $\{d_1, d_2, r_2^{-1}, < d_3, t_3 >, \cdots, < d_u, t_u >\}$ are the CRT factors used to speed up decryption, satisfying:

$$r_2 \cdot r_2^{-1} \equiv 1 \mod r_1$$

$$t_j \cdot \prod_{i=1}^{j-1} r_i \equiv 1 \mod r_j, \ 3 \leq j \leq u$$

$$e \cdot d_i \equiv 1 \mod (r_i - 1), \ 1 \leq i \leq u.$$

Similarly, we introduce $k, k_1, k_2, \cdots, k_u$ and obtain

$$N = \prod_{i=1}^{u} r_i \tag{6}$$

$$e \cdot d = k \cdot \prod_{i=1}^{u}(r_i - 1) + 1 \tag{7}$$

$$e \cdot d_i = k_i \cdot (r_i - 1) + 1, \ 1 \leq i \leq u \tag{8}$$

Performing Hensel lifting on Eq. (6)–(8) we obtain

$$\left(N - \prod_{i=1}^{u} r_i'\right)[j] \equiv \sum_{i=1}^{u} r_i[j] \mod 2 \tag{9}$$

$$\left(ed' - 1 - k \prod_{i=1}^{u}(r_i' - 1)\right)[j + \tau(k)] \equiv d[j + \tau(k)] \mod 2 \tag{10}$$

$$(ed_i - 1 - k_i(r_i' - 1))[j + \tau(k_i)] \equiv r_i[j] + d_i[j + \tau(k_i)] \mod 2, \ 1 \leq i \leq u \tag{11}$$

Since Terada and Villena only use the prime factors in the private key, their work is based on Eq. (10). According to Eq. (10), we get one constraint and u unknowns with their degrees of freedom of $u - 1$ [6]. In the case where every bit in $slice(i)$ is unknown, each Hensel lift will produce 2^{u-1} candidate solutions.

In the complete key, the total number of candidate solutions is then given by $2^{(u-1)\times \frac{n}{u}}$.

Terada and Villena's work is based on the BE model, so their pruning condition is that any partial candidate solution containing bits inconsistent with the corresponding bits in $\overline{sk}$ is discarded. By analyzing the relationship between the erasure rate δ and the size of the candidate solution tree, Terada and Villena derive the bound for the tree recovery algorithm under this model in polynomial time with respect to n as

$$\delta \leq 2^{\frac{1}{u}} - 1.$$

2.4 Limitations and Solutions

The limitation of Terada and Villena's work is mainly in the fact that the noisy leakage model is too idealized. Their key recovery algorithm works well with the BE model, but cannot handle the case with error bit because any candidate solution that does not match a known bit in $\overline{sk}$ is discarded. How to keep the running time of the entire recovery algorithm within an acceptable range while retaining the correct solution is also a challenge we face.

To solve the above problem, we propose a pruning criterion and try to explain the basis of pruning and the theoretical bounds of the algorithm in terms of coding theory. We consider the process by which an adversary acquires a corrupted version of the RSA private key, $\overline{sk}$, after a cold boot attack as the process of converting the correct private key, sk, into $\overline{sk}$ after transmission over a noisy channel, and denote by $\mathbf{s}$ the codeword of the correct private key, sk, and $\mathbf{c}$ the codeword of the private key observation, $\overline{sk}$, acquired over a noisy channel. In coding theory, the conversion of $\mathbf{s}$ to $\mathbf{c}$ is determined by the type of noise in the channel, in [5,16] by the erasure rate δ, and in our leakage model by the erasure rate δ and the error rate (α, β). The model defines $\mathbf{Pr}(\mathbf{c}|\mathbf{s})$ over all possible pairs $(\mathbf{s}, \mathbf{c})$, the problem we face is how to decode $\mathbf{c}$ in and reproduce $\mathbf{s}$ with high probability.

3 Recovering Key from Binary Erasure Error Model

In this section, we present the algorithm for recovering Multi-Prime RSA keys from the Binary Erasure Error model. From Sect. 2.1, we know that the Binary Erasure Error model is divided into symmetric (BESE model) and asymmetric (BEAE model) cases. To simplify the analysis, we will first present the key recovery algorithm under the BESE model, then extend the algorithm to the BEAE model, and finally present the theoretical bounds of the two algorithms.

3.1 BESE Model

In our algorithm, we use the likelihood measure as a criterion for pruning. The higher the probability that a candidate solution is the correct solution, the higher the corresponding likelihood measure. Since the erasure bit $\mathbf{E}$ is skipped during the subsequence acquisition, the erasure rate is not reflected in the likelihood measure.

The most primitive way is to perform Hensel lifting on all n/u slices of the private key at once, and then take the candidate solution with the largest likelihood measure as our correct solution. Recall from Sect. 2.3 that at full size, the total number of candidate solutions obtained by Hensel lifting is given by $2^{(u-1)\times\frac{n}{u}}$. So, our goal is to find the maximum value of :

$$\arg \max_{0 \leq i < 2^{(u-1)\times\frac{n}{u}}} \mathbf{Pr}(\mathbf{s_i}|\mathbf{c}),$$

where $\mathbf{s_i} \in \mathbf{S}$, $\mathbf{S}$ represents the set of complete candidate solutions, and $\mathbf{s_i}$ is the i-th candidate solution.

However, note that it is almost impossible to reconstruct at the scale of $2^{(u-1)\times\frac{n}{u}}$, and indeed any cost over the power of n is unacceptable due to the scale of RSA. Therefore, our goal is to constrain the cost within a polynomial level of n.

Next, we will degrade the idea of finding the correct solution for the entire private key to finding the correct solution for some bits of the private key by slicing, so that the cost is bounded by a polynomial in the power of n. This is because the noise in the channel causes random interference to the private key, then the erroneous and erased bits will be uniformly distributed in the noisy private key sequence. Thus, we can decompose the process of finding the original (correct) value sk of a full-size private key noisy sequence $\overline{sk}$ into the process of finding the original solution subsequence corresponding to a noisy subsequence of length T. When we partition the subsequence, we will skip the erasure bits $\mathbf{E}$ to simplify the impact analysis caused by the error rate. Recall that in Sect. 2.2, the focus of our algorithm is on the expansion phase and the pruning phase.

Expansion Phase. For the private key noisy sequence $\overline{sk}$ there are $\frac{n}{u}$ slices and the total number of bits is $\frac{n}{u} \times u = n$. $\mathbf{E}$ represents erased bits in $\overline{sk}$. Let us take the example of $u = 3$ and $T = 5$ and assume the noisy sequence is:

$$\{r_1[0], r_2[0], r_3[0], r_1[1], E, r_3[1], r_1[2], r_2[2], E, E, r_2[3], r_3[3], r_1[4], \cdots, r_3[\frac{n}{u}]\}$$

So the subsequences are:

$$\{r_1[0], r_2[0], r_3[0], r_1[1], E, r_3[1]\}$$
$$\{r_1[2], r_2[2], E, E, r_2[3], r_3[3], r_1[4]\}$$
$$\cdots$$

To obtain the candidate solution subsequence corresponding to that in the noisy subsequence of the private key, we need to perform several Hensel liftings on the candidate solution $\mathbf{c}$. We denote by t_i the number of Hensel liftings to be performed, and Δ_i the number of candidate solutions of ut_i bits generated after t_i Hensel liftings, corresponding to the erased bits $\mathbf{E}$ in the noisy subsequence. We call the ut_i bits generated by candidate solution expansion nodes. Thus, we have $t_i = \lceil (T + \Delta_i)/u \rceil$ and this step will generate $2^{(u-1) \times t_i}$ candidate solution nodes. This implies that i in the original solution subsequence $\mathbf{s_i}$ is bounded by $0 \leq i < 2^{(u-1) \times t_i}$.

Pruning Phase. We use the likelihood measure as a function of the score for each candidate solution subsequence, keeping only the top L candidates with the highest score and discarding the rest. Finding the correct solution subsequence using the likelihood measure can be simply written as:

$$\arg \max_{0 \leq i < 2^{(u-1) \times t_i}} \mathbf{Pr(s_i | c)}$$

According to Bayes' theorem, we can rewrite it as:

$$\arg \max_{0 \leq i < 2^{(u-1) \times t_i}} \frac{\mathbf{Pr(s_i) Pr(c | s_i)}}{\mathbf{Pr(c)}}$$

For a given noisy private key subsequence $\mathbf{c}$, $\mathbf{Pr(c)}$ is a constant. More generally, we assume that $\mathbf{P(s_i)}$ is also a constant independent of i [11]. Therefore, we can express the likelihood measure as:

$$\arg \max_{0 \leq i < 2^{(u-1) \times t_i}} Pr(c | s_i) = \arg \max_{0 \leq i < 2^{(u-1) \times t_i}} \epsilon^{d_i} (1 - \epsilon)^{1 - d_i}$$

Here, d_i denotes the Hamming distance of the noisy sequence of T-bit bits from the corresponding position of the candidate solution, where the Hamming distance is computed by skipping the erasure bits. We use $\mathbf{G(s_i | c)}$ to denote the fraction of candidate solutions $\mathbf{s_i}$ when the noisy subsequence is known to be $\mathbf{c}$. Considering the simplicity of the calculation, we can express the fraction of candidate solutions in its logarithmic form as follows:

$$\mathbf{G(s_i | c)} := d_i \log \epsilon + (1 - d_i) \log(1 - \epsilon)$$

For a completed private key, the $\mathbf{s_i}$ with the largest log-likelihood measure is the original solution $\mathbf{s}$. Consider that the error probability is not 100% uniformly distributed among the subsequence of T bits, and that too tight a constraint will result in discarding the correct solution. Therefore, we keep the top L solutions with the largest log-likelihood measure and discard the other candidates. L is set to 1 for channels with only erasure noise [16].

Algorithm 1 is a formal representation of our algorithm.

Algorithm 1. Recovering Multi-Prime RSA Key

Input: noisy key sequence $\overline{sk}$, the number of prime factors u, parameters (T, L).

Output: A set of L most likely candidate sequences that represent the original private key.

Initialization Phase: Divide the private key noisy sequence into subsequences of length T, skipping the erasure bit **E**, and calculate t_i, which means that the number of slice need to be candidates for solution expansion for each subsequence, and initialize $slice(0)$ to $\{1, 1, \cdots, 1\}$.

Expansion Phase: For each slice, perform Hensel lifts on candidate solutions to generate a set of candidate nodes. The time of Hensel lifts is determined by $t_i = \lceil (T + \Delta_i)/u \rceil$, where Δ_i represents the number of erased bits in the candidate solution of size ut_i bits. This phase generates $2^{(u-1)t_i}$ candidate nodes for each slice.

Pruning Phase: Calculate the log-likelihood measure for each candidate sequence. Retain the top L candidate solutions based on their log-likelihood measure.

We repeat the expansion and pruning stages until the candidate solutions are elevated to $slice(n/u)$.

Finalization Phase: output the L candidate solutions.

3.2 BEAE Model

In this section, we further consider the case of the BEAE model. We repeat that no previous work on cold boot attacks has considered both erasure and asymmetric errors, whether CRT-RSA or Multi-Prime RSA. Considering this phenomenon not only allows our recovery algorithm to match the actual leakage model but also improves the tolerance for higher error rate.

Our main work is to reflect the inhomogeneity of the error probability in the likelihood measure by modifying the scoring function for the pruning phase. Specifically, higher weights are assigned to directions with higher error probabilities. The extension phase is consistent with that in the BESE model. Following the work of [11], we modified the score function as follows:

$$\mathbf{G}(\mathbf{s_i}|\mathbf{c}) = n_{00}^i \log(1 - \alpha) + n_{01}^i \log \alpha + n_{11}^i \log(1 - \beta) + n_{10}^i \log \beta$$

To recap, $\alpha := Pr(0 \to 1)$ and $\beta := Pr(1 \to 0)$ are the error probabilities. n_{00}^i represents the number of 0-bits in the T-bit subsequence of candidate solution $\mathbf{s_i}$ and the corresponding bit in the private key observation sequence $\mathbf{c}$ are both 0, for the i-th iteration. Similarly, n_{01}^i represents the number of 0-bits in $\mathbf{s_i}$ and 1-bits in $\mathbf{c}$, and vice versa for n_{10}^i.

When α (or β) is 0, we call this case a Z-channel model with erasure. In this case, solutions containing n_{01}^i (or n_{10}^i) candidate solutions can be discarded by replacing $n_{01}^i \log \alpha$ (or $n_{10}^i \log \beta$) in the score function with a penalty function, such as $-1000 n_{01}^i$ (or $-1000 n_{10}^i$).

3.3 Theoretical Bound

Before we begin, let us introduce a well-known fact about combinatorial numbers and Binary Entropy [2].

Lemma 2. *For any positive integer n and $w(\leq n)$, it holds that:*

$$\frac{1}{\sqrt{8w(1-w/n)}} \leq 2^{nH(w/n)} \leq \sum_{i=0}^{w} \binom{n}{i} \leq 2^{nH(w/n)} \tag{12}$$

For the simplicity of analysis, we first consider the case of symmetric error.

BESE Model. In the BESE model, the adversary observes a private key sequence $\overline{sk}$ of length $n(1-\delta)$ bits. Since we retain L candidate solutions during each iteration, if the correct solution exists, there are $L-1$ incorrect solutions within. We consider the impact on the operation of the algorithm caused by the incorrect solutions retained in the previous iteration and the incorrect solution expansion in the new iteration. We follow the assumptions made in the work of [5].

Assumption 1. *The bit slice corresponding to a wrong node consists of random bits.*

According to Assumption 1, if a candidate solution $\mathbf{s}$ satisfies the following criterion, we consider it to be consistent with the observed private key value $\overline{sk}$:

Criteria 1. *The Hamming distance between $\mathbf{s}$ and $\overline{sk}$ is less than $n\epsilon$.*

Therefore, the probability Pr that one candidate $\mathbf{s}$ is consistent with $\overline{sk}$ can be represented as:

$$Pr = \frac{\sum_{i=0}^{n\epsilon} \binom{n(1-\delta)}{i}}{2^{n(1-\delta)}} \tag{13}$$

From Lemma 2, we can obtain the upper bound of Eq. (12).

$$Pr \leq 2^{-n(1-\delta)(1-H(\epsilon/(1-\delta)))} \tag{14}$$

We define $C(\delta;\epsilon)$ as $C(\delta;\epsilon) := (1-\delta)(1-H(\epsilon/(1-\delta)))$, where $H(x)$ denotes the binary entropy function. Therefore, the probability that a candidate solution is consistent with the observed private key $\overline{sk}$ is at most $2^{-nC(\delta;\epsilon)}$. As discussed in Sect. 2.4, the total number of candidate solutions is given by $2^{(u-1) \times \frac{n}{u}}$, so the expected upper bound on the number of candidate solutions that are consistent with $\overline{sk}$ is $2^{n(1-1/u-C(\delta;\epsilon))}$.

If $C(\delta;\epsilon) < 1 - 1/u$, the running time of the algorithm is exponential in n, which is unacceptable as $n \to +\infty$. On the other hand, if $C(\delta;\epsilon) \geq 1 - 1/u$, the algorithm can recover the key in polynomial time of n. Therefore, the requirement for our algorithm to recover the key in polynomial time is:

$$(1-\delta)\left(1 - H\left(\frac{\epsilon}{(1-\delta)}\right)\right) \geq 1 - \frac{1}{u} \tag{15}$$

This bound is represented by Fig. 1(a). We analyze the rationality of our boundaries from the perspective of information theory.

Shannon's Noisy-Channel Coding Theorem. Given a noisy channel with channel capacity **C** and information transmitted at a rate **R**. If **C** > **R** there exists codes that allow the probability of error at the receiver to be made arbitrarily small. If **C** < **R**, an arbitrarily small probability of error is not achievable.

Where the left-hand side of the inequality $C(\delta; \epsilon)$ can be considered as the channel capacity of the BESE channel, and the right-hand side is the communication rate of this channel. Recall from Sect. 2.2 that if we know the $u - 1$ Multi-Prime RSA bits in one slice, then we can determine the unique correct solution for that slice. We can decode the noisy key with an arbitrarily small error probability to recover its original value. When $\delta = 0$, $C(0; \epsilon) = 1 - H(\epsilon)$ is the channel capacity of the BSE channel, which is also consistent with the information we know.

BEAE Model. Combining the above explanations, we can conclude that the condition for successfully decoding a noisy key is that the channel capacity of the noisy channel is greater than the communication rate. In Multi-Prime RSA, we define the communication rate R as $1 - \frac{1}{u}$. Therefore, to obtain the recoverable upper bound of the tree-based recovery algorithm, we need to find the channel capacity C that satisfies $C > R$.

However, there are no studies that illustrate the channel capacity of Binary Erasure Asymmetric Error noisy channels. Therefore, combining with the channel capacity of the Binary Asymmetric Error noisy channel in [7]: $C(\alpha, \beta) = H\left(\frac{1}{2} + \frac{\beta - \alpha}{2}\right) - \frac{H(\alpha)}{2} - \frac{H(\beta)}{2}$, we define the channel capacity of the Binary Erasure Asymmetric Error noisy channel as:

$$C(\delta; \alpha, \beta) := (1 - \delta)\left(H\left(\frac{1}{2} + \frac{\beta - \alpha}{2(1 - \delta)}\right) - \frac{H\left(\frac{\alpha}{1-\delta}\right)}{2} - \frac{H\left(\frac{\beta}{1-\delta}\right)}{2}\right)$$

There will be a demonstration of the reasonableness of BEAE channel capacity in terms of boundary checking.

When $\delta = 0$, $C(0; \alpha, \beta) = H\left(\frac{1}{2} + \frac{\beta - \alpha}{2}\right) - \frac{H(\alpha)}{2} - \frac{H(\beta)}{2} = C(\alpha, \beta)$. When $\alpha = \beta = \epsilon$, $C(\delta; \alpha, \beta) = C(\delta; \epsilon, \epsilon) = (1 - \delta)\left(1 - H\left(\frac{\epsilon}{1-\delta}\right)\right) = C(\delta; \epsilon)$. In particular, although α is a small but non-zero value in our leakage model, we still give the channel capacity when $\alpha = 0$ (in [11], called the Z-channel) and $\delta > 0$ by $C(\delta; 0, \beta) = (1 - \delta)\left(H\left(\frac{1}{2} + \frac{\beta}{2(1-\delta)}\right) - \frac{H\left(\frac{\beta}{1-\delta}\right)}{2}\right)$.

Therefore, the recoverable bound of the maximum likelihood function-based algorithm is $C(\delta; \epsilon) \geq 1 - 1/u$. That is:

$$(1 - \delta)\left(H\left(\frac{1}{2} + \frac{\beta - \alpha}{2(1 - \delta)}\right) - \frac{H\left(\frac{\alpha}{1-\delta}\right)}{2} - \frac{H\left(\frac{\beta}{1-\delta}\right)}{2}\right) \geq 1 - \frac{1}{u} \qquad (16)$$

This bound is represented by Fig. 1(b).

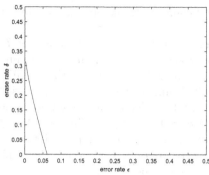
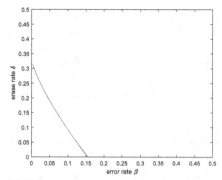

(a) When $u = 3$, the relationship between erasure rate δ and error rate ϵ with polynomial time theoretical bound.

(b) When $u = 3$, $\alpha = 0.001$, the relationship between erase rate δ and error rate β with polynomial time theoretical bound.

Fig. 1. Theoretical bounds of Binary Erasing Symmetric (Asymmetric) Error model

Application to CRT-RSA. Based on the previous law, we infer the theoretical recovery bound of the tree-based recovery algorithm for CRT-RSA under the BEAE channel as $C(\delta; \alpha, \beta) > 1/m$. In fact, we have also demonstrated this through experiments. By using a similar tree-based recovery algorithm as in this study and the Hensel lifting method in [5], we have selected the parameters as $(T = 20, L = 2^8)$ to prove this.

For a CRT-RSA private key with m parameters, each slice in a Hensel lifting needs only one known bit to recover the other bits. Thus, according to Shannon's Noisy-Channel Coding Theorem, correct decoding of noisy private keys can be achieved as long as 1 bit is correctly transmitted for every m bits transmitted, as shown in the work of [7] and [9].

4   Implementation and Performance

We implemented the algorithm in C++ using NTL version 11.5.1 and GMP version 6.2.0 and accelerated it using the OpenMP multithreaded library. Our tests were run in 64-bit mode on an Intel(R) Xeon(R) Gold 5220R processor running at 2.20 GHz. Unless otherwise stated below, our experiments were run 100 times, each time using a randomly generated 1024-bit Multi-Prime RSA key.

In our experiments, we always test the parameters (T, L) first and then select the best result for the experiment based on the test results.

Optimal Parameter Selection. Figure 2 represents the increase in runtime (the right vertical coordinates) and success rate (the left vertical coordinates) as the algorithm's running parameter L is relaxed (the parameter T is also fixed for control variables) with fixed noise, but they do not increase proportionally. Our goal is to find a threshold for the parameter L such that the cost of the increase in runtime does not outweigh the benefit in terms of success rate yet makes the success rate as high as possible.

From Fig. 2(a), we can see that for a fixed noisy $(\delta; \alpha, \beta)$ and parameter T, increasing L from 2^8 to 2^9 increased the success rate by 15%, and the running time doubled. However, increasing L from 2^9 to 2^{10} also doubled the running time, but the success rate only increased by 3%. Similarly, when L was increased to 2^{11}, the increase in success rate was only 1%. Therefore, we selected the optimal parameters $(T = 12, L = 2^9)$ when $\delta = 0$ and $u = 3$. Similarly, based on Fig. 2(b), we selected the optimal parameters $(T = 8, L = 2^8)$ when $\delta = 0.2$ and $u = 3$. Due to space constraints and to avoid redundancy, we use the same method for parameter selection in our subsequent experiments.

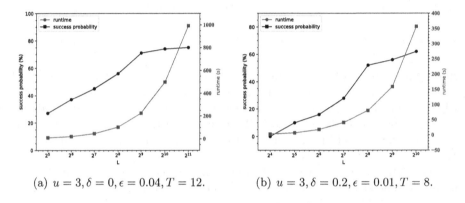

(a) $u = 3, \delta = 0, \epsilon = 0.04, T = 12$.   (b) $u = 3, \delta = 0.2, \epsilon = 0.01, T = 8$.

Fig. 2. Success probability and running time for different parameters at fixed $(\delta; \epsilon)$

Experimental Results. In our experiments, the erasure rate δ and the experimental parameters (T, L) are always fixed. In the symmetric error case, the error rate ϵ is gradually increased and our bounds are verified by observing the decreasing trend of the success rate. And in the asymmetric case, referring to [3] and [11], we fix the error rate α to 0.001 and then gradually increase the error β.

For the BESE model, Table 1 shows that when the erasure rate δ is 0.1, the success rate of the recovery algorithm is over 90% for $\epsilon < 0.15$. However, the success rate drops rapidly for $\epsilon > 0.02$ and converges to 0 at ϵ of 0.039, which corresponds to our theoretical bound.

Table 1. The trend of the success rate when $u = 3$, $\delta = 0.1$, $T = 12$, $L = 2^8$.

ϵ	0.015	0.02	0.025	0.03	0.035	0.036	0.037	0.038	0.039
success rate	90%	74%	41%	25%	11%	7%	4%	3%	3%
average time (seconds)	263	270	266	262	241	254	271	234	249

For the BEAE model, with α fixed at 0.001 according to the settings of [3] and [11], Table 2 reveals that for $\delta = 0$, the success rate is over 90% with $\beta < 0.1$, while for $\beta > 0.1$, success rate gradually decreases and converges to zero at approximately 0.155. In the case of a Z-channel with erasure, with $\delta = 0.1$ and $\alpha = 0$, Table 3 shows that the key recovery algorithm only allows for an error probability β of up to 0.099.

Table 2. The trend of the success rate when $u = 3$, $\alpha = 0.001$, $\delta = 0$, $T = 12$, $L = 2^8$.

β	0.06	0.07	0.08	0.09	0.1	0.11	0.12	0.13	0.14	0.15	0.154
success rate	100%	99%	96%	93%	92%	67%	65%	35%	27%	13%	5%
average time (seconds)	213	212	211	213	212	213	213	212	213	213	212

Table 3. The trend of the success rate when $u = 3$, $\alpha = 0$, $\delta = 0.1$, $T = 12$, $L = 2^9$.

β	0.05	0.055	0.06	0.065	0.07	0.075	0.08	0.085	0.09	0.095	0.100
success rate	75%	72%	71%	66%	50%	41%	32%	15%	13%	2%	0%
average time (seconds)	220	218	240	220	216	221	227	233	224	235	*

In addition to the $u = 3$ case, we have also carried out experimental verification for $u = 2$ and $u = 4$. For reasons of space, only the experimental results for $u = 4$ are given here. Table 4 indicates that when $\delta = 0$, the success rate converges to 0 at approximately $\epsilon = 0.041$. Likewise, Table 5 demonstrates that for $\delta = 0$ and $\alpha = 0.001$, the success rate converges to 0 as β approaches 0.101. These experimental data align with the theoretical results presented in Sect. 3.3.

The results show that for a given δ, the upper bound on the error rate of the recovery algorithm decreases with increasing u. However, the value of u is limited. When the modulus N is fixed length but u is large, the modulus N can be decomposed without additional information by algorithms known as the digital field sieve (NFS)[1] or elliptic curve method (ECM)[2].

---

[1] It is an algorithm to factor an integer N with a very good performance.
[2] It is an algorithm to compute a non-trivial factor of N.

Table 4. The trend of the success rate when $u = 4$, $\delta = 0$, $T = 12$, $L = 2^8$. The theoretical bound for ϵ is 0.041

ϵ	0.005	0.01	0.015	0.017	0.02	0.025	0.03	0.035	0.04	0.041
success rate	100%	100%	96%	94%	80%	58%	31%	20%	6%	2%
average time (seconds)	274	272	272	274	275	275	274	271	267	275

Table 5. The trend of the success rate when $u = 4$, $\delta = 0$, $\alpha = 0.001$, $T = 12$, $L = 2^8$. The theoretical bound for β is 0.101.

β	0.01	0.02	0.03	0.04	0.05	0.06	0.07	0.08	0.09	0.1	0.101
success rate	100%	100%	99%	97%	90%	80%	69%	43%	20%	17%	5%
average time (seconds)	273	273	273	273	272	269	269	262	259	258	257

5   Conclusion

This paper has examined the Multi-Prime RSA key recovery algorithm in the noisy leakage model, specifically in the Binary Erasure Symmetric Error model, and has extended this to the more realistic Binary Erasure Asymmetric Error model. Experimental results demonstrate the feasibility of the algorithm and establish theoretical bounds from an information theoretic perspective.

Our analysis reveals that the security of RSA under cold boot attacks improves to some extent with an increase in the number of prime factors of modulus N. The results of our experiments indicate that at $\delta = 0, \alpha = 0.001$, the erasure rate β tolerated by the tree-based recovery algorithm decreases from 0.289 to 0.155 if we increase u from 2 to 3.

To summarize, our investigation has added to the comprehension of the security of Multi-Prime RSA in a practical noisy leakage model when facing cold boot attacks. Moreover, it supplies significant data that can benefit practitioners in strengthening their encryption schemes. Further investigations could delve into the security of different variants of RSA under the cold boot attacks leakage model.

Acknowledgements. This work is supported in part by National Key R&D Program of China (No. 2022YFB3103800), National Natural Science Foundation of China (No. U1936209, No. 62002353, No. 62202231 and No. 62202230), China Postdoctoral Science Foundation (No. 2021M701726), Jiangsu Funding Program for Excellent Postdoctoral Talent (No. 2022ZB270) and Yunnan Provincial Major Science and Technology Special Plan Projects (No. 202103AA080015).

References

1. Boneh, D., Shacham, H.: Fast variants of RSA. CryptoBytes **5**(1), 1–9 (2002)
2. Cover, T.M., Thomas, J.A.: Elements of Information Theory, 2nd edn. Wiley, Hoboken (2006)

3. Halderman, J.A., Schoen, S.D., Heninger, N., et al.: Lest we remember: cold-boot attacks on encryption keys. Commun. ACM **52**(5), 91–98 (2009)
4. Henecka, W., May, A., Meurer, A.: Correcting errors in RSA private keys. In: Rabin, T. (ed.) CRYPTO 2010. LNCS, vol. 6223, pp. 351–369. Springer, Heidelberg (2010). https://doi.org/10.1007/978-3-642-14623-7_19
5. Heninger, N., Shacham, H.: Reconstructing RSA private keys from random key bits. In: Halevi, S. (ed.) CRYPTO 2009. LNCS, vol. 5677, pp. 1–17. Springer, Heidelberg (2009). https://doi.org/10.1007/978-3-642-03356-8_1
6. Kogure, J., Kunihiro, N., Yamamoto, H.: Generalized security analysis of the random key bits leakage attack. In: Jung, S., Yung, M. (eds.) WISA 2011. LNCS, vol. 7115, pp. 13–27. Springer, Heidelberg (2012). https://doi.org/10.1007/978-3-642-27890-7_2
7. Kunihiro, N.: An improved attack for recovering noisy RSA secret keys and its countermeasure. In: Au, M.-H., Miyaji, A. (eds.) ProvSec 2015. LNCS, vol. 9451, pp. 61–81. Springer, Cham (2015). https://doi.org/10.1007/978-3-319-26059-4_4
8. Kunihiro, N., Honda, J.: RSA meets DPA: recovering RSA secret keys from noisy analog data. In: Batina, L., Robshaw, M. (eds.) CHES 2014. LNCS, vol. 8731, pp. 261–278. Springer, Heidelberg (2014). https://doi.org/10.1007/978-3-662-44709-3_15
9. Kunihiro, N., Shinohara, N., Izu, T.: Recovering RSA secret keys from noisy key bits with erasures and errors. In: Kurosawa, K., Hanaoka, G. (eds.) PKC 2013. LNCS, vol. 7778, pp. 180–197. Springer, Heidelberg (2013). https://doi.org/10.1007/978-3-642-36362-7_12
10. Kunihiro, N., Takahashi, Y.: Improved key recovery algorithms from noisy RSA secret keys with analog noise. In: Handschuh, H. (ed.) CT-RSA 2017. LNCS, vol. 10159, pp. 328–343. Springer, Cham (2017). https://doi.org/10.1007/978-3-319-52153-4_19
11. Paterson, K.G., Polychroniadou, A., Sibborn, D.L.: A coding-theoretic approach to recovering noisy RSA keys. In: Wang, X., Sako, K. (eds.) ASIACRYPT 2012. LNCS, vol. 7658, pp. 386–403. Springer, Heidelberg (2012). https://doi.org/10.1007/978-3-642-34961-4_24
12. Quisquater, J.J., Couvreur, C.: Fast decipherment algorithm for RSA public-key cryptosystem. Electron. Lett. **21**(18), 905–907 (1982)
13. Rivest, R.L., Shamir, A., Adleman, L.: A method for obtaining digital signatures and public-key cryptosystems. Commun. ACM **21**, 120–126 (1978)
14. Shi, G., Wang, G., Gu, D.: Further cryptanalysis of a type of RSA variants. In: Susilo, W., Chen, X., Guo, F., Zhang, Y., Intan, R. (eds.) ISC 2022. LNCS, vol. 13640, pp. 133–152. Springer, Cham (2022). https://doi.org/10.1007/978-3-031-22390-7_9
15. Takayasu, A., Kunihiro, N.: General bounds for small inverse problems and its applications to multi-prime RSA. In: Lee, J., Kim, J. (eds.) ICISC 2014. LNCS, vol. 8949, pp. 3–17. Springer, Cham (2015). https://doi.org/10.1007/978-3-319-15943-0_1
16. Terada, R., Villena, R.C.: Factoring a multiprime modulus N with random bits. In: Desmedt, Y. (ed.) ISC 2013. LNCS, vol. 7807, pp. 185–196. Springer, Cham (2015). https://doi.org/10.1007/978-3-319-27659-5_13
17. Wang, T., Cui, X., Ni, Y., et al.: A practical cold boot attack on RSA private keys. In: AsianHOST 2017, pp. 55–60. IEEE (2017). https://doi.org/10.1109/AsianHOST.2017.8353995

Performance Impact Analysis of Homomorphic Encryption: A Case Study Using Linear Regression as an Example

Thomas Prantl[1(✉)], Simon Engel[1], Lukas Horn[1], Dennis Kaiser[1],
Lukas Ifländer[1], André Bauer[1], Christian Krupitzer[2], and Samuel Kounev[1]

[1] University of Würzburg, Würzburg, Germany
{thomas.prantl,simon.engel,lukas.horn,dennis.kaiser,
lukas.ifflander,andre.bauer,samuel.kounev}@uni-wuerzburg.de
[2] University of Hohenheim, Würzburg, Germany
christian.krupitzer@uni-hohenheim.de

Abstract. In recent years, the trend has increasingly been to store and process data in the cloud. However, this is based on the premise that cloud providers treat the data in a trustworthy manner. One way of using the data in the cloud without the provider having access to it is homomorphic encryption. However, since this encryption has only recently become practicable, analysis of its for practical applications is still in its infancy. Therefore, we investigate the performance of homomorphic encryption using a real-world application, namely linear regression. Our main finding is that although the homomorphic computation of linear regression is in the range of minutes and thus slower than in the non-homomorphic case, linear regression can be computed homomorphic and is therefore suitable for use cases where data security is the top priority.

Keywords: Homomorphic Encryption · Performance Analysis

1 Introduction

In our digital world, the collection and processing of data is of paramount importance to businesses. To provide a flexible and scalable infrastructure for the data, the trend is to utilize cloud computing. In fact, Marc Hurd (former co-CEO of Oracle Corporation) estimates that 80% of enterprise data centers will be moving to the cloud by 2025 [17]. However, to use the cloud and its benefits, the data must be given to a third party that must be trusted. After all, there are many fraud scenarios. For instance, the cloud provider could be active in the same area as the user and use the uploaded data himself. To mitigate these risks, one solution could be to use homomorphic encryption. This encryption allows data to be stored and processed in a public cloud while the provider does not have access to it. Technically, due to the homomorphic encryption, the user can then

W. Meng et al. (Eds.): ISPEC 2023, LNCS 14341, pp. 284–298, 2023.
https://doi.org/10.1007/978-981-99-7032-2_17

run databases or microservices in the cloud as well as train machine learning models and store the data in the cloud without any concerns. Although the idea of homomorphic encryption was introduced in 1978 [16] and the first implementation of this method [4] was presented in 2009, homomorphic encryption has only recently been made available to developers in the form of corresponding libraries. As a result, the performance analysis of homomorphic encryption for everyday uses cases is still in its infancy. Consequently, the goal of this paper is to investigate the performance of this encryption in practice, using linear regression as an example. In summary, our evaluation shows that although the use of homomorphic encryption slows down the computation of linear regression, the computations are still possible in an acceptable time and that homomorphic encryption is thus a way to realise data protection. The remainder of this paper is organized as follows: In Sect. 2, we introduce the concept of homomorphic encryption and linear regression. In Sect. 3, we explain the architectures utilized to assess the performance. Next, we investigate the performance in Sect. 4. Section 5 discusses related work. Finally, Sect. 6 concludes the paper.

2   Background

This section introduces the basic terms and concepts of homomorphic encryption, linear regression, and gradient descent.

2.1   Homomorphic Encryption

For the definition of a homomorphic cryptosystem, we first define the term cryptosystem. For this, however, we first need to define the terms plaintext and ciphertext. We call all things that can be encrypted plaintext. The encryption of a plaintext is called a ciphertext. Based on these terms we can define what a cryptosystem is according to [11].

Definition 1. *A cryptosystem is defined as a tuple* $(\Sigma, \mathcal{G}, \mathcal{E}, \mathcal{D})$ *with the following properties:*

- *Σ is a finite, non-empty set. It is called the "alphabet". The following three sets are subsets of Σ: $\mathcal{P}$ is the "plaintext space", $\mathcal{K}$ is the "key space", $\mathcal{C}$ is the "ciphertext space"*
- *$\mathcal{G}$ is a probabilistic algorithm that outputs a keypair (pk, sk) chosen according to some distribution*
- *$\mathcal{E}$ takes as input a key k and a plaintext message m and encrypts it to a ciphertext c*
- *$\mathcal{D}$ takes as input a key k and a ciphertext c and outputs the plaintext m*

Additionally, a cryptosystem must satisfy the following condition, otherwise it is not guaranteed that a ciphertext can be brought back to it's original form, which would make the cryptosystem quite useless:

$$\forall m \in \mathcal{P} : \forall (pk, sk) \in \mathcal{K} : \mathcal{D}(sk, \mathcal{E}(pk, m)) = m$$

In the following, we denote the key as a pair (pk, sk) where pk is the key for encryption and sk the one for decryption. Now that we have introduced the notion of cryptosystem in general, we extend it with respect to homomorphism. Homomorphic encryption aims to do operations like addition, multiplication, exponentiation, etc. on encrypted data. Therefore, we extend the Definition 1 to fulfill these requirements.

Definition 2. *A homomorphic cryptosystem is defined as a tuple* $(\Sigma, \mathcal{G}, \mathcal{E}, \mathcal{D}, \mathcal{F}, Evaluate)$ *with the following properties [5]:*

- $(\Sigma, \mathcal{G}, \mathcal{E}, \mathcal{D})$ *is a cryptosystem*
- $\mathcal{F}$ *is a set of functions which can be calculated by the cryptosystem*
- *Evaluate is an algorithm that given a key* k, *a function* $f \in \mathcal{F}$ *and a ciphertext* c *calculates a new ciphertext* c' *of the same length*

The last condition is necessary because otherwise it would be possible to just write the desired calculation at the end of the ciphertext and execute it when it is decrypted. We now extend this definition to a fully homomorphic cryptosystem.

Definition 3. *Let* $\mathcal{H} = (\Sigma, \mathcal{G}, \mathcal{E}, \mathcal{D}, \mathcal{F}, Evaluate)$ *be a homomorphic cryptosystem. It is called "fully homomorphic" if* $\mathcal{F}$ *contains all possible functions.*

2.2 Linear Regression with Gradient Descent

We define the linear regression problem according to [13]. The linear regression problem can be simplified described as follows: Based on a set of variables $x_1, \ldots, x_n$ we try to determine the target variable y. In doing so, we assume that we can weight these variables differently and add them up. We also assume that there is a linear relationship between the target and the influencing variables and we also have a corresponding dataset, which depicts concrete influencing variables on the target variable. The problem to be solved now is how to determine the different weights of the influencing variables so that the target variable can be calculated as accurately as possible. More formally defined, we have an influence vector $X = \{x_1, \ldots, x_n\}^T$, a weight vector $\Theta = \{\Theta_1, \ldots, \Theta_n\}^T$ and a target variable y and have to choose Θ in such a way that the scalar product of Θ and X gives y, as shown in Eq. 1a.

$$y = f(X) = \sum_{i=0}^{n} \theta_i x_i \quad \text{(1a)} \qquad J(\Theta) = \frac{1}{2} \sum_{i=0}^{n} (\theta_i x_i - y_i)^2 \quad \text{(1b)}$$

One method to determine Θ is the gradient descent method [13], which requires the existence of a derivable error function, also called cost function. For this purpose, we use the function in Eq. 1b analogous to [13]. The procedure of the gradient descent method can be summarized as follows: An initial random assignment is chosen for Θ. Then, the target variable is predicted for each data point of the dataset and Θ is updated based on the deviation. The update of a concrete $\Theta_j \in \Theta$ is thereby done by according to Eq. 2. Using our cost function

Eq. 2 can be simplified to Eq. 3. In practice, the dataset is not only iterated once but several times to update Θ. In the following, we also refer to an iteration as a learning epoch.

$$\Theta_j := \Theta_j - \alpha \frac{\partial}{\partial \Theta_j} J(\Theta) \tag{2}$$

$$\frac{\partial}{\partial \Theta_j} J(\Theta) = \Theta_j - (\theta_j * x_j - y_j) * x_j \tag{3}$$

3 Evaluation Architectures for Homomorphic Linear Regression

In this section we present our evaluation environment. In doing so, we consider two different architectures. As a metric, we consider the time required for the respective calculations. Since exactly the same result parameters were always calculated for the linear regression in the non-homomorphic and the homomorphic case, we do not go into more detail about the accuracy of both methods.

3.1 Offline Client Architecture

The functionality of the offline architecture is illustrated in Fig. 1a and shows the two parties involved, the client and the server. The client wants the linear regression to be calculated on its dataset, but does not want to perform these calculations itself. Instead, the client wants the server to perform these calculations for it. However, the client wants the server to perform the calculations, but not to see the dataset or know the results of the calculations. For this reason the client encrypts its data homomorph and sends it to the server. The server can perform the required calculations on the homomorphic encrypted data and send the result back to the client. The client then only has to decrypt the result.

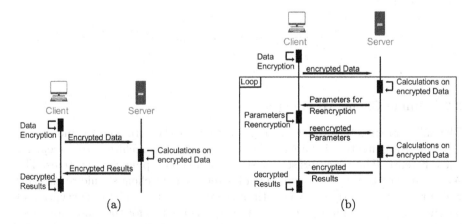

Fig. 1. Illustration of the (a) offline and (b) online architecture.

As metrics for the offline architecture, we use the time $\bar{t}_{prep}$ it takes to encrypt the dataset homomorphic, the time $\bar{t}_{c_e}$ it takes to calculate the linear regression, and the time $\bar{t}_d$ it takes to decrypt the results. We calculate $\bar{t}_{prep}$, $\bar{t}_{c_e}$, and $\bar{t}_d$ respectively by encrypting the original dataset n times in a row, or performing the homomorphic linear regression calculation n times in a row, or decrypting the results n times in a row and averaging over the required times. As an example of these calculations, Eq. 4 gives the calculation of $\bar{t}_{prep}$, where $t_p^{i,1}$ represents the time at which the initial dataset was encrypted for the ith time and $t_p^{i,0}$ represents the time at which the ith encryption process of the initial dataset began. As a measure of accuracy, we use the standard deviation in each case, which is given for $\bar{t}_p$ in Eq. 5 as an example.

$$\bar{t}_{prep} = \frac{1}{n} \sum_{i=0}^{n} t_p^{i,1} - t_p^{i,0} \tag{4}$$

$$\sigma_{prep} = \sqrt{\frac{1}{n-1} * \sum_{i=0}^{n} (t_p^{i,1} - t_p^{i,0} - \bar{t}_{prep})^2} \tag{5}$$

To evaluate the performance impact of homomorphic encryption we consider (1) how do the client computation times behave in the homomorphic case relative to the non-homomorphic case, see Eq. 6a and (2) how does the sum of the computation times of the server and client behave in aggregate in the homomorphic case relative to the non-homomorphic case, see Eq. 6b. The first case indicates the factor by which the client must wait longer for the results of the linear regression if the client homomorphic outsources the calculations to the server than if the client calculates the linear regression itself. The second case describes the factor by which the total calculation times for the client and server increase if the client homomorphic outsources the calculation of the linear regression to the server instead of calculating it itself. In the Eqs. 6a and 6b $\bar{t}_{nh}$ stands for the average time the client would need to compute the linear regression on the unencrypted dataset.

$$O_{Client} = \frac{\bar{t}_{prep} + \bar{t}_d}{\bar{t}_{nh}} \tag{6a} \qquad O_{Total} = \frac{\bar{t}_{prep} + \bar{t}_d + \bar{t}_{c_e}}{\bar{t}_{nh}} \tag{6b}$$

3.2   Online Client Architecture

The online architecture, shown in Fig. 1b, includes the actors client and server. The online architecture is largely identical to the offline architecture, except for one difference. The client assists the server in homomorphic computations. The server can send the client encrypted parameters that the client should re-encrypt, which resets the multiplicative depth of these parameters. The re-encryption of parameters can take place as often as needed. As metrics for the online architecture, we use $\bar{t}_{prep}$, $\bar{t}_{c_e}$, and $\bar{t}_d$ and augment them with the time $\bar{t}_{re}$ required by the client to re-encrypt homomorphic encrypted parameters. The computation of $\bar{t}_{re}$ and its accuracy measure is analogous to the Eqs. 4 and 5. We determine the impact of applying Homomorphic encryption in the case of the online architecture in Eqs. 7a and 7b largely analogous to the corresponding Eqs. 6a and 6b of the offline architecture. The only difference is that $\bar{t}_{re}$ is added to the numerator in each case.

$$O_{Client} = \frac{\bar{t}_{prep} + \bar{t}_d + \bar{t}_{re}}{\bar{t}_{Client}} \quad (7a) \quad O_{Total} = \frac{\bar{t}_{prep} + \bar{t}_d + t_{c_e} + \bar{t}_{re}}{\bar{t}_{Client}} \quad (7b)$$

4 Evaluation

In this section, we present our measurement set up and results.

4.1 Measurement Set up

For the sake of simplicity, we have realized the client and the server on the same hardware. All the measurements for our two architectures were carried out on our HPE ProLiant DL360 Gen9 server. This server has 8 CPU cores with 2.6 GHz each and 32 GB RAM. We used Ubuntu 20.04 LTS as the operating system. For the implementation of the underlying homomorphic cryptosystem, we used the open source library PALISADE [14]. Since PALISADE only provides the operations addition and multiplication, we had to implement the linear regression ourselves using the gradient descent method. As a dataset on which we want to calculate the linear regression we have used the dataset of the Kaggle competition, in which the value of a house is to be learned [9].

4.2 Offline Architecture Evaluation

For the evaluation of our offline architecture, we first look at the times needed to encrypt datasets of different sizes, followed by the time needed to decrypt the results. Then we analyze the computation times of the server as well as the overhead of the client and the total overhead.

Dataset Encryption. Figure 2a shows that the time needed to encrypt a dataset increases with the size of the dataset, as expected, but also with the number of the trained epochs, which is unexpected at first glance. The reason for this is that we encrypt the data with the minimum level of multiplicative depth required for the respective number of epochs. The multiplicative depth indicates how many multiplications are allowed in each case. When allowing more multiplications, more complex data must be encrypted, which leads to longer encryption times. Additionally, it is noticeable in Fig. 2a that encryption

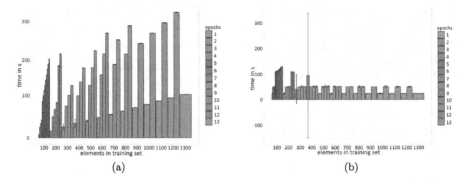

Fig. 2. Times required to (a) encrypt datasets and (b) decrypt results in case of the offline architecture. We used the standard deviation as a measure of accuracy. We have also only given the encryption times of the combinations of number of elements and epochs for which we were able to encrypt the dataset and perform the homomorphic calculations with the given RAM.

times are not given for every combination of dataset size and number of epochs. This is because we have only given the times for the combinations for which we were able to both encrypt the data and perform the subsequent homomorphic calculation of the linear regression with the RAM available on the server. Thus, with a dataset size of 100 elements we were still able to calculate all planned 13 epochs, for 200 elements only 6 epochs, for 300 elements only 4 epochs, for 700 elements only 3 epochs, for 900 elements only 2 epochs and for 1300 elements only one epoch. In summary, we draw the following conclusions for the encryption of the dataset: (1) the encryption times depend not only on the dataset size but also on the complexity of the performed operations (here: the required multiplicative depth), (2) homomorphic encryption has large demands for RAM, which is why the linear regression could not be calculated homomorphic for many combinations, and (3) for the feasible combinations, less than 4 min were required for the encryption in each case. The 4 min alone for preparing the encrypted data before the actual linear regression calculations can begin may seem like a lot at first glance, however, it is important to remember that the encrypted data can also be used for other evaluation and thus represent only a one-time cost.

Results Decryption. The times for decrypting the results also depend on the multiplicative depth, but are independent of the dataset size, which can be seen in Fig. 2b, in which we have again analogously only given the times for the feasible combinations. The independence of the dataset size is due to the fact that the number of result parameters for linear regression is constant. Analogously to the times for encrypting the dataset in Fig. 2a, the times for decrypting the result parameters increase with the number of learning epochs. This is again due to the fact that more complex calculations are required for more learning epochs, which is why the data must be encrypted in a more complex manner to allow a greater multiplicative depth, resulting in longer decryption times. However, since the required decryption times are always less than 200 ms, apart from two outliers, the decryption times are negligible in our opinion.

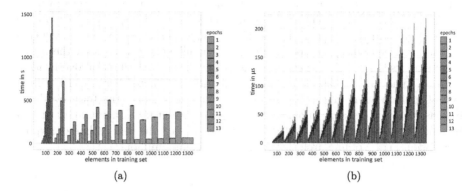

(a)   (b)

Fig. 3. Calculation times of the server for linear regression in (a) case of the offline architecture and (b) the non-homomorphic case. The standard deviation in the form of error bars was given as a measure of accuracy

Homomorphic Calculations. The times required by the server in the case of the offline architecture for calculating the linear regression homomorphic using the gradient descent method can be seen for different dataset sizes in Fig. 3a. In this figure, it is again noticeable that we could not execute the same number of epochs for all dataset sizes with the given RAM of the server. In order to be able to classify the required calculation times in the case of the online architecture, the respective calculation times for the non-homomorphic case are illustrated in Fig. 3b. What is immediately apparent from the Fig. 3a and 3b are the following two observations: (1) in the non-homomorphic case, the server's RAM was sufficient to train 13 epochs each for all dataset sizes and (2) in the non-homomorphic case, always less than 225 μs are required, while in the homomorphic case, the smallest dataset for 13 epochs already requires over 1250 s. Thus, the homomorphic calculation of linear regression using the offline architecture are significantly slower than the non-homomorphic calculation.

Time Overhead. In order to better quantify the overhead already observed, which the homomorphic calculation of the linear regression entails, we additionally consider O_{Client} and O_{Total} in the Figs. 4a and 4b. To do this, we first consider Fig. 4a, in which the overhead O_{Client} of the client in the case of the offline architecture is shown depending on the dataset size and performed learning epochs. To reiterate, the overhead O_{Client} defined in Sect. 2 can be simplified seen as the factor by which the client's computational time is higher due to the use of homomorphic encryption and the corresponding architecture than if the client had computed the linear regression itself non-homomorphic. The time overhead for the client is in all cases at least a factor of more than 4 million but at most a factor of 14 million. The overhead of the client increases the larger the dataset or the number of learning epochs.

The total overhead O_{Total} generated by the use of homomorphic encryption for the client and server is illustrated in Fig. 4b. To recap, the overhead O_{Total} defined in Sect. 2 can be simplified as the factor by which the computation time of the client and the server is higher due to the use of homomorphic encryption and the corresponding architecture than if the client had computed the linear regression itself non-homomorphic. This graph shows that the total overhead in terms of time for the cases considered amounts to a factor between 10 million and 80 million. Similar to the overhead of the client alone, the total overhead increases with increasing number of epochs or dataset size. In summary, it can be said that the overhead in terms of time due to the use of homomorphic encryption in the offline architecture is well over one million.

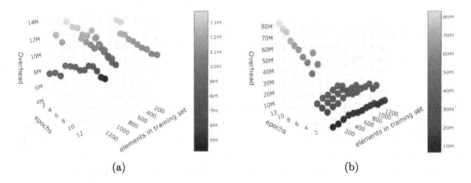

(a)   (b)

Fig. 4. The total time overhead of (a) the client and (b) the client and server in the case of the offline architecture. Again we have also only given the overhead times for those combinations of number of elements and epochs for which we were able to perform the homomorphic calculations with the given RAM

4.3   Online Architecture Evaluation

For the evaluation of our online architecture, we proceed analogously to the evaluation of our offline architecture and start again with the encryption and decryption times. Afterwards, we compare the times for computation before analyzing the introduced overhead.

Dataset Encryption and Results Decryption. Figure 5a and 5b show the encryption and decryption times. Compared to the offline architecture, the encryption times only depend on the size of the dataset and increase linearly with the dataset size. This is because by re-encrypting the data we can reset the multiplicative depth and thus only need the multiplicative depth required for one epoch. This means that we never need more than 2 min to encrypt with the online architecture, whereas we sometimes need almost twice that time with the offline architecture. It is also noticeable that with the online architecture we were able to execute the planned 13 epochs for each dataset size. With less than 2 min, the time required for encryption is also negligible in our opinion, since the encrypted data can also be used for further evaluations. The time needed to decrypt the results is illustrated in Fig. 5b. Analogous to the offline architecture, the decoding times of the results are independent of the dataset size. However, in the case of the online architecture, they are also independent of the number of learning epochs. This is because the multiplicative depth is now independent of the number of learning epochs and we can therefore use the same depth in each case. Since the result decoding times, also within the scope of the error, are below 40 ms in each case, these are again negligible in our opinion in contrast to the required time for the encryption of the dataset.

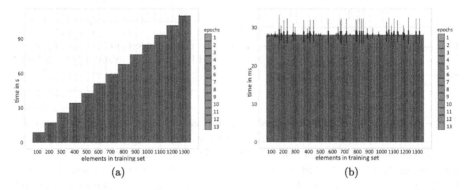

Fig. 5. Times required to (a) encrypt datasets and (b) decrypt the result of the linear regression in case of the online architecture. We used the standard deviation as a measure of accuracy, but it is mostly too small to be visible.

Homomorphic Calculations. Analogous to the evaluation of the offline architecture, we next look at the required calculation times of the server in Fig. 6a. What is striking in comparison to the calculation times of the server in the case of the offline architecture in Fig. 3a is that we were able to train the 13 epochs for all dataset sizes in the case of the online architecture. In addition, the calculation times in the case of the online architecture are significantly shorter than the corresponding times in the offline architecture, but are still significantly greater than the times required in the non-homomorphic case, see Fig. 3b. This means that the online architecture already provides the server with a performance boost in terms of time in contrast to the offline architecture. However, this boost is only achieved because the client is now ready to re-encrypt intermediate results. This results in additional computation time for the client compared to the offline architecture. If we look at Fig. 6b, we can see that this additional effort also increases with the size of the dataset and the number of learning epochs, but we can also see, that this effort has always remained below 1.5 s in total. Thus, in our opinion, this additional effort for the client is negligible, as the 1.5 s is only the cumulative time required, and the client is significantly less burdened for a single re-encryption and is thus still available for other tasks.

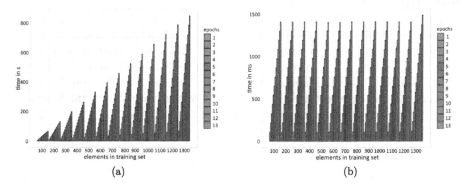

Fig. 6. Calculation times of (a) the server for the linear regression and (b) the client for the re-encryption in the case of the online architecture. The standard deviation is again mostly too small to be visible.

Time Overhead. Finally, we look at how the overhead of the client and the total overhead behave in the case of the online architecture. To do this, we first look at the overhead of the client in Fig. 7a. From this Figure it can be seen that the relationship from the offline architecture, namely that the overhead increases for the client with increasing learning epochs or elements in the data set, does not apply to the online architecture. In the case of online architecture, the overhead for the client decreases as the number of learning epochs increases. Compared to the offline architecture the actual overhead for the client is also lower in each case, even if it is still in the tens of millions. If we look at the total time overhead for the server and client in Fig. 7b, we can draw the same conclusions for the total overhead as for the client overhead. In summary, the online architecture generates less overhead than the offline architecture in that the client not only encrypts the initial dataset and decrypts the results, but also assists the server with the calculations. However, even with the online architecture, the overhead in terms of time is factors of over one million. The greatest advantage of the online architecture is therefore that it allows up to 13 learning epochs to be calculated for larger datasets. More than 13 epochs would have been theoretically possible, but for time reasons we have limited ourselves to a maximum of 13 epochs.

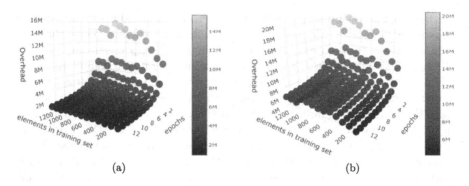

(a)   (b)

Fig. 7. The time overhead of the (a) client and (b) the client and server in the case of the online architecture for the homomorphic calculation of the linear regression.

4.4 Discussion

Our results show that the encryption is feasible in a reasonable amount of time. However, the required time depends not only on the dataset size, but also the operation type. The decryption process requires a negligible amount of time. Furthermore, the computation of the linear regression is significantly slower than the non-homomorphic calculation. In the following, we discuss these findings.

Homomorphic encryption, besides making linear regression slower, is a possibility how to realize data protection. For example, it is extremely difficult to use machine learning in the cloud for research with medical data, because one first need an ethics council and have to comply with all the regulations due to the sensitivity of the data. By means of homomorphic encryption one could share such encrypted data and could also organize, e.g., AI competitions as it is often usual in the AI world. Remarkably, the development of homomorphic libraries is at its beginning. There are already first approaches to adapt homomorphic encryption on GPUs, where already speed ups of the factor 1000 are possible [7]. Optimizing the libraries even further and run on GPU rather than CPU then there is still room for improvements. One possible improvement could be bootstrapping, i.e. that one resets the multiplicative depth of an encrypted vector directly and does not have to decrypt and re-encrypt the vector for this. We have seen that it does not matter how many elements a vector consists of. Thus homomorphic encryption is well suited for applications with parallel computations. Therefore, it would make sense to try homomorphic encryption on neural networks, e.g., by starting with feed forward networks, where one could represent the transition from one layer to the next as a single vector multiplication.

4.5 Threats to Validity

Regarding possible threats to the validity of our statements, we encountered the following points. First, the calculation of overhead depends on the hardware used. For example, in our example, the total time overhead O_{total} could be reduced by using more powerful hardware for the server, which would allow the server to compute the homomorphic linear regression calculations faster. Thus, the term $\bar{t}_{c_e}$ in the Eqs. 6b or 7b would be smaller, making O_{total} smaller overall. We are aware of this fact, however, see this as common practice to report the times and, for reproducibility reasons, we also report the used hardware infrastructure. Further, as we rely an a hardware setup with seems to be realistic for practical usage, We think that we limit this threat by that. The second possible danger for the validity of our statements lies in the used library PALLISADE. During our measurements, we noticed that the library contains minor memory leaks. These memory leaks were not due to us, since they occur even in the PALISADE standard examples. To make sure that these memory leaks do not have any influence on the performance, we have carried out corresponding measurements and could not detect any influence on the calculation times. In addition, to make sure that the measurements are not falsified by the memory leaks, we controlled the measurements via an external script, which manually releases the RAM and resolves the memory leaks.

5   Related Work

In this section, we review related work and highlight the novelty of our contribution. The authors of the papers [8] and [15] analyzed homomorphic linear regression as well. However, they used the Paillier cryptosystem, which is not fully homomorphic. The Paillier cryptosystem allows for the product of two ciphertexts to be decrypted as the sum of the corresponding plaintexts and for a ciphertext raised to the power of a plaintext to be decrypted as the product of the two plaintexts. Thus, to compute the multiplication for linear regression, the data must be in plaintext, which is not the case in our fully homomorphic approach. Using a fully homomorphic cryptosystem allows us to compute the multiplications and additions needed for linear regression directly on the encrypted data. By using a cryptosystem that is not fully homomorphic, the authors also do not have the associated problem of increasing multiplicative depth and the performance issues that come with it. We have analyzed these performance problems using two different architectures. We also consider a different application case. We consider the case where the owner of the data can store it homomorphic encrypted in a cloud and use the computational resources there to perform arbitrary analysis, such as linear regression, on that data. In contrast, the authors in [8] pursue the goal that if the dataset is distributed across multiple parties, it is still possible for the individual parties to compute the linear regression together without having to make their data available to any of the other parties. The authors in [15] have a similar goal.

The authors of [12] have also dealt with homomorphic regression, but with logistic regression. As a cryptosystem, they use the system of Cheon et al. [3], which requires only homomorphic encoded data for the computation of multiplication and addition. The authors circumvent the problem of multiplicative depth on the one hand by rescaling the encrypted values and on the other hand that certain hyperparameters have to be determined beforehand on the unencrypted data. We differ from this approach in that we do not perform precomputations on unencrypted data and analyze the impact of multiplicative depth on performance. In terms of metrics, we additionally consider the overhead incurred by the use of homomorphic encryption and, unlike [12], achieve the same accuracy with our homomorphic encryptions as in the unencrypted case.

In [2], the authors also want to compute the linear regression homomorphic, using Microsoft's SEAL library, which allows multiplication and addition on homomorphic encoded data. The linear regression was computed on different datasets whose size is unknown. Therefore, the performance values given are difficult to classify with regard to the times required for encrypting and decrypting or for calculating the linear regression. In addition, the calculation of the inverse of a matrix, which is necessary for how they calculate the linear regression, is not encrypted. We differ from this approach, among other things, in that all calculations are done homomorphic, we specify the used dataset, and that we analyze the overhead that arises from the use of homomorphic encryption.

The paper [1] is an extension of the work [6] Therefore we focus only on the paper [1]. The authors of [1] make use of the two-server model from [10] and assume that the data owner can outsource the computation of linear regression to two non-colluding servers S1 and S2. In doing so, server S1 combines the data homomorphic encrypted by the data owner and masked them. The data thus encrypted and masked can be decrypted by server S2 to compute the linear regression on the unencrypted but masked data. This approach poses the risk that the servers could collaborate and thus gain access to the data. This is also the main difference with our approach, which performs all computations only on the homomorphic encrypted data. As a result, the data owner retains full control over his data, no matter how many servers of the cloud cooperate.

6   Conclusion

One way of using the data in the cloud without the provider having access to it is homomorphic encryption. However, since this encryption has only been practicable recently, there is only little work that investigates its performance. Therefore, we presented two approaches to realize homomorphic encryption. The first approach is that the client sends its data homomorphic encrypted to the cloud, which is to perform the corresponding calculations. The client does not support the cloud in the calculations and only decrypts the result. The second approach is largely the same as the first approach, except that the client now supports the cloud in the calculations in such a way that it decrypts and re-encrypts individual parameters in order to reset the multiplicative depth of these parameters. We compared those approaches in an linear regression application and analyzed the times required for encryption, decryption and computation as well as the introduced overhead. The results show that the encryption times depend not only on the dataset size, but also the operation type; however, in our scenario, encryption is feasible in a reasonable amount of time. The decryption process requires a negligible amount of time. Furthermore, the computation of the linear regression is significantly slower than the non-homomorphic calculation up to a factor of 80 million.

References

1. Akavia, A., et al.: Linear-regression on packed encrypted data in the two-server model. In: Proceedings of the 7th ACM Workshop on Encrypted Computing & Applied Homomorphic Cryptography (2019)
2. Chen, B., et al.: Implementing linear regression with homomorphic encryption. Procedia Comput. Sci. **202**, 324–329 (2022). International Conference on Identification, Information and Knowledge in the internet of Things, 2021
3. Cheon, J.H., Kim, A., Kim, M., Song, Y.: Homomorphic encryption for arithmetic of approximate numbers. In: Takagi, T., Peyrin, T. (eds.) ASIACRYPT 2017. LNCS, vol. 10624, pp. 409–437. Springer, Cham (2017). https://doi.org/10.1007/978-3-319-70694-8_15
4. Gentry, C.: Fully homomorphic encryption using ideal lattices. In: Proceedings of the Forty-First Annual ACM Symposium on Theory of Computing (2009)
5. Gentry, C.: Computing arbitrary functions of encrypted data. Commun. ACM **53**(3) (2010). https://doi.org/10.1145/1666420.1666444
6. Giacomelli, I., Jha, S., Joye, M., Page, C.D., Yoon, K.: Privacy-preserving ridge regression with only linearly-homomorphic encryption. In: Preneel, B., Vercauteren, F. (eds.) ACNS 2018. LNCS, vol. 10892, pp. 243–261. Springer, Cham (2018). https://doi.org/10.1007/978-3-319-93387-0_13
7. Goey, J.Z., et al.: Accelerating number theoretic transform in GPU platform for fully homomorphic encryption. J. Supercomput. **77**(2), 1455–1474 (2021)
8. Hall, R., et al.: Secure multiple linear regression based on homomorphic encryption. J. Off. Stat. **27**(4), 669 (2011)
9. Kaggle: House Prices - Advanced Regression Techniques. https://www.kaggle.com/competitions/house-prices-advanced-regression-techniques/data. Accessed 29 Oct 2022
10. Kamara, S., Mohassel, P., Raykova, M.: Outsourcing multi-party computation. Cryptology ePrint Archive (2011)
11. Katz, J., et al.: Introduction to Modern Cryptography, 2nd edn. Chapman Hall, CRC Cryptography and Network Security, CRC Press, Boca Raton; London; New York (2015)
12. Kim, M., et al.: Secure logistic regression based on homomorphic encryption: Design and evaluation. JMIR Med. Inform. **6**(2), e8805 (2018)
13. Ng, A.: CS229 lecture notes. CS229 Lect. Notes **1**(1), 1–3 (2000). https://see.stanford.edu/materials/aimlcs229/cs229-notes1.pdf. Accessed 25 Sept 2022
14. PALISADE Project: Palisade Homomorphic Encryption Software Library. https://palisade-crypto.org/. Accessed 17 Jan 2023
15. Qiu, G., et al.: Privacy-preserving linear regression on distributed data by homomorphic encryption and data masking. IEEE Access **8**, 107601–107613 (2020)
16. Rivest, R.L., et al.: On data banks and privacy homomorphisms. Found. Secure Comput. **4**(11), 169–180 (1978)
17. Steve, R., Angus, L.: Oracle ceo hurd says 80% of corporate data centers gone by 2025. https://www.wsj.com/articles/BL-CIOB-11316. Accessed 25 Sept 2022

Chosen Ciphertext Security for Blind Identity-Based Encryption with Certified Identities

Sohto Chiku[1](✉) [iD], Keisuke Hara[1,2] [iD], and Junji Shikata[1]

[1] Yokohama National University, Yokohama, Japan
`chiku-sohto-tw@ynu.jp`
[2] National Institute of Advanced Industrial Science and Technology, Tokyo, Japan

Abstract. Identity-based encryption (IBE) is one of the important extension of public-key encryption (PKE) which can use identities, such as email addresses or phone numbers, as public keys. Due to this aspect, IBE can reduce the cost of maintaining public key infrastructure. However, it has a special issue called the "key escrow problem", which means that the key generation center (KGC) can decrypt all ciphertexts and get all messages in them since it inherently has all user public/private key pairs. To tackle this problem, Emura, Katsumata, and Watanabe recently proposed a variant of IBE called *blind IBE with certified identities* by introducing identity certifying authority (ICA). Their constructions are based on pairing or lattice and secure against chosen plaintext attacks.

In this paper, we introduce security against chosen ciphertext attacks (CCA security) for blind identity-based Encryption with certified identities. More precisely, we formalize definitions of 3-types security against chosen ciphertext attacks (security against corrupted users, KGC, and ICA) for blind IBE with certified identities. Then, we propose the first blind IBE with certified identities schemes. Roughly, we provide a generic construction by applying the Fujisaki-Okamoto transformation to previous CPA secure Blind IBE with certified identities schemes. Through our generic construction, we obtain two instantiations based on pairing or lattice. Finally, we implement our pairing based scheme and demonstrate that it is practically efficient compared with existing schemes.

Keywords: Identity-based Encryption · Chosen Ciphertext Security · Key Escrow Problem · Pairing · Lattice

1 Introduction

Identity-based Encryption (IBE) is one of important notion in cryptography with advanced functionalities proposed by Shamir [17]. IBE can use arbitrary strings, such as e-mail addresses, as public keys. This reduces the cost of using public key infrastructures. In IBE, we have a special entity called the key-generation center (KGC) who maintains a master public/secret key pair. Using this master key, the KGC issues private keys for user IDs after confirming the validity of the IDs. That is, the KGC potentially has the power to decrypt all users' ciphertexts. This critical disadvantage of IBE is called the *key escrow problem*, and this problem is a main barrier when considering real-world use of IBE.

W. Meng et al. (Eds.): ISPEC 2023, LNCS 14341, pp. 299–314, 2023.
https://doi.org/10.1007/978-981-99-7032-2_18

To overcome this problem, several attempts to reduce the amount of trust on the KGC in IBE have already been proposed. One of the solutions is to involve each user in the user secret key generation process, such as certificate-less encryption (CE) [2] and registration-based encryption (RBE) [11]. Another approach is to introduce an independent notion of security against the KGC for (standard) IBE [5,14]. Inspired by the Chow's work [5], Emura, Katsumata, and Watanabe recently proposed a new variant of IBE called *blind IBE with certificated identities* [7,8].[1] The idea of their work is to introduce a new entity called *identity-certifying authority* (ICA) to authenticate the users in the system and realizing anonymous key-issuing protocol between users and the KGC. More precisely, for blind IBE, they formalized three security properties for (corrupted) users, KGC, and ICA, respectively. Then, they provided blind IBE schemes satisfying these properties based on the standard assumptions over pairing or lattice in the random oracle model (ROM).

While their blind IBE deals with the key escrow problem, it captures only security against chosen plaintext attacks (CPA security). From the aspect of abilities for adversaries, we have two flavors of security for encryption schemes (e.g., PKE, IBE): CPA security and chosen ciphertext attacks (CCA) security [3,6,10]. In general, since CCA security captures active adversaries (and implies non-malleability), it is more desirable than CPA security and has been recognized as de facto security requirement.

1.1 Our Contribution

Based on the above motivation, this paper gives the following three contributions.

CCA Security for Blind IBE with Certified Identities. Firstly, we provide new security notions capturing CCA for blind IBE. Specifically, by extending the previous CPA security for blind IBE, we give formal definitions of CCA security for (corrupted) users (IND-ANON-CCA security), KGC (IND-ANON-KGC$_{CCA}$ security), and ICA (IND-ANON-ICA$_{CCA}$ security), respectively.

A Generic Construction of CCA Secure Blind IBE with Certified Identities. As our second technical result, we show a generic construction of CCA secure blind IBE with certified identities from CPA secure blind IBE with certified identities [7,8]. Specifically, we extend the classical Fujisaki-Okamoto (FO) conversion [9], which is a technique to upgrade CPA secure PKE to CCA secure PKE in the ROM, to blind IBE setting, and applies to a CPA secure blind IBE scheme. More precisely, in order to capture the lattice instantiation in [7,8], we consider a variant of the FO conversion preserved even under the presence of correctness errors [13] instead of the original FO conversion. Then, we provide formal security proofs for the obtained blind IBE scheme, and give two instantiations over pairing or lattice.

Implementation of Our Pairing-Based CCA Secure Blind IBE Scheme. Finally, in order to show the practical efficiency of our pairing-based CCA secure blind IBE scheme, we

---

[1] In this work, for the purpose of distinction, we refer to the above variant of IBE as "blind IBE" and the original IBE as "(standard) IBE".

implement and evaluate it in Python. From this experimentation result, even though our scheme has stronger security, we can see that our scheme is as efficient as the previous CPA secure blind IBE scheme [8] and the (most classical and efficient) Boneh-Franklin IBE scheme [4].

1.2   Organization

The remaining part of this paper is organized as follows: In Sect. 2, we introduce preliminaries that will be used later. Then, in Sect. 3, we give the relevant definitions including syntax and security definitions. Next, the construction and proof of our IBE are given in Sect. 4. In Sect. 5, we give two instantiations of our schemes and comparison space cost. Finally, Sect. 6 presents the performance evaluation of pairing-based schemes.

2   Preliminaries

In what follows, we first introduce some notations used in this work. Then, we give a few preliminaries related to bilinear groups and lattice. (Due to the space limitation, we omit the definitions of digital signature and pseudorandom function.)

Notations. In this paper, we use the following notations. For $n \in \mathbb{N}$, we denote $[n] = \{1, .., n\}$. $x \leftarrow X$ denotes the operation of sampling an element x from a finite set X. $y \leftarrow \mathcal{A}(x; r)$ denotes that a probabilistic Turing machine $\mathcal{A}$ outputs y for an input x using a randomness r, and we simply denote $y \leftarrow \mathcal{A}(x)$ when we need not write an internal randomness explicitly. For interactive Turing machines $\mathcal{A}$ and $\mathcal{B}$, $v \leftarrow \langle \mathcal{A}(x_a), \mathcal{B}(x_b) \rangle$ denotes that $\mathcal{A}$ outputs v at the end of an execution of an interactive protocol between $\mathcal{A}$ and $\mathcal{B}$, where $\mathcal{A}$ and $\mathcal{B}$ take x_a and x_b as input respectively. PPT stands for probabilistic polynomial time. $x := y$ denotes that x is defined by y. $\hat{e}$ denotes the base of the natural logarithm. We say a function $\varepsilon(\lambda)$ is negligible in λ, if $\varepsilon(\lambda) = o(1/\lambda^c)$ for every $c \in \mathbb{Z}$, and we write $negl(\lambda)$ to denote a negligible function in λ. $\emptyset$ denotes the empty set. If $\mathcal{O}$ is a function or an algorithm and $\mathcal{A}$ is an algorithm, $\mathcal{A}^{\mathcal{O}}$ means $\mathcal{A}$ has oracle access to $\mathcal{O}$.

Bilinear Groups. Here, we recall some notations for bilinear groups. Let p be a λ-bit prime, $\mathbb{G}$ and $\mathbb{G}_T$ groups of order p, $e : \mathbb{G} \times \mathbb{G} \to \mathbb{G}_T$ a bilinear map (pairing), and g a generator of $\mathbb{G}$. We require that bilinearlity: for all $g_1, g_2 \in \mathbb{G}$ and $a, b \in \mathbb{Z}_p$, $e(g_1^a, g_2^b) = e(g_1, g_2)^{ab}$, and non-degeneracy: $e(g, g) \neq 1$ hold. We say that $(\mathbb{G}, \mathbb{G}_T, g, p, e)$ is a bilinear group.

Lattice. Here, we recall some notations for lattice and the Learning with Error (LWE) assumption. A (full-rank-integer) m-dimensional lattice Λ in $\mathbb{Z}^m$ is a set of the form $\{\Sigma_{i \in [m]} x_i b_i | x_i \in \mathbb{Z}\}$, where $\mathbf{B} = \{b_1, \cdots, b_m\}$ are m linearly independent vectors in $\mathbb{Z}^m$. We call $\mathbf{B}$ the basis of the lattice Λ. For any positive integers n, m and $q \geq 2$, a matrix $\mathbf{A} \in \mathbb{Z}_q^{n \times m}$ and a vector $\mathbf{u} \in \mathbb{Z}_q^n$, we define the lattices $\Lambda^{\perp}(\mathbf{A}) = \{\mathbf{z} \in \mathbb{Z}^m | \mathbf{A}\mathbf{z} = 0 \mod q\}$ and $\Lambda_{\mathbf{u}}^{\perp}(\mathbf{A}) = \{\mathbf{z} \in \mathbb{Z}^m | \mathbf{A}\mathbf{z} = \mathbf{u} \mod q\}$. Furthermore, fix $\mathbf{u} \in \mathbb{Z}_q^n$. Then the conditional distribution of $\mathbf{e} \leftarrow D_{\mathbb{Z}^m, \sigma}$ given $\mathbf{A}\mathbf{e} = \mathbf{u} \mod q$ for a uniformly random $\mathbf{A}$ in $\mathbb{Z}_q^{n \times m}$ is statistically close to $D_{\Lambda_{\mathbf{u}}^{\perp}(\mathbf{A}), \sigma}$. The following lemma states useful algorithms for sampling short vectors from lattices.

Lemma 1 ([12, 15]). *Let $n, m, q > 0$ be integers with $m \leq 2n \log q$.*

TrapGen$(1^n, 1^m, q) \rightarrow (\mathbf{A}, \mathbf{T_A})$: *There exists a randomized algorithm that outputs a matrix $\mathbf{A} \in \mathbb{Z}_q^{n \times m}$ and a full-rank matrix $\mathbf{T_A} \in \mathbb{Z}^{m \times m}$, where $\mathbf{T_A}$ is a basis for $\Lambda^\perp(\mathbf{A})$, $\mathbf{A}$ is statistically close to uniform and $\|\mathbf{T_A}\|_{\mathsf{GS}} = O(\sqrt{n \log q})$.*

SamplePre$(\mathbf{A}, \mathbf{u}, \mathbf{T_A}, \sigma) \rightarrow \mathbf{e}$: *There exists a randomized algorithm that, given a matrix $\mathbf{A} \in \mathbb{Z}_q^{n \times m}$, a vector $\mathbf{u} \in \mathbb{Z}_q^n$, a basis $\mathbf{T_A}$ for $\Lambda^\perp(\mathbf{A})$, and a Gaussian parameter $\sigma > \|\mathbf{T_A}\|_{\mathsf{GS}} \cdot \omega(\sqrt{\log m})$, outputs a vector $\mathbf{e} \in \mathbb{Z}^m$ sampled from a distribution which is $\mathrm{negl}(n)$-close to $D_{\Lambda_{\mathbf{u}}^\perp(\mathbf{A}), \sigma}$.*

3 CCA Security for Blind IBE with Certified Identities

In this section, we recall the syntax of blind IBE with certified identities, then introduce CCA security for it.

3.1 Recap: The Syntax of Blind IBE with Certified Identities

In this section, we recall the definition of blind IBE with certified identities by Emura et al. [7, 8].

Definition 1 (Blind IBE with Certified Identities [7,8]**).** *A Blind IBE scheme with certified identities* IBE *consists of the following PPT algorithms:*

Setup$(1^\lambda) \rightarrow$ params: *The setup algorithm takes as input a security parameter 1^λ, and outputs a public parameter* params. *We assume the identity space $\mathcal{ID}$ and the message space $\mathcal{M}$ are defined by* params. *Moreover, we assume* params *are implicitly provided as input to the following algorithms.*

KGC.KeyGen(params) $\rightarrow$ (mpk, msk): *The KGC key-generation algorithm takes as input* params, *and outputs a master public key* mpk *and a master secret key* msk.

ICA.KeyGen(params) $\rightarrow$ (vk, ik): *The ICA key-generation algorithm takes as input* params, *and outputs a certificate verification key* vk *and a certificate issuing key* ik.

ICA.Cert(vk, ik, ID) $\rightarrow$ (cert, td): *The certificate-issuing algorithm run by ICA takes as inputs a certificate verification key* vk, *a certificate issuing key* ik, *and a identity* ID $\in \mathcal{ID}$, *and outputs a certificate* cert *and a trapdoor information* td.

IBE.Enc(mpk, ID, M) $\rightarrow$ C: *The encryption algorithm run by a sender takes as inputs the master public key* mpk, *an identity* ID $\in \mathcal{ID}$, *and a message* M $\in \mathcal{M}$, *and outputs a ciphertext* C.

IBE.Dec(mpk, sk$_{\mathsf{ID}}$, C) $\rightarrow$ M *or* $\perp$: *The decryption algorithm run by receiver takes as input the master public key* mpk, *a secret key* sk$_{\mathsf{ID}}$, *and a ciphertext* C, *and outputs* M.

⟨ObtainKey(mpk, ID, cert, td), IssueKey(mpk, msk, vk)⟩: *The interactive secret key issuing protocol between a user and the KGC involves two interactive algorithms* ObtainKey *and* IssueKey. *The user and the KGC interactively run the* ObtainKey *algorithm and the* IssueKey *algorithm, respectively as follows.*

    User: *The user takes as input* (mpk, ID, cert, td) *as specified by the input of* ObtainKey, *and sends a first-round message* M$_{\mathsf{user}}$ *to the KGC.*

KGC: *The KGC takes as input* $(\mathsf{mpk}, \mathsf{msk}, \mathsf{vk})$ *as specified by the input of* IssueKey *along with the message* $\mathsf{M}_{\mathsf{user}}$ *sent by the receiver, and returns a second-round message* $\mathsf{M}_{\mathsf{KGC}}$ *to the receiver.*

User: *On input the message* $\mathsf{M}_{\mathsf{KGC}}$ *from the KGC, the receiver (locally) outputs either* $\mathsf{sk}_{\mathsf{ID}}$ *or* $\bot$.

As the correctness, we call a blind IBE scheme IBE is δ-correct if $\mathbf{E}[\max_{\mathsf{M}\in\mathcal{M}}$ $\Pr[\mathsf{IBE}.\mathsf{Dec}(\mathsf{mpk}, \mathsf{sk}_{\mathsf{ID}}, \mathsf{C}) \neq \mathsf{M} | \mathsf{C} \leftarrow \mathsf{IBE}.\mathsf{Enc}(\mathsf{mpk}, \mathsf{ID}, \mathsf{M})]] \leq \delta$, where the expectation is taken over $\mathsf{params} \leftarrow \mathsf{Setup}(1^\lambda)$, $(\mathsf{mpk}, \mathsf{msk}) \leftarrow \mathsf{KGC}.\mathsf{KeyGen}(\mathsf{params})$, $(\mathsf{vk}, \mathsf{ik}) \leftarrow \mathsf{ICA}.\mathsf{KeyGen}(\mathsf{params})$, $(\mathsf{cert}, \mathsf{td}) \leftarrow \mathsf{ICA}.\mathsf{Cert}(\mathsf{vk}, \mathsf{ik}, \mathsf{ID})$, $\mathsf{sk}_{\mathsf{ID}} \leftarrow \langle\mathsf{ObtainKey}(\mathsf{mpk}, \mathsf{ID}, \mathsf{cert}, \mathsf{td}), \mathsf{IssueKey}(\mathsf{mpk}, \mathsf{msk}, \mathsf{vk})\rangle$, and $\mathsf{C} \leftarrow \mathsf{IBE}.\mathsf{Enc}(\mathsf{mpk}, \mathsf{ID}, \mathsf{M})$.

Emura et al. [7,8] formalized three security notions for blind IBE with certified identities against (corrupted) users (IND-ANON-CPA security), KGC (IND-ANON-KGC security), and ICA (IND-ANON-ICA security), respectively.

3.2 Definition of CCA Security

In this section, we introduce CCA security for blind IBE with certified identities. Firstly, we consider security against corrupted users who have chosen ciphertext attacks. We call this IND-ANON-CCA security, to explicitly indicate that it implies anonymity. This differs from IND-ANON-CPA security of blind IBE in that an adversary $\mathcal{A}$ can access the decryption oracle, that will output any message from any identities and ciphertexts. Note that we do not consider an adversary $\mathcal{A}$ that can obtain a certificate for ID^*, since this will allow $\mathcal{A}$ to trivially break security. This corresponds to the assumption that, in practice, an adversary cannot obtain a certificate for the challenge identity ID^*.

Definition 2 (IND-ANON-CCA). *We define* IND-ANON-CCA *security by the following game between a challenger and a PPT adversary* $\mathcal{A}$. *Below, let* CTSamp *be a sampling algorithm that takes a master public key as input and outputs an element in the ciphertext space.*

Setup: *At the outset of the game, the challenger runs* $\mathsf{params} \leftarrow \mathsf{Setup}(1^\lambda)$, $(\mathsf{mpk}, \mathsf{msk}) \leftarrow \mathsf{KGC}.\mathsf{KeyGen}(\mathsf{params})$, $(\mathsf{vk}, \mathsf{ik}) \leftarrow \mathsf{ICA}.\mathsf{KeyGen}(\mathsf{params})$, *and initializes an empty list* $\mathsf{IDList} := \emptyset$. *The challenger further picks a random coin* $\mathsf{coin} \leftarrow \{0, 1\}$ *and keeps it secret. The challenger gives* $(\mathsf{params}, \mathsf{mpk}, \mathsf{vk})$ *to* $\mathcal{A}$. *After this,* $\mathcal{A}$ *can adaptively make the following four types of queries to the challenger in arbitrary order: certificate, secret key, decryption, and challenge queries.* $\mathcal{A}$ *can query the first three arbitrary polynomials many times and the fourth only once.*

Certificate Query: *If* $\mathcal{A}$ *submits* $\mathsf{ID} \in \mathcal{ID}$ *(it must be* $\mathsf{ID} \neq \mathsf{ID}^*$ *after the challenge query) to the challenger, the challenger computes* $(\mathsf{cert}, \mathsf{td}) \leftarrow \mathsf{ICA}.\mathsf{Cert}(\mathsf{vk}, \mathsf{ik}, \mathsf{ID})$ *and returns* $(\mathsf{cert}, \mathsf{td})$ *to* $\mathcal{A}$. *It then stores* ID *to* IDList.

Secret Key Query: *If* $\mathcal{A}$ *submits a first-round message* $\mathsf{M}_{\mathsf{user}}$ *to the challenger, the challenger runs the IssueKey algorithm taking as inputs* $(\mathsf{mpk}, \mathsf{msk}, \mathsf{vk})$ *and the message* $\mathsf{M}_{\mathsf{user}}$, *and obtains a second-round message* $\mathsf{M}_{\mathsf{KGC}}$. *It then returns* $\mathsf{M}_{\mathsf{KGC}}$ *to* $\mathcal{A}$.

Decryption Query: *If $\mathcal{A}$ submits an identity ID and a ciphertext C (it must be ID $\neq$ ID* $\vee$ C $\neq$ C* after the challenge query), the challenger runs M $\leftarrow$ IBE.Dec(mpk, sk$_{ID}$, C) where sk$_{ID}$ $\leftarrow$ $\langle$ObtainKey(mpk, ID, (cert, td) $\leftarrow$ ICA.Cert(vk, ik, ID)), IssueKey(mpk, msk, vk)$\rangle$. Then, the challenger returns M to $\mathcal{A}$.*

Challenge Query: *If $\mathcal{A}$ submits (ID*, M*) to the challenger where ID* $\in$ $\mathcal{ID}$, ID* $\notin$ IDList and M* $\in$ $\mathcal{M}$, the challenger proceeds as follows: If coin $= 0$, the challenger returns C* $\leftarrow$ IBE.Enc(mpk, ID*, M*). Otherwise, if coin $= 1$, the challenger returns C* $\leftarrow$ CTSamp(mpk).*

Guess: *$\mathcal{A}$ outputs a guess $\widehat{\text{coin}}$ $\in$ $\{0, 1\}$ for coin. We say that IBE is IND-ANON-CCA secure if the advantage $\text{Adv}_{\text{IBE}, \mathcal{A}}^{\text{IND-ANON-CCA}}(\lambda) = |\Pr[\text{coin} = \widehat{\text{coin}}] - 1/2|$ is negligible in λ for any PPT adversary $\mathcal{A}$.*

Then, we also define security against the honest-but-curious KGC (KGC follows the protocol but attempts to obtain information about the underlying plaintexts from the observed ciphertexts) who have CCA. We call this IND-ANON-KGC$_{\text{CCA}}$ security. As for user, this differs from IND-ANON-KGC security of blind IBE in that an adversary $\mathcal{A}$ can access the decryption oracle. Security against the KGC guarantees that, when the KGC runs honestly (that is, generates secret keys honestly), it cannot get any information about the corresponding identities or plaintexts from target ciphertexts, even if it uses knowledge obtained via the key-issuing protocol.

Definition 3 (IND-ANON-KGC$_{\text{CCA}}$). *We define IND-ANON-KGC$_{\text{CCA}}$ security by the following game between a challenger and a PPT adversary $\mathcal{A}$. Below, let CTSamp be a sampling algorithm that takes a master public key as input and outputs an element in the ciphertext space.*

Setup: *At the outset of the game, the challenger runs params $\leftarrow$ Setup(1^λ), (mpk, msk) $\leftarrow$ KGC.KeyGen(params), (vk, ik) $\leftarrow$ ICA.KeyGen(params), and initializes an empty list IDList $:= \emptyset$. The challenger further picks a random coin coin $\leftarrow$ $\{0, 1\}$ and keeps it secret. The challenger gives (params, mpk, msk, vk) to $\mathcal{A}$. After this, $\mathcal{A}$ can adaptively make the following four types of queries to the challenger in arbitrary order: certificate, secret key, decryption, and challenge queries. $\mathcal{A}$ can query the first three arbitrary polynomials many times and the fourth only once.*

Encryption Query: *If $\mathcal{A}$ submits an index i and a message m $\in$ $\mathcal{M}$ to the challenger, the challenger first checks if i $\in$ $[Q_{\text{key}}]$ where $[0]$ is defined as the empty set. If not, the challenger aborts and outputs $\widehat{\text{coin}}$ $\leftarrow$ $\{0, 1\}$. Otherwise, the challenger retrieves the $i - th$ entry ID$_i$ $\in$ IDList[i] and returns C $\leftarrow$ IBE.Enc(mpk, ID$_i$, m).*

Decryption Query: *If $\mathcal{A}$ submits a index i and a ciphertext C to the challenger (it must be i $\neq$ i^* $\vee$ C $\neq$ C* after the challenge query), the challenger first checks if i $\in$ $[Q_{\text{key}}]$ where $[0]$ is defined as the empty set. If not, the challenger aborts the game and outputs $\widehat{\text{coin}}$ $\leftarrow$ $\{0, 1\}$. Otherwise, the challenger retrieves the $i - th$ entry ID$_i$ $\in$ IDList[i] and returns M $\leftarrow$ IBE.Dec(mpk, sk$_{ID_i}$, C) to $\mathcal{A}$, where sk$_{ID_i}$ $\leftarrow$ $\langle$ObtainKey(mpk, ID$_i$, (cert, td) $\leftarrow$ ICA.Cert(vk, ik, ID$_i$)), IssueKey(mpk, msk, vk)$\rangle$.*

IssueKey Query: *If $\mathcal{A}$ makes an IssueKey query, the challenger first randomly samples* ID $\leftarrow$ $\mathcal{ID}$ *and computes* (cert, td) $\leftarrow$ ICA.Cert(vk, ik, ID). *It then runs* ObtainKey *on inputs* (mpk, ID, cert, td) *to generate the first-round message* M_{user} *and returns* M_{user} *to $\mathcal{A}$. Finally, the challenger stores* ID *to* IDList$[Q_{key}]$ *and updates* $Q_{key} \leftarrow Q_{key} + 1$.

Challenge Query: *If $\mathcal{A}$ submits* (i^*, M^*) *to the challenger where* $M^* \in \mathcal{M}$, *the challenger first checks if* $i^* \in [Q_{key}]$. *If not, the challenger proceeds as follows: The challenger first retrieves the* $i^* - th$ *entry* $ID_{i^*} \in$ IDList$[i^*]$. *Then, if* coin $=$ 0, *the challenger returns* $C^* \leftarrow$ IBE.Enc(mpk, ID_{i^*}, M^*). *Otherwise, if* coin $=$ 1, *the challenger returns* $C^* \leftarrow$ CTSamp(mpk).

Guess: *$\mathcal{A}$ outputs a guess* $\widehat{coin} \in \{0, 1\}$ *for coin. We say that* IBE *is* IND-ANON-KGC$_{CCA}$ *secure if the advantage* $\text{Adv}_{\text{IBE},\mathcal{A}}^{\text{IND-ANON-KGC}_{CCA}}(\lambda) = |\Pr[coin = \widehat{coin}] - 1/2|$ *is negligible in λ for any PPT adversary $\mathcal{A}$.*

Finally, we consider security against the malicious ICA who have CCA. A malicious ICA can generate certificates for any users, and thereby obtain the corresponding secret keys by impersonating the user and interacting with the (honest) KGC. Therefore, in principle, we do not allow the ICA to have the capability of generating a potentially malicious key pair (vk, ik) in the experiment, while disallowing it to have access to the decryption oracle. As for above two definition, this differs from IND-ANON-ICA security of blind IBE in that an adversary $\mathcal{A}$ can access the decryption oracle.

Definition 4 (IND-ANON-ICA$_{CCA}$). *We define* IND-ANON-ICA$_{CCA}$ *security by the following game between a challenger and a PPT adversary $\mathcal{A}$. Below, let* CTSamp *be a sampling algorithm that takes a master public key as input and outputs an element in the ciphertext space.*

Setup: *At the outset of the game, the challenger runs* params $\leftarrow$ Setup(1^λ), (mpk, msk) $\leftarrow$ KGC.KeyGen(params). *The challenger further picks a random coin* coin $\leftarrow \{0, 1\}$ *and keeps it secret. The challenger gives* (params, mpk) *to $\mathcal{A}$. After this, $\mathcal{A}$ can make the challenge query once.*

Decryption Query: *If $\mathcal{A}$ submits an identity* ID, *issuing key* ik, *verifying key* vk *and a ciphertext* C *(it must be* ID $\neq$ ID* $\vee$ C $\neq$ C* *after the challenge query), the challenger runs* M $\leftarrow$ IBE.Dec(mpk, sk$_{ID}$, C) *where* sk$_{ID}$ $\leftarrow$ $\langle$ObtainKey(mpk, ID, (cert, td) $\leftarrow$ ICA.Cert(vk, ik, ID)), IssueKey(mpk, msk, vk)$\rangle$. *Then, the challenger returns* M *to $\mathcal{A}$.*

Challenge Query: *If $\mathcal{A}$ submits* (ID*, M*) *to the challenger where* M$^* \in \mathcal{M}$. *Then the challenger proceeds as follows: If* coin $= 0$, *the challenger returns* C$^* \leftarrow$ IBE.Enc(mpk, ID*, M*). *Otherwise, if* coin $= 1$, *the challenger returns* C$^* \leftarrow$ CTSamp(mpk).

Guess: *$\mathcal{A}$ outputs a guess* $\widehat{coin} \in \{0, 1\}$ *for coin. We say that* IBE *is* IND-ANON-ICA$_{CCA}$ *secure if the advantage* $\text{Adv}_{\text{IBE},\mathcal{A}}^{\text{IND-ANON-ICA}_{CCA}}(\lambda) = |\Pr[coin = \widehat{coin}] - 1/2|$ *is negligible in λ for any PPT adversary $\mathcal{A}$.*

4 Our Construction of CCA Secure Blind IBE with Certified Identities

In this section, we construct a CCA secure blind IBE scheme with certified identities and give security proofs for it. Section 4.1 gives a generic construction toward CCA security. Section 4.2 shows our construction satisfies security defined in Sect. 3.2.

4.1 Construction

This section gives a generic construction of CCA secure blind IBE with certified identities.

Construction. Let IBE $=$ (Setup, KGC.KeyGen, ICA.KeyGen, ICA.Cert, IBE.Enc, IBE.Dec, $\langle$ObtainKey, IssueKey$\rangle$) be a blind IBE scheme satisfying 3-type security notions IND-ANON-CPA, IND-ANON-KGC, and IND-ANON-ICA. Then, we construct another blind IBE scheme IBE$' =$ (Setup$'$, KGC.KeyGen$'$, ICA.KeyGen$'$, ICA.Cert$'$, IBE.Enc$'$, IBE.Dec$'$, $\langle$ObtainKey$'$, IssueKey$'\rangle$) as follows: Let $\mathcal{M}$ be a message space of IBE, $\mathcal{R}$ a randomness space of IBE.Enc, and $\mathcal{M}'$ a message space of IBE$'$.

- Setup$'$: It works in the following steps:
  1. Run params $\leftarrow$ Setup(1^λ).
  2. Pick two hash functions $H_1 : \mathcal{M} \to \mathcal{R}$ and $H_2 : \mathcal{M} \times \mathcal{C} \to \mathcal{M}'$.
  3. Set params $=$ (params, H_1, H_2).
  4. Output public parameters params.
- KGC.KeyGen$'$: It works in the following steps:
  1. Run (mpk, msk) $\leftarrow$ KGC.KeyGen(params).
  2. Output master public/secret key pair (mpk, msk).
- ICA.KeyGen$'$: It works in the following steps:
  1. Run (ik, vk) $\leftarrow$ ICA.KeyGen(params).
  2. Output certificate issuing/verifying key pair (ik, vk).
- ICA.Cert$'$: It works in the following steps:
  1. Run (cert, td) $\leftarrow$ ICA.Cert(ik, vk, ID).
  2. Output certificate information cert and trapdoor information td.
- IBE.Enc$'$: It works in the following steps:
  1. Samples $k \leftarrow \mathcal{M}$
  2. Computes $C_0 \leftarrow$ IBE.Enc(params, ID, k; $H_1(k)$)
  3. Computes $C_1 \leftarrow M \oplus H_2(k, C_0)$
  4. Outputs $C = (C_0, C_1)$
- IBE.Dec$'$: Let $C = C_0 || C_1$ be a ciphertext to decrypt. It works in the following steps:
  1. Computes $k :=$ IBE.Dec(params, sk$_{\text{ID}}$, C_0).
  2. Computes $M := H_2(k, C_0) \oplus C_1$.
  3. Verifies that Enc(mpk, ID, k; $H_1(k)$) $= C_1$ holds. If not, outputs $\bot$.
  4. Outputs M as the decryption of C.
- $\langle$ObtainKey$'$, IssueKey$'\rangle$: It works between a user and the KGC as follows:
  1. Run sk$_{\text{ID}}/\bot \leftarrow \langle$ObtainKey(mpk, ID, cert, td), IssueKey(mpk, msk, vk)$\rangle$.
  2. Output sk$_{\text{ID}}$ or $\bot$.

Correctness. From a similar argument to [13, Theorem 3.1], if IBE is δ-correct, IBE$'$ is δ_1-correct where $\delta_1 = q_{H_1} \cdot \delta$, where q_{H_1} is the number of H_1 query.

4.2 Security Proofs

In this section, we provide the formal security proofs for our scheme in Sect. 4.1.

Theorem 1. *Suppose that the hash function* H_1 *and* H_2 *are random oracles and IBE is IND-ANON-CPA secure blind IBE scheme, then IBE$'$ is IND-ANON-CCA secure.*

Proof. We show how to construct an adversary $\mathcal{B}$ that breaks IND-ANON-CPA security of IBE by using an adversary $\mathcal{A}$ that breaks IND-ANON-CCA security of IBE$'$ with an advantage $\varepsilon(\lambda)$. The challenger starts an IND-ANON-CPA security game by running params $\leftarrow$ Setup(1^λ), (mpk, msk) $\leftarrow$ KGC.KeyGen(params) and (vk, ik) $\leftarrow$ ICA.KeyGen(params). $\mathcal{B}$ works by interacting with $\mathcal{A}$ in the IND-ANON-CCA game as follows:

Setup: $\mathcal{B}$ gives params, mpk, vk to $\mathcal{A}$. When $\mathcal{A}$ makes oracle queries, $\mathcal{B}$ responds as follows:

H_1 **Query:** $\mathcal{B}$ maintains a list of tuples (x_i, h_i) to responds the queries. We refer to this list as H_1List. The list is initially empty. When $\mathcal{A}$ queries x_i, $\mathcal{B}$ responds as follows:

1. If the query x_i already appears on the H_1List in a tuple (x_i, h_i) then $\mathcal{B}$ responds with $H_1(x_i) = h_i$.
2. Otherwise, $\mathcal{B}$ picks h_i from $\mathcal{R}$ randomly.
3. $\mathcal{B}$ adds the tuple (x_i, h_i) to the H_1List.

H_2 **Query:** $\mathcal{B}$ maintains a list of tuples (y_i, C_0^i, g_i) as explained below. We refer to this list as the H_2List. The list is initially empty. When $\mathcal{A}$ queries (y_i, C_0^i), $\mathcal{B}$ responds as follows:

1. If the query y_i and C_0^i already appears on the H_2List in a tuple (y_i, C_0^i, g_i) then $\mathcal{B}$ responds with $H_2(y_i, C_0^i) = g_i$.
2. Otherwise, $\mathcal{B}$ picks a random element g_i from $\mathcal{M}'$ of IBE.
3. $\mathcal{B}$ adds the tuple (y_i, C_0^i, g_i) to the H_2List and returns g_i.

Certificate Query: Let ID be an certificate query issued by $\mathcal{A}$. $\mathcal{B}$ queries ID to its own certificate oracle and gets the corresponding certification cert and trapdoor td. $\mathcal{B}$ passes (cert, td) to $\mathcal{A}$ as answer of the query.

Secret Key Query: Let M_{user} be an secret key query issued by $\mathcal{A}$. $\mathcal{B}$ inputs M_{user} to its own secret key oracle and gets the corresponding second round message M_{KGC}. $\mathcal{B}$ passes M_{KGC} to $\mathcal{A}$ as answer of the query.

Decryption Query: Let (ID, C $= (C_0, C_1)$) be a decryption query issued by $\mathcal{A}$. $\mathcal{B}$ responds as follows:

1. Find a pair of tuples (x, h) and (x, C_0, g) from the H_1List and H_2List, respectively, such that $C_0 = $ IBE.Enc(mpk, ID, x; h).
2. Outputs $g \oplus C_1$ if there exists such a pair of tuples, or outputs $\perp$ otherwise.

Challenge Query: When $\mathcal{A}$ outputs an identity ID* and message M* on which it wishes to be challenged, $\mathcal{B}$ sends ID* to the challenger and receives a ciphertext C_0^*. Then, $\mathcal{B}$ generates $C_0^*||C_1^*$ where C_1^* is random element in $\mathcal{M}'$. $\mathcal{B}$ gives $C_0^*||C_1^*$ as the challenge to $\mathcal{A}$.

Guess: Once $\mathcal{A}$ decides that Phase 2 is over it outputs a guess $\widehat{\text{coin}}$.

After $\mathcal{A}$ outputs the guess $\widehat{\text{coin}}$, $\mathcal{B}$ chooses a tuple (x, h) or (y, C_0, g) from the H_1List or the H_2List, respectively. Then, $\mathcal{B}$ outputs k in the tuple as the answer of the IND-ANON-CPA game. Now, we define the following three events:

SuccA: The event that $\mathcal{A}$ wins the IND-ANON-CCA game.

AskA: The event that $\mathcal{A}$ asks a query for $H_1(\text{IBE.Dec}(\text{mpk}, \text{sk}_{\text{ID}}, C_0))$ or $H_2(\star, \text{IBE.Dec}(\text{mpk}, \text{sk}_{\text{ID}}, C_0))$ at some point during the game, where $\text{sk}_{\text{ID}} := \langle \text{ObtainKey}(\text{mpk}, \text{ID}, (\text{cert}, \text{td}) \leftarrow \text{ICA.Cert}(\text{vk}, \text{ik}, \text{ID})), \text{IssueKey}(\text{mpk}, \text{msk}, \text{vk})\rangle$ and $\star$ denotes any elements in $\mathcal{M}$.

Fail: The event that the simulation fails before $\mathcal{A}$ submits a query for $H_1(\text{IBE.Dec}(\text{mpk}, \text{sk}_{\text{ID}}, C_0))$ or $H_2(\star, \text{IBE.Dec}(\text{mpk}, \text{sk}_{\text{ID}}, C_0))$.

Then, we have $\Pr[\text{SuccA}|\neg\text{Fail}] \cdot \Pr[\neg\text{Fail}] \geq \varepsilon(k) + \frac{1}{2} - \Pr[\text{Fail}]$. Since $\Pr[\text{SuccA}|\neg\text{Fail}, \text{AskA}] = 1/2$, we also have $\Pr[\text{SuccA}|\neg\text{Fail}] = \Pr[\text{SuccA}|\neg\text{Fail} \wedge \text{AskA}] \cdot \Pr[\text{AskA}] + \frac{1}{2}(1 - \Pr[\text{AskA}]) = \frac{1}{2}\Pr[\text{AskA}] + \frac{1}{2}$. Hence, we have that $(\frac{1}{2}\Pr[\text{AskA}] + \frac{1}{2}) \cdot \Pr[\neg\text{Fail}] \geq \varepsilon(\lambda) + \frac{1}{2} - \Pr[\text{Fail}]$, and therefore, $\Pr[\text{AskA}] \geq 2\varepsilon(\lambda) - \Pr[\text{Fail}]$. Next, we estimate $\Pr[\text{Fail}]$. The event Fail occurs only when either

Case 1. $\mathcal{A}$ submits a decryption query $\text{ID}, C_0 || H_2(x, C_0) \oplus M$ such that $C_0 = \text{IBE.Enc}(\text{mpk}, \text{ID}, x; H_1(x))$ without asking $H_1(x)$, where $x \leftarrow \mathcal{M}$, or

Case 2. $\mathcal{A}$ submits a decryption query $\text{ID}, \text{IBE.Enc}(\text{mpk}, \text{ID}, x; H_1(x)) || C_1$ such that $C_1 = H_2(x, \text{IBE.Enc}(\text{mpk}, \text{ID}, x; H_1(x))) \oplus M$ without asking $H_2(x, \text{IBE.Enc}(\text{mpk}, \text{ID}, x; H_1(x)))$, where $x \leftarrow \mathcal{M}$.

Case 1 and Case 2 happen with probability at most $\frac{q_{H_1}}{|\mathcal{M}|}$ and $\frac{q_{H_2}}{|\mathcal{M}|}$, respectively, and therefore, we have that $\Pr[\text{Fail}] \leq 1 - (1 - \frac{q_{H_1} - q_{H_2}}{|\mathcal{M}|})^{q_D}$. Hence, we have that $\text{Adv}_{\mathcal{B}}(\lambda) \geq \frac{1}{q_{H_1} + q_{H_2}}\Pr[\text{AskA}] \geq \frac{1}{q_{H_1} + q_{H_2}}(2\varepsilon(\lambda) - 1 - (1 - \frac{q_{H_1} - q_{H_2}}{|\mathcal{M}|})^{q_D})) \simeq \frac{1}{q_{H_1} + q_{H_2}}(2\varepsilon(\lambda) - q_D\frac{q_{H_1} - q_{H_2}}{|\mathcal{M}|})$. $\square$

Theorem 2. *Suppose that the hash function* H_1 *and* H_2 *are random oracles and* IBE *is* IND-ANON-KGC *secure blind IBE scheme, then* IBE' *is* IND-ANON-KGC$_{\text{CCA}}$ *secure.*

Proof. We show how to construct adversary $\mathcal{B}$ that breaks IND-ANON-KGC security of IBE by using adversary $\mathcal{A}$ that breaks IND-ANON-KGC$_{\text{CCA}}$ security of IBE' with advantage $\varepsilon(\lambda)$. The challenger starts an IND-ANON-KGC security game by running params $\leftarrow$ Setup(1^λ), (mpk, msk) $\leftarrow$ KGC.KeyGen(params) and (vk, ik) $\leftarrow$ ICA.KeyGen(params). $\mathcal{B}$ works by interacting with $\mathcal{A}$ in the IND-ANON-KGC$_{\text{CCA}}$ game as follows:

Setup: $\mathcal{B}$ gives params, mpk, msk, vk to $\mathcal{A}$. When $\mathcal{A}$ makes oracle queries, $\mathcal{B}$ responds as follows:

H_1 **query:** $\mathcal{B}$ maintains a list of tuples (k_i, h_i) to responds the queries. We refer to this list as H_1List. The list is initially empty. When $\mathcal{A}$ queries x_i, $\mathcal{B}$ responds as following:

    1. If the query x_i already appears on the H_1List in a tuple (x_i, h_i) then $\mathcal{B}$ responds with $H_1(x_i) = h_i$.

2. Otherwise, $\mathcal{B}$ picks h_i from $\mathcal{R}$ randomly.
3. $\mathcal{B}$ adds the tuple (x_i, h_i) to the H_1List.

H_2 **Query:** $\mathcal{B}$ maintains a list of tuples (y_i, C_0^i, g_i) as explained below. We refer to this list as the H_2List. The list is initially empty. When $\mathcal{A}$ queries (y_i, C_0^i), $\mathcal{B}$ responds as follows:

1. If the query y_i and C_0^i already appears on the H_2List in a tuple (y_i, C_0^i, g_i) then $\mathcal{B}$ responds with $H_2(y_i, C_0^i) = g_i$.
2. Otherwise, $\mathcal{B}$ picks a random element g_i from $\mathcal{M}'$ of IBE.
3. $\mathcal{B}$ adds the tuple (y_i, C_0^i, g_i) to the H_2List and returns g_i.

Issue Key Query: When $\mathcal{A}$ makes issue key query, $\mathcal{B}$ runs certificate query issued by $\mathcal{A}$. $\mathcal{B}$ passes M_{user} to $\mathcal{A}$ as answer of the query.

Decryption Query: Let $(j, C = (C_0, C_1))$ be the $i-th$ decryption query issued by $\mathcal{A}$. $\mathcal{B}$ responds as follows:

1. Find a pair of tuples (x, h) and (x, C_0, g) from the H_1List and H_2List, respectively, such that $C_0 = \text{IBE.Enc}(\text{mpk}, \text{ID}, x; h)$.
2. Outputs $g \oplus C_1$ if there exists such a pair of tuples, or outputs $\perp$ otherwise.

Challenge Query: Once $\mathcal{A}$ decides that Phase 1 is over it outputs a index i^* and message M^* on which it wishes to be challenged. $\mathcal{B}$ sends i^* to the challenger and receives a ciphertext C_0^*. Then, $\mathcal{B}$ generates $C_0^*||C_1^*$ where C_1^* is random element in $\mathcal{M}'$. $\mathcal{B}$ gives $C_0^*||C_1^*$ as the challenge to $\mathcal{A}$.

Guess: When $\mathcal{A}$ outputs a guess $\widehat{\text{coin}} \in \{0, 1\}$, $\mathcal{B}$ chooses a tuple σ, M, g or σ, h from the H_1List or the H_2List, respectively. Then, $\mathcal{B}$ outputs σ in the tuple as the answer of the IND-ANON-KGC game.

Similar to the proof of Theorem 1, we have $\text{Adv}_{\mathcal{B}}(\lambda) \geq \frac{1}{q_{H_1}+q_{H_2}}(2\varepsilon(\lambda) - q_D \frac{q_{H_1}-q_{H_2}}{|\mathcal{M}|})$.

$\square$

The security against the ICA is a strictly weaker variant of the security against corrupted users. Therefore, Theorem 1 also ensures IND-ANON-ICA$_{CCA}$ security as the following Corollary 1.

Corollary 1. *Suppose that the hash function H_1 and H_2 are random oracles and IBE is IND-ANON-ICA secure blind IBE scheme, then IBE$'$ is IND-ANON-ICA$_{CCA}$ secure.*

5   Instantiation

In this section, we provide two instantiations of our generic construction given in Sect. 4. In Sect. 5.1 (resp., Sect. 5.2), we provide the formal description of pairing-based construction (resp., the lattice-based construction). In Sect. 5.3, we compare the space costs of each element about our schemes and the existing schemes.

5.1   Instantiation from Pairing

In this section, we show how to construct a CCA secure blind IBE scheme from the CPA secure blind IBE scheme based on pairing [8].

Construction. Let $\mathbb{G}$ and $\mathbb{G}_T$ be groups with prime order p, $g \in \mathbb{G}$ be a generator, and $e : \mathbb{G} \times \mathbb{G} \to \mathbb{G}_T$ be a pairing. Let the identity space $\mathcal{ID}$ of the IBE scheme IBE be $\mathsf{ID} = \mathbb{Z}_p$ and the message space $\mathcal{M}$ of IBE be $\mathcal{M} = \{0,1\}^l$. Finally, let Sig := (Sig.KeyGen, Sig.Sign, Sig.Verify) be a digital signature scheme with message space $\{0,1\}^n$ for some n. We assume that Sig provides the standard security notion of existential unforgeability under an adaptive chosen message attack (EUF-CMA).

Setup(1^λ): : Choose $(\mathbb{G}, \mathbb{G}_T, g, p, e)$ where p be a λ-bit prime number. Output params $= (1^\lambda, (\mathbb{G}, \mathbb{G}_T, g, p, e), \mathsf{H}_0, \mathsf{H}_1, \mathsf{H}_2)$ where $\mathsf{H}_0 : \mathbb{Z}_p \to \mathbb{G}, \mathsf{H}_1 : \mathbb{G}_T \to \mathbb{Z}_p, \mathsf{H}_2 : \mathbb{G}_T \times \mathbb{G}_T \to \{0,1\}^l$ are hash functions modeled as random oracle.

KGC.KeyGen(params): Choose $x \leftarrow \mathbb{Z}_p$ and compute $Y = g^x$. Then, output a master public key mpk $= Y$ and a master secret key msk $= x$.

ICA.KeyGen(params): Run $(\mathsf{vk_{Sig}}, \mathsf{sk_{Sig}}) \leftarrow$ Sig.KeyGen(1^λ). Then, output a certificate verification key vk $= \mathsf{vk_{Sig}}$ and a certificate issuing key ik $= \mathsf{sk_{Sig}}$.

ICA.Cert(vk, ik, ID): Parse ik $= \mathsf{sk_{Sig}}$ and compute $u_{\mathsf{ID}} = \mathsf{H}_0(\mathsf{ID})$. Then, choose $y_{\mathsf{ID},1} \leftarrow \mathbb{Z}_p$ and compute $u_{\mathsf{ID},1} = g^{y_{\mathsf{ID},1}}$. Furthermore, compute $u_{\mathsf{ID},2} = u_{\mathsf{ID}} u_{\mathsf{ID},1} \in \mathbb{G}$ and $\sigma_{\mathsf{Sig}} \leftarrow$ Sig.Sign($\mathsf{sk_{Sig}}, u_{\mathsf{ID},2}$). Finally, output a certificate cert $= (u_{\mathsf{ID},2}, \sigma_{\mathsf{Sig}})$ and trapdoor information td $= y_{\mathsf{ID},1}$.

IBE.Enc(mpk, ID, M): Compute $u_{\mathsf{ID}} = \mathsf{H}_0(\mathsf{ID})$. To encrypt a message M $\in \{0,1\}^l$, sample $k \leftarrow \mathbb{G}_T$, and computes $r = \mathsf{H}_1(k)$. Next, compute $(c_0, c_1, c_2) = (g^r, k \cdot e(u_{\mathsf{ID}}, Y)^r, M \oplus \mathsf{H}_2(k, c_1))$. Finally, output a ciphertext C $= (c_0, c_1, c_2)$.

IBE.Dec(mpk, sk$_{\mathsf{ID}}$, C): Parse C $= (c_0, c_1, c_2)$. Compute $k = c_1/e(\mathsf{sk_{ID}}, c_0)$ and M $= c_2 \oplus \mathsf{H}_2(k, c_1)$. If $k \cdot e(u_{\mathsf{ID}}, Y)^{\mathsf{H}_1(k)} = c_1$, then output M, otherwise output $\perp$.

⟨ObtainKey(mpk, ID, cert, td), IssueKey(mpk, msk, vk)⟩: The user and the KGC interactively runs ObtainKey and IssueKey, respectively.

User: On input (mpk, ID, cert, td), set the first-round message $\mathsf{M_{user}} =$ cert and send $\mathsf{M_{user}}$ to the KGC. Here, cert $= (u_{\mathsf{ID},2}, \sigma_{\mathsf{Sig}})$.

KGC: On input (mpk, msk, vk) and the first-round message $\mathsf{M_{user}}$, parse vk $= \mathsf{vk_{Sig}}$ and $\mathsf{M_{user}} = (u_{\mathsf{ID},2}, \sigma_{\mathsf{Sig}})$. If Sig.Verify($\mathsf{vk_{Sig}}, u_{\mathsf{ID},2}, \sigma_{\mathsf{Sig}}$) $= \perp$, then set $\mathsf{M_{KGC}} = \perp$ and send $\mathsf{M_{KGC}}$ to the user. Otherwise, parse mpk $= Y$ and msk $= x$. Then, compute $y_{\mathsf{ID},2} = u_{\mathsf{ID},2}^x$, set $\mathsf{M_{KGC}} = y_{\mathsf{ID},2}$, and send $\mathsf{M_{KGC}}$ to the user.

User: If $\mathsf{M_{KGC}} = \perp$, then output $\perp$. Otherwise, parse td $= y_{\mathsf{ID},1}$ and $\mathsf{M_{KGC}} = y_{\mathsf{ID},2}$, compute $e_{\mathsf{ID}} = y_{\mathsf{ID},2} \cdot Y^{-y_{\mathsf{ID},1}}$ and (locally) output the secret key sk$_{\mathsf{ID}} = e_{\mathsf{ID}}$.

5.2 Instantiation from Lattice

In this section, we show how to construct a CCA secure blind IBE scheme from the CPA secure blind IBE scheme based on lattice [7].

Construction. Let the identity space $\mathcal{ID}$ of the IBE scheme IBE be $\mathcal{ID} = \{0,1\}^*$. In practice, by using collusion resistant hash functions, we can set $\mathcal{ID} = \{0,1\}^l$ for $l = O(\lambda)$. Here, we occasionally treat elements in $\mathbb{Z}_q^n$ as binary strings over $\{0,1\}^{n \log q}$ through some fixed canonical embedding. Let PRF : $\mathcal{K} \times \mathcal{X} = \mathcal{Y}$ be any pseudorandom function with appropriate domain $\mathcal{X}$ and range $\mathcal{Y}$ (i.e., let $\mathcal{X}$ include $\mathcal{ID}$ and the set of all the first-round messages $\mathsf{M_{user}}$, and let range $\mathcal{Y}$ include an appropriate length of randomness used by algorithms ICA.Cert and IssueKey). Finally, let

Sig = (Sig.KeyGen, Sig.Sign, Sig.Verify) be a deterministic digital signature scheme with message space $\{0,1\}^{n \log q}$ where the randomness used to sign a message is derived deterministically from the signing key and the message. Using PRFs, any digital signature scheme can be derandomized. We assume that Sig provides the standard security notion of existential unforgeability under an adaptive chosen message attack (EUF-CMA).

Setup(1^λ): Choose positive integers n, m and prime q, and output params = $(1^\lambda, 1^n, 1^m, q, \alpha', \sigma, H_0, H_1, H_2)$, where $H_0 : \{0,1\}^* \rightarrow \mathbb{Z}_q^n, H_1 : \{0,1\}^l \rightarrow \mathbb{Z}_q^n, H_2 : \{0,1\}^l \times \{0,1\}^l \rightarrow \{0,1\}^l$ are hash functions modeled as random oracles.

KGC.KeyGen(params): Run $(\mathbf{A}, \mathbf{T_A}) \leftarrow$ TrapGen($1^n, 1^m, q$) and sample a PRF key $s_{KGC} \leftarrow \mathcal{K}$. Then, output a master public key mpk = $\mathbf{A} \in \mathbb{Z}_q^{n \times m}$ and a master secret key msk = $(\mathbf{T_A}, s_{KGC})$.

ICA.KeyGen(params): Run $(vk_{Sig}, sk_{Sig}) \leftarrow$ Sig.KeyGen(1^λ) and sample a PRF key $s_{ICA} \leftarrow \mathcal{K}$. Then, output a certificate verification key vk = vk_{Sig} and a certificate issuing key ik = (sk_{Sig}, s_{ICA}).

ICA.Cert(vk, ik, ID): Parse ik = (sk_{Sig}, s_{ICA}) and compute $u_{ID} = H(ID)$. Then, sample a short vector $y_{ID,1} \leftarrow \{0,1\}^m$ and compute $u_{ID,1} = \mathbf{A}y_{ID,1}$. Furthermore, compute $u_{ID,2} = u_{ID} - u_{ID,1} \in \mathbb{Z}_q^n$ and $\sigma_{Sig} \leftarrow$ Sig.Sign($sk_{Sig}, u_{ID,2}$). Finally, outputs a certificate cert = $(u_{ID,2}, \sigma_{Sig})$ and a trapdoor information td = $y_{ID,1}$. Here, we assume all the randomness used in this algorithm is derived from $r_{ID} \leftarrow$ PRF(s_{ICA}, ID).

IBE.Enc(mpk, ID, M): Compute $u_{ID} = H_0(ID)$. To encrypt a message M $\in \{0,1\}^l$, sample k $\leftarrow \{0,1\}^l$, $\mathbf{x} \leftarrow D_{\mathbb{Z}^m, \alpha', q}$, and $x \leftarrow D_{\mathbb{Z}, \alpha', q}$, and compute s = $H_1(k)$, $c_0 = \mathbf{A}^\top \mathbf{s} + \mathbf{x}$, $c_1^i = u_{ID}^\top \mathbf{s} + x + k_i \lfloor q/2 \rceil$ $(i = 0, \ldots, l-1)$, and $c_2 = M \oplus H_2(k, c_1)$. Finally, output C = (c_0, c_1, c_2).

IBE.Dec(mpk, sk_{ID}, C): Parse, C = (c_0, c_1, c_2) and $sk_{ID} = e_{ID}$. Compute $\omega_i = c_0 - e_{ID}c_1^i$ $(i = 0, \ldots, l-1)$ and if ω_i is closer to 0 than $\lfloor q/2 \rceil$ mod q, then $k_i' = 0$, otherwise $k_i' = 1$. Next, compute M = $c_2 \oplus H_2(k', c_1)$. If $c_1^i = u_{ID}^\top H_1(k) + x + k_i \lfloor q/2 \rceil$ $(i = 0, \ldots, l-1)$, then output M, otherwise output $\perp$.

$\langle$ObtainKey(mpk, ID, cert, td), IssueKey(mpk, msk, vk)$\rangle$: The user and the KGC interactively runs ObtainKey and IssueKey, respectively.

   User: On input (mpk, ID, cert, td), set the first-round message M_{user} = cert and send M_{user} to the KGC. Here, cert = $(u_{ID,2}, \sigma_{Sig})$.

   KGC: On input (mpk, msk, vk) and the first-round message M_{user}, parse vk = vk_{Sig} and M_{user} = $(u_{ID,2}, \sigma_{Sig})$. If Sig.Verify($vk_{Sig}, u_{ID,2}, \sigma_{Sig}$) = $\perp$, then set $M_{KGC} = \perp$ and send M_{KGC} to the user. Otherwise, parse mpk = $\mathbf{A}$ and msk = $(\mathbf{T_A}, s_{KGC})$. Then, sample a short vector $y_{ID,2} \leftarrow$ SamplePre($\mathbf{A}, u_{ID,2}, \mathbf{T_A}, \sigma$), set $M_{KGC} = y_{ID,2}$, and send M_{KGC} to the user. Here, we assume all the randomness used in this algorithm is derived from $r_{M_{user}} \leftarrow$ PRF(s_{KGC}, M_{user}).

   User: If $M_{KGC} = \perp$, then output $\perp$. Otherwise, parse td = $y_{ID,1}$ and $M_{KGC} = y_{ID,2}$, set $e_{ID} = y_{ID,1} + y_{ID,2}$ and (locally) output the secret key $sk_{ID} = e_{ID}$.

5.3   Space Cost Comparison

In this section, we compare the space costs of our CCA secure blind IBE schemes with CPA secure ones by [8]. Table 1 shows a summary of the space costs among them.

In Table 1, in the columns "CPA Lattice" and "CCA Lattice", l denote the length of plaintexts. As we can see in Table 1, compared between a CPA secure scheme and a CCA secure scheme, the costs of a secret key are the exactly same, and the overheads of a ciphertext are the almost same.

Table 1. Evaluation of Space Costs

Element	CPA Pairing	CCA Pairing	CPA Lattice	CCA Lattice
Secret key	$|\mathbb{G}|$	$|\mathbb{G}|$	$|\mathbb{Z}_q^n|$	$|\mathbb{Z}_q^n|$
Plaintext	$|\mathbb{G}_T|$	l	l	l
Ciphertext	$2|\mathbb{G}_T|$	$2|\mathbb{G}_T| + l$	$|\mathbb{Z}_q^n| + l|\mathbb{Z}_q|$	$|\mathbb{Z}_q^n| + l|\mathbb{Z}_q| + l$

6   Implementation of Our Pairing-Based Construction

In this section, we show that our proposed pairing -based scheme does not lose efficiency compared to existing schemes. Specifically, the processing time and data size of our scheme are the almost same as ones of BF-IBE [4] and EKW-Blind-IBE [8]. To this end, we implement a proof of concept in Python 3.7.13 using Charm 0.50 [1], which is a framework for prototyping pairing-based cryptosystems. Our IBE is constructed using symmetric pairings, but for efficiency reasons, we instantiate it with an asymmetric curve with 224-bit base field (curve MNT224 in Charm), which gives approximately 112 bits of security [16]. The experimental platform is performed on a personal computer running 64-bit Ubuntu 22.04 LTS with AMD Ryzen 5-3600 CPU@3.50 GH and 8 GB of RAM. Table 2 presents a comparison result of the cost in milliseconds, associated to the main cryptographic operations among of BF-IBE, CCA version BF-IBE, EKW-Blind-IBE, and CCA version of EKW-Blind-IBE (our scheme). We executed these experiments in 50 different runs of 10 times each, and both the minimum and average timing was taken for each operation; we use the Python module timeit for these measurements. It can be seen that the efficiency of BF-IBE, EKW-Blind-IBE, and our scheme are comparable for the main high-level operations of IBE, namely Encryption and Decryption. Furthermore, the total average processing time of other operations in our scheme is about 37.187 ms, which is considered highly practical, while our scheme has additional security compared to BF-IBE and EKW-Blind-IBE.

Table 2. Evaluation of Time Performance

	BF-IBE-CPA		BF-IBE-CCA		EKW-Blind-IBE		Ours	
	min. (ms)	ave. (ms)	min. (ms)	ave. (ms)	min. (ms)	ave. (ms)	min. (ms)	ave. (ms)
KGC.KeyGen	4.512	4.911	4.990	5.150	4.485	4.887	4.534	5.091
ICA.KeyGen	–	–	–	–	4.011	4.374	3.982	4.456
ICA.Cert	–	–	–	–	1.143	1.251	1.216	1.291
SKGen (Extract)	0.565	0.627	0.553	0.622	7.424	8.075	8.036	8.261
Encryption	11.212	12.327	13.528	14.408	11.222	12.271	13.961	14.505
Decryption	3.176	3.513	3.333	3.609	3.430	3.512	3.498	3.583

Acknowledgement. This research was in part conducted under a contract of "Research and development on new generation cryptography for secure wireless communication services" among "Research and Development for Expansion of Radio Wave Resources (JPJ000254)", which was supported by the Ministry of Internal Affairs and Communications, Japan. This work also was in part supported by JSPS KAKENHI Grant Numbers JP22H03590 and JP21H03395, JST-CREST JPMJCR22M1, and JST-AIP JPMJCR22U5.

References

1. Akinyele, J.A., et al.: Charm: a framework for rapidly prototyping cryptosystems. J. Cryptographic Eng. **3**(2), 111–128 (2013)
2. Al-Riyami, S.S., Paterson, K.G.: Certificateless public key cryptography. In: Laih, C.-S. (ed.) ASIACRYPT 2003. LNCS, vol. 2894, pp. 452–473. Springer, Heidelberg (2003). https://doi.org/10.1007/978-3-540-40061-5_29
3. Attrapadung, N., et al.: Relations among notions of security for identity based encryption schemes. Cryptology ePrint Archive, Report 2005/258
4. Boneh, D., Franklin, M.: Identity-based encryption from the Weil pairing. In: Kilian, J. (ed.) CRYPTO 2001. LNCS, vol. 2139, pp. 213–229. Springer, Heidelberg (2001). https://doi.org/10.1007/3-540-44647-8_13
5. Chow, S.S.M.: Removing escrow from identity-based encryption. In: Jarecki, S., Tsudik, G. (eds.) PKC 2009. LNCS, vol. 5443, pp. 256–276. Springer, Heidelberg (2009). https://doi.org/10.1007/978-3-642-00468-1_15
6. Dolev, D., Dwork, C., Naor, M.: Non-malleable cryptography (extended abstract). In: 23rd ACM STOC, pp. 542–552
7. Emura, K., Katsumata, S., Watanabe, Y.: Identity-based encryption with security against the KGC: a formal model and its instantiation from lattices. In: Sako, K., Schneider, S., Ryan, P.Y.A. (eds.) ESORICS 2019. LNCS, vol. 11736, pp. 113–133. Springer, Cham (2019). https://doi.org/10.1007/978-3-030-29962-0_6
8. Emura, K., Katsumata, S., Watanabe, Y.: Identity-based encryption with security against the KGC: a formal model and its instantiations. Theor. Comput. Sci. **900**, 97–119 (2022)
9. Fujisaki, E., Okamoto, T.: How to enhance the security of public-key encryption at minimum cost. In: Imai, H., Zheng, Y. (eds.) PKC 1999. LNCS, vol. 1560, pp. 53–68. Springer, Heidelberg (1999). https://doi.org/10.1007/3-540-49162-7_5
10. Galindo, D., Hasuo, I.: Security notions for identity based encryption. Cryptology ePrint Archive, Report 2005/253
11. Garg, S., Hajiabadi, M., Mahmoody, M., Rahimi, A.: Registration-based encryption: removing private-key generator from IBE. In: Beimel, A., Dziembowski, S. (eds.) TCC 2018. LNCS, vol. 11239, pp. 689–718. Springer, Cham (2018). https://doi.org/10.1007/978-3-030-03807-6_25
12. Green, M., Hohenberger, S.: Blind identity-based encryption and simulatable oblivious transfer. In: Kurosawa, K. (ed.) ASIACRYPT 2007. LNCS, vol. 4833, pp. 265–282. Springer, Heidelberg (2007). https://doi.org/10.1007/978-3-540-76900-2_16
13. Hofheinz, D., Hövelmanns, K., Kiltz, E.: A modular analysis of the Fujisaki-Okamoto transformation. In: Kalai, Y., Reyzin, L. (eds.) TCC 2017. LNCS, vol. 10677, pp. 341–371. Springer, Cham (2017). https://doi.org/10.1007/978-3-319-70500-2_12
14. Izabachène, M., Pointcheval, D.: New anonymity notions for identity-based encryption. In: Ostrovsky, R., De Prisco, R., Visconti, I. (eds.) SCN 2008. LNCS, vol. 5229, pp. 375–391. Springer, Heidelberg (2008). https://doi.org/10.1007/978-3-540-85855-3_25

15. Micciancio, D., Peikert, C.: Trapdoors for lattices: simpler, tighter, faster, smaller. In: Pointcheval, D., Johansson, T. (eds.) EUROCRYPT 2012. LNCS, vol. 7237, pp. 700–718. Springer, Heidelberg (2012). https://doi.org/10.1007/978-3-642-29011-4_41

16. Miyaji, A., Nakabayashi, M., Takano, S.: New explicit conditions of elliptic curve traces for FR-reduction. IEICE Trans. Fundam. Electron. Commun. Comput. Sci. **84**, 1234–1243 (2001)

17. Shamir, A.: Identity-based cryptosystems and signature schemes. In: Blakley, G.R., Chaum, D. (eds.) CRYPTO 1984. LNCS, vol. 196, pp. 47–53. Springer, Heidelberg (1985). https://doi.org/10.1007/3-540-39568-7_5

A New Gadget Decomposition Algorithm with Less Noise Growth in HE Schemes

Chao Liu[1,2(✉)] and Bozhong Liu[2]

[1] Shenzhen Institutes of Advanced Technology, Chinese Academy of Sciences, Shenzhen, China
[2] Sangfor Technologies Inc., Shenzhen, China
`liuchao@sangfor.com.cn`

Abstract. A gadget decomposition algorithm can invert a specific gadget matrix and produce an output with specific statistical properties. Such algorithms are commonly used in GSW-type homomorphic encryption schemes, like TFHE, to enable homomorphic multiplication on ciphertexts while controlling noise growth.

In this paper, we propose a new decomposition algorithm that has lower noise growth compared to existing algorithms. Our work is inspired by Genise et al.'s algorithm [EUROCRYPT 2018] and can be considered an improved version of their algorithm. Our decomposition procedure is designed using the idea of Babai's nearest plane algorithm. Our experimental result show that both the noise growth and efficiency are superior to Genise et al.'s algorithm, and Zhang-Yu's algorithm [PKC 2022].

Keywords: Gadget decomposition · Subgaussian distribution · Lattice gadget · Implementation · Homomorphic encryption

1 Introduction

Homomorphic Encryption (HE) [5,7,8,11,14] is a crucial technique for protecting sensitive data. In lattice-based homomorphic encryptions, the noise in the ciphertexts grows after performing homomorphic operations. Let $Enc(m; e)$ be the HE encryption ciphertext of message m with noise e. The noise in two ciphertexts sum to the sum of the noise in those two ciphertexts, i.e.

$$Enc(m_1; e_1) + Enc(m_2; e_2) = Enc(m_1 + m_2; e_1 + e_2).$$

When multiplying a ciphertext $Enc(m; e)$ by a constant u, the result is $Enc(um; ue)$, and the noise can become large when u is large.

A solution to obtain a meaningful encryption (with small noise) of um is to use binary digit decomposition of u. Given encryptions

$$\{Enc(2^i m; e_i)\}_{i=0,\cdots,k-1},$$

one can compute $Enc(um)$ by decomposing $u = \sum_i 2^i u_i$ where $u_i \in 0, 1$, and computing

$$\sum_i u_i \cdot Enc(2^i m; e_i) = Enc(\sum_i 2^i u_i m; \sum_i u_i e_i) = Enc(um; \sum_i u_i e_i).$$

In this way, the resulting noise scales linearly with $k = \log_2 u$ but not u. This method is widely used in the GSW-type homomorphic encryption schemes [15] such as FHEW [10], TFHE [8], and the recently proposed NTRU-type scheme [4, 17].

In a paper by Alperin-Sheriff and Peikert [2], it was suggested that when using Subgaussian Decomposition, the resulting noise can be reduced more than the binary digit decomposition. The Pythagorean Additivity property of the subgaussian distribution allows the noise to only increase as $O(\sqrt{k})$. Although Discrete Gaussian Sampling can also result in the Pythagorean growth, its sampling process is significantly more complex, making it unfeasible for use in decomposing a factor in HE schemes. Thus, Subgaussian Decomposition is the preferred option in HE schemes due to its Pythagorean Additivity and reduced noise overhead.

The first practical Subgaussian Decomposition algorithm was proposed by Genise et al. [13]. This algorithm allows for the decomposition of any value $u < q$ into a subgaussian vector, given a modulus q and base b. Testing by Genise et al. [13] showed that using Subgaussian Decomposition improved the implementation performance of the KP-ABE scheme [9] by a factor ranging from 18x to 289x.

The noise produced by the homomorphic multiplication computation $\sum_i u_i \cdot Enc(2^i m; e_i)$ is $\sum_i u_i e_i$. Assuming e_i is independently sampled from a Gaussian distribution with parameter σ (which is typical in homomorphic encryption schemes), then $\sum_i u_i e_i$ can be considered as an element from a Gaussian distribution with parameter $\|u\|_2 \sigma$, where $u = (u_0, \cdots, u_{k-1})$ is the vector of u's decomposition parameters. The magnitude of the noise growth $\sum_i u_i e_i$ largely depends on the length (e.g., l_2 norm) of u.

The algorithm proposed by Genise et al. is a randomized algorithm, meaning that some outputs perform better than others. For example, if $q = 23$, $b = 3$, and $u = 16$, then Table 1 shows all possible decomposition results. As shown, the decomposition $(-1, 1, -1)$ performs better than the others, as it has the smallest $\|u\|_2$. If there were a method that could always produce the decomposition $(-1, 1, -1)$, it would result in smaller noise growth in the homomorphic encryption ciphertexts multiplication. This motivates our work to find a better way to generate smaller decompositions than those produced by Genise et al.'s algorithm.

Table 1. For modulus $q = 23$ and base $b = 3$, the decomposition results ($g^{-1}(u) = u$ in the table) for $u = 16$ using Genise et al.'s algorithm in [13], the Algorithm 2 in this paper and the digit decomposition algorithm.

Algorithm	$g^{-1}(u) = u$	Probability	$\|u\|_2$
Genise et al.'s [13]	$(1, 2, 1)$	4.5%	$\sqrt{6}$
	$(-2, 3, 1)$	2.2%	$\sqrt{14}$
	$(1, -1, 2)$	15.8%	$\sqrt{6}$
	$(-2, 0, 2)$	7.9%	$\sqrt{8}$
	$(-1, 1, -1)$	36.1%	$\sqrt{3}$
	$(2, 0, -1)$	18%	$\sqrt{5}$
	$(-1, -2, 0)$	10.3%	$\sqrt{5}$
	$(2, -3, 0)$	5.2%	$\sqrt{13}$
Digit Decomposition	$(1, 2, 1)$	100%	$\sqrt{6}$
Ours	$(-1, 1, -1)$	100%	$\sqrt{3}$

1.1 Our Works

We give a new decomposition algorithm that generates smaller decompositions than the algorithm proposed by Genise et al. [13]. Unlike Genise et al.'s algorithm [13], our algorithm is deterministic to output those "shorter decomposition vector"[1], resulting in more efficient implementation and lower noise growth for homomorphic encryption schemes.

Our method is to directly use the idea of Babai's algorithm [3] for decomposition, resulting in smaller outputs than Genise et al.'s algorithm. Specifically, the subgaussian parameter of our algorithm's outputs is half that of Genise et al.'s algorithm, i.e., $\frac{b+1}{2}\sqrt{2\pi}$ compared to $(b+1)\sqrt{2\pi}$ when $q \neq b^k$. This means that in a GSW-type [15] homomorphic encryption scheme, the estimated noise growth after ciphertext multiplication using our algorithm is much smaller than using Genise et al.'s algorithm. Furthermore, as our algorithm does not require any randomness generation, it is also more efficient.

We implement our algorithm in Sect. 4 using the PALISADE Library, and compare its performance to Genise et al.'s algorithm and another similar decomposition algorithm [22]. Our experiments show that our decomposition indeed outperforms the other two algorithms in terms of noise growth and efficiency.

1.2 Related Works

Besides the subgaussian decomposition algorithm proposed by Genise et al. [13], Jeon et al. [16] proposed an algorithm that outputs a bounded uniform distribution. Their algorithm consists of two sub-routines: *Decomposition* and *Sampling*.

---

[1] While our algorithm may have lost the "randomness" present in Genise et al.'s algorithm, it is worth noting that in homomorphic encryption algorithms, such as the commonly used Digit Decomposition, "randomness" is not necessary for a decomposition.

However, due to the fact that the noise growth of their algorithm is worse than that of Genise et al.'s algorithm (from Fig. 2 in [16]), we did not implement it for comparison.

Zhang and Yu [22] proposed another decomposition algorithm to address the performance gap observed between Genise et al.'s algorithm for the cases when $q = b^k$ and $q < b^k$. They proposed to first sample the $(k-1)$ lower digits using the subgaussian algorithm for modulus b^{k-1}, and then compute the highest digit independently when $q < b^k$. Their algorithm performs better than Genise et al.'s algorithm and we compare it with our proposed algorithm and Genise et al.'s algorithm in Sect. 4.

1.3   Organization

In Sect. 2, we describe some preliminaries about notations and subgaussian random variables and lattices. In Sect. 3, we present our decomposition algorithm. In Sect. 4, we give the implementation result of our decomposition.

2   Preliminaries

In this paper, $\mathbb{Z}_q = \mathbb{Z}/q\mathbb{Z}$ is denoted as the quotient ring of integers modulo q, and $(\mathbb{Z}_q, +)$ is presented as the additive group of $\mathbb{Z}_q = \mathbb{Z}/q\mathbb{Z}$. We usually indicate numbers with lowercase letters, such that $z \in \mathbb{Z}$, vectors are in bold lower-case letters, $\mathbf{z} \in \mathbb{Z}^n$, matrices are in bold capital letters, $\mathbf{M} \in \mathbb{Z}^{n \times n}$, and denote $\mathbf{I}_n$ as the $n \times n$ identity matrix. We assume that the vector $\mathbf{z} = (z_0, z_1, \ldots, z_{n-1})$ is in column form, and denote its transpose as $\mathbf{z}^T = [z_0, z_1, \ldots, z_{n-1}]$. For vectors $\mathbf{z}_0, \mathbf{z}_1, \ldots, \mathbf{z}_{n-1}$, we denote the horizon concatenation of those vectors as $\mathbf{M} = [\mathbf{z}_0, \mathbf{z}_1, \ldots, \mathbf{z}_{n-1}]$, and the vertical concatenation as $\mathbf{M}^T = (\mathbf{z}_0^T, \mathbf{z}_1^T, \ldots, \mathbf{z}_{n-1}^T)$. We denote the l_2 norm of vector $\mathbf{z}$ by $\|\mathbf{z}\|_2$, the l_∞ by $\|\mathbf{z}\|_\infty$.

For an integer $x \geq 1$ and an integer base $b > 1$ such that $x < b^k$, where $k \geq 1$, then x's b-ary decomposition is a vector $\boldsymbol{x} = [x]_b^k = (x_0, \cdots, x_{k-1}) \in \{0, \cdots, b-1\}^k$ such that $\sum_i b^i x_i = x$.

We use the notation $x \xleftarrow{\$} \chi$ to denote the sampling of a value x according to the probability distribution χ, while $x \xleftarrow{\$} U(\mathbb{Z}_q)$ indicates that x is sampled uniformly from $\mathbb{Z}_q$. We will make use of the Geršgorin Circle Theorem, which is stated as follows.

Theorem 1 ([13], Theorem 2.1). *Let $\mathbf{T}$ be an $n \times n$ matrix with complex entries. For each row j let t_j be the sum of its non-diagonal entries' magnitudes: $t_j = \sum_{j \neq i} |\mathbf{T}(j, i)|$. Then, the eigenvalues of $\mathbf{T}$ are all in $\cup_j \{z \in \mathbb{C} : |z - \mathbf{T}(j,j)| \leq t_j\}$.*

2.1   Subgaussian Random Variables

A real random variable X is subgaussian [19,21] with parameter s if for all $x \in \mathbb{R}$, if its (scaled) moment-generating function satisfies $\mathbb{E}[exp(2\pi x X)] \leq exp(\pi s^2 x^2)$.

Any B-bounded centered random variable X is subgaussian with parameter $B \cdot \sqrt{2\pi}$. Two useful properties for subgaussian random variables are as follows:

- Homogeneity: if X is subgaussian with parameter s, then $t \cdot X$ is subgaussian with parameter $t \cdot s$.
- Pythagorean additivity: if X_1 is subgaussian with parameter s_1, X_2 is subgaussian with parameter s_2, then, $X_1 + X_2$ is subgaussian with parameter $\sqrt{s_1^2 + s_2^2}$.

For a real random vector z, if for all real unit vectors u, their marginal $\langle z, v \rangle$ is subgaussian with parameter s then we say z is subgaussian with parameter s. If one vector is the concatenation of subgaussian variables or vectors, each of which is subgaussian with parameter s and is independent of the prior one, then it is also subgaussian with parameter s. Homogeneity and Pythagorean additivity also hold from the linearity of vectors.

The following two lemmas will be used in our analysis.

Lemma 1 ([13], Lemma 2.2). *Let $v \in \mathbb{R}^n$ be a discrete random vector such that each coordinate v_i is subgaussian with parameter β_i given the previous coordinates take any values. Then v is a subgaussian vector with parameter $\max_i \{\beta_i\}$.*

Lemma 2 ([19],Corollary 2.3, [13], Lemma 2.2). *Let v be a subgaussian vector with parameter β and let $\mathbf{T}$ be a linear transformation. Then, $\mathbf{T}v$ is a subgaussian vector with parameter $\beta\sqrt{\lambda_{max}(\mathbf{T}\mathbf{T}^T)}$ where $\lambda_{max}(\cdot)$ is the largest eigenvalue.*

2.2 Lattices

We denote a lattice Λ with basis $\mathbf{B} = [b_0, \cdots, b_{k-1}] \in \mathbb{Z}^{n \times k}$ as $\Lambda = \mathcal{L}(\mathbf{B}) = \{\sum_{i=0}^{k} z_i b_i : z_i \in \mathbb{Z}\}$. In this paper, we consider only the case where $k = n$ (full-rank lattices). A permutation of the basis vectors is also a lattice basis. If a lattice is a sublattice of $\mathbb{Z}^n$, it is called an integer lattice.

The Gram-Schmidt orthogonalization (GSO) of a lattice Λ's basis $\mathbf{B} = [b_0, \cdots, b_{n-1}]$ is a set of vectors $\tilde{\mathbf{B}} = [\tilde{b}_0, \cdots, \tilde{b}_{n-1}]$, where $\tilde{b}_i$ is the component of b_i orthogonal to $\text{span}(b_0, \cdots, b_{i-1})$. Note that the GSO is not the basis of the lattice. However, for $\mathcal{P}_{1/2}(\tilde{\mathbf{B}}) := \tilde{\mathbf{B}} \cdot (-1/2, 1/2]^n$, the GSO provides a tiling of $\mathbb{R}^n$ such that $\mathbb{R}^n = \cup_{z \in \Lambda}(z + \mathcal{P}_{1/2}(\tilde{\mathbf{B}}))$. In this paper, we will utilize the nearest plane algorithm, also known as Babai's greedy decoding algorithm [3] (given in Appendix).

Theorem 2. *Given $\mathbf{B}, \tilde{\mathbf{B}}, t \in \mathbb{R}^n$, there is an algorithm which returns the unique lattice point in $t + \mathcal{P}_{1/2}(\tilde{\mathbf{B}})$ in time $O(n^2)$ and memory $O(n^3)$[2].*

---

[2] Assumes the GSO has entries each presented in $O(n)$ bits.

q-ary Lattices. In this paper we mostly consider the q-ary lattices. Fix an integer modulus $q > 0$ and let integer $m > n$. We say $\mathbf{B}$ is primitive if $\mathbf{B}\mathbb{Z}_q^m = \mathbb{Z}_q^n$. Given an matrix $\mathbf{B} \in \mathbb{Z}_q^{n \times m}$, define lattices $\Lambda_q^\perp(\mathbf{B}) = \{z \in \mathbb{Z}^m : \mathbf{B}z = 0 \bmod q\}$. When $\mathbf{B}$ is primitive, the cosets of $\Lambda_q^\perp(\mathbf{B})$, $\Lambda_u^\perp := \{z \in \mathbb{Z}^m : \mathbf{B}z = u \bmod q\}$, are in bijection with $\mathbb{Z}_q^n$.

Subgaussian Decomposition. For $m > w > n$, in many lattice crypto-schemes, given a primitive $\mathbf{G} \in \mathbb{Z}_q^{n \times w}$ and an arbitrary $u \in \mathbb{Z}_q^n$ as input, there is need to find a subgaussian vector $x \in \mathbb{Z}^w$ such that $u = \mathbf{G}x \bmod q$. This problem is called the subgaussian decomposition problem or subgaussian sampling. In [2], Alperin-Sheriff and Peikert use a generic adaptation of Babai's algorithm to achieve subgaussian decomposition, which runs in $O(k^2)$ and uses space $O(k^3)$. Then in [13], Genise et al. use a technique developed by Genise and Micciancio [12] to achieve subgaussian decomposition in $O(k)$ time and space. In this paper, we optimize Genise et al.'s work [13].

A $\mathbf{G}$ commonly used is defined as $\mathbf{G} = \mathbf{I}_n \otimes g^T$ (usually called gadget matrix) with blocks $g^T := (1, b, \cdots, b^{k-1})$, where integer $b \in (1, q)$ is the base and $k = \lceil \log_b q \rceil$.

3   Gadget Decomposition Algorithms

In this section, we present our main decomposition algorithms for the gadget matrix $\mathbf{G} = \mathbf{I}_n \otimes g^T$. We demonstrate how to efficiently compute the function $g^{-1} : \mathbb{Z}_q \to \mathbb{Z}^k$ and compute $\mathbf{G}^{-1}(u) = (g^{-1}(u_i))_{i=1}^n$ component by component.

Let the gadget be $g^T := (1, b, \cdots, b^{k-1})$, where $k = \lceil \log_b q \rceil$. In this section, we will present two different decomposition methods based on whether q is a power of b (i.e., when $q = b^k$) or when $q < b^k$. The decomposition algorithms for the case when q and u are given in CRT form are presented in the appendix (Sect. B).

Our main result is presented in the following theorem.

Theorem 3. *For an integer modulus $q > 1$, any integer base $b > 1$, $k = \lceil \log_b q \rceil$, gadget $g^T = [1, b, \cdots, b^{k-1}]$ and a randomly chosen $u \xleftarrow{\$} U(\mathbb{Z}_q)^3$, there exists a decomposition algorithm g^{-1} that outputs a decomposition vector and satisfies the following conditions:*

- *If $q = b^k$, the algorithm runs in linear $O(k)$ time and space, and the subgaussian parameter of the output vector $g^{-1}(u)$ is at most $\frac{b}{2}\sqrt{2\pi}$.*
- *If $q \neq b^k$, the algorithm runs in linear $O(k)$ time and space, and the subgaussian parameter of the output vector $g^{-1}(u)$ is at most $\frac{b+1}{2}\sqrt{2\pi}$.*

A proof of Theorem 3 is provided in the following subsections, Sect. 3.2 and Sect. 3.3.

---

[3] The reason for randomly selecting u from $\mathbb{Z}_q$ is that, in the GSW-type homomorphic encryption scheme [15], the decomposition algorithm typically operates on an element randomly chosen from $\mathbb{Z}_q$ based on the LWE assumption.

3.1 Algorithm Rationale

We outline the construction of our algorithm as follows.

Given a primitive matrix $\mathbf{G} \in \mathbb{Z}_q^{n \times w}$ and an arbitrary input vector $\boldsymbol{u}$, the goal is to find a vector $\boldsymbol{x} \in \mathbb{Z}^w$ with a small l_2 norm such that $\mathbf{G}\boldsymbol{x} = \boldsymbol{u} \mod q$. We define lattices as:

$$\Lambda_q^{\perp}(\mathbf{G}) = \{\boldsymbol{z} \in \mathbb{Z}^w : \mathbf{G}\boldsymbol{z} = \mathbf{0} \mod q\}.$$

Therefore, the problem is equivalent to finding a short vector in the cosets of $\Lambda_q^{\perp}(\mathbf{G})$:

$$\Lambda_{\boldsymbol{u}}^{\perp}(\mathbf{G}) = \{\boldsymbol{z} \in \mathbb{Z}^w : \mathbf{G}\boldsymbol{z} = \boldsymbol{u} \mod q\}.$$

It is important to note that finding the shortest vector in $\Lambda_{\boldsymbol{u}}^{\perp}(\mathbf{G})$, which is known as the Shortest Vector Problem (SVP), is a difficult task. The shortest vector is usually obtained by applying a lattice reduction algorithm, such as LLL [18,20] or BKZ [6] on the lattice basis, and this is impractical for a decomposition algorithm. Instead, our goal is to find a "short" vector, and a feasible way to achieve this is through Babai's algorithm.

Initially, Babai's algorithm can be utilized to find a near vector $\boldsymbol{z}$ of $-\boldsymbol{v}$ in the lattice $\Lambda_q^{\perp}(\mathbf{G})$, where $\boldsymbol{v} \in \Lambda_{\boldsymbol{u}}^{\perp}(\mathbf{G})$, and return $\boldsymbol{v} + \boldsymbol{z}$ as the result. This concept was first presented by Alperin-Sheriff and Peikert in [2]. They employed a randomized version of Babai's algorithm to sample a subgaussian vector from $\Lambda_{\boldsymbol{u}}^{\perp}(\mathbf{G})$. However, one limitation of this approach is that the basis of $\Lambda_q^{\perp}(\mathbf{G})$ is not diagonal or sparse, which makes it challenging to implement Babai's algorithm. As a result, this decomposition method requires time complexity of $O(k^2)$ and space complexity of $O(k^3)$, where k is the dimension of the lattice $\Lambda_q^{\perp}(\mathbf{G})$.

After that, Genise et al. proposed an efficient decomposition algorithm based on the technique of Genise and Micciancio [12]. Genise and Micciancio showed that the basis of $\Lambda_q^{\perp}(\mathbf{G})$ can be represented as $\mathbf{SD}$, where $\mathbf{S}$ and $\mathbf{D}$ are sparse and triangular. In Genise et al.'s algorithm, for a vector $\boldsymbol{v} \in \Lambda_{\boldsymbol{u}}^{\perp}(\mathbf{G})$, instead of sampling a vector in $\Lambda_q^{\perp}(\mathbf{G})$, a randomized version of Babai's algorithm is applied in the lattice $\mathcal{L}(\mathbf{D})$ to find a vector $\boldsymbol{z}$ that is close to $-\mathbf{S}^{-1}\boldsymbol{v}$, and the result is obtained by applying the transform $\mathbf{S}$ on $\boldsymbol{z}$, i.e. returning $\boldsymbol{v} + \mathbf{S}\boldsymbol{z}$. Due to the special structure of the basis of $\mathcal{L}(\mathbf{D})$, the entire algorithm runs in $O(k)$ time and uses $O(k)$ space.

In Genise et al.'s algorithm [13], a randomized version of Babai's algorithm was used to find vector $\boldsymbol{z}$ such that $\boldsymbol{z} + \mathbf{S}^{-1}\boldsymbol{v}$ is a subgaussian vector. The randomized version of Babai's algorithm in Genise et al.'s algorithm rounds to one of two adjacent planes that the target lies in, probabilistically. However, we have discovered that this method can produce some poor results. There is a probability that the returned $\boldsymbol{z}$ is far from the target vector $-\mathbf{S}^{-1}\boldsymbol{v}$, and in this case, the norm of the final decomposition will be large. Additionally, we have found that when always choosing the nearest plane of the two adjacent planes, the norm of the decomposition result is smaller. Therefore, in our algorithm, we choose the nearest plane directly in the Babai's algorithm instead of using a randomized version.

3.2 Power-of-Base Case

As a warm up, we consider the case when $q = b^k$ in this section. The input is a positive coset representative $u \in \{0, 1, \cdots, q-1\}$. The lattice $\Lambda_q^\perp(g^T)$ has a basis represented by:

$$
S = \begin{pmatrix}
b & & & \\
-1 & \ddots & & \\
& \ddots & b & \\
& & -1 & b
\end{pmatrix},
$$

and it has GSO $\tilde{S} = b \cdot I$.

Our goal is to find a short vector in $\Lambda_u^\perp(g^T) = \{z \in \mathbb{Z}^k : g^T z = u \mod q\}$ as described in Sect. 3.1. This can be achieved by finding a $\mathbf{0}$'s nearby vector $v \in \Lambda_u^\perp(g^T)$ in $\Lambda_q^\perp(g^T)$. Given the GSO of $\tilde{S}$ as $b \cdot I$, the Babai's nearest plane algorithm can be easily implemented on it. The resulting algorithm is outlined in Algorithm 1. The algorithm simplifies the above process for efficiency and its correctness and efficiency are straightforward to verify.

Algorithm 1. $g^{-1}(u)$ for $q = b^k$.

Input: $u \in \mathbb{Z}_q$
Output: Decomposition vector $x \in \Lambda_u^\perp(g^T)$
1: Let $x \leftarrow \mathbf{0}$
2: **for** $j = n - 1$ to 0 **do**
3:    Let $y \leftarrow u \mod b \in \{0, \cdots, b-1\}$.
4:    $x_i \leftarrow y - \lfloor \frac{y}{b} \rfloor \cdot b$
5:    $u \leftarrow (u - x_i)/b$
6: **end for**
7: **return** x

3.3 Arbitrary Modulus, Arbitrary Base

Next, we present our algorithm for the case when q is not a power of b. In this scenario, the GSO of S_q in the lattice $\Lambda_q^\perp(g^T)$ is not diagonal and not sparse, making the Babai's nearest plane algorithm difficult to implement on basis S_q. To address this challenge, we employ Genise and Micciancio's technique from their work in [12]. They found the fact that S_q admits a sparse, triangular factorization:

$$
\mathbf{S}_q =
\begin{pmatrix}
b & & & q_0 \\
-1 & \ddots & & \vdots \\
& \ddots & b & q_{k-1} \\
& & -1 & q_{k-1}
\end{pmatrix}
=
\begin{pmatrix}
b & & & \\
-1 & \ddots & & \\
& \ddots & b & \\
& & -1 & b
\end{pmatrix}
\begin{pmatrix}
1 & & & d_0 \\
& \ddots & & \vdots \\
& & 1 & d_{k-2} \\
& & & d_{j-1}
\end{pmatrix}
= \mathbf{SD},
$$

where $[q]_b^k = (q_0, \ldots, q_{k-1})$, and $d_i = \frac{d_{i-1}+q_i}{b}$ with initial condition $d_{-1} = 0$.

Thus, instead of directly sampling a short vector in $\Lambda_u^\perp(\boldsymbol{g}^T)$, we first use the Babai's nearest plane algorithm to find a vector $\boldsymbol{x}$ on the lattice $\mathcal{L}(\mathbf{D})$ that is near the target vector $\boldsymbol{t} = -\mathbf{S}^{-1}\boldsymbol{v}$, where $\boldsymbol{v}$ is a vector on the lattice $\Lambda_u^\perp(\boldsymbol{g}^T)$. Then, we map the vector $\boldsymbol{x}$ back to the original lattice by applying the linear transformation $\mathbf{S}$ to it and adding $\boldsymbol{v}$. It can be demonstrated that if $\boldsymbol{x} - \boldsymbol{t} = \boldsymbol{e}$, then $\mathbf{S}\boldsymbol{x} + \boldsymbol{v} = \mathbf{S}\boldsymbol{e}$, and thus, the norm of $\mathbf{S}\boldsymbol{e}$ is equal to the norm of the output of the decomposition algorithm. We will prove that $\mathbf{S}\boldsymbol{e}$ has a subgaussian parameter of $\frac{b+1}{2}\sqrt{2\pi}$ by using following Lemma 3, 4 (and then Theorem 3 is proven).

The input to our algorithm is $u \in \{0, 1, \ldots, q-1\}$, and the steps are as follows:

1 Compute the element $\boldsymbol{v} \leftarrow [u]_b^k$, which is in $\Lambda_u^\perp(\boldsymbol{g}^T)$.
2 Compute the preimage $\boldsymbol{t} = -\mathbf{S}^{-1}\boldsymbol{v}$.
3 Find the near vector $\boldsymbol{x}$ of $\boldsymbol{t}$ on lattice $\mathcal{L}(\mathbf{D})$ using Babai's nearest plane algorithm.
4 Compute $\mathbf{S}\boldsymbol{x} + \boldsymbol{v}$ to obtain the result vector from $\Lambda_u^\perp(\boldsymbol{g}^T)$.

Since the basis $\mathbf{D}$ has a diagonal Gram-Schmidt orthogonalization (GSO) and $\mathbf{S}$ is sparse and triangular, the nearest plane algorithm in step 3 has an efficient specialization. Additionally, the transformations $\mathbf{S}^{-1}$ and $\mathbf{S}$ can be calculated in linear time.

The proposed algorithm is outlined in Algorithm 2. The algorithm is optimized to avoid the explicit computation of $\mathbf{S}, \mathbf{D}$, and to avoid floating point numbers.

Lemma 3. *Step 2 $\sim$ 7 of Algorithm 2 performs the Babai's nearest plane algorithm on lattice $\mathcal{L}(\mathbf{D})$ around target vector $\boldsymbol{t} := -\mathbf{S}^{-1}[u]_b^k$.*

Proof. The reader can look at Babai's nearest plane Algorithm 3 in the Appendix A first to make a better understanding of the following proofs. Note that

$$
\mathbf{D} =
\begin{pmatrix}
1 & & & \frac{q_0}{b} \\
& \ddots & & \vdots \\
& & 1 & \frac{\sum_{i=0}^{k-2} q_i b^i}{b^{k-1}} \\
& & & \frac{q}{b^k}
\end{pmatrix}
$$

and $\boldsymbol{t} = -\left(\frac{u_0}{b}, \cdots, \frac{\sum_{i=0}^{k-2} u_i b^i}{b^{k-1}}, \frac{u}{b^k}\right)^T$. Then let the i-th column of $\mathbf{D}$ is $\boldsymbol{d}_{i-1}$, so we set

$$
x_{k-1} = \lfloor \langle \boldsymbol{t}, \tilde{\boldsymbol{d}}_{k-1}\rangle / \|\tilde{\boldsymbol{d}}_{k-1}\|_2^2 \rceil = -\lfloor u/q \rceil
$$

in step 2.

Algorithm 2. $g^{-1}(u)$

Input: $u \in \mathbb{Z}_q$
Output: Decomposition vector $x \in \Lambda_u^\perp(g^T)$
 1: Let $u \leftarrow [u]_b^k, q \leftarrow [q]_b^k, x, y \leftarrow 0, x_{-1} = 0$
 2: $x_{k-1} \leftarrow -\lfloor u/q \rceil$
 3: **for** $j = k - 2$ to 0 **do**
 4:     $u \leftarrow u - u_{j+1}b^{j+1}, q \leftarrow q - q_{j+1}b^{j+1}$.
 5:     Let $c \leftarrow -(u + x_{k-1}q)$.
 6:     Set $x_j \leftarrow \lfloor c/b^{j+1} \rceil$
 7: **end for**
 8: **for** $j = 0$ to $k - 2$ **do**
 9:     $y_j \leftarrow b \cdot x_j - x_{j-1} + x_{k-1} \cdot q_j + u_j$.
10: **end for**
11: $y_{k-1} \leftarrow -x_{k-2} + x_{k-1} \cdot q_{k-1} + u_{k-1}$.
12: **return** y

Since the basis of $\mathcal{L}([d_0, \cdots, d_{k-2}])$ is I_{k-1}, so for a given vector $v \in \mathcal{L}([d_0, \cdots, d_{k-2}])$, for the remainder of the loops, the center (c_j in Algorithm 3 step 3) in the Babai's algorithm is $c_j = \lfloor \langle v, \tilde{d}_j \rangle / \|\tilde{d}_j\|_2^2 \rceil = \lfloor v_j \rceil$. Since every two basis vector d_i, d_j for $i \neq j, i, j \in \{0, 1, \cdots, k - 2\}$ is orthogonal to each other, step $v \leftarrow v - c_j d_j$ in Babai's algorithm (Algorithm 3 step 3) need not be performed. Thus, there is only a need to perform $t \leftarrow t - x_{k-1}d_{k-1}$, which can be implemented by the special property of t and d. Since $t_j = -(\sum_{i=0}^{j} u_i \cdot b^i)/b^{j+1}$ and $d_j = (\sum_{i=0}^{j} q_i \cdot b^i)/b^{j+1}$, so in our algorithm the center in every loop is

$$x_j = \lfloor t_j - x_{k-1}d_j \rceil = \lfloor -(\sum_{i=0}^{j} u_i b^i + x_{k-1} \sum_{l=0}^{j} q_l b^l)/b^{j+1} \rceil,$$

which is exactly computed in step $4 \sim 6$ of Algorithm 2. The lemma follows. $\square$

To analysis the subgaussian parameter obtained by our algorithm we give the following lemma.

Lemma 4. *For the target vector* $t := -S^{-1}[u]_b^k$, *and the vector* $x = (x_0, x_1, \cdots, x_{k-1})^T$ *after the nearest plane algorithm (i.e. after step 7) in Algorithm 2, we have that* $e = Dx - t$ *is a subgaussian vector with parameter* $\sqrt{2\pi}/2$.

Proof. Let $v = Dx$, then

$$v_j = x_j + x_{k-1}\frac{\sum_{i=0}^{j-1} q_i b^i}{b^{j+1}}.$$

Since

$$t_j = -\frac{\sum_{i=0}^{j} u_i b^i}{b^{j+1}}$$

and

$$x_j = -\frac{\sum_{i=0}^{j} u_i b^i}{b^{j+1}} - x_{k-1}\frac{\sum_{i=0}^{j} q_i b^i}{b^{j+1}} + \epsilon,$$

where $|\epsilon| < 1/2$, so $v_j + t_j = \epsilon$, and this means that $||e||_\infty < 1/2$. The lemma follows.   □

Proof of Theorem 3. For the case $q = b^k$, for randomly chosen $u \xleftarrow{\$} U(\mathbb{Z}_q)$, Algorithm 1 returns subgaussian vector $x \in \Lambda_u^\perp(g^T)$ with parameter $b/2\sqrt{2\pi}$ in time and space $\log_b q$ by inspection and Lemma 1.

For the case $q \neq b^k$, by Lemma 3, after step 7 in Algorithm 2, x is so that $\mathbf{D}x$ is the output of nearest plane algorithm on $\mathbf{D}$ with target vector $-\mathbf{S}^{-1}u$. By Lemma 4 and Lemma 1,

$$\mathbf{S}_q + u = \mathbf{S}(\mathbf{D}x - t + t) + u = \mathbf{S}(\mathbf{D}x - t)$$

is a subgaussian vector with parameter $\sqrt{\lambda_{max}(\mathbf{S} \cdot \mathbf{S}^T)}\sqrt{2\pi}/2$, where $\sqrt{\lambda_{max}(\mathbf{S} \cdot \mathbf{S}^T)}$ is the maximum eigenvalue of $\mathbf{S} \cdot \mathbf{S}^T$. By Theorem 1 and a routine calculation for $\mathbf{S} \cdot \mathbf{S}^T$'s entries, $\lambda_{max}(\mathbf{S} \cdot \mathbf{S}^T) \leq (b+1)^2$. The theorem follows.   □

4   Implementation Results

All experiments were performed on a computer with an Intel(R) Core(TM) i5-8265U CPU @ 1.60 GHz and 4GB RAM, running Ubuntu 16.04.1 64-bit system. The PALISADE Library [1] was used to compare the results of our algorithm with those of the previous subgaussian decomposition algorithms, GMP19 [13] and ZY21 [22]. We focus on the case when $q < b^k$ just like in [13,22], which is the the typical scenario in cryptography.

4.1   Complexity and Performance

As reported in the paper by Zhang and Yang [22], the integer implementation of the decomposition algorithm outperforms its floating-point counterpart. Therefore, we implemented the integer version of Algorithm 2 to achieve optimal performance. To ensure fairness, we also implemented integer versions of the GMP19 and ZY21 algorithms [13,22]. Additionally, we tested the original floating-point GMP19 algorithm as described in [13]. Our implementation imposes the restriction that the gadget base b must be a power of 2, as noted in [22].

The results of the four algorithms are displayed in Fig. 1, which shows the relationship between gadget decomposition rate and the various algorithms. The figure demonstrates that our algorithm is faster than both GMP19 and ZY21. Specifically, when $b = 2$ and $k = \lceil 60/\log b \rceil = 60$, our algorithm is approximately 4.5 (respectively, 2.7) times faster than the PALISADE (respectively, integer) implementation of GMP19 and around 2 times faster than the integer implementation of ZY21.

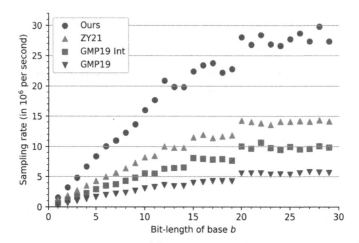

Fig. 1. Runtime of sampling rate for native uniformly random integers (w.r.t a 60-bit modulus). Experimental values measure over 10^8 samplings. In the figure, "Ours" refers to Algorithm 2, "ZY21" represents the integer implementation of algorithm 4 in [22], and "GMP19" (respectively, "GMP19 Int") denotes the floating-point (respectively, integer) implementation of algorithm 2 in [13].

4.2   Quality

Figure 2 displays the differences in the noise growth of GSW-type products using four algorithms: our Algorithm 2, classical binary gadget decomposition (denoted as Binary), algorithm 2 in [13] (denoted as "GMP19"), and algorithm 4 in [22] (denoted as "ZY21"). The comparison method is the same as the one used in [13] and [22], which involves first generating an error vector in R^m and then iteratively multiplying it by $\mathbf{G}^{-1}(\mathbf{U}_i)$, where $\mathbf{U}_i$ is a vector of uniformly random ring elements in ring R^m at level i. Similar to [13,22], a tree multiplication approach is used instead of a sequential evaluation approach, and different $\mathbf{U}_i$ are used at each level.

In Fig. 2, a steeper slope represents a more rapid increase in noise growth. As shown in the figure, the Binary method has the fastest noise growth, while ZY21 is better than GMP19. Our algorithm has the slowest noise growth among the three algorithms. A more detailed comparison between our algorithm, ZY21, and GMP19, when $b = 2^2$ and $b = 2^3$, is illustrated in Figs. 3 and 4, respectively. In either case, the noise growth of our algorithm is the slowest.

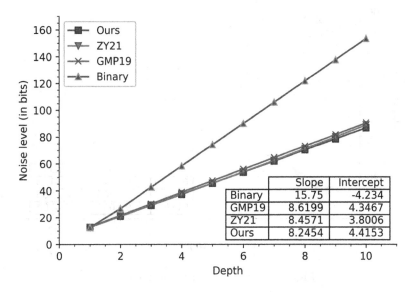

Fig. 2. Noise growth for GSW-type multiplication for case when $b = 2$. The base in the exponentiation is $(mn)^\beta$, where $m = k + 2 = 182$, $n = 1024$ and β represents the rate of noise growth. The slope of the linear interpolation is given by $\beta \log_2(mn)$.

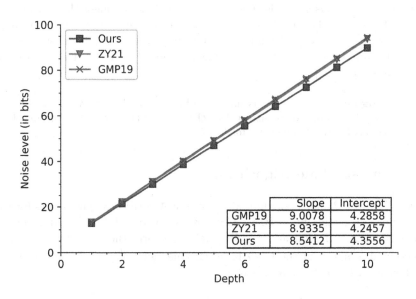

Fig. 3. Figure for the case when $b = 2^2$.

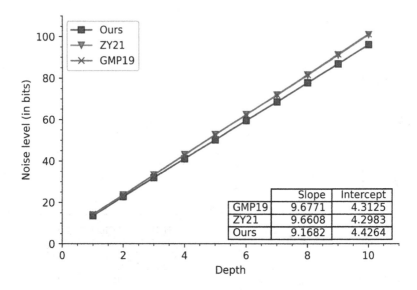

Fig. 4. Figure for the case when $b = 2^3$.

5   Conclusion and Discussion

In this paper, we present a new gadget decomposition algorithm for Homomorphic Encryption (HE) schemes with improved noise growth and performance compared to previous methods. The key insight behind our algorithm is to always choose the nearest plane of the two adjacent planes when using the Babai's algorithm during the decomposition process. Our implementation demonstrates that our algorithm outperforms the algorithms proposed by Genise et al. in [13] and Zhang and Yu in [22].

Acknowledgments. This paper is supported by the Cloud Security Key Technology Research Key Laboratory of Shenzhen (No. ZDSY20200811143600002). Authors thank the anonymous ISPEC'23 reviewers for helpful comments.

A   Nearest Plane Algorithm

Babai's Nearest Plane Algorithm [3] is given in Algorithm 3. The inputs for this algorithm is a lattice basis $\mathbf{B}$, its GSO $\tilde{\mathbf{B}}$, and a target $\boldsymbol{t} \in \mathbb{R}^n$. It returns a lattice point $\boldsymbol{x}$ such that $\boldsymbol{x} - \boldsymbol{t} \in \mathcal{P}_{1/2}(\mathbf{B})$. The correctness can be checked by represented $\boldsymbol{x}$ and $\boldsymbol{t}$ in the GSO basis $\tilde{\mathbf{B}}$. One can verify that the coordinate (coefficient of $\tilde{\boldsymbol{b}}_i$) of $\boldsymbol{x} - \boldsymbol{t}$ is $c_i - \lfloor c_i \rceil < 1/2$.

Algorithm 3. The nearest plane algorithm.

Input: Basis $\mathbf{B} = [\boldsymbol{b}_0, \cdots, \boldsymbol{b}_{n-1}] \in \mathbb{Z}^{n \times n}$; GSO Basis $\tilde{\mathbf{B}} = [\tilde{\boldsymbol{b}}_0, \cdots, \tilde{\boldsymbol{b}}_{n-1}]$; vector $\boldsymbol{t} \in \mathbb{Z}^n$

Output: A vector $\boldsymbol{x} \in \mathcal{L}(\mathbf{B})$ such that $\boldsymbol{x} - \boldsymbol{t} \in \mathcal{P}_{1/2}(\tilde{\mathbf{B}})$
1: $\boldsymbol{b} \leftarrow \boldsymbol{t}$
2: **for** $j = n - 1$ to 0 **do**
3:   $\boldsymbol{b} \leftarrow \boldsymbol{b} - c_j \boldsymbol{b}_j$ where $c_j = \lfloor \langle \boldsymbol{b}, \tilde{\boldsymbol{b}}_j \rangle / \langle \tilde{\boldsymbol{b}}_j, \tilde{\boldsymbol{b}}_j \rangle \rceil$
4: **end for**
5: **return** $\boldsymbol{t} - \boldsymbol{b}$

B Decomposition in CRT Form

For $q = \Pi_{j=1}^r q_j$, each coprime factor q_j fix the base-b_j gadget vector $\boldsymbol{g}_j^T = (1, b_j, \cdots, b_j^{k_j - 1})$ with $k_j = \lceil log_{b_j}(q_j) \rceil$. An element $u \in \mathbb{Z}_q$ can be represented as its Chinese Remainder Theorem form (CRT form) as $(u \bmod q_1, \cdots, u \bmod q_r) = (u_1, \cdots, u_r) \in \mathbb{Z}_{q_1} \times \cdots \times \mathbb{Z}_{q_r}$. Then, for this CRT form, the decomposition algorithm can be performed for every $\boldsymbol{g}_j^{-1}$. Samping in CRT form for $(u_1, \cdots, u_r)$ is given in Algorithm 4. The result is given in the following theorem.

Theorem 4. *Let q have factorization $q = \Pi_{j=1}^r q_j$ into coprime factors $\{q_j\}$, $(b_j)_{j=1}^r$ be an r-tuple of base such that $b_j < q_j$, and let $k = \sum k_j$ with $k_j = \lceil log_{b_j} q_j \rceil$. Then, there exists subgaussian decomposition algorithm can be performed in-parallel with r processors, each using time and space $O(k_i)$ and with parameter at most $\frac{max_j(b_j)+1}{2}\sqrt{2\pi}$.*

Algorithm 4. Decomposition in CRT form.

Input: $(u_1, \cdots, u_r)$
Output: $\boldsymbol{g}_{CRT}^{-1}(u_1, \cdots, u_r)$
1: **for** $i = 1$ to r **do**
2:   $\boldsymbol{x}_i \leftarrow \boldsymbol{g}_i^{-1}(u_i)$.
3: **end for**
4: **return** $\boldsymbol{x} = (\boldsymbol{x}_1, \cdots, \boldsymbol{x}_r)$.

Since except for the $\boldsymbol{g}_j^{-1}$ component, the Algorithm 4 is same with the Algorithm 4 in [13], for more details about the decomposition in CRT form, please see [13].

References

1. PALISADE Lattice Cryptography Library (release 1.11.5) (2021). https://palisade-crypto.org/
2. Alperin-Sheriff, J., Peikert, C.: Faster bootstrapping with polynomial error. In: Garay, J.A., Gennaro, R. (eds.) CRYPTO 2014. LNCS, vol. 8616, pp. 297–314. Springer, Heidelberg (2014). https://doi.org/10.1007/978-3-662-44371-2_17

3. Babai, L.: On Lovász' lattice reduction and the nearest lattice point problem. In: Mehlhorn, K. (ed.) STACS 1985. LNCS, vol. 182, pp. 13–20. Springer, Heidelberg (1985). https://doi.org/10.1007/BFb0023990

4. Bonte, C., Iliashenko, I., Park, J., Pereira, H.V.L., Smart, N.P.: FINAL: faster FHE instantiated with NTRU and LWE. IACR Cryptology ePrint Archive, p. 74 (2022). https://eprint.iacr.org/2022/074

5. Brakerski, Z., Gentry, C., Vaikuntanathan, V.: (Leveled) fully homomorphic encryption without bootstrapping. In: Goldwasser, S. (ed.) Innovations in Theoretical Computer Science 2012, Cambridge, MA, USA, 8–10 January 2012, pp. 309–325. ACM (2012)

6. Chen, Y., Nguyen, P.Q.: BKZ 2.0: better lattice security estimates. In: Lee, D.H., Wang, X. (eds.) ASIACRYPT 2011. LNCS, vol. 7073, pp. 1–20. Springer, Heidelberg (2011). https://doi.org/10.1007/978-3-642-25385-0_1

7. Cheon, J.H., Kim, A., Kim, M., Song, Y.: Homomorphic encryption for arithmetic of approximate numbers. In: Takagi, T., Peyrin, T. (eds.) ASIACRYPT 2017. LNCS, vol. 10624, pp. 409–437. Springer, Cham (2017). https://doi.org/10.1007/978-3-319-70694-8_15

8. Chillotti, I., Gama, N., Georgieva, M., Izabachène, M.: Faster fully homomorphic encryption: bootstrapping in less than 0.1 seconds. In: Cheon, J.H., Takagi, T. (eds.) ASIACRYPT 2016. LNCS, vol. 10031, pp. 3–33. Springer, Heidelberg (2016). https://doi.org/10.1007/978-3-662-53887-6_1

9. Dai, W., et al.: Implementation and evaluation of a lattice-based key-policy ABE scheme. IEEE Trans. Inf. Forensics Secur. **13**(5), 1169–1184 (2018)

10. Ducas, L., Micciancio, D.: FHEW: bootstrapping homomorphic encryption in less than a second. In: Oswald, E., Fischlin, M. (eds.) EUROCRYPT 2015. LNCS, vol. 9056, pp. 617–640. Springer, Heidelberg (2015). https://doi.org/10.1007/978-3-662-46800-5_24

11. Fan, J., Vercauteren, F.: Somewhat practical fully homomorphic encryption. IACR Cryptology ePrint Archive 2012, 144 (2012). http://eprint.iacr.org/2012/144

12. Genise, N., Micciancio, D.: Faster Gaussian sampling for trapdoor lattices with arbitrary modulus. In: Nielsen, J.B., Rijmen, V. (eds.) EUROCRYPT 2018. LNCS, vol. 10820, pp. 174–203. Springer, Cham (2018). https://doi.org/10.1007/978-3-319-78381-9_7

13. Genise, N., Micciancio, D., Polyakov, Y.: Building an efficient lattice gadget toolkit: subgaussian sampling and more. In: Ishai, Y., Rijmen, V. (eds.) EUROCRYPT 2019. LNCS, vol. 11477, pp. 655–684. Springer, Cham (2019). https://doi.org/10.1007/978-3-030-17656-3_23

14. Gentry, C.: Fully homomorphic encryption using ideal lattices. In: Proceedings of the 41st Annual ACM Symposium on Theory of Computing, STOC 2009, Bethesda, MD, USA, 31 May–2 June 2009, pp. 169–178 (2009)

15. Gentry, C., Sahai, A., Waters, B.: Homomorphic encryption from learning with errors: conceptually-simpler, asymptotically-faster, attribute-based. In: Canetti, R., Garay, J.A. (eds.) CRYPTO 2013. LNCS, vol. 8042, pp. 75–92. Springer, Heidelberg (2013). https://doi.org/10.1007/978-3-642-40041-4_5

16. Jeon, S., Lee, H., Park, J.: Efficient lattice gadget decomposition algorithm with bounded uniform distribution. IEEE Access **9**, 17429–17437 (2021)

17. Kluczniak, K.: NTRU-v-um: secure fully homomorphic encryption from NTRU with small modulus. In: Yin, H., Stavrou, A., Cremers, C., Shi, E. (eds.) Proceedings of the 2022 ACM SIGSAC Conference on Computer and Communications Security, CCS 2022, Los Angeles, CA, USA, 7–11 November 2022, pp. 1783–1797. ACM (2022)

18. Lenstra, A.K., Lenstra, H.W., Lov sz, L.: Factoring polynomials with rational coefficients. Mathematische Annalen **261**(4) (1982)
19. Lyubashevsky, V., Peikert, C., Regev, O.: A toolkit for ring-LWE cryptography. In: Johansson, T., Nguyen, P.Q. (eds.) EUROCRYPT 2013. LNCS, vol. 7881, pp. 35–54. Springer, Heidelberg (2013). https://doi.org/10.1007/978-3-642-38348-9_3
20. Nguyen, P.Q.: The LLL Algorithm: Survey and Applications (2010)
21. Vershynin, R.: Introduction to the non-asymptotic analysis of random matrices. In: Eldar, Y.C., Kutyniok, G. (eds.) Compressed Sensing, pp. 210–268. Cambridge University Press (2012)
22. Zhang, S., Yu, Y.: Towards a simpler lattice gadget toolkit. In: Hanaoka, G., Shikata, J., Watanabe, Y. (eds.) PKC 2022. LNCS, vol. 13177, pp. 498–520. Springer, Cham (2022). https://doi.org/10.1007/978-3-030-97121-2_18

Malicious Player Card-Based Cryptographic Protocols with a Standard Deck of Cards Using Private Operations

Tomoya Morooka[1], Yoshifumi Manabe[1(✉)] [iD], and Kazumasa Shinagawa[2,3]

[1] School of Informatics, Kogakuin University, Tokyo, Japan
manabe@cc.kogakuin.ac.jp
[2] Ibaraki University, 4-12-1 Nakanarusawa, Hitachi, Ibaraki 316-8511, Japan
kazumasa.shinagawa.np92@vc.ibaraki.ac.jp
[3] National Institute of Advanced Industrial Science and Technology (AIST),
2-3-26 Aomi, Koto, Tokyo 135-0064, Japan

Abstract. This paper shows new card-based cryptographic protocols to compute Boolean functions using a standard deck of cards when the players are malicious. Card-based cryptographic protocols use physical cards instead of computers. They can be used when the software on computers is not reliable. We discuss protocols that use a standard deck of cards because it is easy to prepare. Though protocols that use private operations tend to be efficient in the number of cards used in the protocols, malicious actions are possible during private operations. This paper shows three-player protocols to prevent malicious actions by watching another player's actions. We show logical AND, XOR, and copy protocols since any Boolean functions can be realized by a combination of the protocols. The numbers of cards used by the protocols are the minimum.

Keywords: card-based cryptographic protocols · Boolean functions · malicious players · standard deck of cards · multi-party secure computation

1 Introduction

Card-based cryptographic protocols [8,22] were proposed in which physical cards are used instead of computers to securely compute values. They can be used when computers cannot be used or users cannot trust the software on the computer. Also, the protocols are easy to understand, thus the protocols can be used to teach the basics of cryptography [4,17] to accelerate the social implementation of advanced cryptography [5]. den Boer [2] first showed a five-card protocol to securely compute the logical AND of two inputs. Since then, many protocols have

The second author was supported by JSPS KAKENHI Grant Number JP23H00479.
The third author was supported during this work by JSPS KAKENHI Grant Numbers
JP21K17702 and JP23H00479, and JST CREST Grant Number JPMJCR22M1.

been proposed to realize primitives to compute any Boolean functions [13,23,33] and specific computations such as millionaires' problem [16,24,28], voting [19, 25,27,37], grouping [6], ranking [35], lottery [34], proof of knowledge of a puzzle solution [3,31], and so on. This paper considers computations of logical AND and logical XOR functions and copy operations since any Boolean function can be realized with a combination of these computations.

Most of the above works are based on a two-color card model. In the two-color card model, there are two kinds of cards, ♣ and ♡. Cards of the same marks cannot be distinguished. In addition, the back of both types of cards is ?. It is impossible to determine the mark in the back of a given card of ?. Though the model is simple, such special cards might not be available. Playing cards are easy to prepare, thus protocols using a standard deck of playing cards and their formal security proofs were shown [7,9,11,12,18,26,32]. Recently, protocols that use private operations were shown [14]. Private operations are executed where the other players cannot see, for example, under the table or in the back. The protocols in [14] achieve the minimum number of cards. Though private operations are effective in card-based protocols, there is a problem with private operations. Since the private operations are executed where the other players cannot see, a player might execute malicious actions during private operations. For example, a malicious player might see the marks of face-down cards. Another malicious player might swap the cards to change the values. We need to prevent or detect such malicious actions.

A countermeasure to the problems is watching private actions and detect malicious actions. When the protocols are executed by two players, Alice and Bob, Alice must not see Bob's private actions. If Alice sees Bob's private operations, Alice can see all operations, thus Alice sees the relationship between the private inputs and the output. If the output cards are opened to see the final result, Alice can know the private input data from the relationship. Thus, another player other than the two players is necessary to watch the private operations. If the watcher sees both Alice and Bob's private operations, the watching player can know all operations and the relationship between the input data and the output data. Thus the watching player knows the private data. This paper shows that three players are sufficient to detect malicious actions and keep the protocol secure, just as in the case of the two-color model [29]. In the three-player protocols shown in this paper, Bob watches Alice's private operations, Carol watches Bob's private operations, and Alice watches Carol's private operations.

Few works are done for the case when some players are malicious or make mistakes [1,10,15,20,21,36]. [20] discusses information leakage at operation errors. The other works are categorized into two groups. The first one is to use additional cards or special items such as envelopes [10,15,21,36]. The second type introduces the watching player. The watching player for the protocol with a two-color card model is shown [15]. Abe et al. showed a three-player majority voting protocol with a malicious player [1]. Note that the above works are done for the two-color card model. There is no work for a standard deck of cards. As long as the author knows, this is the first work that discusses malicious activities in protocols that use a standard deck of cards and private operations.

In Sect. 2, basic notations and the private operations introduced in [29] are shown. Section 3 shows logical AND, copy, and logical XOR protocols.

2   Preliminaries

2.1   Basic Notations

This section gives the notations and basic definitions of card-based protocols with a standard deck of cards. A deck of playing cards consists of 52 distinct mark cards, which are named 1 to 52. The number of each card (for example, 1 is the ace of the spade, and 52 is the king of the club) is common knowledge among the players. The back of all cards is the same $\boxed{?}$. It is impossible to determine the mark in the back of a given card of $\boxed{?}$.

One-bit data is represented by two cards as follows: $\boxed{i}\,\boxed{j} = 0$ and $\boxed{j}\,\boxed{i} = 1$ if $i < j$.

One pair of cards that represents one bit $x \in \{0, 1\}$, whose face is down, is called a commitment of x, and denoted as $commit(x)$. It is written as $\underbrace{\boxed{?}\,\boxed{?}}_{x}$.

The base of a commitment is the pair of cards used for the commitment. If card i and j $(i < j)$ are used to set $commit(x)$, the commitment is written as $commit(x)^{\{i,j\}}$ and written as $\underbrace{\boxed{?}\,\boxed{?}}_{x^{\{i,j\}}}$. When the base information is obvious or unnecessary, it is not written.

Note that when these two cards are swapped, $commit(\bar{x})^{\{i,j\}}$ can be obtained. Thus, logical negation can be computed without private operations.

A set of cards placed in a row is called a sequence of cards. A sequence of cards S whose length is n is denoted as $S = s_1, s_2, \ldots, s_n$, where s_i is i-th card of the sequence. $S = \underbrace{\boxed{?}}_{s_1}\,\underbrace{\boxed{?}}_{s_2}\,\underbrace{\boxed{?}}_{s_3}\,\ldots,\,\underbrace{\boxed{?}}_{s_n}$. A sequence whose length is even is called an even sequence. $S_1 \| S_2$ is a concatenation of sequence S_1 and S_2.

All protocols are executed by three players, Alice, Bob, and Carol. The players are malicious, that is, they might not obey the rule of the protocols and execute any operation. This paper assumes that even malicious players correctly execute misbehavior detection. In the protocols in this paper, a player watches the private operations executed by another player. If a player misbehaves, the watching player detects the malicious action and says that the player misbehaved. The misbehaved player has a punishment for the misbehavior. The detail of the punishment mechanism is out of the scope of this paper. To avoid punishment, malicious players obey the rule of the protocols. Note that the watching player does not output a false misbehavior detection. For the two-color card model, a three-player misbehavior detection protocol without false alarm detection and a four-player misbehavior detection protocol with the ability of false alarm detection was shown [29]. In order to detect false alarms in a standard deck of cards, four players seem to be necessary. False alarm detection is a further study.

There is no collusion among players, otherwise, private input data can be easily revealed.

The inputs of the protocols are given in a committed format, that is, the players do not know the input values. The output of the protocol must be given in a committed format so that the result can be used as input for further computation.

A protocol is secure when the following two conditions are satisfied: (1) If the output cards are not opened, each player obtains no information about the private input values from the view of the protocol for the player (the sequence of the cards opened to the player). (2) When the output cards are opened, each player obtains no additional information about the private input values other than the information by the output of the protocol. For example, if the output cards of an AND protocol for input x and y are opened and the value is 1, the players can know that $(x, y) = (1, 1)$. If the output value is 0, the players must not know whether the input (x, y) is $(0, 0)$, $(0, 1)$, or $(1, 0)$.

2.2 Private Operations

We show three private operations introduced in [29]: private random bisection cuts, private reverse cuts, and private reveals.

Primitive 1 (*Private random bisection cut*)

A private random bisection cut is the following operation on an even sequence $S_0 = s_1, s_2, \ldots, s_{2m}$. A player selects a random bit $b \in \{0, 1\}$ and outputs

$$S_1 = \begin{cases} S_0 & \text{if } b = 0 \\ s_{m+1}, s_{m+2}, \ldots, s_{2m}, s_1, s_2, \ldots, s_m & \text{if } b = 1 \end{cases}$$

In [29], the operation is executed in a place where the other players cannot see. The player must not disclose the bit b.

Note that if the private random cut is executed when $m = 1$ and $S_0 = commit(x)^{\{i,j\}}$, given $S_0 = \boxed{?}\boxed{?}$, The player's output $S_1 = \boxed{?}\boxed{?}$, which is
$x^{\{i,j\}}$ $\qquad x \oplus b^{\{i,j\}}$

$\boxed{?}\boxed{?}$ or $\boxed{?}\boxed{?}$.
$x^{\{i,j\}}$ $\quad \overline{x}^{\{i,j\}}$

Note that a private random bisection cut is the same as the random bisection cut [23], but the operation is not executed in public.

Primitive 2 (*Private reverse cut*)

A private reverse cut is the following operation on an even sequence $S_2 = s_1, s_2, \ldots, s_{2m}$ and a bit $b \in \{0, 1\}$. A player outputs

$$S_3 = \begin{cases} S_2 & \text{if } b = 0 \\ s_{m+1}, s_{m+2}, \ldots, s_{2m}, s_1, s_2, \ldots, s_m & \text{if } b = 1 \end{cases}$$

In [29], the operation is executed in a place where the other players cannot see. The player must not disclose b.

Note that the bit b is not newly selected by the player. This is the difference between the primitive in Primitive 1, where a random bit must be newly selected by the player.

If a player executes a private random bisection cut to S when the random bit is b and then executes a private reverse cut using b, the result is S.

Note that in some protocols below, selecting left m cards is executed after a private reverse cut. The sequence of these two operations is called a private reverse selection. A private reverse selection is the following procedure on an even sequence $S_2 = s_1, s_2, \ldots, s_{2m}$ and a bit $b \in \{0, 1\}$. A player outputs

$$S_3 = \begin{cases} s_1, s_2, \ldots, s_m & \text{if } b = 0 \\ s_{m+1}, s_{m+2}, \ldots, s_{2m} & \text{if } b = 1 \end{cases}$$

Primitive 3 *(Private reveal). A player privately opens a given committed bit. The player must not disclose the obtained value.*

Using the obtained value, the player privately sets a sequence of cards.

Consider the case when Alice executes a private random bisection cut on $commit(x)$ and Bob executes a private reveal on the bit. Since the committed bit is randomized by the bit b selected by Alice, the opened bit is $x \oplus b$. Even if Bob privately opens the cards, Bob obtains no information about x if b is randomly selected and not disclosed by Alice. Bob must not disclose the obtained value. If Bob discloses the obtained value to Alice, Alice knows the value of the committed bit.

2.3 Opaque Commitment Pair

An opaque commitment pair is defined as a useful situation for to design a secure protocol using a standard deck of cards [18]. It is a pair of commitments whose bases are unknown to all players. Let us consider the following two commitments using cards i, j, i', and j'. The left (right) commitment has value x (y), respectively, but it is unknown that (1) the left (right) commitment is made using i and j (i' and j'), respectively, or (2) the left (right) commitment is made using i' and j' (i and j), respectively. Such a pair of commitments is called an opaque commitment pair and written as $commit(x)^{\{i,j\},\{i',j'\}} || commit(y)^{\{i,j\},\{i',j'\}}$.

The protocols in this paper use a little different kind of pair, called semi-opaque commitment pair. A player thinks a pair is an opaque commitment pair but another player knows the bases of the commitments. Let us consider the case when a protocol is executed by Alice and Bob. Bob privately makes the pair of commitments with the knowledge of x and y. For example, Bob randomly selects a bit $b \in \{0, 1\}$ and

$$S = \begin{cases} commit(x)^{\{i,j\}} || commit(y)^{\{i',j'\}} & \text{if } b = 0 \\ commit(x)^{\{i',j'\}} || commit(y)^{\{i,j\}} & \text{if } b = 1 \end{cases}$$

then $S = commit(x)^{\{i,j\},\{i',j'\}}||commit(y)^{\{i,j\},\{i',j'\}}$ for Alice. Such a pair is called semi-opaque commitment pair and written as $commit(x)^{\{i,j\},\{i',j'\}|Alice}||$ $commit(y)^{\{i,j\},\{i',j'\}|Alice}$, where the name(s) of the players who think the pair as a opaque commitment pair is written. Note that a name is not written does not mean the player knows the bases of the commitments. For example, the above example says nothing about whether Bob knows the bases or not. Note that the name of the player is written with the initial when it is not ambiguous.

2.4 Space and Time Complexities

The space complexity of card-based protocols is evaluated by the number of cards. Minimizing the number of cards is discussed in many works.

The number of rounds was proposed as a criterion to evaluate the time complexity of card-based protocols using private operations [30]. The first round begins from the initial state. In most protocols, a player initially has all cards, but the definition assumes general cases when each player initially has some number of cards. The first round is (possibly parallel) local executions by each player using the cards initially given to each player. It ends at the instant when no further local execution is possible without receiving cards from another player. The local executions in each round include sending cards to some other players but do not include receiving cards.

The $i(>1)$-th round begins with receiving all the cards sent during the $(i-1)$-th round. Each player executes local executions using the received cards and the cards left to the player at the end of the $(i-1)$-th round. Each player executes local executions until no further local execution is possible without receiving cards from another player. We can define the number of rounds and average rounds. The number of rounds of a protocol is the maximum number of rounds necessary to output the result among all possible inputs and random values. For randomized (Las Vegas) protocols, the average round is the average number of rounds necessary to output the result. Since each operation is relatively simple, the dominating time to execute protocols with private operations is the time to send cards between players and set up so that the cards are not seen by the other players. Thus the number of rounds is the criterion to evaluate the time complexity of card-based protocols with private operations. If the local execution needs many operations, for example, $O(n)$ operations where n is the size of the problem, we might need another criterion to consider the cost of local executions.

Let us show an example of a protocol execution, its space complexity, and time complexity with the conventional two-color card model. In the two-color card model, there are two kinds of marks, ♣ and ♡. One-bit data is represented by two cards as follows: ♣♡ = 0 and ♡♣ = 1.

Protocol 1 *(AND protocol in [29])*
Input: commit(x) and commit(y).
Output: commit(x ∧ y).

1. *Alice executes a private random bisection cut on commit(x). Let the output be commit(x′). Alice sends commit(x′) and commit(y) to Bob.*

2. *Bob executes a private reveal on* $commit(x')$. *Bob privately sets*

$$S_2 = \begin{cases} commit(y)||commit(0) \; if \; x' = 1 \\ commit(0)||commit(y) \; if \; x' = 0 \end{cases}$$

and sends S_2 *to Alice.*
3. *Alice executes a private reverse selection on* S_2 *using the bit b generated in the private random bisection cut. Let the obtained sequence be* S_3. *Alice outputs* S_3.

The AND protocol realizes the following equation.

$$x \wedge y = \begin{cases} y \text{ if } x = 1 \\ 0 \text{ if } x = 0 \end{cases}$$

Our new AND protocol is also based on this equation. The correctness of the protocol is shown in [29]. The number of cards is four since the cards of $commit(x')$ are re-used to set $commit(0)$.

Let us consider the time complexity of the protocol. The first round ends at the instant when Alice sends $commit(x')$ and $commit(y)$ to Bob. The second round begins with receiving the cards by Bob. The second round ends at the instant when Bob sends S_2 to Alice. The third round begins with receiving the cards by Alice. The number of rounds of this protocol is three.

3   AND, XOR, and Copy with Three Malicious Players

This section shows our new protocols for AND, XOR, and copy executed by three malicious players. Any malicious action during private operations is detected by a watching player, thus the malicious actions are prohibited if there is no collusion between players.

Bob watches Alice's operations, Carol watches Bob's operations, and Alice watches Carol's operations. All operations are executed in the following manner. Initially, all players are in the same room. If the next operation is executed by Alice, first, Carol exits the room. Then, Alice executes the private operations in front of Bob. Thus, Bob knows all private values. For example, if Alice executes a private random bisection cut, Bob knows the random bit Alice selected. If Alice executes a private reveal, Bob knows the value of the cards Alice opened. If Alice misbehaves, Bob detects the fact and terminates the protocol execution. If there is no misbehavior, Alice's private operations are correctly finished. Then Carol comes back to the room and they execute the next step of the protocol. If the next private operation is executed by Bob(Carol), Alice(Bob) exits from the room, Bob(Carol) executes the private operation in front of Carol(Alice), and Alice(Bob) comes back to the room, respectively.

In the following protocol descriptions, we just write "Alice executes a private operation" to mean "Carol exits the room, Alice executes a private operation in front of Bob, and Carol comes back to the room" for simplicity.

Before we show the protocols, we show a subroutine to fix the base of a given commitment.

3.1 Base-Fixed Protocol with Three Players

We show a base-fixed protocol with two inputs $commit(x)$ and $commit(y)$. The base of $commit(x)$ is fixed to $\{1, 2\}$. In the following protocol, the second input value y is not used as the output, but the value must be kept secret.

The protocol needs private reveals and the values of cards are seen. Before a player sees a value of $commit(x)$ and sets cards according to the value, the value must be randomized to hide the value. In the protocol below, Alice sees the value, thus the value must be randomized by the other players. One-player randomization is not enough to hide the private value. Suppose that a player executes a randomization in advance. They obtain $commit(x \oplus r)$ and then Alice executes a private reveal. Since Bob watches Alice's execution, Bob knows $x \oplus r$. If the randomization r is executed by Bob, Bob knows r and $x \oplus r$ and Bob knows secret value x. Then consider the case when the randomization is executed by Carol. Alice watches Carol's private operation and knows r. Since Alice knows $x \oplus r$ and r, Alice knows the secret value x. Therefore, one-player randomization is not enough to hide the private value, and two-player randomizations are necessary. The value must be randomized by Bob and Carol in advance.

Note that the bases of the input commitments are leaked to Alice and Bob during the execution. The protocol can be used only if the information leakage does not cause a security problem, for example, the bases are randomly set by some other player.

Protocol 2 *(Three player base-fixed protocol)*
  Input: $commit(x)^{\{1,2\},\{3,4\}|A}||commit(y)^{\{1,2\},\{3,4\}|A}$.
  Output: $commit(x)^{\{1,2\}}$.

1. Bob executes a private random bisection cut on each pair using two random bits br_1 and br_2, respectively. The result $S_1 = commit(x \oplus br_1)^{\{1,2\},\{3,4\}|A}||commit(y \oplus br_2)^{\{1,2\},\{3,4\}|A}$.
2. Carol executes a private random bisection cut on each pair using two random bits cr_1 and cr_2, respectively. The result $S_2 = commit(x \oplus br_1 \oplus cr_1)^{\{1,2\},\{3,4\}|A}||commit(y \oplus br_2 \oplus cr_2)^{\{1,2\},\{3,4\}|A}$.
3. Alice executes a private reveal on both pairs of S_2. Alice makes $S_3 = commit(x \oplus br_1 \oplus cr_1)^{\{1,2\}}$.
4. Bob executes a private reverse cut using br_1 on S_3. The result $S_4 = commit(x \oplus cr_1)^{\{1,2\}}$.
5. Carol executes a private reverse cut using cr_1 on S_4. The result is $commit(x)^{\{1,2\}}$.

Theorem 1. *The input values are private in the base-fixed protocol.*

Proof. Alice sees $x \oplus br_1 \oplus cr_1$ and $y \oplus br_2 \oplus cr_2$ in Step 3. Since Alice watches Carol's private operations, Alice sees cr_1 and cr_2 in Step 2. Alice obtains no information about x and y since br_1 and br_2 are unknown to Alice.

Bob knows br_1 and br_2 in Step 1. Since Bob watches Alice's private operations, Bob sees $x \oplus br_1 \oplus cr_1$ and $y \oplus br_2 \oplus cr_2$ in Step 3. Bob obtains no information about x and y since cr_1 and cr_2 are unknown to Bob.

Carol knows cr_1 and cr_2 in Step 2. Since Carol watches Bob's private operations, Carol sees br_1 and br_2 in Step 1. Carol obtains no information about x and y.   □

3.2   AND Protocol

In the following AND, copy, and XOR protocols, the bases of the output commitments are fixed to avoid information leakage from the bases when the outputs are opened.

The outline to execute by three players is as follows. The protocol in [14] has two randomizations. The first is the randomization of the bases of the two input values. The second is the randomization of the input values.

Carol executes private reveals in the following protocol. By the same argument written in the description of the base-fixed protocol, the value must be randomized by the other players in advance. Suppose that Alice and Bob use random bits a and b to randomize x, respectively. After Carol's private operation using $x \oplus a \oplus b$, Alice and Bob execute a private reverse cut using a and b, respectively, to undo the randomizations. Such randomizations are executed before every private reveals in the protocol.

Next, we need to randomize the bases of the two pairs to hide the relation between the output and inputs. Initially, $commit(0)$ is made from the cards of $commit(x)$ using $\{1,2\}$ and $commit(y)$ is made using $\{3,4\}$. Suppose that the output of AND is $commit(0)$. It means that $x = 0$. If no base change is executed, the base $\{1,2\}$ of the output reveal $x = 0$. Thus the randomization of bases is necessary. If the base randomization is executed by one player, the private information is known to one player just like the case of randomization of values. Thus the base randomization must be executed by two players.

The detailed protocol is shown below. Note that for the simplicity of description, we write $S \oplus b$ to mean the pair that the left and the right card are swapped if $b = 1$. If $S = commit(x)$, $S \oplus b$ means $commit(x \oplus b)$.

Protocol 3 *(Three player AND protocol)*
  Input: $commit(x)^{\{1,2\}}$ and $commit(y)^{\{3,4\}}$.
  Output: $commit(x \wedge y)^{\{1,2\}}$.

1. *Alice executes a private random bisection cut on $commit(x)^{\{1,2\}}$ using random bit a_1. The result is $S_1 = commit(x \oplus a_1)^{\{1,2\}}$.*
2. *Bob executes a private random bisection cut on S_1 using random bit b_1. The result is $S_2 = commit(x \oplus a_1 \oplus b_1)^{\{1,2\}}$.*
3. *Carol executes a private reveal on S_2. Carol sees $x \oplus a_1 \oplus b_1$. According to the value, Carol sets $S_3 \| S_4$ as*

$$S_3 \| S_4 = \begin{cases} commit(0)^{\{1,2\}} \| commit(y)^{\{3,4\}} & if \ x \oplus a_1 \oplus b_1 = 0 \\ commit(y)^{\{3,4\}} \| commit(0)^{\{1,2\}} & if \ x \oplus a_1 \oplus b_1 = 1 \end{cases}$$

The cards of S_2 are reused to set $commit(0)$.

4. *Alice executes a private random bisection cut on S_3 and S_4 using random bit a_2 and a_3, respectively. The result is $S_3 \oplus a_2 \| S_4 \oplus a_3$.*

5. *Bob executes a private random bisection cut on $S_3 \oplus a_2$ and $S_4 \oplus a_3$ using random bit b_2 and b_3, respectively. The result is $S_3 \oplus a_2 \oplus b_2 \| S_4 \oplus a_3 \oplus b_3$.*

6. *Carol randomly selects bit $c_1 \in \{0,1\}$. Carol executes private reveals on the two pairs and exchanges the bases of two pairs if $c_1 = 1$. Then, Carol executes private random bisection cuts on the two pairs using random bits $c_2, c_3 \in \{0,1\}$. Let the result be $S_5 \| S_6 =$*

$$
\begin{cases}
commit(0 \oplus a_2 \oplus b_2 \oplus c_2)^{\{1,2\}} \| commit(y \oplus a_3 \oplus b_3 \oplus c_3)^{\{3,4\}} \\
\quad if \ x \oplus a_1 \oplus b_1 = 0 \ and \ c_1 = 0 \\
commit(0 \oplus a_2 \oplus b_2 \oplus c_2)^{\{3,4\}} \| commit(y \oplus a_3 \oplus b_3 \oplus c_3)^{\{1,2\}} \\
\quad if \ x \oplus a_1 \oplus b_1 = 0 \ and \ c_1 = 1 \\
commit(y \oplus a_2 \oplus b_2 \oplus c_2)^{\{3,4\}} \| commit(0 \oplus a_3 \oplus b_3 \oplus c_3)^{\{1,2\}} \\
\quad if \ x \oplus a_1 \oplus b_1 = 1 \ and \ c_1 = 0 \\
commit(y \oplus a_2 \oplus b_2 \oplus c_2)^{\{1,2\}} \| commit(0 \oplus a_3 \oplus b_3 \oplus c_3)^{\{3,4\}} \\
\quad if \ x \oplus a_1 \oplus b_1 = 1 \ and \ c_1 = 1
\end{cases}
$$

7. *Bob executes private reveals on $S_5 \| S_6$. Bob randomly selects bit $b_4 \in \{0,1\}$. Bob exchanges the bases of the two commitments if $b_4 = 1$. Then Bob executes private reverse cuts on the pairs using b_2 and b_3, respectively. The result is*

$$
\begin{cases}
commit(0 \oplus a_2 \oplus c_2)^{\{1,2\}} \| commit(y \oplus a_3 \oplus c_3)^{\{3,4\}} \\
\quad if \ x \oplus a_1 \oplus b_1 = 0 \ and \ c_1 \oplus b_4 = 0 \\
commit(0 \oplus a_2 \oplus c_2)^{\{3,4\}} \| commit(y \oplus a_3 \oplus c_3)^{\{1,2\}} \\
\quad if \ x \oplus a_1 \oplus b_1 = 0 \ and \ c_1 \oplus b_4 = 1 \\
commit(y \oplus a_2 \oplus c_2)^{\{1,2\}} \| commit(0 \oplus a_3 \oplus c_3)^{\{3,4\}} \\
\quad if \ x \oplus a_1 \oplus b_1 = 1 \ and \ c_1 \oplus b_4 = 1 \\
commit(y \oplus a_2 \oplus c_2)^{\{3,4\}} \| commit(0 \oplus a_3 \oplus c_3)^{\{1,2\}} \\
\quad if \ x \oplus a_1 \oplus b_1 = 1 \ and \ c_1 \oplus b_4 = 0
\end{cases}
$$

8. *Carol executes private reverse cuts on the pairs using c_2 and c_3, respectively.*

9. *Alice executes a private reverse cut on each of the pairs using a_2 and a_3, respectively.*

Let $S_7 \| S_8$ be the result after the two private reverse cuts. $S_7 \| S_8 =$

$$
\begin{cases}
commit(0)^{\{1,2\}} \| commit(y)^{\{3,4\}} & if \ x \oplus a_1 \oplus b_1 = 0 \ and \ c_1 \oplus b_4 = 0 \\
commit(0)^{\{3,4\}} \| commit(y)^{\{1,2\}} & if \ x \oplus a_1 \oplus b_1 = 0 \ and \ c_1 \oplus b_4 = 1 \\
commit(y)^{\{1,2\}} \| commit(0)^{\{3,4\}} & if \ x \oplus a_1 \oplus b_1 = 1 \ and \ c_1 \oplus b_4 = 1 \\
commit(y)^{\{3,4\}} \| commit(0)^{\{1,2\}} & if \ x \oplus a_1 \oplus b_1 = 1 \ and \ c_1 \oplus b_4 = 0
\end{cases}
$$

Alice then executes a private reverse cut using a_1. The result is

$$
\begin{cases}
commit(0)^{\{1,2\}} \| commit(y)^{\{3,4\}} & if \ x \oplus b_1 = 0 \ and \ c_1 \oplus b_4 = 0 \\
commit(0)^{\{3,4\}} \| commit(y)^{\{1,2\}} & if \ x \oplus b_1 = 0 \ and \ c_1 \oplus b_4 = 1 \\
commit(y)^{\{1,2\}} \| commit(0)^{\{3,4\}} & if \ x \oplus b_1 = 1 \ and \ c_1 \oplus b_4 = 1 \\
commit(y)^{\{3,4\}} \| commit(0)^{\{1,2\}} & if \ x \oplus b_1 = 1 \ and \ c_1 \oplus b_4 = 0
\end{cases}
$$

10. *Bob executes a private reverse selection using b_1. Let T_0 be the result and T_1 be the pair that is not selected.*

$$T_0 = \begin{cases} commit(0)^{\{1,2\}} & \text{if } x = 0 \text{ and } c_1 \oplus b_4 = 0 \\ commit(0)^{\{3,4\}} & \text{if } x = 0 \text{ and } c_1 \oplus b_4 = 1 \\ commit(y)^{\{1,2\}} & \text{if } x = 1 \text{ and } c_1 \oplus b_4 = 1 \\ commit(y)^{\{3,4\}} & \text{if } x = 1 \text{ and } c_1 \oplus b_4 = 0 \end{cases}$$

The value of T_0 is $commit(x \wedge y)$ and its base is randomly set by $c_1 \oplus b_4$. Since Alice does not know b_4, $T_0 = commit(x \wedge y)^{\{1,2\},\{3,4\}|A}$. Similarly,

$$T_1 = \begin{cases} commit(y)^{\{3,4\}} & \text{if } x = 0 \text{ and } c_1 \oplus b_4 = 0 \\ commit(y)^{\{1,2\}} & \text{if } x = 0 \text{ and } c_1 \oplus b_4 = 1 \\ commit(0)^{\{3,4\}} & \text{if } x = 1 \text{ and } c_1 \oplus b_4 = 1 \\ commit(0)^{\{1,2\}} & \text{if } x = 1 \text{ and } c_1 \oplus b_4 = 0 \end{cases}$$

The value of T_1 is $commit(\bar{x} \wedge y)$ and its base is randomly set by $c_1 \oplus b_4$. $T_1 = commit(\bar{x} \wedge y)^{\{1,2\},\{3,4\}|A}$.
Next, execute the base-fixed protocol on these pairs. Then the players obtain $commit(x \wedge y)^{\{1,2\}}$.

The protocol is 14 rounds since the first step of the base-fixed protocol is executed by Bob. The semi-honest two-player AND protocol [14] is 8 rounds. The number of cards is four. Since four cards are necessary to input x and y, the number of cards is the minimum. The correctness of the output value is shown in the protocol, thus we show the security.

Theorem 2. *The AND protocol is secure.*

Proof. First, we show the security for Bob. Since Bob watches Alice, Bob knows the values in Steps 1, 2, 4, 5, 7, 9, 10 and Steps 1, 3, and 4 of the base-fixed protocol. Bob thus sees a_i, b_i, br_i, $x \wedge y \oplus br_1 \oplus cr_1$, $\bar{x} \wedge y \oplus br_2 \oplus cr_2$, and $((0 \oplus a_2 \oplus b_2 \oplus c_2$ and $y \oplus a_3 \oplus b_3 \oplus c_3$ if $x \oplus a_1 \oplus b_1 = 0)$ or $(y \oplus a_2 \oplus b_2 \oplus c_2$ and $y \oplus a_3 \oplus b_3 \oplus c_3$ if $x \oplus a_1 \oplus b_1 = 1))$. Bob can obtain no information about the secret input and output values since the values of cards are randomized by c_2, c_3, cr_1, or cr_2 that are unknown to Bob.

From the bases of the cards, Bob obtains no information since the bases of two randomized values, $0 \oplus a_2 \oplus b_2 \oplus c_2$ and $y \oplus a_3 \oplus b_3 \oplus c_3$ (or $y \oplus a_2 \oplus b_2 \oplus c_2$ and $0 \oplus a_3 \oplus b_3 \oplus c_3$) are randomized by unknown value c_1. The bases of two randomized values, $x \wedge y \oplus br_1 \oplus cr_1$ and $\bar{x} \wedge y \oplus br_2 \oplus cr_2$ are randomized by $c_1 \oplus b_4$ but c_1 is unknown to Bob.

Next, we show the security for Carol. Since Carol watches Bob, Carol knows the values in Steps 2, 3, 5, 6, 7, 8, 10 and Steps 1, 2, 4, and 5 of the base-fixed protocol. Carol thus sees b_i, c_i, br_i, cr_i, $x \oplus a_1 \oplus b_1$, $0 \oplus a_2 \oplus b_2$, $y \oplus a_3 \oplus b_3$, and $((0 \oplus a_2 \oplus b_2 \oplus c_2$ and $y \oplus a_3 \oplus b_3 \oplus c_3$ if $x \oplus a_1 \oplus b_1 = 0)$ or $(y \oplus a_2 \oplus b_2 \oplus c_2$ and $y \oplus a_3 \oplus b_3 \oplus c_3$ if $x \oplus a_1 \oplus b_1 = 1))$. From the cards, Carol obtains no information about the secret input values since the values are randomized by unknown values a_1, a_2, or a_3.

About the bases of the cards, Carol knows whether she set $commit(0)^{\{1,2\}}||commit(y)^{\{3,4\}}$ or $commit(0)^{\{3,4\}}||commit(y)^{\{1,2\}}$ in Step 3 and both two base randomizations by Carol and Bob, thus she knows whether $S_7||S_8$ is $commit(0)||commit(y)$ or $commit(y)||commit(0)$ and each commitment is made by $\{1,2\}$ or $\{3,4\}$. However, Carol cannot see the private reverse cut by Alice in Step 9, Carol cannot know which pair is selected as the final result thus no information is known to Carol. Since Alice sets the base to $\{1,2\}$, Carol cannot know information about the secret input values from the base of the final result.

Last, we show the security for Alice. Alice knows the values in Steps 1, 3, 4, 6, 8, 9, and Steps 2, 3, and 5 of the base-fixed protocol. Alice thus sees a_i, c_i, cr_i, $x \oplus a_1 \oplus b_1$, $x \wedge y \oplus br_1 \oplus cr_1$, and $\bar{x} \wedge y \oplus br_2 \oplus cr_2$, and $((0 \oplus a_2 \oplus b_2 \oplus c_2$ and $y \oplus a_3 \oplus b_3 \oplus c_3$ if $x \oplus a_1 \oplus b_1 = 0)$ or $(y \oplus a_2 \oplus b_2 \oplus c_2$ and $y \oplus a_3 \oplus b_3 \oplus c_3$ if $x \oplus a_1 \oplus b_1 = 1))$. From the revealed cards, Alice obtains no information about the secret input and output values since each value is randomized by unknown value b_1, b_2, b_3, br_1, or br_2.

Alice knows whether $S_3||S_4$ is $commit(0)^{\{1,2\}}||commit(y)^{\{3,4\}}$ or $commit(y)^{\{3,4\}}||commit(0)^{\{1,2\}}$. Alice also knows the bases of each pair of $S_5||S_6$. Though Alice knows the bases of $S_5||S_6$, Bob's base change using b_4 is unknown to Alice. Thus, the bases of T_0 and T_1 are random for Alice because of b_4. When Alice sees $x \wedge y \oplus br_1 \oplus cr_1$ and $\bar{x} \wedge y \oplus br_2 \oplus cr_2$ in Step 3 of the base-fixed protocol, the bases are randomized by $c_1 \oplus b_4$. Thus, Alice obtains no information from the bases of the commitments.   □

3.3   Copy Protocol

Next, we show a new copy protocol by three players.

Protocol 4 *(Three player copy protocol)*
   Input: $commit(x)^{\{1,2\}}$ and two new cards 3 and 4.
   Output: $commit(x)^{\{1,2\}}$ and $commit(x)^{\{3,4\}}$

1. *Alice executes a private random bisection cut on $commit(x)^{\{1,2\}}$ using random bit a. The result is $commit(x \oplus a)^{\{1,2\}}$.*
2. *Bob executes a private random bisection cut on $commit(x \oplus a)^{\{1,2\}}$ using random bit b. The result is $commit(x \oplus a \oplus b)^{\{1,2\}}$.*
3. *Carol executes a private reveal on $commit(x \oplus a \oplus b)^{\{1,2\}}$ and sees $x \oplus a \oplus b$. Carol privately makes $commit(x \oplus a \oplus b)^{\{3,4\}}$.*
4. *Alice executes a private reverse cut on each of the pairs using a. The result is $commit(x \oplus b)^{\{1,2\}}$ and $commit(x \oplus b)^{\{3,4\}}$.*
5. *Bob executes a private reverse cut on each of the pairs using b. The result is $commit(x)^{\{1,2\}}$ and $commit(x)^{\{3,4\}}$.*

The number of cards is the minimum. The protocol is five rounds. The semi-honest two-player copy protocol [14] is three rounds.

Theorem 3. *The copy protocol is secure.*

Proof. Alice sees a and $x \oplus a \oplus b$. Bob sees a and b. Carol sees b and $x \oplus a \oplus b$. Thus no player knows the secret value x.   □

3.4   XOR Protocol

Since AND and copy protocols are shown and NOT is obvious, any Boolean function can be realized by the combination of these protocols. XOR protocol is shown because the realization of XOR is simple.

Protocol 5 *(Three player XOR protocol)*
   Input: $commit(x)^{\{1,2\}}$ and $commit(y)^{\{3,4\}}$.
   Output: $commit(x \oplus y)^{\{1,2\}}$.

1. *Alice executes a private random bisection cut on $commit(x)^{\{1,2\}}$ and $commit(y)^{\{3,4\}}$ using the same random bit $a \in \{0,1\}$. The result is $commit(x \oplus a)^{\{1,2\}}$ and $commit(y \oplus a)^{\{3,4\}}$.*
2. *Bob executes a private random bisection cut on $commit(x \oplus a)^{\{1,2\}}$ and $commit(y \oplus a)^{\{3,4\}}$ using the same random bit $b \in \{0,1\}$. The result is $commit(x \oplus a \oplus b)^{\{1,2\}}$ and $commit(y \oplus a \oplus b)^{\{3,4\}}$.*
3. *Carol executes a private reveal on $commit(y \oplus a \oplus b)^{\{3,4\}}$. Carol sees $y \oplus a \oplus b$. Carol executes a private reverse cut on $commit(x \oplus a \oplus b)^{\{1,2\}}$ using $y \oplus a \oplus b$. The result is $commit((x \oplus a \oplus b) \oplus (y \oplus a \oplus b))^{\{1,2\}} = commit(x \oplus y)^{\{1,2\}}$.*

The protocol is three rounds. The semi-honest two-player XOR protocol [14] is two rounds. The protocol uses four cards. Since any protocol needs four cards to input x and y, the number of cards is the minimum.

Theorem 4. *The XOR protocol is secure.*

Proof. Alice sees a and $y \oplus a \oplus b$. Bob sees a and b. Carol sees b and $y \oplus a \oplus b$. Thus no player knows the secret value y.   □

References

1. Abe, Y., Iwamoto, M., Ohta, K.: How to detect malicious behaviors in a card-based majority voting protocol with three inputs. In: 2020 International Symposium on Information Theory and Its Applications (ISITA), pp. 377–381. IEEE (2020)
2. den Boer, B.: More efficient match-making and satisfiability *the five card trick*. In: Quisquater, J.-J., Vandewalle, J. (eds.) EUROCRYPT 1989. LNCS, vol. 434, pp. 208–217. Springer, Heidelberg (1990). https://doi.org/10.1007/3-540-46885-4_23
3. Bultel, X., et al.: Physical zero-knowledge proof for Makaro. In: Izumi, T., Kuznetsov, P. (eds.) SSS 2018. LNCS, vol. 11201, pp. 111–125. Springer, Cham (2018). https://doi.org/10.1007/978-3-030-03232-6_8
4. Cheung, E., Hawthorne, C., Lee, P.: CS 758 project: secure computation with playing cards (2013). http://cdchawthorne.com/writings/secure_playing_cards.pdf

5. Hanaoka, G., et al.: Physical and visual cryptography to accelerate social implementation of advanced cryptographic technologies. IEICE Trans. Fundam. Electron. Commun. Comput. Sci. (2023). (In Japanese)

6. Hashimoto, Y., Shinagawa, K., Nuida, K., Inamura, M., Hanaoka, G.: Secure grouping protocol using a deck of cards. IEICE Trans. Fundam. Electron. Commun. Comput. Sci. **101**(9), 1512–1524 (2018)

7. Koch, A.: Cryptographic protocols from physical assumptions. Ph.D. thesis, Karlsruhe Institute of Technology, Germany (2019)

8. Koch, A.: The landscape of optimal card-based protocols. Math. Cryptol. **1**(2), 115–131 (2021)

9. Koch, A., Schrempp, M., Kirsten, M.: Card-based cryptography meets formal verification. N. Gener. Comput. **39**(1), 115–158 (2021)

10. Koch, A., Walzer, S.: Foundations for actively secure card-based cryptography. In: Proceedings of 10th International Conference on Fun with Algorithms (FUN 2020). Schloss Dagstuhl-Leibniz-Zentrum für Informatik (2020)

11. Koyama, H., Miyahara, D., Mizuki, T., Sone, H.: A secure three-input and protocol with a standard deck of minimal cards. In: Santhanam, R., Musatov, D. (eds.) CSR 2021. LNCS, vol. 12730, pp. 242–256. Springer, Cham (2021). https://doi.org/10.1007/978-3-030-79416-3_14

12. Koyama, H., Toyoda, K., Miyahara, D., Mizuki, T.: New card-based copy protocols using only random cuts. In: Proceedings of the 8th ACM on ASIA Public-Key Cryptography Workshop, APKC 2021, pp. 13–22. Association for Computing Machinery, New York (2021)

13. Manabe, Y.: Survey: card-based cryptographic protocols to calculate primitives of Boolean functions. Int. J. Comput. Softw. Eng. **27**(1), 178 (2022)

14. Manabe, Y., Ono, H.: Card-based cryptographic protocols with a standard deck of cards using private operations. In: Cerone, A., Ölveczky, P.C. (eds.) ICTAC 2021. LNCS, vol. 12819, pp. 256–274. Springer, Cham (2021). https://doi.org/10.1007/978-3-030-85315-0_15

15. Manabe, Y., Ono, H.: Card-based cryptographic protocols with malicious players using private operations. N. Gener. Comput. **40**(1), 67–93 (2022)

16. Miyahara, D., Hayashi, Y.I., Mizuki, T., Sone, H.: Practical card-based implementations of Yao's millionaire protocol. Theoret. Comput. Sci. **803**, 207–221 (2020)

17. Mizuki, T.: Applications of card-based cryptography to education. In: IEICE Techinical Report ISEC2016-53, pp. 13–17 (2016). (In Japanese)

18. Mizuki, T.: Efficient and secure multiparty computations using a standard deck of playing cards. In: Foresti, S., Persiano, G. (eds.) CANS 2016. LNCS, vol. 10052, pp. 484–499. Springer, Cham (2016). https://doi.org/10.1007/978-3-319-48965-0_29

19. Mizuki, T., Asiedu, I.K., Sone, H.: Voting with a logarithmic number of cards. In: Mauri, G., Dennunzio, A., Manzoni, L., Porreca, A.E. (eds.) UCNC 2013. LNCS, vol. 7956, pp. 162–173. Springer, Heidelberg (2013). https://doi.org/10.1007/978-3-642-39074-6_16

20. Mizuki, T., Komano, Y.: Information leakage due to operative errors in card-based protocols. Inf. Comput. **285**, 104910 (2022)

21. Mizuki, T., Shizuya, H.: Practical card-based cryptography. In: Ferro, A., Luccio, F., Widmayer, P. (eds.) FUN 2014. LNCS, vol. 8496, pp. 313–324. Springer, Cham (2014). https://doi.org/10.1007/978-3-319-07890-8_27

22. Mizuki, T., Shizuya, H.: Computational model of card-based cryptographic protocols and its applications. IEICE Trans. Fundam. Electron. Commun. Comput. Sci. **100**(1), 3–11 (2017)

23. Mizuki, T., Sone, H.: Six-card secure AND and four-card secure XOR. In: Deng, X., Hopcroft, J.E., Xue, J. (eds.) FAW 2009. LNCS, vol. 5598, pp. 358–369. Springer, Heidelberg (2009). https://doi.org/10.1007/978-3-642-02270-8_36

24. Nakai, T., Misawa, Y., Tokushige, Y., Iwamoto, M., Ohta, K.: How to solve millionaires' problem with two kinds of cards. N. Gener. Comput. **39**(1), 73–96 (2021)

25. Nakai, T., Shirouchi, S., Iwamoto, M., Ohta, K.: Four cards are sufficient for a card-based three-input voting protocol utilizing private permutations. In: Shikata, J. (ed.) ICITS 2017. LNCS, vol. 10681, pp. 153–165. Springer, Cham (2017). https://doi.org/10.1007/978-3-319-72089-0_9

26. Niemi, V., Renvall, A.: Solitaire zero-knowledge. Fundam. Inform. **38**(1, 2), 181–188 (1999)

27. Nishida, T., Mizuki, T., Sone, H.: Securely computing the three-input majority function with eight cards. In: Dediu, A.-H., Martín-Vide, C., Truthe, B., Vega-Rodríguez, M.A. (eds.) TPNC 2013. LNCS, vol. 8273, pp. 193–204. Springer, Heidelberg (2013). https://doi.org/10.1007/978-3-642-45008-2_16

28. Ono, H., Manabe, Y.: Efficient card-based cryptographic protocols for the millionaires' problem using private input operations. In: Proceedings of 13th Asia Joint Conference on Information Security (AsiaJCIS 2018), pp. 23–28 (2018)

29. Ono, H., Manabe, Y.: Card-based cryptographic logical computations using private operations. N. Gener. Comput. **39**(1), 19–40 (2021)

30. Ono, H., Manabe, Y.: Minimum round card-based cryptographic protocols using private operations. Cryptography **5**(3), 17 (2021)

31. Sasaki, T., Miyahara, D., Mizuki, T., Sone, H.: Efficient card-based zero-knowledge proof for sudoku. Theoret. Comput. Sci. **839**, 135–142 (2020)

32. Shinagawa, K., Mizuki, T.: Secure computation of any Boolean function based on any deck of cards. In: Chen, Y., Deng, X., Lu, M. (eds.) FAW 2019. LNCS, vol. 11458, pp. 63–75. Springer, Cham (2019). https://doi.org/10.1007/978-3-030-18126-0_6

33. Shinagawa, K., Nuida, K.: A single shuffle is enough for secure card-based computation of any Boolean circuit. Discret. Appl. Math. **289**, 248–261 (2021)

34. Shinoda, Y., Miyahara, D., Shinagawa, K., Mizuki, T., Sone, H.: Card-based covert lottery. In: Maimut, D., Oprina, A.-G., Sauveron, D. (eds.) SecITC 2020. LNCS, vol. 12596, pp. 257–270. Springer, Cham (2021). https://doi.org/10.1007/978-3-030-69255-1_17

35. Takashima, K., et al.: Card-based protocols for secure ranking computations. Theoret. Comput. Sci. **845**, 122–135 (2020)

36. Takashima, K., Miyahara, D., Mizuki, T., Sone, H.: Actively revealing card attack on card-based protocols. Nat. Comput. **21**(4), 615–628 (2022)

37. Watanabe, Y., Kuroki, Y., Suzuki, S., Koga, Y., Iwamoto, M., Ohta, K.: Card-based majority voting protocols with three inputs using three cards. In: Proceedings of 2018 International Symposium on Information Theory and Its Applications (ISITA), pp. 218–222. IEEE (2018)

Cryptanalysis of Human Identification Protocol with Human-Computable Passwords

Maciej Grześkowiak[1], Łukasz Krzywiecki[2(✉)], and Karol Niczyj[3]

[1] Adam Mickiewicz University, Poznań, Poland
`maciej.grzeskowiak@amu.edu.pl`
[2] Wroclaw University of Science and Technology, Wrocław, Poland
`lukasz.krzywiecki@pwr.edu.pl`
[3] Karol Niczyj Software House, Wrocław, Poland
`karol.niczyj@knsh.pl`

Abstract. In this paper we demonstrate effective attacks on *Human Identification Protocol with Human-Computable Passwords* (HIPHCP) presented in ISPEC'22. The protocol, which was designed to allow fast user identification, is vulnerable to both the active and the passive attacks, where the significant amount of the secret key can be learned by the adversary. This subsequently allow to compromise the full secret key via brute-forcing the remaining secret bits.

Keywords: Cryptoanalysis · Human-Computable Passwords · Identification scheme · Short password · Shared secret

1 Introduction

In this paper we address security issue of the Human Identification Protocol with Human-Computable Passwords (HIPHCP) [1] presented in ISPEC'22. In general the protocol could be classified as an Identification Scheme (IS), where a prover and a verifier parties pre-share the same secret. Specifically, the additional requirement is that the secret should be easy to memorize and human computable, and as such, it should be easy to input in the prover's device by the end user. This makes it similar, from the ergonomic perspective, to Password based Authenticated Key agreement Protocols (PAKE), where short passwords input by the parties, are used to pair parties' devices and to establish a strong symmetric session key between them.

Identification Scheme. Identification schemes (IS) are used to prove one's identity to a verifier. Typically, IS are implemented using asymmetric cryptography with keys managed via *Public Key Infrastructure* (PKI). In this scenario, within an interactive zero-knowledge protocol, a prover convinces the knowledge of a secret key to a Verifier holding the corresponding public key. The main security requirements for IS is *impersonation resistance* - no attacker should be able

W. Meng et al. (Eds.): ISPEC 2023, LNCS 14341, pp. 347–364, 2023.
https://doi.org/10.1007/978-981-99-7032-2_21

to successfully complete the protocol, and be positively identified, without the corresponding secret key. Typically, both a prover and a verifier exchanges messages over an open communication channel, but runs their computations locally. The algorithm executed by the prover holding the secret key, and challenged from the the verifier, should correspond with the result of the verifier's algorithm called with the public key and the response from the prover. This involves complex computations over large numbers, and are run on the users' electronic devices, which store sensitive secret keys.

Shared Secret Identification. In some scenarios the prover and the verifier share the same short secret, called *password*, which allows for its fast input into the corresponding devices. This could be used to coin a session secret key, long enough for subsequent secure encrypted communication between the devices paired in this way. However, because short passwords have small entropy, the main threat here is that messages exchanged between parties could be treated as effective oracles for potential password guessing attacks. Therefore *Password Based Authenticated Key Exchange* (PAKE) protocols (see e.g. [2–4]) utilize the asymmetric cryptography, and Diffie-Hellman like key exchange techniques to disperse the short passwords in the large groups of computations, in a way that, it is impossible to brute-force the password from the resulting transcript of the protocol execution.

Human Computable Secrets. In some scenarios it is required that a user actively participate in the identification process. It means the user has to perform a "small human action" which guaranties that the identification process is not fully automated and machine operated. This usually protects against potential brute-force attacks, or "unawareness" attacks, as those "small human actions" should be difficult to software simulate. Usually this involves some specific interface-level actions, like *Completely Automated Public Turing test to tell Computers and Humans Apart* (CAPTCHA) proposed in [5]. In some cases human operator additionally has to apply some basic computations itself, using small numbers and basic mathematical operations. First Human-Generated Password protocol (HGP) was proposed in [6]. The commercially implemented protocols were [7,8], where [7] is slow, while [8] is weak.

Problem Statement. Providing the HGP construction, that is provably secure, and yet which ergonomy and complexity are on acceptable level, is not an easy task. The proposition from [1] was supposed to close the gap between the two requirements (as of [7,8]), being both fast and secure. Here in this paper we discuss some aspects of this scheme, pointing out its vulnerabilities.

1.1 Contribution of the Paper

The contribution of the paper is the following:

- We crypto-analyze the original Human Identification Protocol with Human-Computable Passwords from [1]:

- We demonstrate a very effective active attack, which allows to find out positions in the matrix secret.
- We demonstrate a passive attack. This attack is only slightly slower then the active attack.

Both attacks can be combined. The indexes in the secret matrix, obtained from the active attack, can be used to speed-up the passive attack process.

1.2 Related Work

Identification schemes are typically based on public-key cryptography [9–13]. Several ISes constructions are design to withstand specific attacks [14,15], including statistical attacks [16], reset attacks [17,18], and ephemeral key leakages in three-round (commitment, challenge, response) schemes [19,20].

Password based schemes allow to authenticate low-entropy password holders, to pair their devices and to establish a session encryption key. These schemes are usually based on Diffie-Hellman key exchange, where the fresh generator is created by a deterministic function over the password [2–4,21,22]. Some of the password based constructions has been proposed for Machine Readable Travel Documents (MRTD) [23–25].

In the context of human generated passwords, and human computable secrets, apart from constructions [1,6–8] mentioned above, we refer to reviews [26,27], and the scheme from [28].

1.3 Structure of the Paper

In Sect. 2 we define the system model and the security notion for identification protocols with shared secrets. In Sect. 3 we recall the base construction from [1]. In Sect. 4 we demonstrate our attacks.

2 Preliminaries and Notation

2.1 System Model

We start from the formal definition of identification scheme, where a prover $\mathcal{P}$, traditionally called Alice, identifies in front of a verifier $\mathcal{V}$, called Bob. Here both parties hold the same pre-shared secret S. Thus, a *positive verification* in the scheme means, that Bob concludes that on the other side of the communication channel is a user that holds the same secret.

Definition 1 (Shared Secret Identification Scheme). *A shared secret identification scheme* IS *is a tuple of procedures* $(\mathsf{PG}, \mathsf{KG}, \mathcal{P}, \mathcal{V}, \pi)$:

$\mathsf{par} \leftarrow \mathsf{PG}(1^\lambda)$: *takes the parameter* λ, *and outputs public parameters.*
$S \leftarrow \mathsf{KG}(\mathsf{par})$: *outputs a secret shared between the prover and the verifier.*
$\mathcal{P}(S)$: *denotes the Prover algorithm which interacts with the Verifier* $\mathcal{V}$.

$\mathcal{V}(S)$: *denotes the Verifier algorithm which interacts with the Prover* $\mathcal{P}$.
$\pi(\mathcal{P}, \mathcal{V})$: *denotes the protocol of interactions between* $\mathcal{P}$ *and* $\mathcal{V}$.

IS *has Initialization and Operation Stages. In Initialization Stage, parameters and keys for users are generated. In the latter, a user proves interactively its identity in front of the Verifier:* $\pi(\mathcal{P}(S), \mathcal{V}(S))$. *We write* $\pi(\mathcal{P}, \mathcal{V}) \to 1$ *iff* $\mathcal{P}$ *and* $\mathcal{V}$ *have mutually accepted each other in* π. *The scheme is* correct *iff*

$$\Pr[\text{par} \leftarrow \text{PG}(1^\lambda), S \leftarrow \text{KG}(\text{par}), \pi(\mathcal{P}(S), \mathcal{V}(S)) \to 1] = 1.$$

2.2 Impersonation Resilience

The fundamental security requirement for IS with parameters $\text{par} \leftarrow \text{PG}(1^\lambda)$ is that no malicious algorithm $\mathcal{A}$, without the secret key S, but observing ℓ executions of $\pi(\mathcal{P}(S)), \mathcal{V}(S))$ between a legitimate prover and verifier, should be accepted in protocol π as the observed prover $\mathcal{P}(S)$. In other words, we require that probability $\Pr[\pi(\mathcal{A}(\text{par}), \mathcal{V}(S)) \to 1] \leq \epsilon(\lambda, \ell)$, where $\epsilon(\lambda, \ell)$ is a negligible function. We formally define our security experiment in Sect. 2.4.

2.3 Adversary Model

The process in which an adversary gains knowledge about the attacked protocol is modeled by a *Query Stage* of the security experiment. This means that the adversary runs a polynomial number ℓ of the protocol executions between the prover and the verifier: $\pi(\mathcal{P}(S), \mathcal{V}(S))$. We consider the adversary which can intercept messages from $\mathcal{V}(S)$, modify it according to its will, and forward it to the prover $\mathcal{P}(S)$. The adversary itself can play the role of the verifier, but of course without the access to the secret S.

2.4 Security Experiments

Let the view v_i be the total knowledge $\mathcal{A}$ can gain after i runs of π. These includes the set $\{T_1, \ldots, T_i\}$, where T_i is the transcript of the protocol messages in the ith execution. The IS is secure if such a cumulated knowledge after ℓ executions does not help the Adversary to be accepted by the verifier except with a negligible probability.

Definition 2 (Impersonation Security).
Let IS = (PG, KG, $\mathcal{P}$, $\mathcal{V}$, π). *We define security experiment* $\text{Exp}_{\text{IS}}^{\lambda, \ell}$:
Init Stage : $\text{par} \leftarrow \text{PG}(1^\lambda)$, $S \leftarrow \text{KG}(\text{par})$, $\mathcal{A}(\text{par})$.
Query Stage : *For* $i = 1$ *to* ℓ *run:* $\pi(\mathcal{P}(S), \mathcal{A}(\mathcal{V}(S), v_{i-1})) \to T_i$,
    where $\mathcal{A}(\mathcal{V}(S), v_{i-1})$ *indicate the adversary that has access to challenges from*
    $\mathcal{V}(S)$, *and can modify them using the knowledge* v_{i-1} *from previous executions.*
Impersonation Stage : $\mathcal{A}$ *executes the protocol* $\pi(\mathcal{A}(\text{par}, v_\ell), \mathcal{V}(S))$.

The advantage of $\mathcal{A}$ *in the experiment* $\text{Exp}_{\text{IS}}^{\lambda, \ell}$ *is the probability of acceptance in the last stage:*

$$\mathbf{Adv}(\mathcal{A}, \mathrm{Exp}_{\mathsf{IS}}^{\lambda,\ell}) = \Pr[\pi(\mathcal{A}(\mathsf{par}, v_\ell), \mathcal{V}(S)) \to 1].$$

We say that the IS *is* (λ, ℓ)*-secure if* $\mathbf{Adv}(\mathcal{A}, \mathrm{Exp}_{\mathsf{IS}}^{\lambda,\ell}) \leq \epsilon(\lambda, \ell)$ *and* ϵ *is negligible function of parameters* λ, ℓ.

3   The Original Protocol

3.1   The Protocol Pattern

The original HIPHCP protocol from [1] has typical two-round pattern depicted in Fig. 1. Both parties, Alice and Bob, share a predefined secret S, and locally compute a function $F_S(C)$, where C denotes a challenge from the verifier. Note that usually the choice of the function $F_S(C)$ is related to the requirements and limitations of the parties and their devices. It is worth to mention, that if S is sufficiently large, the function F could be realize via cryptographically secure hash function $\mathcal{H}$ (or via efficient deterministic encryption scheme,). Then, both parties could compute $r = \mathcal{H}(C\|S)$. However, in the case of HIPHCP from [1] the secret S is short. For short secrets one could apply or modify existing PAKE protocols. Yet, in the construction from [1] the function $F_S(C)$ is assumed to input not only short *human-memorable* secret S, but to be easily *human-computable* as well. We abstract from assessing if these requirement are achieved, but we note that the user computed operations, as defined originally in [1], and recalled in subsequent subsections, are quite complex.

Let IS $=$ (PG, KG, $\mathcal{P}$, $\mathcal{V}$, π) be an identification scheme, where (C, r) denotes challenge and response messages. Let S denote a shared secret. Let $F_S(C)$ denote a function on S, C. Let $\pi(\mathcal{P}(S), \mathcal{V}(S))$ define the two-round pattern:

2. $\mathcal{V}$: Prepare a random challange C, $\mathcal{P} \xleftarrow{C} \mathcal{V}$.
3. $\mathcal{P}$: Compute $r = F_S(C)$, $\mathcal{P} \xrightarrow{r} \mathcal{V}$.
4. $\mathcal{V}$: Accept iff $F_S(C) == r$.

Fig. 1. The two-round pattern of the HIPHCP protocol from [1].

3.2   Function F

Here we formally define the function F. We only slightly adjust the notation from [1] for legibility of attacks description. Fix $n \in \mathbb{N}$, $n \geq 10$ and let be the index set $I_n = \{1, 2, \ldots, n\}$. Let $\mathcal{K}$ be the power set of $I_n \times I_n$,

$$\mathcal{K} = P(I_n \times I_n).$$

Fix $q \in \mathbb{N}$. We denote by $M_n(\mathbb{Z}_q)$ the set of $n \times n$ matrices over a ring $\mathbb{Z}_q$. For fixed integer $0 < L \leq 10$ we define the keyed function

$$F : \mathcal{K} \times M_n(\mathbb{Z}_q) \to \mathbb{Z}_q^L.$$

Consider a challenge-response protocol in which users Alice and Bob have a shared secret $S \in \mathcal{K}$ that Alice can use to respond to Bob's challenges in such a way that an adversary cannot easily learn the secret. Suppose that the secret shared between Alice and Bob is a family of sets of $\mathcal{K}$ drawn at random from $\mathcal{K}$,

$$S = \{B^I, B^O\}, \quad B^I = \{B_1^I, \dots B_{b-1}^I\} \quad B^O = \{B_0^O, B_1^O \dots B_{b-1}^O\}.$$

The sets B^O and B^I determine the entries of matrices in $M_n(\mathbb{Z}_q)$. Authentication proceeds as follows: Bob generates a random matrix $C \in M_n(\mathbb{Z}_q)$ and send it to Alice, as a challenge. Alice responds with $r = F(S, C) = F_S(C)$. Bob accepts if r from Alice equals to $F_S(C)$ computed locally by Bob.

3.3   Secret and Challenge

At the beginning of this paragraph we will describe the procedure for choosing a secret S. Fix $n, q \in \mathbb{N}$, $n \geq 10$. For given positive integers $1 \leq b, L \leq 10$ and $1 \leq l_1, \dots, l_{b-1} \leq 10$ we select randomly a secret S from $\mathcal{K}$. The set S is a family of sets

$$S = \{B_0^O, \dots, B_{b-1}^O, B_1^I, \dots, B_{b-1}^I\}, \quad B_i^z, B_j^w \in \mathcal{K},$$

where $z, w \in \{O, I\}$,

$$B_0^O = \{(i_1, j_1), \dots, (i_L, j_L)\},$$
$$B_t^O = \{(i_t, j_t)\},$$
$$B_t^I = \{(i_1, j_1), \dots, (i_{l_t}, j_{l_t})\},$$

for $t = 1, \dots, b-1$. For given matrix $C = [c_{i,j}] \in M_n(\mathbb{Z}_q)$, we determine the sets consisting of the matrix elements

$$B_0^O(C) = \{c_{i_1, j_1}, \dots, c_{i_L, j_L}\},$$
$$B_t^O(C) = \{c_{i_t, j_t}\},$$
$$B_t^I(C) = \{c_{i_1, j_1}, \dots, c_{i_{l_t}, j_{l_t}}\},$$

for $t = 1, \dots, b - 1$. For simplicity of notation, we take $c_w = c_{i_w, j_w}$ and omit the subscripts i_w, j_w of c's. In this way, for given S and C, the elements of the corresponding sets $B_r^O(C)$ and $B_t^I(C)$ can be written in a simplified form

$$B_0^O(C) = \{c_1, \dots, c_L\},$$
$$B_t^O(C) = \{c_t\},$$
$$B_t^I(C) = \{c_1, \dots, c_{l_t}\},$$

for $t = 1, \dots, b - 1$. The element m_w of $B_i^z(C)$ corresponding to the position w is denoted by $B_i^z(C)[w]$, where $i = 0, \dots, b - 1$, $z \in \{O, I\}$. Note that, the sets $B_t^O(C)$ have only one element, which we will denote by $B_t^O(C)[1]$ for $t = 1, \dots, b - 1$.

We illustrate the procedures for selecting the secret key with an example.

Example 1. Suppose that Alice and Bob share a secret with parameters $n = q = 10$, $b = 4$ and $L = 3$, $l_1 = 2$, $l_2 = 3$, $l_3 = 4$. So $\mathcal{K} = P(I_{10} \times I_{10})$ is a set of sets of ordered pairs (i, j) with $i, j \in I_{10}$. Let Alice and Bob share a secret S consisting of sets,

$$S = \{B_0^O, \ldots, B_3^O, B_1^I, \ldots, B_3^I\},$$

where

$$B_0^O = \{(1,1), (2,5), (4,3)\},$$
$$B_1^I = \{(2,9), (4,8)\},$$
$$B_2^I = \{(5,1), (5,2), (5,3)\},$$
$$B_3^I = \{(8,3), (8,4), (9,1), (9,6)\},$$
$$B_1^O = \{(7,7)\},$$
$$B_2^O = \{(8,8)\},$$
$$B_3^O = \{(4,7)\}.$$

Example 2. Let's choose a challenge matrix $C = [c_{i,j}] \in M_{10}(\mathbb{Z}_{10})$,

$$C = \begin{bmatrix} 1 & 2 & 3 & 4 & 5 & 6 & 7 & 8 & 9 & 0 \\ 2 & 7 & 9 & 3 & 5 & 6 & 1 & 1 & 1 & 4 \\ 3 & 3 & 5 & 3 & 4 & 5 & 6 & 4 & 8 & 9 \\ 4 & 5 & 2 & 6 & 4 & 4 & 0 & 1 & 8 & 6 \\ 5 & 4 & 2 & 0 & 3 & 2 & 3 & 7 & 3 & 5 \\ 6 & 9 & 2 & 5 & 4 & 6 & 6 & 1 & 6 & 3 \\ 7 & 8 & 3 & 6 & 9 & 5 & 9 & 7 & 8 & 4 \\ 8 & 6 & 2 & 1 & 4 & 2 & 6 & 8 & 4 & 8 \\ 9 & 1 & 6 & 6 & 5 & 5 & 3 & 0 & 5 & 1 \\ 0 & 3 & 2 & 3 & 4 & 6 & 6 & 5 & 8 & 7 \end{bmatrix}.$$

The sets $B_t^O(C), B_t^I(C)$ corresponding to the matrix C, where $r = 0, 1, 2, 3$, $t = 1, 2, 3$, are of the form

$$B_0^O(C) = \{c_{1,1}, c_{2,5}, c_{4,3}\} = \{1, 5, 2\},$$
$$B_1^I(C) = \{c_{2,9}, c_{4,8}\} = \{1, 1\},$$
$$B_2^I(C) = \{c_{5,1}, c_{5,2}, c_{5,3}\} = \{5, 4, 2\},$$
$$B_3^I(C) = \{c_{8,3}, c_{8,4}, c_{9,1}, c_{9,6}\} = \{2, 1, 9, 5\},$$
$$B_1^O(C) = \{c_{7,7}\} = \{9\},$$
$$B_2^O(C) = \{c_{8,8}\} = \{8\},$$
$$B_3^O(C) = \{c_{4,7}\} = \{0\}.$$

We are now in a position to describe how the function F works. Assume that the secret S has been chosen. Then we are interested in of the algorithm for computing the single-input function

$$F_S : M_n(\mathbb{Z}_q) \to \mathbb{Z}_q^L.$$

In [1] the author uses the following notation, the value of function $F_S(C)$ is denoted by OTP, where OTP is an array with L elements. That is $F_S(C) = OTP[1..L]$.

Algorithm 1. An algorithm for computing F_S

Require: $S = \{B_0^O, \ldots, B_{b-1}^O, B_1^I, \ldots, B_{b-1}^I\}$, $C \in M_n(\mathbb{Z}_q)$, $q, b, L \in \mathbb{N}$, $1 \le b, L \le 10$
Ensure: $OTP \in \mathbb{Z}_q^L$
1: $block = 0$
2: **for** $i = 1, \ldots, L$ **do**
3:    $v_{in} = B_0^O(C)[i]$
4:    $v_{out} = v_{in}$
5:    **for** $u = 0, \ldots, b - 2$ **do**
6:       $j = u + block \pmod{b-1} + 1$
7:       **if** $v_{in} \in B_j^I(C)$ **then**
8:          $v_{out} \leftarrow B_j^O(C)[1]$
9:          $block = j \pmod{b}$
10:            **go to** 13
11:      **end if**
12:   **end for**
13:   $OTP[i] = v_{in} + v_{out} \pmod{q}$
14: **end for**

Important note. In the original paper [1], the author imprecisely defines the steps of the algorithm for computing $F_S(C)$ regarding the order in which the B_j^I-blocks are searched. Therefore, we set this order as in steps 2–12. This does not affect the presented attack's effectiveness but only how it is written.

Example 3. Let us compute $F_S(C) = OTP$, where S is the secret of Example 1 and C is the matrix of Example 2. It is an elementary check that $OTP = 034$.

4   Attacks

4.1   Active Attack Description

Suppose Alice and Bob share a secret S, where S is the set of a family of sets

$$S = \{B_0^O, \ldots, B_{b-1}^O, B_1^I, \ldots, B_{b-1}^I\}, \quad B_i^z, B_j^w \in \mathcal{K},$$

where $z, w \in \{O, I\}$. We present a probabilistic algorithm that finds B_0^O, part of the secret S, with high probability. We assume that Alice and Bob choose

S secretly and that integers $n \geq 10, q$ and L are known to the adversary, say Celine. For convenience of exposition, we assume that n is an even number. Let us fix a secret

$$B_0^O = \{(i_1, j_1), \dots, (i_L, j_L)\}.$$

It is clear that

$$(i_k, j_k) \in I_n \times I_n, \quad 1 \leq k \leq L.$$

Let us fix k. Given $X \subseteq I_n \times I_n$ such that $(i_k, j_k) \in X$, we describe an attack scenario in which Celina locates a set $Y \subset X$ of cardinality $\frac{|X|}{2}$ such that $(i_k, j_k) \in Y$. We start by describing the auxiliary procedure. The procedure takes an arbitrary set $X \subseteq I_n \times I_n$, $n, k \in \mathbb{N}$, and $M = [m_{i,j}] \in M_n(\mathbb{Z}_{10})$. We assume that M is with all entries zero. The procedure returns $Y \subset X$ such that $(i_k, j_k) \in Y$, $|Y| = \frac{|X|}{2}$, and $C = [c_{i,j}] \in M_n(\mathbb{Z}_{10})$.

PROCEDURE DIVSET(n, k, X, M)

1. Celine randomly divides X into two disjoint sets of the same cardinality. Let Y and Z be such a partition of the set X, that is $X = Y \cup Z$, and $|Y| = |Z| = \frac{|X|}{2}$.
2. Alice changes the values of the matrix $M = [m_{i,j}]$ according to the formula

$$\begin{aligned} m_{i,j} = 3 \quad \text{if} \quad (i,j) \in Y, \\ m_{i,j} = 1 \quad \text{if} \quad (i,j) \in Z. \end{aligned} \tag{1}$$

and takes $C = M$.
3. Celine sends the challenge C to Alice. Alice respond with

$$OTP = F_S(C).$$

4. If $OTP[k] = 6$, then Celine concludes that $(i_k, j_k) \in Y$ and she returns (Y, C).
5. If $OTP[k] = 2$, then Celine learns that $(i_k, j_k) \in Z$ and she returns (Z, C).
6. If $OTP[k] = 4$, then Celine randomly re-divides set X and start the procedure from the beginning.

From Lemma 2, it follows that procedure DIVSET will execute on average twice before returning the result.

Example 4. Alice and Bob share the secret S,

$$S = \{B_0^O, B_1^O B_2^O, B_1^I, B_2^I\},$$

where

$$B_0^O = \{(4, 4), (7, 7)\}, \quad B_1^O = \{(1, 8)\}, \quad B_2^O = \{(1, 1)\},$$
$$B_1^I = \{(4, 1), (5, 1), (5, 2)\}, \quad B_2^I = \{(7, 2), (8, 1)\}.$$

To learn in which part of the set X is $(i_1, j_1) \in B_0^O$, Celine executes procedure DIVSET(n, k, X, M) with $k = 1$, $n = 8$, $X = I_8 \times I_8$. $M = [m_{i,j}] \in M_8(\mathbb{Z}_{10})$, and M be with all entries zero.

1. Celine randomly divides X into two disjoint sets, $X = Y \cup Z$,

$$Y = \{(i,j) : i \in [1,4], j \in [1,8]\}, \quad Z = X \backslash Y,$$

2. Celina constructs matrix C,

$$C = \begin{bmatrix} 3\,3\,3\,3\,3\,3\,3\,3 \\ 3\,3\,3\,3\,3\,3\,3\,3 \\ 3\,3\,3\,3\,3\,3\,3\,3 \\ 3\,3\,3\,3\,3\,3\,3\,3 \\ 1\,1\,1\,1\,1\,1\,1\,1 \\ 1\,1\,1\,1\,1\,1\,1\,1 \\ 1\,1\,1\,1\,1\,1\,1\,1 \\ 1\,1\,1\,1\,1\,1\,1\,1 \end{bmatrix},$$

3. Celine sends the challenge C to Alice. Alice respond with

$$OTP = F_S(C) = 64.$$

4. Since $OTP[1] = 6$, then Celine concludes that $(i_1, j_1) \in Y$ and she returns (Y, C).

Vulnerable Subspace. We are now in a position to present the main algorithm that finds part of the secret S. We assume that $n = 2^u$, $u \in \mathbb{N}$. Given $n, u, k \in \mathbb{N}$ and $X = I_n \times I_n$ the algorithm returns $(i_k, j_k) \in B_0^O$.

ALGORITHM FINDSECRET(n, k, X)

1. Take $C_0 = [c_{i,j}] \in M_n(\mathbb{Z}_{10})$ to be the matrix with all entries zero,
2. $X_0 = X$
3. For $i = 1, \ldots 2u$ do
   (a) $(X_i, C_i) :=$ PROCEDURE DIVSET(n, k, X_{i-1}, C_{i-1}),
4. Return X_{2u}.

Lemma 2 shows that procedure DIVSET will execute on average twice before returning the result. It is intuitively clear that the algorithm FINDSECRET performs an average of $4u$ steps, where each step is the running time of procedure DIVSET.

Example 5. In this example we show the execution of algorithm FINDSECRET for the secret S from example 4. To learn the secret $(i_1, j_1) \in B_0^O$, Celine executes algorithm FINDSECRET$(1, 8, X)$ with $k = 1$, $n = 8$, $X = I_8 \times I_8$.

The following parameters calculated by the algorithm are given in the table below. The headings of the table mean respectively: i-iteration, 'input' - input to procedure DIVSET, 'partition'-the partition into two disjoint sets performed in procedure DIVSET, 'matrixa' - challenge sent to Alice by Celine, $OTP[1]$ - first digit of the response sent by Alice, 'output'-the values returned by the procedure DIVSET.

i	input	partition	matrix	$OTP[1]$	output
1	X_0, C_0	$X_0 = Y_0 \cup Z_0$	C_1	6	$X_1 = Y_0, C_1$
2	X_1, C_1	$X_1 = Y_{11} \cup Z_{11}$	C_{21}	4	
2	X_1, C_1	$X_1 = Y_{12} \cup Z_{12}$	C_{22}	2	$X_2 = Z_{12}, C_2 = C_{22}$
3	X_2, C_2	$X_2 = Y_2 \cup Z_2$	C_3	6	$X_3 = Y_2, C_3$
4	X_3, C_3	$X_3 = Y_3 \cup Z_3$	C_4	6	$X_4 = Y_3, C_4$
5	X_4, C_4	$X_4 = Y_4 \cup Z_4$	C_5	2	$X_5 = Z_4, C_5$

Consecutive outputs X_i and C_i of algorithm FINDSECRET o for $i = 1, 2, 3, 4, 5$:

$$X_1 = Y_0 = \{(i,j) : i \in [1,4], j \in [1,8]\},$$
$$Y_{11} = \{(i,j) : i \in [1,4], j \in [1,4]\},$$
$$X_2 = Z_{12} = \{(i,j) : (i \in [1,2], j \in [5,8]) \cap (i \in [3,4], j \in [1,4])\},$$
$$X_3 = Y_2 = \{(i,j) : (i \in [1,2], j \in [7,8]) \cap (i \in [3,4], j \in [3,4])\},$$
$$X_4 = Y_3 = \{(i,j) : (i \in [1,2], j \in [7,8]) \cap (i \in [3,4], j \in [3,4])\},$$
$$X_5 = Z_4 = \{(i,j) : (i \in [1,2], j = 7) \cap (i \in [3,4], j = 3)\},$$

$$C_1 = \begin{bmatrix} 3&3&3&3&3&3&3&3 \\ 3&3&3&3&3&3&3&3 \\ 3&3&3&3&3&3&3&3 \\ 3&3&3&3&3&3&3&3 \\ 1&1&1&1&1&1&1&1 \\ 1&1&1&1&1&1&1&1 \\ 1&1&1&1&1&1&1&1 \\ 1&1&1&1&1&1&1&1 \end{bmatrix}, C_{21} = \begin{bmatrix} 3&3&3&3&1&1&1&1 \\ 3&3&3&3&1&1&1&1 \\ 3&3&3&3&1&1&1&1 \\ 3&3&3&3&1&1&1&1 \\ 1&1&1&1&1&1&1&1 \\ 1&1&1&1&1&1&1&1 \\ 1&1&1&1&1&1&1&1 \\ 1&1&1&1&1&1&1&1 \end{bmatrix}, C_2 = \begin{bmatrix} 3&3&3&3&1&1&1&1 \\ 3&3&3&3&1&1&1&1 \\ 1&1&1&1&3&3&3&3 \\ 1&1&1&1&3&3&3&3 \\ 1&1&1&1&1&1&1&1 \\ 1&1&1&1&1&1&1&1 \\ 1&1&1&1&1&1&1&1 \\ 1&1&1&1&1&1&1&1 \end{bmatrix}.$$

$$C_3 = \begin{bmatrix} 3&3&3&3&1&1&3&3 \\ 3&3&3&3&1&1&3&3 \\ 1&1&3&3&3&3&3&3 \\ 1&1&3&3&3&3&3&3 \\ 1&1&1&1&1&1&1&1 \\ 1&1&1&1&1&1&1&1 \\ 1&1&1&1&1&1&1&1 \\ 1&1&1&1&1&1&1&1 \end{bmatrix}, C_4 = \begin{bmatrix} 3&3&3&3&1&1&3&1 \\ 3&3&3&3&1&1&3&1 \\ 1&1&3&1&3&3&3&3 \\ 1&1&3&1&3&3&3&3 \\ 1&1&1&1&1&1&1&1 \\ 1&1&1&1&1&1&1&1 \\ 1&1&1&1&1&1&1&1 \\ 1&1&1&1&1&1&1&1 \end{bmatrix}, C_5 = \begin{bmatrix} 3&3&3&3&1&1&3&1 \\ 3&3&3&3&1&1&3&3 \\ 1&1&3&1&3&3&3&3 \\ 1&1&3&3&3&3&3&3 \\ 1&1&1&1&1&1&1&1 \\ 1&1&1&1&1&1&1&1 \\ 1&1&1&1&1&1&1&1 \\ 1&1&1&1&1&1&1&1 \end{bmatrix}.$$

Algorithm Analysis. The computational complexity of algorithm FINDSE-CRET depends on the running time of procedure DIVSET. To analyze the procedure we assume that $n = 2^u$, $|X| = 2^{2w}$, where $2^{2w} \mid 2^{2u}$ and $w, u \in \mathbb{N}$. Then $X \subseteq I_n \times I_n$. Let us assume that Alice and Bob share the secret

$$S = \{B_0^O, \ldots, B_{b-1}^O, B_1^I, \ldots, B_{b-1}^I\}.$$

Fix k, $1 \leq k \leq L$, and we denote by

$$(i_k, j_k) \in B_0^O \tag{2}$$

the currently searched an element of set S. If $B_t^I \cap Y \neq \varnothing$, then we denote by $B_{t_1}^I$ be the first block found in step 7 of the Algorithm 1 such that $B_{t_1}^I \cap Y \neq \varnothing$. If $B_t^I \cap Z \neq \varnothing$, then we denote by $B_{t_2}^I$ be the first block found in step 7 of the Algorithm 1 such that $B_{t_1}^I \cap Z \neq \varnothing$. We take

$$t_0 = \min(t_1, t_2),$$

and we define

$$
\begin{aligned}
(i_Y, j_Y) &= \min_s \{(i_s, j_s) \in B_{t_0}^I \cap Y\} \quad \text{if} \quad t_0 = t_1, \\
(i_Z, j_Z) &= \min_s \{(i_s, j_s) \in B_{t_1}^I \cap Z\} \quad \text{if} \quad t_0 = t_2.
\end{aligned}
\tag{3}
$$

Then the element

$$(i_{t_0}, j_{t_0}) \in B_{t_0}^O \tag{4}$$

is uniquely determined. The analysis of the procedure depends on the placement of elements (2), (3), and (4) in the sets Y and Z. With the notation above we have the lemma.

Lemma 1. *Fix $n = 2^u$, $u \in \mathbb{N}$. Let $X \subseteq I_n \times I_n$, and let C be the challenge sent to Alice in step 3 of* PROCEDURE DIVSET. *Alice's response $OTP[k] = 4$ if and only if $(i_k, j_k), (i_Y, j_Y) \in Y$ and $(i_{t_0}, j_{t_0}) \in Z$ or $(i_k, j_k), (i_Z, j_Z) \in Z$ and $(i_{t_0}, j_{t_0}) \in Y$.*

Proof. Let $(i_k, j_k), (i_Y, j_Y) \in Y$ and $(i_{t_0}, j_{t_0}) \in Z$. From (1) we obtain $c_{i_k, j_k} = c_{i_Y, j_Z} = 3$ and $c_{i_{t_0}, j_{t_0}} = 1$. Thus $v_{in} = B_0^O(C)[k] = 3$ in step 3 of Algorithm 1. Moreover, $v_{in} \in B_{t_0}^I(C)$ in step 7 of Algorithm 1, and the corresponding $v_{out} = B_{t_0}^O(C)[1] = 1$. Consequently, $OTP[k] = v_{in} + v_{out} = 4 \pmod{10}$. The proof is identical for the second case. Let $OTP[k] = 4$. This occurs only when ($v_{in} = 3$ and $v_{out} = 1$) or ($v_{in} = 1$ and $v_{out} = 3$). Suppose the first case occurs. Then $3 = v_{in} = B_0^O(C)[k]$ in step 3 of Algorithm 1, $(i_k, j_k) \in Y$. There exist positive integers t, s such that $v_{in} \in B_t^I(C)$ and $B_t^I(C)[s] = v_{in}$ in step 7 of Algorithm 1. By (3) $(i_s, j_s) = (i_Y, j_Y) \in Y$ and $t = t_0$. Since $1 = v_{out} = B_t^O(C)[1] = c_{i_t}, c_{j_t} \in C$ in step 8 of Algorithm 1, so $(i_t, j_t) \in Z$. The proof is identical for the second case.

The analysis of the computational complexity of the procedure is more subtle and requires estimating the probability that $OTP[k] = 4$.

Lemma 2. *Fix $n = 2^u$, $u \in \mathbb{N}$. Let $X \subseteq I_n \times I_n$, and let C be the challenge sent to Alice in step 3 of* PROCEDURE DIVSET. *The probability that Alice's response with $OTP[k] = 4$ is at most equal to $\frac{1}{2} - \frac{1}{2^{l+2}}$ and the probability that she response with $OTP[k] \neq 4$ is at least equal to $\frac{1}{2} + \frac{1}{2^{l+2}}$, where $l = \sum_{t=1}^{b-1} |B_t^I|$.*

Proof. Let us assume that Alice and Bob share the secret

$$S = \{B_0^O, \ldots, B_{b-1}^O, B_1^I, \ldots, B_{b-1}^I\}.$$

and let

$$B^I = \bigcup_{t=1}^{b-1} B_t^I, \quad |B_t^I| = l_t, \quad \sum_{t=1}^{b-1} l_t = l. \tag{5}$$

Suppose $X = I_n \times I_n$. The space of matrix indices

$$X = \{(i, j) \in I_n \times I_n\}$$

is divided into two disjoint sets Y and Z such that $|Y| = |Z|$. The experiment consists of a random choice of elements $(i, j) \in X$. The outcome of the experiment consists of the determination whether $(i, j) \in Y$ or $(i, j) \in Z$. We assume that all such events are independent of each other. We compute the probability that $OTP[k] = 4$. Lemma 1 shows that two possibilities should be considered.

$$(i_k, j_k), (i_Y, j_Y) \in Y, \quad (i_{t_0}, j_{t_0}) \in Z$$

or

$$(i_k, j_k), (i_Z, j_Z) \in Z, \quad (i_{t_0}, j_{t_0}) \in Y.$$

Note that, if $(i_k, j_k) \in Y$, then by (3) $(i_Y, j_Y) \in Y$ if and only if $t_0 = t_1$. Thus $B^I \cup Y \neq \emptyset$. On the other hand, if $(i_k, j_k) \in Z$, then by (3) $(i_Y, j_Y) \in Z$ if and only if $t_0 = t_2$. Then $B^I \cup Z \neq \emptyset$. Now, we compute the probability that $B^I \cup Y \neq \emptyset$ and $B^I \cup Z \neq \emptyset$. Let E_Y be the event that $B^I \cap Y = \emptyset$, and E_Z be the event that $B^I \cap Z = \emptyset$. By (5) we have that the probability that

$$P(E_Y) = P(E_Z) = \frac{1}{2^{l+1}}.$$

Therefore, the probability that

$$P(E_Y \cup E_Z) = \frac{1}{2^l}$$

and consequently, the probability that

$$P(E_Y^c \cap E_Z^c) = 1 - \frac{1}{2^l},$$

where E_Y^c, E_Z^c is the complement of E_Y, E_Z respectively. Moreover, let E_k be the event that the $(i_k, j_k) \in Y$, and let E_{t_0} be the event that the $(i_{t_0}, j_{t_0}) \in Y$. The probability that

$$P(E_k) = P(E_{t_0}) = P(E_k^c) = P(E_{t_0}^c) = \frac{1}{2},$$

where E_k^c, $E_{t_0}^c$ is the complement of E_k, E_{t_0} respectively. By the above and Lemma (1) we obtain that the probability

$$P(OTP[k] = 4) = P(E_Y)P(E_k)P(E_{t_0}^c) + P(E_Z)P(E_k^c)P(E_{t_0})$$
$$+ P\left(E_Y^c \cap E_Z^c\right)P(E_k)P(E_{t_0}^c) + P\left(E_Y^c \cap E_Z^c\right)P(E_k^c)P(E_{t_0})$$
$$= \frac{1}{2}\left(1 - \frac{1}{2^l}\right) + \frac{1}{2^{l+2}} = \frac{1}{2} - \frac{1}{2^{l+2}},$$

and

$$P(OTP[k] \neq 4) = \frac{1}{2} + \frac{1}{2^{l+2}}.$$

It is important to notice, if $X \subseteq I_n \times I_n$ then the number l can only decrease. So the probability $P(OTP[k] \neq 4)$ increase and the probability of $P(OTP[k] = 4)$ decrease, which completes the proof.

Lemma 3. *Let C be the challenge sent to Alice in step 3 of* PROCEDURE DIVSET. *If $OTP[k] = 6$ then $(i_k, j_k) \in Y$.*

Proof. It is clear that $OTP[k] = 6$ if and only if $v_{in} = 3$ and $V_{out} = 3$ in step 13 of Algorithm 1. Moreover, it is easy to see that $v_{in} = B_0^O(C)[k]$, and it follows that $(i_k, j_k) \in Y$.

Lemma 4. *Let C be the challenge sent to Alice in step 3 of* PROCEDURE DIVSET. *If $OTP[k] = 2$ then $(i_k, j_k) \in Z$.*

Proof. The proof follows very closely the proof of Lemma 3.

4.2 Description of Passive Attack

According to authors of [1], the resistance of a system to frequency analysis is attributed to the randomness of the challenge. However, it is important to note that the output of the system is not randomly generated and can be used in combination with the challenge for frequency analysis, which can compromise the security of the system. Here we present a straightforward attack, called NAIVEPASSIVEATTACK, which can be mounted to discover G_0 and B^O, thereby restricting the number of possible OTPs.

The procedure of NAIVEPASSIVEATTACK is as follows: given a history of challenge-output pairs C_i and OTP_i, the algorithm performs the following steps:

1. For each $k \in 1, \ldots, L$:
   (a) For each pair of coordinates $(x_1, y_1), (x_2, y_2) \in I_n \times I_n$, calculate the number of challenge-output pairs where $c_{x_1, y_1} + c_{x_2, y_2} = OTP_i[k] \pmod{q}$, where $c_{x_1, y_1}, c_{x_2, y_2}$ are elements of C_i.
   (b) Select the pair $(x_1, y_1), (x_2, y_2)$ with the highest count calculated in the previous step and fix it as a_k, b_k.

2. For a given challenge C, we can calculate a candidate for $OTP[k]$ as follows:

$$OTP[k] = c_{a_k} + c_{b_k} \pmod{q}.$$

Here, the coordinates a_k and b_k correspond to the k-th element of B_0^O and an element of one of $B_j, j \in \{0, 1, \ldots, b\}$, respectively. Alternatively instead of using values obtained from frequency analysis, the algorithm can use the values obtained from an active attack.

Example 6. Let secret S consisting of sets,

$$S = \{B_0^O, B_1^O, B_1^I, \},$$

where

$$B_0^O = \{(2, 3)\},$$
$$B_1^O = \{(3, 1)\},$$
$$B_1^I = \{(1, 1), (1, 3), (2, 1), (3, 2), (3, 3)\}.$$

Table 1. Values calculated in step 1a

(x, y)	(1,1)	(1,2)	(1,3)	(2,1)	(2,2)	(2,3)	(3,1)	(3,2)	(3,3)
(1,1)	5	1	2	4	2	1	7	5	5
(1,2)	1	0	3	4	2	4	4	1	2
(1,3)	2	3	4	4	2	0	6	6	4
(2,1)	4	4	4	5	1	2	4	3	3
(2,2)	2	2	2	1	3	0	5	2	3
(2,3)	1	4	0	2	0	18	14	1	2
(3,1)	7	4	6	4	5	14	4	3	2
(3,2)	5	1	6	3	2	1	3	1	5
(3,3)	5	2	4	3	3	2	2	5	3

In Table 1 we present values we got in step 1a for 30 challenge-output pairs. We can see that highest value we got for pair $(2, 3), (2, 3)$, which corresponds to $B_0^O[1], B_0^O[1]$. The second highest value is $(2, 3), (3, 1)$ which corresponds to $B_0^O[1], B_1^O[1]$. For

$$C = \begin{bmatrix} 5 & 1 & 8 \\ 9 & 5 & 7 \\ 4 & 1 & 3 \end{bmatrix}$$

$OTP[1]$ candidate should be equal to $c_{2,3} + c_{2,3} = 7 + 7 = 4 \pmod{10}$. For this small example OTP was guessed correctly 46,637 times for 100,000 randomly generated challenges.

By using this naive method with $n = 16$, $m = 300$ challenge-output pairs, and a randomly selected secret with a number of input blocks $b = 7$, where each input block length is equal to 8, we were able to successfully guess OTP 561 for 100,000 randomly generated challenges, which gives a 0.56% success rate. This is significantly more than the expected success rate of 1 success per 10,000,000 tries (0.0001%). This result highlights the vulnerability of the system to frequency analysis attacks.

5   Conclusion

In this paper we demonstrate two attack algorithms, active and passive, on the base construction from [1]. The algorithms allow to find positions in the secret matrix of the prover. This allow to facilitate the subsequent effective brute force attack for the remaining bits of the secret.

Acknowledgment. The research was partially financed from the internal funds of the Department of Fundamentals of Computer Science of the Wrocław University of Science and Technology for conducting research.

References

1. Matelski, S.: Secure human identification protocol with human-computable passwords. In: Su, C., Gritzalis, D., Piuri, V. (eds.) ISPEC 2022. LNCS, vol. 13620, pp. 452–467. Springer, Cham (2022). https://doi.org/10.1007/978-3-031-21280-2_25
2. Jablon, D.P.: Extended password key exchange protocols immune to dictionary attacks. In: Proceedings, IEEE Computer Society 6th Workshop on Enabling Technologies (WET-ICE 1997), Infrastructure for Collaborative Enterprises, 18–20 June 1997, MIT, Cambridge, MA, USA, pp. 248–255(1997) . https://doi.org/10.1109/ENABL.1997.630822
3. Bellare, M., Pointcheval, D., Rogaway, P.: Authenticated key exchange secure against dictionary attacks. IACR Cryptol. ePrint Arch. 14 (2000). http://eprint.iacr.org/2000/014
4. Boyko, V., MacKenzie, P.D., Patel, S.: Provably secure password-authenticated key exchange using diffie-hellman. IACR Cryptol. ePrint Arch. 44 (2000). http://eprint.iacr.org/2000/044
5. von Ahn, L., Blum, M., Hopper, N.J., Langford, J.: CAPTCHA: using hard AI problems for security. In: Biham, E. (ed.) EUROCRYPT 2003. LNCS, vol. 2656, pp. 294–311. Springer, Heidelberg (2003). https://doi.org/10.1007/3-540-39200-9_18
6. Matsumoto, T., Imai, H.: Human identification through insecure channel. In: Davies, D.W. (ed.) EUROCRYPT 1991. LNCS, vol. 547, pp. 409–421. Springer, Heidelberg (1991). https://doi.org/10.1007/3-540-46416-6_35
7. Hopper, N.J., Blum, M.: Secure human identification protocols. In: Boyd, C. (ed.) ASIACRYPT 2001. LNCS, vol. 2248, pp. 52–66. Springer, Heidelberg (2001). https://doi.org/10.1007/3-540-45682-1_4

8. Brostoff, S., Inglesant, P., Sasse, M.A.: Evaluating the usability and security of a graphical one-time PIN system. In: McEwan, T., McKinnon, L. (eds.) Proceedings of the 2010 British Computer Society Conference on Human-Computer Interaction, BCS-HCI 2010, Dundee, United Kingdom, 6–10 September 2010, pp. 88–97. ACM (2010). http://dl.acm.org/citation.cfm?id=2146317

9. Schnorr, C.P.: Efficient signature generation by smart cards. J. Cryptol. **4**(3), 161–174 (1991). https://doi.org/10.1007/BF00196725

10. Fiat, A., Shamir, A.: How to prove yourself: practical solutions to identification and signature problems. In: Odlyzko, A.M. (ed.) CRYPTO 1986. LNCS, vol. 263, pp. 186–194. Springer, Heidelberg (1987). https://doi.org/10.1007/3-540-47721-7_12

11. Feige, U., Fiat, A., Shamir, A.: Zero-knowledge proofs of identity. J. Cryptol. **1**(2), 77–94 (1988). https://doi.org/10.1007/BF02351717

12. Guillou, L.C., Quisquater, J.-J.: A practical zero-knowledge protocol fitted to security microprocessor minimizing both transmission and memory. In: Barstow, D., et al. (eds.) EUROCRYPT 1988. LNCS, vol. 330, pp. 123–128. Springer, Heidelberg (1988). https://doi.org/10.1007/3-540-45961-8_11

13. Okamoto, T.: Provably secure and practical identification schemes and corresponding signature schemes. In: Brickell, E.F. (ed.) CRYPTO 1992. LNCS, vol. 740, pp. 31–53. Springer, Heidelberg (1993). https://doi.org/10.1007/3-540-48071-4_3

14. Kim, H.-K., Yang, H.-S.: Security framework to verify the low level implementation codes. In: Gervasi, O., et al. (eds.) ICCSA 2005. LNCS, vol. 3481, pp. 52–61. Springer, Heidelberg (2005). https://doi.org/10.1007/11424826_6

15. Kurosawa, K., Heng, S.-H.: The power of identification schemes. In: Yung, M., Dodis, Y., Kiayias, A., Malkin, T. (eds.) PKC 2006. LNCS, vol. 3958, pp. 364–377. Springer, Heidelberg (2006). https://doi.org/10.1007/11745853_24

16. Asghar, H.J., Li, S., Steinfeld, R., Pieprzyk, J.: Does counting still count? revisiting the security of counting based user authentication protocols against statistical attacks. In: 20th Annual Network and Distributed System Security Symposium, NDSS 2013, San Diego, California, USA, 24–27 February 2013, The Internet Society (2013). https://www.ndss-symposium.org/ndss2013/does-counting-still-count-revisiting-security-counting-based-user-authentication-protocols

17. Canetti, R., Goldreich, O., Goldwasser, S., Micali, S.: Resettable zero-knowledge (extended abstract). In: Proceedings of the Thirty-second Annual ACM Symposium on Theory of Computing. STOC 2000, New York, NY, USA, pp. 235–244. ACM (2000). http://doi.acm.org/10.1145/335305.335334

18. Bellare, M., Fischlin, M., Goldwasser, S., Micali, S.: Identification protocols secure against reset attacks. In: Pfitzmann, B. (ed.) EUROCRYPT 2001. LNCS, vol. 2045, pp. 495–511. Springer, Heidelberg (2001). https://doi.org/10.1007/3-540-44987-6_30

19. Krzywiecki, Ł: Schnorr-like identification scheme resistant to malicious subliminal setting of ephemeral secret. In: Bica, I., Reyhanitabar, R. (eds.) SECITC 2016. LNCS, vol. 10006, pp. 137–148. Springer, Cham (2016). https://doi.org/10.1007/978-3-319-47238-6_10

20. Krzywiecki, Ł., Kutylowski, M.: Security of okamoto identification scheme: a defense against ephemeral key leakage and setup. In: Wang, C., Kantarcioglu, M., (eds.) Proceedings of the Fifth ACM International Workshop on Security in Cloud Computing, SCC@AsiaCCS 2017, Abu Dhabi, United Arab Emirates, 2 April 2017, pp. 43–50. ACM (2017). https://doi.org/10.1145/3055259.3055267

21. MacKenzie, P.: On the security of the speke password-authenticated key exchange protocol. Cryptology ePrint Archive, Paper 2001/057 (2001). https://eprint.iacr.org/2001/057

22. Hao, F., Shahandashti, S.F.: The SPEKE protocol revisited. IACR Cryptol. ePrint Arch. 585 (2014). http://eprint.iacr.org/2014/585

23. Bender, J., Fischlin, M., Kügler, D.: Security analysis of the PACE key-agreement protocol. IACR Cryptol. ePrint Arch. 624 (2009). http://eprint.iacr.org/2009/624

24. Bender, J., Dagdelen, Ö., Fischlin, M., Kügler, D.: The PACE—AA protocol for machine readable travel documents, and its security. In: Keromytis, A.D. (ed.) FC 2012. LNCS, vol. 7397, pp. 344–358. Springer, Heidelberg (2012). https://doi.org/10.1007/978-3-642-32946-3_25

25. Hanzlik, L., Krzywiecki, Ł, Kutyłowski, M.: Simplified PACE—AA protocol. In: Deng, R.H., Feng, T. (eds.) ISPEC 2013. LNCS, vol. 7863, pp. 218–232. Springer, Heidelberg (2013). https://doi.org/10.1007/978-3-642-38033-4_16

26. Li, S., Shum, H.Y.: Secure human-computer identification (interface) systems against peeping attacks: Sechci. Cryptology ePrint Archive, Paper 2005/268 (2005). https://eprint.iacr.org/2005/268

27. Yan, Q., Han, J., Li, Y., Deng, R.H.: On limitations of designing leakage-resilient password systems: attacks, principals and usability. In: 19th Annual Network and Distributed System Security Symposium, NDSS 2012, San Diego, California, USA, 5–8 February 2012. The Internet Society (2012)

28. Blocki, J., Blum, M., Datta, A., Vempala, S.S.: Towards human computable passwords. In: Papadimitriou, C.H. (ed.) 8th Innovations in Theoretical Computer Science Conference, ITCS 2017, 9–11 January 2017, Berkeley, CA, USA. Volume 67 of LIPIcs., Schloss Dagstuhl - Leibniz-Zentrum für Informatik, pp. 10:1–10:47 (2017). https://doi.org/10.4230/LIPIcs.ITCS.2017.10

A Source Hiding Protocol for Cooperative Intelligent Transportation Systems (C-ITS)

Hannes Salin[1(✉)] and Łukasz Krzywiecki[2]

[1] Swedish Transport Administration, Borlänge, Sweden
hannes.salin@trafikverket.se
[2] Department of Fundamentals of Computer Science, Wrocław University of Science and Technology, Wrocław, Poland
lukasz.krzywiecki@pwr.edu.pl

Abstract. In multi-user scenarios where requirements of privacy are high, we propose a modular, anonymous and source hiding protocol for sending signed messages (SHP). By combining existing cryptographic building blocks, encryption and ring signature schemes, we are able to mitigate traceability and routing attacks on otherwise anonymous participants. Moreover, our protocol is secure without any trusted third party. Our construction is provably secure in our security model, where the adversary controls the communication channels. We illustrate our construction via a Vehicle Ad-Hoc Network (VANET) use-case, where the SHP provide source anonymity to cluster of vehicles exchanging signed safety and security messages to road-side units within Cooperative Intelligent Transportation Systems (C-ITS).

Keywords: Source Hiding · Network Anonymity · Ring Signatures

1 Introduction

In this paper we address a scenario with an ad-hoc group of parties, which exchange signed information that would be collected by a verifier, in a way that provide full anonymity of the original *signer-and-sender*. A common solution for such scenarios are ring signatures. These type of schemes provide functionality that allows a holder of a secret key to generate an anonymously signed message in relation to the group of public keys. A verifier can only conclude that the signature was created by a secret key holder, corresponding to one of the public keys out of the complete set of public keys within a group of potential signers. Here, a typical example is a *whistle blowing* functionality for a group of executives. In a parliament or a committee, there might be a need of information sharing which requires public attention. In many such cases the identity of the whistle-blower should be protected. Although ring signatures provide anonymity of the key holder, it cannot provide a network-layer anonymity if the information

W. Meng et al. (Eds.): ISPEC 2023, LNCS 14341, pp. 365–379, 2023.
https://doi.org/10.1007/978-981-99-7032-2_22

sharing is digital, i.e. the network addresses of the anonymous key holders are not protected by a ring signature scheme since it is used in the upper levels of the technology stack, e.g. the application layer but not the network layer.

1.1 Challenges for Source Hiding

Path-Tracing Attacks: We consider the identity of each participant i in a group $\{1, \ldots, n\}$ of users, both using a public/private signing key-pair $(\mathsf{sks}_i, \mathsf{pks}_i)$, and a logical location L_i, i.e. the network address such as IP address. Ring signatures, although anonymous, are encapsulated in network packets, and thus can be identified with associated source addresses used. A powerful adversary controlling the communication links can try to trace the signer, analyzing e.g. IP source and destination addresses in the network layer, and routing paths of messages. Therefore, even if the participant's cryptographic anonymization via a ring signature scheme (e.g. on the application layer), it is equally important that the network source identity (e.g. on the network layer) is protected.

VANET Use-Case Without a Trusted-Third-Party (TTP): In the connected vehicle and infrastructure context, both moving and stationary nodes can send large volumes of protected and authenticated data, presenting a significant challenge. However, we require that the source identity L_i of a moving vehicle is secured in such ad-hoc groups without the need of a TTP. To clarify, we should not depend on a TTP to provide an anonymization scheme (confusion) for the network layer source addresses where all data packets with ring signatures are traversing. We contrast this to solutions such as ToR-routing [5] and mixnets [2]. The reason is due to enhanced security for the VANET architecture, to not rely on one or several TTP:s that have cryptographic dependent computations in the protocol.

1.2 Network Layer Pseudonyms

Current ETSI standardization efforts [3] lean towards pseudonymizing vehicles in C-ITS due to privacy concerns when sending safety and security messages. Vehicles in a VANET should be able to send anonymous messages within the group and nearby road-side units. Regardless of the scenario, in order to protect each vehicle from traceability and de-anonymization attacks on the network layer [4], the communication procedure must ensure full anonymity. Moreover, when sending messages, the anonymity property must be intact when exposed to both active and passive attacks. Most importantly, a ring signature scheme in itself will only provide anonymity of the identity of the vehicle, but not the (IP) source, hence path routing attacks are still a threat. In some cases, vehicles in a VANET might need to send a security message to a third party, like police or safety RSUs, via a proxy node if the party is remote. This scenario requires an ad-hoc setup between the group and proxy. For untrusted environments, a secure protocol ensuring group authenticity is needed. Given the continuous message sharing in VANETs, a multi-round (interactive) ring signature protocol could leverage the existing communication flow.

1.3   Problem Statement

To maintain privacy in collaborative scenarios like commission board voting, ring signatures are useful. However, network structures like IP addresses can reveal identities during network communication. Thus, a more robust protocol is needed for complete identity privacy and source hiding. In the C-ITS domain, collaboration is often ad-hoc, not allowing for trusted parties to ensure anonymization or location privacy. A robust protocol is required to prevent anonymity and traceability attacks at both the application layer, which transports signature data packets, and the network layer, which uses IP-addresses for routing. From the cryptographic point of view we formulate the following requirements for the messages and signatures:

- A message from different sources (signers) send to a collector should be signed anonymously within a group of potential signers. This can be facilitate by ring signatures. A real signer is hidden in a well defined, however a finite group of users. Later verification allows to conclude that fact.
- Ring signatures over the messages created at sources and routed over an infrastructure network to the collector for verification, should be unlinkable to signers by the adversary overhearing the underlying communication links and nodes.

1.4   Related Work

The notion of ring signatures was introdced by Rivest et al. [11], and allows to sign a message anonymously within a group of potential signers. Ring signatures have also been investigated in the context of C-ITS and VANET, e.g. [1,8–10]. To ensure network communication anonymity and source hiding, the concept of mixed networks, also called mixnets, can be used [2]. A mixnet is a system where an input is cryptographically transformed and permuted, i.e. securely shuffled, and then published in a random order, hence providing untraceability between the input and output. Many different approaches for VANET location privacy has been proposed, and Khan et al. [7] summarizes some of the current proposals. However, to the best knowledge of the authors, no location privacy for source hiding, without a TTP, but using ring signatures and onion-like encryption, has been proposed so far.

1.5   Contribution

In this paper we propose a protocol for secure *source-hiding* delivery of ring signatures from a group of users to a server. We consider the ring signatures that are created by users in distinct locations. Such signatures need to be delivered over the existing network infrastructure, where packets can be traced by the adversary.

- We propose a *source-hiding* protocol immune to routing path tracing and ring signature de-anonymization via source address attacks.

- Our SHP scheme has a modular construction and is based on a secure encryption scheme ES, and an unforgeable anonymous ring signature scheme RS.
- The proposed scheme does not require an additional *trusted-third-party* and is entirely self-contained within the group of users registered to the RS system.
- We propose two versions of the SHP scheme: the basic scheme secure in the *honest-but-curious* adversary model, and the extended version secure against malicious users trying to substitute signed messages with a forged ones.

Our scheme can be used in any system that utilize ring signature for anonymity purposes. We also argue it can be used in specific *ad-hoc* scenarios for VANET:s, where messages from incoming vehicles should be anonymously delivered to RSU:s or external verifiers.

1.6   Structure of Paper

In Sect. 2 we detail systems settings, threat model and necessary notations. In Sect. 3 we describe the proposed schemes with formal security proofs, whereas in Sect. 4 the results from a benchmark analysis is given. In Sect. 5 we conclude our paper.

2   Preliminaries

2.1   System Settings

To illustrate our proposed source hiding protocol, we use a C-ITS scenario where a cluster of vehicles connect and initially authenticate into a VANET. The cluster also establish a pre-defined ordering of the public keys of all participants. We assume n vehicles are connected and need to send a secure or critical message to a verifier outside of the VANET, ensuring full source anonymity of all v_i's. A server (e.g. a RSU) is used for running the interactive ring signature source hiding protocol with the collaborative group of signing vehicles. Each vehicle v_i creates is own message m_i, which needs to be verified at later stages or by remote verifiers. Next, each v_i computes a layered encryption of the message using the pre-determined order of the other vehicles' public keys. In this way each v_i has its own onion-like ciphertext with n layers. The receiving RSU server collects all n onion ciphertexts, and sends iteratively in the reverse the whole collection to all v_i's, that now decrypt their outer layers. This iterates through all n layers for each v_i. After decryption the collection of resulting the onions is re-shuffled. The re-shuffled and down-layered ciphertexts are sent back to the server which now can put forward the messages and ring signatures to a verifier without revealing the origin of the signer. We note that the RSU itself does not need to be trusted since it cannot extract any source data from the vehicles, despite having full access to all messages, onion-ciphertexts and ring signatures. The protocol will ensure that the verifying party, e.g. the police, will successfully verify the message but cannot trace the location or source of the original signer.

2.2   Requirements and Threat Model

Anonymous Signature Verification Requirement: We consider n users with signing public keys $\mathsf{PKS} = \{\mathsf{pks}_i\}_1^n$ at n different locations $\{L_i\}_1^n$. Each user produces a distinct message m_i, and signs it with an anonymous ring signature σ_i, s.t. from any verifier's perspective, each user with a public key in PKS could be a potential signer. Messages and signatures are send from users locations and routed to a chosen collector location for later verification.

Threats: In the given system setting described in Sect. 2.1 we now consider a *curious* adversary $\mathcal{A}$ that is able to intercept all network communication, e.g. controls the underlying network infrastructure. Given any signature-message pair (m_i, σ_i) for verification, the adversary's goal is to find out who is the original signer i and its source address L_i, hence mounting a tracebility attack. Another attack would be for $\mathcal{A}$ to replace some pair (m_i, σ_i) with a fresh one (m_i^*, σ_i^*), that does not originate from the user i at the location L_i. This is feasible as σ_i^* provides full anonymity within a group of potential signers, but is successfully verifiable.

2.3   Cryptographic Building Blocks

Our scheme is build on top of existing secure cryptographic components: an encryption scheme ES, and anonymous ring signature RS. Asymmetric-key algorithm cryptosystems ES are used for securing the communication between the users and the server. For the self-containment of the paper, we recall the *Indistinguishability under Chosen Ciphertext Attack* (IND-CCA2) model for asymmetric-key algorithm cryptosystems from [6].

Definition 1. *A tuple* $\mathsf{ES} = (\mathsf{ParGenE}, \mathsf{KeyGenE}, E, D)$, *is an asymmetric-key encryption system where:*

$\mathsf{epar} \leftarrow \mathsf{ParGenE}(\lambda)$ *takes the security parameter* λ *and outputs parameters* $\mathsf{epar} = (\mathcal{K}, \mathcal{M}, \mathcal{C})$, *where* $\mathcal{K}$ *is a key-pair space,* $\mathcal{M}$ *is a message space,* $\mathcal{C}$ *is a ciphertext space.*

$(\mathsf{sk}, \mathsf{pk}) \leftarrow \mathsf{KeyGen}(\mathsf{par})$ *is a key-pair generation algorithm, which inputs* par *and outputs a key-pair* $(\mathsf{sk}, \mathsf{pk}) \in \mathcal{K}$: *a secret key* sk *and its corresponding public key* pk .

$c \leftarrow E(m, \mathsf{pk})$ *is an encryption algorithm that inputs a message* $m \in \mathcal{M}$, *a public key* pk, *and outputs a ciphertext* $c \in \mathcal{C}$.

$m \leftarrow D(c, \mathsf{sk})$ *is a decryption algorithm that inputs a ciphertext* $c \in \mathcal{C}$, *a secret key* sk, *and outputs the corresponding plaintext* m.

We require that the encryption scheme is correct, i.e. for any $m \leftarrow_\$ \mathcal{M}$:

$$\Pr \begin{bmatrix} \mathsf{ParGenE}(\lambda) \rightarrow \mathsf{epar}, \\ \mathsf{KeyGenE}(\mathsf{epar}) \rightarrow (\mathsf{sk}, \mathsf{pk}) \\ E(m, \mathsf{pk}) \rightarrow c \\ D(c, \mathsf{sk}) \rightarrow m \end{bmatrix} = 1. \tag{1}$$

The IND-CCA2 model is commonly defined by the following experiment:

Definition 2 (Indistingushability under CCA2). *Given an asymmetric-key cryptosystem* $(\mathsf{ParGenE}, \mathsf{KeyGenE}, E, D)$ *we define the chosen ciphertext indistinguishability experiment* IND-CCA2:

Init : epar $\leftarrow$ ParGenE(λ), (sk, pk) $\leftarrow$ KeyGenE(par).
Adversary : *Let the adversary* $\mathcal{A}$, *be a malicious algorithm initialized with parameters* epar, *and the public key* pk.
Decryption Oracle : *Let a decryption oracle* $\mathcal{O}_D$, *be an algorithm initialized with parameters* par, *s.t. when queried with a ciphertext* $c \leftarrow E(m, \mathsf{pk})$, *it outputs the corresponding plaintext* m, *i.e.* $\mathcal{O}_D(c, \mathsf{pk}) \rightarrow m$. *The second argument* pk *is just an indicator, i.e. which public key the ciphertext was computed from. Thus the oracle* $\mathcal{O}_D(c, \mathsf{pk})$ *is an equivalent to the entity holding the appropriate corresponding secret key* $\mathcal{O}_D(c, \mathsf{pk}) = D(c, \mathsf{sk})$.
Guess Game : *This game is the following protocol:*

1. *The adversary can encrypt a number* q_E *of messages* $m \in \mathcal{M}$ *of its choice via* $E(m, \mathsf{pk})$. *The adversary can querry a number* q_D *of ciphertext* $c \in \mathcal{C}$ *of its choice via* $\mathcal{O}_D(c, \mathsf{pk})$.
2. *The adversary generates two messages of its choice:* $(m_0, m_1) \leftarrow \mathcal{A}(\mathsf{par})$ *and sends them to a challenger.*
3. *The challanger generates a random bit* $b \leftarrow_\$ \{0, 1\}$, *encrypts the message* m_b *to the ciphertext* $c_b = E(m_b, \mathsf{pk})$, *and sends* c_b *to* $\mathcal{A}$.
4. *The adversary can encrypt a number* ℓ_E *of messages* $m \in \mathcal{M}$ *of its choice via* $E(m, \mathsf{pk})$. *The adversary can querry a number* ℓ_D *of ciphertext* $c \in \mathcal{C}$ *of its choice via* $\mathcal{O}_D(c, \mathsf{pk})$, *provided that* $c \neq c_b$.
5. *Let* $\mathcal{M}_E, \mathcal{C}_D$ *denote the messages encrypted, and ciphertexts queried to* $\mathcal{O}_D$, *in the steps 1 and 4 respectively. The adversary outputs its own bit* $\hat{b} \leftarrow \mathcal{A}(\mathsf{epar}, m_0, m_1, \mathsf{pk}, \mathcal{M}_E, \mathcal{C}_D)$.

We define the advantage of the adversary $\mathcal{A}$ *in the experiment as the probability that the* $\mathcal{A}$ *outputs the correct bit* $\hat{b} = b$ *indicating the encrypted message* m_b, *i.e.:*

$$\mathbf{Adv}(\mathcal{A}, \mathsf{IND-CCA2}) = |\Pr\left[\hat{b} = b\right] - 1/2|. \tag{2}$$

Let ℓ *denotes the upper limit for the sum of all numbers of queries:* $q_E + q_D + \ell_E + \ell_D$ *in the* Guess Game. *We say that the encryption scheme is* IND-CCA2 *secure if the advantage of the adversary* $\mathcal{A}$ *is negligible in parameters* λ, ℓ *i.e.:*

$$\mathbf{Adv}(\mathcal{A}, \mathsf{IND-CCA2})) \leq \epsilon(\lambda, \ell). \tag{3}$$

Definition 3. *A 4-tuple* RS $=$ (ParGenS, KeyGenS, RingSign, RingVerify) *is a ring signature scheme defined as the following procedures:*

spar $\leftarrow$ ParGenS(λ) *takes the security parameter* λ *and produces parameters of the scheme* spar $= (\mathcal{K}, \mathcal{M}, \mathcal{S})$, *where* $\mathcal{K}$ *is a key-pair space,* $\mathcal{M}$ *is a message space,* $\mathcal{S}$ *is a signature space.*
(sks, pks) $\leftarrow$ KeyGenS(spar) *is a key-pair generation algorithm, which inputs* par *and outputs a key-pair* (sks, pks) $\in \mathcal{K}$: *a secret key* sks *and its corresponding public key* pks.

$\sigma \leftarrow \mathsf{RingSign}(m, \mathsf{sks}_j, \mathsf{PKS})$ – *signing procedure that takes a message m, the secret key sks_j and the set of public keys $\mathsf{PKS} = \{\mathsf{pks}_1, \ldots, \mathsf{pks}_k\}$, $\mathsf{pks}_j \in \mathsf{PKS}$. It returns a ring signature σ.*

$1/0 \leftarrow \mathsf{RingVerify}(\sigma, m, \mathsf{PKS})$ *a signature verification algorithm takes a signature σ, a message m, and the set of public keys PKS. It returns a bit (0 or 1) indicating whether the signature σ is valid, i.e., whether someone having a public key from the set PKS has signed m.*

We require that the signature scheme is correct, i.e. a signature created by signer $j \in \{1, \ldots, n\}$ from a set of n potential signers over any message $m \in \mathcal{M}$, is always positively verifiable:

$$\Pr \begin{bmatrix} \mathsf{ParGenS}(\lambda) \rightarrow \mathsf{spar}, \\ \mathsf{KeyGenS}(\mathsf{spar}) \rightarrow \{(\mathsf{sks}_i, \mathsf{pks}_i)\}_1^n \\ \forall_{(j,m)} : j \in \{1, \ldots, n\}, m \in \mathcal{M} \\ \begin{bmatrix} \mathsf{RingSign}(m, \mathsf{sks}_j, \{\mathsf{pks}_i\}_1^n) \rightarrow \sigma \\ \mathsf{RingVerify}(\sigma, m, \{\mathsf{pks}_i\}_1^n) \rightarrow 1 \end{bmatrix} \end{bmatrix} = 1. \quad (4)$$

Moreover, we assume that above schemes are *unforgeable* in the *chosen-message* scenario: suppose a forger's goal is to produce a verifiable signature σ for a message m which was not previously signed in the query stage. We then say that the forger succeeds, if it can forge σ for m with a non-negligible probability.

Definition 4 (Ring Unforgeability)). *Let $\mathsf{RS} = (\mathsf{ParGen}, \mathsf{KeyGen}, \mathsf{RingSign}, \mathsf{RingVerify})$ be a ring signature scheme. We define a security experiment:*

Init : $\mathsf{spar} \leftarrow \mathsf{ParGen}(\lambda)$, $\{(\mathsf{sks}_i, \mathsf{pks}_i)\}_1^n \leftarrow \mathsf{KeyGen}(\mathsf{spar})$.

Ring Sign Oracle : $\mathcal{O}_{\mathsf{RingSign}}(m, j, \mathsf{PKS}) \rightarrow \sigma$ *takes a message m, the signer indicator $j \in \{1, \ldots, n\}$, and the set of public keys $\mathsf{PKS} = \{\mathsf{pks}_i\}_1^n$ and outputs a ring signature σ, as if generated with the secret key sks_j, and the public keys PKS, s.t. $\mathsf{RingVerify}(\sigma, m, \mathsf{PKS}) = 1$.*

Hash Oracle : *The hash oracle $\mathcal{O}_{\mathcal{H}}$ is modeled in ROM.*

Adversary : *Let the adversary $\mathcal{F}^{\mathcal{O}_{\mathsf{RingSign}}, \mathcal{O}_{\mathcal{H}}}(\mathsf{PKS})$, be a malicious algorithm initialized with the public parameters par and public keys PKS, having access to the oracles $\mathcal{O}_{\mathsf{RingSign}}$ and $\mathcal{O}_{\mathcal{H}}$. It issues ℓ number of queries to the oracles. Let $M = \{m_i\}_1^\ell$, and $\Omega = \{\sigma_i\}_1^\ell$ denote the set of the messages, and the corresponding signatures the oracles process.*

Forgery : *The adversary generates a tuple:*
$(m^*, \sigma^*) \leftarrow \mathcal{F}^{\mathcal{O}_{\mathsf{RingSign}}, \mathcal{O}_{\mathcal{H}}}(\mathsf{PKS})$ for a new $m^* \notin M$, which was not queried to $\mathcal{O}_{\mathsf{RingSign}}$ oracle.

We say that the signature scheme is secure if for each forgery type, the probability that the adversary produces a valid signature is negligible in parameters λ, ℓ:

$$\Pr \begin{bmatrix} \mathsf{ParGenS}(\lambda) \rightarrow \mathsf{spar}, \\ \mathsf{KeyGenS}(\mathsf{spar}) \rightarrow \{(\mathsf{sks}_i, \mathsf{pks}_i)\}_1^n \\ (m^*, \sigma^*) \leftarrow \mathcal{F}^{\mathcal{O}_{\mathsf{RingSign}}, \mathcal{O}_{\mathcal{H}}}(\{\mathsf{pks}_i\}_1^n) \\ \mathsf{RingVerify}(m^*, \sigma^*, \{\mathsf{pks}_i\}_1^n) \rightarrow 1 \\ m^* \notin M \end{bmatrix} \leq \epsilon(\lambda, \ell). \quad (5)$$

Definition 5 (Ring Anonymity RS − A). *Let $\mathcal{D}$ denote a distinguisher algorithm given public parameters* par *and a set of all keys $\{(\mathsf{sks}_i, \mathsf{pks}_i)\}_1^n$. It chooses a message $m \in \mathcal{M}$. A challenger chooses an index $j \leftarrow_\$ \{1, \ldots, n\}$ uniformly at random and creates the signature $\sigma \leftarrow$ RingSign$(m, \mathsf{sks}_j, \{\mathsf{pks}_i\}_1^n)$. We say that the scheme RING is anonymous if the chance of $\mathcal{D}$ for guessing j is negligible different from $1/n$. We define the RS − A experiment:*

Init : spar $\leftarrow$ ParGenS(λ), $\{(\mathsf{sks}_i, \mathsf{pks}_i)\}_1^n \leftarrow$ KeyGenS(spar).
Adversary : *Let the adversary $\mathcal{D}$, be a malicious algorithm initialized with parameters* spar, *and the keys $\{(\mathsf{sks}_i, \mathsf{pks}_i)\}_1^n$.*
Anonymity Game : *This game is the following protocol:*
  1. *The distinguisher generates a message: $m \leftarrow \mathcal{D}(\mathsf{spar}, \{(\mathsf{sks}_i, \mathsf{pks}_i)\}_1^n)$ and sends m to a challenger.*
  2. *The challenger having access to $\{(\mathsf{sks}_i, \mathsf{pks}_i)\}_1^n$ generates a random index $j \leftarrow_\$ \{1, \ldots, n\}$, and a signature $\sigma \leftarrow$ RingSign$(m, \mathsf{sks}_j, \{\mathsf{pks}_i\}_1^n)$, and sends σ to $\mathcal{D}$.*
  3. *The distingusher outputs its own index $\hat{j} \leftarrow \mathcal{D}(\sigma, m, \{(\mathsf{sks}_i, \mathsf{pks}_i)\}_1^n)$.*

We define the advantage of the distinguisher $\mathcal{D}$ in the experiment as the probability that $\mathcal{D}$ outputs the correct index $\hat{j} = j$ indicating the signer:

$$\mathbf{Adv}(\mathcal{D}, \mathsf{RS} - \mathsf{A}) = |\Pr\left[\hat{j} = j\right] - 1/n|. \tag{6}$$

We say that the RS − A scheme is anonymous if the advantage of the distinguisher $\mathcal{D}$ is negligible in the parameter λ i.e.:

$$\mathbf{Adv}(\mathcal{D}, \mathsf{RS} - \mathsf{A})) \leq \epsilon(\lambda). \tag{7}$$

3   Proposed Scheme

3.1   Notation

Assume we have a group of n users identified by indexes $\{1, \ldots, n\}$. Let $(\mathsf{sks}_i, \mathsf{pks}_i)$ and $(\mathsf{ske}_i, \mathsf{pke}_i)$ denote the key pairs used by user i in ring signature RS and encryption ES schemes respectively. Let PKS $= \{\mathsf{pks}_i\}_1^n$, PKE $= \{\mathsf{pke}_i\}_1^n$ denote the sets of public keys for encryption and signing. Assume that each user i is bounded to a unique location L_i. This could be realized by Internet address IP_i of that user, or by any other well accepted unified locator for the network infrastructure used by the users. We assume that any group of users can be efficiently ordered by e.g. encryption public keys - thus forming a sequence of those public keys $\langle \mathsf{PKE} \rangle$. Each user within the sequence knows its own position in that sequence, as well as positions of other users. W.l.o.g. assume that the indexes in the sequence $\langle \mathsf{PKE} \rangle$ are $\langle 1, \ldots, n \rangle$. Moreover we assume that each user uses his own secret random permutation P_i. Let $\mathcal{H}$ denote a secure hash function used for commitments.

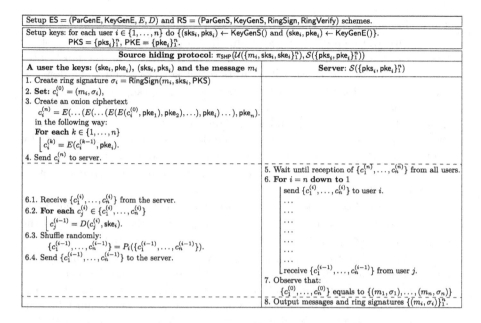

Fig. 1. The proposed Source Hiding Protocol SHP with ring signatures.

3.2   Scheme Description

Here we describe a protocol between a set of users registered in ES, RS schemes i.e. possessing the secret keys of those schemes, denoted by $\mathcal{U}(\{(\mathsf{sks}_i, \mathsf{ske}_i)\}_1^n)$ and a server having public keys $\mathcal{S}(\{(\mathsf{pks}_i, \mathsf{pke}_i)\}_1^n)$. Each user i wants to send anonymously a message m_i, signed with a chosen ring signature scheme RS in a way that the route of messages from the user location L_i would not allow to identify that user. Assume that user i creates a message m_i and signs it to $\sigma_i = \mathsf{RingSign}(m_i, \mathsf{sks}_i, \mathsf{PKS})$. If σ_i is send directly to the server via the communication infrastructure, the adversary controlling the communication links and routers can identify the real signer by the location L_i even though the ring signature used provides the anonymity property. Therefore, in Fig. 1, we propose an *onion* like Source Hiding Protocol SHP using an encryption scheme ES to obfuscate the route for m_i, σ_i messages from L_i to the server:

$$\pi_{\mathsf{SHP}}(\mathcal{U}(\{(m_i, \mathsf{sks}_i, \mathsf{ske}_i)\}_1^n), \mathcal{S}(\{(\mathsf{pks}_i, \mathsf{pke}_i)\}_1^n))$$

– In steps 1–2 the signer signs its own message m_i anonymously with the ring signature into σ_i using all public key from PKS, and sets $c_i^{(0)} = (m_i, \sigma_i)$.
– Then in steps 3–4 the signer creates an onion ciphertext $c_i^{(n)} = E(\dots(E(\dots(E(c_i^{(0)}, \mathsf{pke}_1), \dots), \mathsf{pke}_i)\dots), \mathsf{pke}_n)$, with n layers, by first encrypting the $c_i^{(0)} = (m_i, \sigma_i)$ with the first public key pke_1 from $\langle\mathsf{PKE}\rangle$, and iteratively encrypting the results with the subsequent public keys from $\langle\mathsf{PKE}\rangle$, including its own public key pke_j in the correct iteration. The result of each encryption iteration is the input for the next encryption iteration.

Thus, the only way to get back the content $c_i^{(0)} = (m_i, \sigma_i)$ from the onion $c_i^{(n)}$ is with the help of each user from the group, which has to decrypt its layer with its own secret key. This process should start from the most outer layer n of the user decrypting it with its secret key ske_n, and going down to the most inner ciphertext decrypted by user holding ske_1. The onion $c_i^{(n)}$ is send to the server.

- In step 5 the server awaits for all onion ciphertexts $\{c_1^{(n)}, \ldots, c_n^{(n)}\}$. Obviously these are unreadable, hence they must be decrypted in the correct order by appropriate holders of the secret keys. Thus in a loop 5, the server sends iteratively $\{c_1^{(n)}, \ldots, c_n^{(n)}\}$ to each user according to the reverse order of $\langle \mathsf{PKE} \rangle$, so from n down to 1.

- In the i-th iteration of the loop (step 6), the sequence of onion ciphertexts $\{c_1^{(i)}, \ldots, c_n^{(i)}\}$ are sent to user i, which decrypts with the secret key ske_i the outer i-th layer from all onions $c_i^{(i)} \in \{c_1^{(i)}, \ldots, c_n^{(i)}\}$ into $\{c_1^{(i-1)}, \ldots, c_n^{(i-1)}\}$ (step 6.2), shuffles that sequence randomly (in step 6.3) via a random permutation P_i, and sends it back to the server (step 6.4). Note that each user i has the chance of shuffling, as all onions are encrypted in i-th layer with the public key pke_i. So, in order to decrypt that layer, all onions must be sent to the i-th user holding the corresponding secret key ske_i. Thus the i-th user can execute shuffling in step 6.3.

Note: If we omit the Step 1 in the SHP protocol, and create ciphertexts c_i consisting only of messages, then later, for anyone accessing the server repository, the messages could originate from any source. Ring signatures (used in Step 1) limit the potential origin only to the users with keys in the set PKS.

3.3   Security Analysis

First we analyze our protocol in the *honest-but-curious* adversary model. In this model we assume that the adversary follows the rules, but its goal is to deduce which user produce message m_i and signed it to σ_i. The situation is described by the game in which the only uncorrupted user is the one with index i and the adversary is given all signing keys, secret and public: $\{(\mathsf{sks}_i, \mathsf{pks}_i)\}_1^n$, and all public encryption keys $\{\mathsf{pke}_i\}_1^n$. The adversary denotes here a curious server that wants to find where the message and signature from a chosen j-th user is located in the final list $\{(m_1, \sigma_1), \ldots, (m_n, \sigma_n)\}$, obtained in step 7 of the proposed protocol.

Definition 6 (ASHP - Anonymity Model of SHP). *Let* ES, RS *be set with* $\lambda_{\mathsf{ES}}, \lambda_{\mathsf{RS}}$ *parameters. Assume that each user* i *holding* $\mathsf{sks}_i, \mathsf{ske}_i$ *is bounded to a unique location* L_i *and* $\mathcal{D}$ *knows all the routes for messages transported in the underlying network infrastructure. Let* $\mathcal{D}$ *denote a distinguisher algorithm given public parameters of the schemes:* $\mathsf{par} = (\mathsf{spar}, \mathsf{epar})$, *all* RS *keys:* $\{(\mathsf{sks}_i, \mathsf{pks}_i)\}_1^n$, *and all encryption keys:* $\{\mathsf{pke}_i\}_1^n$. *It chooses* n *messages* $\{m_{\hat{i}}\}_1^n$. *A challenger randomly assigns those messsages to users, i.e. each user* i *gets randomly one message* $m_{\hat{i}}$. *Next, the challenger chooses one index* $\hat{j}$ *indicating the original* *message $m_{\hat{j}}$ assign to user j and sends $\hat{j}$ to the adversary. Then the protocol* SHP *is executed. In the end the adversary outputs its index k. We say that the protocol* SHP *is anonymous and source hiding if the chance of $\mathcal{D}$ for outputting k equal to j that correctly indicates a user given $m_{\hat{j}}$, is negligible different from $1/n$. We define the* ASHP *experiment:*

Init : par $\leftarrow$ ParGenS(λ), $\{(\mathsf{sks}_i, \mathsf{pks}_i)\}_1^n \leftarrow$ KeyGenS(par).

Adversary : *Let the adversary $\mathcal{D}$, be a malicious algorithm initialized with the parameters of* ES, RS *schemes, and the keys:* $\{(\mathsf{sks}_i, \mathsf{pks}_i)\}_1^n$, $\{\mathsf{pke}_i\}_1^n$.

Source Hiding Game : *It is the following protocol:*

1. *The distinguisher generates n messages of its choice:*
   $\{m_{\hat{i}}\}_1^n \leftarrow \mathcal{D}(\mathsf{par}, \{(\mathsf{sks}_i, \mathsf{pks}_i)\}_1^n, \{\mathsf{pke}_i\}_1^n)$ *and sends $\{m_{\hat{i}}\}_1^n$ to a challenger.*

2. *The challenger randomly permutes those messages $\{m_i\}_1^n = P(\{m_{\hat{i}}\}_1^n)$ and assigned them to users, i.e. each user i gets randomly one message $\hat{i}$. Next the challenger generates a random index $\hat{j} \leftarrow_\$ \{1,\ldots,n\}$ indicating a message before permutation, and sends $\hat{j}$ to $\mathcal{D}$.*

3. *The protocol*
   $\pi_{\mathsf{SHP}}(\mathcal{U}(\{m_i, \mathsf{sks}_i, \mathsf{ske}_i\}_1^n, \mathcal{D}(\{(\mathsf{sks}_i, \mathsf{pks}_i)\}_1^n, \{\mathsf{pke}_i\}_1^n))$

4. *The distingusher outputs its own index*
   $k \leftarrow \mathcal{D}(\mathsf{par}, \hat{j}, \{m_{\hat{i}}\}_1^n, \{(\mathsf{sks}_i, \mathsf{pks}_i)\}_1^n, \{\mathsf{pke}_i\}_1^n)$ *indicating which user k was given the message $\hat{j}$ to sign and process in the protocol π_{SHP}.*

We define the advantage of the distinguisher $\mathcal{D}$ in the experiment as the probability that $\mathcal{D}$ outputs the correct index k equal to j indicating the user given $m_{\hat{j}}$ to process in π_{SHP}.

$$\mathbf{Adv}(\mathcal{D}, \mathsf{SHP}) = |\Pr[j = k] - 1/n|. \tag{8}$$

We say that the SHP *scheme is anonymous and source hiding if the advantage of the distinguisher $\mathcal{D}$ is negligible in the parameter $\lambda_{\mathsf{ES}}, \lambda_{\mathsf{RS}}$ i.e.:*

$$\mathbf{Adv}(\mathcal{D}, \mathsf{SHP})) \leq \epsilon(\lambda_{\mathsf{ES}}, \lambda_{\mathsf{RS}}). \tag{9}$$

Theorem 1. *The scheme π_{SHP} given in Fig. 1 is secure in the* ASHP *model as of Definition 6.*

Proof. To prove the theorem it suffices to show that the answer of the distinguisher $\mathcal{D}$ does not depend on the initial assignment of messages to users, and that its output k is equiprobable across all the initial setups. We use a *sequence-of-games* methodology iterating from game G0 to G5. G0 starts with the user i with message $m_{\hat{i}}$, and the user j with message $m_{\hat{j}}$. We modify the subsequent games, to finalize with G5 with the user i with message $m_{\hat{j}}$, and the user j with message $m_{\hat{i}}$. The adversary should not realize about the game changes.

Let **G0** denote the initial security game, where a message of index $\hat{j}$ was assign to user j, and some message $\hat{i}$ was given to another user i. Let p_0 denote the probability that $\mathcal{D}$ outputs index k with that setup in that game.

Setup ES = (ParGenE, KeyGenE, E, D) and RS = (ParGenS, KeyGenS, RingSign, RingVerify) schemes.
Setup keys: for each user $i \in \{1,\ldots,n\}$ do $\{(\text{sks}_i, \text{pks}_i) \leftarrow \text{KeyGenS}()$ and $(\text{ske}_i, \text{pke}_i) \leftarrow \text{KeyGenE}()\}$. $\quad$ PKS = $\{\text{pks}_i\}_1^n$, PKE = $\{\text{pke}_i\}_1^n$.

Modified source hiding protocol: $\pi_{\text{SHP2}}(\mathcal{U}(\{m_i, \text{sks}_i, \text{ske}_i\}_1^n), \mathcal{S}(\{\text{pks}_i, \text{pke}_i\}_1^n))$	
A user the keys: $(\text{ske}_i, \text{pke}_i)$, $(\text{sks}_i, \text{pks}_i)$ and the message m_i	Server: $\mathcal{S}(\{\text{pks}_i, \text{pke}_i\}_1^n)$
1. Each user i generates commitment to message m_i, by: $\quad r_i \leftarrow_\$ R$ and $h_i = \mathcal{H}(m_i, r_i)$.	
2. Execute source hiding protocol: $\quad \pi_{\text{SHP}}(\mathcal{U}(\{h_i, \text{sks}_i, \text{ske}_i\}_1^n), \mathcal{S}(\{\text{pks}_i, \text{pke}_i\}_1^n))$.	
	3. Output resulting commitments H = $\{h_i\}_1^n$.
4. Each user i checks if its commitment h_i is published by the server. $\quad$ If it is not published the user breaks.	
5. Execute the source hiding protocol: $\quad \pi_{\text{SHP}}(\mathcal{U}(\{(m_i, r_i), \text{sks}_i, \text{ske}_i\}_1^n), \mathcal{S}(\{\text{pks}_i, \text{pke}_i\}_1^n))$.	
	6. Output messages and ring signatures $\{((m_i, r_i), \sigma_i)\}_1^n$.
7. Everyone can check if signed messages correspond to signed commitments: $\quad$ If for each $i \in \{1,\ldots,n\}$ $\quad\quad \lfloor \mathcal{H}(m_i, r_i) \in$ H. $\quad$ then accept $\quad$ else reject	

Fig. 2. Modified version of SHP: π_{SHP2} immune against adversary Type 2.

Let **G1** denote a modification of the previous game, where ring signatures are created with switched keys: a message of index $\hat{j}$ is signed with sks_i, and the message $\hat{i}$ is signed with sks_j. Let p_1 denote the probability that $\mathcal{D}$ outputs index k with that setup.

Lemma 1. $|p_0 - p_1| \leq \epsilon_{\text{RS-A}}$, where $\epsilon_{\text{RS-A}}$ is the advantage of breaking the anonymity of ring signature scheme RS.

Proof (Proof of Lemma 1). It is straightforward. Any efficient algorithm $\mathcal{D}$ which outputs k with probability p_1 in G1 non-negligibly different than probablity p_0 for outputting k in the game G0, could be used as a sub-procedure to the attacker algorithm against the anonymity of ring signature RS.

Let **G2** denote a modification of the previous game, where the content of the inner onions $c_i^{(n)}$, is switched to some random values and $c_i^{(0)} = (m_{\hat{r}}, \sigma_r')$, but in the final decrypted list the pair $c_i^{(0)} = (m_{\hat{i}}, \sigma_i')$ appears. Let p_2 denote the probability that $\mathcal{D}$ outputs index k with that setup.

Lemma 2. $|p_1 - p_2| \leq \epsilon_{\text{IND-CCA2}}$, where $\epsilon_{\text{IND-CCA2}}$ is the advantage of breaking the security of encryption scheme ES.

Proof (Proof of Lemma 2). Any efficient algorithm $\mathcal{D}$ which outputs k with probability p_2 in G2 non-negligibly different than probablity p_2 for outputting k in the game G2, could be used as a sub-procedure to the attacker algorithm $\mathcal{A}$ against the security of encryption scheme ES. Assume that $\mathcal{A}$ plays a security experiment IND-CCA2 against the key pk. This pk wil be treated as a public key of user 1 in G2. $\mathcal{A}$ prepares the messages $m_0 = c_i^{(0)} = (m_{\hat{i}}, \sigma_i')$, and $m_1 = c_i^{(0)} = (m_{\hat{r}}, \sigma_r')$ for the experiment IND-CCA2, respectively. After getting a challenge c_b, it simulates the rest of secret keys and public keys for the run of protocol π_{SHP} specifically with the onions: $c_j^{(n)} = E(\ldots(E((m_{\hat{j}}, \sigma_j'), \text{pk}), \ldots), \text{pke}_n)$, $c_i^{(n)} = $

$E(\dots (c_b), \mathsf{pke}_n)$. Now if $\mathcal{D}$ returns k with probability p_1 it behaves like in game G1 and m_b encodes $m_0 = c_i^{(0)} = (m_{\hat{i}}, \sigma_i')$, otherwise it behaves like in G2 and m_b encodes $m_1 = c_i^{(0)} = (m_{\hat{r}}, \sigma_r')$

Let **G3** denote a modification of the previous game, where the content of the inner onions $c_j^{(n)}$, is switched to some random values and $c_j^{(0)} = (m_{\hat{r}'}, \sigma_{r'}')$, but the final decrypted list includes the pair $c_j^{(0)} = (m_{\hat{j}}, \sigma_j'))$. Let p_3 denote the probability that $\mathcal{D}$ outputs index k with that setup.

Lemma 3. $|p_2 - p_3| \leq \epsilon_{\mathsf{IND-CCA2}}$, *where* $\epsilon_{\mathsf{IND-CCA2}}$ *is the advantage of breaking the security of encryption scheme* ES.

Proof (Proof of Lemma 3). Essentially as the proof of Lemma 2.

Let **G4** denote a modification of the previous game, where the content of the inner onions $c_i^{(n)}$, is switched to: $c_i^{(0)} = (m_{\hat{j}}, \sigma_j')$. Let p_3 denote the probability that $\mathcal{D}$ outputs index k with that setup.

Lemma 4. $|p_3 - p_4| \leq \epsilon_{\mathsf{IND-CCA2}}$, *where* $\epsilon_{\mathsf{IND-CCA2}}$ *is the advantage of breaking the security of encryption scheme* ES.

Proof (Proof of Lemma 4). Essentially as the proof of Lemma 2.

Let **G5** denote a modification of the previous game, where the content of the inner onions $c_j^{(n)}$, is switched to $c_j^{(0)} = (m_{\hat{i}}, \sigma_i')$. Let p_3 denote the probability that $\mathcal{D}$ outputs index k with that setup.

Lemma 5. $|p_4 - p_5| \leq \epsilon_{\mathsf{IND-CCA2}}$, *where* $\epsilon_{\mathsf{IND-CCA2}}$ *is the advantage of breaking the security of encryption scheme* ES.

Proof (Proof of Lemma 5). Essentially as the proof of Lemma 2.

Now we have $|p_0 - p_5| \leq \epsilon_{\mathsf{RS-A}} + 4\epsilon_{\mathsf{IND-CCA2}}$, which is negligible. Note that p_0 is the probability of $\mathcal{D}$ outputting k in G0, where the user j was given and signed $m_{\hat{j}}$ with his secret key sks_j, and the user i was given and signed $m_{\hat{i}}$ with his secret key sks_i. However p_5 is the probability of $\mathcal{D}$ outputting k in G5, where the user j was given and signed $m_{\hat{i}}$ with his secret key sks_i, and the user i was given and signed $m_{\hat{j}}$ with his secret key sks_i. Thus $\mathcal{D}$ cannot distinguish between two setups G0 and G5 where the messages $m_{\hat{j}}$ and $m_{\hat{i}}$ were switched between users j and i.

3.4   Enhanced Protocol

In this section we address a stronger adversary that is not only curious, but would like to manipulate onion ciphertexts in a way that results with different final messages and signatures at the server. Here we consider a malicious participant of the signing group $\mathcal{U}(\{\mathsf{sks}_i, \mathsf{ske}_i\}_1^n)$. Observe that in the π_{SHP} protocol any malicious user i, that decrypts (in step 6.2) its layers $c_j^{(i)} \in \{c_1^{(i)}, \ldots, c_n^{(i)}\}$ via $D(c_j^{(i)}, \mathsf{ske}_i)$ into $c_j^{(i-1)}$, can easily substitute any of the decrypted results with a fresh ciphertext onion, e.g.: $\hat{c}_j^{(i-1)} = E(\ldots(E(\hat{c}_j^{(0)}, \mathsf{pke}_1), \ldots), \mathsf{pke}_{(i-1)})$. It just signs its own fresh message $\hat{m}$ anonymously with the ring signature into $\hat{\sigma}$ using public keys from $\{\mathsf{pke}_1, \ldots, \mathsf{pke}_{(i-1)}\}$, and sets $\hat{c}^{(0)} = (\hat{m}, \hat{\sigma})$. Such an onion will be correctly processed by subsequent users, and finally will be received in the decrypted form $(\hat{m}, \hat{\sigma})$ by the server.

To mitigate that we propose an enhanced version of our protocol π_{SHP2} presented in Fig. 2. The idea behind the modification is the following:

- The protocol is executed in two main rounds.
- In the first round (steps 1 and 2) each user i produces its message m_i and a commitment to that messsage $h_i = \mathcal{H}(m_i, r_i)$ for some random value r_i of appropriate size, where $\mathcal{H}$ is a secure hash function. Subsequently, users run the protocol $\pi_{\mathsf{SHP}}(\mathcal{U}(\{(h_i, \mathsf{sks}_i, \mathsf{ske}_i)\}_1^n, \mathcal{S}(\{(\mathsf{pks}_i, \mathsf{pke}_i)\}_1^n)$. The server publishes the commitments (step 3), and each user checks if its commitment is published. A user which commitment is not published breaks (step 4).
- The protocol $\pi_{\mathsf{SHP}}(\mathcal{U}(\{((m_i, r_i), \mathsf{sks}_i, \mathsf{ske}_i)\}_1^n), \mathcal{S}(\{(\mathsf{pks}_i, \mathsf{pke}_i)\}_1^n))$ is run in the second round (steps 5 to 7), where each user ring-signs its message consisting from two parts (m_i, r_i). Subsequently (step 6) the server publishes the resulting messages and signatures: $\{((m_i, r_i), \sigma_i)\}_1^n$. In the end (step 7) everybody can check if the messages complies with the commitments, i.e. if each commitment from the set $\mathsf{H} = \{h_i\}_1^n$ is opened with one published message m_i together with the corresponding randomness r_i.

Corollary 1: *Assuming none of the user breaks, all commitments were correctly processed via π_{SHP} and outputted in step 3 of π_{SHP2}.*

Corollary 2: *Assuming accept in step 7 of π_{SHP2} none of the messages and signatures were replaced in π_{SHP} run in step 5 of π_{SHP2}.*

4   Benchmark

We provide a benchmark analysis of the proposed construction. The analysis of operations is over one participant, together with the total run of the SHP when run over n participants. We used standard RSA encryption, BLS ring signatures and SHA256 hash computations, implemented and run with Python. The benchmark was run on an Apple 2020 M1, 8 GB RAM. Encryption and decryption ran in 0.3790 ms and 3.1679 ms respectively, and a BLS ring signature in 1.6341 ms. A complete run of protocol π_{SHP} with $n = 20$ participants was 75.5721 ms, and for π_{SHP2} it was 73.0341 ms.

5   Conclusion

We have proposed two type of SHP protocols that provides source hiding, hence mitigates traceability attacks and de-anonymization of a single signer within a group of potential signers. We have illustrated the applicability of our protocols via VANET scenarios. We conclude that our protocols are implementable from a performance perspective even in challenging (vehicle) environments which require very fast (near instant) responses.

Acknowledgment. This work was supported by the internal funds of the Department of Fundamentals of Computer Science of the Wrocław University of Science and Technology for the conducted research.

References

1. Bouakkaz, S., Semchedine, F.: A certificateless ring signature scheme with batch verification for applications in VANET. J. Inf. Secur. Appl. **55**, 102669 (2020). https://doi.org/10.1016/j.jisa.2020.102669. https://www.sciencedirect.com/science/article/pii/S2214212620308218
2. Chaum, D.L.: Untraceable electronic mail, return addresses, and digital pseudonyms. Commun. ACM **24**(2), 84–90 (1981). https://doi.org/10.1145/358549.358563
3. European Telecommunications Standards Institute: ETSI TR 103 415 V1.1.1: Intelligent Transport Systems (ITS); Security; Pre-standardization study on pseudonym change management (2018). https://www.etsi.org/standards. Accessed 12 May 2022
4. European Telecommunications Standards Institute: ETSI EN 302 636-6-1 V1.2.0: Intelligent Transport Systems (ITS), Vehicular Communications; GeoNetworking; Part 6: Internet Integration, Sub-part 1: Transmission of IPv6 Packets over GeoNetworking Protocol (2022)
5. Goldschlag, D.M., Reed, M.G., Syverson, P.F.: Hiding routing information. In: Anderson, R. (ed.) IH 1996. LNCS, vol. 1174, pp. 137–150. Springer, Heidelberg (1996). https://doi.org/10.1007/3-540-61996-8_37
6. Katz, J., Lindell, Y.: Introduction to Modern Cryptography, 2nd edn. Chapman Hall/CRC, Boca Raton (2014)
7. Khan, S., Sharma, I., Aslam, M., Khan, M.Z., Khan, S.: Security challenges of location privacy in VANETs and state-of-the-art solutions: a survey. Future Internet **13**(4), 96 (2021). https://doi.org/10.3390/fi13040096. https://www.mdpi.com/1999-5903/13/4/96
8. Liu, F., Wang, Q.: IBRS: an efficient identity-based batch verification scheme for VANETs based on ring signature. In: 2019 IEEE Vehicular Networking Conference (VNC), pp. 1–8 (2019). https://doi.org/10.1109/VNC48660.2019.9062800
9. Liu, L., Wang, Y., Zhang, J., Yang, Q.: Efficient proxy ring signature for VANET. J. Eng. **2019**(9), 5449–5454 (2019)
10. Mundhe, P., Yadav, V.K., Singh, A., Verma, S., Venkatesan, S.: Ring signature-based conditional privacy-preserving authentication in VANETs. Wireless Pers. Commun. **114**(1), 853–881 (2020). https://doi.org/10.1007/s11277-020-07396-x
11. Rivest, R.L., Shamir, A., Tauman, Y.: How to leak a secret. In: Boyd, C. (ed.) ASIACRYPT 2001. LNCS, vol. 2248, pp. 552–565. Springer, Heidelberg (2001). https://doi.org/10.1007/3-540-45682-1_32

A Revocable Outsourced Data Accessing Control Scheme with Black-Box Traceability

Yuchen Yin[1], Qingqing Gan[1], Cong Zuo[2], Ning Liu[1], Changji Wang[1(✉)], and Yuning Jiang[1]

[1] Department of Cyber Security, Guangdong University of Foreign Studies, Guangzhou 510006, China
wchangji@126.com

[2] School of Cyberspace Science and Technology, Beijing Institute of Technology, Beijing 100081, China

Abstract. Ciphertext-policy attribute-based encryption (CP-ABE) is a promising solution to the fine-grained access control problem of encrypted data. Several CP-ABE-based cryptographic cloud storage systems have been proposed in recent years. However, existing CP-ABE schemes still have several limitations that make them not effective to be used in a practical application. Firstly, decryption privileges may be changed when the user revocation happens to prevent the leakage of encrypted data. Secondly, malicious users may delegate decryption keys to unauthorized users for profit. Thirdly, the complex operation of encryption and decryption may bring a huge computational cost and is usually considered to be a heavy burden for system users. Therefore, this paper proposes a new CP-ABE scheme ROBBT-CPABE, which can provide attribute revocation, black-box tracking, outsourcing encryption, and outsourcing decryption. By using the information distribution algorithm and the secure modular exponentiation outsourcing algorithm, the scheme can achieve attribute revocation and outsource some expensive encryption and decryption operations to the cloud server. Based on the construction of indistinguishable traceable ciphertext, the proposed scheme can support black-box tracking. Then the ROBBT-CPABE scheme is formally proved to be selective replay chosen ciphertext attack (RCCA) secure and black-box traceable secure. Performance analysis demonstrates the efficiency and practicality of ROBBT-CPABE.

Keywords: Ciphertext-policy attribute-based encryption · Cloud storage · Revocation · Outsourcing Encryption/Decryption · Black-box traceability

1 Introduction

With the emergence and rapid development of cloud computing, more and more companies or individuals choose to upload their data to cloud servers for utilizing the cloud resources, such as "unlimited" storage space and computing costs.

W. Meng et al. (Eds.): ISPEC 2023, LNCS 14341, pp. 380–398, 2023.
https://doi.org/10.1007/978-981-99-7032-2_23

However, when these data are outsourced to the cloud storage server, the data owner will lose actual control of their data, especially for sensitive data. In order to protect privacy, the data owner tries to encrypt data and then outsources the ciphertexts onto the cloud server. Meanwhile, the data owner should be able to control the access rights of the data for cloud data sharing. Therefore, encrypting data and designing flexible and fine-grained access control mechanisms are crucial for data security protection in the cloud.

To solve the above problem, Sahai and Waters first proposed the concept of At-tribute-based encryption (ABE) to provide flexible and fine-grained access control for cloud data [1]. Generally speaking, ABE can be divided into key-policy (KP-ABE) and ciphertext-policy (CP-ABE) according to the location of the access policy. In CP-ABE, the access structure is embedded in the ciphertext, and the attributes are embedded in the user's private key. In KP-ABE, the attribute is embedded in the ciphertext, and the access structure is embedded in the user's private key. In KP-ABE and CP-ABE systems, a user will be able to decrypt the ciphertext if and only if the attributes set satisfies the access structure. Due to data owners can formulate access policies in CP-ABE, it is more suitable for access control applications in cloud.

Bethencourt et al. [2] proposed the first CP-ABE scheme with support for tree access structure. Cheung and Newport [3] presented how to structure a CP-ABE scheme using an AND-gate policy. Although many CP-ABE schemes have been presented, there are still some limitations in previous CP-ABE constructions. Firstly, the number of users and permissions in the CP-ABE system is constantly changing, and ciphertext updates occur from time to time. This requires an efficient and flexible algorithm to achieve revocation [4]. Secondly, since the user's private key is related to attributes, the user can use his private key to make a decryption black-box device for profit [5–7]. Therefore, the CP-ABE scheme should provide the function of tracking the malicious users who manufacture the decryption device. Thirdly, with the continuous growth of the number of attributes in the system, the overhead of encryption and decryption will increase heavily. Therefore, an algorithm that can outsource encryption and decryption is needed to reduce the computational overhead of users while protecting users' privacy during the outsourcing process. Hence, how to construct an efficient and secure CP-ABE scheme with the functions of revocability, outsourcing, and traceability becomes an essential issue.

1.1 Our Contribution

In this article, we have proposed a novel **R**evocable, **O**utsourcing CP-ABE scheme with **B**lack-**B**ox **T**raceability, named ROBBT-CPABE, for flexible access control in cloud environment. The main innovations of this work are given as follows.

1) Indirect revocation and black-box traceability: The Information Dispersal Algorithm is used to cut the ciphertext into slices. Then using the new access strategy to re-encrypt a random slice to achieve efficient revocation. Once

there is a decryption black-box device, the malicious user who made the black-box can be traced by sending the tracking ciphertext that the black-box cannot recognize.

2) Outsourced encryption, decryption and correctness verification: The divisions of exponent and base with random pairs make the original data unavailable to the cloud encryption server, and use two sets of random pairs to achieve verification of outsourced encryption and decryption.

3) Security and performance: ROBBT-CPABE is proven secure against the selective replay chosen ciphertext attack (RCCA). The black-box traceable secure is also proved in the generic bilinear group model. Performance comparisons illustrate that ROBBT-CPABE is extensible, efficient, and utilizable.

1.2   Related Work

User attribute updates and ciphertext access policy updates occur from time to time in ABE. Therefore, revocation is quite important in ABE to achieve fine-grained access. According to the different executors of revocation, it can be divided into indirect revocation and direct revocation. In indirect revocation, the revocation information is dynamically issued by the authority, and keys are updated for users who have not been revoked. While in the direct revocation, the user needs to add the revocation information to a revocation list and sends it together with the ciphertext when encrypting.

In 2021, Bouchaala et al. [8] presented an indirect revocation scheme using Information Dispersal Algorithm (IDA), the ciphertext slice stored in the cloud server is re-encrypted with the symmetric encryption key to a random data slice of the ciphertext. Although the overhead of this scheme is relatively small, it only supports white-box tracking, which is not applicable in reality. Guo et al. [9] proposed a user attribute revocation scheme in 2023. When user attribute revocation occurs, the attribute manager updates the user's attribute group key. The ciphertext is updated to ensure the forward and backward security of the scheme. Sarma et al. [10] proposed a revocable CPABE scheme in fog computing, and let the fog nodes undertake most of the encryption and decryption operations. Combining proxy re-encryption and version control technology, Zhao et al. [11] proposed the CP-ABE-CPRE scheme where this scheme performs attribute revocation through different version numbers.

In ABE schemes, traceability is an important feature that enables the tracking of vulnerabilities and the delegation of keys. According to the different requirements of the algorithm, traceability research can be divided into white-box and black-box [12]. The white-box traceability is based on a well-formed decryption key as input. Unlike the white-box traceability, the black-box mechanism provides the device with the ciphertext and obtains the decrypted plaintext to ensure that at least one user can be tracked. In 2020, Zhao et al. [11] proposed a publicly accountable black-box tracking CP-ABE scheme. In this paper, all users can track malicious users who create and decrypt black-box devices without the participation of other secret information. But there is still the problem of heavy tracking overhead. Qiao et al. [6] described a CP-ABE scheme based on access tree strategy, which has black-box user traceability. The tracker designs a tracking ciphertext for the decryption device, then the analysis showed the user identity. And the tracking process of [7] is similar with [6]. The authority sends each user's corresponding tuple to the tracer and the tracer analyzes the decryption result of the device to identify the users hidden in the decryption device.

In traditional attribute-based encryption, the computational cost increases linearly with the number of attributes and complexity of the access policies, which brings a huge computational burden to the device terminal, so the outsourcing function is also very important for the ABE scheme. In 2019, Li et al. [13] applied the power exponential security outsourcing algorithm to CP-ABE. However, because the results of multiple random slice calculations cannot be effectively distinguished by the server, the probability of correct verification during verification is only $1/2$. Inspired by [13], Yu et al. [14] proposed a new scheme that supports a verifiable exponentiation security outsourcing with effective verification operation. The proposed scheme can protect data privacy by splitting the data into two sets of different random pairs and sending them to the cloud server for calculation. As a result, it increases the probability of correct verification to "1".

1.3   Organization

The remainder of this paper is organized as follows. In Sect. 2, we introduce related preliminaries. Section 3 describes the model of syntax and security. Our scheme is presented in Sect. 4. In Sect. 5, the security and performance analysis are discussed. Section 6 presents the concluding remarks.

2   Preliminaries

2.1   Bilinear Pairing

Given a multiplicative cyclic group G of order p, and g is the generator of the group G. $e : G \times G \rightarrow G_T$ is a bilinear map that satisfies the following properties:

1. Bilinear: For $\forall a, b \in Z_p$, and $\forall u, v \in G, e\left(u^a, v^b\right) = e(u, v)^{ab}$;
2. Non-degeneracy: $\forall u, v \in G, e\left(u, v\right) \neq 1$;
3. Computability: For $\forall u, v \in G$, it exists a polynomial time algorithm to compute $e(u, v)$.

2.2   Linear Secret Sharing Scheme

A secret sharing scheme Π on a set of participants P is called a linear secret sharing scheme (LSSS) on Z_p if the following conditions are satisfied [15].

1. The secret share shared by each entity constitutes a vector on Z_p.

2. For Π, there exists a matrix M of $\ell \times n$, and the mapping function maps each row of the matrix into a related party. For $i = 1, \ldots, \ell$, $\rho(i)$ is the party associated with row i. We consider a column vector $\boldsymbol{v} = [s, y_2, y_3, \ldots, y_n]^T$, and $s \in Z_p$ represents the shared secret and y_i is randomly chosen where $i = 2, \ldots, n$. In order to conceal the secret s, calculated $\lambda_i = M_i \boldsymbol{v}$ as a shared of s, where λ_i matching the party $\rho(i)$, M_i is the ith row vector of M.

LSSS has the property of linear reconstruction. If $S \in A$ is an accessing authorization set, then there exists a constant $\{\omega_i \in Z_p\}_{i \in I}$ for $\sum_{i \in I} \omega_i \lambda_i = s$, where λ_i denotes the efficient share of secret s and $I = \{i : \rho(i) \in S\}$.

2.3 Complexity Assumptions

The complexity assumption used in our scheme is the decisional q-parallel BDHE.

Definition 1. *Select a group G of prime order p under the security parameters, and randomly choose $a, s, b_1, \ldots, b_q \in Z_p$. Given all of the following terms [16].*

$$\boldsymbol{y} = \{g, g^s, g^a, \ldots, g^{a^q}, g^{a^{q+2}}, \ldots, g^{a^{2q}},$$
$$\forall_{1 \leq j \leq q} g^{s b_j}, g^{a/b_j}, \ldots, g^{a^q/b_j}, g^{a^{q+2}/b_j}, \ldots, g^{2q/b_j}, \tag{1}$$
$$\forall_{1 \leq j, k \leq q, k \neq j} g^{a \cdot s \cdot b_k / b_j}, \ldots, g^{a^q \cdot s \cdot b_k / b_j}\}$$

The algorithm $\mathcal{B}$ guesses by outputting $z \in \{0, 1\}$, if $|\Pr\left[\mathcal{B}\left(\boldsymbol{y}, \psi = e(g, g)^{a^{q+1}s}\right) = 0\right] - \Pr[\mathcal{B}(\boldsymbol{y}, \psi = \delta) = 0]| \geq \epsilon$ where $e(g, g)^{a^{q+1}s}, \delta \in G_T$.

3 Syntax and Security Definitions for ROBBT-CPABE

As illustrated in Fig. 1, there are five participants in the system framework of ROBBT-CPABE:

- Trusted Authority (TA): A trusted authority that sets the public parameters and generates the master secret key of the system. it also produces pre-keys for DUs. Furthermore, it could track malicious users when necessary.
- Data Owner (DO): The owner of the data. Before hosting the data to the CAS, DO has to encrypt the data under a chosen access policy and interact with CAS to generate outsourcing ciphertext.
- Cloud Encryption Server (CES): A cloud server that assists DO in encrypting messages.
- Cloud Auxiliary Server (CAS): A cloud server that stores ciphertext, updates ciphertext and assists DUs in decrypting messages.
- Data User (DU): A person who can recover the plaintext only if the attributes of the user match the embedded access strategy.

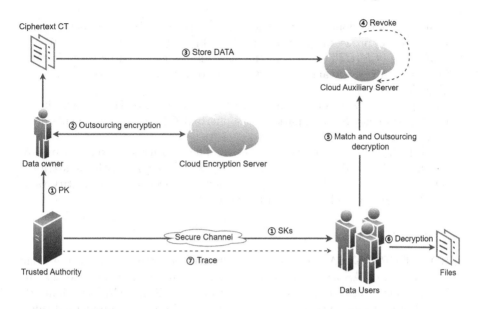

Fig. 1. System architecture of ROBBT-CPABE.

A ROBBT-CPABE scheme includes eight polynomial-time algorithms as follows.

- Setup $(\lambda, \{0,1\}^*) \rightarrow (PK, MSK, T_{id})$. The algorithm is executed by TA. It takes in a security parameter λ and an attribute universe set $\{0,1\}^*$. It returns the system public parameter PK and the corresponding system master secret key MSK. In addition, this algorithm initializes a table $T_{id} = \emptyset$ to track identity.
- KeyGen $(PK, MSK, S, id) \rightarrow (TK, SK)$. The algorithm is executed by TA and DU. It takes in PK, MSK, an attribute set $S \subseteq \{0,1\}^*$ of a user with id. The relevant transform key TK and private key SK are output. Then it stores the id and a tracking parameter into T_{id}.
- Encrypt $(PK, m, \mathbb{A} = (A, \rho)) \rightarrow (CT)$. The algorithm is executed by CES and DO. It takes in PK, a plaintext message m, and an access structure $\mathbb{A}$ over the attribute universe set. DO will hand over part of the encryption work to CES to complete. After the interaction between DO and CES, it outputs a ciphertext CT.
- Revoke $(PK, CT, \mathbb{A}^*) \rightarrow (c_j)$. The algorithm is executed by CES. It takes in PK, a ciphertext CT, and a new access policy $\mathbb{A}^*$. It runs (n, n)-IDA to split ciphertext into n, and chooses a random slice ct_j for re-encryption. It outputs the re-encrypted single random slice c_j.
- Match $(ct_j) \rightarrow 0$ or 1. The algorithm is executed by CAS and DU. If revocation occurs in the system that the ciphertext access policy has been updated, the user should succeed in the matching phase. This algorithm takes in the

ciphertext of random slice ct_j. When the user successfully decrypts to ct_j and the matching process is passed, this algorithm output 1, else outputs 0.

- Transform $(TK, CT) \to (CT')$. The algorithm is executed by CAS. It takes in transform key TK and a ciphertext CT. It outputs the corresponding part of the ciphertext CT'.
- Decrypt $(SK, CT') \to (m)$. The algorithm is executed by DU. It takes in the user's private key SK and part of the ciphertext CT'. It outputs the plaintext message m.
- Trace $(PK, \mathbb{A}_T = (A', \rho), m_T, T_{id}) \to id$. The algorithm is executed by TA. It takes in PK and an access structure $\mathbb{A}_T$ which matches with the attribute set S of the user, a plaintext m_T specified by tracer and the identity table T_{id}. It outputs the identity id of the user.

3.1 Security Model

In ROBBT-CPABE, TA is defined as a fully trusted authority. Both the cloud server CES and CAS are assumed to be semi-trusted and we assume that no collusion occurs between servers. That is to say, CES and CAS will honestly execute the predefined program, but they try to obtain the confidential information of the original data as much as possible. DU is considered untruthful, he/she perhaps makes their key into a decryption black-box device to profit. The specific security requirements of ROBBT-CPABE are shown as follows.

Selective RCCA Secure. The selective replay chosen ciphertext attack (RCCA) security model is defined as follows [17].

- *Init.* Adversary $\mathcal{A}$ chooses a challenge access strategy (A^*, ρ^*) and sends (A^*, ρ^*) to the simulator $\mathcal{B}$.
- *Setup.* $\mathcal{B}$ runs Setup algorithm and sends PK to $\mathcal{A}$.
- *Phase 1.* $\mathcal{B}$ Initializes a blank table T^*, an empty set D and an integer $j = 0$. $\mathcal{B}$ responses to queries of adversary $\mathcal{A}$ by following steps.
- *Create(S):* $\mathcal{B}$ runs $KeyGen$ algorithm to get (SK, TK), sets $j = j + 1$ and stores tuple (j, S, SK, TK) in T^*. Then $\mathcal{B}$ sends TK to $\mathcal{A}$.
- *Corrupt(i):* If there is an entity i in T^*, then $\mathcal{B}$ can obtain this entity $(j, S, SK_{id,S}, TK)$ and sets $D := D \cup S$. $\mathcal{B}$ returns $SK_{id,S}$ to $\mathcal{A}$. Else, output $\perp$.
- *Decrypt(i, CT):* With the input (SK, CT), $\mathcal{B}$ returns the output of Decrypt algorithm to $\mathcal{A}$.
- *Challenge.* $\mathcal{A}$ submits two equal-length messages m_0 and m_1 to $\mathcal{B}$, then $\mathcal{B}$ runs Encrypt algorithm to get ciphertext CT^* of massage m_β where $\beta \in \{0, 1\}$ and returns CT^* to $\mathcal{A}$.
- *Phase 2.* The same thing as Phase 1.
- *Guess.* If the guess of the output of adversary $\mathcal{A}$ is β' and $\beta' = \beta$, then $\mathcal{A}$ wins this game. The probability of $\mathcal{A}$ winning the game is: $Adv_{\mathcal{A}} = |\Pr[\beta' = \beta] - 1/2|$.

Definition 2. *ROBBT-CPABE is selective RCCA secure if $Adv_{\mathcal{A}}$ is negligible.*

Black-Box Traceable Secure. The traced ciphertext and the normal ciphertext should be indistinguishable for black-box traceability. If the adversary can distinguish the ciphertext, he/she can make the tracking algorithm fail by returning an error message. A tracking algorithm is traceable secure only if it is ensured that the decryption device cannot distinguish the tracking ciphertext from the normal ciphertext. The black-box traceable security model is defined as the following attack game played between an adversary $\mathcal{A}$ and a challenger $\mathcal{C}$.

- *Setup.* Challenger $\mathcal{C}$ runs Setup algorithm to generate system public parameter PK and system master secret key MSK then sends PK to $\mathcal{A}$.
- *Phase 1.* $\mathcal{A}$ is allowed to make private key queries on adaptively chosen user attribute set. $\mathcal{C}$ runs KeyGen algorithm to generate the corresponding key SK for $\mathcal{A}$.
- *Challenge.* $\mathcal{A}$ chooses an access structure $\mathbb{A}_T^*$ and sends it to $\mathcal{C}$. $\mathcal{C}$ chooses a massage m and a random value $\beta \in \{0, 1\}$. When $\beta = 0$, $\mathcal{C}$ runs Encrypt $(PK, m', \mathbb{A}_T^* = (A^*, \rho)) \to CT_1$. When $\beta = 1$, $\mathcal{C}$ runs Encrypt $(PK, m', \mathbb{A}_T^* = (A^*, \rho)) \to CT_2$. Finally, $\mathcal{C}$ sends ciphertext CT_β to $\mathcal{A}$.
- *Phase 2.* The same thing as Phase 1.
- *Guess.* If the guess of the output of adversary $\mathcal{A}$ is β' and $\beta' = \beta$, then $\mathcal{A}$ wins this game. The probability of $\mathcal{A}$ winning the game is: $Adv_{\mathcal{A}} = |\Pr[\beta' = \beta] - 1/2|$

Definition 3. *ROBBT-CPABE is black-box traceable secure if $Adv_{\mathcal{A}}$ is negligible.*

4   Construction of ROBBT-CPABE

The goal of the ROBBT-CPABE scheme is to ensure fine-grained access control and enhanced security in cloud environment. It bridges the limitations discussed earlier and provides a revocable, outsourced computing, black-box tracking-enabled access control scheme for cloud storage. We plot the operations of authorities at various stages in Fig. 2.

4.1   System Initialization

Setup $(\lambda, \{0, 1\}^*) \to (PK, MSK, T_{id})$. TA inputs a security parameter λ and a system attribute universe set $\{0, 1\}^*$. It generates a group G of prime order p and generator and makes a bilinear map e. It also randomly chooses $\alpha, a \in Z_p$. Besides, it denotes hash functions $H_1 : \{0, 1\}^* \to Z_p$, $H_2 : \{0, 1\}^* \to G$ and $H_3 : \{0, 1\}^* \to \{0, 1\}^\lambda$. Finally, it sets $T_{id} = \emptyset$ for tracking. The public parameters are published as $PK = (g, e(g, g)^\alpha, g^a, H_1, H_2, H_3)$. g^α is retained as the master secret key MSK.

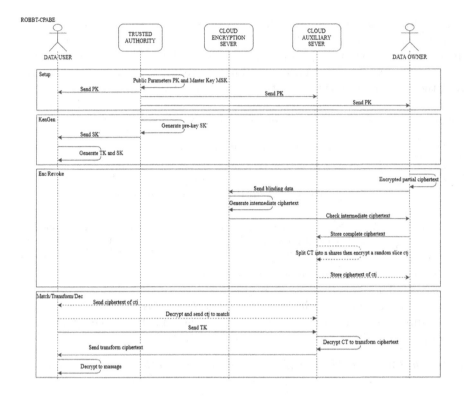

Fig. 2. Sequence diagram of ROBBT-CPABE.

4.2   Key Generation

KeyGen $(PK, MSK, S, id) \rightarrow (TK, SK)$. This algorithm consists of two parts. First, TA generates a pre-key for a user identified as id, and S is a set of attributes owned by the user. TA selects a random number $t' \in Z_p^*$, and computes $I = H_1(id), K' = g^{\alpha I}g^{at'}, L' = g^{t'}, K_i' = H_2(att(i))^{H_1(att(i))t'})_{i \in S}$, then sends SK' to the user, where $SK' = (PK, I, K', L' = g^{t'}, K_i')$. At the same time, TA stores the tuples $(id, ID_{SK} = e(g, g)^{t'/I})$ into T_{id}. After receiving SK', the user selects a random number $z \in Z_p^*$, and generates a transform key $TK = (PK, I, K = (K')^{1/z} = g^{\alpha I/z}g^{at}, L = (L')^{1/z} = g^t, K_i = H_2(att(i))^{H_1(att(i))t})_{i \in S}$ where $t = t'/z$. The user holds the private key $SK = (z, TK)$.

4.3   Encryption

Encrypt $(PK, m, \mathbb{A} = (A, \rho)) \rightarrow (CT)$. First, DO specifies an access policy $\mathbb{A} = (A, \rho)$, and selects a random number $r \in G_T$, computes $s = H_1(r, m), R = H_3(r), C = r \cdot e(g, g)^{\alpha s}, C' = g^s, C'' = m \oplus R$. Let A be a matrix of $l \times n$, and ρ is a single mapping function, mapping each row of matrix A to an attribute. DO selects a random vector $\boldsymbol{v} = (s, y_2 \ldots y_n) \in Z_p^n$ for sharing secret number s and computes $\lambda_i = \boldsymbol{v} \cdot A_i$ that A_i is the ith row of matrix A for $i = 1, \ldots, t$. Furthermore, DO randomly selects $r_1, r_2, \ldots, r_l \in Z_p$. Inspired by [14], DO communicates with CES to compute intermediate ciphertext $CT_{intermedia} = \{C_i = g^{a\lambda_i} H_2(att\,(i))^{-r_i H_1(att(i))}, D_i = g^{r_i}\}_{i \in S}$. The specific process is consisting of three parts.

1. DO generates three random blind pairs $(\gamma_1, g^{\gamma_1}), (\gamma_2, g^{\gamma_2}), (\beta, g^\beta)$ by Random algorithm [18], and computes $\omega_1 = g^a/g^{\gamma_1} \bmod p, \omega_2 = H_2(att\,(i))^{H_1(att(i))}/g^{\gamma_2} \bmod p, c_{i1} = \lambda_i - d_{i1}x_1 \bmod p$, where $d_{i1} \in Z_p^*$, x is a random value that $x \geq 2^\lambda$, λ is a security parameter. The exponent and the base are divided into random slices calculated by the cloud encryption sever (CES):

$$
\begin{aligned}
C_i &= g^{a\lambda_i} H_2(att\,(i))^{-r_i H_1(att(i))} \\
&= (\omega_1 g^{\gamma_1})^{\lambda_i} (\omega_2 g^{\gamma_2})^{-r_i H_1(att(i))} \\
&= g^{\gamma_1 \lambda_i} g^{\gamma_2(-r_i H_1(att(i)))} \omega_1^{\lambda_i} \omega_2^{-r_i H_1(att(i))} \\
&= g^{\gamma_1 \lambda_i - \gamma_2 r_i H_1(att(i))} \omega_1^{c_{i1}+d_{i1}x_1} \omega_2^{c_{i2}-d_{i1}x_1} \\
&= g^\beta g^{\gamma_1 \lambda_i - \gamma_2 r_i H_1(att(i)) - \beta} \omega_1^{c_{i1}} \omega_2^{c_{i2}} (\omega_1 \omega_2^{-1})^{d_{i1}x_1} \bmod p
\end{aligned}
\tag{2}
$$

   The generation process of another division is the same as above. DO generates another three random blind pairs $(\alpha_1, g^{\alpha_1}), (\alpha_2, g^{\alpha_2}), (\eta, g^\eta)$ and the division is shown as $C_i = g^\eta g^{\alpha_1 \lambda_i - \alpha_2 r_i h_i H_1(att(i)) - \eta} \omega_3^{c_{i3}} \omega_4^{c_{i4}} (\omega_3 \omega_4^{-1})^{d_{i2}x_2} \bmod p$.

2. DO sends data to CES and queries in random order as follows.

$$
\begin{aligned}
&U(\omega_1, c_{i1}) \rightarrow \omega_1^{c_{i1}}; \; U(\omega_2, c_{i2}) \rightarrow \omega_2^{c_{i2}}; \\
&U((\omega_1 \omega_2^{-1})^{x_1}, d_{i1}) \rightarrow (\omega_1 \omega_2^{-1})^{d_{i1}x_1}; \\
&U(\gamma_1 \lambda_i - \gamma_2 r_i H_1(att\,(i)) - \beta, g) \rightarrow g^{\gamma_1 \lambda_i - \gamma_2 r_i H_1(att(i)) - \beta}
\end{aligned}
\tag{3}
$$

3. DO verifies the returned calculation result, and the formula is as follows.

$$
\begin{aligned}
&g^\beta g^{\gamma_1 \lambda_i - \gamma_2 r_i h_i H_1(att(i)) - \beta} \omega_1^{c_{i1}} \omega_2^{c_{i2}} (\omega_1 \omega_2^{-1})^{d_{i1}x_1} \\
&= g^\eta g^{\alpha_1 \lambda_i - \alpha_2 r_i h_i H_1(att(i)) - \eta} \omega_3^{c_{i3}} \omega_4^{c_{i4}} (\omega_3 \omega_4^{-1})^{d_{i2}x_2}
\end{aligned}
\tag{4}
$$

The calculation and verification process of D_i is similar to that of C_i. Finally, DO uploads the whole ciphertext $CT = (C, C', C'', C_i, D_i)$ to CAS for storage.

4.4   Revocation

Revoke $(PK, CT, \mathbb{A}^* = (A^*, \rho)) \rightarrow (c_j)$. The revocation phase is based on re-encrypting a random piece. If the data owner wants to update the access policy, he/she sends the new access policy $\mathbb{A}^*$ to CAS. CAS runs (n, n)-IDA to divide CT into n parts, $CT = (ct_1, ct_2, \ldots, ct_n)$ where (n, n)-IDA is a fault-tolerant algorithm for data fragmentation backup [19] and we use it to reduce the computational burden of re-encryption. Then CAS randomly selects $j \in \{1, \ldots, n\}$ and runs encryption$(PK, ct_j, \mathbb{A}^* = (A^*, \rho))$ to re-encrypt the random piece ct_j with a new access structure $\mathbb{A}^* = (A^*, \rho)$ into c_j.

4.5 Match and Transform

If a revocation has occurred in the system, users should successfully pass the matching phase first.

Match $(ct_j) \rightarrow 0$ or 1. A legitimate user can successfully decrypt the updated ciphertext CT only if the following possess. The user should successfully decrypt the c_j with privacy SK, and return ct_j to CAS. Then CAS checks whether ct_j equals the stored ct_j. If true, CAS will run Transform algorithm to decrypt the transform ciphertext.

Transform $(TK, CT) \rightarrow (CT')$. If the user passes the match or there is no revocation occurring in the system. DU sends the transform key TK to CAS, and CAS uses TK to decrypt the transform ciphertext. Suppose the user's attribute set S satisfies the access policy (A, ρ), define $x = \{i : att(i) \in S\}$. There exists a constant set $\{\omega_i \in Z_p\}_{i \in x}$. If λ_i is the effective share of secret s, then there exist $\sum_{i \in x} \omega_i \lambda_i = s$. $CT_{transform}$ is calculated according to the following process.

$$
\begin{aligned}
CT_{transform} &= e(C', K) / \prod_{i \in x} \left(e\left(C_i, L\right) e\left(D_i, K_i\right) \right)^{\omega_i} \\
&= e(g^s, g^{\alpha I/z} g^{at}) / \prod_{i \in x} \left(e(g^a \lambda_i H_2(att\,(i))^{-r_i H_1(att(i))}, g^t) \right. \\
&\qquad \left. e(g^{r_i}, H_2(att(i))^{H_1}(att(i))\,t)_{i \in S}) \right)^{\omega_i} \\
&= e(g, g)^{\alpha s I/z}
\end{aligned}
\tag{5}
$$

4.6 Decryption

Decrypt $(SK, CT') \rightarrow (m)$. The user can calculate $r = C/CT_{transform}^{z/I}$ with the private key SK, then $m = C \oplus H_3(r)$. In addition, he/she can calculate $s = H_1(r, m)$. Then the user can verify the correctness of the results by checking whether two equations $C = r \cdot e(g, g)^{\alpha s}$ and $CT_{transform} = e(g, g)^{\alpha s I/z}$ are held. If held, it means the CAS has executed the outsourced decryption correctly, and the user will accept the plaintext m.

4.7 Trace

Trace $(PK, \mathbb{A}_T = (A', \rho), m_T, T_{id}) \rightarrow id$. If a black box decryption device appears and claims to be able to decrypt any ciphertext that can be accessed by the attribute set S_T, since the decryption key and algorithm are embedded in the black box, the corresponding black box tracking algorithm needs to be used to find the malicious user who made the black box.

TA traces malicious users as a tracer. It specifies an access policy $\mathbb{A}_T = (A', \rho)$ matching S_T, a plaintext m' for tracking, a secret s' and calculate $Trap = s' - s$. It runs Encrypt$(PK, m', \mathbb{A}_T = (A', \rho)) \rightarrow TCT$ where secrete sharing vector $v' = (s', y_2 \ldots y_n) \in Z_p^n$, $\lambda_i' = v' \cdot A_i$ and randomly $\{r_i'\}_{i \in x}$. Note that s' is used as the secret sharing number, and the exponent of C and C' is s.

$$TCT = (C = r \cdot e(g,g)^{\alpha s}, C' = g^s, C'' = m \oplus R,$$
$$\{C'_i = g^{a\lambda'_i} H_2(att\,(i))^{-r'_i H_1(att(i))}, D'_i = g^{r'_i}\}_{i \in I}) \qquad (6)$$

TA disguised as a user of a black box device and sent ciphertext TCT to it. The black-box cannot distinguish TCT from CT, so it would try to decrypt TCT. The decryption process is the same as above. If the black-box is a revoked user, he/she should pass the match process. Else, CAS runs transform algorithm and obtains a transform ciphertext $TCT' = (C, C'', TCT_{transform})$.

$$TCT_{transform} = e(C', K) / \prod_{i \in x} (e\,(C'_i, L)\, e\,(D'_i, K_i))^{\omega_i}) \qquad (7)$$
$$= e(g,g)^{\alpha s I/z + (s - s')at}$$

Now, TCT' and CT' indistinguishable. The black-box runs decryption algorithm and returns the plaintext m' to the tracer. TA calculates as follows.

$$r' = C / TCT_{transform}^{z/I} = r \cdot e(g,g)^{(s-s')atz/I} \qquad (8)$$
$$m' = C \oplus F\,(r')$$

TA can verify the correctness of the results by checking whether the equations $r' \cdot e(g,g)^{s'atz/I} = r \cdot e(g,g)^{satz/I}$. Then TA calculates $(r'/r)^{1/(Trap \cdot at)} = e(g,g)^{t'/I}$, and searches the tracking list T_{id} to reveal id corresponding to the private key used by the black-box.

5   Security and Performance Analysis

5.1   Security Analysis

Theorem 1. *ROBBT-CPABE is selective RCCA secure if the deterministic q-BDHE assumption holds in the group G and G_T.*

Proof. We can construct a simulator $\mathcal{B}$ to solve the decision q-BDHE with a non-negligible advantage if there is a polynomial time adversary $\mathcal{A}$ that can break through the proposed ROBBT-CPABE scheme in the selective RCCA model with a non-negligible advantage ε.

- *Init.* Simulator $\mathcal{B}$ inputs the q-BDHE tuple $(\boldsymbol{y}, \psi)$, $\psi = e(g,g)^{a^{q+1}s} \in G_T$ to challenge. Adversary $\mathcal{A}$ chooses a challenge access strategy (A^*, ρ^*) and sends to the simulator $\mathcal{B}$.
- *Setup.* $\mathcal{B}$ chooses a random $\alpha' \epsilon Z_p$, and implicitly sets $\alpha = \alpha' + a^{q+1}$ by letting $e(g,g)^\alpha = e\,(g^a, g^{a^q})\, e\,(g,g)^{\alpha'}$.
- *Phase 1* $\mathcal{B}$ Initializes four blank tables T_1, T_2, T_3, T_4, an empty set D and an integer $j = 0$. $\mathcal{B}$ responds to an attacker's queries by following steps.
  1. Random Oracle Hash $H_1\,(r, m)$. If an entity (r, m, s) exists in the table T_1, return s. Otherwise, randomly select a value s, (r, m, s) is recorded in table T_1 and returns s.

2. Random Oracle Hash $H_2(r)$. If an entity (r, R) exists in the table T_2, return R. Otherwise, randomly select a value $R \in \{0,1\}^k$, (r, R) is recorded in table T_2 and returns R.

3. Random Oracle Hash $H_2(id)$. If an entity (id, I) exists in the table T_3, return I. Otherwise, randomly select a value $I \in \{0,1\}^k$, (id, I) is recorded in table T_3 and returns I.

– *Create*(S) Suppose S does not satisfy access policy (A^*, ρ^*) and set $j = j+1$. Choose a random $y \in Z_p$ and find a column vector $\boldsymbol{\omega} = [\omega_1, \ldots, \omega_{n^*}]^T \in Z_p^{n^*}$ where $\omega_1 = -1$ and $M_i^* \boldsymbol{\omega} = 0$. Indexes for all i values $att^*(i) \in S$. Setting

$$L' = g^y \prod_{i=1}^{n^*} (g^{a^{q+1-i}})^{\omega_i} = g^t, t = y + \omega_1 a^q + \omega_2 a^{q-1} + \cdots + \omega_{n^*} a^{q+1-n^*}, K' =$$

$g^{\alpha' I} g^{ar} \prod_{i=2}^{n^*} (g^{a^{q+2-i}})^{\omega_i}$. For K_x $(\forall x \in S)$, if there is no i satisfying the equation $att^*(i) = x$, random oracle response $K'_x = H_2(att(x))^{H_1(att(x))t}$, else,

$$K'_x = \prod_{i=1}^{n^*} \left(H_2(att(x))^{(a^j/b_i)y} \prod_{k=1, k\neq j}^{n^*} \left(H_2(att(x))^{a^{q+1-i}/b_i} \right)^{\omega_k} \right)^{M_{i,j}^*} \cdot$$

$$H_2(att(x))^{H_1(att(x))t}$$

$$= (H_2(att(x))^{H_1(att(x))} H_2(att(x))^{aM_{i,1}^*/b_i} \cdots H_2(att(x))^{a^{n^*} M_{i,n^*}^*/b_i})^t$$

(9)

$\mathcal{B}$ runs KeyGen to get $SK' = (PK, I, K', L', \{K_x'\}_{x \in S})$. The algorithm selects a random value $z \in Z_p$, set $TK_{id} = (PK, I, K = (K')^{1/z}, L = (L')^{1/z}, \{K_x\}_{x \in S} = \{K_x'\}_{x \in S}$ and $SK_{id,S} = (z, TK_{id})$. If S satisfies the access policy, then select a 'false' transformed key, and the process is similar to the above. Select a random value $d \in Z_p$, run KeyGen to get SK', $TK = SK'$, $SK_{id,S} = (d, TK_{id})$, where if $z = \alpha/d$, regenerate TK. Finally, store $(j, S, SK_{id,S}, TK, ID_{SK} = e(g,g)^{t'/I})$ in T_4 and return TK to $\mathcal{A}$.

– *Corrupt*(i). $\mathcal{A}$ is restricted to query the key associated with access policy (A^*, ρ^*). If there is an entity in T_3 and T_4, then $\mathcal{B}$ can obtain this entity $(j, S, SK_{id,S}, TK, id, I, ID_{SK})$ and $D = D \cup S$. $\mathcal{B}$ returns $SK_{id,S}$ to $\mathcal{A}$. Else, output $\bot$.

– *Decrypt*(i, CT). Suppose the inputted ciphertext has been partially decrypted. ciphertext $CT = (C, C'', CT_{transform})$ is related to access strategy, and $\mathcal{A}$ can query $(j, S, SK_{id,S}, TK, id, I, ID_{SK})$ in T_3 and T_4. If not query or $S \notin (A^*, \rho^*)$, output $\bot$ to $\mathcal{A}$. If the key does not satisfy the challenge access policy (A^*, ρ^*) in the i-th entity, form the following process:

1. Parse $SK_{id,S} = (z, TK_{id})$, compute $r = C/CT_{transform}^{z/I}$.
2. Get the record (r, m_i, s_i) from T_1. If it does not exist, return $\bot$ to $\mathcal{A}$.
3. If there is $y \neq x$ in a set and $(r, m_{y'}, s_{y'}), (r, m_{x'}, s_{x'}), m_{y'} \neq m_{x'}, s_{y'} \neq_{x'}$ in T_1, $\mathcal{B}$ then outputs $\bot$.
4. Otherwise, query (r, R) from table T_2. If it does not exist, output $\bot$.
5. For each element i, test whether the equation is satisfied: $C = r \cdot e(g,g)^{\alpha s}, C'' = m \oplus R, CT_{transform} = e(g,g)^{\alpha s I/z}$.
6. If there is i that passes the above steps, the message m_i is output; otherwise, output $\bot$.

If the key does not satisfy the challenge access policy (A^*, ρ^*) in the i-th entity, form the following process:

1. Parse $SK_{id,S} = (d, TK_{id})$, compute $r = CT_{transform}$.
2. Test whether record (r, m_i, s_i) satisfies equation $\beta = e(g, g)^{s_i}$.
3. $\mathcal{B}$ outputs $\perp$, if no matching is found.
4. $\mathcal{B}$ aborts the simulation, if more than one matching is found.
5. Else let (r, m_i, s_i) becoming the unique match, query (r, R) from T_2, and if it does not exist, $\mathcal{B}$ outputs $\perp$.
6. Test whether the equation is satisfied: $C = r \cdot e(g, g)^{\alpha s}$, $C'' = m \oplus R$, $CT_{transform} = e(g, g)^{\alpha s I / z}$.
7. Output m, if all steps pass, else output $\perp$.

- *Challenge.* $\mathcal{A}$ propose two equal-length plaintexts m_0 and m_1 to $\mathcal{B}$, then $\mathcal{B}$ chooses a massage m_β where $\beta \in \{0, 1\}$ and gets the r_β associated with m_β. Compute $C = r_\beta \cdot \psi \cdot e(g^s, g^{\alpha'})$, $C' = g^s$ and randomly choose $y_2, \ldots, y_{n^*}$. Then share secret s by vector $\boldsymbol{v} = (s, sa + y_2, \ldots, sa^{n+1} + y_{n^*}) \in Z_p^{n^*}$ and randomly choose $r_1, \ldots, r_l$. For $i = 1, \ldots, n^*$, compute $D_i = g^{-r'_i} g^{-sb_i}$,

$$C_i = H1_{att^*_{(i)}}^{r'_i} \Big(\prod_{j=2,\ldots,n^*} (H_2(att(x))^a)^{M^*_{i,j} y'_j} \Big)(H_2(att(x))^{b_i \cdot s})^{-z_{att^*_i}} \Big(\prod_{k \in 1, \cdots, n^*}$$

$\prod_{j=1,\cdots,n^*} (H_2(att(x))^{a^j s (b_i / b_k)})^{M^*_{k,j}}$. Finally, $\mathcal{B}$ choose $C'' \in \{0, 1\}^k$ and sends

$CT^* = (C, C', C'', C_i, D_i)$ to $\mathcal{A}$.

- *Phase 2.* The same thing as Phase 1.
- *Guess.* The adversary $\mathcal{A}$ outputs a guess bit β'. If $\beta' = \beta$ and $\psi = e(g, g)^{a^{q+1}s}$, the simulator $\mathcal{B}$ will give a valid simulation, we have $\Pr[B(\boldsymbol{y}, \psi = e(g, g)^a q + 1s) = 0] = 1/2 + Adv_{\mathcal{A}}$. The message m_β is completely hidden by the adversary when ψ is a random group element. We have $\Pr[B(\boldsymbol{y}, \psi = \delta) = 0] = 1/2$ where δ is randomly chosen from group G_T. Thus, $|\Pr[B(\boldsymbol{y}, \psi = e(g, g)^a q + 1s) = 0] - \Pr[B(\boldsymbol{y}, \psi = \delta) = 0]| = Adv_{\mathcal{A}} = \varepsilon$.

Therefore, $\mathcal{B}$ can break the decisional q-BDHE problem with non-negligible advantage.

Theorem 2. *ROBBT-CPABE is black-box traceable secure in the generic bilinear group model if the adversary $\mathcal{A}$ queries at most q times in following games and wins the game with an advantage of $\varepsilon = O(q^2 / p)$.*

The detailed proof is given in the Appendix.

5.2   Performance Analysis and Implementation Evaluation

Functionality Comparisons. Table 1 shows that schemes [8,9] support attribute revocation, but only achieve white-box traceability which is inapplicable in the real world. Scheme [7] supports black box tracking, but this scheme is a conventional CP-ABE scheme, which cannot afford complex functions like revocation and outsourcing. Scheme [10] supports revocation and outsourcing, but there is no design for tracking function in the scheme. To sum up, our solution can support revocation, outsourcing and black-box tracking, which can efficiently track malicious users and revoke them.

Table 1. Functionality Comparisons.

Schemes	Security assumption	Attribute revocation	Traceability	Outsourcing
[7]	q-type	×	Black-box	×
[8]	BDH	✓	White-box	×
[9]	CDH	✓	White-box	✓
[10]	DBDH	✓	×	✓
ours	decisional q-parallel BDHE	✓	Black-box	✓

Efficiency Comparisons. Table 2 gives a comparison of the computational cost of key generation, encryption, decryption and tracking. Let E be the exponent operation in groups, P denotes one pairing operation. Let s be the number of attributes that the user owns and l be the number of attributes. The number of attributes satisfying the accessing strategy is represented by n. And user number is represented by $|U|$. '–' indicates that the scheme does not have the corresponding function.

Table 2. Efficiency Comparisons.

Schemes	Key generation	Encryption		Decryption		Trace
		DO	CES	DU	CAS	
[7]	$(5+3s)E$	$(2+7l)E$	-	$(2+n)E+(1+4n)P$	-	$(2+14l+|U|)E$
[8]	$(6+s)E$	$(5+3l)E$	-	$(3+n)E+(4+n)P$	-	$2P$
[9]	$(4+3s)E$	$(2+3l)E$	$2l$	$(1+n)E+(1+n)P$	$2nE+(2+n)P$	-
[10]	$(4+4s)E$	$4E$	$(2+4l)E$	P	$(2+3n)P$	-
ours	$(6+s)E+P$	$6E$	$8lE$	$2E$	$nE+(2n+1)P$	$8E$

Our scheme and [8] have fewer exponent computations during the key generation phase, but one more bilinear pairing operation is computed due to our need for black-box tracking. Since [9,10] support outsourced computing in the encryption and decryption stages, we compare ROBBT-CPABE with [9,10]. It is clear that our scheme requires fewer exponential operations to be computed by the user during the encryption phase. And the reason the server is more computationally expensive than [9,10] is that we implement verification and [9,10] does not. The same is true for a large amount of computation in the decryption phase. In the tracking phase, we compare with [7]. Since we can outsource some ciphertext calculations, the calculation amount of the tracer is relatively small.

Implementation Evaluation. In order to further evaluate the performance of our scheme, we implement [8–10] and ROBBT-CPABE on Intel(R) Core(TM) i5-7300HQ CPU at 2.50 GHz and 4.00 GB RAM. We used the JPBC library of JAVA to complete the simulation experiment. The Type A elliptic curve with a group order bit length of 512 bits is selected, where $y^2 = x^3 + x$. We do consider the computation overhead of exponential operation and bilinear pairing in the systems.

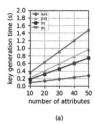 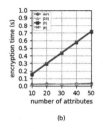 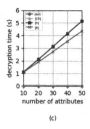

| (a) | (b) | (c) |

Fig. 3. Comparisons of Computation time. (a) KeyGen. (b) Encryption. (c) Decryption.

Figure 3 describes the execution results of the computation time experience in key generation, encryption, and decryption. The number of attributes in the access policy increases from 10 to 50, and the number of user attributes that satisfy the access policy also increases from 10 to 50. And the results of the conducted experiments are the average of 5 trials. Figure 3(a) shows the key generation time of all schemes is linearly related to the number of attributes, but the slope of our scheme is small and the performance is within a certain range. Figure 3(b) shows the time required for users encryption in [8,9] is linear with the number of attributes, but the encryption time of our scheme is stable between 0.024 s and 0.029 s, and the encryption efficiency has been greatly improved, which effectively reduces the consumption of computing resources by data owners. Figure 3(c) shows the decryption time of [8,9] is linear with the number of attributes, while most of the decryption operations of [10] and our scheme are outsourced to the cloud server. The decryption time of local data users is constant. Although the decryption time of our scheme is slightly higher than [10], our scheme has the function of verifying outsourcing decryption and has better performance.

6 Conclusion

In this paper, we propose a novel CP-ABE scheme called ROBBT-CPABE, for revocability, outsourced computation, and black-box traceability. It performs revocation by re-encrypting the ciphertext slice and matching, makes the original data unavailable to the encryption server and enables verification by splitting the exponent and base with random pairs, and guarantees black-box traceability by using tracking ciphertexts and tracking lists. And we prove that ROBBT-CPABE is secure and show the practicality and efficiency of the scheme through the comparative analysis.

Acknowledgements. This research is funded by Science and Technology Program of Guangzhou (Grant No. 202201010067,2023A04J0330) and Guangdong Basic and Applied Basic Research Foundation (Grant No. 2022A1515110980).

A   Black-Box Security Proof for ROBBT-CPABE

Definition 4. *The generic bilinear group model [2]: We consider two random encodings ψ_0, ψ_1 of a group Z_p^*, that is injective maps $\psi_0, \psi_1 : Z_p^* \to \{0,1\}^m$ where $m > 3\log(p)$. Set $G = \psi_1(x), x \in Z_p^*, G_T = \psi_2(x), x \in Z_p^*$ and an oracle to compute a non-degenerate bilinear map $e : G \times G \to G_T$. We refer to G_T as a generic bilinear group.*

Theorem 3. *ROBBT-CPABE is black-box traceable secure in the generic bilinear group model if the adversary $\mathcal{A}$ queries at most q times in following games and wins the game with an advantage of $\varepsilon = O(q^2/p)$.*

Proof. $\mathcal{A}$ can win the game with a negligible advantage when the order p of group is large enough. When ψ_0, ψ_1, G, G_T are generic bilinear groups, elements in G, G_T can be mapped to a random string by function ψ_0, ψ_1 where $g = \psi_1(1), g^x = \psi_1(x), e(g,g)^y = \psi_2(y)$.

- *Setup.* Challenger $\mathcal{C}$ randomly chooses $\alpha, a \in Z_p^*$. The public parameters are published as $PK = (g, e(g,g)^\alpha, g^a, H_1, H_2)$. g^α is kept as the master secret key MSK.
- *Phase 1.* Adversary $\mathcal{A}$ is allowed to make q' private key queries on adaptively chosen user attribute set $S_1, \ldots, S_{q'}.\mathcal{C}$ runs KeyGen algorithm to generate corresponding key SK for $\mathcal{A}$. And $SK = (z, K = g^{\alpha I/z}g^{at}, L = g^t, K_x = H_2(att(x))^{H_1(att(x))t})_{x \in S})$.
- *Challenge.* $\mathcal{A}$ chooses a challenge access structure $\mathbb{A}^*$ and sends to $\mathcal{C}$. $\mathcal{C}$ randomly chooses a massage $m \in G_T, s \in Z_p^*$ and $\mu \in \{0,1\}$. When $\mu = 0$, $s' = s$, else, random chooses $s' \in Z_p^*$. $\mathcal{C}$ runs Encrypt algorithm, randomly chooses vector $v = (s', y_2, \ldots, y_n) \in Z_p^{n+1}$ where s' is the secret. Get $\lambda = (\lambda_1, \lambda_2, \ldots, \lambda_l) \in Z_p^{l \times 1}$ through $\lambda_i = A_i v$. $\mathcal{C}$ sends CT to $\mathcal{A}$. And $CT = (C = r \cdot e(g,g)^{\alpha s}, C' = g^s, C'' = m \oplus R, C_i = g^{a\lambda_i}H_2(att(i))^{-r_i H_1(att(i))}, D_i = g^{r_i}{}_{i \in S})$
- *Phase 2.* The same thing as Phase 1. $\mathcal{A}$ continues to access the key SK corresponding to the attribute set S, where the attribute set S has at least one query that satisfies the access strategy $\mathbb{A}^*$.
- *Guess.* Only if the adversary $\mathcal{A}$ can judge $s' = s$, we assume he/she wins the game. When the results of the two queries are consistent, the adversary can distinguish whether $s' = s$ holds or not, else, we say it is no 'unexpected collisions'. The probabilities of two types of unexpected collisions are discussed below.

In the first case, variables such as $\alpha, s\alpha, at$ are unknown parameters for $\mathcal{A}$. $\mathcal{A}$'s query process can be abstracted into a rational function $\mathcal{F}(var)$ where var is the known parameters of $\mathcal{A}$. An unexpected collision would occur when two queries correspond to two distinct formal rational functions. An unexpected collision would be when two queries corresponding to two distinct formal rational functions $\mathcal{F}_1 = \mathcal{F}_2$, but where due to the random choices of these variables' values, we have that the values of $\mathcal{F}_1|_{s'=s}$ and $\mathcal{F}_2|_{s'=s}$ coincide. Since the unknown parameters are all exponentials, the known parameters can only be linearly transformed to construct a function of the form $\mathcal{F} = \gamma s + \theta$, where θ, γ are constant and $\gamma \neq 0$. It follows that $\mathcal{F}_1 - \mathcal{F}_2$ means that $\mathcal{A}$ conducts a pair of $\gamma s = \mathcal{F}_1 - \mathcal{F}_2 + \gamma s'$ and $\gamma s' = \mathcal{F}_2 - \mathcal{F}_1 + \gamma s$ query. The following will prove that it is impossible for $\mathcal{A}$ to create such a pair of queries in the game.

- Let a non-empty set $\Gamma = \{x : S_x\}$, where S_x satisfies the access structure $\mathbb{A}^*$. The adversary $\mathcal{A}$ decrypts ciphertext with $[SK_{S_x} = \prod_{i \in I, i \neq j} (e(C_i, L)e(D_i, K_{\rho(i)}))^{\omega_i} = e(g, g)^{s'at}]$, where $s' = \lambda_x \omega_x$. So, if $\mathcal{A}$ want to get $\gamma s = \gamma s'$, he/she needs to make index $\sum_{x \in \Gamma'} (\xi_x at)s = s'at$, where $\Gamma' \in \Gamma$. Since it is impossible for $\mathcal{A}$ to eliminate index at, it is not possible to create a collision for $\gamma s' = \gamma s$.

In the second case, due to the nature of the system causing unexpected collisions, the outputs of the two queries of challenger $\mathcal{C}$ are consistent. By the Schwartz-Zippel lemma [20,21], the probability of this event is $O(1/p)$. By a union bound, the probability that any such collision happens is at most $O(q^2/p)$. Therefore, we can assume that such a collision does not occur and maintain $1 - O(q^2/p)$ of the probability mass. Thus, the probability of $\mathcal{A}$ winning this game is negligible, when p is large enough.

References

1. Sahai, A., Waters, B.: Fuzzy identity-based encryption. In: Cramer, R. (ed.) EUROCRYPT 2005. LNCS, vol. 3494, pp. 457–473. Springer, Heidelberg (2005). https://doi.org/10.1007/11426639_27
2. Bethencourt, J., Sahai, A., Waters, B.: Ciphertext-policy attribute-based encryption. In: 2007 IEEE Symposium on Security and Privacy (SP 2007), pp. 321–334 (2007). https://doi.org/10.1109/SP.2007.11
3. Cheung, L., Newport, C.: Provably secure ciphertext policy ABE. In: Proceedings of the 14th ACM Conference on Computer and Communications Security, pp. 456–465. ACM, Alexandria Virginia USA (2007). https://doi.org/10.1145/1315245.1315302
4. Li, Q., Xia, B., Huang, H., Zhang, Y., Zhang, T.: TRAC: traceable and revocable access control scheme for mHealth in 5G-enabled IIoT. IEEE Trans. Industr. Inf. 18(5), 3437–3448 (2022). https://doi.org/10.1109/TII.2021.3109090
5. Liu, Z., Cao, Z., Wong, D.S.: Blackbox traceable CP-ABE: how to catch people leaking their keys by selling decryption devices on ebay. In: Proceedings of the ACM Conference on Computer and Communications Security, pp. 475–486 (2013). https://doi.org/10.1145/2508859.2516683
6. Qiao, H., Ren, J., Wang, Z., Ba, H., Zhou, H.: Compulsory traceable ciphertext-policy attribute-based encryption against privilege abuse in fog computing. Futur. Gener. Comput. Syst. 88, 107–116 (2018). https://doi.org/10.1016/j.future.2018.05.032
7. Liu, Z., Ding, Y., Yuan, M., Wang, B.: Black-box accountable authority CP-ABE scheme for cloud-assisted e-health system. IEEE Syst. J. 17(1), 756–767 (2023). https://doi.org/10.1109/JSYST.2022.3175244

8. Bouchaala, M., Ghazel, C., Saidane, L.A.: Trak-CPABE: a novel traceable, revocable and accountable ciphertext-policy attribute-based encryption scheme in cloud computing. J. Inf. Secur. Appl. **61**, 102914 (2021). https://doi.org/10.1016/j.jisa.2021.102914

9. Guo, L.F., Xing, X.M., Guo, H.: An efficient traceable and revocable attribute-based encryption scheme in cloud storage. J. Cryptol. Res. **10**(1), 131–145 (2023). https://doi.org/10.13868/j.cnki.jcr.000584

10. Sarma, R., Kumar, C., Barbhuiya, F.A.: PAC-FIT: an efficient privacy preserving access control scheme for fog-enabled IoT. Sustain. Comput. Inform. Syst. **30**, 100527 (2021). https://doi.org/10.1016/j.suscom.2021.100527

11. Zhao, Q., Wu, G., Ma, H., Zhang, Y., Wang, H.: Black-box and public traceability in multi-authority attribute based encryption. Chin. J. Electron. **29**(1), 106–113 (2020). https://doi.org/10.1049/cje.2019.10.006

12. Liu, Z., Cao, Z., Wong, D.S.: White-box traceable ciphertext-policy attribute-based encryption supporting any monotone access structures. IEEE Trans. Inf. Forensics Secur. **8**(1), 76–88 (2013). https://doi.org/10.1109/TIFS.2012.2223683

13. Li, Z., Li, W., Jin, Z., Zhang, H., Wen, Q.: An efficient ABE scheme with verifiable outsourced encryption and decryption. IEEE Access **7**, 29023–29037 (2019). https://doi.org/10.1109/ACCESS.2018.2890565

14. Yu, J., He, G., Yan, X., Tang, Y., Qin, R.: Outsourced ciphertext-policy attribute-based encryption with partial policy hidden. Int. J. Distrib. Sens. Netw. **16**(5), 155014772092636 (2020). https://doi.org/10.1177/1550147720926368

15. Beimel, A.: Secure Schemes for Secret Sharing and Key Distribution. Ph.D. thesis, Technion - Israel Institute of Technology, Israel (1996)

16. Waters, B.: Ciphertext-policy attribute-based encryption: an expressive, efficient, and provably secure realization. In: Catalano, D., Fazio, N., Gennaro, R., Nicolosi, A. (eds.) PKC 2011. LNCS, vol. 6571, pp. 53–70. Springer, Heidelberg (2011). https://doi.org/10.1007/978-3-642-19379-8_4

17. Green, M., Hohenberger, S., Waters, B.: Outsourcing the decryption of ABE ciphertexts. pp. 34–34 (2011)

18. Wang, Y., et al.: Securely outsourcing exponentiations with single untrusted program for cloud storage. In: Kutyłowski, M., Vaidya, J. (eds.) ESORICS 2014. LNCS, vol. 8712, pp. 326–343. Springer, Cham (2014). https://doi.org/10.1007/978-3-319-11203-9_19

19. Rabin, M.O.: Efficient dispersal of information for security, load balancing, and fault tolerance. J. ACM **36**(2), 335–348 (1989). https://doi.org/10.1145/62044.62050

20. Schwartz, J.T.: Fast probabilistic algorithms for verification of polynomial identities. J. ACM **27**(4), 701–717 (1980). https://doi.org/10.1145/322217.322225

21. Zippel, R.: Probabilistic algorithms for sparse polynomials. In: Ng, E.W. (ed.) Symbolic and Algebraic Computation. LNCS, vol. 72, pp. 216–226. Springer, Heidelberg (1979). https://doi.org/10.1007/3-540-09519-5_73

LocKey: Location-Based Key Extraction from the WiFi Environment in the User's Vicinity

Philipp Jakubeit[1]([✉])[iD], Andreas Peter[1,2][iD], and Maarten van Steen[1][iD]

[1] University of Twente, Drienerlolaan 5, 7522 Enschede, NB, The Netherlands
p.jakubeit@utwente.nl
[2] University of Oldenburg, Ammerländer Heerstraße 114-118,
26129 Oldenburg, Germany

Abstract. We investigate extracting persistent information from semi-volatile signals in the user's vicinity to extend existing authentication factors. We use WiFi as a representative of semi-volatile signals, as WiFi signals and WiFi receiver hardware are ubiquitous. WiFi hardware is mostly bound to a physical location and WiFi signals are semi-volatile by nature. By comparing different locations, we confirm our expectation that location-specific information is present in the received WiFi signals. In this work, we study whether and how this information can be transformed to satisfy the following properties of a cryptographic key so that we can use it as an extension of an authentication factor: it must be uniformly random, contain sufficient entropy, and the information must be secret. We further discuss two primary use cases in the authentication domain: using extracted low-entropy information (48 bits) for password hardening and using extracted high-entropy information (128 bits and 256 bits) as a location-specific key. Using the WiFi-signal composition as an authentication component increases the usability, introduces the factor of 'location' to the authentication claims, and introduces another layer of defense against key or password extraction attacks. Next to these advantages, it has intrinsic limitations, such as the need for the receiver to be in proximity to the signal and the reliance on WiFi signals, which are outside the user's control. Despite these challenges, using signals in the proximity of a user works in situations with a fallback routine in place while increasing usability and transparency. LocKey is capable to extract low-entropy information at all locations measured, and high-entropy from 68% locations for 128-bit keys (48% of the locations respectively for 256-bit keys). We further show that with an initial measurement time of at most five minutes, we can reconstruct the key in at least 75% of the cases in less than 15, 30, and 40 s depending on the desired key strength.

Keywords: Location-based Authentication · Fuzzy Key Extractions · WiFi Signals

1   Introduction

Authentication is a crucial component of ensuring the security of online transactions and information. It describes the 'provision of assurance that a claimed characteristic of an entity is correct' [16]. There are three main types of authentication factors distinguished by the claim made: knowledge factors, possession factors, and inherence factors. *Knowledge factors* involve something the user knows (e.g., password, PIN, or an answer to a security question). These are most prevalent in practice and are often used as the primary factor in multi-factor authentication. *Possession factors* involve something the user has (e.g., a smart card, a physical token, or a mobile phone). These factors are becoming more common in modern authentication methods, as users are increasingly relying on their mobile devices for authentication. *Inherence factors* involve something the user is, represented by biometric data (e.g., fingerprints, facial recognition, or iris scans). These factors are becoming more popular as a means to access a physical token or a mobile phone. Multi-factor authentication combines two or more of these factors to provide increased security. For example, a bank might use a combination of a password (knowledge factor) and an SMS (possession factor) to authenticate a user.

Location-based authentication is another type of claim that can be used during the authentication process. It is different from the other authentication factors as it is not about the user but the environment the user is in. Traditionally, a location-based authentication factor is used to localize a user (e.g., IP address ranges, GPS). However, we do not intend to localize a user but to recognize the environment the user is in. For the purpose of authentication, to validate a location claim, it is sufficient to validate that the claimed location is indeed a location associated with the user. Where the location is located is no required knowledge to validate the claim.

We propose the recognition of WiFi measurements of a location as an additional factor. In today's traditional setup, a user accesses a device either by knowledge or inherence claims to authenticate from the device towards a service with a combination of knowledge and possession claims. The user provides their password and a token or a challenge-response authentication based on a key the user owns. Our goal is to extend these factors with a claim of location in terms of WiFi measurements. Such a measurement must contain sufficient information for the desired use case. As each location differs in the information available, we choose the amount of information to extract on a per-location basis. With this, we are capable of either extending the information present in a password/key-based authentication claim or replacing an entire authentication factor. In the banking example given above, it might suffice to know that a user logging in with the correct credentials is at a typical location for this user. E.g., credit card usage consistency checks rely largely on such behavioral consistencies.

Especially in urban environments, wireless protocols based on the IEEE 802.11 standard (WiFi) and hence WiFi signals, and WiFi hardware are ubiquitous and ever-increasing. WiFi signals are known in the literature to be suited for various use cases such as indoor positioning [26], area selection [8], distance binding [10], behavioral profile construction [21], location fingerprinting [18], and key extraction [7]. In this paper, we look at the latter: extracting information from the WiFi signals surrounding us which share properties of a cryptographic key. What distinguishes our work from previous work is that we only rely on measurements without changing the existing infrastructure. By this, we introduce an extension that can be applied seamlessly (see Sect. 8 for more details on the differences with the related work). At first glance this might seem easy to achieve, however, it turned out to be more intricate. First, as our work is motivated by the quest for seamless authentication, we do not consider having control over or changing the behavior of access points (APs). We only consider the WiFi hardware of the user, the sensor. Second, as we observe electromagnetic signals, there are fluctuations and disturbances, which result in signals being inconsistently present. Third, as WiFi signals are emitted into the world we are required to find a way to make the derived information secret.

Our assumed WiFi infrastructure builds on stationary access points (APs), which constantly emit signals to indicate their presence, the so-called beacon frame. We use the information in the periodically sent beacon frames to derive location-specific information from the vicinity of a user. The setting is that we only observe signals, we need to account for inconsistencies in the volatile signals, and we need to make at least some information from the publicly available signals secret. The approach we take is (as done in biometrics e.g., [17]) not to store the information, but to generate and later reproduce it from a semi-persistent source. This is appealing as it reduces the attack surface because an adversary cannot extract this information from the hardware. Due to the potential volatility of the signals we require a backup procedure or fallback routine to be in place. To make the observed information secret, we require another source of randomness such that a vicinity key derived from the environment becomes uniformly random, and secret, and contains sufficient entropy in the information-theoretic sense. With LocKey:

- We show how to use a vicinity key to strengthen existing secret information (key or password).
- We increase the usability of multi-factor authentication.
- We get location as a claimed characteristic while preserving privacy.

To do so, we describe how to construct a WiFi measurement by observing only available APs by processing the available beacon frame features as an environmental entropy source and show how to precisely reconstruct such a WiFi measurement from a sufficiently similar measurement. Next, we show how to derive a vicinity key from such a WiFi measurement by introducing a device component. While doing so, we identify entropy estimates and evaluate the performance of our proposed method by using our real-world dataset and analyze our method in terms of the system's security. We observe that a low-entropy vicinity key of 48-bit can be extracted at all considered locations, while we can extract high-entropy vicinity keys of 128-bit at 68% of the locations, and 256-bit vicinity keys at 48% of the locations considered. We further show that with initial WiFi measurements of up to five minutes, we can reconstruct a key in less than 40 s for all vicinity key strengths. Further, LocKey adds an extra layer of security on top of knowledge and possession factors. When a password or key gets compromised in traditional schemes, the adversary broke the system, while with LocKey in place, an adversary is required to derive a composition of WiFi APs that is sufficiently similar to the AP composition at the user's location.

2   Foundations

In this section, we describe the two underlying foundations of LocKey. First, we focus on WiFi beacon frames, what they entail, and by which circumstances they are impacted. Second, we focus on fuzzy extractors, what they are, and why they are a perfect fit for the inconsistent AP compositions we observe.

2.1   WiFi Beacon Frames

The WiFi beacon frame is a management frame defined in the IEEE 802.11 standard [14]. A periodically sent beacon frame advertises the presence of the base station. The WiFi beacon frame entails information about the network, like the physical address and capabilities of the network. Which fields to use is limited by two aspects; the presence in the beacon frame itself and the receiver's operating system (OS). *The presence of the information* in the beacon frame itself is not guaranteed, as a frame contains mandatory and optional fields. *The OS of the receiver* matters, as different OSs provide different levels of access to beacon frame fields in general and based on access rights within the system itself. In the case of the Linux OS, the accessible fields are the network's name called the service set identifier (SSID), the media access control address (MAC address), a general flag, the maximum bandwidth to use, the security and capability flags, the frequency used, and the mode of the AP [12]. These fields combined have a theoretical maximum of 63 bits; entropy analyses on real-world data suggest a minimum of 9 bits [18]. Privileged access on Linux (root space) and Windows allows access to more beacon-frame fields, while OSX and mobile operating systems are more restrictive in accessing beacon-frame fields.

2.2   Fuzzy Extractors

The authors of [9] coined the term fuzzy extractor. However, the idea of using sets to lock a vault goes back to [20]. One way to look at fuzzy extractors is as error-tolerant and nonuniformity-tolerant key-encapsulation mechanisms for a secret key. They can generate a uniformly random string R from an input w. This extraction process is error-tolerant, so a sufficiently similar input $w' \sim w$ reproduces the same uniformly random string R. The inputs' similarity can be expressed on the bit level by the inputs' Hamming distance. Sufficiently similar means that the Hamming distance is not greater than t, the number of errors that can be corrected. The generate and reproduce functions are the two building blocks of a fuzzy extractor and can be constructed from two components: a secure sketch and a strong extractor, as shown in Fig. 1.

Secure Sketches. A secure sketch is a function that recreates an input w from another input w' with a small Hamming distance to w. A secure sketch consists of two main components. The secure sketch and the reconstruct function. The secure sketch receives an input w and produces a sketch s such that a similar input w' together with that sketch s can be used by the reconstruct function to output the original input w.

Strong Extractor. The strong extractor function is not fuzzy in itself. It generates a defined output based on its defined inputs. A family of hash functions is used to extract a uniformly random string from an input and an entropy source. The extraction process uses the input w and an additional entropy source r. The authors of [9] show that a 2-wise independent hash function produces an optimal result, as the length of the random input r is less critical in the scenario of o fuzzy extractor. We will describe what family of hash functions we chose in our instantiation section.

Building a Fuzzy Extractor from a Secure Sketch and a Strong Extractor. In Fig. 1, we show a schematic of the components from a fuzzy extractor and how to construct it from a secure sketch and a strong extractor. The input w is used as input to the secure sketch to create a sketch s. This sketch, together with internally generated randomness r, forms the output, helper data $P = (s, r)$. This randomness r is used together with the input w as input to the strong extractor to create the uniformly distributed string R. To reproduce this R created by the generator function, the reproduce function receives the helper

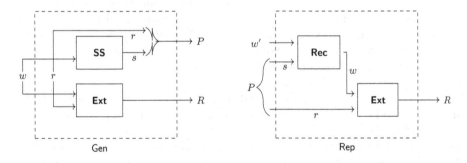

Fig. 1. Schematic of a fuzzy extractor constructed of a secure sketch (SS) and a strong extractor (Ext). The generate function takes w as input. The secure sketch creates a sketch, while the strong extractor uses the input and internally generated randomness to generate a uniformly random string R. The generator function outputs the string R and helper data P, which consists of the sketch s and internal randomness r. The reproduce function takes an input w' similar to w and the helper data P as input. Internally, a reconstruct function takes the input w' and the s element of the helper data P and outputs the reconstructed w. The reconstructed w is used together with the r part of the helper data P as input to the strong extractor, which outputs the same uniform random string R as outputted by the generator function if the Hamming distance of w and w' is sufficiently small ($\leq t$).

data P and a similar input w' as inputs. It inputs the sketch part s included in P and the input w' into the reconstruct function. The reconstruct function reconstructs from both its inputs the original input w. The reconstructed w is used with the random r component of the helper data P as input to the strong extractor. This strong extractor performs exactly as its counterpart in the generation construction and outputs R.

3   Overview on LocKey

In this work, we focus on the IEEE 802.11 standard [14], which we will refer to as WiFi. However, we assume that the principle we describe will also hold for other wireless standards and somewhat persistent electromagnetic signals in general. We consider a *sensor*, a wireless receiver, capable of observing the beacon frames sent by WiFi APs. We assume both, the sensor and the APs, to be spatially static. We assume standard laptop hardware (e.g., [15]) as the sensor. The sensor gathers measurements of APs over time. We describe each AP by an AP representation (APR). We call a specific composition (set) of APRs measured at one location a WiFi measurement.

We want to see how the composition of measured WiFi signals in the vicinity of a user can be used to derive a vicinity key. The main challenge lies in the fact that the WiFi composition is fluctuating. Already a small physical area is subject to heavy fluctuations (an illustration of the fluctuation of WiFi signals in a right square prism of dimensions 36 cm^2 by 18 cm can be seen at [22]). To compensate for the signal fluctuations, we choose to work with a fuzzy extractor. This works by conducting initial measurements and deriving a vicinity key and helper data. With this helper data, it is possible to derive the same vicinity key from sufficiently similar measurements. Sufficiently similar refers to two measurements differing in at most t elements. We derive t from the initial measurements as it influences the entropy of our derived key and we need to know before how much entropy is available at a location.

We focus especially on usability and transparency. An authentication system using the WiFi environment of a user does not impose a serious burden on the user. During the first generation of a vicinity key, the user is required to stay in place for the time required to measure the environment. However, afterward, the authentication can be conducted from the service and software on the user's device alone. This becomes even more prominent in the before-mentioned scenario of a confirmation SMS. Instead of retyping a code, the user is not required to engage at all. It suffices that the user resides at a known location. This leads to further applications such as transparent authentication schemes in which the service authenticates a user continuously.

We split a vicinity key into two components, the measurement component, and the device component. The helper data P forms the device component and the input set forms the measurement component. A fuzzy extractor is constructed such that P leaks only a predefined amount of information about the input set. The input set leaks no information about the helper data. Only in combination do they produce the desired, uniformly random string, the vicinity key. Contrary to the default assumption of fuzzy extractors, we propose for our application to treat both components as confidential.

To derive a key once and again, we distinguish the generation and reproduction phases. In Fig. 2, we give a visual overview of the extraction process of a vicinity key in both phases.

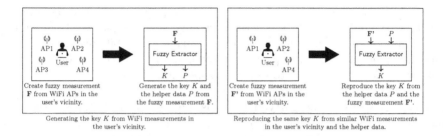

Fig. 2. A visualized overview of LocKey.

Generation Phase. During the generation phase, we scan the environment for a fuzzy measurement $\mathbf{F}$, which we input into the generate function of a fuzzy extractor. Internally, this results in inputting $\mathbf{F}$ into a secure sketch and inputting $\mathbf{F}$ together with freshly generated randomness r into a strong extractor. The secure sketch produces the sketch s, which we combine with r to the helper data $P=(s,r)$. The strong extractor produces the vicinity key K. Due to being based on the fuzzy measurement $\mathbf{F}$, the vicinity key K is location specific. The fuzzy measurement $\mathbf{F}$ forms the measurement component and r, internally created randomness, forms the device component.

Reproduction Phase. During the reproduction phase, we scan the environment for a fuzzy measurement $\mathbf{F'}$. We input $\mathbf{F'}$ and $P = (s, r)$ into the reproduce function of a fuzzy extractor. Internally, this results in inputting $\mathbf{F'}$ and the sketch part s of the helper data P into a reconstruction function which outputs $\mathbf{F}$. This $\mathbf{F}$ forms, together with the r part of the helper data, the input for a strong extractor, which produces the vicinity key K. The vicinity key K is identical to the vicinity key K produced in the generation phase if $\mathbf{F}$ and $\mathbf{F'}$ differ in at most t APs.

The challenging aspect of deriving a key from WiFi measurements is the size of the universe and the fact that we have an unstable amount of APs in each WiFi measurement. Thus, we require for LocKey a solution that can deal with varying input sizes and perform well even in large universes of potential input sizes. However, before we find a fitting solution, we first discuss our goals for LocKey and how it can be utilized.

3.1 Application and Integration Suggestions

We intend to use the vicinity key K derived from the WiFi environment of the user as a claim in an authentication scheme. We discuss the use of LocKey in password hardening and challenge-response-based authentication and present further use cases in Sect. 7. In general a vicinity key can be seen as secure salt with a location component.

Password Hardening. The user extends the entropy in a password by appending the extracted bits from the derived vicinity key. For password hardening, we require only a low amount of entropy; for example, 48 bits may suffice. This application increases the entropy of a password almost for free. The only requirement we impose on a user is to reside in a specific location.

Challenge-Response. The party the user is authenticating towards presents a question (challenge) and the user must provide a valid answer (response). For a challenge-response scheme, we require a higher amount of entropy; 128-bit or 256-bit are standard key sizes. Which key size to choose depends on the context of the authentication and the available entropy at a measured location. A vicinity key K could be used to prove that the environment at a specific location was measured. The two choices of challenge-response authentication are to either use a message authentication code-based approach [23] or an approach that uses asymmetric cryptography and requires the user to sign a message [11].

4 Instantiating LocKey

In this section, we elaborate on the information present in the data and our choices for the fuzzy extractor and its components, the secure sketch, and the strong extractor.

4.1 Data Representation

We build an access-point representation (APR) from the features provided by the AP. To do so, we need to estimate the information conveyed in each feature. The theoretical maximum amount of MAC address information is 48 bits [14], constructed from a 24-bit organizationally unique identifier (OUI) and a 24-bit network interface controller. As MAC addresses are assumed to be unique, we can interpret them as an index of APs. Assuming at least 10-bit for the OUI, the maximum of information has a cap of 2^{34} considering the APs min-entropy. The *min-entropy* is the negative logarithm of the probability of the most likely outcome. We choose the min-entropy, as we need to consider the most conservative entropy estimate for the strong extractor to guarantee the chosen key strength. The definition of min-entropy is:

$$H_{min} = -\log(\max_i p_i)$$

To represent the entropy of an APR in a real measurement, we considered the data observed. We measured only a fraction of potential MAC addresses with a min-entropy of 7.15 bits. We choose one byte as APR length, as we use the extendable output function SHAKE (Secure Hash Algorithm with KEccak [5]) to generate the APR by digesting the plain beacon frame features. We use SHAKE-128 with a security strength of 128 bits when it is sufficient. Also, we show the results for higher security, in which case we opt for SHAKE-256.

4.2   Fuzzy Extractor

We construct our fuzzy extractor as described in Sect. 2.2 by combining a secure sketch with a strong extractor. For the secure sketch, we choose PinSketch [9], and for the strong extractor, we choose the original universal hash function proposed by Carter and Wegman [6].

Secure Sketch. We choose PinSketch as the secure sketch for our instantiation, as it fits our requirements perfectly. PinSketch conducts error correction on a set of elements. It can handle arbitrarily many errors, even though each error it can correct reduces the entropy. Therefore, we choose t, the number of errors to correct, tight on a per-location basis. However, PinSketch is optimal with a loss of $t \, log(n + 1)$. What distinguishes PinSketch from other set-based sketches is that it can handle varying set sizes and can deal with large universes due to its optimized nature.

Assuming a universe $\mathcal{U}$, PinSketch creates a binary vector of $n = |\mathcal{U}|$ bits to represent a set. From there, it becomes equivalent to the error correction of two vectors in that space. The problematic part is the size of the universe $\mathcal{U}$. If it becomes too large, other secure sketches become infeasible. PinSketch uses two tricks to change that. PinSketch stores only the support of a vector and builds on BCH codes for error correction.

Support of a Vector. The support of a vector v, $supp(v)$, lists only the positions on which a vector is nonzero. Using only the support of a vector makes the description of small words very efficient. In the case of fuzzy WiFi measurements, each APR consists of 8 bits. Therefore, we can describe each APR by a vector of size $|APR| = 2^8$. To list all possible APRs and set only the APRs present in a specific WiFi measurement to 1 while all other values are 0 requires a vector of size $2^{|APR|}$. Listing only the positions present is obviously much more efficient.

BCH Codes. BCH codes [13] are a class of cyclic error-correcting codes constructed using polynomials over a finite field. BCH codes can correct multiple-bit errors and provide highly efficient decoding using syndrome decoding. To describe syndrome decoding, we need to dive a bit deeper into the inner workings of linear codes. We assume linear code C and a message x. The length of each code word in C is n, and the dimension of C as a vector subspace is k. To derive a code word $c = Gx$ of the linear code C corresponding to message x, we multiply x with a generator matrix G of size $k \times n$ whose rows form a basis for a linear code. G can be written in the standard form with I_k being the $k \times k$ identity matrix and P being a $k \times (n - k)$ matrix as $G = [I_k|P]$. From G the parity-check matrix H can be constructed as $H = [P^\top|I_{n-k}]$ such that $GH^\top = 0$.

A *syndrome* s of any vector y of the ambient vector space is defined to be $s = Hy^\top$. Due to the construction of H, the syndrome s is zero if and only if the vector y is a code word.

Syndrome decoding makes use of the fact that $Hz = He$, the syndrome of an error pattern e is equal to the syndrome of an observation $z = c + e$ consisting of the code word c observed with this error pattern e, as we know from the definition of a syndrome that $Hc = 0$.

The equality implies that a table of error patterns can be pre-computed. In the case of an observation of a value y, we know that y is no code word if $Hy^\top \neq 0$. Further, we can look up the error pattern in the generated table to retrieve the bits to correct. Deducing and correcting an error can be implemented in logarithmic time complexity.

Both choices make PinSketch quite efficient with time complexity of $poly(|w| \log n)$ [9] and also provide an optimal storage complexity of $t \, log(n+1)$. In words, this means that in a setting capable of correcting up to t errors, for a set w which consists of several $l = log(n + 1)$ bit vectors, a sketch consists of only t binary vectors of length l. $t \, log(n + 1)$ is also the amount of entropy loss, which makes sense as the sketch makes $t \times l$ bits public. The authors of PinSketch focused on the time complexity required. They reduced it to polynomial time based on the set size of the input set $|w|$ and being only logarithmically in the size of the universe n. Most other secure sketch solutions working on sets are time bound by the size of the universe, therefore, being dependent only on the input-set size is an improvement. In the following, we list the workings of PinSketch in the generation and reproduction phase.

Strong Extractor. As a strong extractor, we choose the 2-wise independent family of universal hash function proposed by Carter and Wegman [6], which is defined by:

$$h_{a,b}(x) = ((ax + b) \mod p) \mod m$$

We construct x from hashing all elements, the APRs, of an observed set w, a WiFi measurement $\mathbf{F}$, with SHAKE-128 (respectively SHAKE-256) and create an output of size $|x| \in \{128, 256\}$, based on approved key sizes by the NIST [4]. The output size determines the desired security level. However, the number of APs available determines an upper bound for the security level per location.

PinSketch [9]

Generation phase:
  Input: w, **Output:** s
Compute the syndrome $syn(w)$ of w.
Output the syndrome as sketch $s = syn(w)$.

Reproduction phase:
  Input: w',s, **Output:** w
Compute the syndrome $syn(w')$ of w'.
Compute $\sigma = syn(w) - syn(w')$, the difference between both syndromes.
Find a vector v such that $syn(v) = \sigma$ for which holds that $|supp(v)| \leq t$.
As the vector v is equal to the difference of the inputs $v = w - w'$, output $v + w' = w$.

As we intend to extract sufficient entropy, we choose our universe for hashing U_h depending on the security guarantees desired such that $|U_h| = |x|$.

It applies to the moduli that p must be a prime and $p \geq |U_h|$ and that m specifies the output range of numbers of the strong extractor. As p needs to be larger or equal to the size of the universe, we decide to go for a prime expressible by $2^z - k$ for tuples of $(z, k) \in \{(129, 25), (257, 93)\}$ such that p is greater than U_h, and we have a reasonably tight bound for the coefficients. We randomly choose the coefficients a and b modulo p except for $a \neq 0$. This choice implies that we have two z bit numbers as part of the helper data and hence as the device component of the key. We choose $m = |U_h|$ as we use the strong extractor to get only a uniformly distributed string based on the entropy we derived from our input x.

5   Evaluation

Data sets available online provide MAC addresses and other information. However, they do not include the capability features of WiFi beacon frames, which we need for measuring the environment. Therefore, we created our own, ethics-committee approved, data set from 37 locations measured in offices and flats[1]. We conducted the measurements with ordinary WiFi hardware from laptops (e.g., [15]) in the Linux OS. In total, we measured 1167 different APs in these locations, with the number of APs measured by the sensor varying from 1 to 100 APs in one measurement for the duration of one second. A beacon frame is received every 5 ms to 1 s. This interval is configurable by the user and device-specific. Therefore, not all available APs are present in each measurement.

The main questions are whether there is sufficient entropy at a location, and for how long we need to measure to derive the desired amount of entropy. Both questions must be asked during the generation phase and during the reproduction phase. During the generation phase, we determine the locations suitable for a specific key strength. With the measured duration, we set the stage for the reproduction phase. We discuss the inherent tradeoff and parameter choices later

---

[1] https://gitlab.com/lockey1/scandata.

in this section. During the reproduction phase, we determine the measurements at a location suitable for reconstruction and the duration required to reconstruct successfully.

Generation Phase – Location Suitability. First, we determined what sufficient entropy entails. Recall that we have a set of measurements per location. Each measurement is represented by a set of APs. We represent each AP by an 8-bit APR and each AP contains at least 7.15 bits of entropy we can harvest. The key size as well as the error correction require entropy. The *key size* determines the entropy required to derive a key of the desired size. Hence, we require at least $\lceil 48/7.15 \rceil = 7$ APs to derive the low-entropy key and 18 (respective 35) APs to derive the high-entropy keys of 128 and 256 bits. The *error correction* requires additional entropy. We described in Sect. 4.2 that PinSketch has the optimal amount of entropy loss, $t \, \log(n+1)$ for n being the size of the universe $|\mathcal{U}| = 2^{|APR|}$. As we determined the length of an APR to be 8 bits, the entropy loss is $t * 8$ bits. As each AP has a min-entropy of 7.15 bits we require 1.12 additional APs for each AP to correct.

We considered 37 locations with each a total length of one hour divided into 3600 one-second measurements. We chose the first measurement as starting point for the generation phase. This represents the real-world scenario: a user enters a location and checks whether it is suited for the use of LocKey by starting to measure WiFi signals. With this procedure, we determined the number of locations providing sufficient entropy per desired key strength (see Table 1).

Table 1. The number of locations from our test set of 37 locations from which we can extract sufficient entropy to guarantee the desired key strength with at least one AP to correct using the first measurement as starting point.

No. of suitable locations (out of 37)	Key strength in bits
37	48
25	128
17	256

Generation Phase – Duration. We analyzed our dataset and chose generation-phase measurement lengths of 3, 4, and 5 min for the 48, 128, and 256-bit key extractions. We chose these measurement lengths as they provide sufficient entropy for a maximum of locations with sufficient entropy for error correction. However, at the end of this section, we discuss the implications and other choices.

Reproduction Phase. The helper data generated during the generation phase entails the number of APs and the number of APs we can correct. Therefore, we aggregated measurements until we have sufficient APs to attempt a reconstruction of the generation-phase WiFi measurements. This condition is met as soon as we observe at least the number of APs we are capable to correct subtracted from the total number of APs used in the generation phase. Our choices for measurement times during the generation phase imply that we have $3600 - 180 = 3420$ s of measurements for the 48-bit scenario, 3360 s for the 128-bit scenario, and 3300 s for the 256-bit scenario remaining to analyze the reconstruction capabilities. We chose every measurement of these remaining measurements as starting point and aggregate measurements until the condition is met to attempt a reconstruction.

Reproduction phase – measurement suitability. In Fig. 3 we show the success rate of the attempted reconstructions. Note that missing bars indicate that the specific location has not sufficient entropy for the desired key strengths. We divided the bar plot into three focus areas. We reconstructed the vast majority of locations in more than 99%. For the 48-bit scenario, only locations L11 and L12 had a slightly lower performance than 99% but still more than 98%. For the 128-bit scenario, less locations provide sufficient entropy at all, but only locations L11 and L22 had fewer than 99% of starting points from which we can reconstruct. In the 256-bit scenario, even fewer locations had sufficient entropy, but also most locations had more than 99% of successful reconstructions. Only location L30 had about 98% of correct reconstruction. Locations L11 and L32 are outliers and only allowed for about 75% and 85% of the starting points to reconstruct successfully. These reconstruction performances show that LocKey performs with more than 99% of successful reconstruction for the vast majority of locations and starting measurements.

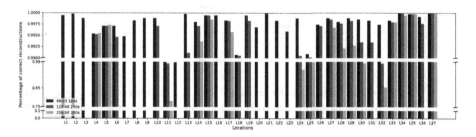

Fig. 3. These bar plots show the reconstruction performance per location for each possible starting measurement in the remaining set of valid measurements for the reproduction phase. Missing bars show that the specific location does not provide sufficient entropy for the location in question. The broken axis allows us to focus on the relevant performances.

Reproduction phase – Duration. The crucial follow-up question is how long it takes to conduct these reconstructions. In Fig. 4, we show box plots to convey the varying length of measurements required. For clarity, we omit the outliers in our visualization. In the 48-bit scenario we observed between 0.7% and 7.1% of outliers at all locations except L7 and L9 with the highest outlier requiring 262 s at location L4. In the 128-bit scenario we observed between 0.02% and 9.3% of outliers at all locations, with the highest outlier requiring 253 s at location

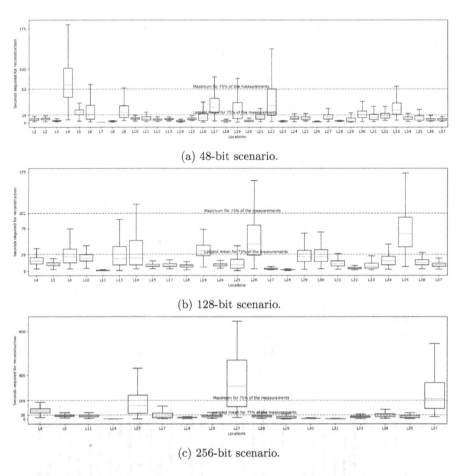

Fig. 4. The three box plots show the required time for reconstructing the set of APs in all scenario. We highlighted the average and maximum time required to reconstruct 75% of the measurements of all locations.

L35. In the 256-bit scenario we observed between 0.3% and 6.4% of outliers at all locations except L27 with the highest outlier requiring 750 s at location L37. Per figure, we show the largest average and maximum time required to restore two-thirds of all measurements. We can reconstruct a set of APs on average for 75% of the measurements in less than 15, 30, and 40 s and require a maximum of 65, 103, and 170 s for the respective key sizes of 48, 128, and 256 bits. We also observed that we require less than three minutes in the 48 and 128 bits scenarios and that for most of the locations five minutes are sufficient for the 256 bits scenario, while two locations require up to 15 min to reconstruct. This is a direct consequence of the 5 min we used in the generation phase. During these 5 min, many APs can be aggregated, which we need to measure before attempting the reconstruction.

Tradeoff. Having longer generation-phase measurements introduces a tradeoff for the reproduction phase. More generation-phase measurements lead to a higher percentage of successful reconstructions, however, require longer measurement times during the reproduction phase for several locations. Less generation-phase measurements imply a shorter measuring duration required during the reproduction phase. This reduced duration implies that the reconstruct is less often successful. From our analysis, we observed that as a bare minimum, we required only generation-phase measurement lengths of 40, 60, and 160 s (for 48, 128, 256-bit key strength scenarios). Choosing these shorter generation-phase measurements, we required less time to gather enough APs during the reconstruction (the outliers in the 256-bit scenario take at most 200 s), which makes sense as we considered fewer measurements. Therefore, we are not required to measure for that long when trying to reconstruct. The disadvantage is that fewer locations provide sufficient entropy. Additionally, the performance drops significantly for some locations as the APs not taken into consideration are still present and could poison our reconstruction attempts.

We determined how long to measure during the generation phase. This impacts the performance and measurement times of the reconstruction phase. We suggest deciding on a per-location basis for an optimal strategy. Looking at the four locations with a mean above 20 s for the 48-bit case in Figure 4a we observed strong signal fluctuations at the location. Therefore, we must also decide on a per-location basis how stable the signals are and whether the signal stability is sufficient for the desired use case.

6   Security Model and Analysis

We consider a user and an adversary. The user conducts WiFi measurements and executes either the generate or reproduce function to construct the vicinity key K. We assume that the user is trusted, that the user's hardware is not compromised, and that the user does not deliberately provide any information to the adversary.

We consider two different scenarios, the first in which the attacker is assumed to have no knowledge of the device component, the helper data P and the second in which the attacker has knowledge of P. We assume for both scenarios that the adversary's goal is to retrieve the vicinity key K.

No access to P Without access to the device component, the adversary is required to guess the correct key K or the WiFi measurements $\mathbf{F}$ the user used during the generation phase and the random coefficients of the strong extractor. Due to our choice of key derivation, the key K is either of size 48-bit, 128-bit, or 256-bit and is uniformly distributed. This implies that an attacker has a chance of $\frac{1}{|K|}$ for $|K| \in \{2^{48}, 2^{128}, 2^{256}\}$ to guess a key correctly.

An adversary could compromise a WiFi capable device near the user, or be on-site to conduct WiFi measurements. However, without knowing the information in the helper data P the adversary has no means to know whether the

WiFi measurement conducted is the WiFi measurement used during the generation phase. Without knowing the random coefficients a and b from the universal hash function, it is infeasible to extract the correct vicinity key K. Therefore, we conclude that an adversary is required to brute force at least the number of bits of the freshly generated vicinity key and that doing so is infeasible.

With access to P This entails that the adversary got access to the user's device and circumvented security mechanisms in place. Traditional standalone solutions (e.g., password or key) would be broken at this point. Therefore, this is a worst-case analysis, which focuses on the question: if the adversary has access to the device component, the helper data P, how likely is it for an adversary to also derive the measurement component? From P the adversary knows a, b, t and $|\mathbf{F}|$. As PinSketch is capable of correcting up to t APs the task at hand for an adversary becomes to sample the correct set of APs such that together with P the vicinity key K can be reconstructed. The minimum set size to have for a correct reconstruction has size $k = |\mathbf{F}| - t$. The chance for an adversary to choose the correct k APRs is $\binom{n}{k}$. The question becomes what the knowledge of the AP composition of the adversary is. We express the adversary's domain knowledge by n. If the adversary has no information, then $n = 2^{48}$, which is the theoretical upper bound from the specification. An adversary with access to a service like Wigle, which lists one billion APs, reduces this number already to $n = 2^{30}$. However, if an adversary is capable of constructing a scan on-site the size of n could be decreased significantly. If the adversary misses only one AP, having observed only $k - 1$ correct APs, the missing AP can be from the whole domain (at least 2^{30}). However, if the adversary happens to measure at least k correct APs the chance becomes smaller. As soon as the adversary scans at least one AP not in the measurement component of size k, the adversary has to try at least k combinations. Therefore, this can be mitigated by asking the service to allow only a strict number of authentication attempts. The only chance the adversary has is to scan k correct APs as $\binom{n}{k} = 1$ for $n = k$. Considering the fluctuation of APs, this is highly improbable and works only if the adversary has access to P and the location's WiFi composition.

7   Discussion

In this section, we discuss our results and its limitation as well as the privacy considerations that come with it.

Results. We deliberately chose the bare minimum of information per APR and showed that all locations provide sufficient entropy in the measurable beacon frames for the scenario of password hardening and that between 46% and 68% percent of the locations provide sufficient entropy to derive a high-entropy key. Further, we showed that we are capable to determine whether LocKey can be applied at a given location and which measurement times we require per specific location.

Limitations. The limitations of our approach are twofold. On the one hand, we observe outliers (Sect. 5), which require long (up to 15 min) reconstruction times. These locations with specific key strengths might not yet be suited for the application of LocKey. On the other hand, we consider WiFi measurements, which are inherently mostly out of the control of the user. Therefore, changes in the AP composition could deny key reconstruction. However, we observe two general and one specific mitigation. First, being capable of correcting t errors gives us some flexibility regarding a changing environment. Second, we assume application only when a fallback mechanism is present. In the case of the password and the challenge-response mechanism, a second factor would enable an alternative confirmation of identity and allow for a re-enrollment with the new WiFi environment.

Local Attacks. Jamming, flooding or AP pool poisoning describes an adversary who deliberately changes the AP environment of a user. This can happen during the generation phase and during the reconstruction phase. Therefore, we assume a trusted generation phase. The system checks anyways that sufficient APs are present. During the reconstruction phase manipulating the WiFi environment could result in a denial of service. As a countermeasure, we have the assumption that LocKey should only be used in conjunction with a fall-back factor.

Privacy. The privacy considerations are relevant as personally identifiable information (PII) is present in the beacon frame. For the features accessible on the Linux OS, the SSID and the MAC address classify as PII. The EU classifies a MAC address belonging to a user, even in its hashed form, as PII [24]. However, it is impossible for an adversary to retrieve the PII because we process the PII only locally and combine it with high entropy randomness. An adversary on-site could conduct a WiFi measurement and obtain the PII, such as every entity conducting WiFi measurements at a specific location. For an adversary, even holding the correct vicinity key K, there is no stable ground truth to derive relevant PII.

8   Related Work

In our work, we use WiFi beacon frame features measured for a certain period to derive a vicinity key by fuzzy extraction. To our knowledge, we are the first to promote the idea of using the semi-volatile signals of a user as key storage from a read-only perspective. We do require that a backup mechanism is present, due to the volatile nature of the signals.

The authors of [1] approach the problem from the perspective of spatial role-based access control and the authors of [7] discuss position-based cryptography also in terms of a user's claimed characteristic. Both are examples of plenty solutions which require control of the sensor and the APs. With these, the authors prove that in the Bounded Retrieval Model position-based secret communication and position-based authentication and signatures are possible. In contrast, we offer the user an increase in security and the reduced burden of a second authentication factor only by access to the sensor. However, we most likely require occasional re-enrollments of the user.

The authors of [3] use error correction to create a shared key separately on two WiFi nodes, focusing on reducing the computation and communication overhead. They achieve this by elevating signal interference. Explicitly, the authors use deep fades, a strong and destructive interference. They measure deep fades occurring in the signal transmitted to the node for a particular duration and encode their occurrence in a bit string. If two nodes are sufficiently close to one another, the bit string is similar enough that both nodes can reconstruct the same key by communicating verification information. The approach presented differs from ours, as two nodes are required to compute the same key, and they create the key from signal interference. Instead, we want to reproduce a key at the same device and location later from information sent in a beacon frame. However, we consider the work sufficiently relevant as might offer a path for future work to look into the information transmitted by the WiFi standard and in interference or error behavior.

The authors of [25] also use WiFi signals to create a shared key between two devices. In their case, two devices are in a body area network. What makes their publication interesting is that it focuses on the RSSI only. They create a fixed-length binary vector between two WiFi devices based on the signal strength of the communication between these two devices. The authors of [2] go one step further and use next to the RSSI, the link quality indicator. Another metric produced by the sensor not by the AP. They show that the method is suited to 'verify the location of an IoT node within a small area with high probability of success'. Using other sensor metrics might help to extend LocKey in the future or use a similar concept on small IoT devices.

Unrelated to fuzzy extractors is the concept of [18] in which the authors fingerprint a location only in terms of WiFi signals. They draw a line between capability and PII aspects of a WiFi beacon frame and recognize a location in terms of only the previously mentioned six capability features available in the Linux OSs. Their work shows that the surrounding WiFi signals accurately define a location. However, they focus on the average entropy by applying the Shannon entropy as they are not required to harvest the entropy for key generation. Hence, they could leave out the higher entropy sources of MAC address and SSID to opt for more privacy, as they intend to share a template of the WiFi location with a service to allow for authentication which requires a heightened focus on PII.

9   Conclusion

The signals in a user's environment provide sufficient reconstructable information to derive a key even when having access only to the sensor and focusing only on particular WiFi features. The density of the electromagnetic signals determines the amount of information that is extractable at a location. We showed that it is possible to extract the information once and also to some certainty *reconstruct* the extracted information. However, it is possible that the required composition is not achievable. Therefore, we focused only on use cases with a fallback mechanism in place. We further showed that combining the measured component with the device component in a secure extraction step generates uniformly random key material. The extent to which we can successfully extract a key is dependent on the location. We were able to extract a low-entropy key of 48-bit for all locations we considered. Extracting a 128-bit key succeeded for nearly 68% of the locations while extracting a 256-bit key succeeded for nearly 46% of the locations we considered.

Future work includes applying LocKey in practice, to increase the entropy available and to decrease the measurement time. More WiFi data could be captured to increase the entropy available and decrease the measurement time. This can either be achieved by including more features like the RSSI or by deriving different stable features from the beacon frame. Additionally, different data sources can be used to extract the required entropy. Different aspects of WiFi could be gathered, e.g., interference or error behavior as done by [3] or WiFi could be used to read other signals in the user's vicinity as done by [19]. Next to WiFi, different wireless data sources like Bluetooth, Lora, or alike can be aggregated. Finally, we expect a 'natural' increase in electromagnetic signals available over time due to the adaptation of more wireless devices, which increases the applicability of authentication-factor extensions like LocKey.

References

1. Agudo, I., Rios, R., Lopez, J.: A privacy-aware continuous authentication scheme for proximity-based access control. Comput. Secur. **39**, 117–126 (2013)
2. Aman, M.N., Basheer, M.H., Sikdar, B.: Two-factor authentication for IoT with location information. IEEE Internet Things J. **6**(2), 3335–3351 (2018)
3. Azimi-Sadjadi, B., Kiayias, A., Mercado, A., Yener, B.: Robust key generation from signal envelopes in wireless networks. In: Proceedings of the 14th ACM Conference on Computer and Communications Security, pp. 401–410 (2007)
4. Barker, E., Dang, Q.: Nist special publication 800–57 part 1, revision 5: Recommendation for key management: Part 1-general, May 2020. Cited on, page 58 (2020)
5. Bertoni, G., Daemen, J., Peeters, M., Van Assche, G.: The keccak sponge function family: Specifications summary (2011). http://keccak.noekeon.org/specs_summary.html
6. Carter, J.L., Wegman, M.N.: Universal classes of hash functions. In: Proceedings of the Ninth Annual ACM Symposium on Theory of Computing, pp. 106–112 (1977)
7. Chandran, N., Goyal, V., Moriarty, R., Ostrovsky, R.: Position based cryptography. In: Halevi, S. (ed.) CRYPTO 2009. LNCS, vol. 5677, pp. 391–407. Springer, Heidelberg (2009). https://doi.org/10.1007/978-3-642-03356-8_23
8. Cho, Y., Bao, L., Goodrich, M.T.: LAAC: a location-aware access control protocol. In: 2006 3rd Annual International Conference on Mobile and Ubiquitous Systems-Workshops, pp. 1–7 (2006)
9. Dodis, Y., Reyzin, L., Smith, A.: Fuzzy extractors: how to generate strong keys from biometrics and other noisy data. In: Cachin, C., Camenisch, J.L. (eds.)

EUROCRYPT 2004. LNCS, vol. 3027, pp. 523–540. Springer, Heidelberg (2004). https://doi.org/10.1007/978-3-540-24676-3_31

10. Fakhreddine, A., Tippenhauer, N.O., Giustiniano, D.: Design and large-scale evaluation of WiFi proximity metrics. In: European Wireless 2018; 24th European Wireless Conference, pp. 1–6. VDE (2018)

11. Foti, J.: Entity authentication using public key cryptography (1997)

12. GNOME. org.freedesktop.networkmanager.accesspoint (2021). https://developer. gnome.org/NetworkManager/1.2/gdbus-org.freedesktop.NetworkManager. AccessPoint.html

13. Hocquenghem, A.: Codes correcteurs d'erreurs. Chiffers **2**, 147–156 (1959)

14. IEEE Standard. Wireless lan medium access control (mac)and physical layer (phy) specifications (2007). https://www.iith.ac.in/~tbr/teaching/docs/802.11-2007.pdf

15. Intel. Dual band wireless-ac 8265 (2021). https://ark.intel.com/content/www/us/ en/ark/products/94150/intel-dual-band-wireless-ac-8265.html

16. ISO 27000. Information technology, security techniques, information security management systems, overview andvocabulary (2018)

17. Jagadeesan, A., Thillaikkarasi, T., Duraiswamy, K.: Cryptographic key generation from multiple biometric modalities: fusing minutiae with iris feature. Int. J. Comput. Appl. **2**(6), 16–26 (2010)

18. Jakubeit, P., Peter, A., van Steen, M.: The measurable environment as nonintrusive authentication factor on the example of WiFi beacon frames. In: Saracino, A., Mori, P. (eds.) ETAA 2022. LNCS, vol. 13782, pp. 48–69. Springer, Cham (2022). https://doi.org/10.1007/978-3-031-25467-3_4

19. Jeong, W., et al.: SDR receiver using commodity wifi via physical-layer signal reconstruction. In: Proceedings of the 26th Annual International Conference on Mobile Computing and Networking, pp. 1–14 (2020)

20. Juels, A., Sudan, M.: A fuzzy vault scheme. Des. Codes Crypt. **38**(2), 237–257 (2006)

21. Li, G., Bours, P.: Studying WiFi and accelerometer data based authentication method on mobile phones. In: Proceedings of the 2018 2nd international Conference on Biometric Engineering and Applications, pp. 18–23 (2018)

22. Lohr, C.: A WebGL-based raytraced voxel engine with transparency of WiFi signal over a 360mm x 360mm x 180mm area (2016). https://cnlohr.github.io/ voxeltastic/

23. Turner, J.M.: The keyed-hash message authentication code (HMAC). Federal Inf. Process. Standards Publ. **198**(1), 1–13 (2008)

24. WP29. Opinion 01/2017 on the proposed regulation for the eprivacy regulation (2002/58/ec). (2017). http://ec.europa.eu/newsroom/document.cfm?doc_ id=44103

25. Yang, W., Sun, Y., Zhan, L., Ji, Y.: Low mismatch key agreement based on wavelet-transform trend and fuzzy vault in body area network. Int. J. Distrib. Sens. Netw. **9**(6), 912873 (2013)

26. Yang, C., Shao, H.-R.: WiFi-based indoor positioning. IEEE Commun. Mag. **53**(3), 150–157 (2015)

BAHS: A Blockchain-Aided Hash-Based Signature Scheme

Yalan Wang⬤, Liqun Chen$^{(\boxtimes)}$⬤, Long Meng⬤, and Yangguang Tian⬤

University of Surrey, Guildford, UK
liqun.chen@surrey.ac.uk

Abstract. Hash-based one-time signatures are becoming increasingly important as they are post-quantum safe and have been used in multi-cast communication and other applications. However, managing the state of such signatures can present a significant challenge, as signers are typically responsible for ensuring that the state cannot be reused. Recently, blockchain, as a public platform, is used to design revocation management and status verification systems. While blockchain revocation is attractive, many well-known blockchains make use of ECDSA as their underlying signature scheme, and this is not post-quantum safe. Researchers have been working on replacing ECDSA with post-quantum signature schemes but they are much more costly. In this paper, we introduce a new one-time signature scheme, called Blockchain-Aided Hash-based Signature (BAHS), in which a hash-based commitment scheme acts as the building block, and signers' commitments and opened commitments are publicly accessible via a distributed blockchain. A signature is formed from the commitment/opened commitment and blockchain. Unlike existing blockchain systems, the commitment in BAHS is simpler than that in most existing hash-based one-time signature schemes or other post-quantum signature schemes. We provide a formal security model for the BAHS scheme and give the security proof. Finally, we have implemented our BAHS scheme and the result shows its practicality.

Keywords: Digital signature · Hash function · Blockchain · Cryptographic protocols

1 Introduction

Digital signatures are a cryptographic primitive for verifying the authenticity of digital data. A one-time hash-based signature, as proposed by Lamport in [21], is a special type of digital signature, in which each signing key can be used only once and one-way functions without trapdoors are applied. One-time hash-based signatures can be used in multi-cast communications, such as wireless sensor networks [26] and smart grids [24]. In these applications, signatures are used to achieve demand response, operation and control. The deployment of hash-based one-time signature schemes faces a significant challenge, i.e., state management. This refers to the process of ensuring that a signature cannot be reused.

© The Author(s), under exclusive license to Springer Nature Singapore Pte Ltd. 2023
W. Meng et al. (Eds.): ISPEC 2023, LNCS 14341, pp. 419–439, 2023.
https://doi.org/10.1007/978-981-99-7032-2_25

The problem of state management was discussed in [15]. A comprehensive assessment of the security impact of reusing a one-time signature private key was provided in [9]. Based on the research on this topic, ISO/IEC 14888-4 2nd Committee Draft [2] provides the following recommendations to implement robust state management mechanisms:

- The state used in hash-based one-time signatures is a piece of information, which should be stored, maintained, and updated for the whole lifespan of the private key.
- One way to reduce the chances of state reuse is to prevent the copy or extraction of the private key from the signing module. Assuming this way can be guaranteed, the issue of state management is simplified to a single signing environment, rather than having to manage multiple signing environments. Consequently, the problem of state management is replaced by a more intricate issue: the state synchronization problem.
- During the signing, the signer will first update the state and then start the signing procedure. If this process was done in a reverse order, there is a risk that the signature is produced but the state remains in its previous value.

In accordance with these recommendations, a signer is responsible for ensuring state management. Nevertheless, the signer may either lack the ability or may not be trustworthy enough to assume full responsibility.

Recently, blockchain is used to design revocation management and status verification systems [3,13]. In these blockchain-based systems, the blockchain acts as data storage. During signature verification, verifiers must examine the key status to determine if the signer has been revoked or not. Obviously, a risk is that a malicious signer will not revoke their key. As a result, these blockchain-based schemes are still unable to effectively implement state management. Recently, in [23], they took the public ledger to assist the threshold signature scheme and the state management, but the underlying signature scheme is based on classical signature algorithms, which is complicated and not post-quantum secure. Generally, most existing blockchains make use of a traditional signature scheme, ECDSA, or its variants, e.g., [8,25], as an underlying signature scheme. This type of signature scheme is not post-quantum secure. Recently, NIST has announced to standardize three post-quantum signatures, Dilithium [20], Falcon [7] and SPHINCS+ [11]. They are being considered to replace the traditional RSA- and EC-based signatures. There has been some research on considering the use of post-quantum secure signatures in blockchains (cryptocurrency) [7,11,12,14]. However, based on the result of Holmes' work [17], all the well-known post-quantum signatures are quite expensive to be implemented in blockchains.

Now, the question is whether we can use the state verification capability in a blockchain to create a simpler one-time signature scheme. In this paper, by leveraging the Merkle tree in the blockchain to generate commitments, we enable state management through the public accessibility of keys, commitments/opened commitments. Therefore, we develop a straightforward post-quantum one-time signature scheme. We call this new scheme *blockchain-aided hash-based signature* (BAHS). In the BAHS scheme, there are three types of entities, a set of signers, a blockchain, and a set of verifiers. To sign a message m using the signing key sk, the signer creates a commitment input $cInput$ ($cInput = H(m,\ sk)\|H(sk)$) and sends it to a blockchain. Before accepting this input, the blockchain checks whether the signing key has been used before. If not, $cInput$ will be appended to the blockchain to be time-stamped and the commitment com is formed. At a later time (block), the signer needs to open the commitment by sending the input $oInput$, $oInput = (m, sk, cInput)$ to the blockchain. And the opened commitment on the blockchain is denoted by $\widetilde{com}$. Finally, com and $\widetilde{com}$ form a signature. During verification, the verifier retrieves the signature from the blockchain and checks whether the signature is valid or not. The aid of the blockchain guarantees the key state management in the scheme.

Our contributions can be summarized as follows:

- We propose a BAHS scheme, which is the first hash-based one-time signature scheme that achieves key state management without entirely relying on the signer.
- Our BAHS scheme only makes use of hash functions and blockchain (Merkle tree) to generate the commitment, which is post-quantum secure and more efficient and simpler than traditional signatures and other post-quantum signatures.
- We introduce a formal definition of the security model for our proposed BAHS scheme and provide concrete security proof. This security analysis indicates that the BAHS scheme holds the properties of correctness and unforgeability.
- We provide a proof of concept implementation of the BAHS scheme. The implementation and evaluation confirm its practicality.

The rest of this paper is structured as follows. We introduce preliminaries in Sect. 2. We present the syntax for a generic BAHS scheme in Sect. 3. Based on the generic BAHS definition, we present our BAHS scheme in detail in Sect. 4. In Sect. 5, we introduce the security model and provide the security proof. In Sect. 6, implementation results are given. Finally, in Sect. 7, we present the conclusion.

2 Preliminaries

2.1 Hash Functions

Definition 1. *A secure hash function maps a string of bits of variable length (but usually upper bounded) to a fixed-length string of bits.*

The properties of hash functions are one-wayness, second preimage-resistance and collision-resistance [1], which are described as follows:

- **One-wayness.** Given a hash function H and a hash value $H(m)$, it is computationally infeasible to get the input message m.
- **Second Preimage-resistance.** Given a hash value $H(m)$ of a message m, it is computationally infeasible to find a second input m' which maps to the same output $H(m)$.
- **Collision-resistance.** Given a Hash function H, it is computationally infeasible to find a pair of messages m and m' to make $H(m) = H(m')$.

2.2   Commitment Scheme

In a commitment scheme [10,19], there are two phases, i.e., committing and opening. Here we give a definition of these two phases as follows:

- Committing: To commit a data string b, the prover P chooses r randomly $r \leftarrow \{0,1\}^l$ and computes the commitment $com \leftarrow$ commit(r, b), where commit is a function:$\{0,1\}^l \times \{0,1\}^l \rightarrow \{0,1\}^l$. Then the prover can send com to the verifier V.
- Opening: The prover can reveal r, b to the verifier V. Then the verifier V computes $com' =$ commit(r, b) and checks whether $com' = com$ or not.

Hash functions can be used to design commitment scheme [4,6]. In our scheme, we follow the Merkle tree method to compute signers' commitments.

2.3   Blockchains

A blockchain is a distributed digital blockchain of signed transactions that are grouped into blocks. As shown in Fig. 1, a block header contains a block index number bid_i, a nonce non_i, a hash value of the previous block header hbh_{i-1}, a time-stamp ts_i, and a Merkle tree root r_i of all block data. The block data contains a list of transactions along with their corresponding digital signatures. The generation of block b_i and the process of connecting with the block b_{i+1} are described as follows:

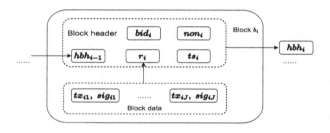

Fig. 1. A general block structure for a blockchain

- Assume there are J transactions in block i, each transaction $tx_{ij} (j \in [1, J])$ is signed using a signature scheme SIG, i.e., $sig_{ij} \leftarrow SIG(tx_{ij})$. Then block data bd_i, i.e., $bd_i = ([tx_{i1}, sig_{i1}], ..., [tx_{iJ}, sig_{iJ}])$.
- The consensus nodes aggregate bd_i with a Merkle Tree (MT) by using a hash function H. i.e., $r_i \leftarrow MT(H; bd_i)$. Then consensus nodes calculate the hash value hbh_{i-1} of the previous block header bh_{i-1}, i.e., $hbh_{i-1} = H(bh_{i-1})$.
- The block header bh_i is formed, i.e., $bh_i = (hbh_{i-1}, r_i, bid_i, non_i, ts_i)$. The block b_i is formed as $b_i = (bd_i, bh_i)$.
- The consensus nodes calculate the hash value of the block header of the block b_i, $hbh_i = H(bh_i)$, which is recorded in the next block b_{i+1}.

Then the process of calculating the hash value of the block header hbh_i using a blockchain algorithm Blc is defined as follows:

$$(a_p, \ hbh_i) \leftarrow Blc(..., [tx_{ip}, \ sig_{ip}], ...)$$

where $p \in [1, \ J]$ and a_p is the authentication path from the transaction $[tx_{ip}, \ sig_{ip}]$ to hbh_i.

Blockchain Integrity. Let a blockchain be an entity that maintains an auditable database **L**. We model the capability of an adversary against a blockchain as corrupted users or power-limited consensus nodes (no more than 49% malicious nodes). A successful adversary could launch the following attacks that bypass the blockchain auditing check:

- **Tampering attack.** The adversary changes, adds, or removes information in the blockchain without being audited.
- **Back-dating attack.** The adversary claims any non-existed information on the blockchain.

Then we define the data integrity property of **L** as follows:

Definition 2. *A blockchain **L** holds data integrity, if for any Probabilistic Polynomial Time (PPT) adversary $\mathcal{A}$, the probability of making either a tampering attack or a back-dating attack is negligible.*

2.4 Quantum Random Oracle

In this scheme, we are concerned with its post-quantum security. On a classical computer, we can model a hash function as an random oracle F. Based on Boneh's work [5], hash functions used in this work meet the *history free* reduction. Therefore, we can model the hash function as a quantum random oracle. Formally, for the case of an random oracle F, executions of the unitaries describing the adversary are interleaved with executions of an oracle unitary:

$$\mathcal{O}_f : \sum_{x,y} \alpha_{x,y} \, |x\rangle \, |y\rangle \rightarrow \sum_{x,y} \alpha_{x,y} \, |x\rangle \, |y \oplus f(x)\rangle . \tag{1}$$

For q queries, the adversary is described by a sequence of unitaries $U_0,...,U_q$ and executed as $U_q \mathcal{O}_f U_{q-1} \mathcal{O}_f ... \mathcal{O}_f U_0 \, |0\rangle$.

3   Generic Definitions for a Blockchain-Aided Hash-Based Signature Scheme (BAHS)

Let $com = \mathsf{commit}(sk, m)$ be a hash-based commitment scheme. The function of commit can be realized by the Merkle tree in the blockchain. The main concept behind our one-time signature scheme is for a signer to commit to both the private signing key and the message and store the commitment on one block of a blockchain. At a later time, the signer opens the commitment with the message and private key and stores the opened commitment on another block of the blockchain. Each signer's commitment and opened commitment form a signature, which can then be verified by anyone who can access the blockchain. In our BAHS scheme, each block generation happens at a time epoch. Authentication of signers is application-oriented, i.e., some applications only allow legitimate users to submit their keys and signatures; some applications allow any users to do so. The choice of user authentication is out the scope of this paper.

3.1 Notation

The notation is listed in Table 1.

Table 1. Notation used in the BAHS scheme

Notation	Meaning
$\mathcal{S}$	signer space
$i \in \mathcal{S}$	signer identity
sk_i	signer i's signing key
pk_i	signer i's public key
m_i	message to be signed by i
$cInput_i$	signer i's commitment input
$oInput_i$	signer i's opened commitment input
com_i	signer i's commitment
$\tilde{com}_i$	signer's opened commitment
σ_i	signer i's signature
β	epoch index associated with a block in the blockchain
$\mathbf{L}_\beta$	blockchain database from the genesis block to β-th block

BAHS Players. A BAHS scheme consists of three types of players: a **blockchain**, a set of **signers**, and a set of **verifiers**.

- By maintaining its database $\mathbf{L}$, the blockchain aids signers by storing their commitments, opened commitments and signatures. The blockchain also maintains the status information of those commitments.
- Let $\mathcal{S}$ be the space of signers. Given a message m_i, a signer $i \in \mathcal{S}$ generates their one-time secret signing key sk_i, input $cInput_i$ to commitment com_i and $oInput_i$ input to the opened commitment $\tilde{com}_i$ and submits $cInput_i$ and $oInput_i$ to the blockchain in two different blocks. The outputs on the blockchain can become com_i and $\tilde{com}_i$, respectively. Finally, signature is $\sigma_i = (cInput_i, com_i, oInput_i, \tilde{com}_i)$.
- A verifier retrieves a signature from the blockchain and verifies the signature.

BAHS Key Management. Let $\mathcal{S}_\beta \subset \mathcal{S}$ be the set of signers whose commitments have appeared in the blockchain's database up to the start of epoch β. The blockchain maintains information about the status of $cInput_i$ (because it is computed by signing key sk_i), $i \in \mathcal{S}_\beta$, for each epoch β, and this information is denoted by info_β^i. We write info_β for the set of all these info_β^i with different i and info^i for the set of all these info_β^i with different β. We give the definition of info_β as follows:

Definition 3. *The key status information* info_β *can be retrieved from the blockchain. It can be used to obtain the status,* status_β^i, *of any given* $cInput_i$. *This status will be as follows :*

$$\mathsf{status}_\beta^i \in \{(cInput_i, +), (cInput_i, -), (cInput_i, \bot)\},$$

where $(cInput_i, +)$ *means that* $cInput_i$ *has been submitted to the blockchain and the signer* i *is allowed to sign,* $(cInput_i, -)$ *means that* $cInput_i$ *has been submitted to the blockchain but the signer* i *is not allowed to sign,* $(cInput_i, \bot)$ *means that* $cInput_i$ *has not yet been submitted to the blockchain.*

3.2 Description of a Generic Construction of BAHS

A generic construction of BAHS is described in a timeline with multiple epochs and it consists of the following algorithms/protocols. Note that during signing, the signer will generate the signing key and message to be signed, in which both sk and m are random numbers.

- Setup(1^λ) $\rightarrow$ $(pp, \mathsf{info}_0, \mathbf{L})$: In epoch 0, the blockchain nodes run the Setup algorithm by taking as input a security parameter λ and outputting the system parameters pp, the initial system information info_0 and database $\mathbf{L}$.
- Sign$\{\beta, \mathsf{info}_\beta, (sk_i, m_i)_{i \in [Q]}, \mathbf{L}_\beta\} \rightarrow (\sigma_i, \mathbf{L}_{\beta+1}, \mathsf{info}_{\beta+1})$: In epoch β, a set of Q users and the blockchain nodes run the Sign protocol as follows. We assume $Q = M + N$, M is the number of users submitting the commitment onto the blockchain, N is the number of users opening their commitment onto the blockchain. The nodes take as inputs system information info_β, and the database $\mathbf{L}_\beta$. A user is in one of the two following stages:
  1. Committing. For a user i_b ($i_b \in [M]$), who wants to commit, given a private key sk_{i_b} and a message m_{i_b}, he/she computes the input to the commitment $cInput_{i_b}$ and submits it to the blockchain. If $cInput_{i_b}$ does not exist on the blockchain database $\mathbf{L}$, the blockchain nodes will record it and the record of this transaction is called commitment com_{i_b}.
  2. Opening. To make a signature publicly verifiable, user $j_d \in [N]$ releases sk_{j_d} on the blockchain to open the commitment. Upon receiving sk_{j_d}, the blockchain nodes check the status of $cInput_{j_d}$. If sk_{j_d} has not been used before, the blockchain nodes store $oInput_{j_d} = (cInput_{j_d}, m_{j_d}, sk_{j_d})$ to the blockchain datebase $\mathbf{L}$, and the record of this transaction is called opened commitment $\tilde{com}_{j_d}$.

After the signing protocol, the outputs include a signature $\sigma_i = (cInput, com_i, oInput, \tilde{com}_i)$, the updated database $\mathbf{L}_{\beta+1}$, in which public information for verification forms signer i's public key pk_i, and system information $\mathsf{info}_{\beta+1}$ for the next epoch. From a signer's view, the Committing and Opening stages are run in sequence in two different blocks. From the blockchain's view, these two stages are run simultaneously in every block for different signers.

- Verify$(\sigma_i, \mathsf{info}^i) \to 0/1$: In any epoch after a signature σ_i is generated and available on the blockchain database $\mathbf{L}$, a verifier can retrieve σ_i together with the system information info^i and verify it. The verifier outputs 0 for rejecting the signature and 1 for accepting it.

3.3 Security Model for BAHS

We adopt a security model modified based on [18] for the BAHS scheme. The capability of an adversary against the BAHS scheme can be modeled as corrupted signers who can generate signing keys by themselves or outside attackers who cannot obtain signing keys. A successful adversary can launch any one of the following attacks:

- Tampering attack. The adversary changes, adds, or deletes existing records on the blockchain.
- Forging attack. The adversary claims a valid signature that is generated or released by an entity using a signing key more than once or is not generated by an entity.

The security of a BAHS scheme can be captured through two properties: correctness and unforgeability. The unforgeability is defined as an experiment, which is performed between an adversary $\mathcal{A}$ and a challenger $\mathcal{C}$. Several global variables are used in experiments: h records the honest signer, M is the number of signers who are invoked in the experiment, and K is the number of honest signers who attempt to submit commitments onto the blockchain. β_{Current} and β_{Revoke} denote the current epoch as well as the epoch in which the honest signer is revoked. $\mathcal{R}$ is the set of signers to be revoked. The adversary can access the blockchain database $\mathbf{L}$ and the system information info_β for any epoch β.

Note that we need to model hash functions as oracles. It is common practice to model hash functions as random oracles [22], specifically, with a random value space, and a table T to record values. Furthermore, Boneh *et al.* [5] formalized the notion of quantum-accessible random oracle model (QROM), where the adversary can query the classical random oracle (RO) with quantum states. They introduced a concept called history-free reduction, showing that certain lattice-based schemes in the random oracle model (ROM) can be proven secure in QROM, such as GPV'08 [16]. Specifically, if a simulator can decide the classical RO answers independently of the history of previous queries, then it implies security in the QROM. Therefore, in our scheme, the hash function can be modeled as a quantum random oracle because it meets the *history-free* reduction requirements and the scheme can be proved post-quantum secure. A simple definition of executions in quantum random oracle is given in Sect. 2.4.

Correctness. In general, correctness means a signature generated by an honest signer should always be valid (if the signer has not been revoked). We give the definition of correctness as follows:

Definition 4. *A BAHS scheme is correct that we get the result* $1 \leftarrow$ Verify$(\sigma_i, info^i)$, *where* λ *is the security parameter, if* $(info_{\beta+1}, L_{\beta+1}, \sigma_i) \leftarrow$ Sign $\{\beta, info_\beta, (sk_i, m_i)_{i \in [Q]}, L_\beta\}$ *and* $(pp, info_0, L) \leftarrow$ Setup(1^λ).

Unforgeability. It means that the adversary can corrupt any number of signers except for one honest signer h. The adversary can query signatures from h on any messages at the adversary's choice, but can not generate a new valid signature of h. The adversary can generate a valid signature σ_i for a corrupted signer i but this signature generation must be with the assistance of the blockchain. Formally, unforgeability is defined as an experiment in Fig. 2.

Experiment $Exp_{BAHS,\mathcal{A}}^{Unforge}(\lambda)$

- $h = \perp$; $iS = \emptyset$; $cS = \emptyset$.
- $(pp, \mathbf{L}, info_0) \leftarrow$ Setup(1^λ), $\mathbf{L} = \emptyset$, $info_0 = \emptyset$.
- $(\mathbf{L}_{\beta+1}, \sigma_i, info_{\beta+1}) \leftarrow \mathcal{A}^{AddHU,AddCU,Update,Revoke,H}(pp, \mathbf{L}, info_0)$
- If $i = h$:
  - If $(cInput_h, m) \in iS \wedge (\sigma_h, m) \in cS$ return 0.
- Else:
  - If $(\sigma_i, m) \in cS$ return 0.
- Return Verify$(\sigma_i, info^i)$.

Fig. 2. The unforgeability experiment for the BAHS scheme

The adversary can have access to the following oracles and the details of oracles are shown in Fig. 6 in Appendix A. We present details of the random oracle **H** and it can be modelled as the corresponding quantum random oracle following the definition in Sect. 2.4.

- **AddHU()**: This oracle allows the adversary to add a single honest signer in the experiment. In each call, this oracle executes the submission of the commitment onto the blockchain by simulating the honest signer and the blockchain. This oracle can be called at most $k(\lambda)$ times where $k(\cdot)$ is any polynomial. Once the commitment is submitted successfully, further calls will be ignored. This oracle only returns the honest signer's input to the commitment $cInput_h$.

- **AddCU**(i, $cInput_i$): This oracle allows the adversary to add a corrupt signer i to the system. The adversary can choose the corrupted signer's signing key sk_i and the corresponding input $cInput_i$ to the commitment.
- **Revoke**($\mathcal{R}$): This oracle allows the adversary to update the information list from $\text{info}_{\beta_{\text{Current}}}$ to $\text{info}_{\beta_{\text{Current}+1}}$, by revoking the set of signers $\mathcal{R}$ and keeping the remaining. If h is revoked in this oracle query, set β_{Revoke} to β_{Current}.
- **Update**(): This oracle allows the adversary to query the signature associated with a signer i which is recorded in the list cS. Note that the signer i can be an honest signer h or a corrupted signer $i \neq h$, who was created by the adversary via the **AddCU**(i, $cInput_i$) oracle.
- **H**(): On input a string x, the oracle checks if x has been queried before. If yes, it returns $T[x]$. If no, a random string h can be returned and be recorded as $T[x] = h$.

Based on the above definitions, we define unforgeability as follows:

Definition 5. *A BAHS scheme is unforgeable, if for any p.p.t. (quantum) adversary $\mathcal{A}$, the following condition holds:*

$$\Pr\left[\text{Exp}_{BAHS,\mathcal{A}}^{Unforge}(1^\lambda) = 1\right] \leq \text{negl}(\lambda) \tag{2}$$

4 The Blockchain-Aided Hash-Based Signature Scheme (BAHS)

We now present a concrete BAHS scheme. In this scheme, we need the following three extra hash functions: $H_1 : \{0,1\}^\lambda \rightarrow \{0,1\}^l$; $H_2 : \{0,1\}^* \times \{0,1\}^\lambda \rightarrow \{0,1\}^l$; $H_3 : \{0,1\}^l \times \{0,1\}^l \times \{0,1\}^\lambda \times \{0,1\}^* \rightarrow \{0,1\}^l$, where λ is the system security level and l is the length of hash outputs. It is required that H_1, H_2, and H_3 hold the properties of one-wayness and collision-resistance. Note that in this scheme, the key status information can be instantiated by the status of $H_1(sk)$, which is part of the input $cInput$. In the following proof, we will apply this instantiation.

4.1 BAHS Algorithms/Protocols

Following the BAHS syntax in Sect. 3.2, the concrete BAHS algorithms/protocols are instantiated in detail as follows:

---

protocol 1: Sign protocols for BAHS

Input: β, **L**, $info_\beta$, $cInput_{[M]}$, $oInput_{[N]}$, /* $(M, N) \in \mathbb{N} \times \mathbb{N}$, $[M] = \{i_1, \ldots, i_M\}$,
$[N] = \{j_1, \ldots, j_N\}$, $(i_b, j_d) \in \mathcal{S} \times \mathcal{S}$, $[M] \cap [N] = \emptyset$. */
Output: **L** (updated), $info_{\beta+1}$.

1 initiate $info_{\beta+1} = \emptyset$, $z_{[M+N]} = \emptyset$; /* A set storing leaf values */
2 initiate $a_{[M+N]} = \emptyset$; /* A set storing authentication path */
3 initiate $r_\beta = \emptyset$; /* This is used to store the root value. */, /*
    $status_\beta^k \in \{(H_1(sk_k), +), (H_1(sk_k), -), (H_1(sk_k), \perp)\}$*/.
4 $\forall k \in \mathcal{S}_\beta$, set $info_{\beta+1}^k = info_\beta^k$;
5 **for** $b = 1;\ b \le M;\ b{+}{+}$ **do**
6 $\quad$ initiate $\sigma_{i_b} = \emptyset$;
7 $\quad$ obtain $status_\beta^{i_b}$ from $info_\beta^{i_b}$; /* $A = H_1(sk_{i_b})$ and $B = H_2(m_{i_b}, sk_{i_b})$. */
8 $\quad$ parse $cInput_{i_b} = A||B$;
9 $\quad$ **if** $status_\beta^{i_b} = (A, \perp)$ **then**
10 $\quad\quad$ | set $status_{\beta+1}^{i_b} = (A, +)$, $\sigma_{i_b} = \sigma_{i_b} \cup cInput_{i_b}$; compute $z_b = H_2(cInput_{i_b})$;
11 $\quad$ **else**
12 $\quad\quad$ | reject this entry;
13 $\quad$ **end**
14 **end**
15 **for** $d = 1;\ d \le N;\ d{+}{+}$ **do**
16 $\quad$ initiate $\sigma_{j_d} = \emptyset$, $num.H_1(sk_{j_d}) = 0$, /* $num.H_1(sk_{j_d})$ is the number of $H_1(sk_{j_d})$; */;
    $\quad$ obtain $status_\beta^{j_d}$ from $info_\beta^{j_d}$; /* $C = H_1(sk_{j_d})$, $D = H_2(m_{j_d}, sk_{j_d})$, $E = sk_{j_d}$, and
    $\quad$ $F = m_{j_d}$; */
17 $\quad$ parse $oInput_{j_d} = C||D||E||F$;
18 $\quad$ **if** $status_\beta^{j_d} = (C, \perp) \vee (C, -)$ **then**
19 $\quad\quad$ | reject this entry;
20 $\quad$ **else**
21 $\quad\quad$ **if** $status_\beta^{j_d} = (C, +)$ **then**
22 $\quad\quad\quad$ | retrieve $cInput_{j_d} = C||D'$ from **L**;
23 $\quad\quad$ **else**
24 $\quad\quad\quad$ **if** $D = D' \wedge H_1(E) = C \wedge H_2(F, E) = D$ **then**
25 $\quad\quad\quad\quad$ | $num.H_1(sk_{j_d}){+}{+}$;
26 $\quad\quad\quad$ **else**
27 $\quad\quad\quad\quad$ | reject this entry;
28 $\quad\quad\quad$ **end**
29 $\quad\quad$ **end**
30 $\quad\quad$ **if** $num.H_1(sk_{j_d}) == 1$ **then**
31 $\quad\quad\quad$ | set $status_{\beta+1}^{j_d} = (C, -)$;
32 $\quad\quad\quad$ | set $\sigma_{j_d} = \sigma_{j_d} \cup oInput_{j_d}$;
33 $\quad\quad\quad$ | compute $z_{d+M} = H_3(oInput_{j_d})$;
34 $\quad\quad$ **else**
35 $\quad\quad\quad$ | reject this entry;
36 $\quad\quad$ **end**
37 $\quad$ **end**
38 **end**
39 compute a block β by using the Blc algorithm: $(a_i, hbh_\beta) \leftarrow Blc(z_1, \ldots, z_i, \ldots, z_{M+N})$;
40 **for** $b = 1;\ b \le M;\ b{+}{+}$ **do**
41 $\quad$ | set $\sigma_{i_b} = \sigma_{i_b} \cup z_b \cup a_b \cup hbh_\beta$; **L**=**L**$\cup\sigma_{i_b}$;
42 **end**
43 **for** $d = 1;\ d \le N;\ d{+}{+}$ **do**
44 $\quad$ | set $\sigma_{j_d} = \sigma_{j_d} \cup z_{d+M} \cup a_{d+M} \cup hbh_\beta$; **L**=**L**$\cup\sigma_{j_d}$;
45 **end**

- Setup(1^λ) $\to$ (pp, $info_0$, **L**): The blockchain nodes run this algorithm Setup to initiate the system. Given a security parameter λ, choose three hash functions H_1, H_2 and H_3, initiate the system public parameters pp, the beginning epoch as epoch 0, the associated system information $info_0$ and the database **L** to be empty.

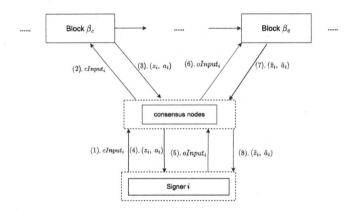

Fig. 3. The signature generation protocol from the signer's view

- Sign(β, info$_\beta$, $(sk_i, m_i)_{i \in [Q]}$, $\mathbf{L}_\beta$) $\rightarrow$ (σ_i, $\mathbf{L}_{\beta+1}$, info$_{\beta+1}$): From a signer's view, the process of this protocol can be seen in Fig. 3. From s ledger's view, the process of this protocol can be shown in Fig. 4. All steps are also arranged in protocol 1.
    - Committing: For user i_b ($i_b \in [M]$), the commitment input is computed as $cInput_{i_b} = A||B$, $A = H_1(sk_{i_b})$ and $B = H_2(m_{i_b}, sk_{i_b})$. Then the user sends the $cInput_{i_b}$ to the blockchain nodes. The blockchain nodes need to check the validity of A based on info$_\beta$. If the check result is positive, the blockchain nodes add $cInput_{i_b}$ to the corresponding signer's commitment com_{i_b} recorded by the blockchain by time-stamping the input $cInput_{i_b}$. Note that $com_{i_b} = (cInput_{i_b}, z_b, a_b, hbh_\beta)$, where z_b is a leaf value, a_b is the authentication path, hbh_β is the hash value of the block header. Otherwise, reject it.
    - Opening: To make a signature publicly verifiable, user j_d ($j_d \in [N]$) releases $oInput_{j_d} = (cInput_{j_d}, m_{j_d}, sk_{j_d}) = (H_1(sk_{j_d})||H_2(m_{j_d}, sk_{j_d})|| sk_{j_d}||m_{j_d}) = C||D||E||F$ on the blockchain. Upon receiving the $oInput_{j_d}$, the blockchain nodes use C to retrieve $cInput_{j_d}$. Then the blockchain nodes check the validity of $oInput_{j_d}$. If the check is positive, the blockchain nodes add $oInput_{j_d}$ to the corresponding signer's opened commitment $c\tilde{o}m_{j_d}$ recorded by the blockchain by time-stamping the $oInput_{j_d}$. Note that $c\tilde{o}m_{j_d} = (oInput_{j_d}, \tilde{z}_d, \tilde{a}_d, hbh_\beta)$, where $\tilde{z}_d$ is a leaf value, $\tilde{a}_d$ is the authentication path, hbh_β is the hash value of the block header. Otherwise, reject it.

    For a signer i, the signature $\sigma_i = (cInput_i, com_i, oInput_i, c\tilde{o}m_i)$ ($\beta < \beta'$). The public key for the signer i is $pk_i = (a_b, hbh_\beta, \tilde{a}_b, hbh_{\beta'})$. Finally, the blockchain outputs the updated database $\mathbf{L}_{\beta+1}$ and information list info$_{\beta+1}$.
- Verify(σ_i, info^i) $\rightarrow$ 0/1: A verifier runs the algorithm Verify to verify a signature. The verifier works as follows:
    - Parses σ_i as $(com_i, c\tilde{o}m_i)$, where $\beta' < \beta$.
    - Computes $z_i' = H_2(cInput_i)$ and checks whether z_i' equals z_i or not.

- Use z_i and a_i to recompute the Merkle tree root in the block β', and then compute $hbh'_{\beta'}$. Finally checks whether $hbh'_{\beta'}$ equals $hbh_{\beta'}$ or not.
- Computes $z'_i = H_3(oInput_i)$ and checks whether $\tilde{z}'_i$ equals $\tilde{z}_i$ or not.
- Use $\tilde{a}_i$, $\tilde{z}_i$ to recompute the Merkle tree root and hbh'_β. Checks whether hbh'_β equals hbh_β or not.
- If all previous checks pass, outputs 1 for "accept". Otherwise, outputs 0 for "reject".

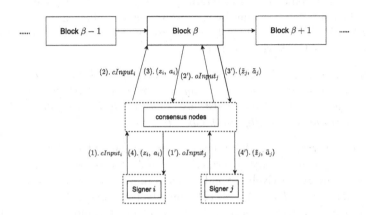

Fig. 4. The signature generation protocol from the blockchain's view

5   Security Analysis

Following the security model defined in Sect. 3.3, we need to clarify three random oracles $\mathbf{H}_1$, $\mathbf{H}_2$ and $\mathbf{H}_3$ for hash functions H_1, H_2 and H_3, respectively. Details of these oracles are similar to the definition in Sect. 3.3. Due to the page limit, we omit details here. In the unforgeability experiment, these three oracles can not only be accessed by the adversary but also internally be called by the simulation of the **AddHU** and **Update** oracles. The oracle **AddHU** includes the process of Committing while **Update** includes the process of Sign.

Because the simulator of each RO $\mathbf{H}_i$, $i \in \{1, 2, 3\}$, can decide the RO answers independently of the history of previous queries, hash functions meet the *history-free* reduction requirements. These three ROs can be modeled as QROs.

Theorem 1. *The BAHS scheme is correct, assuming the hash function H_1 is collision-resistant and the blockchain follows the BAHS scheme description correctly.*

Proof. On one hand, if a signer $\mathcal{A}$ is corrupt, there will be two cases. Firstly, he can predict the honest signer's signing key sk_h and the corresponding commitment is successfully submitted with the same $H_1(sk_h)$ in a previous session. However sk_h must be selected at random, and the probability of $\mathcal{A}$ picking the same signing key, i.e., $sk_i = sk_h$, is negligible in the security parameter. Except this, the only probability is that $sk_h \neq sk_i$ but $H_1(sk_h) = H_1(sk_i)$ – when this happens, the collision of the hash function H_1 is found, which contradicts to the assumption that the function H_1 is collision-resistant. Therefore, the probability of this case happening is negligible. Secondly, there is another signer i created by $\mathcal{A}$ with $sk_i = sk_h$ and this signer i is revoked when h is valid. If the adversary attempts to add i with $sk_i = sk_h$ after the signer h, it will be rejected by the blockchain. Therefore, the adversary's attempt will always fail.

On the other hand, based on $\text{status}_\beta^h = (H_1(sk_h), +)$, we can get that at epoch β, the honest signer h has been submitted and is allowed to sign. Following the BAHS scheme description, the signature on the blockchain for this valid signer h can pass the Verify algorithm.

Theorem 2. *The BAHS scheme is unforgeable if the hash function H_1 holds properties of one-wayness and collision-resistance, the hash functions H_2 and H_3 hold properties of collision-resistance, and the blockchain follows the BAHS scheme descriptions correctly and holds integrity.*

Proof. The adversary wins the unforgeability experiment in any one of the two scenarios: (1) The adversary generates $(\sigma_h, \text{info}^h)$ for an honest signer h, where com_h and σ_h are respectively a valid signer commitment and signature for m at epoch β, $\text{status}_\beta^h = (H_1(sk_h), +)$. (2) The adversary generates $(\sigma_i, \text{info}^i)$ for a corrupted signer i, who is controlled by the adversary, and the adversary does not get help from the blockchain. The proof for unforgeability is as follows.

In scenario (1), The adversary outputs $(\sigma_h, \text{info}^h)$, which meets following conditions:

- $\text{status}_\beta^h = (H_1(sk_h), +) \wedge \text{Verify}(\text{info}^h, \sigma_h) = 1$.
- $(cInput_h, m) \notin iS \vee (\sigma_h, m) \notin cS$.

This may happen in any one of the following cases:

1. The honest signer h generated an input to the commitment $cInput_h$ and $H_1(sk_h)$, which have been recorded on the blockchain. If the adversary wins the game, there are some sub-cases described as follows:
   - **Case 1.** Given certain record $H_1(sk_h)$ on the blockchain, the adversary gets the right signing key sk_h. Using sk_h and a different message m', the adversary can create a valid commitment input $cInput' = H_1(sk_h)||H_2(m', sk_h)$ by querying the oracle $\mathbf{H_2}$. Then the commitment input $cInput'$ can pass the blockchain's check and the algorithm Verify. This means the one-wayness of the hash function H_1 is broken which is contradicted with the assumption that the hash function H_1 is one-way. Therefore, the probability of this sub-case happening is negligible.
   - **Case 2.** The adversary can use a different pair of sk' and m' to query oracles H_1 and H_2 to get $H_1(sk_h) = H_1(sk')$, $H_2(m_h, sk_h) = H_2(m', sk')$. Then the adversary can forge a valid commitment input and open it on the blockchain before the honest signer h opens it. This means two scenarios happened at the same time: (1) the challenger can find a collision

sk' and sk_h in the oracle H_1, which contradicts the assumption that the function H_1 is collision-resistant; (2) the challenger can find a collision $m'\|sk'$ and $m_h\|sk_h$ in the oracle H_2, which contradicts to the assumption that the function H_2 is collision-resistant; Therefore, the probability of this case happened is negligible.

2. The honest signer h has send the input to the opened commitment $oInput_h = (cInput_h,\ m_h,\ sk_h)$ to the blockchain. In this case, the adversary can get the signing key sk_h directly. Using the signing key sk_h, the adversary can use a different message m' to generate the commitment input $cInput' = H_1(sk_h)\|H_2(m',\ sk_h)$, which can be submitted to the blockchain. However, this is contradicted with the assumption the blockchain follows the scheme description. Therefore, the probability of this case happening is negligible.

3. During computing the Merkle tree, the adversary can have access to the blockchain to change some input value of hash function H_2. For example, the adversary changes certain leaf values z_h to be z'. If the final record on (including the authentication path a_i) the blockchain can keep the same, which means the challenger finds a collision for the hash function H_2. This is contradicted to the assumption the hash function H_2 is collision-resistant. Or the final record on the blockchain can be changed. This is contradicted to the assumption that the blockchain is trusted. Therefore, the probability of this case happening is negligible.

In scenario (2) $i \neq h$, the adversary outputs $(\sigma_i, \mathsf{info}^i)$ and there are some cases, which meet the following conditions:

- $\mathsf{Verify}(\sigma_i, \mathsf{info}^i) = 1$
- $(\sigma_i,\ m) \notin cS$.

This may happen in any one of the following cases:

1. The adversary uses a different signing key sk_i to query oracles $\mathbf{H}_1$ and $\mathbf{H}_2$ to make $H_1(sk_i) = H_1(sk_j)$ and $H_2(m,\ sk_i) = H_2(m,\ sk_j)$, then submits the commitment input $cInput_j$ on the blockchain to claim that this commitment is valid for an uncorrupt signer j. This means the challenger can find a collision in oracles $\mathbf{H}_1$ and $\mathbf{H}_2$, which is contradicted to the assumption that hash functions H_1 and H_2 are collision-resistant. Therefore, the probability of this case happening is negligible.

2. The adversary can use a different pair of sk_i and m_i to query oracles H_1 and H_2 to get $H_1(sk_i) = H_1(sk_j)$, $H_2(m_i,\ sk_i) = H_2(m_j,\ sk_j)$. Then the adversary can forge a valid commitment input and submit it on the blockchain, which is considered as a valid commitment input generated by the signer j. This means two scenarios happened at the same time (1) the challenger can find a collision sk_i and sk_j in the oracle H_1, which contradicts to the assumption that the function H_1 is collision-resistant; (2) the challenger can find a collision $m_i\|sk_i$ and $m_j\|sk_j$ in the oracle H_2, which contradicts to the

assumption that the function H_2 is collision-resistant; Therefore, the probability of this case happened is negligible.

3. Because the adversary can control a corrupted signer to get the signer's signing key sk_i. The adversary can send a number of commitment inputs $cInput_j$, $j \in [1, R]$ with one signing key sk_i and different messages m_j, $j \in [1, R]$ to the blockchain in one block. These commitment inputs can be recorded on the blockchain. Then the adversary can try to open these commitments to the blockchain. However, this is contradicted to the assumption that one signing key can be used only once. If there is more than one commitment input using the same signing key recorded on the blockchain, all of these commitment inputs will be rejected. So the probability of this case happening is negligible.

4. Considering a signer i has submitted the input to the opened commitment $(cInput_i, m_i, sk_i)$ to the blockchain, the adversary uses a different pair of (m', sk') to generate the input to the opened commitment $cInput_i' = H_1(sk')||H_2(m', sk') = cInput_h$ to make $H_1(sk_h) = H_1(sk')$, $H_3(H_1(sk')||H_2(m',sk')||m'||sk') = H_3(H_1(sk_h)||H_2(m_h,sk_h)||m_h||sk_h)$. This means the challenger finds a collision in H_1, H_2 and H_3, which is contradicted to the assumption that hash functions H_1, H_2 and H_3 are all collision-resistant. Therefore, the probability of this case happening is negligible.

5. During computing the Merkle tree, the adversary can have access to the blockchain to change some input value of hash function H_2. The adversary changes a certain leaf value z_h to be z'. If the final record (including the authentication path a_i) on the blockchain can keep the same, which means the challenger finds a collision for the hash function H_2. This is contradicted to the assumption the hash function H_2 is collision-resistant. Or then the final record on the blockchain can be changed. This is contradicted to the assumption that the blockchain is trusted. Therefore, the probability of this case happening is negligible.

Overall, the BAHS scheme provides unforgeability.

6   Implementations

We have made a prototype implementation, in which we only measure the communication and computational overhead of our commitment scheme rather than the cost or transaction overhead on the blockchain.

Implementation of a Specific Blockchain. We implement our BAHS scheme in Python. Note that the signing time includes the time for the blockchain to generate the whole Merkle tree in one block and the corresponding hash value of the block header. The programs were compiled using Pycharm and executed on a laptop (processor: 2.6 GHz, 6-Core, Intel Core i7; Memory: 16GB 2667 MHz) with the macOS operating system. We set the security level as 256-bit. As shown in Table 2, J is the number of signers in a block. For simplicity, we assume $\frac{J}{2}$ signers to submit commitments and the other $\frac{J}{2}$ signers to open signatures. We implement two blocks as an example of blockchains. We choose 2^{10},..., 2^{15},...,2^{20} as different parameters for the number of signers, which are larger than that in Bitcoin. According to Table 2, we can see that the signing time is far less than 15 s in Ethereum or 10 min in Bitcoin. Our scheme is practical.

Fig. 5. The returned proof from the OriginStamp service

Implementation Based on Public Blockchains. In this implementation, we want to test performance of the BAHS scheme on known blockchain platforms. Therefore, classic signature algorithms, such as ECDSA, used in existing blockchain does not influence our implementation. Considering existing blockchains, we use the platform "OriginStamp" to publish and timestamp our opened signature, which contains three typical blockchains, i.e., Bitcoin, Ethereum, and Aion. Due to the page limit, we take the Bitcoin as an example. We upload data to Bitcoin and each time the web server calculates the Merkle tree root value and inserts it into a Bitcoin transaction. After the transaction is committed, the web server returned a proof for verification, which is shown in Fig. 5. Also, the information on the certificate can be accessed at the website https://verify.originstamp.com.

Our BAHS scheme is the first blockchain-aided hash-based signature scheme and it is different from any traditional digital signature schemes, so we do not compare the BAHS scheme with other signature schemes.

Table 2. The implementation results for the signature scheme

Parameters	SS(KB)[a]	CIG(ms)[b]	ST(ms) [c]
$J = 2^{10}$	1.69	$5.42 * 10^{-3}$	3.38
$J = 2^{11}$	1.81	$5.36 * 10^{-3}$	5.94
$J = 2^{12}$	1.93	$5.79 * 10^{-3}$	11.55
$J = 2^{13}$	2.06	$6.03 * 10^{-3}$	23.15
$J = 2^{14}$	2.19	$5.61 * 10^{-3}$	53.23
$J = 2^{15}$	2.31	$5.26 * 10^{-3}$	102.04
$J = 2^{16}$	2.43	$2.82 * 10^{-3}$	258.52
$J = 2^{17}$	2.55	$1.3 * 10^{-3}$	499.65
$J = 2^{18}$	2.67	$0.68 * 10^{-3}$	1123.12
$J = 2^{19}$	2.79	$0.32 * 10^{-3}$	2131.42
$J = 2^{20}$	2.91	$0.16 * 10^{-3}$	4337.23

[a] SS stands for the signature size and KB means kilobytes.
[b] CIG stands for the commitment input generation time and ms stands for millisecond.
[c] ST stands for the signing time and ms stands for millisecond.

7   Conclusion

In this paper, we propose a new one-time signature scheme, i.e., BAHS, in which signing keys, commitments and opened commitments are publicly accessible via a distributed blockchain. The BAHS scheme is much simpler than traditional signature schemes and other post-quantum signature schemes. We also provide a formal definition of the security model for the BAHS scheme and security proof. Finally, we implement this scheme and show its practicality.

Acknowledgments. We thank the European Union's Horizon research and innovation program for support under grant agreement numbers: 101069688 (CONNECT), 101070627 (REWIRE), 952697 (ASSURED), 101019645 (SECANT) and 101095634 (ENTRUST). These projects are funded by the UK government's Horizon Europe guarantee and administered by UKRI. The first author thanks the China Scholarship Council (CSC) for providing the research scholarship. We also thank the anonymous reviewers from ISPEC for their valuable comments.

Appendix

A   Oracles for the Unforgeability

AddHU()

- If $K = k(\lambda)$ return $\bot$.
- $K = K + 1$.
- If $h = \bot$: $N = N + 1$; $h = N + 1$.
- $com_h \leftarrow$ Committing(sk_h, m).
- If $cInput_h \neq \bot$:
    - $\beta_{\mathsf{Add}} = \beta_{\mathsf{Current}}$.
    - $K = k(\lambda)$.
    - Set $\mathsf{status}^h_{\beta_{\mathsf{Current}}} = (cInput_h, +)$ and let $\mathbf{L} = \mathbf{L} \cup com_h$.
- Return $(sk_h, cInput_h)$.

AddCU(i, $cInput_i$)

- If $i \notin [N+1] \vee i = h$, return $\bot$.
- If $\mathsf{status}^i_{\beta_{\mathsf{Current}}} \neq (cInput_i, \bot)$, return $\bot$.
- If $i = N + 1$: $N = N + 1$.
- Set $\mathsf{status}^i_{\beta_{\mathsf{Current}}} = (cInput_i, +)$ and let $\mathbf{L} = \mathbf{L} \cup cInput_i$.

Revoke($\mathcal{R}$)

- If $\mathcal{R} \not\subseteq [N]$ return $\bot$.
- $\beta_{\mathsf{Current}} = \beta_{\mathsf{Current}} + 1$.
- $\forall i \in \mathcal{R}$, set $\mathsf{status}^i_{\beta_{\mathsf{Current}}} = (cInput_i, -)$.
- If $h \in \mathcal{R}$ and $\beta_{\mathsf{Revoke}} = \infty$ set $\beta_{\mathsf{Revoke}} = \beta_{\mathsf{Current}}$.

Update (β, info_β, $\mathbf{L}$, ..., $cInput_{i_b}/oInput_{j_d}$, ...)

- If inputs=(β, info_β, $\mathbf{L}$, ..., $cInput_i$, ...)
    - $(\sigma_{i_b}, \mathbf{L}_{\beta+1}, \mathsf{info}_{\beta+1}) \leftarrow$ Committing(β, info_β, $\mathbf{L}$, ..., $cInput_{i_b}$, ...).
    - Return σ_i.
- If inputs=(β, info_β, $\mathbf{L}$, ..., $oInput_{j_d}$, ...)
    - $(\sigma_{j_d}, \mathbf{L}_{\beta+1}, \mathsf{info}_{\beta+1}) \leftarrow$ Opening(β, info_β, $\mathbf{L}$, ..., $oInput_{j_d}$, ...).
    - Return σ_{j_d}

Fig. 6. Oracles for the unforgeability

References

1. ISO/IEC 10118–1. Information technology - Security techniques - Hash functions - Part 1: General. Standard (2016)
2. ISO/IEC CD 14888–4.2. Information technology - Security techniques - Digital signatures with appendix - Part 4: Stateful hash-based mechanisms (2022)

3. Yakubov, A., Shbair, W., Wallbom, A.: A blockchain-based PKI management framework. In: The First IEEE/IFIP International Workshop on Managing and Managed by Blockchain (Man2Block) colocated with IEEE/IFIP NOMS (2018)

4. Becker, G.: Merkle signature schemes, merkle trees and their cryptanalysis. Ruhr-University Bochum, Technical report, 12:19 (2008)

5. Boneh, D., Dagdelen, Ö., Fischlin, M., Lehmann, A., Schaffner, C., Zhandry, M.: Random oracles in a quantum world. In: Lee, D.H., Wang, X. (eds.) ASIACRYPT 2011. LNCS, vol. 7073, pp. 41–69. Springer, Heidelberg (2011). https://doi.org/10.1007/978-3-642-25385-0_3

6. Catalano, D., Fiore, D.: Vector commitments and their applications. In: Kurosawa, K., Hanaoka, G. (eds.) PKC 2013. LNCS, vol. 7778, pp. 55–72. Springer, Heidelberg (2013). https://doi.org/10.1007/978-3-642-36362-7_5

7. Cozzo, D., Smart, N.P.: Sharing the LUOV: threshold post-quantum signatures. In: Albrecht, M. (ed.) IMACC 2019. LNCS, vol. 11929, pp. 128–153. Springer, Cham (2019). https://doi.org/10.1007/978-3-030-35199-1_7

8. Johnson, D., Menezes, A., Vanstone, S.: The elliptic curve digital signature algorithm (ECDSA). Int. J. Inf. Secur. 1, 36–63 (2001)

9. McGrew, D., Kampanakis, P., Fluhrer, S., Gazdag, S.-L., Butin, D., Buchmann, J.: State management for hash-based signatures. In: Chen, L., McGrew, D., Mitchell, C. (eds.) SSR 2016. LNCS, vol. 10074, pp. 244–260. Springer, Cham (2016). https://doi.org/10.1007/978-3-319-49100-4_11

10. Damgård, I.: Commitment schemes and zero-knowledge protocols. In: Damgård, I.B. (ed.) EEF School 1998. LNCS, vol. 1561, pp. 63–86. Springer, Heidelberg (1999). https://doi.org/10.1007/3-540-48969-X_3

11. Bernstein, D.J., Hülsing, A.: The SPHINCS$^+$ signature framework. In: ACM CCS, pp. 2129–2146 (2019)

12. Bernstein, D.J., et al.: SPHINCS: practical stateless hash-based signatures. In: Oswald, E., Fischlin, M. (eds.) EUROCRYPT 2015. LNCS, vol. 9056, pp. 368–397. Springer, Heidelberg (2015). https://doi.org/10.1007/978-3-662-46800-5_15

13. Adja, Y.C.E., Hammi, B., Ahmed, S., Zeadally, S.: A blockchain-based certificate revocation management and status verification system. Comput. Secur. 104, 102209 (2021)

14. El Bansarkhani, R., Mohamed, M.S.E., Petzoldt, A.: MQSAS - a multivariate sequential aggregate signature scheme. In: Bishop, M., Nascimento, A.C.A. (eds.) ISC 2016. LNCS, vol. 9866, pp. 426–439. Springer, Cham (2016). https://doi.org/10.1007/978-3-319-45871-7_25

15. Groot Bruinderink, L., Hülsing, A.: "Oops, I Did It Again" – security of one-time signatures under two-message attacks. In: Adams, C., Camenisch, J. (eds.) SAC 2017. LNCS, vol. 10719, pp. 299–322. Springer, Cham (2018). https://doi.org/10.1007/978-3-319-72565-9_15

16. Gentry, C., Peikert, C., Vaikuntanathan, V.: Trapdoors for hard lattices and new cryptographic constructions. In: STOC, pp. 197–206 (2008)

17. Holmes, S.: Impact of post-quantum signatures on blockchain and DLT systems. In: DLT (2023)

18. Bootle, J., Cerulli, A., Chaidos, P., Ghadafi, E., Groth, J.: Foundations of fully dynamic group signatures. J. Cryptol. 33(4), 1822–1870 (2020)

19. Juels, A., Wattenberg, M.: A fuzzy commitment scheme. In: ACM CCS, pp. 28–36 (1999)

20. Ducas, L., Lepoint, T., Lyubashevsky, V., Schwabe, P., Seiler, G., Stehlé, D.: Crystals-dilithium: digital signatures from module lattices (2018)

21. Lamport, L. : Constructing digital signatures from a one way function (1979)
22. Bellare, M., Rogaway, P.: Random oracles are practical: a paradigm for designing efficient protocols. In: ACM CCS (1993)
23. Marco, L., Talayhan, A., Vaudenay, S.: Making classical (threshold) signatures post-quantum for single use on a public ledger. Cryptology ePrint Archive (2023/420)
24. Li, Q., Cao, G.: Multicast authentication in the smart grid with one-time signature. IEEE Trans. Smart Grid **2**(4), 686–696 (2011)
25. Gennaro, R., Goldfeder, S., Narayanan, A.: Threshold-optimal DSA/ECDSA signatures and an application to bitcoin wallet security. In: Manulis, M., Sadeghi, A.-R., Schneider, S. (eds.) ACNS 2016. LNCS, vol. 9696, pp. 156–174. Springer, Cham (2016). https://doi.org/10.1007/978-3-319-39555-5_9
26. Chang, S.M., Shieh, S., Lin, W.W., Hsieh, C.M.: An efficient broadcast authentication scheme in wireless sensor networks. In: ASIACCS, pp. 311–320 (2006)

Lever: Making Intensive Validation Practical on Blockchain

Mingming Wang[1] and Qianhong Wu[2]([envelope])

[1] School of Electronic and Information Engineering, Beihang University,
Beijing 100191, China
wangmingming@buaa.edu.cn
[2] School of Cyber Science and Technology, Beihang University, Beijing 100191, China
qianhong.wu@buaa.edu.cn

Abstract. Blockchain heralds the dawn of decentralized applications that coordinate proper computations without the need for prior trust. Existing blockchain solutions, however, are incapable of dealing with intensive validation. Duplicated execution leads to limited throughput and unacceptable expenses. Furthermore, the absence of secure incentive mechanisms derives undesired dilemmas among rational verifiers. This work presents Lever, the first off-chain solution that makes intensive validation cost-efficient and scalable among rational verifiers. To achieve the best scalability, Lever curtails the scale of each validation to a single node and introduces novel challenge-response games between potential adversaries and rational stakeholders, optimizing validation redundancy according to the practical adversarial capability confronted. Meanwhile, compelling incentive design efficiently transfers adversary collateral to specialized rewards for honest participants, therefore allowing the user to lever sufficient endorsement with minimum cost. A backstop protocol is designed to resolve intractable disputes and circumvent the well-known Verifier's Dilemma. Experiments show that Lever significantly improves the throughput and reduces expenses of intensive validation with a slight tradeoff in latency. It is also robust to conceivable attacks on validation and performs distinguishable ability to purify Byzantine participants.

Keywords: Blockchain · Crypto-economic Protocols · Verifiable Computation · Incentive Compatibility

1 Introduction

In modern computation and application systems, it is difficult to obtain reliable public services without a trusted third party. Public blockchain thrives to remove such dependency with the help of permission-less consensus and ingenious incentive mechanisms. Furthermore, the innovation of smart contract endows it with the potential to subvert most existing applications, processing computational tasks in a fair and ordered manner.

Validation, as the inevitable procedure to ensure the correctness of computation, is the most fundamental functionality of blockchain. Advanced backbone

W. Meng et al. (Eds.): ISPEC 2023, LNCS 14341, pp. 440–461, 2023.
https://doi.org/10.1007/978-981-99-7032-2_26

frameworks based on Byzantine Agreement [1,2] plus Sharding [3,4] have significantly improved its efficiency, enabling strong consistency and linear optimizations on scalability. Yet, they have to assume negligible workload during execution. The restriction stems from two sides. On the one hand, all nodes are potentially required to independently verify every transaction in their region. Such redundancy makes the execution of intensive workload extremely inefficient and expensive. To prevent resultant congestion, complexity limits like GasLimit [5] have to be set up, which sacrifices the applicability of the system. On the other hand, altruism is heavily relied. The lack of fair and secure incentive mechanisms fails to allocate rewards according to the actual workload of verifiers. When the overhead becomes increasingly high, rational nodes choose to skip or refuse validation, which leads to the Verifier's Dilemma [6]. No guarantee for validity or liveness is available in this state of affairs.

State-of-the-art research trend focuses on off-chain solutions to circumvent the problem. By moving intensive workloads elsewhere off the blockchain, the solutions decouple costly operations from the backbone. According to the major trade-off imported, they can be roughly classified into three types. 1. Contract-specific solutions [7–10] necessitate a significant amount of effort from stakeholders, the set of nodes with an initial vested interest in the task. The requirements could include frequent interactions [7,11], a high amount of collateral [7,8,10,11] and strict on-line response [7–9,11]. Once not satisfied, protocols will be aborted or taken over by the adversary. 2. Resource-dominant solutions [12–16] introduce costly procedures such as duplicated executions with high redundancy [12] and zero-knowledge proof generation [13–16], which is difficult to scale and too expensive for users. 3. The other existing solutions resort to extra trust dependencies from TEE [17,18] or TTP [19] to break such limitations, which is fragile and not practical in many scenarios. It is also noteworthy that the validity of most solutions builds on the altruism of verifiers. The abandoning of rationality may render plausible incentive design pointless since rational players have full motive to freeload the rewards from altruists. To date, there lack of sound designs and secure arguments ensuring a compatible reward for every honest verifier.

To tackle the above challenges, we intend to build a self-contained off-chain solution with the following intuitions. Let redundancy denote the times of duplicated validation required to finalize a transaction in a blockchain framework. Intuitively, to make intensive validation scalable, the uppermost target is to remove unnecessary redundancy for each task. Our approach is to simplify the actual redundancy of a task by tracing the capability of its adversary. Concretely, we add sequential rounds of single validation before a backstop scheme driven by the costly SNARK execution. Stakeholders of each incoming task can report a dispute by proposing challenges whenever the validation result is invalid. In the worst-case scenario, the adversary has to persistently endorse the wrong verdict until his budget runs out. Otherwise, the task gets finalized in early rounds with no further challenge proposed. For tasks without a wealthy and stubborn adversary, a correct execution could be achieved with optimized redundancy under single validation. Only intractable disputes will be resolved by the powerful but costly backstop. This promises the scalability of the system.

In terms of incentive, each round of single validation brings about a nature confrontation between the verifier and the challenger who hold verdicts contradictive to each other. By imposing an exponentially round-increasing collateral on every participant, the forfeit of the adversary can not only cover the reward of honest verifiers and stakeholders, but also leads to the rapid incentive accumulation of the task itself. The user only needs to pay the minimal expense for the initial validation and then waits for the adversary to cover the incentive gaps of subsequent duplicated executions. Meanwhile, every honest participant can receive a compatible and undisputed reward for his efforts. As a result, the design is both cost-effective and incentive-compatible. As the game evolves, the increasing reward will entice more rational nodes into participation. We adopt randomly-select neutral nodes as the subject of validation, which naturally expands the bounds of the stakeholder set. Incumbent Byzantine verifiers will also be timely evicted from the system for their misbehaviors, resulting in a major relief on the protocol's collateral and interaction requirements.

Combining the inspirations, we present Lever, the first scalable and incentive compatible off-chain framework specialized for intensive validation. Besides, Lever achieves cost-efficiency and perfect applicability that are usually absent in related works. Lever can tolerate at most $n/4$ Byzantine participants and can be deployed on top of current backbone frameworks underlying the classical Byzantine Agreement [20, 21]. Suitable examples are Solida [1], Algorand [2].

Contributions

- **Creation of Lever-Boost Game, a pattern for optimized execution and incentive accumulation.** The pattern iteratively organizes multiple rounds of single validation with randomly selected verifiers. Nodes can report disputes and evolve the game by proposing challenges. Incentive designs transform the forfeits of the adversary to make an exponentially growing of reward. Validation gets efficiently finalized when no challenge occurs, which greatly reduces the redundancy of the framework. Disputes can at most last for logarithmic rounds since adequate incentives will be accumulated for dispute resolution. The game makes cost-efficiency and scalability of the framework.
- **Construction of secure backstop, an incentive-compatible pattern for dispute resolution.** The pattern employs rational nodes in a Sybil-resistant group to bid for chances to finalize the task once a handsome reward is accumulated. The winner then builds costly SNARK proof off-chain to indisputably assert the correct verdict on the backbone. We combine the backstop with a robust incentive design that enables Lever to handle the adversary with unlimited budget and ensures honest validation as the unique dominant strategy. The backstop pledges validity and finality of the framework.
- **Game-theoretic analyses and implementation.** We provide convincing proofs and build a proof-of-concept implementation to evaluate Lever. Experimental results suggest that, Lever linearly scales the throughput with the increase of nodes and resolves over 98.3% workload via single validation even

in the worst-case configuration. Let E_b denote the cost ratio between backstop execution and single validation execution, it ensures the scheme's reliable finalization within $\mathcal{O}(\log E_b)$ rounds. Also, Lever reduces the user expense to a single validation and provides any honest participant an attractive incentive linear with his collateral.

Table 1. Comparison of Lever with state-of-the-art solutions (Let P_g denote the total number of instructions in the intensive validation program. As for payoff, a denotes the expense for a single validation, F denotes the transaction fee per time to anchor a digest to the backbone. Let B_A be the budget of adversary to commit attack. We use $A|B$ where A denotes the average case, B refers to the worst case. In Yoda's scheme, k' denotes the number of nodes in an execution set. In ACE's scheme, contract owners have full rights to choose the number of verifiers x when deploying their contracts)

Protocol	Assumption	IC[b]	Redundancy	Finality[a]	Cost	Applicability
State Channels [9]	BA	No	$\mathcal{O}(1)|\mathcal{O}(n)$	$\mathcal{O}(1)|Inf$	$0|\log n \cdot a$	Restricted
Arbitrum [7]	BR	No	$\mathcal{O}(1)$	$\mathcal{O}(1)|\mathcal{O}(B_A \log(P_g))$	$0|\frac{1}{P_g}a + \log(P_g)F$	Restricted
ACE [10]	BA	No	$\mathcal{O}(x)$	$\mathcal{O}(1)|Inf$	xa	Restricted
Truebit [11]	BR	No	$\mathcal{O}(1)$	$\mathcal{O}(1)|Inf$	$a|a + \log(P_g)F$	Complete
Yoda [12]	Semi-honest	No	$\mathcal{O}(k')$	$\mathcal{O}(1)$	$k'a$	Complete
BDR [19]	BR+TTP	Yes	$\mathcal{O}(1)$	$\mathcal{O}(1)$	$2a$	Restricted
Lever	BR	Yes	$\mathcal{O}(1)|\mathcal{O}(\log \mathcal{E}_B)$	$\mathcal{O}(1)|\mathcal{O}(\log \mathcal{E}_B)$	a	Complete

[a] The rounds expected to achieve finality, the metric reflects the latency of each solution.
[b] Incentive Compatibility.

2   Definitions and Background

2.1   Intensive Validation on Blockchain

Blockchain maintains an open and distributed ledger through a peer-to-peer network, which provides data immutability and computation verifiability. Smart contract extends its functionality to general-purpose computation. Prominent platforms like Ethereum [5] equip Turing-complete languages to make sophisticated logic executable on-chain. A smart contract is defined by a prescribed collection of code, while its execution is triggered by transactions, which can be parsed as a successful transition of state: $Tx : o_i \rightarrow o_f$. In Lever, we denote each attempt for state transition as a Task $\mathcal{T}$.

Inspired by Chainspace [4], we adopt an asymmetric model to simplify the validation workload. The fulfillment of every task is dissolved into two parts. An private computation procedure Com for user to derive the final state of the contract in advance and obtain the necessary data to form a transaction:

$$\mathcal{T}.\mathsf{Com}(o_i) \rightarrow o_f, data;$$

$$Tx := \langle o_i, o_f, data \rangle_{\mathsf{sk}}$$

and a deterministic validation procedure Ver for nodes to check the correctness
of execution on-chain:

$$\mathcal{T}.\mathsf{Ver}(Tx) \rightarrow \{valid, invalid\}$$

Other than being obfuscated with the execution of contracts, validation is
reduced to a decision problem with optimized complexity which provides better
privacy concerns.

We further define the difficulty of a task $\eta_{\mathcal{T}}$ as the precise complexity mea-
surement of its validation procedure weighted by a prescribed instruction set.
The workload is considered as *intensive* if its difficulty is beyond a fixed bound η'.
Accordingly, we name the transaction carrying intensive workload as *Validation
Intensive Transaction* (VIT).

When handling intensive validation with non-trivial cost, the behavior of a
player can be described by his initial interest relevance towards the task. We
introduce a private valuation $v_{\mathcal{T}}$ to describe his preference in conducting the
correct execution of $\mathcal{T}$. Accordingly, all players involved in validation can be
classified into three types:

- Stakeholder $\mathcal{S}$: nodes who have $v_{\mathcal{T}} > 0$ will actively safeguard the correct
  result if their cost does not exceed $v_{\mathcal{T}}$.
- Disinterest $\mathcal{D}$: nodes who have $v_{\mathcal{T}} = 0$ will participate in validation only for
  chasing the reward of execution due to rationality.
- Adversary $\mathcal{A}$: nodes who have $v_{\mathcal{T}} < 0$ will make every effort to keep the correct
  result from being accepted on-chain. This type also includes Byzantine nodes
  that could be irrational in launching attacks to break the system.

The intention of our design is to lever disinterest but rational verifiers to perform
correct validation on $\mathcal{T}$ against the potential adversary with minimal cost from
the stakeholders.

2.2   Challenge Response Pattern

We review the classical challenge response pattern [22] which serves as the building block of Lever. In this pattern, a task is privately executed by a proposer who
signs the VIT as his endorsement on its validity. After it is broadcast, any stakeholder of the task can submit a challenge within a predetermined time limit to
declare against the proposal. Whenever a challenge is collected, a dispute occurs,
and the timeout resets. The VIT can only be accepted if no disputes arise before
the time limit expires.

The pattern's safe deployment is clearly contingent on the safe and timely
resolution of disputes. Existing solutions, such as Truebit [11] and Arbitrum [7],
use an interactive bisection scheme between the proposer and the challenger to
resolve every dispute instantaneously. Let P_g denote the total number of instructions in the intensive validation program. It takes $\mathcal{O}(\log P_g)$ rounds of bisection
to narrow their disagreement down to the execution of a single instruction, which
can be easily checked on-chain to assert the validity of the challenge.

We consider the construction far from efficient and jeopardizes validation finality owing to the abuse of the challenge interface. The scheme entails $\mathcal{O}(2 \log P_g)$ interactions from disputers to the backbone to maintain the integrity of the bisection operation, incurring significant latency benchmarked by the consensus interval. Stakeholders endure heavy collateral and strict online demand throughout the process. What's worse, the adversary may endlessly restart the dispute by persistently challenging the same proposal until his budget $B_\mathcal{A}$ runs out, which further compromises the finality to $\mathcal{O}(B_\mathcal{A} \log(P_g))$. In terms of incentive, though heavy forfeits are imposed to compensate the honest disputer, sly adversaries can get around most penalties by challenging each other.

In Sect. 4, our design accordingly figures out the above drawbacks. Instead of handling the dispute at once, we exploit the prolonged dispute to gather incentives for subsequent executions. All confirmed proposals are merged into two conflicting parties by their verdicts and every new challenge potentially increases the reward of VIT by consuming the adversarial ones. Even if an adversary has an unlimited budget, it only takes a limited number of challenges to accumulate adequate incentives and thoroughly resolve the dispute by backbone in one shot. Finality is thus well preserved, and the entire procedure entails no dense interaction or extra expense on honest participants.

2.3   Related Works

Many prominent works have been proposed to handle intensive workload with blockchain, which we create a systematic taxonomy below and compare with Lever in Table 1.

Contract-Specific Solutions. The pattern treats each contract as an independent validation system and introduces stakeholders' participation in optimizing the validation procedure. State channels [8,9] simply define stakeholders as verifiers of the contract. If all members remain honest, state transitions can be achieved with the best performance via unanimous assertions on each proposal. Otherwise, execution has to move back to the backbone, which indicates the loss of finality over intensive workloads. Arbitrum [7] allows stakeholders to challenge wrong proposals and employs the bisection protocol to resolve possible disputes off-chain. However, a wealthy and stubborn adversary can dramatically deteriorate the finality of the scheme by abusing the challenge interface. ACE [10] attains efficiency by importing trust in contract creators to decide the verifier set and threat model for their contracts. Hence a malicious contract creator could fully manipulate the validation result of his contract. It is noteworthy that existing contract-specific solutions suffer from heavy applicability restrictions. Applications with dynamic membership, large stakeholder sets, and competitive trigger requests could stop the protocols from working properly. To compare, with the same level of optimized redundancy and cost-efficiency, Lever achieves robust finality in all cases, maintains full applicability, and remains trustless to any participant. Moreover, Lever largely remits the stakeholders' burden in interaction and collateral by importing rational disinterests into validation.

Competition-Driven Solutions. The pattern promotes active competition from rational disinterests to safeguard the validity of tasks. A typical solution is Truebit [11], which allows multiple verifiers to compete for the validation incentive of a VIT, incorporating the challenge response game to reflect disputes and bisection protocol to resolve them. Unfortunately, it is vulnerable to the Participation Dilemma [7]. The adversary could generate several Sybil identities and burst to engage in one task, making the incentive become negligible to rational verifiers which results in the loss of task validity. Comparatively, Lever realizes a scheduled and robust task arrangement, achieves Sybil resistance over verifiers, and conducts fair workload coordination to give every honest execution a compatible reward.

Resource-Dominant Solutions. Such solutions consume intensive computation resources to gain undisputable evidence for VIT's validity and finality. Powerful schemes like zkSNARKs [14,16] and zkSTARKs [13,15] simplify arbitrary computation to a zero-knowledge proof with fast validation time and short proof size. However, the proof generation introduces considerable expenses on either computation or storage from stakeholders of the task, which is not cost-efficient. In Yoda [12], VITs are repetitively executed among several groups of randomly-selected disinterests, and task finality is decided by threshold voting. However, by releasing the BR model assumption to Quasi-Honest, the protocol avoids discussing possible defective behaviors from rational nodes. Also, rewards could become incompatible if termination cannot be attained as expected within certain groups. By contrast, Lever is more cost-effective and removes any dependency on altruism. Both solutions can be integrated into Lever as a secure backstop, reducing user expenses to a single validation reward.

Other Solutions. TEE-based solutions like Eriken [17] and POSE [18] provide support over confidentiality and intensive execution towards smart contracts. Tasks are conducted off-chain in SGX or TrustZone enclaves with extremely low redundancy. However, system validity along with finality depends on every enclave executing the stored code correctly. A compromised enclave will cause catastrophic effects like invalid blockchain states and privacy leakage. Dong *et al.* [19] present a game-theoretic solution to obtain cost-effective outsourced computing on blockchain. Unfortunately, it assumes the existence of a trusted third party as the guarantee of validity. Lever eliminates any reliance on trust and delivers substantially stronger resistance against compromised entities with average redundancy that is comparably effective.

3   System Overview

3.1   Actors

Lever considers a system with the following actors:

- **Transaction Founder** - privately executes the task, packs his result in a VIT, and broadcasts it to the blockchain.

- **Verifiers** - register themselves on-chain and chase rewards by undertaking validation tasks. After each validation, a verdict $vd \in \{\text{valid}, \text{invalid}\}$ is given to the VIT.
- **Challengers** - propose challenges to oppose the verdict of a verifier.
- **Judges** - are incentivized to resolve intricate disputes on intensive workloads.

Every actor is uniquely identified by a public/private key pair. However, nodes may play different roles at the same time and create multiple identities over challengers or verifiers. We will prove such behaviors cannot interfere with the validity of the protocol. Also, the adversary may take over any actor to launch attacks. As a result, each participant is required to take collateral before taking action, which will be forfeited once their malicious conduct is detected.

3.2 Methodologies

As shown in Fig. 1, in Lever, the intensive workload is taken by two phases:

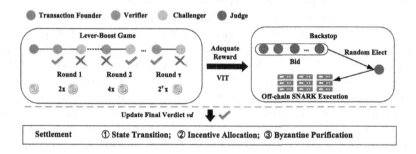

Fig. 1. Overview of Lever

In Lever-Boost Game π_L, a VIT takes at most τ rounds of single validation. In each round, a randomly selected verifier submits his verdict on $\mathcal{T}$ while anyone can serve as a challenger refuting him to revive the next game round. If no challenge is received within a pre-defined time limit, the protocol takes the result of the last verifier as the *final verdict*. Otherwise, forfeits from the adversary double the task reward for every new round, which swiftly covers the incentive demand for dispute resolution. Workloads troubled with intricate disputes automatically trigger the backstop scheme π_B, in which a group of judges runs for eligibility to create SNARK proof for the task to get the accumulated incentive. A *final verdict* vd is accepted only if the SNARK proof w.r.t. the statement $\mathcal{T}.\text{Ver}(\text{VIT}) = vd$ approved by the backbone. Once finality is achieved, Lever conducts settlement to: 1) update the status of contracts, 2) distribute incentives to participants, and 3) remove Byzantine participants from the system.

In Lever, the utility of a participant P is defined by the following equation:

$$u_P = \begin{cases} i_P - c_P + v_{\mathcal{T}} & vd = \mathcal{T}.\text{Ver}(\text{VIT}) \,. \\ i_P - c_P - v_{\mathcal{T}} & vd \neq \mathcal{T}.\text{Ver}(\text{VIT}) \,. \end{cases} \tag{1}$$

Where i_P denotes the incentive he obtains from Lever (possibly be a reward or a forfeit), c_P denotes the computation cost he consumes on the intensive workload. To evaluate the behaviors among various types of players, the initial interest of the task is also counted according to the correctness of *final verdict*.

Essentially, Lever is a crypto-economic protocol [23]. It encodes an incentive mechanism, seeking to promote honest validation of VIT among rational stakeholders and disinterests. We aim to propose a dominant-strategy-incentive-compatible (DSIC) mechanism that honest validation stays as a weakly dominant strategy for every rational player. This means regardless of what any other players do, the strategy earns a player a payoff at least as high as any other strategy.

3.3   Assumptions

We assume a well-connected network with dynamic membership. Incumbent participants can establish Sybil-resistant identities at backbone by mechanisms like [24,25]. We adopt the Byzantine-Rational model (BR) as Lever's threat model. When dealing with intensive workloads, non-Byzantine nodes are assumed to be rational and would take foremost interest in maximizing their payoffs. We assume there exist at most $f < n/4$ Byzantine players out of n incumbent nodes. They can behave arbitrarily to deviate from the protocol, including but not limited to aborting, freeloading, taking bribes, or collusion. The adversary is computationally bounded such that cryptographic primitives are secure. We also assume the existence of random oracle $\mathcal{R}_\mathcal{O}$. Let c denote the cost to conduct an honest validation. Regarding each task, we assume at least one rational stakeholder who initially has $v_T > c$ exists. Our design is simplified from external economic risks by assuming the relatively stable value of the currency.

3.4   System Properties

Lever achieves intensive validation with the following properties:

- *Validity:* For any VIT accepted by Lever, $\mathcal{T}.\mathsf{Ver}(VIT) = valid$ always holds.
- *Finality:* Each VIT will get finalized within δ_f w.h.p.
- *Agreement:* All non-Byzantine nodes agree on the validity of a VIT.
- *Incentive Compatibility:* Lever ensures the honest validation is DSIC throughout the game. All participants who follow the strategy will get the best positive payoffs. On the contrary, any strategy that deviates from the protocol only ends up with a negative payoff.
- *Scalability:* System throughput grows linearly with the number of verifiers.
- *Efficiency:* Each VIT only incurs $\mathcal{O}(1)$ times of validation on average and $\mathcal{O}(\log \mathcal{E}_B)$ times to reach finality in the worst case.
- *Cost-efficiency:* Transaction founder only needs to pay a minimal reward to proxy the intensive workload on-chain.
- *Self-reinforcement:* Lever efficiently confiscates the budget of the adversary as well as purifies incumbent Byzantine nodes, thus adaptively performing lower latency and redundancy on validation with the decline of the adversary.

4 Lever-Boost Game

4.1 Preparation

Lever provides each VIT with an execution time-limit T_e, which encodes the time limit for endorsement collection, and an incentive benchmark a, which stays the base payment for a single validation. The two factors are closely related to the difficulty of the task η_T. In Lever, nodes lock up their stake to join in validation. Specific accounts bound with public keys are built up to uniformly manage their collaterals in the prevention of double-spending. After execution, a node makes an endorsement for his verdict by sending a proposal:

$$proposal := \langle txid, vd, deposit \rangle_{\mathsf{sk}}$$

The proposal links with the unique identifier of VIT and transfers the collateral to his account. During settlement, rewards or forfeits will also be directly applied to the balance. Only when a VIT gets finalized, its related deposits are spendable. Especially, verifiers are required to pre-store stakes for undertaking validation tasks. We denote the set of incumbent verifiers as $\{V\}$.

Our design also entails the underlying functionalities from backbone which will be realized in Sect. 6. We require the existence of a global clock that cuts the whole timeline into multiple *periods* which are relatively even. The clock is employed to measure T_e and we denote the average time duration of a *period* as T_p. At the beginning of each period, a fresh, unbiased random seed rnd is generated. In each period, nodes from a Sybil-resistant committee reach Byzantine agreement on the proposals with strong consistency.

4.2 Construction

We present the Lever-Boost Game π_L, a scalable off-chain pattern dominant by single validation. The construction can be disassembled into underlying stages:

- (**Lock**) On receiving a VIT, committee members checks to assure: *i.* it carries adequate reward and collateral according to η_T. *ii.* input state o_i has no conflict with any proposed transactions. The VIT will be discarded if any of the checks fail. Otherwise, it will be anchored by backbone with o_i locked to secure the consistency of the game.
- (**Task Assignment**) In the next period, a verifier $V \in \{V\}$ is randomly selected to take the task with the required deposit frozen in his account. An execution time-limit of $\lceil T_e/T_p \rceil$ periods is activated.
- (**Verify**) V obtains vd by executing $\mathcal{T}.\mathsf{Ver}(\mathsf{VIT})$ and then broadcasts his *proposal* to the backbone. Once it is confirmed, the game evolves into the challenge stage. If the timeout expires, the committee will forfeit his collateral and restart the task assignment.
- (**Challenge**) Within a new execution time limit, any node could propose a challenge refuting the verdict of the last verifier. It will be instantly recorded by the committee if an adequate deposit is pledged. Note that, it is possible

when two or more challenges emerge at the same time. By next period, the fresh random seed rnd will be used to fairly confirm one of them and abort the others. The game iteratively undergoes the same assign-verify-challenge circle and finally converges to the following two outcomes: 1. In case the dispute remains unsolved for complete τ rounds, it is regarded as *intricate* and protocol resorts to the backstop scheme for a final verdict. 2. In any round if no valid proposal is collected, the task efficiently finalizes with the verdict from the last verifier.

- (**Settlement**) Lever transits the contract state to o_f if the final verdict equals valid, otherwise unlocks o_i to enable the next trigger. Towards those who have made wrong *proposals*, deposits are forfeited to recursively award truthful verifiers and challengers in each round, while other collaterals automatically get unfrozen. Misbehaved verifiers are expelled from $\{V\}$, no longer assigned any task. The alteration of membership and incentive is confirmed by the backbone consensus for every new block.

Note that, a vital point in our design is to make the validation and challenge unique in each round of the game. Validation thus evolves in an exclusive branch with better consistency. It further prevents fierce competition or Sybil Attack to impair the reward of execution. Each honest participant is promised a fair and stable payoff, preventing the game from falling to the Participation Dilemma [7].

4.3 Incentive Design

Table 2 depicts the collateral and expenses required by π_L where $s \in [1, \tau]$ denotes the round number. The user only needs to pay the initial reward and deposit which are both a to start the first execution. A transaction *fee* is also required to anchor any information on backbone. We consider the cost for intensive validation $c \gg fee$ by default, and obviously $a > c + fee$. As for verifiers and challengers, the required deposit doubles for every new round. Since they hold contradictive verdicts towards each other, there always exists a share of the deposit to double the incentive of $\mathcal{T}$. Hence, validation reward of round $I_R(s)$ is decided by the validity of last challenge proposal,[1] which we denote as σ.

Table 2. Incentive Design of the Lever-Boost Game

Role	Deposit	Expense	Incentive-Correct	Incentive-Wrong
TxFounder	a	$a + fee$	$-a - fee$	$-2a - fee$
Verifier	$2^s a$	fee	$I_R(s)$[a]	$-2^s a - fee$
Challenger	$2^{s+1} a$	fee	$I_R(s)$	$-2^{s+1} a - fee$

[a]
$$I_R(s) = \begin{cases} 2^{s-1}a - fee & \sigma = valid \\ 2^s a - fee & \sigma = invalid \end{cases} \qquad (2)$$

---

[1] In the first round, it is determined by the correctness of VIT.

The effect can be explicitly demonstrated in Fig. 2. Let u_F, u_V, u_C respectively denote the incentive of transaction founder, verifier, and challenger. The surplus incentive of the game can be calculated as $-(u_F + u_V + u_C)$. In case the challenger makes a wrong verdict, an extra reward of $4a$ is generated.[2] While this value becomes $2a$ in honest cases, it combines to encapsulate the task with double reward and collateral.

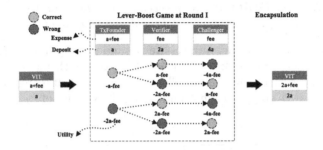

Fig. 2. Role Utility of Lever-Boost Game at Round I

In general, the evolving of π_L leads to an exponentially boosting incentive for honest participants: $u_P \geq 2^{s-1}a - c$. As the validation cost is constant, more rational disinterests will be attracted to the game and help honest user leverage adequate endorsements for his task. While the adversary covers up all expenses of extra executions, their forfeits become explosively expensive. Thus we conclude the following theorem.

Theorem 1. *Lever achieves cost-efficiency and efficiently confiscates the budget of the adversary.*

4.4 Properties

The security threats of π_L mainly come from two aspects. Malicious incumbent verifiers could abort or take bribes to return a wrong verdict. Besides, external adversaries could make false challenge proposals to delay the correct execution. We define those who have the worst behaviors as:

Definition 1. *External Stubborn Adversary. Potential malicious nodes who exhaust their budgets to propose false challenges whenever the VIT receives correct verdicts in Verify phase of the game.*

Below we analyze the game considering the threats, assuming the backstop π_B can always return a correct final verdict within finite periods.

Validity. Towards any task, the maintenance of a correct final verdict requires all invalid *Verify* proposals to get timely challenged. While at least one stakeholder initially has such motivation, they could avoid any loss, meanwhile, obtain

---

[2] Here, *fees* are extracted as commissions for backbone confirmation.

attractive rewards from malicious nodes. Even in the worst case, the secure back-stop will be triggered to enforce correct execution. The key boils down to how much collateral is required. We refer $\rho \in [0, 1]$ to the Byzantine ratio of $\{V\}$, to defend the validity of the game, the average deposit d_h can be calculated as:

$$d_h = a + \sum_{s=1}^{\tau} \rho^s \cdot 2^{s+1} a. \tag{3}$$

Theorem 2. *Lever-Boost Game performs Sybil resistance over verifiers and will never output a wrong final verdict if stakeholders own a collateral of* $(2^{\tau+2} - 3)a$.

Proof. Suppose all incumbent verifiers are Byzantine, according to Eq. (3) with $\rho = 1$, stakeholders can still keep reporting disputes and then obtain the correct verdict from π_B with the maximum collateral. It also indicates creating arbitrary Sybil identites over verifiers cannot undermine the validity of π_L.

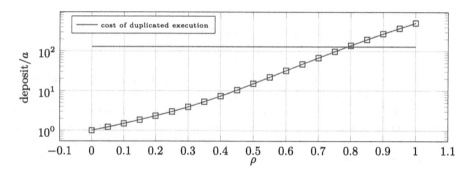

Fig. 3. Average deposit required for validity under various Byzantine ratios.

Although the worst situation entails substantial collateral from stakeholders, such pressure is greatly released considering the following observations. Figure 3 shows the overall variation of the deposit requirement. If we deploy Sybil-resistant mechanisms over the registration of verifiers to suppress ρ within a moderate level (like $\rho < 1/4$), the deposit will be trivial and friendly to the user. Moreover, since the game timely evicts Byzantine verifiers, the requirement will be consistently released as more tasks are taken. We testify such effect by experiment in Sect. 7. In addition, π_L releases the threats from collateral exhaustion or being off-line by enlarging the scale of stakeholders. Consider a disinterest verifier V who has conducted honest execution at round s. In subsequent rounds, by proposing a correct challenge, he will gain an extra payoff $u_V \geq 2^s a -$ fee. If no one defends the task, he will instead lose his collateral and execution cost $u'_V = -2^s a - c -$ fee. This adjusts his interest relevance to $v_T = u_V - u'_V > 0$, which will drive him to firmly defend the task as a stakeholder.

Finality and Scalability. Suppose π_B requires $\mathcal{E}_B$ times of exra execution cost, the adequate incentive could be rapidly accumulated within $\tau = \lceil \log \mathcal{E}_B \rceil$

rounds. This keeps the Lever-Boost Game from endless collateral competition. Let B_A denote the budget of the adversary, in Lever-Boost Game, a task will take $y \leq \tau$ times of execution to obtain a final verdict if:

$$B_A < \sum_{s=1}^{y} (2^s \cdot a + fee) = (2^{y+1} - 2)a + y \cdot fee. \tag{4}$$

Recall the execution cost $c < a$, most intensive workloads could get optimized execution, which helps the system to achieve significantly better scalability. Even an extremely wealthy adversary cannot prevent finality by abusing the challenge interface. The latency of the game is strictly bounded within $2\tau \lceil T_e/T_p \rceil$ periods and adaptively reduced with the budget exhaustion of the adversary.

Incentive Compatibility. With the guarantee of validity and finality, we could further derive the utility expectation of roles according to their strategies. Let p_σ refer to $Pr[\sigma = valid]$. As for stakeholders and disinterests, staying as honest verifiers or challengers respectively earn them stable, positive payoffs, which stay linear with their collaterals:

$$u_V = (p_\sigma \cdot 2^{s-1} + (1 - p_\sigma) \cdot 2^s)a - c - fee + v_T > a - c - fee > 0$$

$$u_C = (p_\sigma \cdot 2^{s-1} + (1 - p_\sigma) \cdot 2^s)a + v_T - fee > a - fee > 0$$

Whereas strategies without a correct verdict including taking bribes, aborting and making false challenges only converge to negative expectations:

$$u_{bribe} = u_{abort} = -2^s a - fee \leq -2a < 0$$

$$u_{stubborn} = -2^{s+1}a - fee \leq -4a < 0$$

Lazy verifiers who deviate by randomly guessing the verdict will suffer more forfeits than their income:

$$u_{guess} = 1/2 \cdot p_\sigma \cdot (2^{s-1} - 2^s)a - fee \leq -p_\sigma \cdot a/2 < 0$$

Similar to the mechanism of Nothing at Stake Attack [26], a lazy verifier could make collaterals on both verdicts. He could instantly challenge his own Verify proposal, leaving the dispute to subsequent rounds. Suppose such an attempt is made in round s, his total payoff expectation can be described as:

$$u_P = \begin{cases} (p_\sigma \cdot 2^{s-1} + (1 - p_\sigma) \cdot 2^s)a - 2^{s+1}a - fee & \mathcal{T}.\mathsf{Ver}(\mathsf{VIT}) = valid \\ (p_\sigma \cdot 2^{s-1} + (1 - p_\sigma) \cdot 2^s)a - 2^s a - fee & \mathcal{T}.\mathsf{Ver}(\mathsf{VIT}) = invalid \end{cases}$$

Such attempts only bring him losses no matter which verdict outperforms. In terms of the game, the strategy upgrades the incentive of task for a wider range of executions with the attacker's own collateral.

Obviously, honest validation is the unique dominant strategy of π_L.

To conclude, Lever-Boost Game keeps the validity, finality, and incentive compatibility of tne system if a secure backstop is served. It also significantly reduces the expense and collateral required from stakeholders and simplifies the dense interactions compared to the classical challenge-response pattern.

5   Backstop Construction

In this section, we utilize succinct non-interactive arguments of knowledge, often known as SNARK [13–16], to construct a secure backstop scheme π_B for the Lever-Boost Game. The scheme is executed among a group of Sybil-resistant judges who hold the responsibility to figure out all *intricate* disputes in the system. At any time, the ratio of incumbent Byzantine players satisfies $\rho < 1/4$.

SNARK allows one party to generate a succinct proof to another that a given statement x is true. It is a triple of algorithms $(Setup, \mathcal{SP}, \mathcal{SV})$, where $Setup(\lambda, \mathsf{rnd}, \mathcal{C})$ takes the security parameter λ and secure randomness rnd to pre-process the circuit $\mathcal{C}$ derived from the statement, and public parameters S_P, S_V are then generated respectively for the prover and the verifier. The prover $\mathcal{SP}(S_P, x, w)$ additionally takes the statement x and the witness w and outputs a proof π. The verifier $\mathcal{SV}(S_V, x, \pi)$ is a decisional deterministic algorithm that checks the proof to assert whether the statement is true. SNARK is succinct because its proof size should be $\mathcal{O}(\log |\mathcal{C}|)$ and the verifier's running time should be $\mathcal{O}(|x| + \log |\mathcal{C}|)$. By contrast, the prover algorithm $\mathcal{SP}$ is computationally intensive and can only be deployed off-chain. A SNARK is said to be transparent if it requires no trusted setup.

Below, we showcase the design of π_B with a transparent SNARK:

- (**Init**) Upon detecting any task $\mathcal{T}$ involved in the dispute, a rational judge assesses the expense upper-bound c_B of its SNARK construction according to the complexity of the validation procedure and the size of VIT. The expense covers the proof generation cost c_{BP} off-chain as well as the duplicated $\mathcal{SV}$ execution cost c_{BV} on-chain.
- (**Bid**) Starting with round $s \geq 2$, the Lever-Boost Game π_L leaves an extra period before the task assignment for judges' possible intervention to resolve the dispute. A rational judge will make bid proposals when his own assessment satisfies $c_B < 2^{s-1}a - c$. To prevent abuse, a valid bid should include a deposit of $2^{s+1}a$. When the backbone confirms one or more valid bids, it fairly chooses one as the winner using public randomness rnd and releases the rest. A new execution timeout T_e is activated for the execution of SNARK.
- (**Construct**) The selected judge first obtains the correct verdict vd by running the validation procedure, and then builds the circuit $\mathcal{C}$ based on the statement $x : \mathcal{T}.\mathsf{Ver}(\mathsf{VIT}) = vd$. Next, he completes $Setup(\cdot)$ and $\mathcal{SP}(\cdot)$ to generate the verifier parameter S_V along with the proof π. Finally, before T_e expires, he signs the proof proposal $\langle \pi, S_V, vd \rangle$ and delivers it to the backbone.
- (**Resolve**) Participants of the backbone run $\mathcal{SV}(\cdot)$ on-chain. In case π is valid, the task gets finalized with the verdict vd, leading to the settlement of π_L. Meanwhile, the truthful judge has his bid released with an additional reward of $I_R(s) - c_{BV} + f_B$. Otherwise, the judge gets ejected from the group with his bid deposit forfeited as the surplus reward f_B for the dispute's subsequent resolution. Since the forfeits directly doubles the current task incentive, π_L starts from round $s + 1$.

Note that, the integration of π_B with the other types of SNARK is entirely feasible. The only difference is that a trusted setup is launched before the Construct step. The imported reliance on trust results in the possibility to achieve a constant execution cost of $\mathcal{SV}$ and constant proof size. With the rise of universal SNARKs, a single trusted setup can now support multiple circuits. Making the tradeoffs will considerably improve the cost-efficiency of the backstop scheme.

The following theorem adapts to π_B with any secure SNARK instance:

Theorem 3. π_B *is* DSIC *and finalizes with the correct verdict within* $\delta_f = \lceil (2T_e/T_p + 1) \cdot (\log \mathcal{E}_B - \lambda/\log \rho) \rceil$ *periods w.h.p.*

Proof. For validity, given completeness of SNARK, the backbone accepts the proof proposal w.h.p. from any truthful judge. Given knowledge soundness of SNARK, the adversary cannot forge a valid π for the wrong statement. Thus, π_B always finalizes with the verdict vd that meets $\mathcal{T}.\mathsf{Ver}(\mathsf{VIT}) = vd$.

For finality, assume the stubborn adversary has an unlimited budget, he can continually propose bids with forged proofs to delay π_B. Before π_L accumulates adequate incentive for π_B, the adversary's defection creates an extra execution timeout T_e. However, his forfeits facilicate the progression of π_L by skipping the entire round of game, saving $2T_e$ instead. As a result, the finality of π_L is well-protected. When the task incentive fulfills the rational judges' assessment, the adversary only has the probability $P = \rho^{s^*} < 10^{-\lambda}$ to delay π_B for extra $s^* = -\lambda/\log \rho$ rounds of T_e until a rational judge wins the bid. To summarise, recall $\mathcal{E}_B = c_B/c$, incentive accumulation takes at most $\tau = \log \mathcal{E}_B$ rounds of π_L. The worst-case finality parameter of Lever is bounded by $\lceil (2T_e/T_p+1) \cdot (\tau + s^*) \rceil$.

For incentive compatibility, truthful judges' utility equals $u_J = I_R(s) - c_{BV} + f_B - c_{BP} - c \geq 2^{s-1}a - c_B - c > 0$, whereas the defected judges' utility equals $u_\mathcal{A} = -2^{s+1}a < 0$. Honest execution is the unique dominant strategy of π_B.

Combining Theorem 3 with analyses in Sect. 4.4, we can conclude that Lever achieves validity and DSIC tolerance of at most $n/4$ Byzantine participants.

6   Integration with Backbone

Difficulty Model. For the safe deployment of Lever, the primary thing is to obtain the truthful difficulty of the task. In Lever, the transaction founder is required to measure η_T in advance and attach η_T to VIT. To prevent possible misstatements, the accuracy of this value is integrated into the validity of the task. In other words, $\mathcal{T}.\mathsf{Ver}(\mathsf{VIT})$ outputs Invalid if there is a mismatch between η_T and the actual workload. As for intensive validation, uncertainty on the initial task incentive may arouse catastrophic effects. An adversary could launch bribing [27] and frontrunning [28,29] to disincentive faithful execution from rational nodes. Other than allowing users to customize the incentive of a transaction, we employ difficulty as the exclusive factor in configuration. For any VIT, we set its incentive benchmark as $a = \gamma_1 \cdot \eta_T$. Also, its execution time limit is stipulated as $T_e = \gamma_2 \cdot \eta_T$. Here, γ_1 and γ_2 are system-defined constants that remain steady for a relatively long time. We assume they are reasonably set up, which makes a attractive to most rational disinterests, and makes T_e adequate for them to independently finish the execution with high probability. The design ensures the same initial yield in the initial task incentive, VITs are thus treated indiscriminately in the execution order. Additionally, any participant in Lever could obtain a compatible reward from honest validation.

Theorem 4. *Any node could predicate the validity of a transaction carrying a reward $\gamma_1 \cdot \eta$ within the execution cost c, where $c < \gamma_1 \cdot \eta$, regardless of whether there is a difficulty misstatement.*

Proof. If an adversary attempts to cover up η_T with η, let η_x denote $min(\eta_T, \eta)$. $\mathcal{T}.Ver(VIT)$ will terminate after finishing operations weighted η_x, and marks the VIT as *invalid*. Since $c/\gamma_1 < \eta_x \leq \eta$ always holds, verifiers will never undertake workloads with insufficient incentive or execution time limit.

Global Clock and Randomness. We set up the global clock with existing committee-based consensus, Solida [1], as the backbone. It manages the committee membership in a sliding window fashion with PoW as the election source. Every time a mining winner gets rolled into the committee, system time is driven to the next period. Other than the use of Nakamoto consensus, it confirms the election with strong consistency by creating a novel Byzantine consensus led by external miners. Meanwhile, fresh randomness sources rnd can be timely extracted from PoW of the winner. Note that, this is not the exclusive way to realize such features. For instance, in frameworks like Algorand [2] which achieves full swap reconfiguration with PoS, a clock can be established referring to the view number of consensus. And secure randomness can be obtained by periodically running algorithms [30] for distributed randomness generation despite a higher overhead being served.

Confirmation of Lever. In Lever, participants independently take intensive validation and output a series of proposals to endorse their verdicts. Each proposal can be viewed as a variant of ledger transfer with negligible overhead. On receiving tasks or proposals, members of backbone conduct incentive and confliction checks, then reach Byzantine agreement to anchor the eligible ones. Whenever detecting a new period from election consensus, they first use the fresh randomness and the collected proposals to derive the state of tasks and then filter out finalized VITs w.r.t. the global clock. Meanwhile, settlement is achieved based on the final verdict. Finally, the states of the game will be updated by the next round of consensus. Thus, the safety of backbone consensus pledges the consistency of Lever.

7   Evaluation

Experimental Setup. We have implemented a proof-of-concept prototype to evaluate Lever under more realistic scenarios. We employ uniform distribution to bootstrap the difficulty of transactions as well as the power of verifiers, while Pareto distribution is used to simulate the deposits of verifiers and the budgets of adversaries. Unless otherwise noted, we deploy the following tests under the worst-case configuration, where there exist exactly $\lfloor n/4 \rfloor$ Byzantine incumbent nodes, who always take bribes to propose the wrong verdict.

Performance. As for intensive validation, the concrete value on throughput is heavily affected by the relative relationship between deposit level of verifiers and the average difficulty of the tasks. Without loss of generality, we evaluate the performance of Lever by setting comparative experiments with frameworks deploying the duplicated execution pattern. We conduct the underlying tests on the same sets of randomized nodes and VITs.

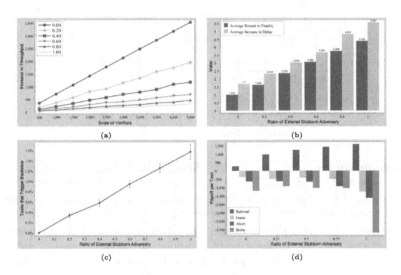

Fig. 4. (*a*) Increase in throughput brought by Lever ($n \in [500, 5000]$). (*b*) Average rounds of game to achieve finality and the increase in latency introduced by Lever.(*c*) Average percent of tasks triggering the backstop. (*d*) Average payoff per validation for various roles ($\gamma_1 = 10$, $\eta_{max} = 50$, $c = \gamma_1 \cdot \eta/2$, $n = 1000$, $\mathcal{E}_B \in [2^{10}, 2^{13}]$).

By consistently infusing excessive VITs to both frameworks in one epoch, we obtain the magnification on throughput incurred by Lever and distinguish the cases with varying scales of verifiers and ratios of the external stubborn adversary. As Fig. 4a shows, Lever scales linearly in the number of verifiers, and the effect is adaptive to the number of external stubborn adversaries.

In terms of latency, we set a fixed scale of verifiers and infuse $5 \cdot 10^4$ randomized VITs into both frameworks. For comparison, we set the latency of duplicated pattern as the execution time limit. As Fig. 4b tells, a task could be finalized at the first round of Lever-Boost Game w.h.p. if no external stubborn adversary is attached to it, this reflects the high efficiency of Lever under the most general case. By contrast, the worst-case latency is finite and affordable, the adversary can averagely delay the task for no more than 4.5 rounds of game.

The backstop scheme is inherently inefficient due to the limited scale of judges and the heavy computation cost for producing SNARK proofs, which could be viewed as the bottleneck of the framework. However, we measure the average percent workload triggering the game by 10^5 VITs verified in Lever. As Fig. 4c shows, even in the worst case with extreme external pressure, over 98.3% of intensive workload gets finalized in Lever-Boost game, which further embodies the superior scalability of Lever and its robustness against DoS attack.

Table 3. Average tasks taken by various strategies in Lever.

R_{st}^* \ Role	Rational	Guess	Abort	Bribe
0.00	107.31	2.4	63.03	1.00
0.25	164.98	1.77	63.69	1.00
0.50	219.18	1.95	60.67	1.00
0.75	274.99	2.00	43.73	1.00
1.00	331.17	2.13	25.10	1.00

* Ratio of external stubborn adversary.

Self-reinforcement. To evaluate the effect of the game in restraining various malicious behaviors, we build three groups of comparative tests, which respectively equips Byzantine verifiers with typical deviated strategies of guessing, aborting, and bribing. After handling 10^5 VITs, we measure the state of nodes and illustrate their average validation opportunities in Table 3, and payoffs in Fig. 4d. As we can see, rational verifiers undertake most chances of validation and steadily obtains a positive payoff, whereas Byzantine nodes suffer substantial forfeits. The ones who guess or bribe make trivial influence before being ejected from the committee. The ones who abort the game exhaust their budget and suffer from maximal losses. Noticeably, the increase of stubborn adversaries greatly raises the incentive for honest validation as well as the severity of punishment.

8   Conclusion and Future Works

To the best of our knowledge, Lever is the first validation framework that supports intensive validation while being incentive-compatible, which makes comprehensive improvements compared to the existing solutions. We prove that the optimized and secure single validation can be fit to blockchain without any dense interaction by making execution redundancy flexible to the budget of the adversary. With the subtle collateral pattern excavated, fair and incentive-compatible mechanisms are proposed to incentivize verifiers according to their actual workload, avoiding any unfavourable dilemma on validation. Furthermore, we demonstrate how Lever significantly releases excessive off-chain efforts from stakeholders and eliminates the brittle dependency on altruism.

Lever also offers several intriguing areas for additional research. Constructing the backstop with duplicated validation can further optimize the off-chain cost ratio $\mathcal{E}_B$ and reduce the collateral needed, the key is to tolerate more abundant defection strategies from parallelly working rational judges. Consider Lever employs pessimistic locking to ensure the atomic execution of every VIT, a substitution of deterministic concurrency control (DCC) [10, 31] will provide better serializability and concurrency for the system. Inspired by Pisa [32], our subsequent work will show that safe escrow-based contracts can be designed to outsource such obligation to rational nodes with optimized expenses. This will completely release all extra efforts required from stakeholders.

Acknowledgements. This paper is supported by the National Key R&D Program of China through project 2020YFB1005600, the Natural Science Foundation of China through projects U21A20467, 61932011, 61972019 and Beijing Natural Science Foundation through project M21031 and CCF-Huawei Huyanglin Foundation through project CCF-HuaweiBC2021009.

References

1. Abraham, I., Malkhi, D., Nayak, K., Ren, L., Spiegelman, A.: Solida: a blockchain protocol based on reconfigurable byzantine consensus. In: 21st International Conference on Principles of Distributed Systems, pp. 25:1–25:19 (2017)
2. Gilad, Y., Hemo, R., Micali, S., Vlachos, G., Zeldovich, N.: Algorand: scaling byzantine agreements for cryptocurrencies. In: Proceedings of the 26th Symposium on Operating Systems Principles, pp. 51–68 (2017)
3. Zamani, M., Movahedi, M., Raykova, M.: Rapidchain: scaling blockchain via full sharding. In: Proceedings of the 2018 ACM SIGSAC Conference on Computer and Communications Security, pp. 931–948 (2018)
4. Al-Bassam, M., Sonnino, A., Bano, S., Hrycyszyn, D., Danezis, G.: Chainspace: a sharded smart contracts platform. In: 25th Annual Network and Distributed System Security Symposium (2018)
5. Wood, G.: Ethereum: a secure decentralised generalised transaction ledger (2017). Accessed 03 Jan 2018
6. Luu, L., Teutsch, J., Kulkarni, R., Saxena, P.: Demystifying incentives in the consensus computer. In: Proceedings of the 22nd ACM SIGSAC Conference on Computer and Communications Security, pp. 706–719 (2015)
7. Kalodner, H.A., Goldfeder, S., Chen, X., Weinberg, S.M., Felten, E.W.: Arbitrum: scalable, private smart contracts. In: 27th USENIX Security Symposium, pp. 1353–1370 (2018)
8. Dziembowski, S., Faust, S., Hostáková, K.: General state channel networks. In: Proceedings of the 2018 ACM SIGSAC Conference on Computer and Communications Security, pp. 949–966 (2018)
9. Miller, A., Bentov, I., Bakshi, S., Kumaresan, R., McCorry, P.: Sprites and state channels: payment networks that go faster than lightning. In: Goldberg, I., Moore, T. (eds.) FC 2019. LNCS, vol. 11598, pp. 508–526. Springer, Cham (2019). https://doi.org/10.1007/978-3-030-32101-7_30

10. Wüst, K., Matetic, S., Egli, S., Kostiainen, K., Capkun, S.: Ace: asynchronous and concurrent execution of complex smart contracts. In: Proceedings of the 2020 ACM SIGSAC Conference on Computer and Communications Security, pp. 587–600 (2020)
11. Teustch, J., Reitwießner, C.: A scalable verification solution for blockchains (2017)
12. Das, S., Ribeiro, V.J., Anand, A.: YODA: enabling computationally intensive contracts on blockchains with byzantine and selfish nodes. In: 26th Annual Network and Distributed System Security Symposium abs/1811.03265 (2019)
13. Wahby, R.S., Tzialla, I., Shelat, A., Thaler, J., Walfish, M.: Doubly-efficient zksnarks without trusted setup. In: 2018 IEEE Symposium on Security and Privacy, pp. 926–943. IEEE (2018)
14. Couteau, G., Katsumata, S., Ursu, B.: Non-interactive zero-knowledge in pairing-free groups from weaker assumptions. In: Canteaut, A., Ishai, Y. (eds.) EUROCRYPT 2020. LNCS, vol. 12107, pp. 442–471. Springer, Cham (2020). https://doi.org/10.1007/978-3-030-45727-3_15
15. Setty, S.: Spartan: efficient and general-purpose zkSNARKs without trusted setup. In: Micciancio, D., Ristenpart, T. (eds.) CRYPTO 2020. LNCS, vol. 12172, pp. 704–737. Springer, Cham (2020). https://doi.org/10.1007/978-3-030-56877-1_25
16. Chen, B., Bünz, B., Boneh, D., Zhang, Z.: Hyperplonk: Plonk with linear-time prover and high-degree custom gates. In: Hazay, C., Stam, M. (eds.) EUROCRYPT 2023. LNCS, vol. 14005, pp. 499–530. Springer, Cham (2023). https://doi.org/10.1007/978-3-031-30617-4_17
17. Zhang, F., et al.: The ekiden platform for confidentiality-preserving, trustworthy, and performant smart contracts. IEEE Secur. Priv. 18(3), 17–27 (2020)
18. Frassetto, T., et al.: Pose: practical off-chain smart contract execution. In: 30th Annual Network and Distributed System Security Symposium (2023)
19. Dong, C., Wang, Y., Aldweesh, A., McCorry, P., van Moorsel, A.: Betrayal, distrust, and rationality: smart counter-collusion contracts for verifiable cloud computing. In: Proceedings of the 2017 ACM SIGSAC Conference on Computer and Communications Security, pp. 211–227 (2017)
20. Castro, M., Liskov, B.: Practical byzantine fault tolerance. In: Proceedings of the Third USENIX Symposium on Operating Systems Design and Implementation, pp. 173–186 (1999)
21. Duan, S., Zhang, H.: Foundations of dynamic BFT. In: 2022 IEEE Symposium on Security and Privacy (SP), pp. 1317–1334 (2022)
22. Eberhardt, J., Tai, S.: On or off the blockchain? Insights on off-chaining computation and data. In: De Paoli, F., Schulte, S., Broch Johnsen, E. (eds.) ESOCC 2017. LNCS, vol. 10465, pp. 3–15. Springer, Cham (2017). https://doi.org/10.1007/978-3-319-67262-5_1
23. Harz, D., Gudgeon, L., Gervais, A., Knottenbelt, W.J.: Balance: dynamic adjustment of cryptocurrency deposits. In: Proceedings of the 2019 ACM SIGSAC Conference on Computer and Communications Security, pp. 1485–1502 (2019)
24. Kiayias, A., Russell, A., David, B., Oliynykov, R.: Ouroboros: a provably secure proof-of-stake blockchain protocol. In: Katz, J., Shacham, H. (eds.) CRYPTO 2017. LNCS, vol. 10401, pp. 357–388. Springer, Cham (2017). https://doi.org/10.1007/978-3-319-63688-7_12
25. Andrychowicz, M., Dziembowski, S.: PoW-based distributed cryptography with no trusted setup. In: Gennaro, R., Robshaw, M. (eds.) CRYPTO 2015. LNCS, vol. 9216, pp. 379–399. Springer, Heidelberg (2015). https://doi.org/10.1007/978-3-662-48000-7_19

26. Li, W., Andreina, S., Bohli, J.-M., Karame, G.: Securing proof-of-stake blockchain protocols. In: Garcia-Alfaro, J., Navarro-Arribas, G., Hartenstein, H., Herrera-Joancomartí, J. (eds.) ESORICS/DPM/CBT -2017. LNCS, vol. 10436, pp. 297–315. Springer, Cham (2017). https://doi.org/10.1007/978-3-319-67816-0_17
27. SECBIT: How the winner got Fomo3d prize - a detailed explanation (2018)
28. Daian, P., et al.: Flash boys 2.0: frontrunning in decentralized exchanges, miner extractable value, and consensus instability. In: 2020 IEEE Symposium on Security and Privacy (SP), pp. 910–927. IEEE (2020)
29. Tjiam, K., Wang, R., Chen, H., Liang, K.: Your smart contracts are not secure: investigating arbitrageurs and oracle manipulators in ethereum. In: CYSARM@ CCS, pp. 25–35 (2021)
30. Schindler, P., Judmayer, A., Stifter, N., Weippl, E.: Hydrand: efficient continuous distributed randomness. In: 2020 IEEE Symposium on Security and Privacy (SP), Los Alamitos, CA, USA, pp. 73–89. IEEE Computer Society (2020)
31. Peng, Z., et al.: Neuchain: a fast permissioned blockchain system with deterministic ordering. Proc. VLDB Endow. **15**(11), 2585–2598 (2022)
32. McCorry, P., Bakshi, S., Bentov, I., Meiklejohn, S., Miller, A.: Pisa: arbitration outsourcing for state channels. In: Proceedings of the 1st ACM Conference on Advances in Financial Technologies, AFT 2019, pp. 16–30. Association for Computing Machinery, New York (2019)

Tikuna: An Ethereum Blockchain Network Security Monitoring System

Andres Gomez Ramirez[1,2]($\boxtimes$), Loui Al Sardy[2,3], and Francis Gomez Ramirez[1,2]

[1] Edenia, Edificio Trifami, 10104 San José, Costa Rica
andres@edenia.com, andres.gomez@sakundi.io
[2] Sakundi, Sepapaja tn 6, 15551 Tallinn, Estonia
loui.alsardy@fau.de
[3] Friedrich-Alexander-Universität Erlangen-Nürnberg, Faculty of Engineering, Department of Computer Science, Martensstr. 3, 91058 Erlangen, Germany

Abstract. Blockchain security is becoming increasingly relevant in today's cyberspace as it extends its influence in many industries. This paper focuses on protecting the lowest level layer in the blockchain, particularly the P2P network that allows the nodes to communicate and share information. The P2P network layer may be vulnerable to several families of attacks, such as Distributed Denial of Service (DDoS), eclipse attacks, or Sybil attacks. This layer is prone to threats inherited from traditional P2P networks, and it must be analyzed and understood by collecting data and extracting insights from the network behavior to reduce those risks. We introduce Tikuna, an open-source tool for monitoring and detecting potential attacks on the Ethereum blockchain P2P network, at an early stage. Tikuna employs an unsupervised Long Short-Term Memory (LSTM) method based on Recurrent Neural Network (RNN) to detect attacks and alert users. Empirical results indicate that the proposed approach significantly improves detection performance, with the ability to detect and classify attacks, including eclipse attacks, Covert Flash attacks, and others that target the Ethereum blockchain P2P network layer, with high accuracy. Our research findings demonstrate that Tikuna is a valuable security tool for assisting operators to efficiently monitor and safeguard the status of Ethereum validators and the wider P2P network.

Keywords: Ethereum blockchain · security · P2P network · deep learning · anomaly detection · vulnerabilities · eclipse attacks

1 Introduction

Ethereum was formally introduced by Vitalik Buterin in his whitepaper in 2014 [3] and launched in 2015 as a public cryptocurrency blockchain platform that supports smart contract functionality with Ether (ETH or Ξ) as its native cryptocurrency and Solidity as its programming language [37]; it is the second largest cryptocurrency after Bitcoin, with around \$200 billion as of March 2023 [7, 41].

Even though blockchain technology is highly secure and decentralized, it still offers attack opportunities. For example, in blockchain networks, there are cases, such as the

© The Author(s), under exclusive license to Springer Nature Singapore Pte Ltd. 2023
W. Meng et al. (Eds.): ISPEC 2023, LNCS 14341, pp. 462–476, 2023.
https://doi.org/10.1007/978-981-99-7032-2_27

ones mentioned in [8, 20, 26, 27], in which the dApps, average users, or the network itself are exposed to risks due to particular vulnerabilities [4, 8, 20, 21, 24, 26, 40, 42, 43]. Therefore, understanding the risks associated with blockchain networks and effectively developing security-focused solutions is essential to any blockchain.

Peer-to-peer (P2P) networks are decentralized networks that include many nodes storing and distributing data collectively, and each node operates as an individual peer. The communication is carried out without a central authority; hence, all nodes obtain the same amount of power and are responsible for the same activities. The P2P network is one of the fundamental components of the blockchains that enable the creation and operation of cryptocurrencies [28].

In the blockchain, the P2P network enables nodes (clients) to exchange data, for instance, transactions and blocks. In general, there is an economic incentive for participants to behave honestly. Given their public and distributed nature, blockchain components are especially exposed to attackers who can easily reach and interact with the different layers. Such adversaries may use a malicious node, tool, or software to take advantage of specific weaknesses in the P2P network layer and launch several attacks on the blockchain, like the ones described in [20, 26, 43]. The security of the entire blockchain relies on the reliability of its P2P network.

The Ethereum P2P protocol [36] was influenced by the kademlia Distributed Hash Table (DHT) design. Although kademlia possesses valuable properties, it has several limitations in terms of its security [4, 22]. There are several known attacks for such a protocol, including the eclipse attacks [20, 43], where it is possible to perform manipulations against the Ethereum P2P network participants, and deanonymization attacks, as presented in [14]. Other types of vulnerabilities are also present (s. Section 3.2). Nevertheless, employing multiple detection and mitigation approaches [10, 11] can significantly reduce or eliminate the severity of these risks.

This research paper introduces the following three main contributions:

- A Machine Learning (ML) approach that can detect several attacks at the Ethereum P2P layer using peer message trace data in a testing simulation environment using the libp2p testground framework;
- The detection of eclipse attacks on the mainnet is demonstrated by extracting custom-generated discovery connection log data from the Ethereum client Prysm and utilizing the LSTM neural network;
- A custom exploit of an eclipse attack was developed and tested against a modified Prysm client on the mainnet. The peer table buckets could be fulfilled by a single attacking machine, overcoming the limitation of a single peer per IP address by using virtual addresses and Docker containers. With this exploit, the effectiveness of the Tikuna approach can be tested.

Moreover, as a contribution to the Ethereum and blockchain security research communities, we have made the Tikuna code publicly available as an open-source resource at our GitHub repository [38].

This paper is organized as follows: Sect. 2 provides an overview of alternative and related approaches. Next, in Sect. 3, the various types of blockchain P2P network attacks are discussed, and the Tikuna approach, consisting of three primary steps, is introduced. The efficacy of the Tikuna approach is evaluated in Sect. 4, utilizing a simulation and mainnet connection dataset. Finally, Sect. 5 concludes the paper by summarizing the proposed work, drawing conclusions, and identifying potential future research directions.

2   Related Work

Researchers have recently started focusing on the solution to address the different attack vectors on the Ethereum platform and the P2P network security vulnerabilities. The following are some of the most recent works that address the security challenges of the Ethereum blockchain P2P networks:

Kabla et al. [21] focus on the security issues of each layer in the Ethereum blockchain, such as the network layer, by providing an in-depth analysis covering the following three areas:

- Its potential attacks include eclipse attacks and account hijacking attacks.
- The vulnerabilities that lead to them are unlimited node creation and uncapped incoming connections.
- Each incident's consequences include double spending or a denial of service.

Furthermore, the work presents an overview of the effectiveness and limitations of the current Intrusion Detection Systems (IDS) as a defense technique against various Ethereum-based attacks.

Vyzovitis et al. [40] propose two different hardening measures for the GossipSub protocol, the mesh construction and the score function. The authors describe some of the countermeasures featured in the GossipSub protocol. However, the proposed methods use fixed rules that should be manually parametrized, which has limited their widespread usage in the different Ethereum clients. We suggest the use of machine learning to select parameters for the detection of attacks automatically.

The report from Least Authority [23] details the results of a security audit they conducted on the next-generation node discovery protocol of the Ethereum P2P network stack. It also reveals areas for improvement in the DevP2P specification, particularly the lack of a proof-of-X scheme for identity generation, disjoint paths in the lookup operation, and broken handshake authentication. Finally, the report indicates that launching eclipse attacks against the Ethereum clients using the current peer discovery specification is trivial.

Marcus et al. [24] highlight the possibility of eclipse attacks on Ethereum nodes, which could be carried out using only two hosts and could result in the victim's view of the blockchain being filtered or their computing power being co-opted. The authors' contributions include a detailed explanation of the network and its relationship with the kademlia protocol, two off-path eclipse attacks, and one involving time manipulation. Furthermore, they have proposed countermeasures to prevent these attacks, such as using a combination of IP address and public key for node identification and making design decisions to harden Ethereum. Some of these countermeasures have been implemented in Geth v1.8. Those measures restrict the number of peers connecting to a victim from the same IP. We show that it is still possible to fulfill buckets from the peer table from a single attacking server with a unique public IP address.

Xu et al. [43] discuss the eclipse attacks on the Ethereum P2P Network. The authors developed an ETH-EDS eclipse-attack detection model targeting the Ethereum platform.

This model used a random forest classification technique to examine the network's regular and attack data packets. The collected data packets included details like the size of the tag packets, the frequency with which they were accessed, and the access time. The findings of the experiments show that malicious network nodes could be identified with a high degree of precision. We further propose using deep learning techniques to automatically select features in the data and improve detection accuracy. We use this research to compare our results. The details of our approach are discussed in the following sections.

3 Tikuna Approach

3.1 Tikuna Terminology

Tikuna is a proof-of-concept peer-to-peer network security monitoring system developed initially for the Ethereum blockchain. It uses deep learning to extract security and performance insights for the early detection of incidents [16, 30]. Our goal with Tikuna is to support the Ethereum community by providing a cutting-edge open-source tool capable of collecting security-related data from the state of the P2P network and improving network visibility by providing insights about the network's current state.

The Ethereum peer-to-peer (P2P) discovery protocol [13, 36] enables nodes on the network to locate and connect with other peers. With this protocol, nodes on the Ethereum network can share information about transactions, blocks, and other network events. The DevP2P architecture includes the discovery protocol as an essential component of the communication system among Ethereum nodes.

Ethereum uses a discovery algorithm similar to Kademlia [25], a Distributed Hash Table (DHT) communication protocol used before for other technologies such as torrents. This protocol enables peers to identify and interact with each other in a decentralized network without having to rely on a central server. Every node in the network is responsible for its routing table, organized in the form of a binary tree with the node's ID at the tree's root. Other peers are listed as leaf nodes. An existing peer can assist a new peer in joining the network by checking its routing table to locate the node relatively closest to the new peer's ID. This is accomplished by utilizing a distance metric based on the peer IDs' XOR operation. This process of gathering information about other peers in the network is repeated iteratively until the new peer has collected data on a significant number of peers in the network. The distance metric is the reason for both the effectiveness and the scalability of kademlia's routing tables, even when applied to extremely large networks.

The unsupervised anomaly detection method selected for this work is the long short-term memory. These algorithms are commonly used for analyzing time series data and natural language processing. Below is a brief introduction to these neural network algorithms.

Recurrent Neural Network. Recurrent neural networks [26] are frequently utilized for processing sequential data, such as time series. RNN is specialized for processing a sequence of values that are a function of time. We can define a data sequence as follows:

$$x(1), \ldots, x(T) \tag{1}$$

where T is the number of available data samples. RNN can scale to long sequences that would not be practical for networks without sequence-based specialization. Most recurrent networks can also process sequences of variable length. One of these models is especially interesting for this research. The long short-term memory model [1, 5, 26, 29, 34] uses a gating mechanism to propagate information through many time steps properly. LSTM networks have a specific memory cell and can capture long-term dependencies in sequential data. They are valuable tools for language modeling problems. These models are a version of recurrent neural networks useful for long interrelated sequences of data [1, 5, 26, 29, 34]. LSTM was chosen in this research for anomaly detection to find malicious connections to an Ethereum client. They can be defined with the following set of equations:

$$\overrightarrow{f}_t = \sigma_g(W_f \overrightarrow{x}_t + U_f \overrightarrow{h}_{t-1} + \overrightarrow{b}_f) \tag{2}$$

$$\overrightarrow{i}_t = \sigma_g(W_i \overrightarrow{x}_t + U_i \overrightarrow{h}_{t-1} + \overrightarrow{b}_i) \tag{3}$$

$$\overrightarrow{o}_t = \sigma_g(W_o \overrightarrow{x}_t + U_o \overrightarrow{h}_{t-1} + \overrightarrow{b}_o) \tag{4}$$

$$\overrightarrow{c}_t = \overrightarrow{f}_t \circ \overrightarrow{c}_{t-1} + \overrightarrow{i}_t \circ \sigma_c(W_c \overrightarrow{x}_t + U_c \overrightarrow{h}_{t-1} + \overrightarrow{b}_c) \tag{5}$$

$$\overrightarrow{h}_t = o_t \circ \sigma_h(c_t) \tag{6}$$

Similarly to the common RNN, $\overrightarrow{x}_t$ is the input vector at a given iteration t, $\overrightarrow{h}_t$ is an output vector of the hidden layer, and $\overrightarrow{c}_t$ is a cell state. In this case, W and U are parameter matrices, and $\overrightarrow{b}$ are bias vectors. $\overrightarrow{f}_t$ is a forget gate vector, $\overrightarrow{i}_t$ is the input gate vector and $\overrightarrow{o}_t$ is the output gate vector. The operator $\circ$ is the entrywise product of matrices.

In the next section, some attacks that can be detected using the described unsupervised anomaly detection model are explained in detail.

3.2 Types of P2P Network Attacks

Adversaries can exploit some vulnerabilities in the blockchain's P2P networks to. perform a variety of attacks [4, 8, 20, 21, 24, 26, 40, 42, 43], including the following:

(1) **Eclipse Attack** [20, 24, 42]. An eclipse attack is an attack that can be carried out against a single victim node or the whole network, where the adversary isolates the victim node within the P2P network by gaining complete control of the node's access to information or control over everything that the node sees.
(2) **Censorship Attack** [40]. During this type of attack, the adversaries will use the nodes on the network that they have created with fake identities (i.e., Sybil nodes) to propagate all messages, except for those the peer published that they are trying to attack. In addition, the primary objective of the attacker is to censor the target and stop its messages from being transmitted to the rest of the network.

(3) **Sybil Attack** [2, 12]. Which is also known as pseudo-spoofing, is an attack that can target any P2P network, such as blockchain networks, in which a single adversary creates a large number of nodes on the network with fake identities to gain a more significant presence in the network and eventually take control of the network. This attack might also be used to carry out other types, such as an eclipse or censorship attack.

(4) **Cold Boot Attack** [40]. In this type of attack, honest nodes and nodes with fake identities (so-called Sybil nodes) join the network simultaneously; genuine peers attempt to build their network while connecting to both Sybil and genuine peers. Since there is no information about honest nodes to secure the network, the Sybils can seize control. There are two possible scenarios for the attack: (1) when the network bootstraps with Sybils joining from the start or (2) when new nodes join the network when it is under attack.

(5) **Flash and Covert Flash Attack** [40]. Sybils will simultaneously connect and launch attacks against the targeted network in a Flash attack. On the other hand, in the Covert Flash Attack, Sybils join the network and act normally for some time to build up their score. Then, they carry out a coordinated attack in which they stop propagating messages altogether to disrupt the network entirely. Furthermore, as the adversaries act appropriately up until that point and establish a valid profile, it is difficult to identify the attack.

Our goal with Tikuna is to identify the described attacks using the anomaly detection approach, that is, by finding peer connections to a victim that deviates from the expected behavior of honest peers. We describe in detail the different components of Tikuna, starting with the data collection and concluding with the anomaly detection module.

3.3 Tikuna Methodology

Figure 1 shows the methodology of Tikuna, which comprises three main steps: (1) data extraction from a simulation environment using the testground [35] framework and the Ethereum mainnet; (2) training and classification analysis; and (3) P2P security incident detection. The following subsections provide a detailed explanation of these steps.

Step 1: Data Extraction from Testground Simulation and Ethereum 2.0 Mainnet. Data extraction refers to extracting data from a simulation or mainnet environment. It may include patterns that are challenging to identify without suitable analysis and converting it into a format ideal for the training part, i.e., for training our LSTM model. However, before this step, the dataset must be preprocessed to extract the pertinent features and convert the data into a format the AI model can interpret.

Every second, the measurement system gathers a sequence of monitoring data from the participating peers in the network. The extracted data is parsed into structured data represented by vectors of integers that are later normalized by applying the MinMaxScaler method from Sklearn. The used data includes timestamps and gossip message event traces. The data extraction process in LSTM [1, 5, 6, 26, 29, 34] involves four main steps: (1) the data cleaning step filters out any data from the simulation da-taset considered irrelevant or corrupt; (2) the feature extraction step involves identify-ing and extracting the relevant features from the dataset, which will be used to train the LSTM model; (3)

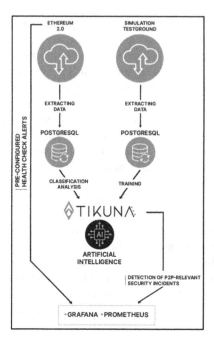

Fig. 1. Overview of the proposed Tikuna Architecture.

The data normalization step scales the extracted features to a standard range, ensuring that the LSTM model can handle them most effectively, and (4) in the sequence formation step, the extracted and normalized features are grouped into a time-series sequence that can be utilized to train the LSTM model.

Step 2: Training and Classification Analysis. The model is fed with input sequences and output labels corresponding to only normal data in the training phase. The model's weights and biases are then iteratively updated to reduce the difference between its predictions and the actual outputs. This enables the model to understand the underlying relationships in the data. in the evaluation part, on the other hand, the trained LSTM model is utilized to predict new, unseen input sequences. The model receives a sequence of input data and generates an output prediction based on the learning patterns during the training process. This prediction may then be compared to the actual label to determine the model's accuracy. As illustrated in Fig. 2, the training data for Tikuna AI are the output data from the preprocessing stage for regular peer communication within the network. In addition, Tikuna uses this data to train the model and extract features that the artificial neural network in the subsequent stage will utilize.

Step 3: Detection of P2P-Relevant Security Incidents. In this step, detecting security incidents related to the P2P network involves identifying and recognizing connection patterns that characterize the threats described in Sect. 3.2. The goal is to quickly identify and respond to such incidents, minimize damage, and maintain network infra-structure security. As shown in Fig. 2, an LSTM method [1, 5, 26, 29, 34] is used by Tikuna. Such a model is based on a recurrent neural network, and it can remember long-term dependencies over the input data (i.e., a series of connection monitoring data). In addition, a forecasting loss function is used to evaluate how well the neural network models the training data by comparing the target and predicting output values to minimize this function (i.e., to train the model to detect anomalies based on previous observations under the assumption that honest peers monitoring data follow a consistent pattern). Consequently, Tikuna detects P2P-relevant security incidents when the peers' connection data deviates from typical behavior.

Finally, Fig. 2 displays the essential steps of the process flow of tikuna that ensure the model is thoroughly trained and capable of precisely detecting data anomalies.

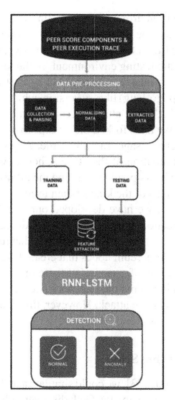

Fig. 2. Tikuna AI Flow Diagram

4   Evaluation

4.1   Experiment Design

Experiments were conducted in two distinct network environments: one using the Protocol Labs simulation tool testground [35] and the other using the Ethereum mainnet to evaluate the effectiveness and performance of the Tikuna approach thoroughly. In this research, we utilized simulations to demonstrate that Tikuna is a practical approach to detecting Ethereum blockchain P2P network attacks.

For all the experiments performed, we have used a set of five dedicated root Hetzner servers in different locations worldwide. They all had 64 GB of DDR4 RAM, two 512GB NVMe SSDs, and an AMD Ryzen CPU as hardware characteristics.

As mentioned before, we have only used the Ethereum mainnet client Prysm [31] because it is the most popular node software at the time of writing. In future research, we plan to explore other prevalent clients.

4.2 Attack Simulation Setup

Since we have two different environments for testing and the mainnet, we have used various strategies to simulate the attacks we wanted to detect. The reason for using two different settings is that the attacks are less complex and less harmful to evaluate first in an isolated yet realistic testing environment. In the testing environment, we used this repository [18], created from a research project by Protocol Labs aimed to recreate several attacks on the libp2p (go-lang) library version, which is the one used by Ethereum (Prysm), Filecoin, and IPFS. All the attacks described in Sect. 3.2 are executed in such a simulation environment. We have forked the gossipsub-hardening repository [19] and modified it to store the peer message traces in a file. A considerable amount of traces are produced during the simulation of the attacks; hence, we have grouped the traces between the 12 types [17] of gossip-sub events and the number of events seen every 300 ms. In Fig. 3, we show samples of the kind of data used.

For the mainnet scenario, we have developed our own eclipse attack code to test the effectiveness of our detection approach in a production environment. The exploit is based on the work in [9] using the Rust programming language. It uses the testground framework to run a series of Ethereum nodes that create fake node IDs specially crafted to be located in specific buckets of a victim's Ethereum client peer table. We have not simulated the other attacks in the mainnet network because they are considerably more complex to deploy than the eclipse attack. However, this attack shows the effectiveness of Tikuna under real conditions.

4.3 Deep Learning Algorithm Setup

With the developed exploit code [33], we could simulate a realistic eclipse attack scenario against a modified Prysm client (using the Geth discovery library). We have changed the code of both projects so the victim node will not advertise the simulated fake peer IDs to other honest peers in the network. We also added new logging features to collect the UDP discovery connections and the gossip-sub message traces received and sent by the victim client. The code forks are in the following repositories [15, 32]. Figure 4 shows a sample of the collected UDP discovery connection data from the honest and attacking peers. The data was collected from the debugging logs of a single victim Ethereum node. Each line has several input features, including a timestamp, IP, and port removed from the peer table, IP and port added to the peer table, and bucket where the peer is added.

Forecasting loss was utilized to model the sequences of peer traces and connection log data and predict the subsequent observed event using the previous observations. By

	timestamp	0	2	3	4	5	6	7	9	11	peer	honest
3652	2022-11-24 23:35:40.100	0	0	0	0	0	0	0	1	0	1	False
3653	2022-11-24 23:35:40.700	0	0	0	1	0	0	0	0	0	1	False
3654	2022-11-24 23:35:40.800	0	0	0	1	0	2	0	0	0	1	False
3655	2022-11-24 23:35:40.900	0	0	0	1	0	0	0	0	0	1	False
3656	2022-11-24 23:35:41.000	0	0	0	4	1	3	0	0	0	1	False
...		...	...	...	...	...	...	...	...	...	...	...
5403	2022-11-24 23:39:04.400	1	141	7	0	0	151	81	0	0	1	False
5404	2022-11-24 23:39:04.500	0	98	19	0	0	117	234	0	0	1	False
5405	2022-11-24 23:39:04.600	1	54	5	0	0	58	56	0	0	1	False
5406	2022-11-24 23:39:04.700	0	150	15	0	0	166	166	0	0	1	False
5407	2022-11-24 23:39:04.800	1	2	9	0	0	11	101	0	0	1	False

Fig. 3. Example data extracted from testground simulations.

learning event patterns from regular series, we could automatically detect anomalies when the event pattern deviates from the ordinary operation [5]. We divide the data into fixed-length sequences to give the machine learning algorithm its inputs. Each input sequence should correspond to a single output label, in our case, the following token in the sequence. Then we needed to transform input sequences into tensors.

The tensors should have the shape (batch_size, time_steps, input_features), where batch_size represents the number of input sequences in a single batch, time_steps represents the length of each input sequence, and input_features represents the number of features in each input data point.

	Timestamp	Removed IP	Removed Port	Added IP	Added Port	Bucket	label
0	[2023-02-03|21:53:11.906]	149.56.240.35	9000	16.0.186.130	9000	252	abnormal
1	[2023-02-03|21:53:11.907]	35.207.99.26	9000	16.0.53.120	9000	255	abnormal
2	[2023-02-03|21:53:11.909]	43.135.40.73	12000	16.0.160.76	9000	252	abnormal
3	[2023-02-03|21:53:11.909]	100.27.30.226	9000	16.0.65.129	9000	256	abnormal
4	[2023-02-03|21:53:11.910]	34.229.79.57	39085	16.0.170.200	9000	255	abnormal
...		...	...	...	...	...	...
1420	[2023-02-04|05:07:00.092]	16.0.61.29	12000	205.185.120.171	12651	254	abnormal
1421	[2023-02-04|07:51:06.105]	54.238.108.184	33311	16.0.61.29	12000	254	abnormal
1422	[2023-02-04|07:51:38.907]	16.0.61.29	12000	162.55.134.100	49429	254	abnormal

Fig. 4. Sample of normal and eclipse attack mainnet data

Formally, for an event e_i at time step t, an input window W is created, which contains m connection events preceding e_i, i.e., $W = [e_{t-m}, \ldots, e_{t-2}, e_{t-1}]$. This is achieved by splitting event sequences into subsequences. Window size and step size are the parameters that control the division process.

The model is then trained to learn a conditional probability distribution $P(e_t = e_i | W)$ for all e_i in the set of distinct log events $E = \{e_1, e_2, \ldots, e_n\}$. In the detection phase, the trained model predicts a new input window, which will be compared against the actual event. An anomaly is seen if the ground truth is not one of the most k probable events predicted by the model.

Given the numerical labels, the trace data collected in the testground simulation attacks required a mean squared error (squared $L2$ norm) loss function. On the other hand, the discovery connection data collected from the mainnet attacks required a cross-entropy loss function because of the categorical labels (the most probable following tokens).

Table 1. Parameters selected for the LSTM model.

Parameters/ Data type	Testground trace data	Mainnet discovery connection data
hidden_size	20	128
num_layers	2	2
num_directions	2	2
embedding_dim	5	10
epochs	100	100
batch_size	1000	1024
learning_rate	0.01	0.01
topk	-	5
patience	5	30
ranxdom_seed	50	42

Table 1 summarizes the various parameters that may be adjusted in the LSTM model for the specific type of data modeled. The hidden_size, num_layers, num_directions, and the embedding_dim were all fixed, and the suggested model defined the values for each parameter. The parameters max_token_len, min_token_count, epochs, batch_size, learning_rate, topk, patience, and random_seed had their values predetermined, and the relevant experimental experience was used to identify their appropriate ranges.

4.4 Experiment Results

Regarding the eclipse attack on a mainnet client, it was possible to overcome the Prysm restriction by adding many nodes from the same public IP address into the same peer table bucket. We used the ECDSA signatures using the secp256k1 curve to generate fake peer IDs and craft many Ethereum Node Records (ENR) for nodes that communicated with the victim's Prysm client. The exploit code will be published once it is reviewed by the Ethereum Foundation to confirm whether a fix is needed. We include in this paper the ML detection results for three different attacks in the testground simulation environment: (1) multiple Sybil nodes launching eclipse attacks against a single node; (2) various nodes trying covert attacks against several honest peers; and (3) several attackers trying to eclipse an entire peer network. For the mainnet environment, we show the detection results for multiple nodes trying to eclipse a single victim node, and we compare the results with a previous approach using random forest classification over network packets [29]. Refer to Sect. 3.2 for an explanation of such attacks.

The results include standard measures like precision, recall, F1 score, and accuracy, using the equations listed in Table 2 to evaluate the models with the different data types.

Table 2. Standard measures equations used to evaluate the models

Equation
$precision = \frac{TP}{TP+FP}$
$Recall = \frac{TP}{TP+FN}$
$F1score = \frac{2*precision*recall}{precision+recall}$
$Accuracy = \frac{TP+TN}{TP+TN+FP+FN}$

Table 3 presents the results of applying our Tikuna anomaly detection approach for detecting attacks in simulated testground runs, including the described metrics, the number of attackers, and the number of victims.

The results were collected after several LSTM iterations with training and evaluation data. As can be seen in Table 3, the best results were obtained for the multiple attacker single victim scenario, with metrics close to 100% of performance. For the other two scenarios, the metrics indicate a lesser optimal performance, especially in recall and accuracy metrics, but still, our approach shows good detection ability.

Table 3. Summary of Tikuna results using the simulation test data

Attack / Metric	Attackers	Victims	Precision	Recall	F1 score	Accuracy
Eclipse Single Victim	100	1	1.00	0.99	0.99	0.99
Covert Attack	100	20	1.00	0.80	0.89	0.80
Eclipse Network	200	50	1.00	0.79	0.88	0.79

Table 4 presents the results of applying our Tikuna approach to the Ethereum mainnet discovery connection data, including precision, recall, F1 score, and accuracy. For completeness, we have also included the results we obtained using the popular transformer deep learning architecture [39]. Four Hetzner servers were used for creating attacking Ethereum nodes, and one was used as a victim node. Except for recall, the Tikuna LSTM anomaly detection approach presented better results than the comparable work in [43], using Random Forest Classification (RFC) over network packets in all the metrics, especially the F1 metric that represents a better balance among true and false positives. The recall measure was the only metric where the RFC work performed better. The transformer model performed similarly to the RFC technique, indicating that it did not outperform the LSTM model. This result is surprising given transformers' success in natural language processing.

Table 4. Summary of Tikuna results using the Ethereum mainnet

Approach / Metric	Precision	Recall	F1 score	Accuracy
Tikuna	0.81	0.88	0.85	0.87
RFC	0.71	0.95	0.62	-
Transformer	0.74	0.99	0.6	0.6

If we compare the results from the testground environment to the mainnet one, more optimal results were obtained for the simulation case with connection trace data. However, that same approach did not work for mainnet detection. Furthermore, the selected discovery connection log data model performed well, making it appropriate for usage in Ethereum blockchain validators.

Furthermore, we conducted experiments to assess the processing time of Tikuna for evaluating new data. On the hardware setup described, our approach demonstrated an average processing time of 3 ms to analyze 20 consensus client log lines. This finding highlights the suitability of our approach for real-time attack detection.

5   Conclusion and Future Work

This paper presents Tikuna, an Ethereum blockchain network security monitoring and anomaly detection system, using a long short-term memory-based neural network model. We introduced three main contributions: our method can detect several attacks at the P2P layer using peer message trace data in a testing simulation environment using the testground tool. We demonstrate the detection of eclipse attacks on the Ethereum mainnet by extracting discovery connection log data from the Prysm client. In addition, a custom exploit implementing an eclipse attack was developed and tested against a modified Prysm client on the mainnet.

Tikuna learns and encodes the expected behavior and the interaction between peers within the network, including timestamps, gossip-sub connection features, and discovery connection log data. It tries to classify this data as normal or malicious based on several attack patterns, such as eclipse and Covert attacks. Moreover, we presented the results of applying our approach to the Ethereum P2P network. We still need to work on reducing the number of false positives in the detection task, a classical problem faced by ML-based intrusion detection systems.

In future work, our team will continue with the development of Tikuna. Our ongoing efforts will be focused on identifying additional attacks, minimizing false positives, detecting real-world incidents, and incorporating different Ethereum clients. Finally, we will explore using our approach in other P2P networks based on the same technology and libraries used by Ethereum, like Filecoin and IPFS.

Acknowledgment. The authors gratefully acknowledge that the Ethereum Foundation Academic Research Grants supported the work presented. We also acknowledge all the support and helpful suggestions from our colleagues on the Edenia team.

References

1. Bengio, Y., Ducharme, R., Vincent, P., Jauvin, C.: A neural probabilistic language model. J. Mach. Learn. Res. **3**, 1137–1155. ACM (2003)
2. Bit2Me: https://academy.bit2me.com/en/que-es-un-ataque-sybil/
3. Buterin, V.: Ethereum: a next-generation smart contract and decentralized application platform (2014). https://ethereum.org/en/whitepaper/
4. Chen, H., Pendleton, M., Njilla, L., Xu, S.: A survey on Ethereum systems security: vulnerabilities, attacks, and defenses. ACM Comput. Surv., **53**(3), 1–43, ACM (2021). https://doi.org/10.1145/3391195
5. Chen, Z., et al.: Experience report: deep learning-based system log analysis for anomaly detection. arXiv (2022). https://doi.org/10.48550/arXiv.2107.05908
6. C. Liu, et al.: Augmented LSTM framework to construct medical self-diagnosis android. In: 2016 IEEE 16th International Conference on Data Mining (ICDM), pp. 251–260. IEEE (2016). https://doi.org/10.1109/ICDM.2016.0036
7. CoinMarketCap: Today's cryptocurrency prices by market cap (2023). https://coinmarketcap.com/
8. Cortes-Goicoechea, M., Bautista-Gomez, L.: Discovering the Ethereum2 p2p network. In: BCCA, pp. 81–88 (2021). https://doi.org/10.1109/BCCA53669.2021.9657041
9. Discv5-testground. https://github.com/ackintosh/discv5-testground. Accessed 15 Mar 2023
10. Du, M. Li, F. Zheng, G., Srikumar, V.: Deeplog: anomaly detection and diagnosis from system logs through deep learning. In: ACM SIGSAC, ACM (2017)
11. Ede, T.V., et al.: DeepCASE: semi-supervised contextual analysis of security events. In: 2022 IEEE Symposium on Security and Privacy (SP), pp. 522–539. IEEE (2022)
12. Eisenbarth, J.P., et al.: Ethereum's peer-to-peer network monitoring and sybil attack prevention. J. Netw. Syst. Manage. **30**, 65. Springer (2022)
13. Ethereum peer-to-peer (P2P) discovery protocol. https://github.com/ethereum/devp2
14. Gao, Y., Shi, J., Wang, X., Shi, R., Yin, Z., Yang, Y.: Practical deanonymization attack in Ethereum based on P2P network analysis. In: ISPA/BDCloud/SocialCom/SustainCom, pp. 1402–1409. IEEE (2021)
15. Go-ethereum. https://github.com/sakundi/go-ethereum. Accessed 15 Mar 2023
16. Paszke, A., et al.: PyTorch: an imperative style, high-performance deep learning library. In: Advances in Neural Information Processing Systems. arXiv (2019)
17. Go-libp2p-pubsub. https://github.com/libp2p/go-libp2p-pubsub/blob/master/pb/trace.pb.go. Accessed 15 Mar 2023
18. Gossipsub-hardening. https://github.com/libp2p/gossipsub-hardening/tree/master/test. Accessed 15 Mar 2023
19. Gossipsub-hardening. https://github.com/sakundi/gossipsub-hardening. Accessed 15 Mar 2023
20. Heilman, E., Kendler, A., Zohar, A., Goldberg, S.: Eclipse attacks on bitcoin's peer-to-peer network. In: USENIX Security 2015, pp. 129–144. USENIX Association (2015)
21. Kabla, A.H.H., et al.: Applicability of intrusion detection system on ethereum attacks: a comprehensive review. In: IEEE Access, **10**, 71632–71655. IEEE (2022)
22. König, L., Unger, S., Kieseberg, P., Tjoa, S.: The risks of the blockchain: a review on current vulnerabilities and attacks. JISIS **10**, 110–127 (2020)
23. Least Authority: node discovery protocol, node discovery protocol, Ethereum foundation (2019). https://leastauthority.com/blog/audits/audit-of-ethereum-foundations-node-discovery-protocol/
24. Marcus, Y., Heilman, E., Goldberg, S.: Low-resource eclipse attacks on Ethereum's peer-to-peer network. In: IACR Cryptology ePrint Archive, vol. 2018, p. 236 (2020). https://eprint.iacr.org/2018/236

25. Maymounkov, P., Mazières, D.: Kademlia: a peer-to-peer information system based on the XOR metric. In: Druschel, P., Kaashoek, F., Rowstron, A. (eds.) IPTPS 2002. LNCS, vol. 2429, pp. 53–65. Springer, Heidelberg (2002). https://doi.org/10.1007/3-540-45748-8_5

26. Mikolov, T., Karafiát, M., Burget, L., Cernocký, J., Khudanpur, S.: Recurrent neural network based language model. In: Interspeech, vol. 2(3) (2010)

27. Saad, M., et al.: Exploring the attack surface of blockchain: a comprehensive survey. IEEE Commun. Surv. Tutorials, **22**, 1977–2008. IEEE (2020)

28. Neudecker, T., Hartenstein, H.: Network layer aspects of permissionless blockchains. IEEE Commun. Surv. Tutorials **21**, 838–857. IEEE (2019)

29. Olah, C.: Understanding LSTM Networks (2015). http://colah.github.io/posts/2015-08-Understanding-LSTMs

30. Pedregosa, F., et al.: Scikit-learn: machine learning in Python. In: JMLR **12**, 2825–2830. arXiv (2011). https://doi.org/10.48550/arXiv.1201.0490

31. Prysm. https://github.com/prysmaticlabs/prysm. Accessed 15 Mar 2023

32. Prysm. https://github.com/sakundi/prysm. Accessed 15 Mar 2023

33. Sakundi. https://github.com/sakundi/discv5-testground/tree/sakundi. Accessed 08 July 2023

34. Sundermeyer, M., Schlüter, R., Ney, H.: LSTM neural networks for language modeling. In: Interspeech, pp. 194–197 (2012)

35. Testground. https://docs.testground.ai/master/#/. Accessed 15 March 2023

36. The Ethereum Foundation: Devp2p—Ethereum peer-to-peer networking specifications. https://github.com/ethereum/devp2p

37. The Solidity Authors. https://docs.soliditylang.org/en/v0.8.19/

38. Tikuna. https://github.com/edenia/tikuna. Accessed 08 July 2023

39. Vaswani, A., et al.: Attention is all you need. In: Advances in Neural Information Processing Systems, vol. 30, arXiv (2017). https://doi.org/10.48550/arXiv.1706.03762

40. Vyzovitis, D., et al.: GossipSub: attack-resilient message propagation in the filecoin and ETH2.0 networks. arXiv (2020). https://doi.org/10.48550/arXiv.2007.02754

41. Wood, D.D.: Ethereum: a secure decentralised generalised transaction ledger (2014). http://paper.gavwood.com/

42. Wüst, K., Gervais, A.: Ethereum eclipse attacks. Technical Report, ETH Zurich (2016)

43. Xu, G., et al.: Am I eclipsed? A smart detector of eclipse attacks for Ethereum. Comput. Secur. 88, 101604. Elsevier (2019). https://doi.org/10.1016/j.cose.2019.101604

Isogeny-Based Multi-signature Scheme

Mathieu de Goyon[1]([✉]) and Atsuko Miyaji[1,2]

[1] Osaka University, Osaka, Japan
mathieu@cy2sec.comm.eng.osaka-u.ac.jp, miyaji@comm.eng.osaka-u.ac.jp
[2] Japan Advanced Institute of Technology, Ishikawa, Japan

Abstract. Multi-signatures are protocols that allow multiple signers to produce a joint signature on the same message. They are used in areas such as blockchains for cryptocurrencies. In recent years, multi-signature schemes have been proposed in lattice-based cryptography as well as pairing-based cryptography but there are currently no multi-signature schemes in isogeny-based cryptography.

In this paper, we propose a multi-signature scheme by extending the Commutative Supersingular Isogeny based Fiat-Shamir signature (CSI-FiSh), as well as its variant CSI-FiSh with Sharing-friendly Keys (CSI-SharK) to the multiple signers setting. To adapt our scheme to the isogeny setting, we use a round-robin during both the key aggregation and the signature aggregation. We also prove the security of our scheme in the Random Oracle Model (ROM) by using the Double Forking Lemma Technique.

Keywords: Isogenies · Multi-Signature · CSI-FiSh · Hard homogeneous spaces

1 Introduction

Isogenies - Isogeny-based cryptography was first introduced in 1997 by Couveignes [8], and later independently rediscovered by Stolbunov and Rostovtsev [21,22] a few years later. They used isogenies between ordinary-elliptic curves to obtain an identification scheme (CRS) and a Diffie-Hellman type key agreement scheme. However, those schemes were impractical and later proven to be insecure by Childs et al. [7].

Isogeny only started gaining attention again in 2011 and 2014 after Jao et al. [14,16] proposed a new Diffie-Hellman type key exchange scheme using supersingular elliptic curves instead. The scheme was later named Supersingular Isogeny Diffie Hellman (SIDH) and attracted most of the attention in isogeny-based cryptography for a few years. However, SIDH is not a direct translation of CRS but a completely different scheme which compensates the non-commutativity of the endomorphism ring in the case of supersingular elliptic curves by revealing the image of specific points. This later proved to be an issue as Castryck and Decru [5] and Maino and Martindale [18] were able to exploit those points to break Supersingular Isogeny Key Encapsulation (SIKE), the SIDH-based submission

© The Author(s), under exclusive license to Springer Nature Singapore Pte Ltd. 2023
W. Meng et al. (Eds.): ISPEC 2023, LNCS 14341, pp. 477–491, 2023.
https://doi.org/10.1007/978-981-99-7032-2_28

to the National Institute of Standards and Technology (NIST). Robert [20] later extended their attack to break SIDH in all instances.

The other isogeny-based key exchange scheme, Commutative Supersingular Isogeny Diffie Hellman (CSIDH), was proposed by Castryck et al. [6] in 2018. It is a direct adaptation of CRS to the supersingular setting by restricting the endomorphism ring to $\mathbb{F}_p$, making the key-exchange more efficient while improving the security. CSIDH is still believed to be secure under Quantum Computers and is the main key exchange protocol in isogeny-based cryptography.

Two signature schemes were proposed based on CSIDH, SeaSign [13] by de Feo and Galbraith and Commutative Supersingular Isogeny based Fiat-Shamir signature(CSI-FiSh) [3] by Beullens et al. Both of them are obtained by applying a Fiat-Shamir transform on an isogeny-based identification scheme, which is an idea originally proposed by Stolbunov in his PhD thesis [23]. While SeaSign suffers some efficiency problem, CSI-FiSh managed to propose an efficient signature scheme by achieving a record-time computation of the underlying ideal-class group, making it one of the first practical isogeny-based signature scheme.

As research on isogeny-based cryptography only started recently and schemes that were built using SIDH have been broken, some useful primitives have still not been adapted to isogeny-based cryptography. When considering signature schemes, while there are currently two main isogeny-based signature schemes, some specific types of signature schemes have still not been adapted to the isogeny-setting. One of the missing primitives is an isogeny-based multi-signature, which we attempt to build in this paper. We first work on a protocol in the Random Oracle model (ROM), while hoping to modify the protocol to be secure in the Quantum Random Oracle Model (QROM) in the future.

Multi-signatures - A multi-signature scheme is a scheme in which n parties with key pairs pk_i, sk_i ($i \in \{1, \cdots, n\}$) sign on a common message and output a multi-signature σ of size independent from n. This is commonly done by having each party output a signature σ_i and aggregating them to obtain the multi-signature. However, this becomes an issue in the isogeny setting as there is no way to combine elliptic curves without knowing the corresponding isogeny. To compensate this fact, we use a round-robin so that all signers participate in the computation together instead of compiling everything.

There are several interesting properties that one might want to achieve when constructing a multi-signature scheme. The first one, which is called **Key Aggregation** [19] is to allow a verifier to verify a multi-signature against an aggregated public key instead of the public key of each signer. As a result, the verification function used in the multi-signature is the same one as in the signature which it originated from. The second one is to achieve security in the **Plain Public Key Model (PPK)** [2]. This requires that each participant publishes his public key in the clear without a dedicated key generation protocol and that an adversary is unable to convince a verifier that an honest party has participated in signing any message unless the party has agreed to it. An alternative to PPK is to have each signer generate a proof of knowledge of their secret key by using a Trusted Third Party.

Many multi-signatures schemes have been proposed based on Schnorr Signature schemes such as KAIAS [17], pairing signature schemes such as Pixel [11] or Lattice signature schemes such as MuSig-L [4]. Threshold signature schemes are another type of signature schemes generated by multiple signers. A threshold signature k out of n can only be generated if k out of the n participants agree to compute the signature together. As a result, multi-signatures share many similarities with n out of n threshold signatures as they are both signatures generated by n signers. However, while threshold signature schemes commonly generate a secret and then distribute shares to each participant by using the Shamir Secret Sharing [15] or alternatives such as Replicated Secret Sharing [10], multi-signatures uses the same Key Generation algorithm as the base signature. Moreover, threshold signature are verified by recomputing the secret if enough people have agreed to sign and then verifying the signature, so the secret can only be used once. In a multi-signature scheme, the same key pair can be used several times, and if the scheme supports Key Aggregation, the verification algorithm is the same as in the base signature scheme. While several threshold signatures have been proposed in isogeny based cryptography such as by de Feo and Meyer [15] or Cozzo and Smart [10] and their variant versions using CSI-FiSh with Sharing-friendly Keys (CSI-SharK) [1], there are currently to our knowledge no multi-signatures in isogeny-based cryptography.

Our Contribution - We construct a multi-signature scheme, which supports Key Aggregation by extending CSI-FiSh to multiple signers. The resulting scheme is proven secure in the Random Oracle Model (ROM) in the Plain Public Key Model (PPK) in a honest-but-curious setting by using the Double Forking Lemma in a similar way to [19]. We also extend the variant of CSI-Fish, CSI-SharK.

We first introduce multi-signature schemes, isogeny-based cryptography and relevant signature schemes in Sect. 2. We introduce the multi-signature protocol in Sect. 3 and prove its security in Sect. 4. Finally, we compare the computations of the multi-signature scheme to CSI-FiSh in Sect. 5.

2   Preliminaries

In this section, we briefly introduce multi-signature schemes, Isogeny-based cryptography, as well as CSI-FiSh [3] and CSI-SharK [1] which form the basis of our multi-signature schemes.

2.1   Multi-signature

We describe the notion of multi-signature schemes and their security. We take the approach taken in [4,17,19] where signers compute an aggregated public key which is used during Verification. Each signer will output a signature on the same message which is aggregated to obtain the multi-signature. We define the algorithms as Key Aggregation and Signature Aggregation. A multi-signature scheme is generally composed of the following algorithms:

- **Param**$(1^\lambda) \longrightarrow params$: given the security parameter λ, output the parameters $params$
- **Keygen**$(params) \longrightarrow (pk, sk)$: given the parameters, output a key pair (pk, sk) with pk public key and sk secret key.
- **KeyAgg**$(params, L_{pk}) \longrightarrow Agg$: given the parameters and a list of all public keys, output the aggregated public key Agg.
- **Sign**$(params, L_{pk}, sk, m) \longrightarrow \sigma$: given the parameters, a list of public keys of all signers L_{pk} and the secret key, output a signature σ
- **SignAgg**$(params, L_\sigma \longrightarrow \Sigma$: given the parameters and a list of signatures of all signers, output the multi-signature Σ
- **Verif**$(params, Agg, m, \Sigma) \longrightarrow b$: given the parameters, the aggregated public key and the multi-signature, output a bit b. If the multi-signature is valid output 1, otherwise output 0.

We define the notion of unforgeability for multi-signature by the following three-stage game:

Setup: Challenger generates $params \longleftarrow \text{Param}(1^\lambda)$ and let $(pk^*, sk^*) \longleftarrow$ Keygen$(params)$ be a challenge key pair. It runs the adversary $\mathcal{A}(params, pk^*)$.

Signature queries: $\mathcal{A}$ has access to the sign oracle for any message m and any set of signer public keys $L_{pk} = \{pk_1, \cdots, pk_n\}$ where $pk_i = pk^*$ for any i. Oracle will simulate the honest signer and output the forgery signature σ_i.

Output: Adversary outputs a forged multi-signature Σ^* on a message m^* not previously queried and a set L_{pk} including pk^*. Adversary wins if the following equation is satisfied:

$$Verif(params, KeyAgg(params, L_{pk}, m^*), \Sigma^*) = 1 \qquad (1)$$

We also introduce the notions of Generalized Forking Lemma [2] and Rogue Key Attacks.

Definition 1. Generalized Forking Lemma- *Fix integers q and l. Let $\mathcal{A}$ be a randomized algorithm which takes as input some main input inp and l-bit strings $\{h_1, \cdots, h_q\}$ and returns either $\perp$ or a pair (i, out), where $i \in \{1, \cdots, q\}$ and out is some side output. The accepting probability of $\mathcal{A}$, denoted $acc(\mathcal{A})$, is defined as the probability, over the random draw of inp (according to some well-understood distribution), $\{h_1, \cdots, h_q\} \longleftarrow \{0,1\}^l$ and the random coins of $\mathcal{A}$, that $\mathcal{A}$ returns a non-$\perp$ output. Consider algorithm ForkA, taking as input inp, described in Algorithm 1. Let frk be the probability (over the draw of inp and the random coins of ForkA) that ForkA returns a non-$\perp$ output. Then*

$$frk \geq acc(\mathcal{A}) \left(\frac{acc(\mathcal{A})}{q} - \frac{1}{2^l} \right) \qquad (2)$$

One of the principal issues when dealing with multi-signature schemes is rogue-key attacks, where a subset of corrupted signers $1 \leq t < n$, uses public keys $pk'_{n-t+1}, \cdots, pk'_n$ computed as functions of public keys of honest users $pk_{n-t+1}, \cdots, pk_n$ to produce forgeries on the set $\{pk_1, \cdots, pk_{n-t}, pk'_{n-t+1}, \cdots, pk'_n\}$.

Algorithm 1. Forking Algorithm

```
 1: pick random coins ρ for 𝒜
 2: h₁, ⋯ , h_q ⟵ {0,1}ˡ
 3: α ⟵ 𝒜(inp, h₁, ⋯ , h_q, ρ)
 4: if α = ⊥ then
 5:     return ⊥
 6: else
 7:     parse α as (i, out)
 8:     h'₁, ⋯ , h'_q ⟵ {0,1}ˡ
 9:     α' ⟵ 𝒜(inp, h₁, ⋯ , h_q, h'₁, ⋯ , h'_q ρ)
10:     if α' = ⊥ then
11:         return ⊥
12:     else
13:         parse α' as (i', out')
14:         if i = i' and h_i ≠ h'_i then
15:             return (i, out, out')
16:         else
17:             return ⊥
18:         end if
19:     end if
20: end if
```

2.2 Isogenies

A good introduction to Isogeny-based cryptography can be found in the Lecture Notes by De Feo [12]. Let E be an elliptic curve over a finite field $\mathbb{F}_p$ with p a large prime. E is supersingular if and only if $\#E = p+1$ and ordinary otherwise.

Let E, E' be two elliptic curves over $\mathbb{F}_p$. An isogeny $\phi : E \longrightarrow E'$ is a morphism from E to E' such that $O_E = \phi(0_{E'})$. An endomorphism ϕ is an isogeny from an elliptic curve to itself. For an elliptic curve E, the set of endomorphisms forms a ring, denoted $\mathrm{End}(E)$ and called the endomorphism ring. We denote $\mathrm{End}(E)_{\mathbb{F}_p}$ the restriction of $\mathrm{End}(E)$ to the base field. In the supersingular case, we have a strict inclusion $\mathrm{End}(E)_{\mathbb{F}_p} \subsetneq \mathrm{End}(E)$, where $\mathrm{End}(E)$ is an order in a quaternion algebra while $\mathrm{End}(E)_{\mathbb{F}_p}$ is an order in an imaginary quadratic field $\mathbb{Q}(\sqrt{-p})$. In the rest of the paper, the endomorphism ring we will refer to is $\mathrm{End}(E)_{\mathbb{F}_p}$, which we will denote as $\mathcal{O}$.

The ideal class group of $\mathcal{O}$ is the quotient of fractional invertible ideals in $\mathcal{O}$ by the principal fractional invertible ideals, denoted as $\mathrm{Cl}(\mathcal{O})$. Let $\mathfrak{a} \subset \mathcal{O}$ be an ideal, we define the $\mathfrak{a}$-torsion group of E elliptic curve as $E[\mathfrak{a}] = \{P \in E | \alpha(P) = 0$ for all $\alpha \in \mathfrak{a}\}$. Using this torsion group, we can define the isogeny $\phi_\mathfrak{a} : E \longrightarrow E_\mathfrak{a}$ with $E_\mathfrak{a} = E/E[\mathfrak{a}]$, which we denote as $\mathfrak{a} \star E$. This isogeny is well-defined and unique up to $\mathbb{F}_p$-isomorphism and the group $\mathrm{Cl}(\mathcal{O})$ acts via $\star$ on the set $\mathcal{E}$ of $\mathbb{F}_p$-isomorphism classes of elliptic curves with endomorphism ring $\mathcal{O}$. It is possible to show that $\mathrm{Cl}(\mathcal{O})$ acts freely and transitively on $\mathcal{E}$, i.e. $\mathcal{E}$ is a principal homogeneous space for $\mathrm{Cl}(\mathcal{O})$. In the rest of paper, we will assume that $\mathrm{Cl}(\mathcal{O})$ is cyclic of order N, generated by the class of an ideal $\mathfrak{g}$.

2.3   CSIDH

As stated in Sect. 1, CSIDH is the main key exchange protocol in Isogeny-based Cryptography. It was proposed by Castryck et al. [6] in 2018 and uses an efficient commutative group action $\star$ by using supersingular elliptic curves with many small $\mathbb{F}_p$-rational subgroups.

Given $\#E(\mathbb{F}_p) = p + 1$ for supersingular elliptic curves, CSIDH uses p of the form $p = 4 \cdot l_1 \cdots l_n - 1$ such that $\#E(\mathbb{F}_p) = 4 \cdot l_1 \cdots l_n$ with l_i small distinct odd primes. In $\mathbb{Q}(\sqrt{-p})$, l_i splits as $(l_i) = < l_i, \pi - 1 > < l_i, \pi + 1 >$ where $\pi = \sqrt{-p}$ is the $\mathbb{F}_p$-Frobenius endomorphism. We denote the first ideal factor $< l_i, \pi - 1 >$ as $\mathfrak{l}_i$.

CSIDH uses ideals of the form $\prod \mathfrak{l}_i^{e_i}$ with e_i exponents chosen uniformly from some interval $] - B, B[$. Let $E_0 : y^2 = x^3 + x$ over $\mathbb{F}_p$. Each isomorphism class of a curve with endomorphism ring $\mathcal{O} = \mathbb{Z}[\pi]$ can be represented by its coefficient A defining the curve $E_A : y^2 = x^3 + Ax^2 + x$. We denote $\mathcal{A}$ the set of such coefficients, the ideal class group $\mathrm{Cl}(\mathcal{O})$ acts freely and transitively on $\mathcal{A}$ via the class group action $\star : \mathrm{Cl}(\mathcal{O}) \times \mathcal{A} \longrightarrow \mathcal{A}$, or given $\mathrm{Cl}(\mathcal{O})$ is of order N, $[] : \mathbb{Z}_N \times \mathcal{A} \longrightarrow \mathcal{A}$. In the rest of the paper, we will refer to a curve E_A with its isomorphic class by the corresponding coefficient A.

2.4   CSI-FiSh

In this section, we briefly describe CSI-FiSh and its variant CSI-SharK. CSI-FiSh is an improved version of the signature scheme proposed by Stolbunov. Both CSI-FiSh and CSI-SharK can be obtaining by applying a Fiat-Shamir Transform on a basic three-pass ID Protocol. The starting curve is the same as for CSIDH, as defined previously. CSI-FiSh uses several optimization such as using several secret keys and including the quadratic twist to increase the soundness.

The protocol is given in Algorithms 2, 3, 4 more details can be found in [3]:

Algorithm 2. CSI-FiSh Key Generation

    Input E_0, N
    Output pk, sk
1: **for** $i = 1, \cdots, S - 1$ **do**
2:     sample $x_i \longleftarrow \mathbb{Z}_N$ and compute $Y_i = [x_i]E_0$
3: **end for**
4: return $sk = (x_1, \cdots, x_{k-1}), pk = (Y_1, \cdots, Y_{k-1})$

CSI-Shark (short for CSI-FiSh with Sharing-friendly Keys) is an alternative to CSI-FiSh proposed by Atapoor et al. [1]. The scheme is almost identical to CSI-FiSh but the authors managed to reduce the size of the secret keys by using an exceptional set instead of using $k - 1$ distinct secret keys.

Definition 2. Exceptional Set: *An exceptional set modulo N is a set $\mathbb{C}_{k-1} = \{c_0, \cdots, c_{k-1}\} \subseteq \mathbb{Z}_N$ where the pairwise difference $c_i - c_j$ of all elements $c_i \neq c_j$ is invertible modulo N.*

Algorithm 3. CSI-FiSh Sign

    Input sk, m
    Output σ
1: **for** $i = 1, \cdots, t$ **do**
2:     sample $b_i \longleftarrow \mathbb{Z}_N$ and compute $E_i = [b_i]E_0$
3: **end for**
4: Set $(c_1, \cdots, c_t) = H(E_1 \cdots E_t \| m)$
5: **for** $i = 1, \cdots, t$ **do**
6:     set $r_i = b_i - sign(|c_i|) \cdot x_{|c_i|} \pmod{N}$
7: **end for**
8: return $\sigma = (r_i, c_i)_{i=1}^{t}$

Algorithm 4. CSI-FiSh Verif

    Input pk, σ, m
    Output bit b
1: **for** $i = 1, \cdots, t$ **do**
2:     Compute $E_i' = [r_i]Y_{c_i}$
3: **end for**
4: Set $(c_1', \cdots, c_t') = H(E_1' \cdots E_t' \| m)$
5: **if** $(c_1', \cdots, c_t') = (c_1, \cdots, c_t)$ **then**
6:     return 1
7: **end if**
8: return 0

Definition 3. Super-Exceptional Set: *A super-exceptional set modulo N is an exceptional set $\mathbb{C}_{k-1} = \{c_0, \cdots, c_{k-1}\} \subseteq \mathbb{Z}_N$ where also the pairwise sum $c_i + c_j$ of all elements c_i, c_j is invertible modulo N.*

We briefly highlight the differences between CSI-FiSh and CSI-SharK. In the key generation protocol, only one secret key a is sampled, as well as an exceptional set $\mathbb{C}_{S-1} = \{c_1, \cdots, c_{k-1}\}$. The public key is calculated as $Y_i = [c_i \cdot x]E_0$. In the Signing and Verification, $(c_1, \cdots, c_t)$ is changed to $(d_1, \cdots, d_t)$ to prevent confusion with the exceptional set. Finally, r_i is calculated as $r_i = b_i - sign(|d_i|)c_{|d_i|}x \pmod{N}$.

Both signature schemes rely on the hardness of inverting a group action, more specifically random instances of a multi-target inversion problem :

Definition 4. Multi-Target Group Action Inverse Problem (MT-GAIP): *Given k curves E_i, with $End(E_1) = \cdots = End(E_k) = \mathcal{O}$, find an ideal $\mathfrak{a} \subset \mathcal{O}$ such that $E_i = \mathfrak{a} \star E_j$ for some $i, j \in \{1, \cdots, k\}$ with $i \neq j$.*

Definition 5. $\mathbb{C}_{k-1}$-Vectorization Problem with Auxiliary Inputs ($\mathbb{C}_{k-1}$-VPwAI): *Given an element $E \in \mathcal{E}$ and the pairs $(c_i, [c_ix]E)_{i=1}^{k-1}$, where $\mathbb{C}_{k-1} = \{c_0 = 0, c_1 = 1, \cdots, c_{k-1}\}$ is an exceptional set, find $x \in \mathbb{Z}_N$*

CSI-FiSh is sEUF-CMA secure in the QROM under the MT-GAIP assumption, while CSI-Shark is sEUF-CMA secure in the QROM under the MT-GAIP assumption and the $\mathbb{C}_{k-1}$-VPwAI assumption. See [1] for the full explanation. Both signature schemes achieve similar running times, which vary depending on the parameters t, k, λ chosen, satisfying $t = \lambda \log_2(k)$. The hash function used $H : \{0,1\}^* \longrightarrow \mathcal{C}$ is modeled as a random oracle. $\mathcal{C}$ is the challenge space, with for $i \in [1,t], c_i \in [-k+1, k-1]$.

2.5   Hard-Homogeneous Spaces

Hard Homogeneous Spaces (HHS) were introduced by Couveignes in [9] as a generalization of Diffie-Hellman schemes. A principal homogeneous space is a set $\mathcal{E}$ that is acted upon transitively by a group $\mathbb{G}$. It is defined by the following map

$$\mathbb{G} \times \mathcal{E} \longrightarrow \mathcal{E}$$

$$g \star E = E'$$

satisfying the following properties:

- *Compatibility*: $g' \star (g \star E) = (g'g) \star E$ for any $g, g' \in \mathbb{G}$ and $E \in \mathcal{E}$;
- *Identity*: $e \star E = E$ if and only if $e \in \mathbb{G}$ is the identity element;
- *Transitivity*: For any $E, E' \in \mathcal{E}$ there exists a unique $g \in \mathbb{G}$ such that $g \star E = E'$.

Couveignes defines a HHS as a finite principal homogeneous space with some additional algorithmic properties. He requires that the following problems can be solved efficiently (e.g., in polynomial time):

- *Group operations*: decide whether a string g represents an element of $\mathbb{G}$, decide whether $g = g'$, compute g^{-1} and gg';
- *Sampling*: sample uniformly random elements from $\mathbb{G}$;
- *Membership*: decide whether a string E represents an element of $\mathcal{E}$, decide whether $E = E'$;
- *Action*: Given g and E, compute $g \star E$.

Furthermore, the following problems should be hard (e.g., not known to be solvable in polynomial time):

- *Vectorization*: Given $E, E' \in \mathcal{E}$, find $g \in \mathbb{G}$ such that $g \star E = E'$;
- *Parallelization*: Given $E, E', F \in \mathcal{E}$, such that $E' = g \star E$, find $F' = g \star F$.

CSI-FiSh is currently the only known instance of HHS in Isogeny-based cryptography, with $\mathcal{E}$ the set of supersingular elliptic curves over $\mathbb{F}_p$ and $Cl(\mathcal{O})$ the group acting on $\mathcal{E}$.

3   Multi-signature Protocols

In this section, we introduce our multi-signature scheme, which is based on CSI-FiSh and highlight how to adapt it to CSI-SharK. In the rest of this section, we consider n parties $P_1, \cdots, P_n$ attempting to generate a multi-signature. We will denote as S the set $\{1, \cdots, n\}$. For readability, we represent the indexes representing the parties as (i) and the others as i. We use the notations of HHS as defined in Sect. 2. Let $\mathbb{G}$ be the group acting on the set $\mathcal{E}$. We will write $[a]$ for g^a and $[a]E$ for $g^a \star E$.

We introduce two different Hash Functions $H_{agg} : \{0,1\}^* \longrightarrow \mathbb{G}$ and $H_{sign} : \{0,1\}^* \longrightarrow \mathcal{C}$ which will be used during key aggregation and signing respectively, and later during the proof. $\mathcal{C}$ represents the challenge space which is identical to CSI-FiSh, for $i \in [1,t], c_i \in [-k+1, k-1]$. The parameters satisfy the same relation as in CSI-FiSh, for a security level of λ, we have $t = \lambda / \log_2(k)$.

We briefly detail the protocol. The Key Aggregation, Signing and Signing Aggregation can be found in Algorithm 5 to Algorithm 7. The Key Generation and Verification is identical to CSI-FiSh.

Params - Pick E_0 the starting curve as in CSIDH and compute $N = \#G$.

Key Generation - As in CSI-FiSh, sample $k - 1$ secret keys $(x_1, \cdots, x_{k-1}) \longleftarrow \mathbb{G}$ and compute the corresponding public keys $(Y_1, \cdots, Y_{k-1})$ with $Y_i = [x_i]E_0$.

KeyAgg - The first difficulty in constructing an isogeny-based protocol is in the Key Aggregation. As there is no group operation $\mathcal{E} \times \mathcal{E} \longrightarrow \mathcal{E}$, in isogenies, it is impossible to simply have each signer output their public keys and combine them. As proposed by de Feo in his threshold signature scheme [15], the participants will participate in a round robin where a party will execute the required computations before sending it to the next party. The algorithm is as follows:

The curves are initialized as $\left(\overline{Y}_1^{(0)}, \cdots, \overline{Y}_{k-1}^{(0)}\right) \longleftarrow (E_0, \cdots, E_0)$. For $j \in S$, $i \in [1, k-1]$, P_j will first compute the aggregation coefficients $a_i^{(j)} = H_{agg}(Y_i^{(j)} \| L_{pk})$.

For $j \in S$, P_j will then receive $\left(\overline{Y}_1^{(j-1)}, \cdots, \overline{Y}_{k-1}^{(j-1)}\right)$ from P_{j-1} and compute $\overline{Y}_i^{(j)} = [a_i^{(j)} \cdot x_i^{(j)}]\overline{Y}^{(j-1)}$ for $i \in [1, k-1]$ by using his secret keys $\{x_1^{(j)}, \cdots, x_{k-1}^{(j)}\}$. At the end, P_n computes

$$\overline{Y}_i = \overline{Y}_i^{(n)} = [a_i^{(1)} \cdot x_i^{(1)}] \cdots [a_i^{(n)} x_i^{(n)}]E_0 = [a_i^{(1)} x_i^{(1)} + \cdots + a_i^{(n)} x_i^{(n)}]E_0$$

for $i \in [1, k-1]$ and broadcast $Agg = (\overline{Y}_1, \cdots, \overline{Y}_{k-1})$ to the other parties.

Signing - The Signing encounters the same issue as the Key Aggregation, since it is impossible to combine the different public keys directly. As a result, the parties will once again need to go through a round robin to compute the aggregated public key. The Signing follows the same steps as the original signature scheme.

- Commitments: For $j \in S$, P_j will sample $\left(b_1^{(j)}, \cdots, b_t^{(j)}\right) \longleftarrow \mathbb{G}$. However, in order to compute $(E_1, \cdots, E_t)$ as in CSI-FiSh, the parties will have to participate in a round robin. The curves are initialized as $\left(E_1^0, \cdots, E_t^0\right) \longleftarrow$ $(E_0, \cdots, E_0)$. Then, each P_j for $j \in S$ will receive $\left(E_1^{(j-1)}, \cdots, E_t^{(j-1)}\right)$, compute $E_i^{(j)} = [b_i^{(j)}]E_i^{(j-1)}$ and send it to the next one. At the end, P_n will compute

$$E_i^{(n)} = [b_i^{(n)}]E_i^{(n-1)} = [b_i^{(1)}] \cdots [b_i^{(n)}]E_0 \tag{3}$$

for $i \in [1, t]$ and broadcast $(E_1, \cdots, E_t) = \left(E_1^{(n)}, \cdots, E_t^{(n)}\right)$ to the other participants.

- Challenges: Compute $(c_1, \cdots, c_t) = H_{sign}(E_1 \cdots E_t \| m)$.
- Response: For $j \in S$, P_j will compute their signature. Compute $r_i^{(j)} = b_i^{(j)} - sign(c_i)a_{|c_i|}^{(j)}x_{|c_i|}^{(j)} \pmod{N}$ for $i \in [1, n]$.
- Signature: P_j outputs his signature $\sigma^{(j)} = (r_1^{(j)}, \cdots, r_t^{(j)}, c_1, \cdots, c_t)$.

SignAgg - The multi-signature is computed by aggregating the signatures. For $i \in [1, t]$, $r_i = \sum_{j=1}^n r_i^{(j)}$. Output $\Sigma = (r_1, \cdots, r_t, c_1, \cdots, c_t)$.

Verification - The verification is the same as CSI-FiSh but verifies the multi-signature against the aggregated public key instead. For $i \in [1, t]$, compute $E_i^* = [r_i]\overline{Y}_{c_i}$. Compute $(c_1^*, \cdots, c_t^*) = H_{sign}(E_1^* \cdots E_t^* \| m)$ and check if $(c_1^*, \cdots, c_t^*) = (c_1, \cdots, c_t)$

Algorithm 5. Key Agg

Input L_{pk}, m
Output Agg
Set $(\overline{Y}_1^{(0)}, \cdots, \overline{Y}_t^{(0)}) \longleftarrow (E_0, \cdots, E_0)$
for $j \in S$ **do**
    for $i = 1, \cdots, k-1$ **do**
        $a_i^{(j)} = H_{agg}(Y_i^{(j)} \| L_{pk})$
    end for
end for
for $j \in S$ **do**
    for $i = 1, \cdots, k-1$ **do**
        $\overline{Y}_i^{(j)} = [a_i^{(j)}x_i^{(j)}]\overline{Y}_i^{(j-1)}$
    end for
end for
Return $\left(\overline{Y}_1^{(n)}, \cdots, \overline{Y}_t^{(n)}\right)$

The CSI-SharK version can be made in the same way by adding a super-exceptional set and sampling a single secret key during Key Generation. The challenges also need to be changed to $(d_1, \cdots, d_t)$ to fit with the original scheme. Both signatures are of the same size as CSI-FiSh, and depend on the parameter chosen for k and t.

Algorithm 6. Sign

    Input sk, m

    Output σ

    Set $(E_1^{(0)}, \cdots, E_t^{(0)}) \longleftarrow (E_0, \cdots, E_0)$ ▷ Initialize the curves to E_0

    for $j \in S$ **do**   ▷ Round Robin to compute the commitments

        for $i = 1, \cdots, t$ **do**

            sample $b_i^{(j)} \longleftarrow \mathbb{G}$

            compute $E_i^{(j)} = [b_i^{(j)}]E_i^{(j-1)}$ ▷ Send to P_{j+1}

        end for

    end for

    Set $(c_1, \cdots, c_t) = H_{sign}(E_1^{(n)} \cdots E_t^{(n)} \| m)$ ▷ Challenges

    for $j \in S$ **do**

        for $i = 1, \cdots, t$ **do**

            set $r_i^{(j)} = b_i^{(j)} - sign(c_i) \cdot a_{|c_i|}^{(j)} \cdot x_{|c_i|}^{(j)} \pmod{N}$

        end for

        set $\sigma^{(j)} = (r_i^{(j)}, c_i)_{i=1}^t$

    end for

    return $(\sigma^{(j)})_{j \in S}$

Algorithm 7. Sign Agg

    Input L_σ, m

    Output Σ

    for $i = 1, \cdots, t$ **do**

        $r_i = \sum_{j \in S} r_i^{(j)}$

    end for

    $\Sigma = (r_1, \cdots, r_t, c_1, \cdots, c_t)$

    return Σ

---

4 Security

In this section, we discuss first prove the correctness of the scheme before analyzing the security of the scheme.

4.1 Correctness

As in Sect. 3, we consider n-signers with public key $\left(E_1^{(j)}, \cdots, E_{k-1}^{(j)}\right)$ and secret key $(x_1^{(j)}, \cdots, x_{k-1}^{(j)})$ with $j \in S$.

For $j \in S$, $i \in [1, k-1]$, P_j will first compute the aggregation coefficients $a_i^{(j)} = H_{agg}(Y_i^{(j)} \| L_{pk})$.

The aggregated public keys $Agg = (\overline{Y}_1, \cdots, \overline{Y}_{k-1})$ will satisfy the following equation:

$$\overline{Y}_i = [a_i^{(1)} \cdot x_i^{(1)}] \cdots [a_i^{(n)} \cdot x_i^{(n)}]E_0 = [a_i^{(1)} \cdot x_i^{(1)} + \cdots + a_i^{(n)} \cdot x_i^{(n)}]E_0 \quad (4)$$

During Signing, each signer P_j for $j \in S$ will sample $b_1^{(j)}, \cdots, b_t^{(j)} \longleftarrow \mathbb{G}$. They will then go through a round robin. At the end, $(E_1, \cdots, E_t)$ will satisfy the following equation:

$$E_i^{(n)} = [b_i^{(1)}] \cdots [b_i^{(n)}] E_0 = [b_i^{(1)} + \cdots + b_i^{(n)}] E_0 \tag{5}$$

The challenges will be computed in the following way with m the chosen message:

$$(c_1, \cdots, c_t) = H_{Sign}(E_1 \cdots E_t \| m)$$

For $j \in S$, P_j computes $r_i^{(j)} = b_i^{(j)} - sign(c_i) a_{|c_i|}^{(j)} \cdot x_{|c_i|}^{(j)} \pmod{N}$ for $i \in [1, t]$. Each party then outputs $\sigma^{(j)} = (r_i^{(j)}, c_i)_{i=1}^{t}$. To aggregate the signatures, compute $r_i = \sum_{j=1}^{n} r_i^{(j)}$ for $i \in [1, t]$ and output $\Sigma = (r_i, c_i)_{i=1}^{t}$.

During verification, the verifier will compute

$$(c_1', \cdots, c_t') = H_{sign}\left([r_1]\overline{Y}_{c_1}, \cdots, [r_t]\overline{Y}_{c_t} \| m\right) \tag{6}$$

For $c_i < 0$, we take the quadratic twist as in CSI-FiSh:

$$\overline{Y}_{c_i} = \left[sign(c_i) \sum_{j=1}^{n} (a_{|c_i|}^{(j)} \cdot x_{|c_i|}^{(j)}) \pmod{N} \right] E_0 \tag{7}$$

The verifier will then check if $(c_1', \cdots, c_t') = (c_1, \cdots, c_t)$.

Indeed we have:

$$[r_i]\overline{Y}_{c_i} = \left[\sum_{j=1}^{n} (b_i^{(j)} - sign(c_i) a_{|c_i|}^{(j)} \cdot x_{|c_i|}^{(j)}) \pmod{N} \right] \left[sign(c_i) \sum_{j=1}^{n} a_{|c_i|}^{(j)} \cdot x_{|c_i|}^{(j)} \right] E_0$$

$$= \left[\sum_{j=1}^{n} b_i^{(j)} \right] E_0$$

$$= E_i^{(n)}$$

As a result, $\left([r_1]Y_{c_1}^{(n)}, \cdots, [r_t]Y_{c_t}^{(n)}\right) = \left(E_1^{(n)}, \cdots, E_t^{(n)}\right)$ and so the equality $(c_1', \cdots, c_t') = (c_1, \cdots, c_t)$ will hold.

4.2   Security

In this section, we analyze the security of both of our schemes. We consider **honest-but-curious** adversaries, which is also called passive security, which is the approach taken in [15]. In order to achieve active security, a Zero-Knowledge proof would be required during the Key Aggregation and signing to ensure the protocol is done correctly, in a similar way to Sashimi [10] but we do not develop it in this paper.

Theorem 1. *Under MT-GAIP Assumption, the multi-signature scheme is EUF-CMA in the Random Oracle Model (ROM).*

Proof Sketch - We use the Double-Forking technique as described in [19]. We adapt the notations to our setting. The parameters $(E_0, \mathbb{G}, N)$ are fixed and the key pair (pk^*, sk^*) are generated for the honest signer with $pk^* = \left(Y_1^*, \cdots, Y_{k-1}^*\right)$ and $sk^* = (x_1^*, \cdots, x_{k-1}^*)$. The target public key is given to the forger $\mathcal{F}$, which will then be able to interact with the honest signer by choosing a message m and a list of public keys L_{pk} with $pk^* \in L_{pk}$ and simulating all signer except an instance of pk^*. To do so, we consider $\mathcal{F}$ has access to a interactive signing oracle as follows:

$\mathcal{F}$ sends L_{pk} to the signing oracle which parses L_{pk} as $\{pk^*, pk_2, \cdots, pk_n\}$ and computes $a_i^{(j)} = H_{agg}(Y_i^{(j)} || L_{pk})$ for $i \in [1, k-1], j \in S$.

The oracle will then sample $(b_1^{(1)}, \cdots, b_t^{(1)}) \longleftarrow \mathbb{G}$, compute $E_i^{(1)} = [b_i^{(1)}]E_0$ for $i \in [1, t]$ and send $E_1^{(1)}, \cdots, E_t^{(1)}$ to $\mathcal{F}$.

The forger $\mathcal{F}$ will sample $(b_1^{(j)}, \cdots, b_t^{(j)}) \longleftarrow \mathbb{G}$ for $j \in [2, n]$ and compute $E_i = [b_t^{(2)} + \cdots + b_t^{(n)}]E_i^{(1)}$ for $i \in [1, t]$ and sends it to the oracle.

The oracle will then compute

$$(c_1, \cdots, c_t) = H_{agg}(E_1, \cdots, E_t || m),$$
$$r_i^{(1)} = b_i^{(1)} - sign(c_i)a_{|c_i|}^{(1)} \cdot x_{|c_i|}^{(1)} \pmod{N}$$

for $i \in [1, t]$ and return $\sigma^{(1)} = (c_1, \cdots, c_t, r_1^{(1)}, \cdots, r_t^{(1)})$ to the forger. The forger will complete the remaining steps by computing $(\sigma^{(2)}, \cdots, \sigma^{(n)})$ and sending them to the oracle which outputs $\Sigma = (r_1, \cdots, r_t, c_1, \cdots, c_t)$.

We invoke the general forking lemma twice, one at the return value of H_{agg} and the second at the return value of H_{sign}. We obtain two valid forgeries $(r_1', \cdots, r_t', c_1', \cdots, c_t')$ and $(r_1, \cdots, r_t, c_1, \cdots, c_t)$ for the same set of public keys L_{pk} and on the same message m. H_{sign} is programmed such that $H_{sign}(E_1, \cdots, E_t || m)$ outputs the same value $(c_1, \cdots, c_t)$ and H_{agg} is programmed such that $H_{agg}(Y_i^{(j)} || L_{pk})$ outputs the same value $a_i^{(j)}$ for $i \in [1, k-1]$ and $j \in S, j \neq 1$ and distinct values $a_i^{(1)'}, a_i^{(1)}$ for $H_{agg}(Y_i^* || L_{pk})$.

At the end, we get the following results for $i \in [1, t]$:

$$r_i = (b_i^{(1)} + \cdots + b_i^{(n)}) + sign(c_i)(a_{|c_i|}^* x_{|c_i|}^* + (a_{|c_i|}^{(2)} x_{|c_i|}^{(2)} + \cdots + a_{|c_i|}^{(n)} x_{|c_i|}^{(n)}) \pmod{N}$$
$$r_i' = (b_i^{(1)} + \cdots + b_i^{(n)}) + sign(c_i)(a_{|c_i|}^{*'} x_{|c_i|}^* + (a_{|c_i|}^{(2)} x_{|c_i|}^{(2)} + \cdots + a_{|c_i|}^{(n)} x_{|c_i|}^{(n)}) \pmod{N}$$

By subtracting the two equations, it's possible to extract

$$(a_{|c_i|}^* - a_{|c_i|}^{*'})x_{c_i}^* = r_i - r_i'$$

and retrieve the value of $x_{|c_i|}$ for $i \in [1, t]$ which would solve the MT-GAIP Problem.

5   Comparison

In this section, we compare the computations of our schemes to CSI-FiSh and the threshold signature of de Feo and Meyer [15]. We assume the threshold signature uses the same optimizations as the other two schemes by using $(k-1)$ public keys, in which Key aggregation corresponds to recomputing the shared secret. Table 1 shows the computation from the point of view of one of the signers. I corresponds to the isogenies, Inv to inverses H to the hashing, M to multiplication and Mod to the modulo.

Table 1. Comparison between the number of computation of our protocol compared to the CSI-FiSh

	CSI-Fish	Our Scheme	Threshold Signature
Key Generation	$(k-1)$ I	$(k-1)$ I	$(k-1)$ I
Key Aggregation	/	$(k-1)$ I $+ (n \cdot k)$ H	$(k-1)$ I $+ (k-1)M$
Signing	t I $+ t$ Mod	t I $+ t$ Mod	t I $+ t$ Mod
Signing Aggregation	/	/	/
Verification	t I	t I	t I

6   Conclusion

We propose a multi-signature scheme by extending the isogeny-based signature CSI-FiSh as well as its variant CSI-SharK. Our scheme supports key aggregation, which allows the scheme to use the same verification algorithm as the base signature. To adapt the scheme to the isogeny-setting, we use a round robin during both the signature aggregation and the key aggregation. We then prove the sEUF-CMA of our scheme by using the Double Forking Technique, and compare the computations to the base scheme CSI-FiSh.

Acknowledgment. This work is partially supported by JSPS KAKENHI Grant Number JP21H03443 and SECOM Science and Technology Foundation.

References

1. Atapoor, S., Baghery, K., Cozzo, D., Pedersen, R.: CSI-SharK: CSI-FiSh with sharing-friendly keys. In: IACR Cryptol. ePrint Arch, p. 1189 (2022)
2. Bellare, M., Neven, G.: Multi-signatures in the plain public-key model and a general forking lemma, pp. 390–399 (2006)
3. Beullens, W., Kleinjung, T., Vercauteren, F.: CSI-FiSh: efficient isogeny based signatures through class group computations. In: IACR Cryptol. ePrint Arch, p. 498 (2019)
4. Boschini, C., Takahashi, A., Tibouchi, M.: MuSig-L: lattice-based multi-signature with single-round online phase. Cryptology ePrint Archive, Paper 2022/1036 (2022)

5. Castryck, W., Decru, T.: An efficient key recovery attack on SIDH (preliminary version). In: IACR Cryptol. ePrint Arch, p. 975 (2022)
6. Castryck, W., Lange, T., Martindale, C., Panny, L., Renes, J.: CSIDH: an efficient post-quantum commutative group action. In: IACR Cryptol. ePrint Arch, p. 383 (2018)
7. Childs, A.M., Jao, D., Soukharev, V.: Constructing elliptic curve isogenies in quantum subexponential time. J. Math. Cryptol. **8**(1), 1–29 (2014)
8. Couveignes, J.M.: Hard homogeneous spaces. In: IACR Cryptol. ePrint Arch, p. 291 (2006)
9. Couveignes, J.M.: Hard homogeneous spaces. Cryptology ePrint Archive, Paper 2006/291 (2006)
10. Cozzo, D., Smart, N.P.: Sashimi: cutting up CSI-FiSh secret keys to produce an actively secure distributed signing protocol. In: Ding, J., Tillich, J.-P. (eds.) PQCrypto 2020. LNCS, vol. 12100, pp. 169–186. Springer, Cham (2020). https://doi.org/10.1007/978-3-030-44223-1_10
11. Drijvers, M., Gorbunov, S., Neven, G., Wee, H.: Pixel: multi-signatures for consensus. In: 29th USENIX Security Symposium (USENIX Security 2020), pp. 2093–2110. USENIX Association (2020)
12. Feo, L.D.: Mathematics of isogeny based cryptography. CoRR abs/1711.04062 (2017)
13. De Feo, L., Galbraith, S.D.: SeaSign: compact isogeny signatures from class group actions. In: Ishai, Y., Rijmen, V. (eds.) EUROCRYPT 2019. LNCS, vol. 11478, pp. 759–789. Springer, Cham (2019). https://doi.org/10.1007/978-3-030-17659-4_26
14. Feo, L.D., Jao, D., Plut, J.: Towards quantum-resistant cryptosystems from supersingular elliptic curve isogenies. J. Math. Cryptol. **8**(3), 209–247 (2014)
15. Feo, L.D., Meyer, M.: Threshold schemes from isogeny assumptions. IACR Cryptol. ePrint Arch, p. 1288 (2019)
16. Jao, D., De Feo, L.: Towards quantum-resistant cryptosystems from supersingular elliptic curve isogenies. In: Yang, B.-Y. (ed.) PQCrypto 2011. LNCS, vol. 7071, pp. 19–34. Springer, Heidelberg (2011). https://doi.org/10.1007/978-3-642-25405-5_2
17. Kojima, R., Yamamoto, D., Shimoyama, T., Yasaki, K., Nimura, K.: A new schnorr multi-signatures to support both multiple messages signing and key aggregation. J. Inf. Process. **29**, 525–536 (2021)
18. Maino, L., Martindale, C.: An attack on SIDH with arbitrary starting curve. In: IACR Cryptol. ePrint Arch, p. 1026 (2022)
19. Maxwell, G., Poelstra, A., Seurin, Y., Wuille, P.: Simple schnorr multi-signatures with applications to bitcoin. Cryptology ePrint Archive, Paper 2018/068 (2018)
20. Robert, D.: Breaking SIDH in polynomial time. In: IACR Cryptol. ePrint Arch, p. 1038 (2022)
21. Rostovtsev, A., Stolbunov, A.: Public-key cryptosystem based on isogenies. In: IACR Cryptol. ePrint Arch, p. 145 (2006)
22. Stolbunov, A.: Constructing public-key cryptographic schemes based on class group action on a set of isogenous elliptic curves. Adv. Math. Commun. **4**(2), 215–235 (2010)
23. Stolbunov, A.: Cryptographic schemes based on isogenies. Ph.D. thesis (2012)

Security Analysis of WAGE Against Division Property Based Cube Attack

Bijoy Das[✉], Abhijit Das, and Dipanwita Roy Chowdhury

Indian Institute of Technology Kharagpur, Kharagpur, India
mantunsec@gmail.com, {abhij,drc}@cse.iitkgp.ac.in

Abstract. In recent years, as more Internet of Things (IoT) devices are connected to the internet, lightweight cryptography has become more and more important. WAGE is a LFSR-based authenticated encryption algorithm and one of the candidates in the NIST standard Lightweight Cryptography competition. It offers 128-bit security. In the literature, the best cryptanalytic estimates available for WAGE pertain to a correlation power attack that recovers the secret key up to 12 out of 111 rounds. In this paper, we evaluate the security of this cipher following the (bit-based) division property based cube attack using mixed-integer-linear-programming (MILP) models. Specifically, we investigate the security of the nonlinear feedback based initialization phase. To the best of our knowledge, our attack is the first one that investigates the security of the nonlinear feedback-based initialization phase of WAGE cipher. Theoretically, the results of our attack enable us to recover the secret key up to the reduced 18-round of the initialization phase utilizing 2^{123} time complexity and $2^{6.32}$ keystream bits.

Keywords: Authenticated Encryption · WAGE · Lightweight cipher · Division Property · Cube Attack

1 Introduction

Inspired by the initialization stage of the Welch-Gong (WG) cipher [5], WAGE [1] is designed with a state size of 259 bits. It operates in a unified duplex sponge mode [2] to offer authenticated encryption with associated data (AEAD) functionality. It is intended to develop efficient hardware implementation for AEAD while still providing adequate security margins. WAGE includes 37-stage LFSR with each stage working over the finite fields $\mathbb{F}_{2^7}$. In addition, it consists of two nonlinear functions such as Welch-Gong permutation (WGP) and Sbox (SB). The LFSR is first loaded with 128-bit secret key and 128-bit nonce and the remaining bits are set to zero. Next, the LFSR with its nonlinear components is run for 111 rounds. Then the cipher generates the keystreams that are used for message encryption. The cipher is mainly designed for encryption in resource-constrained environments such as mobile phones, smart cards, and RFID applications.

W. Meng et al. (Eds.): ISPEC 2023, LNCS 14341, pp. 492–506, 2023.
https://doi.org/10.1007/978-981-99-7032-2_29

The only cryptanalysis on WAGE available in the literature is proposed by [4]. Here, Fei et al. [4] applied Correlation Power Analysis (CPA) technique. In this attack model, they chose the Hamming Weight of the Status Register as the leakage model to evaluate the security of WAGE. According to their attack model's studies, the secret key information can be found in the power traces for up to 12 out of 111 rounds of the WAGE permutation.

Our attack targets the first 18 rounds of the WAGE permutation after loading the 128-bit key and 128-bit nonce in the initialization phase. To the best of our knowledge, our attack is the first one to investigate the security of the non-linear feedback-based initialization phase of the WAGE lightweight AE scheme. The running environment of our attack includes Python language and Gurobi optimizer (as MILP solver).

Our Contribution. The cube attack is mounted on the initialization phase of the reduced 18 rounds of WAGE. A 7-bit S-box trail is used to represent the division trail that propagates through both WG-permutation (WGP) function and SB function of WAGE. In order to model Linear Transformation function $x \otimes w$, we chose $\mathcal{S}$ method [6]. Generally, $\mathcal{S}$ method has some restrictions over $\mathcal{ZR}$ method [9] but it is simple and efficient in terms of the number of constraints. Moreover, in WAGE, we verified that $\mathcal{S}$ method does not produce any invalid trail for the function $x \otimes w$. Hence, our optimizations lead to a full key recovery using only $2^{6.32}$ bits in the keystream after 18 rounds of the initialization phase. This approach is suited for realistic scenarios in lightweight constrained applications where acquiring significant amounts of data is challenging, due to its small data complexity.

The rest of the paper is organized as follows. In Sect. 2.1, we review the concepts of cube attack. Section 2.2 presents a brief overview of division property, bit-based division property, and how to model the division trails using Mixed Integer Linear Programming (MILP). The specification of WAGE is provided in Sect. 3. Section 4 elaborates our proposed cube attack on the initialization phase of WAGE. We also provide a discussion on the results obtained from our experiments. Section 5 concludes the paper.

2 Preliminaries

Here, we give the notations and definitions that are used in this paper.

2.1 Cube Attack

The cube attack was proposed by Dinur and Shamir in EUROCRYPT [3] to recover secret key. For an n_1-bit key $k = (k_1, k_2, \ldots, k_{n_1})$ and m_1-bit IV $v = (v_1, v_2, \ldots, v_{m_1})$, let $f(x)$ be a boolean function from $\mathbb{F}_2^n$ to $\mathbb{F}_2^1$ such that $x = k||v$ and $n = n_1 + m_1$. Let $u \in \mathbb{F}_2^n$ be a constant vector with $u \leftarrow \{u_0, u_1, \ldots, u_{n-1}\}$. Then the algebraic normal form (ANF) of $f(x)$ is defined as $f(x) = x^u \times p(x) + q(x)$, where each term of $q(x)$ is not divisible by x^u. For a set of *cube indices* $I = \{0 \leq i \leq n-1 : u_i = 1\} \subset \{0, 1, \ldots, n-1\}$, x^u represents the corresponding monomial. Therefore, the summation of $f(x)$ over all values of $C_I = \{x \in \mathbb{F}_2^n : u \succeq x\}$ is given by

$$\bigoplus_{x \in C_I} f(k, v) = \bigoplus_{x \in C_I} (x^u \times p(x) + q(x)) = p(x). \tag{1}$$

where $p(x)$ is called the *superpoly* of C_I, and it only involves the variables x_j such that $u_j = 0$ for $0 \le j \le n - 1$.

Equation (1) implies that if the attacker gets a superpoly that is simple enough, she can query the encryption oracle feeding C_I. All the first keystream bits returned are summed to evaluate the right-hand side of Eq. (1). Subsequently, she recovers the secret key bits by solving a system of equations.

2.2   MILP-Aided Bit-Based Division Property

Bit Product Function $\pi_u(x)$. For any $u \in \mathbb{F}_2^n$, let $\pi_u(x)$ be a function from $\mathbb{F}_2^n$ to $\mathbb{F}_2$. For any input $x \in \mathbb{F}_2^n$ with $x \leftarrow \{x_0, x_1, \ldots, x_{n-1}\}$, $\pi_u(x)$ is the AND of x_i satisfying $u_i = 1$. It is defined as $\pi_u(x) = \prod_{i=0}^{n-1} x_i^{u_i}$

Definition 1 (*Division Property*). *Let X be a multi-set whose elements take values from $\mathbb{F}_2^{l_0} \times \mathbb{F}_2^{l_1} \times \cdots \times \mathbb{F}_2^{l_{m-1}}$. The multi-set X has the division property $D_{\mathbb{K}}^{l_0, l_1, \ldots, l_{m-1}}$, where $\mathbb{K}$ denotes a set of m-dimensional vectors whose i-th elements take values between 0 and l_i, if it fulfills the following condition:*

$$\bigoplus_{x \in X} \pi_u(x) = \begin{cases} unknown, & if\ there\ exist\ k \in \mathbb{K}\ such\ that\ wt(u) \succeq k, \\ 0, & otherwise. \end{cases}$$

If there are $k, k' \in \mathbb{K}$ such that $k \succeq k'$ in the division property $D_{\mathbb{K}}^{l_0, l_1, \ldots, l_{m-1}}$, then k can be removed from $\mathbb{K}$ because it is redundant. When $l_0, l_1, \ldots, l_{m-1}$ are restricted to 1, we talk about *bit-based division property*. The main idea of MILP-aided bit-based division property is to model the propagation rules as a series of linear (in)equalities. We adopt the MILP models for **copy**, **AND** and **XOR** from [7]. We rewrite these as follows:

Model 1 (copy): Let $(a) \overset{copy}{\rightarrow} (b_0, b_1)$ be a division trail of the **copy** function. The following constraints are sufficient to describe the division propagation of **copy**.

$$\left\{ a - b_0 - b_1 = 0, \text{where } a, b_0, b_1 \text{ are binary variables} \right.$$

Model 2 (AND): By $(a_0, a_1) \overset{AND}{\rightarrow} (b)$, denote a division trail of the **AND** function. The following inequalities are sufficient to describe the division propagation of **AND**.

$$\left\{ b - a_i \ge 0 \text{ for } i \in \{0, 1\}, \text{where } a_0, a_1, b \text{ are binary variables} \right.$$

Model 3 (XOR): Let $(a_0, a_1) \overset{XOR}{\rightarrow} (b)$ be a division trail of the **XOR** function. The following inequalities are sufficient to describe the division propagation of **XOR**.

$$\left\{ a_0 + a_1 - b = 0, \text{ where } a_0, a_1, b \text{ are binary variables} \right.$$

3   Description of WAGE

Following the same notations from [1], we give a description of WAGE. The WAGE permutation in the unified sponge duplex mode, a 111-round iterative permutation with a state of 259 bits. Two separate S-boxes (WGP and SB) along with a linear feedback function defined over $\mathbb{F}_{2^7}$ are the nonlinear components of this cipher. In addition, the design contains five word-wise XORs and 111 pairs of 7-bit round constants (rc_1, rc_0). One round of WAGE permutation is shown in Fig. 1.

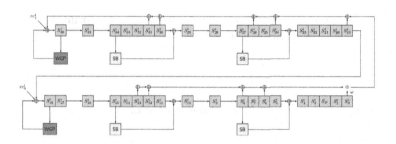

Fig. 1. The i-th Round of WAGE Permutation [1]

Nonlinear Components of WAGE. WAGE uses two different 7-bit S-boxes, called WGP and SB, where SB is built iteratively at the bit level using quadratic functions and WGP is specified over a finite field, $\mathbb{F}_{2^7}$.

Welch-Gong Permutation (WGP). The WGPerm, denoted by WGP7, is defined over $\mathbb{F}_{2^7}$ which is given by

$$WGP7(x) = x + (x + 1)^{33} + (x + 1)^{39} + (x + 1)^{41} + (x + 1)^{104}, \ x \in \mathbb{F}_{2^7}$$

where $\mathbb{F}_{2^7}$ is defined by the primitive polynomial $x^7 + x^3 + x^2 + x + 1$. WGP is constructed from WGP7 by applying decimation $d = 13$ as WGP(x) = WGP7(x^{13}). The hexadecimal representation of the WG permutation is given in a row-major order.

SB S-box. The 7-bit S-box SB is constructed in an iterative way using the nonlinear transformation and the bit permutation. The hexadecimal representation of the S-box is given in a row-major order.

Hex Representation of WGP for WAGE
00 12 0a 4b 66 0c 48 73 79 3e 61 51 01 15 17 0e
7e 33 68 36 42 35 37 5e 53 4c 3f 54 58 6e 56 2a
1d 25 6d 65 5b 71 2f 20 06 18 29 3a 0d 7a 6c 1b
19 43 70 41 49 22 77 60 4f 45 55 02 63 47 75 2d
40 46 7d 5c 7c 59 26 0b 09 03 57 5d 27 78 30 2e
44 52 3b 08 67 2c 05 6b 2b 1a 21 38 07 0f 4a 11
50 6a 28 31 10 4d 5f 72 39 16 5a 13 04 3c 34 1f
76 1e 14 23 1c 32 4e 7b 24 74 7f 3d 69 64 62 6f

Hex Representation of S-box for WAGE
2e 1c 6d 2b 35 07 7f 3b 28 08 0b 5f 31 11 1b 4d
6e 54 0d 09 1f 45 75 53 6a 5d 61 00 04 78 06 1e
37 6f 2f 49 64 34 7d 19 39 33 43 57 60 62 13 05
77 47 4f 4b 1d 2d 24 48 74 58 25 5e 5a 76 41 42
27 3e 6c 01 2c 3c 4e 1a 21 2a 0a 55 3a 38 18 7e
0c 63 67 56 50 7c 32 7a 68 02 6b 17 7b 59 71 0f
30 10 22 3d 40 69 52 14 36 44 46 03 16 65 66 72
12 0e 29 4a 4c 70 15 26 79 51 23 3f 73 5b 20 5c

State Update Function of WAGE. The state of WAGE comprises 37 words, each consisting of 7 bits, resulting in a total state size of 259 bits. The symbol $S = (S_{36}, \ldots, S_0)$ represents these 37 words, where S_i indicates the number of bits in a word. The state update function consists of the following three steps:

– **Computing Linear Feedback.** $fb \leftarrow \mathrm{FB}(S)$. The following primitive polynomial of degree 37 over $\mathbb{F}_{2^7}$ is used as a feedback function

$$\ell(y) = y^{37} + y^{31} + y^{30} + y^{26} + y^{24} + y^{19} + y^{13} + y^{12} + y^8 + y^6 + \omega$$

where ω is a root of $x^7 + x^3 + x^2 + x^1 + 1$, which is also a primitive polynomial over $\mathbb{F}_{2^7}$. Now the feedback computation is given by

$$fb = S_{31} + S_{30} + S_{26} + S_{24} + S_{19} + S_{13} + S_{12} + S_8 + S_6 + (\omega \otimes S_0) \quad (2)$$

For an input $x \in \mathbb{F}_{2^7}$, the ANF representation of $\omega \otimes x$ is given by

$$(x_0, x_1, x_2, x_3, x_4, x_5, x_6) \otimes \omega \rightarrow (x_6, x_0 \oplus x_6, x_1 \oplus x_6, x_2 \oplus x_6, x_3, x_4, x_5) \quad (3)$$

– **Updating Intermediate Words.**

$$\begin{aligned} S_5 &\leftarrow S_5 \oplus SB(S_8), & S_{11} &\leftarrow S_{11} \oplus SB(S_{15}) \\ S_{19} &\leftarrow S_{19} \oplus WGP(S_{18}) \oplus rc_0, & S_{24} &\leftarrow S_{24} \oplus SB(S_{27}) \quad (4) \\ S_{30} &\leftarrow S_{30} \oplus SB(S_{34}), & fb &\leftarrow fb \oplus WGP(S_{36}) \oplus rc_1 \end{aligned}$$

– **Shifting register contents and update the last word.**

$$S_j \leftarrow S_{j+1},\ 0 \leq j \leq 35 \text{ and } S_{36} \leftarrow fb \quad (5)$$

Applying the state update function 111 times to an input state S yields the WAGE permutation's output. Notably, only the Eq. (4) transformation carries out the nonlinear operations; all other operations are linear.

4 Cube Attack on WAGE

Our attack technique exploits the concept of division property based cube attack using MILP. The attack consists of the following three phases.

Offline Phase: The objective of this phase is to recover the preferable superpoly that involves only the secret variables in the cube indices I. The steps are given below.
  - Create an MILP model $\mathcal{M}$ for the cipher whose initialization is reduced to R rounds.
  - The model checks the feasibility of all R-round division trails by propagating the division properties of all the basic operations employed in each round. The model returns *infeasible* if there is no feasible solution.
  - The model takes the cube indices $I = \{i_1, i_2, \ldots, i_{|I|}\}$ as the chosen input prepared by the attacker. The secret variables involved in the superpoly are then computed. Let $J = \{k_{j_1}, k_{j_2}, \ldots, k_{j_{|J|}}\}$ be the computed key bits involved in the superpoly. This operation is computationally feasible using the MILP approach.
  - The attacker chooses the IV, and computes $\bigoplus_{C_I} f(k, v) = p_{\bar{v}}(\bar{k})$, where $\bar{v} = \{v_0, v_1, \ldots, v_{n-1}\} \setminus \{v_{i_1}, v_{i_2}, \ldots, v_{i_{|I|}}\}$ and $\bar{k} = \{k_{j_1}, k_{j_2}, \ldots, k_{j_{|j|}}\}$. Then, all possible combinations of the secret variables $k_{j_1}, k_{j_2}, \ldots, k_{j_{|J|}}$ are tried, and the superpoly is recovered. The complexity of this step is $2^{|I|+|J|}$.

Online Phase: The goal of this phase is to recover the subset of the secret key bits. Once the superpoly is recovered in the offline phase, the attacker queries the cube C_I to the encryption oracle, and gets one bit $p_{\bar{v}}(\bar{k})$ by summing all the first keystream bits returned by the encryption oracle. So the attacker gets one polynomial about the involved key bits. Since the superpoly is balanced, about half of the values of the involved key bits are discarded.

Brute-Force search phase: The attacker gets the remaining bits of the secret key by guessing.

4.1 Cube Attack on the Initialization Phase of WAGE Using MILP

We begin the cube attack by simulating the propagation of the division property for each of the WAGE cipher's functions in each round.

MILP model for the WG-permutation (WGP) and S-box (SB). We find that the degree of each component of $WGP(x)$ and $SB(x)$ is six. A large number of MILP variables and constraints are needed if we model this function based on its ANF representation. As an alternative approach adopted from [8], we represent these function as a 7-bit S-box, where $(x_0, x_1, x_2, x_3, x_4, x_5, x_6)$ and $(y_0, y_1, y_2, y_3, y_4, y_5, y_6)$ are the input and the output of both WGP and SB, respectively. Using Algorithms 1 and 2 in [8] and the *inequality_generator()* function in Sage[1], we discover that just 22 and 49 inequalities are necessary to

---
[1] http://www.sagemath.org/.

represent the transmission of the division property across the WGP and SB, respectively. The reduced inequalities for WGP are given by:

$$x_0 + x_1 + x_2 + 25x_3 + x_4 + x_5 + x_6 - 5y_0 - 5y_1 - 5y_2 - 5y_3 - 5y_4 - 5y_5 - 5y_6 \geq -4$$

$$6x_1 - y_0 - y_1 - y_2 - y_3 - y_4 - y_5 - y_6 \geq -1$$

$$29x_0 + x_1 + x_2 + x_3 + x_4 + x_5 - x_6 - 6y_0 - 6y_1 - 5y_2 - 6y_3 - 6y_4 - 5y_5 - 6y_6 \geq -5$$

$$x_0 + x_1 + x_2 + x_3 + x_4 + 25x_5 + x_6 - 5y_0 - 5y_1 - 5y_2 - 5y_3 - 5y_4 - 5y_5 - 5y_6 \geq -4$$

$$x_0 + x_1 + x_2 + x_3 + x_4 + x_5 + 28x_6 - 6y_0 - 6y_1 - 5y_2 - 6y_3 - 5y_4 - 65y_5 - 5y_6 \geq -5$$

$$- x_0 - x_1 - x_3 - x_5 - 2x_6 - y_0 - 2y_1 - y_2 - 2y_3 - 3y_4 - y_5 + 8y_6 \geq -8$$

$$x_0 - x_2 + x_5 - 2x_6 - 3y_0 - 4y_1 - 2y_2 + 12y_3 - 2y_4 - 3y_5 - 4y_6 \geq -7$$

$$- x_0 - x_1 - x_3 - x_4 - x_5 + y_0 + y_1 + y_2 - 4y_3 + y_4 + y_5 - 5y_6 \geq -9$$

$$-3x_0 - x_1 - 2x_2 - x_3 - x_4 - 3x_5 - x_6 - y_0 + 7y_1 - 2y_2 - 2y_3 - 2y_4 - y_5 \geq -13$$

$$x_0 + x_1 + x_2 + x_3 + 24x_4 + x_5 + x_6 - 5y_0 - 5y_1 - 5y_2 - 5y_3 - 4y_4 - 5y_5 - 5y_6 \geq -4$$

$$-x_0 - 3x_1 - 2x_2 - 2x_3 - 3x_4 - x_5 - 3x_6 + 3y_0 + 3y_1 + 2y_2 + 2y_3 + 3y_4 + y_5 + 3y_6 \geq -11$$

$$- x_0 - x_1 - 2x_2 - x_4 - x_6 - 2y_0 - y_1 - y_2 + 4y_3 - y_4 + y_5 - y_6 \geq -7$$

$$-2x_0 - 3x_1 - 3x_3 - 3x_4 - 3x_5 - x_6 + 3y_0 + 4y_1 + y_2 + 4y_3 + 2y_4 + 3y_5 + 2y_6 \geq -11$$

$$- 2x_0 - x_2 - 2x_3 - 2x_4 - 2x_5 - 2x_6 + y_0 + y_2 + y_3 + y_4 + y_5 - y_6 \geq -10$$

$$- 4x_1 - 5x_2 - 5x_3 - 4x_4 - 4x_6 - y_0 - y_1 + 4y_2 + 4y_3 - y_4 - 5y_5 - y_6 \geq -23$$

$$- x_0 - x_1 - x_2 - x_3 - x_5 - y_4 + y_6 \geq -5$$

$$- x_1 - x_2 - x_3 - x_5 - x_6 - 2y_2 + y_3 - y_4 + y_5 + y_6 \geq -6$$

$$- x_0 - x_2 - x_3 - x_4 - x_5 + y_0 + y_2 + y_3 + y_4 + y_5 + y_6 \geq -4$$

$$- 2x_1 - x_2 - x_3 - 2x_4 - x_5 - 2x_6 + y_0 + y_1 + 2y_2 + y_3 + y_4 - y_5 + y_6 \geq -8$$

$$x_2 + x_4 + x_5 + 9y_0 - 3y_1 - 2y_2 - 3y_3 - 2y_4 - 2y_5 - 3y_6 \geq -3$$

$$-2x_0 - 4x_1 - 3x_2 - x_3 - 4x_4 - 3x_5 - 4x_6 + 3y_0 + 4(y_1 + y_2) + 2y_3 + 4y_4 + y_5 + 4y_6 \geq -16$$

$$-4x_0 - 3x_1 - 2x_2 - 4x_3 - 2x_4 - 4x_5 - x_6 + 19y_0 + 18y_1 + 17y_2 + 19y_3 + 17y_4$$
$$+19y_5 + 16y_6 \geq 0$$
$$(6)$$

Using these 22 inequality constraints, the MILP model for the WG-permutation (WGP) is constructed as shown in Algorithm 1.

Similarly, the reduced inequalities for SB are given as follows:

$$2x_0 + 2x_1 + 2x_2 + 36x_3 + 3x_4 + 3x_5 + 2x_6 - 9y_0 - 9y_1 - 6y_2 - 9y_3 - 6y_4 - 9y_5 - 9y_6 \geq -7$$

Algorithm 1. MILP model for the WG-permutation in WAGE

1: **function** WGP(S, *index*)
2:     $\mathcal{M}.var \leftarrow s'_{index+i}$, x_i , y_i as binary for $0 \leq i \leq 6$
3:     $\mathcal{M}.con \leftarrow s_{index+i} = s'_{index+i} + x_i$ for $0 \leq i \leq 6$
4:     Add constraints to $\mathcal{M}$ based on the reduced set of inequalities WGP_I
5:     **for** $j = 0$ to 36 **do**
6:         $S'[j] = S[j]$ ▷ $S'[j] = (s'_{7j}, s'_{7j+1}, s'_{7j+2}, s'_{7j+3}, s'_{7j+4}, s'_{7j+5}, s'_{7j+6})$
7:     **return** $(\mathcal{M}, S', [y_0, y_1, y_2, y_3, y_4, y_5, y_6])$

$$9x_0 + 3x_1 + 3x_4 + 70x_5 + x_6 - 15y_0 - 21y_1 - 14y_2 - 21y_3 - 14y_4 - 6y_5 - 16y_6 \geq -21$$

$$9x_0 - 3y_0 - 3y_1 - y_2 - y_3 - y_4 - 2y_5 - y_6 \geq -3$$

$$x_0 + 6x_2 + 8x_3 + 2x_4 - 8x_5 + 5x_6 - 16y_0 - 20y_1 + 48y_2 - 22y_3 - 15y_4 - 15y_5 - 4y_6 \geq -30$$

$$5x_0 + x_1 + 24x_4 + x_5 + 2x_6 - y_0 - 8y_1 - 5y_2 - 8y_3 - 5y_4 - 6y_5 - 8y_6 \geq -8$$

$$19x_0 + 2x_1 + x_2 - x_3 + 5x_4 + 5x_5 - 17y_0 - 23y_1 - 17y_2 + 48y_3 - 13y_4 - 14y_5 - 19y_6 \geq -24$$

$$-x_1 - 5x_2 + 3x_3 - x_4 - x_5 + 6x_6 - y_0 - 5y_1 + 2y_2 - 8y_3 - 10y_4 - 7y_5 + 12y_6 \geq -16$$

$$-x_1 - x_2 + 4x_3 - x_4 + 6x_5 - 2x_6 + 3y_0 - 8y_1 + 23y_2 - 14y_3 - 11y_4 - 10y_5 - 7y_6 \geq -19$$

$$-3x_0 - 5x_1 - 2x_2 - x_3 - x_4 - 4x_5 - x_6 + 11y_0 + 7y_1 - 11y_2 - 4y_3 + 9y_4 + 7y_5 + 7y_6 \geq -20$$

$$3x_0 + 3x_1 + x_2 + x_3 + x_4 + 3x_5 + 10x_6 - 8y_0 - 10y_1 - 8y_2 - 10y_3 - 8y_4 - 8y_5 + 21y_6 \geq -9$$

$$-3x_0 - x_2 - x_3 - 4x_4 - 3x_5 + x_6 + 2y_0 + y_1 + 7y_2 - 5y_3 + y_4 - 2y_5 - 7y_6 \geq -17$$

$$2x_0 + 2x_1 + 2x_2 + 36x_3 + 3x_4 + 3x_5 + 2x_6 - 9y_0 - 9y_1 - 6y_2 - 9y_3 - 6y_4 - 9y_5 - 9y_6 \geq -7$$

$$4x_1 + 5x_2 + 9x_3 + x_4 + x_5 + x_6 - 9y_0 - 9y_1 - 8y_2 + 16y_3 - 4y_4 - 8y_5 - 8y_6 \geq -9$$

$$-x_1 - x_2 - 3x_3 - 7x_4 - 7x_5 - 7x_6 + 5y_0 + 6y_1 + 4y_2 + 2y_3 + 7y_4 + 6y_5 - 2y_6 \geq -21$$

$$x_2 + 2x_3 + x_5 + 4x_6 - 10y_0 + 9y_1 - 3y_2 - 5y_3 - 3y_4 - 3y_5 - 3y_6 \geq -10$$

$$12x_0 + 4x_1 + 4x_3 + x_4 + x_5 - 15y_0 + 11y_1 - 11y_2 - 7y_3 - 7y_4 - 14y_5 + 6y_6 \geq -15$$

$$-5x_0 - 3x_1 - 4x_2 - x_3 - 4x_4 - 2x_5 - 2x_6 + 4y_0 - 5y_1 + 3y_2 - y_3 + y_4 - 4y_5 + 2y_6 \geq -21$$

$$8x_0 - x_1 - x_2 + 4x_4 - 2x_5 + 3x_6 - 6y_0 + 7y_1 + 2y_2 - 6y_3 - 8y_4 - 5y_5 - 5y_6 \geq -10$$

$$-2x_0 - 2x_1 - 2x_2 - x_4 + x_5 - 2x_6 - 3y_0 + 2y_1 + 2y_2 - y_3 + 2y_4 + y_5 + y_6 \geq -10$$

$$-3x_0 + 3x_1 + 3x_2 - 3x_3 + 9x_4 + 3x_5 + x_6 - y_0 - 7y_1 - 9y_2 - 7y_3 - 9y_4 + 5y_5 \geq -15$$

$$x_0 + 4x_1 + x_2 + 5x_3 - 2x_4 - 2x_6 - 4y_0 - 3y_3 - 6y_4 - 3y_5 + 2y_6 \geq -8$$

$$-5x_0 - x_1 - 2x_2 - 3x_3 - 3x_5 - 2x_6 + 3y_0 + 4y_1 + 5y_2 + 5y_3 + 3y_4 + 5y_5 + 2y_6 \geq -9$$

$$6x_0 - 4x_1 - 4x_2 - 3x_4 - 3x_5 + 3x_6 - 11y_0 - 10y_1 - 8y_2 - 5y_3 + 26y_4 - 7y_5 - 6y_6 \geq -26$$

$$x_2 + 6x_3 + 5x_4 + 2x_5 + x_6 - 3y_0 - 10y_1 + 21y_2 - 10y_3 - 7y_4 - 9y_5 - 7y_6 \geq -10$$

$$-x_0 - 4x_1 - x_2 - 4x_4 - 2x_5 - 2x_6 + 3y_0 + 3y_1 - 7y_2 - 2y_3 + 6y_4 + 5y_5 + 5y_6 \geq -16$$

$$-x_0 + 2x_1 - x_2 + 3x_3 - x_4 + 3x_5 - x_6 - y_0 - y_1 - 3y_2 - 2y_3 + y_4 - 2y_5 - 2y_6 \geq -6$$

$$-2x_0 + x_1 + 2x_2 - 2x_3 + x_5 + 5x_6 + y_0 - 4y_1 + y_2 - 8y_3 + 2y_4 + y_5 - 10y_6 \geq -12$$

$$-x_0 - 3x_1 - 2x_2 - 3x_3 - 4x_4 - 3x_5 - x_6 + 2y_0 - y_1 + y_2 + y_3 + y_4 - 3y_5 - 2y_6 \geq -18$$

$$-4x_0 - x_1 - x_2 - 4x_3 - 2x_5 - x_6 + 4y_0 + 6y_1 + 3y_2 + 7y_3 + 3y_4 + 4y_5 + 5y_6 \geq -5$$

$$-3x_0 - 4x_3 - x_4 - 3x_5 - x_6 + 4y_0 + 5y_1 + 3y_2 + 5y_3 + y_4 + y_5 + 4y_6 \geq -6$$

$$-x_0 + x_1 + x_2 - x_3 + 3x_6 - 2y_1 - 2y_2 - 2y_3 - 2y_4 + y_5 \geq -4$$

$$-x_0 + x_1 - x_2 + 2x_3 + 2x_4 - x_5 + x_6 - y_0 - 2y_1 - 3y_2 - 2y_3 + y_4 - y_5 \geq -5$$

$$-4x_0 - 2x_1 - 4x_3 - x_5 - 2x_6 + 5y_0 + 7y_1 + 3y_2 + 8y_3 + y_4 + 4y_5 + 7y_6 \geq -5$$

$$3x_1 + 2x_3 - 2y_0 - y_1 - y_2 - 2y_3 + 2y_4 - 2y_5 - y_6 \geq -2$$

$$x_0 - x_1 - x_4 + x_5 + x_6 - y_1 - y_3 - 2y_4 \geq -3$$

$$-x_0 - x_1 - x_4 + 2x_5 - 2x_6 - y_0 - 2y_2 - 3y_3 + 2y_4 - 3y_5 + 2y_6 \geq -8$$

$$x_0 + 2x_1 + 2x_2 + x_3 + x_4 + x_5 + x_6 - y_0 - 3y_1 - 3y_2 - 3y_3 - 3y_4 + 2y_6 \geq -2$$

$$-x_0 - x_3 - x_6 + y_0 + 2y_1 + y_2 + 2y_3 + y_4 + y_5 + y_6 \geq -1$$

$$-11x_0 - 6x_1 - x_2 - 10x_3 - 4x_4 - 5x_5 - 5x_6 + 20y_0 + 22y_1 + 11y_2 + 23y_3 + 3y_4 + 14y_5$$
$$+ 20y_6 \geq -14$$

$$3x_0 + 4x_1 + 3x_2 + 24x_3 + 6x_4 + 5x_5 + 6x_6 - 21y_0 - 24y_1 - 21y_2 - 28y_3 + 68y_4 -$$
$$29y_5 - 22y_6 \geq -26$$

$$-17x_0 + x_1 + 3x_2 + 4x_3 - 6x_4 + 2x_5 + 2x_6 - 5y_0 + y_1 - 12y_2 - 26y_3 - 17y_4 + 34y_5$$
$$- 13y_6 \geq -49$$

$$-8x_0 - 2x_1 - 2x_2 - 6x_3 - x_4 - 3x_5 - 2x_6 + 17y_0 + 20y_1 + 15y_2 + 22y_3 + 12y_4 + 17y_5$$
$$+ 15y_6 \geq 0$$

$$-17x_0 - 4x_1 - x_2 - 16x_3 - 14x_4 - 15x_5 - 16x_6 + 14y_0 + 15y_1 + 2y_2 + 6y_3 + y_4 +$$
$$3y_5 + 5y_6 \geq -62$$

$$-3x_0 - 7x_1 - x_2 - 2x_3 - x_4 - 4x_5 - 6x_6 + 8y_0 + 6y_1 + 11y_2 + 13y_3 - 5y_4 + 11y_5 +$$
$$12y_6 \geq -15$$

$$-5x_0 + 3x_1 + 3x_2 - 5x_3 - 2x_4 - 6x_5 - x_6 + 11y_0 + 7y_1 + 3y_2 + 7y_3 - 4y_4 + 7y_5 +$$
$$11y_6 \geq -11$$

$$-12x_0 - x_1 - 3x_2 - 12x_3 - 4x_4 - 7x_5 - 12x_6 + 8y_0 + 9y_1 - 3y_2 + 3y_3 + 5y_4 +$$
$$y_5 + 9y_6 \geq -41$$

$$x_0 + 12x_1 + 3x_2 + x_3 + x_4 + 7x_5 + 8x_6 - 17y_0 - 26y_1 - 12y_2 + 38y_3 - 7y_4 -$$
$$17y_5 - 17y_6 \geq -25$$

$$(7)$$

$$-11x_0 - 2x_1 - x_2 - 10x_3 - 4x_4 - 2x_5 - 8x_6 + 11y_0 + 13y_1 + 4y_2 + 15y_3 + 6y_4$$
$$+ 5y_5 + 9y_6 \geq -21$$

$$7x_0 + 3x_1 + 2x_2 + 2x_3 + 2x_4 + 4x_5 + 43x_6 - 11y_0 - 11y_1 - 10y_2 - 11y_3 - 8y_4 -$$
$$11y_5 - 10y_6 \geq -9$$

$$(8)$$

Algorithm 2. MILP model for the S-box in WAGE

1: **function** SB(S, *index*)

2:     $\mathcal{M}.var \leftarrow s'_{index+i}$, x_i , y_i as binary for $0 \leq i \leq 6$

3:     $\mathcal{M}.con \leftarrow s'_{index+i} = s_{index+i} + x_i$ for $0 \leq i \leq 6$

4:     Add constraints to $\mathcal{M}$ based on the reduced set of inequalities SB_I

5:     **for** $j = 0$ to 36 **do**

6:         $S'[j] = S[j]$ $\triangleright S'[j] = (s'_{7j}, s'_{7j+1}, s'_{7j+2}, s'_{7j+3}, s'_{7j+4}, s'_{7j+5}, s'_{7j+6})$

7:     **return** $(\mathcal{M}, S', [y_0, y_1, y_2, y_3, y_4, y_5, y_6])$

Using these 49 inequality constraints, the MILP model for the S-box (SB) is constructed as shown in Algorithm 2.

MILP Model for the Feedback Function (FBK). In WAGE, the function FBK is expressed as $S_{31} + S_{30} + S_{26} + S_{24} + S_{19} + S_{13} + S_{12} + S_8 + S_6 + (\omega \otimes S_0)$. We first rewrite $x \otimes \omega = (x_0, x_1, x_2, x_3, x_4, x_5, x_6) \otimes \omega \rightarrow (x_6, x_0 \oplus x_6, x_1 \oplus x_6, x_2 \oplus x_6, x_3, x_4, x_5)$. In order to model this function $x \otimes \omega$, we have two methods such as $\mathcal{S}$ method [6] and $\mathcal{ZR}$ method [9]. However, $\mathcal{S}$ method cannot handle the cancellation phenomenon between terms, so it may introduce some invalid trails. In WAGE, we verified that $\mathcal{S}$ method is enough as it does not produce any invalid trail for this function. Using the technique [6], we get the following system of equations by introducing 10 intermediate binary variables t_i for $1 \leq i \leq 10$ (see Eq. (9)).

$$\begin{cases} x_0 = t_1 \\ x_1 = t_2 \\ x_2 = t_3 \\ x_3 = t_4 \\ x_4 = t_5 \\ x_5 = t_6 \\ x_6 = t_7 + t_8 + t_9 + t_{10} \end{cases} \qquad \begin{cases} y_0 = t_7 \\ y_1 = t_1 + t_8 \\ y_2 = t_2 + t_9 \\ y_3 = t_3 + t_{10} \\ y_4 = t_4 \\ y_5 = t_5 \\ y_6 = t_6 \end{cases} \qquad (9)$$

Algorithm 3 elaborates the MILP model.

Now, we describe the overall MILP model for the WAGE whose initialization is reduced to R rounds. The function **WAGEEval** in Algorithm 4 computes all the division trails.

Algorithm 3. MILP model for FBK operation in WAGE

1: **function** FBK(S, *IndexSet*)
2:     $\mathcal{M}.var \leftarrow z_j$ as binary for $0 \leq j \leq 6$
3:     Add constraints to $\mathcal{M}$ based on Equation (9) to model $\omega \otimes S_0$
4:     **for** $i \in IndexSet$ **do**
5:         $\mathcal{M}.var \leftarrow s'_{7i+j}$, x_{7i+j} as binary for $0 \leq j \leq 6$
6:     temp $= 0$
7:     **for** $j \in [0, 1, 2, 3, 4, 5, 6]$ **do**
8:         **for** $i \in IndexSet$ **do**
9:             temp $\leftarrow$ temp $+ x_{7i+j}$
10:        $\mathcal{M}.con \leftarrow z_j = y_j + temp$ ▷ see Equation (9) for y_j
11:    **for** $j \in \{0, 1, \ldots, 37\} \setminus IndexSet$ **do**
12:        $S'[j] = S[j]$ ▷ $S'[j] = (s'_{7j}, s'_{7j+1}, s'_{7j+2}, s'_{7j+3}, s'_{7j+4}, s'_{7j+5}, s'_{7j+6})$
13:    **return** $(\mathcal{M}, S', [z_0, z_1, z_2, z_3, z_4, z_5, z_6])$

4.2   Evaluate Secret Bits Involved in the Balanced Superpoly

We prepare a cube $C_I(IV)$ to start the evaluation using all feasible combinations of $\{v_{I_1}, v_{I_2}, \ldots, v_{I_{|I|}}\}$. Then, using Algorithm 5 from [7], we extract the relevant secret variables $J = \{k_{j_1}, k_{j_2}, \ldots, k_{j_{|J|}}\}$ from the preferred superpoly. The cube indices $I = \{I_1, I_2, \ldots, I_{|I|}\}$ of the WAGE cipher and the MILP model $\mathcal{M}$ serve as the algorithm's inputs. The initial division property is used to calculate all R-round division trails with the following values: $v_i = 1$ for $i \in I$ and $v_i = 0$ for $i \in \{0, 1, 2, \ldots, m - 1\} \setminus I$. Table 1 summarize all the secret bits involved in the preferable superpoly. Table 1 is built for 13 to 18 rounds of the initialization phase based on our chosen cubes of Table 1.

Table 1. Involved Key bits in the Superpoly for the Cube $C_{\{I_1, I_2, \ldots, I_{15}\}}$

Cube Sequence	Cube Indices	Output bit	#Rounds	Involved Secret Key Variables (J)	$|J|$	Time
I_1	7,21,24,25	60	13	127,133,134,…,195	65	2^{65+4}
I_2	8,21,24,25		14			
I_3	9,21,24,25		15			
I_4	10,21,24,25		16			
I_5	11,21,24,25		17			
			18	0,1,…,13,42,43,…,62,126,127,133,134,…,195	100	2^{100+4}
I_6	21,24,25,109	65	13	127,133,134,…,195	65	2^{65+4}
I_7	21,24,25,97		14			
I_8	24,25,97,109		15			
I_9	21,25,106,109		16			
I_{10}	21,24,25,106		17	0,1,…,6,42,43,…,48, 56,57,…,62,127,133,134,…,195	86	2^{86+4}
			18	0,1,…,13,42,43,…,62,126,127,133,134,…,195	100	2^{100+4}
I_{11}	21,22, 23, 35	66	13	127,133,134,…,195	65	2^{65+4}
I_{12}	21,22, 24, 35		14			
I_{13}	21,22, 25, 35		15			
I_{14}	21,22, 26, 35		16			
I_{15}	21,22, 27, 35		17	0,1,…,6,42,43,…,48, 56,57,…,62,127,133,134,…,195	86	2^{86+4}
			18	0,1,…,13,42,43,…,62,126,127,133,134,…,195	100	2^{100+4}

Searching Cubes. We pick the cube I so that 2^{I+J} has the smallest possible value. The cubes that we select for this attack meet the aforementioned requirement are displayed in Table 1 as $I_1, I_2, \ldots, I_{15}$. There are a total of $|I|$ cubes of size $|I|$ that can be created. The selection of so many cubes is computationally infeasible. We do not have the reasonable evidence that our choice of cube indices are appropriate. However, we have tested many different cubes (see

---

Algorithm 4. MILP model for the Initialization Round of WAGE Cipher

---

1: **function** WAGEEVAL(R, OutputBit)
2:      Prepare an empty MILP model $\mathcal{M}$
3:      $\mathcal{M}.var \leftarrow S_i^0$ for $0 \leq i \leq 37$ ▷ $S_i^0 = (s_{7i}, s_{7i+1}, \ldots, s_{7i+6})$ and $S_i^0[j] = s_j$
4:      **for** $r \in \{1, 2, \ldots, R\}$ **do**
5:          $(\mathcal{M}, S^1, a_1) \leftarrow SB(S^{r-1}, 8)$
6:          $(\mathcal{M}, S^2, a_2) \leftarrow SB(S^1, 15)$
7:          $(\mathcal{M}, S^3, a_3) \leftarrow WGP(S^2, 18)$
8:          $(\mathcal{M}, S^4, a_4) \leftarrow SB(S^3, 27)$
9:          $(\mathcal{M}, S^5, a_5) \leftarrow SB(S^4, 34)$
10:          $(\mathcal{M}, S^6, a_6) \leftarrow WGP(S^5, 36)$
11:          $(\mathcal{M}, S^7, b) \leftarrow FBK(S^6, [0, 6, 8, 12, 13, 19, 24, 26, 30, 31])$
12:          **for** $i \in [5, 11, 19, 24, 30]$ **do**
13:              $\mathcal{M}.var \leftarrow s_{7i+j}^r$, x_{7i+j}^r as binary for $0 \leq j \leq 6$
14:          **for** $i \in [5, 11, 19, 24, 30]$ **do**
15:              $\mathcal{M}.con \leftarrow S_i^7[j] = s_{7i+j}^r + x_{7i+j}^r$ for $0 \leq j \leq 6$
16:          $b_1 = a_1 + X_5$
17:          $b_2 = a_2 + X_{11}$
18:          $b_3 = a_3 + X_{19}$ ▷ $X_i = \{x_{7i}^r, x_{7i+1}^r, \ldots, x_{7i+6}^r\}$
19:          $b_4 = a_4 + X_{24}$
20:          $b_5 = a_5 + X_{30}$
21:          $fb = a_6 + b$
22:          $S_5^r = b_1$
23:          $S_{11}^r = b_2$
24:          $S_{19}^r = b_3$
25:          $S_{24}^r = b_4$
26:          $S_{30}^r = b_5$
27:          **for** $i = 0$ to $35 \setminus \{5, 11, 19, 24, 30\}$ **do**
28:              $S_i^r = S_{i+1}^7$
29:          $\mathcal{M}.con \leftarrow S_0^7 = 0$
30:          $\mathcal{M}.var \leftarrow S_{36}^r$ as binary
31:          $\mathcal{M}.con \leftarrow S_{36}^r = fb$
32:      **for** $i = 0$ to $258 \setminus \{OutputBit\}$ **do**
33:          $\mathcal{M}.con \leftarrow S^7[j] = 0$
34:      $\mathcal{M}.con \leftarrow OutputBit = 1$

Algorithm 5. Evaluate secret variables in superpoly by MILP [7]

1: **function** EVALUATEKEYBITS(MILP model $\mathcal{M}$, Cube Indices I)
2:     $\mathcal{M}.var \leftarrow k_i$ for $0 \leq i \leq n-1$ ▷ $k_0, k_1, \ldots, k_{n-1}$ are secret variables
3:     $\mathcal{M}.var \leftarrow v_j$ for $0 \leq j \leq m-1$ ▷ $v_0, v_1, \ldots, v_{m-1}$ are secret variables
4:     $\mathcal{M}.con \leftarrow v_i = 1$ for $i \in I$
5:     $\mathcal{M}.con \leftarrow v_j = 0$ for $j \in \{(0, 1, \ldots, m-1) \setminus I\}$
6:     $\mathcal{M}.con \leftarrow \sum_{i=0}^{n-1} k_i = 1$
7:     **do**
8:         Solve MILP model $\mathcal{M}$
9:         **if** $\mathcal{M}$ is feasible **then**
10:            pick an index $j \in \{0, 1, \ldots, n-1\}$ such that $k_j = 1$
11:            $J = J \cup \{j\}$
12:            $\mathcal{M}.con \leftarrow k_j = 0$
13:     **while** $\mathcal{M}$ is feasible
14:     **return** J

Table 1 and Table 2) at random. Our tests suggest that the cubes of Table 1 are the most effective for this cipher. How to choose appropriate cubes is still an open question.

Table 2. Involved Key bits in the Superpoly for the Cube $C_{\{I'_1, I'_2\}}$

Cube Sequence	Cube Indices	Output bit	#Rounds	Involved Secret Key Variables (J)	$|J|$	Time
I'_1	25,26,39,41	70	13	126,127,133,134,…,195	65	2^{65+4}
I'_2	25,26,39,93		14			
			15			
			16	0,1,…,13,42,43,…,62,126,127,133,134,…,195	100	2^{100+4}
			17			

Extract a Balanced Superpoly. In order to find the superpoly $p(J, \bar{v})$, for $\bar{v} = \{v_0, v_1, \ldots, v_{m-1}\} \setminus I$, we randomly select the constant part of the IV and test a total of $2^4 \times 2^{100}$ potential permutations (see Table 1 for the reduced 18-round of the cipher for each output bit $\in \{60, 65, 66\}$. Let J be one of the 2^{100} possible values represented by $\hat{J}$. During the offline phase, we calculate the values of $p(J, \bar{v})$, store them in a table $T1$ with an index of $\hat{J}$, and then evaluate the ANF in accordance with those values. If $p(J, \bar{v})$ becomes constant, we choose a new random IV and repeat the process described above until we discover a suitable one that ensures that $p(J, \bar{v})$ is not constant.

To sum up, after computing 2^{4+100} operations, we compute a table $T1$ of size $\hat{J}$. If the attacker can quickly locate the right IVs, the attack is feasible. We suppose that for each of the cubes in Table 1, we can recover the balanced superpoly in just one trial. In fact, there are $128-4 = 124$ bits available to set the constant portion of the IV because each of these cubes has a size of 4. Because of this, we assume that Assumption 1 (which is indicated in [7]) is true with a high degree of probability and derive the complexity numbers appropriately.

4.3 Key Recovery for 18-Round Initialization Phase

For the cubes $I_1, I_2, \ldots, I_{15}$, we employ the balanced superpolys. For each $i \in \{1, 2, \ldots, 15\}$, the following procedures are performed during the online phase.

- Query the encryption oracle with C_{I_i} and compute $S = \bigoplus_{C_{I_i}} f(k, v)$
- Compare S with each entry of T_1. The values of $\bar{k} = \{k_{j_1}, k_{j_2}, \ldots, k_{j_{100}}\}$ for which S does not match T_1 are discarded. Given that the superpoly is balanced, we observe that for 2^{99} values of $\bar{k}$, $p(k_{j_1}, k_{j_2}, \ldots, k_{j_{100}}, \bar{v}) = 0$. Conversely, for the remaining 2^{99} values of $\bar{k}$, $p(k_{j_1}, k_{j_2}, \ldots, k_{j_{100}}, \bar{v}) = 1$. Therefore, we can recover one bit of information in the secret variables.

For each output bit $\in \{60, 65, 66\}$, we can recover one bit of secret information for each cube only in one trial. Since we work with five cubes, we recover five secret variables. The remaining secret bits ($128 - 5 = 123$ of them) are recovered by guessing involving a brute-force complexity of 2^{123}. The total time complexity for the attack is therefore $5 \times 2^{104} + 2^{123} \equiv 2^{123}$. The data complexity for the total computation is $5 \times 2^4 = 2^{6.32}$.

4.4 Discussion on Experimental Results

The initialization phase of WAGE involves 111 numbers of rounds. As the number of rounds increases, the output function's degree in WAGE also grows, and when utilizing the full 111 rounds, it is anticipated to be considerably high. Consequently, if one aims to identify a cube after 111 rounds, the size of the cube is also expected to be large. Such a task necessitates a significant amount of computational time. Considering these factors, a cube attack was conducted on reduced round versions of WAGE instead. Due to the large time complexity involved in searching for larger cubes, our experiments focused on smaller cube sizes. It is worth noting that the identified cubes for the 18 initialization rounds are only of size 4, even though the degree of the output function after 18 rounds is expected to be significantly higher. This observation indicates that the key and the initialization vector are not thoroughly mixed yet after the completion of the 18 rounds. However, the experimental results (small data complexity) demonstrate that our proposed approach is well-suited for realistic scenarios in lightweight constrained applications where gathering large amounts of data is difficult.

5 Conclusion

The security of the nonlinear feedback-based initialization phase of the lightweight stream cipher WAGE is examined in this study. By assuming that the cipher's structure is a non-blackbox polynomial, we can mount a division-property-based cube attack. For the initialization phase of this cipher, our attack suggests a MILP model. We work out the details of the model as specific to the WAGE cipher. To the best of our knowledge, there exist only one correlation power attack against this cipher, and it is mounted up to 12 out of 111 rounds. Our method is able to attack this cipher to 6 more rounds, that is the 18-round of the cipher.

References

1. AlTawy, R., Gong, G., Mandal, K., Rohit, R.: WAGE: an authenticated encryption with a twist. IACR Trans. Symmetric Cryptol. **2020**(S1), 132–159 (2020)
2. AlTawy, R., Rohit, R., He, M., Mandal, K., Yang, G., Gong, G.: sLiSCP: simeck-based permutations for lightweight sponge cryptographic primitives. In: Adams, C., Camenisch, J. (eds.) SAC 2017. LNCS, vol. 10719, pp. 129–150. Springer, Cham (2018). https://doi.org/10.1007/978-3-319-72565-9_7
3. Dinur, I., Shamir, A.: Cube attacks on tweakable black box polynomials. In: Joux, A. (ed.) EUROCRYPT 2009. LNCS, vol. 5479, pp. 278–299. Springer, Heidelberg (2009). https://doi.org/10.1007/978-3-642-01001-9_16
4. Fei, Y., et al.: Correlation power analysis and higher-order masking implementation of WAGE. In: Dunkelman, O., Jacobson, Jr., M.J., O'Flynn, C. (eds.) SAC 2020. LNCS, vol. 12804, pp. 593–614. Springer, Cham (2021). https://doi.org/10.1007/978-3-030-81652-0_23
5. Gong, G., Youssef, A.M.: Cryptographic properties of the welch-gong transformation sequence generators. IEEE Trans. Inf. Theory **48**(11), 2837–2846 (2002)
6. Sun, L., Wang, W., Wang, M.Q.: MILP-aided bit-based division property for primitives with non-bit-permutation linear layers. IET Inf. Secur. **14**(1), 12–20 (2019)
7. Todo, Y., Isobe, T., Hao, Y., Meier, W.: Cube attacks on non-blackbox polynomials based on division property. In: Katz, J., Shacham, H. (eds.) CRYPTO 2017. LNCS, vol. 10403, pp. 250–279. Springer, Cham (2017). https://doi.org/10.1007/978-3-319-63697-9_9
8. Xiang, Z., Zhang, W., Bao, Z., Lin, D.: Applying MILP method to searching integral distinguishers based on division property for 6 lightweight block ciphers. In: Cheon, J.H., Takagi, T. (eds.) ASIACRYPT 2016. LNCS, vol. 10031, pp. 648–678. Springer, Heidelberg (2016). https://doi.org/10.1007/978-3-662-53887-6_24
9. Zhang, W., Rijmen, V.: Division cryptanalysis of block ciphers with a binary diffusion layer. IET Inf. Secur. **13**(2), 87–95 (2019)

When MPC in the Head Meets VC

Li Liu[1,2] and Puwen Wei[1,2,3(✉)]

[1] Key Laboratory of Cryptologic Technology and Information Security, Ministry of Education, Shandong University, Qingdao, China
sdu_liuli@mail.sdu.edu.cn
[2] School of Cyber Science and Technology, Shandong University, Qingdao, China
[3] Quancheng Laboratory, Jinan, China
pwei@sdu.edu.cn

Abstract. In this paper, we investigate zero-knowledge proof systems based on the "MPC-in-the-head" paradigm (MPCitH), which presents the advantage of offering fast proof generation and post-quantum security. However, current constructions suffer from the drawbacks of large proof sizes and high memory consumption. Particularly, as the underlying circuit increases in size, the proof size grows significantly, and the machine that executes MPCitH-based protocol quickly surpasses its memory bounds due to the multiple parallel executions of MPC. To overcome this challenge, we present the VC-then-MPCitH paradigm, which integrates verifiable computation (VC) techniques into MPCitH. We implement our protocol using concrete VC protocol Virgo++ and MPCitH protocol BN++. Leveraging the properties of the underlying protocols, we can embed Virgo++ into BN++ efficiently. The resulting protocol can significantly reduce the memory consumption and the cost of both computation and communication of MPCitH for large circuits. We conduct our evaluation on a circuit over the field $\mathbb{F}_{2^{128}}$ consisting of 40,006 multiplication gates and almost 100000 gates in total. With soundness error of 2^{-128}, our protocol can generate proofs of size 8891 KB in 86 ms, and verify in 70 ms. Furthermore, our protocol outperforms BN++ with the same parameter settings by reducing the proof size by a factor of 10 and shortening both the prover and verifier time by 13 times. On a resource-constrained device that offers 10 GB of memory, our protocol can handle effectively circuits with up to 10 million gates, while BN++ only supports circuits with up to 330,000 gates.

Keywords: Zero-knowledge · MPC-in-the-head · Post-quantum

1 Introduction

Zero-knowledge (ZK) proof enables the prover to demonstrate the correctness of a statement to the verifier without revealing additional information. Since its proposal by Goldwasser, Micali, and Rackoff [16], zero-knowledge proof has become an essential cryptographic primitive, which is widely used to construct privacy-preserving protocols, e.g., anonymous transactions, verifiable voting, identification protocols, etc. During the past decades, researchers have proposed quite a

W. Meng et al. (Eds.): ISPEC 2023, LNCS 14341, pp. 507–526, 2023.
https://doi.org/10.1007/978-981-99-7032-2_30

few efficient constructions of ZK protocols for arithmetic circuits. In particular, Ishai et al.'s seminal work [20] presented the MPC-in-the-head (MPCitH) paradigm which can construct ZK proofs using secure multi-party computation (MPC). Then a series of works have shown concrete ZK protocols following the MPCitH paradigm, e.g., ZKBoo [15], KKW [24], BN [4], Limbo [28], etc. Due to the properties of MPCitH, the resulting ZK protocols do not need to rely on structured (or number-theoretic) assumptions, and hence can offer post-quantum security. Furthermore, these protocols can be transformed to post-quantum digital signatures via Fiat-Shamir transformation, e.g., Picnic 1/2/3 [10,11,21], BBQ [29], Banquet [5], Rainer [13], the security of which only rely on the underlying symmetric key primitives. Compared with zk-SNARKs especially the popular "poly-IOP"-based schemes [12,14], constructions based on MPCitH typically have a significant advantage in prover time, not only the asymptotic complexity of which is linear in the circuit size $O(|\mathcal{C}|)$, where $|\mathcal{C}|$ represents the number of multiplication gates of circuit $\mathcal{C}$, but can achieve outstanding concrete efficiency. Recently, TurboIKOS [19] and BN++ [22] further optimized the proof size of BN while preserving proving efficiency.

However, the proof size of the current MPCitH-based ZK protocols increased significantly with the number of multiplication gates of the circuit. In particular, when the circuit has tens of thousands of multiplication gates, the resulting proof size would be tens of megabytes. Another concern is the high memory consumption which may limit the practical applicability of MPCitH. For large circuits with over 10^5 gates, the memory cost of the current MPCitH-based protocol, say BN++, would be prohibitive or even cause downtime, especially for resource-constrained devices. This is also important in large-scale computational scenarios, such as machine learning with privacy protection. In such scenarios, the service provider needs to prove that a computationally intensive process of the machine learning model is correct without disclosing sensitive data. As the scale of the computation grows, it can become challenging for the service provider to provide the proof in a timely manner.

Contributions. In this work, we introduce "VC-then-MPCitH", a novel paradigm for creating post-quantum zero-knowledge proofs. Our approach integrates verifiable computation (VC) techniques with MPCitH and offers substantial reductions in proof size, computational overhead, and memory consumption when compared to current MPCitH-based constructions. The basic idea is to make use of the efficient verification capabilities of VC methods to compress the circuit size within the MPCitH process, which allows for faster and more efficient operations. However, integrating VC and MPCitH comes with additional consistency-proof requirements that may negate the advantages of using VC in terms of communication and computation costs. To address this problem, we investigate the characteristics of the concrete VC protocol Virgo++ [32] and MPCitH, and devise a simple method of committing to the prover's messages in each round of Virgo++. This allows us to embed Virgo++ into the state-of-the-art MPCitH-based proof system, BN++ [22], efficiently. It is worth noting that for fixed-size circuits, our protocol's proof size and running time are independent of the multiplication gate density. Our protocol inherits the security of the MPCintH protocols and relies only on symmetric primitives instead of other structured or number-theoretic assumptions, providing sufficiently plausible post-quantum security.

We have implemented our protocol using a circuit defined over $\mathbb{F}_{2^{128}}$, containing 40,006 multiplication gates and almost 100,000 gates in total. With the soundness error of 2^{-128}, generating proofs of size 8891 KB takes 86 ms, while verification occurs within 70 ms. Compared to BN++ with the same parameter settings, our proof size is 10× smaller, with prover and verifier time sped up by 13×. Contrasting Virgo++ with ZK implementation, our overall prover time is between 1.2× to 4× faster, while our proof size is larger. It is also worth mentioning that our protocol supports large circuits over any finite fields, whereas the ZK Virgo++ requires special restrictions of finite fields. More importantly, our protocol offers superior scalability concerning memory consumption when compared to BN++. Specifically, BN++ is unable to handle circuits with more than 330,000 gates on devices with limited memory of 10 GB. In contrast, our protocol can support circuits with up to 10 million gates, allowing for high efficiency in proving circuits over a wide range, and is compatible with large-scale computations.

Related Works. Many existing (zk-)SNARKs [12,18,31] use VC [1] as a building block to achieve succinct proof. However, the prover time comes with significant computational overheads due to operations such as FFT and multi-exponentiation. As the circuit scales in large outsourced verifiable computations, generating proofs becomes significantly delayed and inefficient. To address this issue, some studies [9,25] leverage recursive combinations of proof systems to iteratively construct verifiable computations incrementally. In recent years, Interactive Proof (IP) has become an attractive tool for constructing VCs with its superior prover time and statistical soundness. The IP protocols based on GKR [17] and its variants [30,31] are crucial components in the construction of doubly efficient ZK protocols. In the latest results, Virgo++ [32] achieves a strict prover time ($O(|\mathcal{C}|)$) for generic circuits. Recent work [6] utilizes a similar idea to ours. It embeds a GKR-like VC into Groth's SNARK [18] to reduce SNARK's prover time. However, their approach does not account for secret inputs, and constructions that rely on trusted setups make it difficult to add ZK functionality. Ligero++ [8], which offers post-quantum security, achieves a trade-off between proof size and prover time by combining Ligero [3] and Aurora [7]. However, similar to Virgo [33], Ligero++ has constraints on the finite field of the circuit to achieve the low degree test (LDT), and its prover time is marginally higher than Ligero, the asymptotic prover time of which is $O(|\mathcal{C}| \log |\mathcal{C}|)$.

2   Preliminaries

Notations. We use κ as the security parameter and $\mathsf{negl}(\cdot)$ as the negligible function. Let x_i denote the i-th variable of the vector x. $[n]$ denotes the set

$\{1, \ldots, n\}$ and $[a, b]$ stands for the interval from a to b. We formalize the statement for the protocol as the arithmetic circuit satisfiability problem. A fan-in-2 arithmetic circuit $\mathcal{C}$ defined over any finite field $\mathbb{F}$ can be considered as a directed acyclic graph (DAG) $\mathcal{G}$, where gates and wires in $\mathcal{C}$ correspond to points and edges in $\mathcal{G}$, respectively. We assume that there are d layers in $\mathcal{C}$, where d is exactly the longest path of $\mathcal{G}$. Layer d and layer 0 are the input layer and the output layer, respectively. Following the notations of Virgo++, we use S_i to denote the number of gates at layer i and assume that $S_i = 2^{s_i}$ for simplicity. Each layer has a function $V_i : \{0, 1\}^{s_i} \to \mathbb{F}$ to map a gate label to its output value. The wiring-predicate functions $add_{i,j}/mult_{i,j} : \{0, 1\}^{s_{i-1} \times s_i \times s_j} \to \{0, 1\}$ output 1 iff gate z in layer $i-1$ is an addition/multiplication gate and takes the outputs of gate x in layer i and gate y in layer $j (j \geq i)$ as inputs.

We write probabilistic polynomial time Turing machine as "PPT iTM" for short. $\langle \mathcal{P}(\mathsf{in}_p), \mathcal{V}(\mathsf{in}_v) \rangle(x)$ denotes a random variable describing the output of $\mathcal{V}$ when running an interactive protocol with $\mathcal{P}$ on common input x, where $\mathcal{P}, \mathcal{V}$ are PPT iTM, and they take $\mathsf{in}_p, \mathsf{in}_v$ as auxiliary inputs. Let $\mathsf{View}\langle \mathcal{P}(\mathsf{in}_p), \mathcal{V}(\mathsf{in}_v) \rangle(x)$ be the distribution of the entire transcript of the interaction. Let $\mathbf{w} \in \mathbb{F}^{S_d}, \mathbf{y} \in \mathbb{F}^{S_0}$ denote the inputs and outputs of the circuit $\mathcal{C}$, respectively. The relation on $\mathcal{C}$ is defined as $R = \{\langle x = (\mathcal{C}, \mathbf{y}); \mathbf{w} \rangle : \mathcal{C}(\mathbf{w}) = \mathbf{y}\}$.

Definition 1 (Interactive arguments and proofs). $\langle \mathcal{P}, \mathcal{V} \rangle(\mathbf{w}, x)$ *is an interactive argument for the relation R if the following conditions hold:*

- **Completeness**: *For every* $\mathbf{w}$ *s.t.* $\mathcal{C}(\mathbf{w}) = \mathbf{y}$, $\Pr[\langle \mathcal{P}, \mathcal{V} \rangle(\mathbf{w}, x) = \mathsf{acc}] = 1$.
- **Soundness**: *For any* $\mathbf{w}$ *s.t.* $\mathcal{C}(\mathbf{w}) \neq \mathbf{y}$ *and any malicious PPT iTM* $\mathcal{P}^*$, $\Pr[\langle \mathcal{P}^*, \mathcal{V} \rangle(\mathbf{w}, x) = \mathsf{acc}] \leq \mathsf{negl}(|x|)$. *If* $\mathcal{P}^*$ *is computationally unbounded, then* $\langle \mathcal{P}, \mathcal{V} \rangle(\mathbf{w}, x)$ *is an interactive proof (IP).*

Definition 2 (Honest Verifier Zero-Knowledge Argument of Knowledge (HVZKAoK)). $\langle \mathcal{P}(\mathbf{w}), \mathcal{V} \rangle(x)$ *is an HVZKAoK for the relation R with knowledge error ξ if the following conditions hold:*

- **Completeness**: *For every* $\mathbf{w}$ *s.t.* $\mathcal{C}(\mathbf{w}) = \mathbf{y}$, $\Pr[\langle \mathcal{P}, \mathcal{V} \rangle(\mathbf{w}, x) = \mathsf{acc}] = 1$.
- **Knowledge soundness**: *There exists a probabilistic extractor algorithm $\mathcal{E}$ which takes x as input and holds that: for any malicious PPT iTM* $\mathcal{P}^*$, *if the probability $\delta(x)$ that V accepts on input x satisfies $\delta(x) > \xi$, given oracle access to* $\mathcal{P}^*$, $\mathcal{E}$ *outputs* $\mathbf{w}$ *s.t.* $\mathcal{C}(\mathbf{w}) = \mathbf{y}$ *in the expected time* $O(\frac{1}{\delta(x)-\xi})$.
- **Honest Verifier Zero-Knowledge**: *there exists a PPT simulator $\mathcal{S}$ that can access to the randomness used by $\mathcal{V}$ s.t.* $\mathcal{S}(x) \approx \mathsf{View}\langle \mathcal{P}(\mathbf{w}), \mathcal{V} \rangle(x)$.

Commitment. A commitment scheme Com allows a user to commit to a message m with randomness r. The user can open the commitment $\mathsf{Com}(m; r)$ later by revealing (m, r). The commitment should satisfy properties called hiding and binding. Simply speaking, the hiding property requires that it is hard to distinguish between commitments of m_0 and m_1, while binding requires that it is hard to find two different messages m_0 and m_1 such that $\mathsf{Com}(m_0; r_0) = \mathsf{Com}(m_1; r_1)$.

In this work, the commitment scheme is instantiated by a hash function that can be modeled as a random oracle.

Multi-linear Extension (MLE). Any ℓ-variable function $V : \{0,1\}^\ell \to \mathbb{F}$ has a unique MLE $\tilde{V} : \mathbb{F}^\ell \to \mathbb{F}$ that is a multilinear polynomial such that $\tilde{V}(x_1, x_2, \ldots, x_\ell) = V(x_1, x_2, \ldots, x_\ell)$ for all $x_1, \ldots, x_\ell \in \{0,1\}$. $\tilde{V}$ can be expressed as below.

$$\tilde{V}(x_1, x_2, \ldots, x_\ell) = \sum_{b_1, \ldots, b_\ell \in \{0,1\}} \prod_{i=1}^{\ell} \left((1 - x_i)(1 - b_i) + x_i b_i\right) \cdot V(b_1, b_2, \ldots, b_\ell)$$

MPC-in-the-Head and BN++. The main idea of MPC-in-the-head to construct ZK is as follows. For the statement $\mathcal{C}(\mathbf{w}) = \mathbf{y}$ where $\mathbf{w}$ is the witness, the prover simulates N parties of an MPC protocol "in the head". Each party "in his head" takes as input the secret-sharing of $\mathbf{w}$ and runs the MPC protocol to evaluate $\mathcal{C}$ gate-by-gate. The prover commits to the inputs as well as each party's view and related randomness, and opens some of these commitments based on the verifier's challenges. The verifier checks the consistency of all the parties' views and the correctness of the output. Due to the privacy of the underlying MPC, the resulting protocol can achieve zero-knowledge.

BN++ improves the MPCitH paradigm with "lifting" strategies. Instead of evaluating $\mathcal{C}$ gate-by-gate, BN++ takes advantage of the "sacrificing" technique. In particular, shares of results of multiplication gates had been injected by the prover at the beginning and the verifier needs to additionally select random coefficients to run the *Dot-Product Checking*, which is a sub-protocol used for checking the evaluation of L multiplication gates in batch. More precisely, to prove that all $(x_\ell, y_\ell, z_\ell)_{\ell=1}^L$ are multiplication triples, the prover hides them by an auxiliary random dot product $(\{a_\ell, b_\ell\}_{\ell \in L}, c)$ such that $c = \sum_{\ell=1}^L a_\ell \cdot b_\ell$, where all $b_\ell = y_\ell$ are fixed for optimization. Since in the MPCitH, each party holds one share of each of these values (we write $m^{(p)}$ to indicate the share of m held by party p), they run the following process:

a. The verifier chooses random challenge $\epsilon = (\epsilon_1, \ldots, \epsilon_L) \in \mathbb{F}^L$.
b. Each party p sets $\alpha_\ell^{(p)} = \epsilon_\ell \cdot x_\ell^{(p)} + a_\ell^{(p)}$.
c. Each party p open $\{\alpha_\ell\}$ by broadcasting, i.e., $\alpha_\ell = \sum_{p \in [N]} \alpha_\ell^{(p)}$.
d. Each party p sets $v^{(p)} = \sum_{\ell=1}^L (\epsilon_\ell \cdot z_\ell^{(p)} - \alpha_\ell \cdot y_\ell^{(p)}) - c^{(p)}$.
e. The verifier will accept iff $\sum_{p \in [N]} v^{(p)} = 0$.

The soundness of *Dot-Product Checking* is guaranteed by the General Schwartz-Zippel lemma [22].

Sumcheck Protocol and Virgo++. Sumcheck Protocol [27] is a multi-round IP that allows the prover to convince the verifier of a claimed correct evaluation of the sum of a polynomial $f : \mathbb{F}^\ell \to \mathbb{F}$ on the boolean hypercube: $\sum_{b_1, b_2, \ldots, b_\ell \in \{0,1\}} f(b_1, b_2, \ldots, b_\ell) = a$, where the variable degree of f is at most

d. Obviously, computing the sum directly requires exponential time in ℓ due to 2^ℓ combinations of $b_1, \ldots, b_\ell$. The sumcheck protocol provides a more efficient way for the verifier to check the correctness of the evaluation. The protocol proceeds for ℓ rounds. In the i-th ($1 \leq i \leq \ell$) round, the prover sends a d-degree polynomial $f_i(X)$ claiming equal to $\sum_{b_{i+1}, \ldots, b_\ell \in \{0,1\}} f(r_1, \ldots, r_{i-1}, X, b_{i+1}, \ldots, b_\ell)$. The verifier checks if $f(0) + f(1) = f(r_{i-1})$ and sends a random challenge $r_i \in \mathbb{F}$ for the next round. In the last round, the verifier evaluates $f(r_1, \ldots, r_\ell)$ with an oracle query to f and will accept the statement iff $f_\ell(r_\ell) = f(r_1, \ldots, r_\ell)$. The soundness error of the sumcheck protocol is at most $\frac{d\ell}{|\mathbb{F}|}$.

Using sumcheck as the major building block, GKR [17] provides an efficient IP for the verification of the evaluation of layered circuits. Virgo++ is a variant of GKR. As in Virgo++, $S_{i,j}$ denotes the size of the set of gates at layer j connected to layer i, and $s_{i,j} = \lceil \log S_{i,j} \rceil$. The function $V_{i,j} : \{0,1\}^{s_{i,j}} \to \mathbb{F}$ maps the labels of gates in the above set to their output value. With these symbol definitions, the function V_i in layer i can be expressed in terms of $V_{i,i+1}, \ldots, V_{i,d}$ of all layers above the layer i. For a fixed $g_i \in \mathbb{F}^{s_i}$, w.l.o.g., assuming that $s_{i,i+1}$ is the largest, the expression of the function V_i can be formalized with MLEs as following summation on 2-degree polynomial in Eq. (1), a sumcheck protocol will be applied on it to prove the evaluation claim.

$$
\begin{aligned}
\tilde{V}_i(g_i) = &\sum_{x,y \in \{0,1\}^{s_{i,i+1}}} \widetilde{add}_{i+1,i+1}(g,x,y)(\tilde{V}_{i,i+1}(x) + \tilde{V}_{i,i+1}(y_1, \ldots, y_{s_{i,i+1}})) \\
&+ y_{s_{i,i+2}+1} \cdots y_{s_{i,i+1}} \cdot \widetilde{add}_{i+1,i+2}(g,x,y_1, \ldots, y_{s_{i,i+2}})(\tilde{V}_{i,i+1}(x) + \tilde{V}_{i,i+2}(y_1, \ldots, y_{s_{i,i+2}})) \\
&+ \ldots + y_{s_{i,d}+1} \cdots y_{s_{i,i+1}} \cdot \widetilde{add}_{i+1,d}(g,x,y_1, \ldots, y_{s_{i,d}})(\tilde{V}_{i,i+1}(x) + \tilde{V}_{i,d}(y_1, \ldots, y_{s_{i,d}})) \quad (1) \\
&+ y_{s_{i,i+1}+1} \cdots y_{s_{i,i+1}} \cdot \widetilde{mult}_{i+1,i+1}(g,x,y)(\tilde{V}_{i,i+1}(x)\tilde{V}_{i,i+1}(y_1, \ldots, y_{s_{i,i+1}})) \\
&+ y_{s_{i,i+2}+1} \cdots y_{s_{i,i+1}} \cdot \widetilde{mult}_{i+1,i+2}(g,x,y_1, \ldots, y_{s_{i,i+2}})\tilde{V}_{i,i+1}(x)\tilde{V}_{i,i+2}(y_1, \ldots, y_{s_{i,i+2}}) \\
&+ \ldots + y_{s_{i,d}+1} \cdots y_{s_{i,i+1}} \cdot \widetilde{mult}_{i+1,d}(g,x,y_1, \ldots, y_{s_{i,d}})\tilde{V}_{i,i+1}(x)\tilde{V}_{i,d}(y_1, \ldots, y_{s_{i,d}})
\end{aligned}
$$

In Virgo++, the sumcheck protocol on Eq. (1) consists of two $s_{i,i+1}$-round phases that sum on x and y respectively. At the end of sumcheck, the prover sends claims about all layers above the layer i: $\tilde{V}_{i,i+1}(v^{(i,i+1)}), \ldots, \tilde{V}_{i,d}(v^{(i,d)})$ and $\tilde{V}_{i,i+1}(u^{(i,i+1)})$, where $v^{(i,i+1)}, \ldots, v^{(i,d)}, u^{(i,i+1)}$ are randomness determined round by round during the sumcheck. At this point, the verifier receives $i + 2$ claims about the layer $i + 1$. To reduce the multiple claims to a single claim, the verifier will choose random coefficients $\{\alpha_{k,i+1}\}_{k \in [0,i]}, \alpha'_{i,i+1}$ to combine them linearly as the left side of the Eq. (2), which can be simplified to a sum of the hypercube $\{0,1\}^{s_{i+1}}$ on the right side. Then another sumcheck will be applied to the Eq. (2). Since $q_{i+1}(x)$ can be computed locally by the verifier, the resulting claim about the next layer will be $\tilde{V}_{i+1}(g_{i+1})$ for some fixed random g_{i+1}.

$$
\sum_{k=0}^{i} \alpha_{k,i+1} \tilde{V}_{k,i+1}(v^{(k,i+1)}) + \alpha'_{i,i+1}\tilde{V}_{i,i+1}(u^{(i,i+1)}) = \sum_{x \in \{0,1\}^{s_{i+1}}} \tilde{V}_{i+1}(x)q_{i+1}(x) \quad (2)
$$

The protocol will be run iteratively until the claims are reduced to layer d, and the verifier who knows the input can directly check it.

3   Our Construction

Technique Overview. In the MPCitH-based ZK protocol Π_{mpc}, each multiplication gate requires the calculation of $O(M \cdot N)$ multiplications in $\mathbb{F}$ [4], where M and N denote the number of instances and parties in MPCitH, respectively. This leads to significant computation and communication costs for both the prover and the verifier when $|\mathcal{C}|$ is large. To mitigate proof size and reduce verification costs, an intuitive method is to apply VC to the verification circuit of Π_{mpc}, where the proof generated by Π_{mpc} serves as the witness of VC. We denote such method as MPCitH-then-VC. However, the verification circuit of Π_{mpc}, denoted as $\mathcal{C}^{\mathsf{vrfy}}_{mpc}$, is at least $M \cdot N$ times larger than $|\mathcal{C}|$. Thus, MPCitH-then-VC incurs significant computation and communication costs for the prover, negating the benefits of using VC. As a result, we consider the alternative solution VC-then-MPCitH.

Our idea is to apply VC to the original circuit $\mathcal{C}$ and obtain the corresponding verification circuit, denoted as $\mathcal{V}_{IP}$ of VC. Then the prover runs an MPCitH protocol on $\mathcal{V}_{IP}$, which is much the smaller than both $\mathcal{C}^{\mathsf{vrfy}}_{mpc}$ and $\mathcal{C}$. Note that executing VC requires the verifier to have the knowledge of the witness for each round of VC. Therefore, the prover needs to commit to the relevant knowledge of each round to guarantee the zero-knowledge. Thus, we require a modified VC wherein the prover's message in each round is the corresponding commitment. Nevertheless, this necessitates additional consistency proofs for these commitments in a zero-knowledge manner, which may result in an inefficient solution as in MPCitH-then-VC. Fortunately, we can leverage the properties of the concrete MPCitH and VC protocols to mitigate these additional costs. Specifically, we consider BN++ and Virgo++ as the concrete instantiations of MPCitH and VC, respectively. We observe that the "offset" of the prover's messages in Virgo++, which is obtained from the secret sharing of BN++, can serve as a commitment, which will be sent to the verifier during each round of Virgo++. The "offset" does not disclose any secret information and is bound to a unique "witness" provided the relevant randomness commits correctly. As a result, we insert the modified Virgo++ between the offline phase (commit to witness and secret sharing) and the online phase (MPC for $\mathcal{V}_{IP}$) of BN++. Therefore, we can execute the MPCitH protocol on the verification circuit of Virgo++, where the primary operations are linear and multiplication gates are sparse.

3.1   VC-then-MPCitH

In this section, we introduce our VC-then-MPCitH protocol Π which uses BN++ and Virgo++ as major building blocks. The main idea is that the prover and the verifier run a modified VC protocol for $\mathcal{C}(\mathbf{w}) = \mathbf{y}$, where the prover's messages (proofs) are sent as a commitment. Then the prover proves that the committed proofs in VC satisfy the verification circuit of VC for $\mathcal{C}(\mathbf{w}) = \mathbf{y}$ using MPCitH ZK protocol. VC and MPCitH ZK are instantiated with Virgo++ and BN++, respectively. Formal descriptions of Π are shown in Fig. 1, 2, 3 and 4, where Commit denotes a commitment scheme. The function Sample samples values from random tapes in order. ExpandTape denotes a function that expands the random tapes. $\mathsf{H}_0, \mathsf{H}_1$ and H_2 denote hash functions, which can be modeled as random oracles.

Protocol Π

Public Parameters: The number of parallel repetitions M, the number of parties N, and the security parameter κ.

Input: The prover $\mathcal{P}$ and verifier $\mathcal{V}$ hold the description of circuit $\mathcal{C}$ defined on $\mathbb{F}$, the outputs $\mathbf{y} \in \mathbb{F}^{S_0}$, and the description of verification circuit $\mathcal{V}_{IP}$. $\mathcal{P}$ holds the witness $\mathbf{w} \in \mathbb{F}^{S_d}$ such that $\mathcal{C}(\mathbf{w}) = \mathbf{y}$.

Phase 1 (Offline): MPCitH.Commit to witness and seeds

1. $\mathcal{P}$ samples $salt \xleftarrow{\$} \{0,1\}^{2\kappa}$.
2. **for** $e \in [M]$ **do**
3. $\mathcal{P}$ samples a master seed: $\mathsf{seed}_e \leftarrow \{0,1\}^\kappa$.
4. $\mathcal{P}$ uses seed_e as a binary tree root to derive the leaves $\mathsf{seed}_e^{(1)}, ..., \mathsf{seed}_e^{(N)}$.
5.   **for** $p \in [N]$ **do**
6. $\mathcal{P}$ expands random tape: $\mathsf{tape}_e^{(p)} \leftarrow \mathsf{ExpandTape}(salt, p, e, \mathsf{seed}_e^{(p)})$.
7. $\mathcal{P}$ samples randomness $r_e^{(p)} \leftarrow \mathsf{Sample}(\mathsf{tape}_e^{(p)})$.
8. $\mathcal{P}$ commits to seed: $\mathsf{com}_e^{(p)} \leftarrow \mathsf{Commit}(salt, e, p, \mathsf{seed}_e^{(p)}; r_e^{(p)})$.
9. $\mathcal{P}$ samples witness share: $\mathbf{w}_e^{(p)} \leftarrow \mathsf{Sample}(\mathsf{tape}_e^{(p)})$.
10.   **for** $i = 0, ..., d-1$ **do**
11.   **for** $k \in [2s_{i,i+1}]$ **do**
12. $\mathcal{P}$ samples polynomial share: $(\boldsymbol{\pi}_{i,k})_e^{(p)} \leftarrow \mathsf{Sample}(\mathsf{tape}_e^{(p)})$.
13. $\mathcal{P}$ samples claim share: $(\boldsymbol{\pi}_{i,claim})_e^{(p)} \leftarrow \mathsf{Sample}(\mathsf{tape}_e^{(p)})$.
14.   **for** $k \in [s_{i+1}]$ **do**
15. $\mathcal{P}$ samples polynomial share: $(\boldsymbol{\pi}_{i+1,k}^*)_e^{(p)} \leftarrow \mathsf{Sample}(\mathsf{tape}_e^{(p)})$
16. $\mathcal{P}$ samples claim share: $(\boldsymbol{\pi}_{i+1,0})_e^{(p)} \leftarrow \mathsf{Sample}(\mathsf{tape}_e^{(p)})$.
17. $\mathcal{P}$ computes witness offset $\Delta\mathbf{w}_e \leftarrow \mathbf{w} - \sum_{p \in [N]} \mathbf{w}_e^{(p)}$.
18. $\mathcal{P}$ adjusts the first share: $\mathbf{w}_e^{(1)} \leftarrow \mathbf{w}_e^{(1)} + \Delta\mathbf{w}_e$.
19. $\mathcal{P}$ computes $h^{(0)} \leftarrow \mathsf{H}_0\left(\{\mathsf{com}_e^{(p)}\}_{p \in [N], e \in [M]}\right)$ and sends $h^{(0)}, \{\Delta\mathbf{w}_e\}_{e \in [M]}$ to $\mathcal{V}$.

Fig. 1. Phase 1: MPCitH.Commit to witness and seeds.

In **Phase 1**, $\mathcal{P}$ follows BN++ to commit to witness and seeds, which are used to generate the randomness of secret sharing and commitments. We denote the VC proofs for $\mathcal{C}(\mathbf{w}) = \mathbf{y}$ using Virgo++ as $\boldsymbol{\pi}$, which is considered as the parts of the witness in BN++. So the prover needs to sample random shares for both $\mathbf{w}$ (step 9) and $\boldsymbol{\pi}$ (steps 10–16). According to Virgo++ [32], $\boldsymbol{\pi}$ consists of 4 parts: (a) 2-degree polynomials $\{\boldsymbol{\pi}_{i,k}\}_{i \in [0,d-1], k \in [2s_{i,i+1}]}$ created in each round of the sumcheck on Eq. (1) in each layer, (b) $\{\boldsymbol{\pi}_{i,claim}\}_{i \in [0,d-1]}$ containing claims $\tilde{V}_{i,i+1}(v^{(i,i+1)}), ..., \tilde{V}_{i,d}(v^{(i,d)})$ and $\tilde{V}_{i,i+1}(u^{(i,i+1)})$, (c) 2-degree polynomials $\{\boldsymbol{\pi}_{i,k}^*\}_{i \in [0,d-1], k \in [s_{i+1}]}$ that generated in each round of the sumcheck on Eq. (2) between every two layers, and (d) $\{\boldsymbol{\pi}_{i+1,0}\}_{i \in [0,d-1]}$ containing all claims $\tilde{V}_{i+1}(g_{i+1})$ about "the next layer". Each party's random shares for the above 4 parts are computed in steps 10–16. We denote by $(c_{i,k,2}, c_{i,k,1}, c_{i,k,0})$ and $(c^*_{i,k,2}, c^*_{i,k,1}, c^*_{i,k,0})$ the coefficients of 2-degree polynomials $\pi_{i,k}, \pi^*_{i,k}$, respectively.

Phase 2 (Online): Modified VC for $\mathcal{C}(\mathbf{w}) = \mathbf{y}$

1. $\mathcal{V}$ sends random challenge $g_0 \in \mathbb{F}^{s_0}$ to $\mathcal{P}$.
2. $\mathcal{V}$ computes $a_0 = \tilde{V}_{\mathbf{y}}(g)$ and $\mathcal{P}$ computes $a_0 = \tilde{V}_0(g)$.
3. **for** $i = 0, ..., d - 1$ **do**
4.   **for** $k \in [2s_{i,i+1}]$ **do**
5. $\mathcal{P}$ runs the sumcheck protocol on Equation (1) to creat $\pi_{i,k} = (c_{i,k,2}, c_{i,k,1}, c_{i,k,0})$.
6.   **for** $e \in [M]$ **do**
7. $\mathcal{P}$ computes offsets: $(\Delta\pi_{i,k})_e = \pi_{i,k} - \sum_{p\in[N]} (\pi_{i,k})_e^{(p)}$.
8. $\mathcal{P}$ adjusts the first share:$(\pi_{i,k})_e^{(1)} \leftarrow (\pi_{i,k})_e^{(1)} + (\Delta\pi_{i,k})_e$.
9. $\mathcal{P}$ sends $\{(\Delta\pi_{i,k})_e\}_{e\in[M]}$ to $\mathcal{V}$.
10. $\mathcal{V}$ sends random challenge $r_{i,k}$ to $\mathcal{P}$.
11. $\mathcal{P}$ computes $\pi_{i,claim} = \{\tilde{V}_{i,i+1}(u^{(i,i+1)}), \tilde{V}_{i,i+1}(v^{(i,i+1)}), ..., \tilde{V}_{i,d}(v^{(i,d)})\}$.
12.   **for** $e \in [M]$ **do**
13. $\mathcal{P}$ computes offsets: $(\Delta\pi_{i,claim})_e = \pi_{i,claim} - \sum_{p\in[N]} (\pi_{i,claim})_e^{(p)}$.
14. $\mathcal{P}$ adjusts the first share: $(\pi_{i,claim})_e^{(1)} \leftarrow (\pi_{i,claim})_e^{(1)} + (\Delta\pi_{i,claim})_e$.
15. $\mathcal{P}$ sends $\{(\Delta\pi_{i,claim})_e\}_{e\in[M]}$ to $\mathcal{V}$.
16. $\mathcal{V}$ sends the random coefficients $\alpha_{0,i+1}, ..., \alpha_{i,i+1}, ..., \alpha'_{i,i+1}$ to $\mathcal{P}$.
17.   **for** $k \in [s_{i+1}]$**do**
18. $\mathcal{P}$ runs the sumcheck on Equation (2) to create $\pi^*_{i+1,k} = (c^*_{i,k,2}, c^*_{i,k,1}, c^*_{i,k,0})$
19.   **for** $e \in [M]$ **do**
20. $\mathcal{P}$ computes offsets: $(\Delta\pi^*_{i+1,k})_e = \pi^*_{i+1,k} - \sum_{p\in[N]} (\pi^*_{i+1,k})_e^{(p)}$.
21. $\mathcal{P}$ adjusts the first share: $(\pi^*_{i+1,k})_e^{(1)} \leftarrow (\pi^*_{i+1,k})_e^{(1)} + (\Delta\pi^*_{i+1,k})_e$.
22. $\mathcal{P}$ sends $\{(\Delta\pi^*_{i+1,k})_e\}_{e\in[M]}$ to $\mathcal{V}$.
23. $\mathcal{V}$ sends random challenge $r^*_{i+1,k}$ to $\mathcal{P}$.
24. $\mathcal{P}$ sets $g_{i+1} = (r^*_{i+1,1}, ..., r^*_{i+1,s_{i+1}})$ and updates $a_{i+1} = \pi_{i+1,0} = \tilde{V}_{i+1}(g_{i+1})$.
25.   **for** $e \in [M]$ **do**
26. $\mathcal{P}$ computes offsets:$(\Delta\pi_{i+1,0})_e = \pi_{i+1,0} - \sum_{p\in[N]} (\pi_{i+1,0})_e^{(p)}$.
27. $\mathcal{P}$ adjusts the first share:$(\pi_{i+1,0})_e^{(1)} \leftarrow (\pi_{i+1,0})_e^{(1)} + (\Delta\pi_{i+1,0})_e$.
28. $\mathcal{P}$ sends $\{(\Delta\pi_{i+1,0})_e\}_{e\in[M]}$ to $\mathcal{V}$.

Fig. 2. Phase 2: Modified VC for $\mathcal{C}(\mathbf{w}) = \mathbf{y}$

In **Phase 2**, $\mathcal{P}$ and $\mathcal{V}$ run a modified VC protocol for $\mathcal{C}(\mathbf{w}) = \mathbf{y}$. Our modified VC protocol is similar to Virgo++, with the exception that, instead of sending the proofs π directly, the prover sends the commitments to π. (Hence $\mathcal{V}$ cannot check the validity of the messages from $\mathcal{P}$ in this phase.) Here, the "offsets" (steps

7, 13, 20, 26) can be used as the commitments to simplify subsequent consistency proofs, which will be explained later. More precisely, whenever a proof message of π is generated, $\mathcal{P}$ computes its offset and sends it to $\mathcal{V}$. Upon receiving an offset, $\mathcal{V}$ sends a random challenge. As in Virgo++, the random challenges of all rounds are merged into random vectors at the end of each sumcheck. For example, at the end of layer i, x and y in Eq. (1) will be replaced by $(r_{i,1}, \ldots, r_{i,s_{i,i+1}})$ and $(r_{i,s_{i,i+1}+1}, \ldots, r_{i,2s_{i,i+1}})$ respectively after removing the summation symbol. For simplicity, let $u^{(i,i+1)} = (r_{i,1}, \ldots, r_{i,s_{i,i+1}})$ and $v^{(i,j)} = (r_{i,s_{i,i+1}+1}, \ldots, r_{i,s_{i,i+1}+j})$ for $j \in [i+1, d]$.

Phase 3: MPCitH.Simulate MPC for $\mathcal{V}_{IP}$

1. **for** $e \in [M]$ **do**
2.   **for** gate $g_\ell \in \mathcal{V}_{IP}$ **do** //with input $x_{e,\ell}, y_{e,\ell}$
3.   **if** g_ℓ is an addition gate **then**
4.   Party p locally computes the output share: $z_{e,\ell}^{(p)} = x_{e,\ell}^{(p)} + y_{e,\ell}^{(p)}$.
5.   **if** g_ℓ is a multiplication gate **then**
6.   **for** $p \in [N]$ **do**
7. $\mathcal{P}$ samples the share: $z_{e,\ell}^{(p)}, a_{e,\ell}^{(p)} \leftarrow \mathsf{Sample}(\mathsf{tape}_e^{(p)})$.
8. $\mathcal{P}$ computes the offset $\Delta z_{e,\ell} = x_{e,\ell} \cdot y_{e,\ell} - \sum_{p=1}^{N} z_{e,\ell}^{(p)}$.
9. $\mathcal{P}$ adjusts the first share: $z_{e,\ell}^{(1)} \leftarrow z_{e,\ell}^{(1)} + \Delta z_{e,\ell}$.
10. $\mathcal{P}$ computes $a_{e,\ell} = \sum_{i=1}^{N} a_{e,\ell}^{(p)}$ and sets $b_{e,\ell} = y_{e,\ell}$.
11.   **for** $p \in [N]$ **do**
12. $\mathcal{P}$ samples the random inner-prod share: $c_e^{(p)} \leftarrow \mathsf{Sample}(\mathsf{tape}_e^{(p)})$.
13. $\mathcal{P}$ computes $\Delta c_e = \left(\sum_{\ell=1}^{V_m} a_{e,\ell} \cdot b_{e,\ell} \right) - \sum_{p \in [N]} c_e^{(p)}$.
14. $\mathcal{P}$ adjusts the first share: $c_e^{(1)} \leftarrow c_e^{(1)} + \Delta c_e$
15. $\mathcal{P}$ computes $h^{(1)} \leftarrow \mathsf{H}_1\left(salt, \{o_e^{(p)}\}_{p \in [N], e \in [M]}, \{\Delta c_e, (\Delta z_{e,\ell})_{\ell \in [V_m]}\}_{e \in [M]}\right)$
    where $o_e^{(p)}$ is the circuit output share. $\mathcal{P}$ sends $h^{(1)}$ to $\mathcal{V}$.
16. $\mathcal{V}$ sends random coefficients $(\epsilon_{e,\ell})_{e \in [M], \ell \in [V_m]}$ to $\mathcal{P}$.

Phase 4: MPCitH.Check multiplicative triple

1. **for** $e \in [M]$ **do**
2.   **for** $p \in [N]$ **do**
3. $\mathcal{P}$ runs the *Dot-Product Protocol* with multiplicative triple $(x_{e,\ell}^{(p)}, y_{e,\ell}^{(p)}, z_{e,\ell}^{(p)})$, dot-product triple $(a_{e,\ell}^{(p)}, b_{e,\ell}^{(p)}, c_e^{(p)})$, and $\alpha_{e,\ell}^{(p)}$ to compute $v_e^{(p)}$.
4. $\mathcal{P}$ computes $h^{(2)} \leftarrow \mathsf{H}_2\left(salt, \{(\alpha_{e,\ell}^{(p)})_{\ell \in [V_m]}, v_e^{(p)}\}_{p \in [N], e \in [M]}\right)$ and sends $h^{(2)}$ to $\mathcal{V}$.
5. $\mathcal{V}$ sends random challenges $(\bar{p}_e \in [N])_{e \in [M]}$ to $\mathcal{P}$.

Phase 5: MPCitH.Open views

1. **for** $e \in [M]$ **do**
2. $\mathcal{P}$ sets $\{\mathsf{seeds}_e\}$ to be the adjacent nodes of $\mathsf{seeds}^{(\bar{p}_e)}$ in the path of the binary tree, used for deriving the leaf nodes $(\mathsf{seeds}^{(p)_e})_{p \in [N] \setminus \bar{p}_e}$
3. $\mathcal{P}$ sends $salt, \left(\{\mathsf{seeds}_e\}, \mathsf{com}_e^{(\bar{p}_e)}, (\alpha_{e,\ell}^{(\bar{p}_e)})_{\ell \in [V_m]} \right)_{e \in [M]}$ to $\mathcal{V}$.

Fig. 3. MPCitH for $\mathcal{V}_{IP}$

Phase 3, Phase 4 and Phase 5 follow the corresponding procedures of BN++ to show that $\mathcal{P}$ knows the witness $\hat{\mathbf{w}} = (\mathbf{w}, \boldsymbol{\pi})$ of the verification circuit $\mathcal{V}_{IP}$, which is described in Fig. 5. Specifically, $\mathcal{P}$ and $\mathcal{V}$ in Phase 3 simulate the MPC protocol of BN++ for the verification circuit $\mathcal{V}_{IP}$ for relation $R' : \{\langle x' = (\mathcal{V}_{IP}, \mathbf{y}); \hat{\mathbf{w}} \rangle : \mathcal{V}_{IP}(\hat{\mathbf{w}}, \mathbf{y}) = 0\}$. In Phase 4, $\mathcal{P}$ and $\mathcal{V}$ run Dot-Product Checking of BN++ to verify all multiplication gates in $\mathcal{V}_{IP}$, the number of multiplication gates is V_m. $\mathcal{P}$ opens the challenged views of $N - 1$ parties in Phase 5.

Output: $\mathcal{V}$ outputs acc iff the following checks pass.

Check 1:

1. for $e \in [M]$ do
2. $\mathcal{V}$ derives $\{\mathsf{seed}_e^{(p)}\}_{p \in [N] \backslash \bar{p}_e}$ from the $\log N$ nodes in $\{\mathsf{seeds}_e\}$.
3.   for $p \in [N] \backslash \bar{p}_e$ do
4. $\mathcal{V}$expands random tape: $\mathsf{tape}_e^{(p)} \leftarrow \mathsf{ExpandTape}(salt, p, e, \mathsf{seed}_e^{(p)})$.
5. $\mathcal{V}$ samples randomness $r_e^{(p)} \leftarrow \mathsf{Sample}(\mathsf{tape}_e^{(p)})$.
6. $\mathcal{V}$ recomputes $\mathsf{com}_e^{(p)} \leftarrow \mathsf{Commit}(salt, e, p, \mathsf{seed}_e^{(p)}; r_e^{(p)})$.
7. $\mathcal{V}$ computes $h^{(0)\prime} \leftarrow \mathsf{H}_0(\{\mathsf{com}_e^{(p)}\}_{p \in [N], e \in [M]})$, checks that $h^{(0)\prime} \overset{?}{=} h^{(0)}$.

Check 2:

1. for $e \in [M]$ do
2. $\mathcal{V}$ sets $\Delta \hat{\mathbf{w}}_e \leftarrow (\Delta \mathbf{w}_e, \Delta \boldsymbol{\pi}_e)$ where $\Delta \boldsymbol{\pi}_e$ are messages received from $\mathcal{P}$.
3.   for $p \in [N] \backslash \bar{p}_e$ do
4. $\mathcal{V}$ samples the merged witness share: $\hat{\mathbf{w}}_{(e)}^{(p)}$.
5.   if $p = 1$ then $\mathcal{V}$ adjusts the share: $\hat{\mathbf{w}}_e^{(1)} \leftarrow \hat{\mathbf{w}}_e^{(1)} + \Delta \hat{\mathbf{w}}_e$.
6.   for gate $g_\ell \in \mathcal{V}_{IP}$ do //with input $x_{e,\ell}, y_{e,\ell}$
7.   if g_ℓ is an addition gate then
8. $\mathcal{V}$ computes the output share: $z_{e,\ell}^{(p)} = x_{e,\ell}^{(p)} + y_{e,\ell}^{(p)}$.
9.   if g_ℓ is a multiplication gate then:
10. $\mathcal{V}$ samples the share: $z_{e,\ell}^{(p)} \leftarrow \mathsf{Sample}(\mathsf{tape}_e^{(p)})$.
11.   if $p = 1$ then $\mathcal{V}$ adjusts $z_{e,\ell}^{(1)} \leftarrow z_{e,\ell}^{(1)} + \Delta z_{e,\ell}$.
12. $\mathcal{V}$ samples the share: $a_{e,\ell}^{(t)} \leftarrow \mathsf{Sample}(\mathsf{tape}_e^{(p)})$.
13. $\mathcal{V}$ sets $b_{e,\ell}^{(p)} = y_{e,\ell}^{(p)}$.
14. $\mathcal{V}$ samples the random inner-prod share: $c_e^{(p)}$.
15.   if $p = 1$ then $\mathcal{V}$ adjusts $c_e^{(1)} \leftarrow c_e^{(1)} + \Delta c_e$.
16. $\mathcal{V}$ computes $\mathbf{o}_e^{(\bar{p}_e)} = \mathbf{0} - \sum_{i \neq i_e} \mathbf{o}_e^{(p)}$ where $\mathbf{o}$ is the circuit outputs.
17. $\mathcal{V}$ computes $h^{(1)\prime} = \mathsf{H}_1(salt, \{\mathbf{o}_e^{(p)}\}_{t \in [T], e \in [M]})$, checks that $h^{(1)\prime} \overset{?}{=} h^{(1)}$.

Check 3:

1. for $e \in [M]$ do
2.   for $p \in [N] \backslash \bar{p}_e$ do
3. $\mathcal{V}$ runs the Dot-Product Protocol as $\mathcal{P}$ to compute $v_e^{(p)}$.
4. $\mathcal{V}$ computes $h^{(2)\prime} = \mathsf{H}_2(salt, \{(\alpha_{e,\ell}^{(p)})_{\ell \in [V_m]}, v_e^{(p)}\}_{p \in [N], e \in [M]})$, checks that $h^{(2)\prime} \overset{?}{=} h^{(2)}$.

Fig. 4. MPCitH.Verification for $\mathcal{V}_{IP}$

Finally, $\mathcal{V}$ will accept the proof iff all the checks described in Fig. 4 can hold. Unlike BN++, the "offsets" Δw and $\Delta \pi$ are sent to the verifier in **Phase 1** and **Phase 2** instead of **Phase 5**. The verifier needs to merge received offsets in $\Delta \hat{w}$ and run verification. And the verifier must first check h_0 to ensure the commitments are generated correctly. Since the verifier can only get $N-1$ witness shares, the "offset" does not reveal any secrets. Assuming that the seed is committed correctly, the offset can be uniquely bound to a fixed witness due to the binding of the commitment. Hence the offset together with the commitment of the seed can serve as the commitment to the witness.

Description of Circuit $\mathcal{V}_{IP}$

Input: $\hat{w} = (w, \pi)$ and y.

1. Set $a_0 \leftarrow \tilde{V}_y(g_0)$ //$\mathcal{P}$ sets $\tilde{V}_0(g_0)$ directly.
2. **for** $i = 0, \ldots, d-1$ **do**
3.   Set the claim of sumcheck on equation (1): $e \leftarrow a_i$.
4.   **for** $k \in [2s_{i,i+1}]$ **do**
5. $e' \leftarrow \pi_{i,k}(0) + \pi_{i,k}(1) = 2c_{i,k,0} + c_{i,k,1} + c_{i,k,2}$
6. $o_{i,k} \leftarrow e - e'$.
7.   Update $e \leftarrow \pi_{i,k}(r_{i,k}) = c_{i,k,0} + c_{i,k,1} \cdot r_k + c_{i,k,2} \cdot r_{i,k}^2$.
8.   Compute the claims as equation (3) to obtain e'.
9. $o_{i,claim} \leftarrow e - e'$.
10.   Set the sumcheck claim of the equation (2):
11.   Update $e \leftarrow \sum_{k=0}^{i} \alpha_{k,i+1} \tilde{V}_{k,i+1}(v^{(k,i+1)}) + \alpha'_{i,i+1} \tilde{V}_{i,i+1}(u^{(i,i+1)'})$.
12.   **for** $k \in [s_{i+1}]$ **do**
13. $e' \leftarrow \pi^*_{i+1,k}(0) + \pi^*_{i+1,k}(1) = 2c^*_{i+1,k,0} + c^*_{i+1,k,1} + c^*_{i+1,k,2}$.
14. $o^*_{i+1,k} \leftarrow e - e'$.
15.   Update $e \leftarrow \pi_{i+1,k}(r^*_{i,k}) = c^*_{i+1,k,0} + c^*_{i+1,k,1} \cdot r^*_{i,k} + c^*_{i+1,k,2} \cdot r^{*}_{i,k}{}^2$.
16.   Set $g_{i+1} = (r^*_{i+1,1}, \ldots, r^*_{i+1,s_{i+1}})$.
17.   Update $e' \leftarrow \tilde{V}_{i+1}(g_{i+1}) \cdot q_{i+1}(g_{i+1})$.
18. $o_{i+1,0} \leftarrow e - e'$.
19.   Set $a_{i+1} \leftarrow \tilde{V}_{i+1}(g_{i+1})$.
20. $e' \leftarrow \tilde{V}_w(g_d)$, $o_{d,claim} \leftarrow a_d - e'$.

Output: $o = ((\{o_{i,k}\}_{k \in [0,2s_{i,i+1}]}, o_{i,claim}, \{o^*_{i+1,k}\}_{k \in [s_{i+1}]}, o_{i+1,0})_{i \in [0,d-1]}, o_{d,claim})$.

Fig. 5. Description of $\mathcal{V}_{IP}$

The description of $\mathcal{V}_{IP}$ is shown in Fig. 5. $\mathcal{V}_{IP}$ takes as input $\hat{w} = (w, \pi)$ and y s.t. $\mathcal{C}(w) = y$. $\mathcal{V}_{IP}$ is similar to the verification procedure of Virgo++, where the verifier runs the sumcheck for each layer and utilizes the claims from the prover to verify the correctness of linear combinations. In $\mathcal{V}_{IP}$, all terms $\tilde{add}_{i,j}, \tilde{mult}_{i,j}, q_{i+1}(g_{i+1})$ and $\tilde{V}_y(g_0)$ are constants used for linear operations, which can be computed by $\mathcal{P}, \mathcal{V}$ locally. Notice that the evaluation of these constant terms does not require to be proven by the MPCitH protocol. $\mathcal{V}$ can pre-compute these constants since the random challenges can be generated offline. All $a\tilde{d}d_{i,j}, m\tilde{u}lt_{i,j}$ only depend on the circuit wiring instead of the inputs. $q_{i+1}(g_{i+1})$ identifies the correspondence of gate indexes in the subset of some layer with the actual ones. $\tilde{V}_\mathbf{y}$ is the MLE of $\mathbf{y}$ and it should be equal to $\tilde{V}_0$ if the circuit is evaluated correctly. So these constants can be obtained simply from the instance $(\mathcal{C}, \mathbf{y})$ and the randomness. More details of these constants can be found in [30,32]. If π is a valid VC proof for $\mathcal{C}(\mathbf{w}) = \mathbf{y}$, the output $\mathbf{o}$ of $\mathcal{V}_{IP}$ must be a zero-vector $\mathbf{0}$.

Proof Size. We emphasize that the number of multiplication gates which dominates the proof size of Π is only related to the number of layers of $\mathcal{V}_{IP}$ instead of $\mathcal{C}$. The reason is that the multiplication gates to which BN++ is applied only appear in step 8 of $\mathcal{V}_{IP}$. Let $r_{[j..]}$ represent the product $r_{s_{i+1}+s_{i,j}+1} \cdots r_{2s_{i,i+1}}$. We give the expression of the claim at step 8 in Eq. (3). Note that the multiplication gate here means that two inputs are both variables (excluding the multiply-constant operation which is a linear operation). Since there are $d-i$ multiplication gates in the layer i: $\tilde{V}_{i,i+1}(u^{(i,i+1)}) \cdot \tilde{V}_{i,i+2}(v^{(i,j)})$ for $j \in [i+1, \ldots, d]$, we have the number of multiplication gates $V_m = d + (d-1) + \ldots + 1 = \frac{d(d+1)}{2}$.

$$
\begin{aligned}
e' &= a\tilde{d}d_{i+1,i+1}(g_i, u^{(i,i+1)}, v^{(i,i+1)})(\tilde{V}_{i,i+1}(u^{(i,i+1)}) + \tilde{V}_{i,i+1}(v^{(i,i+1)})) \\
&+ r_{[i+2..]} \cdot a\tilde{d}d_{i+1,i+2}(g_i, u^{(i,i+1)}, v^{(i,i+2)})(\tilde{V}_{i,i+1}(u^{(i,i+1)}) + \tilde{V}_{i,i+2}(v^{(i,i+2)})) \\
&+ \ldots + r_{[d..]} \cdot a\tilde{d}d_{i+1,d}(g_i, u^{(i,i+1)}, v^{(i,d)})(\tilde{V}_{i,i+1}(u^{(i,i+1)}) + \tilde{V}_{i,d}(v^{(i,d)})) \\
&+ m\tilde{u}lt_{i+1,i+1}(g_i, u^{(i,i+1)}, v^{(i,i+1)})\tilde{V}_{i,i+1}(u^{(i,i+1)})\tilde{V}_{i,i+1}(v^{(i,i+1)}) \\
&+ r_{[i+2..]} \cdot m\tilde{u}lt_{i+1,i+2}(g_i, u^{(i,i+1)}, v^{(i,i+2)})\tilde{V}_{i,i+1}(u^{(i,i+1)})\tilde{V}_{i,i+2}(v^{(i,i+2)}) \\
&+ \ldots + r_{[d..]} \cdot m\tilde{u}lt_{i+1,d}(g_i, u^{(i,i+1)}, v^{(i,d)})\tilde{V}_{i,i+1}(u^{(i,i+1)})\tilde{V}_{i,d}(v^{(i,d)})
\end{aligned}
\tag{3}
$$

All the messages sent by $\mathcal{P}$ during the protocol constitute the proof:

$$
\left\{ h^{(0)}, h^{(1)}, h^{(2)}, salt, (\{\mathsf{seeds}_e\}, \mathsf{com}_e^{(\bar{p}_e)}, \Delta\mathbf{w}_e, \Delta\pi_e, \Delta c_e, \{\Delta z_{e,\ell}, \alpha_{e,\ell}^{(\bar{p}_e)}\}_{\ell \in [V_m]})_{e \in [M]} \right\}.
$$

where $\Delta\pi = \{(\Delta\pi_{i,k})_{k \in [2s_{i,i+1}]}, (\Delta\pi_{i,claim}), (\Delta\pi_{i+1,k}^*)_{k \in [s_{i+1}]}, (\Delta\pi_{i+1,0})\}_{i \in [0,d-1]}$ stands for the messages sent by $\mathcal{P}$ in **Phase 2**. The proof size of Π is

$$
|\mathsf{proof}| = 8\kappa + M\left(\kappa \cdot \log N + 2\kappa + (2V_m + 1) \cdot \log |\mathbb{F}| + |\Delta\mathbf{w}| + |\Delta\pi|\right).
$$

Compared to BN++ [22], the proof size of which is $|\mathsf{proof}'| = 6\kappa + M(\kappa \cdot \log N + 2\kappa + |\Delta\mathbf{w}| + (2|\mathcal{C}| + 1) \cdot \log |\mathbb{F}|)$, our protocol may reduce the proof size of BN++ by $M(2C_m - 2V_m - |\Delta\pi|) \cdot \log |\mathbb{F}|$ for larger circuits with dense multiplication gates. Furthermore, the advantage of our proof size becomes more obvious for wider and shallower circuits since $V_m < O(d^2)$ which is always bounded by $O(|\mathcal{C}|)$, and $|\Delta\pi|$ is bounded by $O(d\log |\mathcal{C}| + d^2)$. More comparisons on concrete efficiencies are shown in Sect. 5. Besides, our protocol preserves the flexibility of BN++, allowing for a trade-off between proof size and proof time by adjusting the parameters M and N.

Non-interactive Protocol. Our protocol Π is a multi-round interactive protocol which is "public coin". Following the "so-far digest" model [6] and the

Fiat-Shamir paradigm, our interactive protocol can be transformed into a non-interactive version. Notice that, when the protocol in **Phase 2** is transformed to be non-interactive, $\mathcal{V}$ cannot directly check the challenges of the random oracle by the final verification algorithm. The evaluation of challenges will be encoded into the circuit $\mathcal{V}_{IP}$. To improve the performance in practice, the random oracle can be instantiated with hash functions with low multiplication gate density, such as MiMC [2].

4   Security Analysis

Theorem 1. *Assume that* Commit *is a random oracle-based commitment scheme and* H_0, H_1, H_2 *are collision-resistant Hash functions that are modeled as random oracles. The protocol Π is an HVZKoK with knowledge error $\xi \leq \xi_a + \xi_b$ where ξ_a is the knowledge error of* BN++ *and ξ_b is the soundness error of* Virgo++. *More precisely,*

$$\xi \leq \left(\frac{N + |\mathbb{F}| - 1}{N \cdot |\mathbb{F}|} \right)^M + \frac{\sum_{i=0}^{d}(4\lceil \log S_{i,i+1} \rceil + 2\lceil \log S_{i+1} \rceil) + \sum_{i=1}^{d}(i+2)}{|\mathbb{F}|}.$$

Due to space limitation, the proof sketch of Theorem 1 is shown in Appendix A and detailed proofs are available in the full paper.

5   Implementation

Our interactive ZK protocol Π is implemented in C++. We run experiments on a Virtual Machine with an Intel i7-8700 CPU with 3.20 GHz, 4 cores, and 10 GB of RAM. We choose the field $\mathbb{F}_{2^{128}}$ for Π, which could provide comparable security with BN++ on $\mathbb{F}_{2^{128}}$ and Virgo++ with the Virgo commitment working on its optimal choice $\mathbb{F}_{p^2}$ and $p = 2^{61} - 1$. Notice that, to run LDT, Virgo requires that the field either be an extension of $\mathbb{F}_2$ or contain a multiplicative subgroup of order 2^k where k should be large enough. Our protocol which is compatible with any finite field has no such restrictions on the field.

We compare the performance of our protocol with BN++ and Virgo++. For fair comparisons, we modify BN++ based on the open source code [23] so that the modified BN++ is interactive and can prove general circuits parsed from DAGs. In our experiments, $\mathcal{P}$ proves the knowledge of the preimage of SHA-256. The general circuit of SHA-256 follows the code of Virgo++, which has 40006 multiplication gates and 99,949 gates in total.

As shown in Table 1, our protocol only takes 86 ms to generate a proof when $N = 4, M = 64$, which is 13.2× faster than BN++ with the same parameters, and the proof size is close to 10× shorter than BN++. Furthermore, it is 1.2× ∼ 4× faster than Virgo++ with the Virgo commitment. As mentioned in [26], their implementation of Virgo++ does not fully realize zero-knowledge. Virgo++ only commits to the circuit inputs, without considering the commitments to the secret messages generated during the interaction. In addition, realizing ZK for

Virgo++ also requires replacing the MLE with a low-degree extension. So the actual running time and proof size of ZK Virgo++ will be slightly larger than the data in Table 1.

Table 1. Performance Comparison.

	M	N	Field	Prover time	Verifier time	Proof size
Virgo++(ZK)	–	–	$\mathbb{F}_{(2^{61}-1)^2}$	$\gtrsim$324 ms	$\gtrsim$6 ms	$\gtrsim$100.4 KB
BN++	64	4	$\mathbb{F}_{2^{128}}$	1140 ms	1090 ms	87273.1 KB
	43	8		1422 ms	1370 ms	58647.8 KB
	32	16		2002 ms	1950 ms	43652.6 KB
	25	32		3060 ms	3010 ms	34109.9 KB
	20	64		3 min	4 min	27292.9 KB
This work	64	4	$\mathbb{F}_{2^{128}}$	86 ms	70 ms	8891.1 KB
	43	8		102 ms	88 ms	5974.4 KB
	32	16		137 ms	124 ms	4446.6 KB
	25	32		202 ms	185 ms	3474.3 KB
	20	64		307 ms	288 ms	2779.8 KB

Memory Bound and Circuit Size. The machine that executes MPCitH-based ZK will quickly exceed its memory bounds as $M \cdot N$ increases. In the setting of $M = 20, N = 64$ and 8 GB memory, the process of original BN++ will be killed due to out-of-memory. Even allocating more memory, say 10 GB or 12 GB, still takes a few minutes to run BN++.

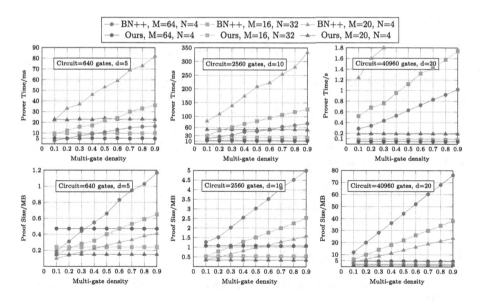

Fig. 6. Comparison at different multiplication gate densities

Moreover, we compare our protocol with BN++ at different multiplication gate densities by randomly generating layered circuits with the width of powers of 2. The comparison for random circuits of various sizes and multiplication gate densities is shown in Fig. 6 (the verifier time in two protocols are both close to the prover time). Obviously, the performance of our protocol is independent of the multiplication gate density, while the prover time and proof size of BN++ increase linearly with the multiplication gate density.

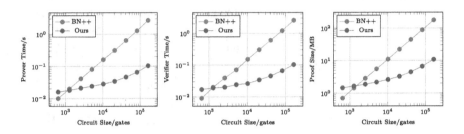

Fig. 7. Comparison at different circuit sizes

We also consider the performance for different circuit sizes at a fixed multiplication gate density of 0.5. We set depth $d = 20$ and width from 2^5 to 2^{13} in the instance of $M = 64, N = 4$. So the size of circuits scales from 640 to 1.6×10^5 gates. As shown in Fig. 7, the advantages of our protocol are obvious when the circuit is larger and multiplication gates are denser. On devices that offer limited memory of 10 GB, our protocol allows the circuit with up to 10 million gates, while BN++ is only applicable to circuits with up to 330,000 gates.

6   Conclusion

We propose the "VC-then-MPCitH" technique to improve the proving efficiency of existing post-quantum ZK protocols. By applying our technique to specific MPCitH protocol BN++ and Virgo++, the resulting ZK protocol reduces the concrete prover and verifier time significantly while expanding the range of supported circuit sizes with restricted memory consumption. Furthermore, our protocol supports circuits over any finite fields without special restrictions, providing high performance in proving circuits over a wide range and making it compatible with large-scale computations.

Acknowledgements. This work was supported by the National Key R&D Program of China (Grant No. 2022YFB2701700, 2018YFA0704702) and Shandong Provincial Natural Science Foundation (Grant No. ZR2020MF053).

A   Proof of Theorem 1

Completeness. The completeness of Π follows from the completeness of Virgo++ and BN++.

HVZK. The HVZK property of Π is ensured by the underlying MPCitH-based ZK protocol, which is HVZK for the statement $\mathcal{V}_{IP}(\hat{\mathbf{w}}, \mathbf{y}) = \mathbf{0}$. So the construction of simulator $\mathcal{S}$ for Π follows the main idea of the ZK simulator for BN++. In the simulation, the offsets of $\mathbf{w}, \boldsymbol{\pi}, c, z, \alpha$ in the protocol are randomly chosen instead of computing from the secret shares. Due to the randomness of shares and the hiding property of Commit, the transcript output by $\mathcal{S}$ is indistinguishable from the real script in distribution.

Knowledge Soundness. Under the premise that $\mathsf{Commit}, \mathsf{H}_0, \mathsf{H}_1$ and H_2 are modeled as random oracles, the following lemmas hold.

Lemma 1. Π *is an argument of knowledge for the relation:* $R' = \{\langle x' = (\mathcal{V}_{IP}, \mathbf{y}); \hat{\mathbf{w}} \rangle : \mathcal{V}_{IP}(\hat{\mathbf{w}}, \mathbf{y}) = \mathbf{0}\}$ *with knowledge error*

$$\xi_a = \left(\frac{N + |\mathbb{F}| - 1}{N \cdot |\mathbb{F}|} \right)^M.$$

Proof Sketch. The knowledge soundness of the relation R' is inherited from BN++. In one of the M independent executions, a malicious $\mathcal{P}^*$ can cheat $\mathcal{V}$ by first adjusting the output shares of multiplication gates, and then adjusting one of the parties' views if the challenges received from $\mathcal{V}$ cannot result in acc. According to Lemma 2 of [22], the probability that $\mathcal{P}^*$ successfully cheats is at most $\frac{1}{|\mathbb{F}|}$ in the first stage, and at most $\frac{1}{N}$ in the second stage due to the opening of $N - 1$ views. Thus the total success probability of P^* is at most $(\frac{1}{|\mathbb{F}|} + (1 - \frac{1}{|\mathbb{F}|}) \cdot \frac{1}{N})^M = \xi_a$. The extractability of knowledge can be proven by listing all possible challenges in **Phase 3** and **Phase 4** and their responses in a $N \times |\mathbb{F}|^{V_m}$ matrix for each execution. The extractor $\mathcal{E}$ can extract the valid witness by tracking entries in the expected time $O(\frac{1}{\delta(x) - \xi_a})$ where $\delta(x)$ is the probability that $\mathcal{P}^*$ passes verification check. More details about the process of knowledge extraction can be found in [4].

Lemma 2. *If Lemma 1 holds and the event causing the knowledge error never happened, then* $\mathbf{w}$ *in the extracted* $\hat{\mathbf{w}} = (\mathbf{w}, \boldsymbol{\pi})$ *will satisfy* $\mathcal{C}(\mathbf{w}) = \mathbf{y}$ *except the probability*

$$\xi_b = \frac{\sum_{i=0}^{d}(4\lceil \log S_{i,i+1} \rceil + 2\lceil \log S_{i+1} \rceil) + \sum_{i=1}^{d}(i+2)}{|\mathbb{F}|}.$$

When $|\mathbb{F}|$ *is large enough,* $\xi_b < \mathsf{negl}(\kappa)$.

Proof Sketch. The proof of Lemma 2 follows the main idea of the soundness analysis of Virgo++. The soundness error ξ_b consists of 3 parts: the soundness error of the sumcheck protocol applied respectively in each layer of the circuit and the linear combination between the adjacent layers, as well as the soundness error of the linear combination itself.

According to Lemma 1, Π is knowledge-soundness for the relation $R' = \{\langle x' = (\mathcal{V}_{IP}, \mathbf{y}); \hat{\mathbf{w}} \rangle : \mathcal{V}_{IP}(\hat{\mathbf{w}}, \mathbf{y}) = \mathbf{0}\}$ with knowledge error ξ_a. Then we can invoke the extractor $\mathcal{E}$ in Lemma 1 to extract the witness $\hat{\mathbf{w}}$ such that $\mathcal{V}_{IP}(\hat{\mathbf{w}}, \mathbf{y}) = \mathbf{0}$ in $O(\frac{1}{1-\xi_a})$ steps, and the intercepted $\mathbf{w}$ from $\hat{\mathbf{w}}$ satisfies $\mathcal{C}(\mathbf{w}) = \mathbf{y}$ with the probability at least $1 - \xi_b$ by Lemma 2. Considering the knowledge error for the whole protocol, it is sufficient to ensure the consistency of the extracted witness in the relation R with R'. Suppose $\mathcal{P}^*$ holds $\mathbf{w}_1, \mathbf{w}_2$ trying to convince the verifier of $\mathcal{C}(\mathbf{w}) = \mathbf{y}$ and $\mathcal{V}_{IP}((\hat{\mathbf{w}}), \mathbf{y}) = \mathbf{0}$. Conditioned on the verifier of Π outputs acc, if $\mathbf{w}$ does not consist with $\hat{\mathbf{w}}$, the cases in which $\mathcal{P}^*$ passes the verification are always reduced to the case that leads to the knowledge error ξ_a or ξ_b. Therefore, Π is knowledge-soundness for the relation $R = \{\langle x = (\mathcal{C}, \mathbf{y}); \ \mathbf{w} \rangle : \mathcal{C}(\mathbf{w}) = \mathbf{y}\}$ with knowledge error at most $\xi \leq \xi_a + \xi_b$.

References

1. Ahmad, H., et al.: Primitives towards verifiable computation: a survey. Front. Comput. Sci. **12**, 451–478 (2018)
2. Albrecht, M., Grassi, L., Rechberger, C., Roy, A., Tiessen, T.: MiMC: efficient encryption and cryptographic hashing with minimal multiplicative complexity. In: Cheon, J.H., Takagi, T. (eds.) ASIACRYPT 2016. LNCS, vol. 10031, pp. 191–219. Springer, Heidelberg (2016). https://doi.org/10.1007/978-3-662-53887-6_7
3. Ames, S., Hazay, C., Ishai, Y., Venkitasubramaniam, M.: Ligero: lightweight sublinear arguments without a trusted setup. In: Proceedings of the 2017 ACM SIGSAC Conference on Computer and Communications Security (CCS), pp. 2087–2104 (2017)
4. Baum, C., Nof, A.: Concretely-efficient zero-knowledge arguments for arithmetic circuits and their application to lattice-based cryptography. In: Kiayias, A., Kohlweiss, M., Wallden, P., Zikas, V. (eds.) PKC 2020. LNCS, vol. 12110, pp. 495–526. Springer, Cham (2020). https://doi.org/10.1007/978-3-030-45374-9_17
5. Baum, C., de Saint Guilhem, C.D., Kales, D., Orsini, E., Scholl, P., Zaverucha, G.: Banquet: short and fast signatures from AES. In: Garay, J.A. (ed.) PKC 2021. LNCS, vol. 12710, pp. 266–297. Springer, Cham (2021). https://doi.org/10.1007/978-3-030-75245-3_11
6. Belling, A., Soleimanian, A., Bégassat, O.: Recursion over public-coin interactive proof systems; faster hash verification. Cryptology ePrint Archive (2022). https://eprint.iacr.org/2022/1072
7. Ben-Sasson, E., Chiesa, A., Riabzev, M., Spooner, N., Virza, M., Ward, N.P.: Aurora: transparent succinct arguments for R1CS. In: Ishai, Y., Rijmen, V. (eds.) EUROCRYPT 2019. LNCS, vol. 11476, pp. 103–128. Springer, Cham (2019). https://doi.org/10.1007/978-3-030-17653-2_4
8. Bhadauria, R., Fang, Z., Hazay, C., Venkitasubramaniam, M., Xie, T., Zhang, Y.: Ligero++: a new optimized sublinear IOP. In: Proceedings of the 2020 ACM SIGSAC Conference on Computer and Communications Security (CCS), pp. 2025–2038 (2020)
9. Bowe, S., Grigg, J., Hopwood, D.: Recursive proof composition without a trusted setup. Cryptology ePrint Archive (2019). https://eprint.iacr.org/2019/1021
10. Chase, M., et al.: The picnic signature scheme, design document v2.2 (2020)
11. Chase, M., et al.: Post-quantum zero-knowledge and signatures from symmetric-key primitives. In: Proceedings of the 2017 ACM SIGSAC Conference on Computer and Communications Security (CCS), pp. 1825–1842 (2017)

12. Chiesa, A., Hu, Y., Maller, M., Mishra, P., Vesely, N., Ward, N.: Marlin: preprocessing zkSNARKs with universal and updatable SRS. In: Canteaut, A., Ishai, Y. (eds.) EUROCRYPT 2020. LNCS, vol. 12105, pp. 738–768. Springer, Cham (2020). https://doi.org/10.1007/978-3-030-45721-1_26

13. Dobraunig, C., Kales, D., Rechberger, C., Schofnegger, M., Zaverucha, G.: Shorter signatures based on tailor-made minimalist symmetric-key crypto. In: Proceedings of the 2022 ACM SIGSAC Conference on Computer and Communications Security (CCS), pp. 843–857 (2022)

14. Gabizon, A., Williamson, Z.J., Ciobotaru, O.: Plonk: permutations over lagrange-bases for oecumenical noninteractive arguments of knowledge. Cryptology ePrint Archive (2019). https://eprint.iacr.org/2019/953

15. Giacomelli, I., Madsen, J., Orlandi, C.: ZKBoo: faster zero-knowledge for boolean circuits. In: 25th USENIX Security Symposium (USENIX Security), pp. 1069–1083 (2016)

16. Goldwasser, S., Micali, S., Rackoff, C.: The knowledge complexity of interactive proof-systems. In: Proceedings of the Seventeenth Annual ACM Symposium on Theory of Computing (STOC), pp. 291–304 (1985)

17. Goldwasser, S., Kalai, Y.T., Rothblum, G.N.: Delegating computation: interactive proofs for muggles. J. ACM (JACM) **62**(4), 1–64 (2015)

18. Groth, J.: On the size of pairing-based non-interactive arguments. In: Fischlin, M., Coron, J.-S. (eds.) EUROCRYPT 2016. LNCS, vol. 9666, pp. 305–326. Springer, Heidelberg (2016). https://doi.org/10.1007/978-3-662-49896-5_11

19. Gvili, Y., Ha, J., Scheffler, S., Varia, M., Yang, Z., Zhang, X.: TurboIKOS: improved non-interactive zero knowledge and post-quantum signatures. In: Sako, K., Tippenhauer, N.O. (eds.) ACNS 2021. LNCS, vol. 12727, pp. 365–395. Springer, Cham (2021). https://doi.org/10.1007/978-3-030-78375-4_15

20. Ishai, Y., Kushilevitz, E., Ostrovsky, R., Sahai, A.: Zero-knowledge from secure multiparty computation. In: Proceedings of the Thirty-Ninth Annual ACM Symposium on Theory of Computing (STOC), pp. 21–30 (2007)

21. Kales, D., Zaverucha, G.: Improving the performance of the picnic signature scheme. IACR Transactions on Cryptographic Hardware and Embedded Systems, pp. 154–188 (2020)

22. Kales, D., Zaverucha, G.: Efficient lifting for shorter zero-knowledge proofs and post-quantum signatures. Cryptology ePrint Archive (2022). https://eprint.iacr.org/2022/588

23. Kales, D., et al.: BN++ implementation. https://github.com/IAIK/bnpp_helium_signatures

24. Katz, J., Kolesnikov, V., Wang, X.: Improved non-interactive zero knowledge with applications to post-quantum signatures. In: Proceedings of the 2018 ACM SIGSAC Conference on Computer and Communications Security (CCS), pp. 525–537 (2018)

25. Kothapalli, A., Setty, S., Tzialla, I.: Nova: recursive zero-knowledge arguments from folding schemes. In: Dodis, Y., Shrimpton, T. (eds.) CRYPTO 2022. LNCS, vol. 13510, pp. 359–388. Springer, Cham (2022). https://doi.org/10.1007/978-3-031-15985-5_13

26. Liu, T., et al.: Virgo++ implementation. https://github.com/TAMUCrypto/virgo-plus

27. Lund, C., Fortnow, L., Karloff, H., Nisan, N.: Algebraic methods for interactive proof systems. J. ACM (JACM) **39**(4), 859–868 (1992)

28. Delpech de Saint Guilhem, C., Orsini, E., Tanguy, T.: Limbo: efficient zero-knowledge MPCitH-based arguments. In: Proceedings of the 2021 ACM SIGSAC Conference on Computer and Communications Security (CCS), pp. 3022–3036 (2021)

29. de Saint Guilhem, C.D., De Meyer, L., Orsini, E., Smart, N.P.: BBQ: using AES in picnic signatures. In: Paterson, K.G., Stebila, D. (eds.) SAC 2019. LNCS, vol. 11959, pp. 669–692. Springer, Cham (2020). https://doi.org/10.1007/978-3-030-38471-5_27

30. Wahby, R.S., et al.: Full accounting for verifiable outsourcing. In: Proceedings of the 2017 ACM SIGSAC Conference on Computer and Communications Security (CCS), pp. 2071–2086 (2017)

31. Wahby, R.S., Tzialla, I., Shelat, A., Thaler, J., Walfish, M.: Doubly-efficient zksnarks without trusted setup. In: 2018 IEEE Symposium on Security and Privacy (SP), pp. 926–943. IEEE (2018)

32. Zhang, J., et al.: Doubly efficient interactive proofs for general arithmetic circuits with linear prover time. In: Proceedings of the 2021 ACM SIGSAC Conference on Computer and Communications Security (CCS), pp. 159–177 (2021)

33. Zhang, J., Xie, T., Zhang, Y., Song, D.: Transparent polynomial delegation and its applications to zero knowledge proof. In: 2020 IEEE Symposium on Security and Privacy (SP), pp. 859–876. IEEE (2020)

Quantum Key Distribution as a Service and Its Injection into TLS

Sergejs Kozlovičs(✉) , Krišjānis Petručeņa , Dāvis Lāriņš ,
and Juris Vīksna

Institute of Mathematics and Computer Science, University of Latvia, Riga, Latvia
{sergejs.kozlovics,krisjanis.petrucena,davis.larins,
juris.viksna}@lumii.lv

Abstract. Quantum key distribution (QKD) is a key agreement method
that relies on the laws of physics and ensures that the keys have not
been eavesdropped on or modified by a third party. While commercial
QKD devices are available, they are expensive, require specific infrastructure, and have high operational expenses. In this paper, we propose an architecture and a set of protocols that allow us to implement
QKD as a service (QaaS). End users communicate with QaaS via classical TLS channels secured with post-quantum cryptography (PQC). We
show how to further strengthen the security of these classical links to
make them sustainable to active attacks (classical and quantum) on any
single segment of QaaS. We also show how to integrate QaaS into the
state-of-the-art TLS 1.3 protocol. As a result, QKD becomes available
for a larger community of end-users. Furthermore, we show how QaaS
can reduce the number of digital signatures within a TLS 1.3 handshake,
which is essential since post-quantum signatures are much longer than
the conventional RSA/ECC-based ones.

Keywords: quantum key distribution · post-quantum cryptography ·
transport layer security · PQC · QKD · TLS · QaaS

1 Introduction

Quantum key distribution (QKD) is the first step on our way to a universal
Quantum Internet. QKD is a state-of-the-art technology that allows two distant
parties to agree on encryption keys. The key distribution process involves a
quantum channel (usually implemented via optical fiber transmitting photons),
but the agreed keys are intended to be used in classical internet communication.

The properties of quantum mechanics (in particular, the no-cloning theorem)
along with quantum key distribution protocols such as BB84 (and its successors
B92, SARG04, Lo05) and COW[1] ensure that if some key has been eavesdropped
on or altered, the parties can notice that and discard the key [2,6].

Since it is difficult to emit single photons and to deal with attenuation over
long distances, certain attacks (such as photon number splitting, PNS, and other

---

[1] Coherent One-Way protocol, patented by IDQ.

W. Meng et al. (Eds.): ISPEC 2023, LNCS 14341, pp. 527–545, 2023.
https://doi.org/10.1007/978-981-99-7032-2_31

side-channel attacks against physical QKD implementations) are theoretically possible [17]. However, these attacks are either hard to exploit on short distances or can be impeded by modified versions of algorithms such as BB84 Decoy State [16]. Thus, for practical purposes, we can assume a short- to midterm security of modern QKD technology with the hope for near-to-perfect security of future QKD devices.

Sadly, the state-of-the-art commercial QKD devices are expensive, require specific infrastructure (high-quality optical fiber links), and have high operational expenses (such as energy costs for cooling down the devices) [13]. In order to make QKD available to a wider community of users, we deliver QKD as a service (QaaS). With QaaS, end users are able to securely obtain a shared secret from two remote key distribution centers (KDCs), where each KDC is directly connected to the corresponding endpoint of the QKD link. KDCs may be located in two cities with an established quantum channel between them. With QaaS, the inhabitants of both cities have the ability to obtain quantumly distributed keys without the need for a direct connection to QKD equipment. QaaS is a technology for connecting end users to existing QKD networks that are now being deployed all over the world [19,22].

The end users connect to KDCs via classical TLS channels, which, from the QKD point of view, are the weakest links in the key distribution process. In order to strengthen the security of classical links used in QaaS, we use post-quantum cryptography (PQC). However, PQC algorithms still have to withstand the test of time,—new attacks are constantly emerging, and the NIST standardization process is not yet finished [1,3,5,7,8]. Thus, we strengthen the security even further by proposing the architecture and a set of protocols that make QaaS sustainable to active attacks (classical and quantum) on any single communication segment. In particular, the full key is not sent via any single classical channel. Thus, a successful man-in-the middle attack would require compromising two independent TLS communication links.

The QaaS architecture and a set of underlying protocols are described in Sects. 2 and 3. In Sect. 4, we offer QaaS-specific authentication options for all involved parties. This is a noticeable contribution, since pure QKD does not offer any authentication mechanism. In Sect. 5, we give insight into some implementation detail and show how to integrate the proposed QaaS into the state-of-the-art TLS 1.3 protocol. We also show how QaaS can be used to reduce the number of digital signatures within a TLS 1.3 handshake, which is essential since post-quantum signatures are much longer than the conventional RSA/ECC-based ones. We conclude by discussing the related work and further research directions (Sects. 6 and 7).

2   The Overall QaaS Architecture

Figure 1 depicts the overall architecture of the proposed QaaS.

At the bottom of Fig. 1, two QKD devices (called Alice and Bob) are connected by multiple links implementing the quantum channel and the service

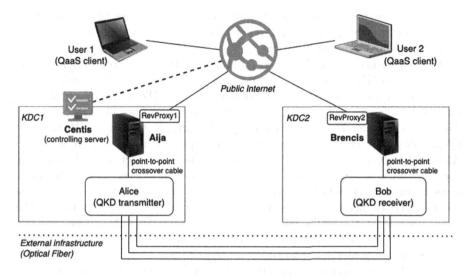

Fig. 1. The architecture of the proposed QaaS.

channel (both channels are needed in most QKD protocols). Depending on the protocol and hardware choice, there can be 2–3 optical links or a mix of a direct optical link and a classical (routed) internet connection [11].

There are multiple QKD devices available in the market.[2] While we conduct our experiments with IDQ Clavis[3] devices, our architecture can be applied to other devices as soon as they meet the following assumptions:

- Alice and Bob are pre-paired at the factory (e.g., with several one-time symmetric keys) and are able to establish a secure service channel as well as the quantum channel (the process of synchronizing the quantum channel usually takes several minutes).
- Once the secure channels are established, both Alice and Bob are able to generate two potentially infinite[3] identical streams of symmetric keys. Some of the shared keys can be used by Alice and Bob for technical purposes, e.g., to replace the pre-paired factory keys for subsequent re-initializations.
- Each key is of the same bit length (256 bit for IDQ Clavis[3]) and has an associated unique truly random key ID, which is near to impossible to guess (IDQ Clavis (See footnote 3) uses 128-bit key IDs; keys and IDs are generated using the built-in QRNG[4] chip).

---

[2] e.g., Toshiba Multiplexed and Long Distance, IDQ Clavis and Cerberis series, QTI Quell-X, LuxQuanta NOVA LQ, KEEQUANT Andariel, SeQre Aurora and Eclipse.

[3] unless the link is physically broken, a hardware failure occurs, or there is constant eavesdropping or intrusion.

[4] quantum random number generator.

From the architectural point of view, Alice and Bob are black boxes that simultaneously produce synchronized key-identifier pairs (K_{id}, id) that are secure against man-in-the-middle attacks.

We place Alice and Bob at two physically distant key distribution centers (KDCs). Each KDC also has a physical server that is directly attached (e.g., by a short crossover cable) to the corresponding QKD device. We call these servers Aija and Brencis (in order to distinguish them from the QKD devices, Alice and Bob); we also call them **KDC endpoints**. Both Aija and Brencis run QaaS server software that takes the stream of quantumly exchanged keys from Alice and Bob, respectively, and implements the QaaS protocols (discussed in Sect. 3), which securely forward the keys to end users, User 1 and User 2. In order to simplify the QaaS server software and strengthen the security of Aija and Brencis, we introduce two reverse proxies, RevProxy1 and RevProxy2. The reverse proxies authenticate end users and ensure encrypted TLS connections with them via the public internet. For such TLS connections, we utilize quantum-safe key exchange methods and signature algorithms.

All backend connections within the boundaries of a KDC (e.g., RevProxy1 ↔ Aija ↔ Alice) are not encrypted; however, we assume that the corresponding physical links are isolated from the external world, and no wiretapping is possible within a KDC.

For technical reasons, we need also a controlling server (called Centis in Fig. 1) that synchronizes key reservations at Aija and Brencis. Centis can be an internal server (located at the premises of one of the KDCs) or an external (cloud) server. Centis needs specific user credentials to pass through RevProxy1 and RevProxy2.

3   QaaS Protocols

The purpose of QaaS is to ensure that end users (User 1 and User 2 in Fig. 1) obtain a shared key that has been quantumly exchanged between Alice and Bob. The main issue is that, in QaaS, we are able to use only classical (i.e., non-quantum) channels between end users and KDCs.

In this section, we introduce two protocols: the Butterfly Protocol and the Control Protocol. The former allows QaaS to tolerate active attacks on any single classical link (even if TLS is decrypted). The latter is used by the controlling server Centis in order to manage key reservations at Aija and Brencis.

3.1   The Butterfly Protocol

Figure 2 depicts message flows between the users and KDCs used in the Butterfly Protocol (hence, the name).

The protocol allows User 1 and User 2 to agree on a shared key and ensures that the full key is not transmitted via any of the classical links. During the protocol, one KDC endpoint (Aija) sends only the first half of the key, and the other (Brencis) sends the second half.

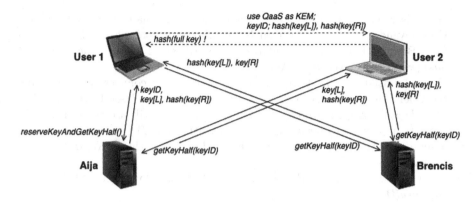

Fig. 2. Message flows in the Butterfly protocol.

There are two types of connections: **the butterfly connections** (straight lines in Fig. 2) and **the user connection** (dashed lines between User 1 and User 2).

All butterfly connections are implemented as bidirectional TLS sockets secured with PQC key exchange mechanisms (KEMs) and digital signature algorithms (for authentication). The butterfly connections require both server and client authentication (see Sect. 4).

The user connection is also implemented as a bidirectional socket. However, instead of a PQC KEM, we use the message flow of the Butterfly Protocol. Since no key material but hashes are sent via the user connection, KEM-like (Diffie-Hellman-like) encryption is unnecessary (although possible). Like in the traditional client-server architecture, client authentication is optional for the user connection. Server authentication can be performed either by a PQC signature algorithm or our novel approach described in Sect. 4.2.

The protocol starts when User 1 wants to communicate with User 2 via a TLS socket.

$1\rightarrow$ Before initiating a TLS handshake with User 2, User 1 chooses one of the two KDCs (say, Aija) and sends the *reserveKeyAndGetKeyHalf* message to it. An alternative (symmetric) scenario, when User 1 chooses Brencis, is also possible. Thus, Aija and Brencis can participate equally in key reservations. We call it the **equivalence property** of KDCs.[5]

$1\leftarrow$ Aija chooses one of the quantumly shared keys *key* and replies with *keyID*, the first (left) half of the key *key[L]*, and the hash of the second (right) half of the key *hash(key[R])*.

$2\rightarrow$ User 1 asks Brencis for the second half of the key by sending the *getKey-Half(keyID)* message.

---

[5] One of the benefits of the equivalence property is that there is no advantage in attacking either of KDCs. Another benefit is the ability to design algorithms and protocols that can purposely choose the first receiver of the *reserveKeyAndGetKey-Half* message.

2← Brencis replies with $hash(key[L])$ and the second half of the key $key[R]$. User 1 validates $key[L]$ (received from Aija) against $hash(key[L])$ received from Brencis. User 1 also validates $key[R]$ (received from Brencis) against $hash(key[R])$ received from Aija.

3→ User 1 initializes the TLS handshake of the user connection by sending the Client Hello message to User 2. In the handshake, User 1 sends $keyID$, $hash(key[L])$, and $hash(key[R])$ to User 2. (User 2 will use these hashes as proof that User 1 has been authenticated within KDC1).

4→ User 2 asks Aija for the first half of the key by sending the *getKeyHalf(keyID)* message.

5→ User 2 asks Brencis for the second half of the key by sending the *getKey-Half(keyID)* message.

4← Aija replies with $key[L]$ and $hash(key[R])$.

5← Brencis replies with $hash(key[L])$ and $key[R]$. User 2 validates $key[L]$ against the two copies of $hash(key[L])$ (received from User 1 and from Brencis) and $key[R]$ against the two copies of $hash(key[R])$ (received from User 1 and from Brencis).

3← User 2 computes $hash(full\ key)$ and sends it in the Server Hello message to User 1. User 1 validates its $full\ key$ against this hash. Since $hash(full\ key)$ cannot be efficiently computed by User 2 without communicating to Aija and Brencis, it serves as proof for User 1 that User 2 has been authenticated within both KDC1 and KDC2.

Step 3 can be launched in parallel with step 2; steps 4 and 5 can be launched in parallel as well.

The strength of the protocol relies on the underlying hash function (e.g., SHA-256 or SHAKE-128, used in our experiments) and PQC algorithms used for the butterfly connections. Besides, the protocol is able to sustain an active attack on any single link. By an active attack we mean the ability to decrypt or wiretap the TLS session key.

- The quantum link is assumed to be secure against wiretapping by the law of Physics.
- If Eve can decrypt *one* of the butterfly links (say User 1 to Aija), she can get the key ID and the first half of the key. However, Eve would be unable to connect also to Brencis (without breaking another butterfly link) since a new connection to Brencis needs client authentication, and Eve lacks the private keys owed by Users 1 and 2.
- If Eve attacks the user link (between User 1 and 2), she cannot wiretap the session key since only key ID and hashes are transmitted there. If Eve alters the key ID that is being sent to User 2, Aija and Brencis won't reply to User 2 for a non-reserved key ID. In an unlikely case when the modified key ID has also been reserved (e.g., by other QaaS users), the hashes won't match.

3.2   User Connection Management

The user connection is a TLS 1.3 connection with the distinction that we inject the Butterfly Protocol as a new key share "group"[6] in the TLS Key Share extension (see more detail on page 14 in Sect. 5). If all butterfly connections finish successfully, and all Butterfly Protocol checks (e.g., hash validations) are passed, both User 1 and 2 get the keys. On any failure (TCP, TLS, or Butterfly Protocol error) within any of the butterfly connections between User1/User2 and Aija/Brencis, the TLS between User 1 and User 2 closes with an exception. That may happen due to security checks (e.g., Aija or Brencis could not authenticate the user, TLS error) or when Aija or Brencis is temporarily down (TCP error). Besides, Aija or Brencis can reply with an error when they have been (re-)launched but are not serving the keys yet (more on that in Sect. 3.4).

3.3   Key Reservation in the Butterfly Protocol

Since both Aija and Brencis can be used for key reservation (Step 1), they need some distributed algorithm that resolves conflicts between them. Besides, if some key has been reserved at one KDC, both KDCs must be ready to send their key halves to Users 1 and 2 and to delete the used key afterward (even if the protocol has started but not finished, e.g., due to a network interruption).

Our idea is to divide the keys into two classes depending on their parity ($keyID$ bit sum). Aija is allowed to reserve those keys for which parity is even, and Brencis—those with odd parity; thus, no collision is possible. However, in order to ensure the eventual consistency of key sets between Aija and Brencis, we also need the following time constants:

- ε is a small time interval ($\varepsilon < 1$ second) that must pass before a newly quantumly exchanged key can be reserved by end users. The need for ε arises from the fact that new keys do not appear in the QaaS software of Aija and Brencis simultaneously. Waiting for the time ε ensures that both KDC endpoints receive the key (thus, ε can be compared to the cycle time in CPUs);
- the key reservation timeout T ($T \approx 90$ seconds)[7]. If a key has been reserved for User 1, but no $getKeyHalf$ message has been received from User 2 during the time T, the key is deleted. At the other KDC endpoint, T is the maximal waiting time between the two $getKeyHalf$ messages expected from Users 1 and 2;
- TTL (time-to-live ≈ 1 day) is the maximal time the key is available for reservation. TTL limits the size of the key buffer and ensures that "zombie" keys are eventually deleted.[8]

---

[6] TLS 1.3 terminology; actually, it is a key exchange method.

[7] We choose T such that each of the three connections at the longest path (Aija $\leftrightarrow$ User 1 $\leftrightarrow$ User 2 $\leftrightarrow$ Brencis) can survive the maximal TCP back-off; $T \approx 3 \times 30$ s $\approx 3\times$ TCP re-transmission timeout for five tries.

[8] A key is called a "zombie" if it is being stored at one KDC endpoint but is not present at the other, i.e., it has been reserved and deleted or hasn't been received

Each KDC endpoint has three disjoint dictionaries that map $keyID$-s to keys: $PreMy$, My, and $NotMy$. New keys with the corresponding parity p are placed temporarily to $PreMy$ (for time ε) before they are moved to My. All the keys with parity $p - 1$ are moved to $NotMy$ without any delay. Therefore, when Aija reserves a key, the time ε has already passed, and Brencis should contain the same key in its $NotMy$ dictionary (even if the key appeared at Brencis later than at Aija but within the allowed ε time slot).

Keys in the My dictionary are stored for the $TTL - \varepsilon$ time. Keys in the $NotMy$ dictionary are stored for the $TTL + T$ time. Thus, if a key is reserved at one KDC endpoint, it will still be available at the other endpoint while the Butterfly Protocol is running. On the other hand, the reserved keys are eventually deleted even if the protocol is aborted.

3.4   The Control Protocol

After the QKD initialization, Aija and Brencis start to receive identical streams of keys from their corresponding QKD devices (Alice and Bob). However, due to system reboots, hardware failure, or network interruptions, one or both KDC endpoints can stop receiving keys from Alice and/or Bob. While it is possible to re-initialize the QKD channels, the process takes a long time (e.g., up to 30 min in IDQ Clavis[3]), and QKD devices consume more power than during normal operation. The purpose of the Control Protocol (executed by the controlling server Centis in Fig. 1) is to ensure that Aija and Brencis have the same streams of QKD keys after they re-connect to Alice and Bob.

For Aija and Brencis, we define the following three states:

EMPTY—when there are no keys received from the QKD device yet;
RECEIVING—when at least one key has been received and put into the My map;
RUNNING—when keys can be reserved by the users. If at some point in time $My \cup PreMy$ becomes empty[9], the state is automatically changed to EMPTY.

When launched, both KDC endpoints are in the EMPTY state. They can change their state to RECEIVING or EMPTY, depending on the keystream from the QKD device. The RUNNING state can be set only by Centis, when both KDC endpoints are in the RECEIVING state.

Centis can send two types of messages to Aija and Brencis:

– **getState** is a no-argument message that asks for the current state; if the state is RECEIVING or RUNNING, the KDC endpoint also sends two key IDs in the reply: $keyID_0$ and $keyID_1$ corresponding to the first key IDs (the oldest) of each parity;

---

at all (due to server restart or network interruption). "Zombie" keys can also be deleted before TTL expires, e.g., by the Control Protocol.

[9] e.g., due to too many key reservation requests or due to some technical failure, when new keys stop appearing from the QKD device.

– **setState**($state, keyID_0, keyID_1$) instructs the KDC endpoint to change its state and remove the unnecessary keys depending on $keyID_0$ and $keyID_1$.

On a regular basis, Centis sends the *getState* message to both KDC endpoints. If one of them is in the EMPTY state or is not reachable, Centis sends the *setState*(EMPTY) to the other endpoint (thus, clearing the keys, if any). However, if both Aija and Brencis are in the RECEIVING state, Centis gets four key IDs (two from each endpoint): $keyID_{0,Aija}, keyID_{1,Aija}, keyID_{0,Brencis}$, and $keyID_{1,Brencis}$. Then Centis sends

– setState(RUNNING, $keyID_{0,Aija}$, $keyID_{1,Aija}$) to Brencis and
– setState(RUNNING, $keyID_{0,Brencis}$, $keyID_{1,Brencis}$) to Aija.

When receiving $keyID_{parity,opponent}$, the endpoint looks up for this key ID in the corresponding dictionary. We distinguish three cases:

– The key is not found. In this case, no keys are deleted because our endpoint has fewer keys than the opponent. Keys will be deleted at the opponent's side, where our first key will be found.
– The key is found, and the parity is ours (corresponding to the keys we can reserve). In this case, keys with the IDs received prior to the found one can be deleted. The opponent does not have them and will not be able to reply to *getKeyHalf* messages for those key IDs.
– The key is found, and the parity is the opponent's parity. In this case, keys received prior to $currentTime - T$ can be deleted. We keep a few older keys (within the time frame T) since they could have been reserved and deleted at our opponent while the Butterfly protocol is still running (thus, Users 1 and 2 can send us *getKeyHalf* requests for those keys).

In any case, the endpoint changes its state to RUNNING, meaning that it can start serving Butterfly protocol requests from users 1 and 2.

While communicating with Aija and Brencis, Centis uses TLS with PQC. Centis certificate is signed by CA_{Centis}, which differs from the CA that signs certificates for Users 1 and 2; thus, reverse proxies can authorize Centis to execute the Control Protocol if Centis possesses the corresponding private key. Since only four key IDs are sent in the Control Protocol, no single bit of the keys themselves is compromised. Though, an active attacker can use these key IDs to impede the Butterfly Protocol. In order to mitigate such attacks, the keys corresponding to the four key IDs are deleted and not distributed to end users.

4   Authentication

In the Butterfly and Control Protocols, User 1, User 2, and Centis act as clients, which initiate the corresponding connections. Obviously, the clients need to validate the authenticity of both KDC endpoints, which have control over all quantumly shared keys. Since the speed of generating new shared keys is limited, KDC endpoints (the servers) have to identify their clients in order to distribute the keys between them. Client authentication is a must if QaaS is offered as a paid service, where different clients may have different payments (e.g., depending on a subscription plan or the number of keys shared).

In addition, depending on the application, User 1 and User 2 (acting as the client and the server in the user connection) may need to validate each other.

First, we show how both client and server authentication can be established by means of PQC signatures. Since PQC signatures are much longer than traditional RSA/ECC-based ones, we also show how to minimize the number of signatures used in the Butterfly and Control Protocols.

4.1   Authentication via PQC Signatures

At one extreme, there could be a single certification authority (CA) that signs the public keys of all involved parties. At another extreme, there could be a separate CA for each node from Fig. 1 with potential intermediate CA-s. A more realistic model, though, is having two trusted root certification authorities (CA-s), CA_1 and CA_2, which are parts of KDC1 and KDC2, respectively. In this model (which we stick to), KDC1 and KDC2 are located in different places (e.g., cities) and managed by different organizations (e.g., city authorities).

Each QaaS client (User 1 and User 2 in Fig. 1) applies for a client certificate either at CA_1 or at CA_2 (e.g., depending on the client's city of residence).[10]. The chosen CA verifies the client payment and issues a client certificate valid for the time period paid up. Each of RevProxy1 and RevProxy2 from Fig. 1 accepts client certificates signed by both CA_1 and CA_2. Besides, the reverse proxies identify themselves with server certificates signed by CA_1 and CA_2, respectively.

The client key pair (generated), the client certificate (signed after receiving payment), and both server certificates (public) are delivered to the client. We call these data client bundle.

Authentication of the controlling server (Centis) is performed similarly. However, its certificate is signed by a specific CA (CA_{Centis}), which is trusted by both RevProxy1 and RevProxy2. CA_{Centis} is used to sign public keys of controlling servers only.

The servers (the reverse proxies) need only CA_1, CA_2, and CA_{Centis} to be configured as trusted root CA-s. Since client authentication is performed by validating digital signatures, no client database is required. However, in a rare case when QaaS access has to be revoked from some client, the corresponding client is added to the server-side certificate revocation list (CLR), which is delivered to both RevProxy1 and RevProxy2.

Client and server authentication is performed via the normal TLS v1.3 flow, following the traditional signed key exchange approach. However, in our case, both the client and the server negotiate a post-quantum KEM and send certificates signed with a PQC algorithm (see Sect. 5). After the handshake, TLS continues as usual using a symmetric cipher suite (e.g., AES in GCM mode).

---

[10] A client can generate a key pair by himself and send a certificate signing request (CSR) to the CA, or the whole process can be performed by the CA.

While the user connection (between Users 1 and 2 in Fig. 2) can also use PQC certificates to authenticate the client and the server, the following section proposes a more elegant approach.

4.2   Reducing the Number of Post-Quantum Signatures

Eliminating Signatures in Client Certificates. Client certificates used in butterfly connections can be replaced by arbitrary tokens. In this case, TLS starts with server-only authentication, and the client sends its token in the encrypted application data. Sending the token *after* the TLS handshake prevents its eaves-dropping.

In the naïve approach, the issued tokens are stored in a database, shared or replicated between both KDCs. In order to ensure database consistency, a classical connection is needed between KDCs (a pre-shared symmetric key can be used for it; KDCs may also update this key with quantumly exchanged keys on a regular basis).

A more advanced approach is to rely on tokens with hash-based signatures such as HMAC-SHA256-based JSON web tokens, JWTs[11]. Each KDC has a secret key used to sign the header and payload (e.g., the client name + expiration date + salt) of JWT tokens. Signed tokens are distributed to QaaS clients. Both KDCs must have secret keys of each other in order to verify tokens signed by either KDC. While not requiring a database, JWTs need a CRL alternative in order to revoke previously issued tokens.

Since JWT tokens support only non-PQC RSA and ECDA asymmetric signature schemes, we suggest using the symmetric HMAC algorithm (considered quantum-safe), where both KDC endpoints know the symmetric keys of each other.

Reducing the Number of Server Signatures to Be Transmitted. Public keys of both KDCs can be added to the client bundle (from Sect. 4.1). Thus, the server can send only its public key instead of the full certificate chain. However, albeit rarely, the client still has to download and verify the full chain after the server key is renewed.

Eliminating Server Signatures in the User Connection. As we explained in Sect. 3.1, the hash values for the full quantumly exchanged key and its halves can be used by User 1 and User 2 as proofs that the counterparty has been authenticated within one or both KDCs. We use this property to extend the Butterfly Protocol with the support for server authentication. We consider the idea of domain-based authentication, traditionally used in TLS certificates.[12]

When requesting a client certificate (or a JWT token), a QaaS client can specify its domain name. This scenario is useful for QaaS clients that will play

---

[11] https://jwt.io.

[12] Technically, any string, e.g., a URI, can be used to identify the communicating parties. In this paper, we use the term "domain name" to represent such strings.

the server role in the user connection (i.e., User 2 in Fig. 2). The signing KDC associates the issued certificate (or a token) with the client domain name (it has to be done only at one KDC, which we call a "domain registrar" for the given QaaS client).

For domain name validation, we introduce the following modifications to the Butterfly Protocol (called the Butterfly Protocol with Domain Validation):

- User 1 (from Fig. 2) appends the domain name of User 2 (application server) to each *reserveKeyAndGetKeyHalf* and *getKeyHalf* request.
- User 1 sends the *reserveKeyAndGetKeyHalf* and *getKeyHalf* messages to Aija and Brencis *before* the handshake with User 2.
- After receiving the domain name in a request sent by User 1, the domain registrar for User 2 associates the reserved key with the domain name and waits for a *getKeyHalf* request from User 2. The other KDC endpoint (which is not the registrar for User 2) just replies as usual and appends the domain check result value of *false*.
- User 2 sends the *getKeyHalf* requests to Aija and Brencis. Each endpoint checks whether the key has been associated with a domain name. If no, the reply to User 2 is sent as usual. If yes, the registrar checks that the domain name is indeed associated with User 2 and sends the requested half of the key to User 2 only if the check returned *true*.[13] In any case, the result of this domain check is sent back to User 2. Thus, if the check fails, User 2 doesn't receive one half of the key and is not able to compute *hash(full key)*.
  After finishing processing the *getKeyHalf* request, the registrar (which was waiting for it) can now reply to User 1 with the check result.
- After receiving both key halves from Aija and Brencis, User 2 validates both hashes received from User 1 and computes *hash(full key)* to be sent to User 1.
- (Check 1) User 1 computes the OR function on both domain check results received from Aija and Brencis. The value of *true* corresponds to the case when the domain name of User 2 has been recognized by one of the KDC endpoints.
- (Check 2) User 1 also validates *hash(full key)* received from User 2 (see Fig. 2). The correct hash value means that User 2 received key halves from both KDCs; thus, User 1 (application client) can now trust that it is talking to User 2 (application server), having the corresponding domain name.

Notice that two checks associate the butterfly connections with the user connection: Check 1 validates that fact of domain registration, while Check 2 validates that User 2 possesses the full key (i.e., the two butterfly links between User 2 and KDCs have been executed).

---

[13] In the case of client certificates, the traditional certificate-based domain name validation is performed. In the case of JWT tokens, the check is performed by a database lookup or by verifying the hash-based JWT signature.

5   Implementation and Integration into TLS 1.3

The QaaS service software that runs on Aija and Brenics has been developed using the Go programming language, which has built-in concurrency support. The QaaS software implements the server-side part of both the Butterfly Protocol and the Control Protocol. In order to support QKD devices from different vendors, we created a Go interface named *KeyGatherer* that is used to obtain streams of indexed keys, i.e., tuples $(keyID, key, timestamp)$. Currently, we have three *KeyGatherer* implementations: one for the IDQ Clavis[3] device (used in our real testbed), another for fetching keys from the file system (e.g., when keys from the QKD device are stored as files; a shared folder can also be used to simulate a QKD device), and the third one for generating random keys on-the-fly inside a single process used to simulate both Aija and Brencis.

The Go code implements the Butterfly Protocol and the Control Protocol via non-TLS web sockets. Post-quantum key and certificate management and TLS implementation on the server side are provided by reverse proxies. We have implemented our own reverse proxy in Java by relying on the TLS implementation provided by the BouncyCastle library[14]. Alternatively, HAProxy based on OpenSSL 1.1.1 with embedded PQC algorithms from the OpenQuantumSafe project can be used [23].[15]

The QaaS client library (used by User 1, User 2, and Centis) has been implemented in Java using the BouncyCastle library. A pure-Java client implementation allows us to deploy the QaaS client library for Linux, macOS, and Windows by compiling it with GraalVM Native Image [25].[16] For the PQC butterfly connections, our Java implementation is interoperable with LibOQS (written in C); thus, we can use any LibOQS-based reverse proxy to provide PQC to backend endpoints.

Sadly, BouncyCastle, out of the box, does not support PQC algorithms in TLS. Thus, we implemented a set of additional classes that allow us to inject PQC KEMs and signature schemes into TLS 1.3 flow in the BouncyCastle code.[17] We call it **TLS Injection Mechanism**. In particular, we extend the Bouncy-Castle PQC JCA/JCE provider and add the ability to inject and invoke new algorithms. These can be PQC algorithms from the BouncyCastle distribution, PQC algorithms implemented in LibOQS (accessible via the liboqs-java Java

---

[14] BouncyCastle provides pure Java implementations of cryptographic primitives, including the majority of PQC algorithms from NIST Rounds 3 and 4 in the latest releases. BouncyCastle can be downloaded from https://www.bouncycastle.org/java.html.

[15] Our scripts for building such HAProxy are available at https://github.com/LUMII-Syslab/oqs-haproxy.

[16] We used the same approach in our quantum random number generator service https://qrng.lumii.lv [15].

[17] We use TLS v1.3 since it supports KEMs and reduces the number of round-trips in a TLS handshake. KEMs are promoted by NIST, while TLS is an IETF standard supported by all browsers and networking libraries.

wrapper[18]), or other algorithms (such as our "virtual" KEM below). We are working hard on merging our code into the main BouncyCastle distribution. Implementation of the TLS Injection Mechanism is not straightforward and has several non-trivial pitfalls, such as:

- modifying the lists of default KEMs and signature schemes (these lists are sent in the TLS Client Hello message);
- aligning BouncyCastle KEM and signature scheme code points with those used by the OpenQuantumSafe project. Since code points for PQC algorithms are not standardized yet, we stick to the reserved-for-private-use ranges, i.e., 0xFE00..0xFEFF for KEMs and 0xFE00..0xFFFF for signature schemes;
- aligning BouncyCastle and OpenQuantumSafe X.509/X.660 object identifiers (OIDs) for PQC algorithms. These OIDs are used in binary representations of keys and certificates in the ASN.1 notation;
- creating converters between the ASN.1 notation and the internal BouncyCastle representation of keys;
- adding support for PQC keys and certificates (in the ASN.1 DER notation) retrieved from Java key stores, where client private keys and certificates, and CA certificates, are located.

For the butterfly connections, currently, we use the SPHINCS+[19] algorithm for signatures and FrodoKEM[20] as KEM in TLS 1.3. We use AES256-GCM-SHA384 as a cipher suite. For application data, instead of using pure TCP+TLS sockets, we use web sockets since 1) they can be used from client-side code running in web browsers and 2) they are compatible with HTTP(s) traffic (important when configuring firewalls and proxies). All messages in the Butterfly Protocol and Control Protocol are encoded in the ASN.1 binary notation[21], with traditional object identifiers (OIDs) for denoting hash functions.[22]

For the user connection (between User 1 and User 2), we introduce a "virtual" KEM called QKD KEM (we reserve the 0xFEFF code point for it). Unlike in traditional KEMs, no key material is sent via the user connection (hence, KEM is "virtual"); the Butterfly Protocol is executed instead. However, from the BouncyCastle point of view, QKD KEM is treated like any other KEM. We use our TLS Injection Mechanism to add QKD KEM support to BouncyCastle.

In order to implement a KEM, three KEM primitives (*KeyGen*, *Encapsulate*, *Decapsulate*) have to be provided. For some KEMs, each of these primitives is called twice (all six calls are intertwined between the client and the server). In QKD KEM, each of the three KEM primitives is needed once: *KeyGen* and *Decapsulate* on the client side and *Encapsulate* on the server side. The primitives are implemented as follows:

---

[18] https://github.com/open-quantum-safe/liboqs-java.

[19] NIST PQC Round 3 winner, to be standardized.

[20] NIST PQC Round 3 candidate, not participating in Round 4 but invented by renowned scientists.

[21] since it is a standard, which is already being used for keys and certificates.

[22] thus, hash functions can be upgraded in the future.

- **KeyGen()** at User 1: sends *reserveKeyAndGetKeyHalf* to Aija and *getKey-Half* to Brencis (see Fig. 2).
  Returns $pk_1 = (keyID, hash(key[L]), hash(key[R]))$ as a public key and $sk_1 = full\ key$ (a concatenation of the key halves) as a secret key. The public key is sent to User 2 in a TLS Client Hello message.
- **Encapsulate**(pk_1) at User 2: sends *getKeyHalf* to Aija and Brencis.
  Returns $sk_2 = full\ key$ (a concatenation of the key halves) as a shared session key for User 2 and $ct_2 = hash(full\ key)$ as a (virtual) ciphertext to be sent back to User 1 in the reply (=TLS Server Hello message).
- **Decapsulate**(sk_1, ct_2) at User 1: validates the hash ct_2 (and performs other checks if domain validation is used).
  Returns the first argument $sk_1 = full\ key$ as is (sk_1 has already been obtained during **KeyGen**). It will serve as a shared session key for User 1. Notice that in the true KEM, sk_1 would be used to decrypt the shared key from the server cipher text (ct_2). In our "virtual" KEM, however, we do not need to perform any actions with sk_1 since the shared key has already been exchanged quantumly and ct_2 contains only the hash.

Our QaaS implementation is available at https://qkd.lumii.lv[23]. So far, we have implemented all required modules and protocols described in this paper except the extra features mentioned in Sect. 4.2.

With our current implementation, we could obtain some preliminary performance test results. Notice that our current implementation has not been optimized and contains some debug code. In our setup, we used BouncyCastle TLS implementation with injected PQC algorithms from LibOQS (via the Java wrapper) and our own pure-Java implementation of the QaaS protocols. We also used our reverse proxies written in Java.

Establishing one PQC TLS link, serializing and sending a short message (a few bytes long), and receiving the result from the server takes 1.57 s on average (on the i7-2600 CPU). TLS-related computations take 96% of that time. Establishing one TLS link with QaaS (by executing the whole Butterfly Protocol) and sending/receiving a message takes 3.75 s on average. Thus, the whole QaaS introduces the 2.38 slowdown factor compared to a single PQC TLS link. With optimizations, we plan to achieve the performance of running the whole QaaS cycle in less than a second on modern CPUs. Thus, using QaaS in the real-world setup seems realistic.

6   Related Work

Multiple attempts to apply the QKD technology in practice have been made. Most software-based solutions are based on re-keying, when the initial symmetric AES keys are replaced by or combined with the QKD keys [18,20]. Both proprietary protocols (such as IDQ Dual-Key agreement) and open modifications to TLS and IPSec have been proposed [4,10]. Such approaches introduce

---

[23] See also: https://github.com/LUMII-Syslab/qkd-as-a-service.

significant modifications to existing protocols or require the ability to replace AES keys at runtime. In contrast, our QaaS architecture keeps the TLS protocol almost intact (with the exception of reserving the 0xFEFF code point for QKD KEM). However, we factor out the key exchange flow (with the two proposed protocols) as a pluggable KEM.

Several attempts have been made to strengthen TLS security with hardware security modules (HSMs) such as IDQ HSMs and SafeNet Ethernet Encryptors [9]. Currently, HSMs can be integrated into QaaS by developing the corresponding drivers manually. While we anticipate more QKD-certified HSMs, the need for common APIs that ensure HSM interoperability becomes more apparent.

Since QKD devices are expensive, the idea of QKD simulation naturally appeared with QKDNetSim as a representative implementation [18].[24] It correlates with our idea of defining a common Go interface for different QKD implementations, where some implementations act as drivers for real QKD devices while others are used as simulated test environments. Technically, QKDNetSim-like simulators can be plugged into our QaaS software, though our Go interface is very simple and cannot be used to tune simulation parameters—a preconfigured simulator is expected.

KEMTLS is probably the most prominent attempt to eliminate the need for long PQC signatures from the TLS handshake [21]. In KEMTLS, additional KEM invocations are used to authenticate the client and the server implicitly at the cost of non-standard TLS flow. While pursuing the same goal, our Butterfly Protocol differs from KEMTLS in two points:

- We do not modify TLS but introduce a new KEM (QKD KEM).
- We use hash functions, not KEMs, for implicit authentication.

Another goal of KEMTLS is to reduce the number of round-trips used in a TLS handshake. In contrast, our goal was to implement an architecture that is sustainable for active attacks on any single segment. That has been achieved at the cost of a larger number of round-trips in the Butterfly protocol. Still, if we consider the user connection only, the number of round trips remains the same as in TLS 1.3 (i.e., 3 for server-only authentication).

Our idea of domain name verification (in the Butterfly Protocol with Domain Validation) involves checks performed by Aija and Brencis. That resembles the Online Certificate Status Protocol (OCSP), which eliminates the need for certificates and certificates revocation lists (CLRs) on the client side but requires an internet connection to the trusted server [12].

Currently, the QKD technology lacks its own authentication mechanism. In 2021, Wang et al. proposed a PQC-based mutual authentication of multiple QKD network users that trust the same CA [24]. The authentication mechanism is based on PQC signatures that are exchanged via a shared classical link. The process is basically the same as TLS with PQC KEMs and signatures. In our QaaS mechanism, we assume that QKD devices (Alice and Bob) authenticate each other via factory pre-shared keys that can be extended/replaced by new

---

[24] See also: https://www.qkdnetsim.info and http://open-qkd.eu.

quantumly exchanged keys. Otherwise, if Alice and Bob were relying on PQC, we would get a chicken and egg situation with the User 1↔User 2 connection that relies on the security of the Alice↔Bob link.

7   Conclusion

In this paper, we proposed the "QKD as a service" (QaaS) architecture, two protocols (and the Domain Validation extension to the Butterfly Protocol), the distributed key reservation algorithm, and several authentication mechanisms for QaaS, including some ideas for reducing the number of (very long) post-quantum signatures.

We hope our work will make QKD available for a larger community of end-users. Still, a lot of work is yet to be done, including the development of formal proofs of the proposed protocols, analysis of potential threats and attacks to QaaS, standardization, supporting and extending our reference implementation by reacting to new developments and standards in the PQC field, and developing multi-hop (multi-node) QKD and QaaS (a very large field of research). Besides, we think that PQC algorithms should find their way to Java chip cards, which can be used for more secure user authentication.

We also look forward to integrating the proposed QaaS into our web application infrastructure webAppOS [14].

Acknowledgements. Research supported by the European Regional Development Fund, project No. 1.1.1.1/20/A/106 "Applications of quantum cryptography devices and software solutions in computational infrastructure framework in Latvia".

References

1. Alagic, G., et al.: Status report on the third round of the NIST post-quantum cryptography standardization process. Technical report, NISTIR 8413, NIST (2022)
2. Bennett, C.H., Brassard, G.: Quantum cryptography: public key distribution and coin tossing. In: Proceedings of IEEE International Conference on Computers, Systems and Signal Processing, vol. 175, p. 8 New York (1984)
3. Castryck, W., Decru, T.: An efficient key recovery attack on SIDH (2022). https://eprint.iacr.org/2022/975. Cryptology ePrint Archive, Paper 2022/975
4. Dervisevic, E., Mehic, M.: Overview of quantum key distribution technique within IPsec architecture. In: Proceedings of the 18th International ISCRAM Conference, pp. 391–403 (2021)
5. Dubrova, E., Ngo, K., Grtner, J.: Breaking a fifth-order masked implementation of CRYSTALS-Kyber by copy-paste (2022). https://eprint.iacr.org/2022/1713. Cryptology ePrint Archive, Paper 2022/1713
6. Gao, R.Q., et al.: Simple security proof of coherent-one-way quantum key distribution. Opt. Express **30**(13), 23783–23795 (2022)
7. Guo, Q., Johansson, A., Johansson, T.: A key-recovery side-channel attack on classic McEliece implementations. IACR Trans. Cryptographic Hardw. Embed. Syst., 800–827 (2022). https://doi.org/10.46586/tches.v2022.i4.800-827

8. Guo, Q., Nabokov, D., Nilsson, A., Johansson, T.: SCA-LDPC: a code-based framework for key-recovery side-channel attacks on post-quantum encryption schemes (2023). https://eprint.iacr.org/2023/294. Cryptology ePrint Archive, Paper 2023/294

9. IDQ: Telecom Service Provider: 100G encryption with OKD (use case brochure) (2017). https://www.idquantique.com/resource_type/quantum-safe-security/

10. IDQ: ID Quantique partners with ADVA to commercialise a quantum-safe encryption solution (press release) (2019). https://www.idquantique.com/id-quantiquepartners-with-adva-to-commercialise-a-quantum-safe-encryption-solution/

11. IDQ: Redefining Security: Clavis XG QKD System (2022). https://www.idquantique.com/quantum-safe-security/products/clavis-xg-qkdsystem/

12. IETF Standard: X.509 Internet Public Key Infrastructure: Online Certificate Status Protocol - OCSP (RFC 6960) (2013)

13. Jacak, M., Jacak, J., Jwiak, P., Jwiak, I.: Quantum cryptography: theoretical protocols for quantum key distribution and tests of selected commercial QKD systems in commercial fiber networks. Int. J. Quantum Inf. **14**(02), 1630002 (2016)

14. Kozlovis, S.: The web computer and its operating system: a new approach for creating web applications. In: Proceedings of the 15th International Conference on Web Information Systems and Technologies (WEBIST 2019), Vienna, Austria, pp. 46–57. SCITEPRESS (2019)

15. Kozlovis, S., Vksna, J.: POSTER: a transparent remote quantum random number generator over a quantum-safe link. In: Zhou, J., et al. (eds.) Applied Cryptography and Network Security Workshops. LNCS, vol. 13285, pp. 595–599. Springer International Publishing, Cham (2022). https://doi.org/10.1007/978-3-031-16815-4_32

16. Lo, H.K., Ma, X., Chen, K.: Decoy state quantum key distribution. Phys. Rev. Lett. **94**(23), 230504 (2005). https://doi.org/10.1103/PhysRevLett.94.230504

17. Mailloux, L.O., Hodson, D.D., Grimaila, M.R., Engle, R.D., Mclaughlin, C.V., Baumgartner, G.B.: Using modeling and simulation to study photon number splitting attacks. IEEE Access?: Pract. Innovations Open Solutions **4**, 2188–2197 (2016)

18. Mehic, M., Maurhart, O., Rass, S., Voznak, M.: Implementation of quantum key distribution network simulation module in the network simulator NS-3. Quantum Inf. Process. **16**(10), 253 (2017)

19. Mehic, M., et al.: Quantum key distribution: a networking perspective. ACM Comput. Surv. **53**(5), 1–41 (2021)

20. Neppach, A., et al.: Key management of quantum generated keys in IPsec. In: Proceedings of the 3rd International SECRYPT Conference, pp. 177–183 (2008)

21. Schwabe, P., Stebila, D., Wiggers, T.: Post-quantum TLS without handshake signatures. In: Proceedings of the 2020 ACM SIGSAC Conference on Computer and Communications Security, pp. 1461–1480. ACM, Virtual Event USA (2020)

22. Stanley, M., Gui, Y., Unnikrishnan, D., Hall, S., Fatadin, I.: Recent progress in quantum key distribution network deployments and standards. J. Phys: Conf. Ser. **2416**(1), 012001 (2022)

23. Stebila, D., Mosca, M.: Post-quantum key exchange for the internet and the open quantum safe project. In: Avanzi, R., Heys, H. (eds.) SAC 2016. LNCS, vol. 10532, pp. 14–37. Springer International Publishing, Cham (2017). https://doi.org/10.1007/978-3-319-69453-5_2

24. Wang, L.J., et al.: Experimental authentication of quantum key distribution with post-quantum cryptography. npj Quantum Inf. **7**(1), 67 (2021)
25. Wimmer, C.: GraalVM native image: large-scale static analysis for Java (keynote). In: Proceedings of the 13th ACM SIGPLAN International Workshop on Virtual Machines and Intermediate Languages, pp. 3–3. ACM (2021)

XFedGraph-Hunter: An Interpretable Federated Learning Framework for Hunting Advanced Persistent Threat in Provenance Graph

Ngo Duc Hoang Son[1,2] , Huynh Thai Thi[1,2] , Phan The Duy[1,2] ,
and Van-Hau Pham[1,2(✉)]

[1] Information Security Laboratory, University of Information Technology, Ho Chi
Minh city, Vietnam
{19522137,19522256}@gm.uit.edu.vn, {duypt,haupv}@uit.edu.vn
[2] Vietnam National University, Ho Chi Minh city, Vietnam

Abstract. Advanced persistent threats (APT) are increasingly sophisticated and pose a significant threat to organizations' cybersecurity. Detecting APT attacks in a timely manner is crucial to prevent significant damage. However, hunting for APT attacks requires access to large amounts of sensitive data, which is typically spread across different organizations. This makes it challenging to train effective APT detection models while preserving data privacy. To address this challenge, this paper proposes XFedGraph-Hunter, an interpretable federated learning framework for detecting APT attacks in provenance graphs. The framework leverages federated learning to train APT attack hunting models collaboratively on decentralized data stored on multiple devices. This approach helps to preserve data privacy and security while improving the model's performance. The machine learning (ML) model employed in the framework is GraphSAGE. Moreover, a pre-trained transformer model is leveraged into the feature preprocessing process to enhance GraphSAGE's performance. Additionally, GNNexplainer is employed to provide explanations for the APT attack hunting model's predictions, thereby increasing transparency and interpretability. The proposed framework is evaluated on DARPA TCE3 datasets, using FedAvg as the federated learning algorithm. The results indicate that the proposed framework can effectively detect APT attacks, achieving high accuracy and F1 scores. The interpretability provided by GNNexplainer helps in understanding the features contributing to the detection of APT attacks. The collaborative approach to APT attack hunting presented in this paper enables multiple parties to contribute their data while preserving privacy, providing an effective and scalable solution for APT detection.

Keywords: Federated Learning (FL) · Intrusion Detection System (IDS) · Explainable Artificial Intelligence (XAI) · Graph Neural Network (GNN) · Advanced Persistent Threat (APT) · Provenance Graph · Transformers

W. Meng et al. (Eds.): ISPEC 2023, LNCS 14341, pp. 546–561, 2023.
https://doi.org/10.1007/978-981-99-7032-2_32

1   Introduction

Recently, the Advanced Persistent Threat (APT) has become a crucial issue, using the most sophisticated techniques to exploit and lurk in the targeted system in the long term, which could last for years. APT attacks are carefully planned and primarily performed by well-resourced adversaries, usually nation-states or state-sponsored groups, using advanced tactics, techniques, and procedures [1,7,16]. Because significant resources and expertise are invested in APT attacks, they typically focus on high-value targets like the government, large business entities, and many other institutions with the objective of obtaining intelligence-related and financial information. Cyber experts and researchers are working towards finding efficient solutions to detect and prevent APT attacks. Among state-of-the-art cybersecurity solutions, the Intrusion Detection System (IDS) maintains a concrete position in cyberwarfare against APT attacks. While Network-based IDS (NIDS) fail to analyze malicious activities in network traffic because obfuscation and encryption techniques are commonly used by attackers, the Host-based IDS (HIDS) provide more capacity to detect APT attacks by monitoring the hosts' activities. Leveraging the HIDS advantage, the Provenance-based IDS (PIDS), especially the provenance graph approach, shows powerful semantic expression and correlation analysis capabilities that effectively detect APT-style multistep attacks, as evidenced by many studies [6,8,10,20].

To perform the intrusion analysis process, PIDS represents the data flow and data origin within a system in a graph format that can be processed by a cyber security expert or some graph analysis techniques. However, provenance graphs are particularly enormous and contain intricate interconnections among objects, which are difficult to analyze. To accomplish this issue, Graph Neural Network (GNN) offers a promising approach that can handle enormous provenance graphs while maintaining its performance to make quick predictions. As a result, GNN can be incorporated with the IDS in order to enhance performance and accuracy when working with provenance graphs, especially for APT detections.

Unfortunately, the internal data of an organization contains deficient or no APT attack activities, which can be a huge problem for training GNN-based IDS, and the public data is not good enough because of privacy concerns and organizations' data-sharing policies. Federated Learning (FL) has arisen due to its decentralized training capabilities without sharing internal data. Organizations participating in the FL training process train local models using their internal data and then aggregate these models into the global model. From there, all participants can use the global model and profit from it. Although some studies have used the FL approach to train Artificial Intelligence (AI)-based IDS systems, only a limited number of studies have worked on this approach in the context of GNN-based IDS.

Another issue with the GNN-based IDS and other DL-based IDS is the lack of transparency and interpretability, which makes it difficult for both users and developers to understand and troubleshoot the IDS's operations. In addition, comprehending how the AI model makes decisions would aid in detecting cyber threat activities and creating a more accurate and effective DL-based IDS system. Despite this, there have been few investigations into the interpretability of these systems, especially GNN-based IDS systems with FL.

Inspired by the aforementioned difficulties, we present XFedGraph-Hunter, an interpretable FL framework for APT attack detection using provenance graph data. Our framework features an FL-based IDS system that utilizes GNN to handle provenance graph data challenges. Then, we leverage a pre-trained transformer model into the framework to enhance FL-based IDS system performance. Finally, to comprehend AI's inference process, we utilize GNNExplainer [22], a model-agnostic approach [14] for interpreting GNN's predictions. By conducting experiments on the DARPA Transparent Computing Engagement 3 (TCE3), we show the performance and capability of our framework to explain our FL-based IDS against APT attacks and provide a better view of understanding IDS predictions.

Our contributions in this work are summarized as follows:

– Propose a robust collaborative APT hunting framework using federated learning. Our framework features an effective PIDS system employing GNN to detect APT attacks using provenance graph data.
– Propose a robust methodology that leverages edge attributes into node representation by utilizing the pre-trained transformer model. This approach demonstrates its capacity to enhance the GraphSAGE model's performance and reduce the number of convergence rounds in the FL training process.
– Explore the factors that affect the decisions made by GNN-based APT attack detectors by integrating Explainable AI (XAI) into the APT detection process using the GNNExplainer methodology.

This article's remaining sections are organized as follows: Related works of APT detection utilizing explainable AI are introduced in Sect. 2. The proposed framework and methodology are then covered in Sect. 3. The experimental setups, analysis results of the APT detectors after being trained using the FL method, and methodologies used to explain a detector choice are all described in Sect. 4. In Sect. 5, we finally wrap up the paper.

2   Related Work

Numerous studies have been conducted to tackle the challenges posed by APT attacks using provenance graphs. For instance, Xie et al. [21] proposed a PIDS system known as Pangoda, which considers both the anomaly degree of an individual path and the entire provenance graph to achieve fast and accurate detection in large data environments. Likewise, Wu and his colleagues [20] proposed Paradise, a real-time, generalized, and distributed intrusion detection system that exploits the characteristics of provenance graphs by analyzing various types and quantities of dependency relationships collected by SPADE [3], a cross-platform distributed data provenance collection, filtration, storage, and querying service. The system prunes and stores them in a highly efficient memory database, constructs vectors for different events in provenance graphs without extra data conversion.

Despite the various techniques proposed in previous studies to deal with the complex and large provenance graph, the graph's complexity remains a major obstacle. In order to tackle this challenge, Hamilton et al. [4] proposed Graph-SAGE, an inductive framework that utilizes node feature information, such as text attributes, to create node embeddings for new data efficiently. Instead of training embeddings for individual nodes, the framework learns a function that generates embeddings by aggregating features from a node's local neighborhood through sampling. In another work, Lo et al. [9] have introduced a new approach called E-GraphSAGE that employs the GNN method to capture both the edge features and topological information of a graph to detect network intrusions in IoT networks based on NetFlow data. In a different approach, Velickovic et al. [18] presents Graph Attention Networks (GATs), which are convolution-style neural networks that work on graph-structured data using masked self-attentional layers. The GATs are computationally efficient, allow assigning different importance to different nodes in a neighborhood, and do not require knowing the entire graph structure upfront. In another study, Wei et al. [19] presented a GNN-based graph pattern-matching approach for cyber threat hunting named DeepHunter that can capture provenance graph behaviors and compare them with known APT attack behaviors despite the inconsistency. Although the prior mentioned studies prove the benefits of employing GNN in detecting and preventing APT attacks, none of them utilize the FL technique to overcome the training data shortage.

In an effort to solve the interpretability issues of GNN models, Ying et al. [22] introduced GNNExplainer, a model-agnostic method that identifies a concise subgraph structure and a limited number of node features that significantly impact the GNN's prediction. In another study, Huang and his colleagues [5] proposed a model-agnostic explainable GNN approach named GraphLIME. The method explains a prediction for a node by generating a nonlinear interpretable model from the explaining node and outputting most features that play a crucial role in the prediction using LIME [15]. Another attempt was XGNN, a method introduced by Yuan et al. [23] that explains the GNN models by generating graph patterns that can maximize the model's predictions using Reinforcement Learning. These investigations exhibit the effectiveness of using various explanation methods for interpreting GNN models. However, there is a shortage of studies that tackle the interpretability of predictions generated by FL-based models.

This study presents a framework that utilizes GNNExplainer to interpret and clarify the outcomes of an FL-based APT detector. The proposed framework also aims to enhance the detection accuracy of the detector by incorporating a cutting-edge GNN-based PIDS in the context of a provenance graph.

3   Methodology

3.1   The APT Hunting System Architecture

Designing a completely robust APT hunting system involves a significant amount of work, which could be too much for the scope of this research. Therefore, to ensure that our proposed framework is efficient while avoiding overwhelming tasks, we develop our APT hunting system from the scheme proposed by [17], which has already proven to be effective in detecting APT attacks. Our proposed system consists of zones and a centralized server, as shown in Fig. 1. Each zone is a participant joining the FL training process and has four components: the SDN network, the SIEM system, the FL-based IDS model, and the explainer module. The details of each component's architecture are discussed below.

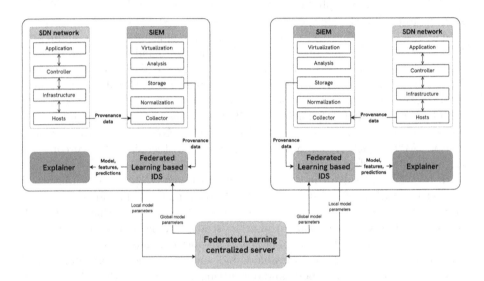

Fig. 1. The architecture of XFedGraph-Hunter

SDN Network: In our proposed architecture, the SDN network plays a crucial role as it may contain malicious activity in the provenance data on the host. To collect and analyze these data, we utilize the SIEM agent, software installed on a host or endpoint device that gathers and forwards system logs to the SIEM collector of the SIEM system, to collect the log data necessary for generating provenance graph data.

SIEM System: Before being stored in the SIEM storage, the data gathered from the SDN network is standardized to meet the requirements of the FL-based IDS system. The stored data can be utilized to visualize and analyze potentially malicious hosts, enabling organizations to promptly respond to potential APT attacks. Moreover, to avoid missing any attacks, the stored data is transmitted to the FL-based IDS system for advanced APT detection.

FL-Based IDS Model: To determine the malicious event from the provenance graph data obtained from the collected system log data, we employ GraphSAGE integrated with a pre-trained transformer model namely TGraphSAGE, as shown in Fig. 2. First, the logs collected by the SIEM system are transformed into the original provenance graph G. However, features of nodes and edges in the graph are usually heterogeneous (difference in the number of features) and challenging to process (exist in multiple types and have values in infinite ranges). Additionally, traditional GraphSAGE models can only learn based on node features and disregard important information from edges. To address these issues, the Transformer model is introduced to standardize the features across nodes and incorporate the edge features into the nodes to form the embedded graph G'. The newly created graph consists of homogeneous features (equal in the number of features between nodes) and is easier to process (features are real numbers that can be easily learned by DNN). Then, the GraphSAGE model analyzes and detects anomalous nodes in the graph G'. The specifics of the utilized DNNs will be given in Sect. 4.2. The GraphSAGE model is also trained using the FL approach outlined in Sect. 3.2.

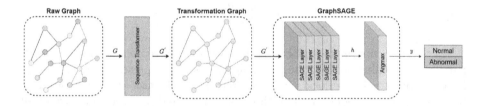

Fig. 2. The architecture of TGraphSAGE

Explainer Module: We utilize the GNNExplainer in this module to interpret the prediction decisions made by the IDS and to validate the accuracy of the model's outputs. However, using the GNNExplainer requires frequent interaction with the IDS, which can have a substantial impact on the performance of the IDS system. Therefore, the module should include a copy of the original IDS model to conduct explanations on that model instead. We will provide a comprehensive discussion of the module architecture in Sect. 3.3.

3.2 Federated Learning Scheme for Hunting Model

To enable decentralized training among participants, we propose an FL model as depicted in Fig. 1, which employs the FedAvg algorithm [11] for model aggregation. During the training phases, each participant communicates with the centralized server using the FL-based IDS system. Each iteration of the FL training process is summarized as follows:

- The participants will communicate with the centralized server to obtain federated parameters. These parameters, according to the FedAvg algorithm, can either be the weights of the global model or the weights of a randomly generated model.
- Then, the participants will use the parameters obtained from the centralized server to train their local models with their internal dataset.
- Once the local training process is complete, the participants will send the local parameters to the centralized server. The local parameters include the local model's weights after being trained and the dataset's size used to train the local model.
- The received local parameters from all participants are utilized on the centralized server to compute a new set of global model weights. This is achieved using Eq. (1).
- The server sends the new global model's weights to the participants. These weights will serve as the federated parameters for continuous training or application of the model.

The aggregation function of the FedAvg algorithm is defined as Eq. (1):

$$w = \sum_{k=1}^{K} \frac{n_k}{n} w_k \tag{1}$$

where w represents the new global model's weights, K represents the number of participants joining the federated training process, w_k represents weights for the k-th collaborator in the local model, n_k represents the size of the dataset used to train the local model for the k-th collaborator, and n is the total size of all clients' datasets.

3.3   Explainer Module

In order to enhance the transparency of the FL-based IDS system predictions, we leveraged GNNExplainer and proposed a methodology described in Fig. 3. Additionally, the explanation outputs are crucial for future security actions on the network. As a result, we decided to validate the explanation outputs by domain experts to maintain the accuracy and performance of the Explainer Module.

Explaining Predictions with GNNExplainer: The goal of GNNExplainer is to identify a minimal subgraph that can explain a GNN prediction. In order to accomplish this, GNNExplainer tries to maximize the mutual information (MI) between the input graph G and the minimal graph G_s to explain the prediction made by the model ϕ:

$$\max_{G_s} MI(Y, (G_S, X_S)) = H(Y) - H(Y|G = G_S, X = X_S) \quad (2)$$

where X_S denotes the associated features with the G_S. Since ϕ is fixed, and so is the entropy $H(Y)$, the MI is maximized when conditional entropy $H(Y|G = G_S, X = X_S)$, which is represented as Eq. 3, is minimized:

$$H(Y|G = G_S, X = X_S) = -E_{Y|G_S, X_S}[log P_\phi(Y|G = G_S, X = X_S)] \quad (3)$$

The input graph can be different and depend on which task is focused on. For our node classification task, our input graph is the k-hops neighbor of the node that needs to be interpreted. Additionally, GNNExplainer presents important factors using difference masks such as the feature mask, which represents features that are crucial to the explained node, and the edge mask, which acts for the minimal subgraph. In this study, we use the edge mask to explain the FL-IDS predictions.

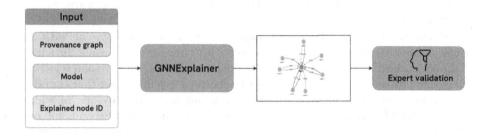

Fig. 3. The architecture of the Explainer Module

4   Experimental Evaluation

4.1   Dataset and Preprocessing

Dataset: In order to conduct experiments that closely resemble real-world scenarios, we utilize the real-life APT dataset named DARPA TCE3[1] dataset. The DARPA TCE3 was conducted as an exercise involving multiple hosts, whose activities were monitored and recorded to create provenance data. These hosts were attacked by various attackers using APT attacks to steal proprietary and personal information from the targeted organization. For our experiments, we selected the CADETS FreeBSD host provenance data as our evaluation dataset, which contains 13,880,763 events generated by benign activities and Nginx backdoors with Drakon APT attacks.

---

[1] DARPA   TCE3:   https://github.com/darpa-i2o/Transparent-Computing/blob/master/README-E3.md.

Table 1. Sentence patterns for each object types

Type	Pattern
net_flow	A net flow object has the local address of {{local_address}}:{{local_port}} and the remote address of {{remote_address}}:{{remote_port}}
file	A file object has the subtype named {{sub_type}}
subject	A subject object has the subtype named {{sub_type}}
unnamed pipe	An unnamed piped object has no properties

Preprocessing: The DARPA TCE3 provenance data consists of objects and events. Objects refer to entities that exist on the host, such as files, folders, and unnamed pipes. Events are generated when these objects interact with each other in some way. As a result, we decided to select objects as nodes and events that feature both source and destination objects as edges for graph presentation. Subsequently, objects' features are transformed into sentences as shown in Table 1, which is embedded using the pre-trained *sentence_transformers* [12] model called *all-MiniLM-L6-v2* [13].

When working with the dataset, there are two issues that come up with us. First, because the number of malicious events is extremely small, using the whole dataset can lead us to model training performance issues. Rather than selecting all events present in the dataset, we opt to choose a specific subset that contains the majority of the malicious activities, resulting in 237,721 events, of which 236,160 (99.3%) are benign, and 1,561 (0.7%) are malicious. Second, for our classification task using GraphSAGE, which utilizes only node features, most of the dataset's objects contain too simple features like type and subtype. To solve this problem, we construct strings from events' features, as shown in Table 2.

Table 2. String patterns for each incorporating event types

Type	Pattern for source node	Pattern for Destination node	Common pattern
execute	executed	was executed	using {{exec}} with the command line "{{cmd_line}}"
accept	accepted the connection from	was accepted to connect with the address	{{address}} using {{exec}}
create_object	created an object	was created	using {{exec}}
modify_process	modified a process	was modified	using {{exec}}
rename	renamed an object	was renamed	using {{exec}}
add_attributes	added attributes to an object	attributes was added	-
flows_to	flowed	was flowed	to another object

These event strings are concatenated with object sentences into complete node sentences. To demonstrate the effectiveness of incorporated node features, we compare them with standalone node features in Sect. 4.4.

4.2 Experimental Settings

We conducted a training simulation for the Federated Learning (FL) model using 10 clients over 10 rounds on an Ubuntu 20.04 virtual machine equipped with 6 core CPUs and 32 GB of RAM. The IDS model architecture that utilizes GraphSAGE is outlined in Table 3. Through experimentation, we trained all clients and found that optimal performance could be achieved with the following configuration: *Adam optimizer* with a *learning_rate* of 0.001 and 100 epochs. To prevent bias in the evaluation process, we ensured that the malicious and benign samples were in the correct ratio while selecting 70% of samples for the training set and the remaining 40% for the testing set. Lastly, we divided the training dataset equally and distributed it to all clients.

Table 3. The architecture of IDS model

Layer (ID)	Activation	Output shape	Connected to
Input (1)	-	(384)	-
SAGELayer (2)	ReLU	(256)	(1)
SAGELayer (3)	ReLU	(256)	(2)
SAGELayer (4)	ReLU	(128)	(3)
SAGELayer (5)	-	(2)	(4)

4.3 Performance Metrics

Detection Metrics: To appropriately assess the model's predictions, we established the following definitions for ground truth values: True Positive (TP) denotes the number of correct predictions assigned to the malicious class, while True Negative (TN) denotes the number of correct predictions assigned to the benign class. False Positive (FP) denotes the number of benign labels that were miscategorized as belonging to the malicious class, and False Negative (FN) denotes the number of malicious labels that were miscategorized as belonging to the benign class.

Accordingly, we use the following metrics for our experiments:

– *Accuracy* refers to the proportion of correct predictions out of the total number of predictions made..

$$Accuracy = \frac{TP + TN}{TP + TN + FP + FN} \tag{4}$$

- *Precision* is the ratio of correct predictions with an malicious label to the total number of predictions that were assigned to the malicious class.

$$Precision = \frac{TP}{TP + FP} \tag{5}$$

- *Recall* is determined by dividing the number of correct predictions with an malicious label by the sum of correct predictions with an malicious label and those that were miscategorized as belonging to the benign class.

$$Recall = \frac{TP}{TP + FN} \tag{6}$$

- *F1-score* is computed by multiplying the product of precision and recall by two, and then dividing this result by the sum of precision and recall.

$$F1 - score = 2 \cdot \frac{Recall \cdot Precision}{Recall + Precision} \tag{7}$$

Interpretability Metrics: According to Gilpin et al. [2], explanations can be evaluated using three methods: application-level evaluation, human-level evaluation, and functionality-level evaluation. However, assessing the quality of explanations can be challenging when relying on data that is difficult to evaluate for non-experts. Moreover, the methods used to generate explanations, such as the GNNExplainer and many other explanation methods for deep learning models, lack established mathematical formulas or methods for assessing the interpretability of their generated explanations. Therefore, we will evaluate explanations using the application-level evaluation method. Specifically, we will analyze the explanations generated by explanation generation methods and utilize our domain knowledge to evaluate the explanations based on the input data and the structure of the model.

4.4 Evaluation Result

Detection Performance Evaluation: Table 4 provides the training results of the TGraphSAGE model on the DARPA TCE3 dataset, evaluated according to the criteria mentioned in Sect. 4.3. Overall, the TGraphSAGE achieved very high performance, with all metrics exceeding 0.9 and the lowest score being 0.9173 (when using only node attributes). Moreover, the TGraphSAGE model outperformed the GraphSAGE model using doc2vec, word2vec, and fasttext in terms of overall performance. Additionally, despite the severe class imbalance in the DARPA TCE3 dataset, with benign samples accounting for 99.3% of the data, both the TGraphSAGE and GraphSAGE models integrated with fast-text achieved perfect scores in the *Recall* criterion (1.0). This demonstrates the impressive performance of TGraphSAGE and the GraphSAGE model integrated with fasttext in detecting malicious events, particularly in scenarios where these

Table 4. Evaluation results for FL-based GraphSAGE in different data preprocessing models

Model	Accuracy	Precision	Recall	F1-Score
d2v+GraphSAGE	0.9976	0.9587	0.5946	0.7339
w2v+GraphSAGE	0.9992	0.8824	0.9984	0.9368
fasttext+GraphSAGE	0.9995	0.9258	1	0.9615
TGraphSAGE (node feature only)	0.9995	0.9173	0.9952	0.9547
TGraphSAGE	**0.9996**	**0.9313**	**1**	**0.9645**

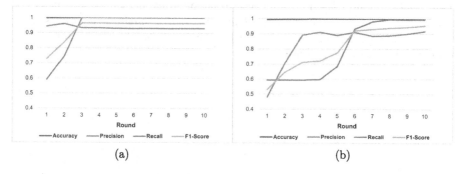

Fig. 4. Convergent performance for TGraphSAGE utilizing (a) both node and edge features and (b) only node features

events are a small fraction compared to benign events occurring daily in the system. However, our proposed model excels in terms of *Precision* score, resulting in a lower false-positive rate.

Beside that, it is worth noting that our approach, which uses both node and edge features, converges faster and achieves the highest performance from round 3 (as depicted in Fig. 4a), while the traditional approach, which uses only node features, gives a fluctuating performance until the final round (as depicted in Fig. 4b).

Explanation Evaluation: We visualize the explanation results as shown in Fig. 5 and Fig. 6. These results are subgraphs whose center node (the green node) is the explained node. Surrounding the explained node are k-hops neighbors with their labels and edges with their importance score from the edge mask, which is within the range $[0, 1]$. By setting the threshold value to 0.5, we can determine crucial pathways for message-passing to propagate and aggregate information, which are blue edges and have an importance score greater than the threshold value, as opposed to gray edges, which are not essential. Additionally, the change in color from light blue to dark blue, as well as the transition from thin to thick edges, signifies an augmentation in the importance score.

Figure 5 shows the explanation result of a benign node. Except for the two bottom nodes, all the rest of the nodes show their importance for the explanation by associating with edges that have an importance score greater than 0.6. To gain a better understanding of the explanation, we analyze the original values of the nodes. All single connections surrounding nodes have a value of "*A subject object has the subtype named process, and it modified a process using sshd.*". The reason why the explanation does not care about two bottom nodes is that GNNExplainer generates a minimal subgraph, not an able one, so the minimal subgraph is transparent enough without bottom nodes. Moreover, the value of the center node is "*A file object has the subtype named file, and it was modified using find, ...*", and the four-connection surrounding node has a value of "*A subject object has the subtype named process, and it modified a process using find, ...*". These original values are all benign behaviors, so the center node is truly classified as a benign node.

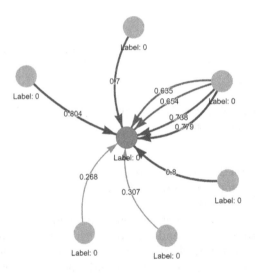

Fig. 5. The explanation for a prediction of a benign object produced by the FL-based GraphSAGE model

Figure 6 shows the explanation result of a malicious node. All surrounding malicious nodes have a certain degree of influence on the center node. Examining the original values of the center node, it contains some malicious files in the dataset, such as "*/var/log/sendmail*", "*/tmp/font*" and "*/tmp/minions*". Thus, we can deduce that the central node is unequivocally classified as malicious.

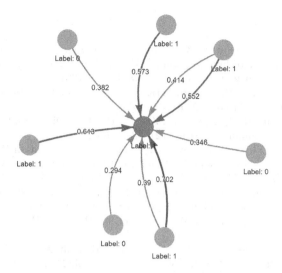

Fig. 6. The explanation for a prediction of a malicious object produced by the FL-based GraphSAGE model

5   Conclusion

In conclusion, this paper proposed XFedGraph-Hunter, an interpretable federated learning framework for detecting advanced persistent threats (APT) attacks in provenance graphs. The proposed framework leverages federated learning to train APT attack hunting models collaboratively on decentralized data stored on multiple devices, preserving data privacy and security while improving the model's performance. The results of the evaluation on the DARPA TCE3 dataset, using FedAvg as the federated learning algorithm, showed that XFedGraph-Hunter can effectively detect APT attacks, achieving high accuracy and F1 scores. The interpretability provided by GNNexplainer helps in understanding the features contributing to the detection of APT attacks, increasing transparency and interpretability. The proposed collaborative approach to APT attack hunting enables multiple parties to contribute their data while preserving privacy, providing an effective and scalable solution for APT detection. XFedGraph-Hunter has the potential to enhance the security and privacy of organizations by detecting APT attacks in a timely and effective manner.

Acknowledgement. This research is funded by Vietnam National University HoChiMinh City (VNU-HCM), Viet Nam under grant number DS2022-26-02.

References

1. Alshamrani, A., Myneni, S., Chowdhary, A., Huang, D.: A survey on advanced persistent threats: techniques, solutions, challenges, and research opportunities. IEEE Commun. Surv. Tutorials **21**(2), 1851–1877 (2019)
2. Doshi-Velez, F., Kim, B.: Towards a rigorous science of interpretable machine learning. arXiv preprint arXiv:1702.08608 (2017)
3. Gehani, A., Ahmad, R., Irshad, H., Zhu, J., Patel, J.: Digging into big provenance (with spade). Commun. ACM **64**(12), 48–56 (2021)
4. Hamilton, W., Ying, Z., Leskovec, J.: Inductive representation learning on large graphs. In: Advances in Neural Information Processing Systems, vol. 30 (2017)
5. Huang, Q., Yamada, M., Tian, Y., Singh, D., Yin, D., Chang, Y.: Graphlime: local interpretable model explanations for graph neural networks (2020)
6. Jenkinson, G., et al.: Applying provenance in APT monitoring and analysis. In: Proceedings of the USENIX Workshop Theory Practice Provenance, pp. 16–16 (2017)
7. Khaleefa, E.J., Abdulah, D.A.: Concept and difficulties of advanced persistent threats (APT): survey. Int. J. Nonlinear Anal. Appl. **13**(1), 4037–4052 (2022)
8. Kurniawan, K., Ekelhart, A., Kiesling, E., Quirchmayr, G., Tjoa, A.M.: Krystal: knowledge graph-based framework for tactical attack discovery in audit data. Comput. Secur. **121**, 102828 (2022)
9. Lo, W.W., Layeghy, S., Sarhan, M., Gallagher, M., Portmann, M.: E-graphsage: a graph neural network based intrusion detection system for IoT. In: NOMS 2022–2022 IEEE/IFIP Network Operations and Management Symposium, pp. 1–9. IEEE (2022)
10. Lv, Y., Qin, S., Zhu, Z., Yu, Z., Li, S., Han, W.: A review of provenance graph based APT attack detection: applications and developments. In: 2022 7th IEEE International Conference on Data Science in Cyberspace (DSC), pp. 498–505 (2022)
11. McMahan, B., Moore, E., Ramage, D., Hampson, S., Arcas, B.A.: Communication-efficient learning of deep networks from decentralized data. In: Artificial Intelligence and Statistics, pp. 1273–1282. PMLR (2017)
12. Nils, R., Gurevych, I.: Sentence-BERT: sentence embeddings using Siamese BERT-networks. arXiv:1908.10084 (2019)
13. Reimers, N., Iryna, G.: Making monolingual sentence embeddings multilingual using knowledge distillation. arXiv: 2004.09813 (2020)
14. Ribeiro, M.T., Singh, S., Guestrin, C.: Model-agnostic interpretability of machine learning. arXiv preprint arXiv:1606.05386 (2016)
15. Ribeiro, M.T., Singh, S., Guestrin, C.: "why should i trust you?" explaining the predictions of any classifier. In: Proceedings of the 22nd ACM SIGKDD international conference on knowledge discovery and data mining, pp. 1135–1144 (2016)
16. Stojanović, B., Hofer-Schmitz, K., Kleb, U.: Apt datasets and attack modeling for automated detection methods: a review. Comput. Secur. **92**, 101734 (2020)
17. Thi, H.T., Son, N.D.H., Duy, P.T., Pham, V.H.: Federated learning-based cyber threat hunting for apt attack detection in SDN-enabled networks. In: 2022 21st International Symposium on Communications and Information Technologies (ISCIT), pp. 1–6. IEEE (2022)
18. Velickovic, P., et al.: Graph attention networks. Stat **1050**(20), 10–48550 (2017)
19. Wei, R., Cai, L., Zhao, L., Yu, A., Meng, D.: DeepHunter: a graph neural network based approach for robust cyber threat hunting. In: Garcia-Alfaro, J., Li, S., Poovendran, R., Debar, H., Yung, M. (eds.) SecureComm 2021. LNICST, vol. 398, pp. 3–24. Springer, Cham (2021). https://doi.org/10.1007/978-3-030-90019-9_1

20. Wu, Y., et al.: Paradise: real-time, generalized, and distributed provenance-based intrusion detection. IEEE Trans. Dependable Secure Comput. **20**(2), 1624–1640 (2023)
21. Xie, Y., Feng, D., Hu, Y., Li, Y., Sample, S., Long, D.: Pagoda: a hybrid approach to enable efficient real-time provenance based intrusion detection in big data environments. IEEE Trans. Dependable Secure Comput. **17**(6), 1283–1296 (2018)
22. Ying, Z., Bourgeois, D., You, J., Zitnik, M., Leskovec, J.: GNNExplainer: generating explanations for graph neural networks. In: Advances in Neural Information Processing Systems, vol. 32 (2019)
23. Yuan, H., Tang, J., Hu, X., Ji, S.: XGNN: towards model-level explanations of graph neural networks. In: Proceedings of the 26th ACM SIGKDD International Conference on Knowledge Discovery & Data Mining. ACM (2020)

XSS Attack Detection by Attention Mechanism Based on Script Tags in URLs

Yuki Nakagawa[✉] and Mamoru Mimura[iD]

National Defense Academy of Japan, Yokosuka, Kanagawa 2398686, Japan
{em61009,mim}@nda.ac.jp

Abstract. XSS (Cross-Site Scripting) attacks exploit vulnerabilities in web applications, and many victims have been reported. As a countermeasure for this, existing studies propose methods to detect XSS attacks by combining natural language processing techniques and machine learning models. Few studies reveal the features that contribute to the classification and the validity of the dataset. In this study, we analyzed the weights of words in the attention mechanism to identify the features that contribute to classification. Our models are combinations of LSTM (Long Short Term Memory) and attention mechanism. Validation experiments were conducted on two different datasets. The experimental result shows that typical features such as script tags and text-encoded hex strings contribute to the classification. In addition, when the benign sample of the test data was increased by a factor of 5, the f1 score was found to decrease to a maximum of 0.55. Since the focused features depend on the dataset, the generality and practicality of the classification model are still to be evaluated. In other words, the utility of the classification model based on the dataset is not high, and it is necessary to verify the model to improve its utility.

Keywords: XSS · LSTM · attention mechanism · NLP

1 Introduction

In recent cyber attacks, XSS (Cross Site Scripting) vulnerabilities called CWE-79 [4] in web applications continue to occur frequently and various damages have been reported. CWE-79 is still a vulnerability that needs to be addressed, as it ranks second in the overall score of the 2022 Top 25 list of weaknesses. [23]. XSS attacks are mainly carried out by inserting scripts into web pages. Therefore, as countermeasures against XSS attacks, input value restrictions and script disabling are used in the operational field. For example, Fang et al. [5,6], Lei et al. [12], Mokbal et al. [15,16] Raed et al. [19], Krishnan et al. [11] and Gulit et al. [7], have proposed using machine learning models to detect XSS attacks for various features including scripts and other linguistic features found in XSS attacks. However, few studies have addressed how machine learning models detect XSS attacks. The validity of the dataset has also not been adequately

W. Meng et al. (Eds.): ISPEC 2023, LNCS 14341, pp. 562–578, 2023.
https://doi.org/10.1007/978-981-99-7032-2_33

verified. This is because the datasets used are rarely made public due to legal and ethical issues, and it is often difficult to mention the utility of the dataset or the number of samples. In other words, many of the studies on XSS attack detection are open to validation with respect to the credibility of the results.

Therefore, this study will examine two methods.

The first method is to classify the datasets used in each previous study that use linguistic features such as URLs using a machine learning model with the attention mechanism. From the classification results, we clarify which words among the linguistic features of XSS attacks the machine learning model focuses on to detect the attacks. If it can be shown that the machine learning model's classification is based on words that are typical linguistic features of XSS attacks, it can be evaluated as a practical detection result with higher accuracy and more credibility. The reason for targeting URLs is that they are in a simple text format and it is easy to extract words and other linguistic features. To the best of our knowledge, there have been few reports of machine learning models visually indicating the words they focus on as important for classification. As a result, we found that the model focused on symbols such as <> that make up scripts.

The second method investigates the change in detection rate when the number of benign samples in the test data is increased. This is based on the method of Mimura [14] and assumes a situation similar to the actual environment in which attacks are detected. By increasing the number of benign samples, it is possible to simulate the case of detecting a small number of malicious samples among a huge number of benign samples. Therefore, we believe that the detection accuracy results allow us to verify the utility of the classification model. As a result, increasing the number of benign samples in the test data by a factor of 5 reduced to a F1 score as low as 0.45. We believe that this will allow us to verify the practicality of this method in terms of detection accuracy when detecting a small number of malicious samples from a large number of benign samples.

The contributions of this paper are as follows:

1. The practicality of the detection method based on linguistic features has been enhanced by the confirmation that the machine learning model using the attention mechanism detects XSS attacks by focusing on words used in typical XSS attacks, such as "<>".
2. Comparison of the top 20 words that the classification model focused on when it detected the words correctly across datasets showed that only 7 to 10 words matched, and that there was variation across datasets, confirming that the words focused on by the classification model are influenced by the dataset.
3. Increasing the number of benign samples in the test data relative to the data set decreased the detection rate, indicating that the practicality of the classification model in a real-world environment is low.

2   Related Work

Various studies have been proposed to detect XSS attacks, as surveyed by Sarmaha et al. [21], Rodríguez et al. [20] and Jasleen et al. [10]. Examples of various methods include detection by domain knowledge and threat intelligence by Zhou et al. [25] and detection based on natural and programming language processing by Maurel et al. [13].

In this chapter, we present key related studies that specifically focus on URLs or natural language features.

Mokbal et al. proposed a method for detecting XSS attacks with the XGBoost Model by selecting features from features based on URL, HTML and JavaScript in the document of a webpage using a sequential backward selection method called SBS [16]. As a result, accuracy, precision, recall, and f1 scores are all greater than 0.99. However, there are concerns about the practicality and generality of the classification model, as only the source of collection and the number of samples are given for the dataset used.

Raed et al. proposed a detection method using Word2vec and CNN-LSTM models after performing various pre-processing procedures on the textual data of each URL, both normal URLs and URLs containing XSS attacks [19]. The various preprocessing steps include encoding the text data, replacing numbers, URL hosts, scheme parts and String characters, and decoding into a readable format. As a result, the accuracy, precision, recall, and f1 scores are all greater than 0.99. However, it does not mention the characteristics of XSS attacks, and the source of collection of benign samples is unknown. In addition, there are concerns about the practicality and generality of the classification model due to the many transformations of the dataset, such as the decoding process.

The method of Fang et al. [6] performs pre-processing on the dataset of XSS attacks and on the dataset of benign samples collected from the database of an open directory project called DMOZ [1]. The preprocessing is done by decoding HTML-encoded and URL-encoded parts, replacing numbers, URL hosts, and scheme parts, and then classifying scripts frequently used in XSS attacks into six categories. The detection process is then performed using Word2vec and LSTM-based classification models. The detection accuracy is 0.995, 0.979, and 0.987 for precision, recall, and f1 scores, respectively. Lei et al. used a similar approach, increasing the number of datasets and changing the classification model to an LSTM-Attention-based classification model for detection [12]. The resulting precision, recall, and f1 scores are 0.993, 0.982, and 0.985, respectively. However, obfuscated language features are lost, as the dataset is only published by Fang et al. [6] and only the decoding process is performed on the dataset. In other words, the utility and versatility of the classification model are also open to validation.

In summary, each of the related studies compared detection accuracy using classification models that were devised with features to be acquired and trained against machine learning models, without sufficient mention of the dataset. However, this method has not sufficiently validated the utility and versatility of the classification model.

In this study, we examine the practicality and versatility of the classification model by clarifying words that have a large impact on classification focusing on character features, i.e., words, and by examining changes in detection rates as the number of benign samples increases.

First, a classification model using the attention mechanism is constructed to detect XSS attacks focusing on character features. Then, we confirm whether the classification model comprehensively focuses on the typical features of XSS attacks by analyzing the contribution of the features that have a high contribution to the detection of XSS attacks. Thus, we clarify the basis for the classification model to detect XSS attacks and analyze whether the model detects XSS attacks in a practical manner. In addition to this, the utility is tested from the accuracy of the classification model with reference to Mimura's method [14]. In this method, performance is compared by increasing the number of benign samples against the utility of the classification model. Although malware is the target of the study in this literature, we believe that the same method can be used to validate the classification model in this study.

3   Related Technique

3.1   LSTM

LSTM (Long Short Term Memory) [8] is a type of RNN (Recurrent Neural Network), and is one of the models that solved the gradient vanishing problem of RNN. RNN is a Neural Network that uses hidden layers and uses the previous output as the next output. However, there was a problem that information could not be handled over a long time horizon. LSTM solves this problem by using forget gates (1), input gates (2), candidate storage cells (3), storage cells (4), output gates (5), and hidden layers (6). The repeating module in an LSTM is shown in Fig. 1, and the equations for each gate in the figure are shown below [17].

The forgetting gate f_t determines how much information to discard from the input x_t and one previous state hidden layer h_{t-1} and is defined by the following equation, where W is the weight vector and b is the bias.

$$f_t = \sigma(W_f \cdot [h_{t-1}, x_t]) + b_f \tag{1}$$

The input gate i_t determines which information is to be stored in the cell and is defined by the following equation

$$i_t = \sigma(W_i \cdot [h_{t-1}, x_t]) + b_i \tag{2}$$

The candidate memory cell $\tilde{C}_t$ represents candidate values to be added to the memory cell to be stored as long-term memory, and is defined by the following equation

$$\tilde{C}_t = tanh(W_C \cdot [h_{t-1}, x_t]) + b_C \tag{3}$$

The memory cell C_t is updated by the forgetting gate f_t, the previous state memory cell C_{t-1}, the input gate i_t and the candidate memory cell $\tilde{C}_t$, defined by the following equation

$$C_t = f_t * C_{t-1} + i_t * \tilde{C}_t \tag{4}$$

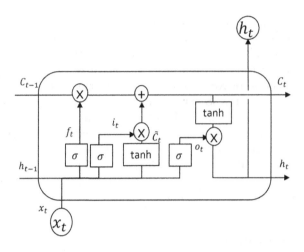

Fig. 1. The repeating module in an LSTM

The output gate o_t is used to determine the output value in combination with the memory cell C_t and is defined by the following equation

$$o_t = \sigma(W_o \cdot [h_{t-1}, x_t]) + b_o \tag{5}$$

The hidden layer h_t is also the output value for the input x_t and is defined by the output gate o_t and the storage cell C_t by the following equation

$$h_t = o_t * tanh(C_t) \tag{6}$$

3.2   Attention Mechanism

The attention mechanism is a mechanism that learns the relationship between elements introduced in the Encoder-Decoder model and the points of attention. It implements an Encoder-Decoder model called Transformer. Among these, this study utilizes a mechanism called self-attention [24]. Self-attention is a method of acquiring the correspondence in the input data using the same input data. First, three vectors called Query, Key and Value are calculated from the input data. The similarity of Query and Key is calculated as weights by the Softmax function. From these weights, the correspondence between Query and Value is obtained and output. Assuming that Query is Q, Key is K, and Value is V, the similarity is defined by the following equation.

$$Attention(Q, K, V) = Softmax(\frac{Q \cdot K^T}{\sqrt{d_k}}) \cdot V \tag{7}$$

3.3   Type of XSS Attacks

XSS attacks can be categorised into three main types. Reflected XSS in which the attacker creates a malicious link containing a script to lure the victim into clicking on it. Inevitably, the victim's request to the server will also contain malicious strings. This means that the server response will also contain malicious code, and the attack will be completed when the script containing this malicious code is executed by the victim's browser. Stored XSS allows attackers to inject malicious code into vulnerable servers, e.g. via message forums. When the victim navigates to this compromised server, the attack is established when malicious code is executed as a script as part of the web page. DOM-based XSS is an attack that primarily resides on the client's browser caused by exploiting script write operations. The attack is established when malicious code injected by the attacker is executed as a script by normal DOM operations on the client's browser.

4   Proposed Method

4.1   Outline

This section describes the validation procedure to describe the utility of the detection methods and the validity of the data sets. The validation is carried out by two methods on two different datasets. The first is validation by classification using a machine learning model combining LSTM and an attention mechanism and extraction of linguistic features based on the classification results. This confirms whether the detection results focus on the features of XSS attacks and refers to the validity of the dataset. Figure 2 shows the validation procedure. The second is to verify the change in detection accuracy with an increase in the number of benign samples. This makes reference to the usefulness of the dataset and the classification model in a real-world environment. Each detail method is presented.

4.2   Dataset

The assumption is that the data used for the validation target is the textual data of the URLs. In other words, Reflected XSS is mainly targeted for detection. However, even Stored XSS and DOM-Based XSS may also be subject to this method under conditions where server-client communication occurs in which the URL contains malicious scripts. Note that a benign sample refers to the URL text when it does not contain scripts by the attacker, while a malicious sample refers to the URL text in which the scripts by the attacker have been inserted. Three different datasets are used in this verification. To ensure validity and reproducibility, we used datasets that use textual data from URLs and are publicly available in the literature on XSS attack detection.

Examples of each are shown with the host part and other parts omitted. Benign samples include those that refer to html files such as " https://***.**/2010/1 0/october-19-1851-death-of-marie-therese.html", which refers to an html file. Malicious samples include " http://***.**/find.jsp?f=" "> < script> alert(1)< /scr ipt>"

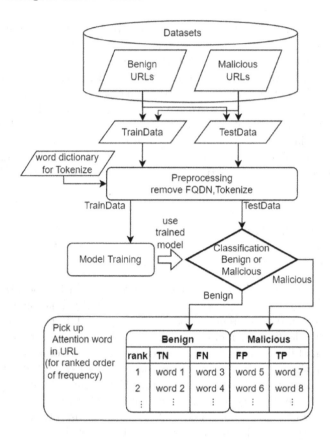

Fig. 2. Procedure flow of the proposed method

with the script inserted. Others, such as " http://*****.**/%22%3E%3C
script%3Ealert%28%22 XSS_BY_C37HUN%22%29%3C/script%3E".

Three datasets were prepared. The number of benign and malignant samples
in the dataset used is shown in Table 1. The first is the dataset used by Fang et al.
[6], consisting of 33,426 malicious samples collected by cloning from XSSed.com
and 31,407 benign samples generated from the DMOZ data. This is designated
as dataset A. However, fewer directories and parameters are included in the
normal data, and classification by data length is considered easier. The second
is the dataset we created, consisting of 13,586 malicious samples collected by
crawling from XSSed.com and 32,070 benign samples extracted from the CIC-
IDS2017 dataset [22]. This is designated as dataset B. This dataset is considered
more difficult to classify than the first dataset because the benign samples also
contains directories and parameters. The third is a dataset that only collected
benign samples. This is designated as dataset C. This is a data set collected from
proxy logs and other sources for use in increasing the number of benign samples
and consists of 482,780 benign samples.

Table 1. Number of samples in the data set

dataset	benign	malicious
Dataset A [6]	31407	33426
dataset B (we created)	32070	13586
dataset C	482780	–

This dataset was collected in 2017 from benign traffic logs of a Class B university network. This network has over 5000 computers connected to it. It also has various security devices connected to it and has been verified as benign traffic by several experts. Of the three datasets, we perform validation experiments on datasets A and B. First, each dataset is divided into training and test data. For the partitioning, k-fold cross-validation was used and the data was divided into 5 parts. In other words, the ratio of training data to test data is 8:2. The ratio of benign samples to malicious samples was kept the same for both the training data and the test data. In this way, the linguistic features are extracted repeatedly so that all samples in the data set used become test data.

4.3   Preprocessing

In preprocessing, data cleaning and tokenization are performed on the data. Preparation for the tokenization process is the creation of a dictionary. The dictionary consists of 452,020 words, which are derived from the text data of 450,176 URL lists of benign and malicious URLs collected from Kaggle [9] and divided into unique words using the Tokenizer module of the Keras library, and 453,020 words with 1,000 special characters that indicate the starting position of the text, etc. The 453,020 words were obtained by adding 1,000 special characters to the 452,020 words that were divided into unique words using the Tokenizer module of the Keras library. In addition, symbols such as ".", "%", "/", and other symbols are also set as one word in the dictionary.

Data Cleaning. The textual treatment is performed as data cleaning for the input data. Only the host and scheme portions of the URL are removed, and the text input to the URL is used directly for the query portion that describes other parameters and directories. For obfuscation by encoding into other character codes, which is often done in XSS attacks, we decided to use the HTTP communication log at the time of communication without processing decryption. This is because it cannot be denied that the unreadability of strings due to obfuscation may also be a linguistic feature of XSS attacks. This is also to make the dataset structure closer to the actual environment in which XSS attacks occur.

Tokenize. As a tokenization process for the input data, the Tokenizer module of the Keras library is used to divide the text of the input data into the smallest units based on the created dictionary, and assign a unique number to each unique word. This converts the text data into numerical data on which the classification model can be trained.

4.4   Machine Learning Model

Referring to the method of Lei et al. [12], we use a classification model that combines LSTM and attention mechanism for classification. The reason for the combined LSTM and attention structure is to take into account the pre- and post-relationships of the words that split the text. The machine learning model used in this experiment was implemented using Tensorflow 2.4 [2], Keras 2.4.3 [3], Python-3.8.9, and scikit-learn 1.0.2 [18]. Parameter tuning of the classification model was performed by selecting the best of the values set by grid search. As a result, the input vector length was set to 128 out of 64, 128, and 256, and the batch size to 16 out of 16, 32, 64, 128, and 256. In addition, the dropout value of the classification model was set to 0.05, and the hidden layer was fixed at 128 dimensions. The maximum number of epochs during training was set to 50, and training was terminated when the loss value no longer varied.

The model was configured as shown in Fig. 3 using the Keras library.

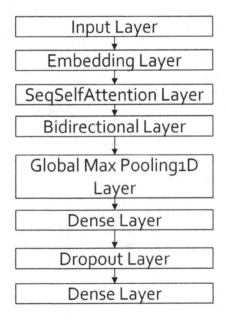

Fig. 3. Machine learning model structure

First, determine the length of the sequence to be input by the Input layer. Next, the Input layer is fed into the Embedding layer, which maps the input words to vectors. In this study, the vector is a 128-dimensional vector. Then, the SeqSelfAttention layer enables weight processing by the attention mechanism. After that, the LSTM is trained on the Bidirectional layer and downsized on the GlobalMaxPooling layer. The downsized vectors are combined in the Dense layer to suppress over-training by the Dropout layer, and the results are output in the last Dense layer. A sigmoid function is used as the activation function.

4.5   Aggregation of Focus Points by the Attention Mechanism

Each sample of input test data is detected by binary classification of a trained classification model. The detection results are classified by the confusion matrix class. In this process, each token of the tokenized sample is assigned a weight for classification by the attention mechanism of the classification model. The tokens with the highest weights are selected from the top 10 tokens in each sample. Special tokens are excluded if they are included in the total. This is done for all classified samples, and the extracted tokens are sorted in order of frequency of occurrence. The tokens at the top of the list are considered more important to the classification of the dataset, and the classification results are discussed. If, as a result of the extraction and aggregation of the tokens and words with high weights, we find that the words characteristic of XSS attacks are at the top of the list, we can assume that the classification model focuses on the linguistic features unique to XSS and performs the classification.

4.6   Change in Detection Rate When Benign Data Increases

In an environment where actual XSS attack detection techniques are required, it is necessary to find a few malicious samples among many benign samples. Therefore, the detection rate must be high even if the number of benign samples increases. Therefore, we investigate the change in detection rate when the number of benign samples in the test data is increased. We increase the number of benign samples in the test data by randomly adding benign samples from dataset C to datasets A and B. The dataset is divided into five parts by k-fold cross-validation, and the ratio of training data to test data is 8:2. Only benign samples are added to the test data after the division, and the change in detection rate is verified. The number of samples to be added is N times the number of benign samples in the test data.

5   Result

5.1   Performance Evaluation Method

In our experiments, we consider benign samples to be benign and malicious samples to contain malicious scripts used in XSS attacks, and test whether each

Table 2. Benign and malicious prediction

		Predict	
		benign	malicious
Actual	benign	True Negative (TN)	False Positive (FP)
	malicious	False Negative (FN)	True Positive (TP)

of them is correctly predicted. The relationship between them is shown in Table 2 as a confusion matrix.

We used accuracy, precision, recall, and f1 as evaluation indices. Each evaluation index is expressed by the following equation.

$$Accuracy = \frac{TP + TN}{TP + FP + FN + TN} \tag{8}$$

$$Precision = \frac{TP}{TP + FP} \tag{9}$$

$$Recall = \frac{TP}{TP + FN} \tag{10}$$

$$f1 = \frac{2Recall \times Precision}{Recall + Precision} \tag{11}$$

5.2 Environment

The environment used in the experiment is shown in Table 3.

Table 3. Test environment

CPU	Core i7-8700 K 3.70 GHz
GPU	NVIDIA GeForce RTX 2080 Ti
Memory	64 GB
OS	Windows10 Home
Programming Language	Python3.8.9

5.3 Change in Detection Rate When Benign Data Increase

As in the previous section, the data set is divided into training and test data. Then, only benign samples are added to the test data, the test data is classified, and the detection rates are compared. The number of benign samples to be added is increased by a number equal to the number of samples in the test data. In this experiment, the number of samples was increased by 6,000 up to 36,000.

The experiment was repeated so that all malignant samples were tested. The detection rate was calculated as the average of the results of repeated experiments. The evaluation indices were similarly validated using accuracy, precision, recall, and f1, respectively.

5.4 Verification of Detection Rate and Linguistic Features by Attention Mechanism

First, the detection accuracies of datasets A and B are shown in the Table 4, along with the detection accuracies of other previous studies.

Table 4. Accuracy comparison

study(used dataset)	Accuracy	Precision	Recall	f1
Proposed Method(dataset A)	0.983	0.995	0.971	0.983
Proposed Method(dataset B)	0.999	0.999	1.0	0.999
Mokbal et al. [16]	0.996	0.995	0.990	0.993
Mokbal et al. [15]	0.993	0.992	0.984	0.988
Methaq et al. [19]	0.991	0.999	0.995	0.993
Lei et al. [12]	–	0.993	0.982	0.985
Fang et al. [6]	–	0.995	0.979	0.987

Repeated experiments were conducted so that all samples in the datasets were tested. The detection rate was calculated as the average of the results of repeated experiments. Detection accuracy was high for both data sets. Compared to the detection accuracies of other studies, there was no significant difference in detection. Although dataset B is an unbalanced dataset with a large benign sample size, no significant difference in detection accuracy was confirmed.

Next, we review the linguistic features extracted from datasets A and B. The top 20 types for each class of TN, FP, FN, and TP, which are the detection results, are shown in the Table 5 and 6.

In dataset B, there was only one sample classified as FP and FN, and the top 20 were not tabulated. Therefore, the fields that did not correspond were left blank. The table shows that for all classes, URL-specific symbols such as "/", "." and "=". The table also shows that at least 50% of the words in one class overlapped with other words in the other class. The corresponding parts are colored in gray in the tables. However, we also found that the samples classified as Malicious TP focused on the symbols "<" and ">" that represent script tags used in XSS attacks, as well as the hexadecimal components such as "3e" and "3c" when the character encoding of these symbols is shown in the table. In addition, a comparison of the data sets A and B shows that 10 of the top 20 words focused on in the TP class, including "<" and ">", overlap, although the malignant samples were collected from the same source. The corresponding areas are colored in dark gray in the tables.

Table 5. Classification featured token in dataset A

rank	TN	FP	FN	TP
1	=	amp	=	>
2	amp	;	&	<
3	&	=	/	3c
4	;	.	.	&
5	id	/	d	"
6	_	&	_	3e
7	/	_	:	alert
8	-	%	com	/
9	soo	search	http	script
10	selected	1	1	)
11	+	id	search	(
12	beschr	www	xss	xss
13	menu	http	page	+
14	.	html	www	cookie
15	ring	-	action	2f
16	page	com	;	'
17	cid	+	(	=
18	1	2f	-	search
19	amg	@	url	22
20	p	:	alert	http

Table 6. Classification featured token in dataset B

rank	TN	FP	FN	TP
1	-	&	id	.
2	/	;	email	/
3	.	2015	<	>
4	com	page	br	<
5	=	index	>	th
6	_	/	?	3c
7	the	amp	amp	-
8	&	5b	;	?
9	2015			com
10	to			php
11	%			=
12	html			-
13	d9			+
14	of			search
15	net			script
16	+			3e
17	a			lt
18	in			22
19	05			asp
20	?			amp

5.5 Transition of Detection Rate with the Increase of Benign Samples

The change in detection rate when the number of benign samples in the test data is increased in datasets A and B is shown in the Fig. 4 and 5.

The number of benign samples to be added was increased from the benign sample size of the test data by 6,000 samples up to 36,000 samples for comparison. The experiment was repeated so that all malignant samples were tested. The detection rate was calculated as the average of the results of repeated experiments. The evaluation indices were similarly validated using accuracy, precision, recall, and f1.

In both datasets A and B, the accuracy, precision, and f1 values decreased as the number of benign samples increased, but the recall value remained almost constant. In addition, there was a difference in the range of decline in the scores of the evaluation indices between datasets A and B. The accuracy value continued to decrease in accordance with the precision value in dataset A, while it remained around 0.9 in dataset B. For the f1 score, increasing the benign sample size of the test data by 24,000 resulted in a decrease to 0.55 for dataset A and 0.70 for dataset B.

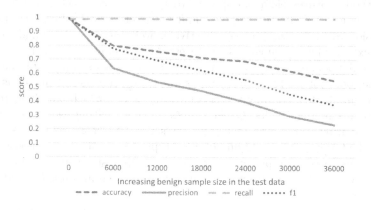

Fig. 4. Transition of accuracy on the dataset A

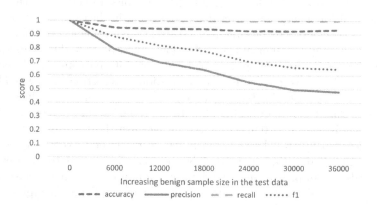

Fig. 5. Transition of accuracy on the dataset B

6   Discussion

6.1   Detection Rate and Linguistic Features by Attention Mechanism

It was confirmed that the detection using natural language processing and machine learning correctly learned and detected the features of malicious samples based on the given dataset, with a high accuracy. This accuracy is comparable to that of other previous studies, suggesting that the method is quantitatively effective. In addition, the results confirming the linguistic features suggest that the method captures elements specific to typical XSS attacks, which are the characteristics of malicious samples, and thus detection by linguistic features are considered to be qualitatively effective as well. On the other hand, comparing the extracted words among the datasets, the agreement rate of the top words is not as high as 50% even for the datasets of malicious samples obtained from the same collection source. This could be due to the influence of the dataset that was configured when training the classification model, which may have resulted in differences in the results. Other results include multiple words overlapping when comparing words extracted from the same dataset across classes. In particular, the top words focused on are often typical symbols that compose URLs. This is considered to represent a trend where linguistic features effective for classification are detected from the relationship between multiple focused words.

6.2   Transition of Detection Rate with the Increase of Benign Samples

When benign samples were increased, the detection rate decreased except for the recall score. This indicates that the number of cases in which the added benign samples were erroneously determined to be malicious was high. In other words, this is a situation where many over-detections occur in the case of unknown data, and is not considered to be practical in a real environment. Another possible reason for the high number of over-detections could be that the composition of the datasets used for training did not include a sufficient range and may have been biased. This was inferred from the variation in detection rates when benign samples were increased in datasets A and B. The rate of decline in dataset B was slower than the rate of decline in dataset A. The accuracy score for dataset B also remained around 0.9. This may be because the features of the benign samples learned by the classification model were closer to those of the added benign samples, resulting in fewer false positives compared to dataset A. In other words, it can be said that the datasets had an impact on the classification results, and that dataset B consisted of more generally benign samples.

6.3   Research Ethics

Although this research attempts to elucidate the principles of XSS attack detection, there is a large dependency on the training data of the classification model. Therefore, we consider that it does not lead to avoiding the detection of attacks.

6.4   Research Limitations

The malicious sample of the dataset used in this study is textual data of URLs collected from XSSed.com. Therefore, the XSS attacks targeted by this validation are limited. Moreover, these malicious samples are detoxified and not truly strings used in actual attack input. In other words, there is room for mentioning differences from actual attacks. In addition, the benign samples are data extracted from two different datasets. Since the classification model is affected by the datasets, there is room to examine the bias of the data.

7   Conclusion

In this study, we attempted to elucidate the features to focus on when detecting XSS attacks from the weights of the attention mechanism using a machine learning model that combines the LSTM and attention mechanisms. We also tested the utility of the classification model by increasing the number of benign samples. Experimental results confirmed that the classification model focused on words such as "<" and ">" used in typical XSS attacks and detected XSS attacks. However, even using malicious samples from the same collection source, we found that only 10 of the top 20 words focused on by the TP class matched. In other words, the words focused on by the classification model are influenced by the dataset used, and there is room for validation of the dataset. In addition, when the benign sample of the test data was increased by a factor of 5, the f1 score was found to decrease to a maximum of 0.55. In other words, detection methods based on machine learning models using vocabulary-based features of URLs [6,12,19] are considered to be of low utility when a realistic and valid dataset cannot be constructed, due to the high influence of the dataset used. This could potentially affect all URL-based detection methods, including unauthorized access detection as well as XSS attacks.

Future work is to verify the versatility and practicality of the dataset and the classification model, and to improve the detection performance when the number of benign samples is large.

References

1. AOL Inc. : Dmoz open directory project (2017). https://dmoz-odp.org/
2. Abadi, M., et al.: TensorFlow: large-scale machine learning on heterogeneous systems (2015). https://www.tensorflow.org/. Software available from tensorflow.org
3. Chollet, F., et al.: Keras (2015). https://keras.io
4. Corporation, T.M.: Cwe-79: improper neutralization of input during web page generation ('cross-site scripting') (2006–2022). https://cwe.mitre.org/data/definitions/79.html
5. Fang, Y., Huang, C., Xu, Y., Li, Y.: RLXSS: optimizing XSS detection model to defend against adversarial attacks based on reinforcement learning. Future Internet **11**(8), 177 (2019). https://www.mdpi.com/1999-5903/11/8/177
6. Fang, Y., Li, Y., Liu, L., Huang, C.: DeepXSS: cross site scripting detection based on deep learning. In: Proceedings of the 2018 International Conference on Computing and Artificial Intelligence, ICCAI 2018, pp. 47–51. Association for Computing Machinery, New York (2018). https://doi.org/10.1145/3194452.3194469
7. Habibi, G., Surantha, N.: XSS attack detection with machine learning and n-Gram methods. In: 2020 International Conference on Information Management and Technology (ICIMTech), pp. 516–520 (2020)

8. Hochreiter, S., Schmidhuber, J.: Long short-term memory. Neural Comput. **9**(8), 1735–1780 (1997)
9. Kaggle Inc. : kaggle (2017). https://www.kaggle.com/
10. Kaur, J., Garg, U.: A detailed survey on recent XSS web-attacks machine learning detection techniques. In: 2021 2nd Global Conference for Advancement in Technology (GCAT), pp. 1–6 (2021)
11. Krishnan, M., Lim, Y., Perumal, S., Palanisamy, G.: Detection and defending the XSS attack using novel hybrid stacking ensemble learning-based DNN approach. Digit. Commun. Netw. (2022). https://www.sciencedirect.com/science/article/pii/S2352864822001997
12. Lei, L., Chen, M., He, C., Li, D.: XSS detection technology based on LSTM-attention. In: 2020 5th International Conference on Control, Robotics and Cybernetics (CRC), pp. 175–180 (2020)
13. Maurel, H., Vidal, S., Rezk, T.: Statically identifying XSS using deep learning. Sci. Comput. Progr. **219**, 102810 (2022). https://www.sciencedirect.com/science/article/pii/S0167642322000430
14. Mimura, M.: Impact of benign sample size on binary classification accuracy. Expert Syst. Appl. **211**, 118630 (2023). https://www.sciencedirect.com/science/article/pii/S0957417422016773
15. Mokbal, F.M.M., Dan, W., Imran, A., Jiuchuan, L., Akhtar, F., Xiaoxi, W.: MLPXSS: an integrated XSS-based attack detection scheme in web applications using multilayer perceptron technique. IEEE Access **7**, 100567–100580 (2019)
16. Mokbal, F.M.M., Dan, W., Xiaoxi, W., Wenbin, Z., Lihua, F.: XGBXSS: an extreme gradient boosting detection framework for cross-site scripting attacks based on hybrid feature selection approach and parameters optimization. J. Inf. Secur. Appl. **58**, 102813 (2021). https://www.sciencedirect.com/science/article/pii/S2214212621000533
17. Olah, C.: Understanding LSTM Networks (2015). http://colah.github.io/posts/2015-08-Understanding-LSTMs/. Accessed 28 July 2022
18. Pedregosa, F., et al.: Scikit-learn: machine learning in python. J. Mach. Learn. Res. **12**, 2825–2830 (2011)
19. Raed, W.K., Methaq, T.G.: A hybrid of CNN and LSTM methods for securing web application against cross-site scripting attack. Indonesian J. Electr. Eng. Comput. Sci. **21**(2), 1022–1029 (2021)
20. Rodríguez, G.E., Torres, J.G., Flores, P., Benavides, D.E.: Cross-site scripting (XSS) attacks and mitigation: a survey. Comput. Netw. **166**, 106960 (2020). https://www.sciencedirect.com/science/article/pii/S1389128619311247
21. Sarmah, U., Bhattacharyya, D., Kalita, J.: A survey of detection methods for XSS attacks. J. Netw. Comput. Appl. **118**, 113–143 (2018). https://www.sciencedirect.com/science/article/pii/S1084804518302042
22. Sharafaldin, I., Lashkari, A.H., Ghorbani, A.A.: Toward generating a new intrusion detection dataset and intrusion traffic characterization. ICISSp **1**, 108–116 (2018)
23. The MITRE Corporation's Common Weakness Enumeration Program: 2022 cwe top 25 most dangerous software weaknesses (2022). https://cwe.mitre.org/top25/archive/2022/2022_cwe_top25.html. Accessed 28 Feb 2023
24. Vaswani, A., et al.: Attention is all you need. In: Advances in Neural Information Processing Systems, vol. 30 (2017)
25. Zhou, Y., Wang, P.: An ensemble learning approach for XSS attack detection with domain knowledge and threat intelligence. Comput. Secur. **82**, 261–269 (2019). https://www.sciencedirect.com/science/article/pii/S0167404818306370

Mining for Better: An Energy-Recycling Consensus Algorithm to Enhance Stability with Deep Learning

Zhen Xia[1], Zhenfu Cao[1,2]([✉]), Jiachen Shen[1]([✉]), Xiaolei Dong[1,2], Jun Zhou[1], Liming Fang[3,4], Zhe Liu[2], Chunpeng Ge[5], and Chunhua Su[6]

[1] Shanghai Key Laboratory of Trustworthy Computing,
East China Normal University, Shanghai, China
jcshen@sei.ecnu.edu.cn
[2] Zhejiang Lab, Hangzhou, China
zfcao@sei.ecnu.edu.cn
[3] College of Computer Science and Technology, Nanjing University of Aeronautics and Astronautics, Nanjing, China
[4] Science and Technology on Parallel and Distributed Processing Laboratory (PDL), Changsha, China
[5] Shandong University, Jinan, China
[6] University of Aizu, Fukushima, Japan

Abstract. As the most popular consensus algorithm for blockchain, the Proof-of-Work (PoW) is suffering from the inability of handling computing power fluctuations. Meanwhile, PoW consumes a significant amount of energy without producing actual value. To address these issues, this paper proposes a deep learning-based consensus framework called Proof-of-Improvement (PoI), which recycles the energy from mining blocks to improve the blockchain itself. In PoI, a new reward mechanism is used to encourage miners to include the high-accuracy model in their blocks. Then, based on PoI, a difficulty adjustment algorithm is designed. Experiments are done on real-world data and the result shows the proposed algorithm's proficiency in preserving block time stability with fluctuating hash rates. To the best of the authors' knowledge, PoI is the first to handle both energy recycling and difficulty adjustment concurrently.

Keywords: Blockchain · Consensus algorithm · Computing power utilization · Difficulty adjustment algorithm · Deep learning

1 Introduction

Since Bitcoin [21]'s proposal, permissionless blockchain technology brings endless possibilities to various fields with its extreme decentralization, high transparency, and verifiability, and is considered the core technology for realizing the next generation of Web. The consensus algorithm is the cornerstone to achieving these features, and it also affects the performance, stability, and security of the

© The Author(s), under exclusive license to Springer Nature Singapore Pte Ltd. 2023
W. Meng et al. (Eds.): ISPEC 2023, LNCS 14341, pp. 579–594, 2023.
https://doi.org/10.1007/978-981-99-7032-2_34

blockchain. As the most successful application of blockchain, Bitcoin uses the Proof-of-Work (PoW) algorithm. So far, PoW and its variants have been adopted by more than 430 cryptocurrencies [1].

Even the most common consensus algorithm, PoW, has some weaknesses. Firstly, the difficulty adjustment algorithm (DAA) of PoW lacks the ability to cope with fluctuations in computing power. For example, the Price of Bitcoin, a digital currency used PoW, has fluctuated wildly in recent years, leading to large swings in the total hash rate of all miners, which in turn affects the stability of block times. The average block time by the end of June 2021 was 1.5 times the desired block time due to a large decline in the price of Bitcoin. The substantial variances in block time will have a significant impact on transaction processing speed, which is a critical performance metric for the user experience of a digital currency. Simply shortening the block time is not a solution because fewer computed blocks will result in inaccurate estimates of computing power and difficulty targets.

Furthermore, since PoW consumes a huge amount of energy to calculate a valid proof of work, no actual value is produced. The minimum yearly electricity consumption for mining Bitcoin is 23.38 TWh [17]. Several new schemes have been put up to address this issue. On the one hand, many new consensus algorithms have been proposed, such as Proof-of-Stake (PoS) [13]. However, a notable concern associated with PoS is its potential impact on the democratic nature of the system due to the influence of wealth concentration. On the other hand, meaningless hash computation in the PoW is transformed into actual tasks in blockchain consensus. Consensus mechanisms constructed based on this idea are generally referred to as Proof-of-Useful-Work (PoUW). These new algorithms not only address the issue of wasted energy but also make it possible to use blockchain in more scenarios. The paper intends to take this one step further and apply it to more scenarios of the blockchain.

Motivation. Although PoUW has reduced energy consumption and used computing resources in various scenarios, the blockchain remains suffering from the instability of block time. It's resulting in a poor transaction experience for cryptocurrencies, which is at present the most widely used application of blockchain. Is it possible to improve the blockchain itself through PoUW? The paper aims to start from this point and recycle the power of computation during the mining process to strengthen the blockchain itself.

Contribution. In this paper, we propose a consensus framework based on deep learning, named Proof-of-Improvement (PoI), which recycles the energy from mining blocks to improve the blockchain itself. Moreover, based on PoI, a new difficulty adjustment algorithm is proposed to improve the stability of block time, enabling the improvement of stability while reusing wasted computational power. To the best of our knowledge, PoI is the first to handle both energy recycling and difficulty adjustment at the same time. The main contributions of this paper are as follows:

1. Proposes a consensus framework, PoI, by combining deep learning with blockchain. PoI utilizes the wasted computing power of PoW to yield actual value. A new block structure is also designed to support block validation without adding participants and minimizing changes to PoW.
2. Designs a difficulty adjustment algorithm based on PoI to adjust the network difficulty target in real-time environments with fluctuating computing power.
3. Discusses the extension of PoI to more scenarios for improving blockchain performance and security.

The remaining part of the paper proceeds as follows. We will present the related work in Sect. 2. In Sect. 3 we present PoI in detail. And we perform simulation experiments and analysis in Sect. 4. In Sect. 5, we discuss the scalability of PoI for application scenarios. Finally, the paper is summarized in Sect. 6.

2   Related Work

2.1   Difficulty Adjustment Algorithm

To increase the stability of block time, researchers proposed a number of improvements based on the Bitcoin [21] difficulty adjustment algorithm. Related studies can be categorized into two types: active adjustment and passive adjustment. Active adjustment algorithms involve miners actively reporting their computational power and adjusting the network difficulty target based on aggregated results. This approach requires miners to commit computational power through pledge shares and involves highly complex algorithms to identify and defend against attacks from malicious nodes [6].

On the other side, passive adjustment algorithms need nodes to estimate the network's overall computational capacity based on information in the chain and then adjust the difficulty target accordingly. Some studies optimize hash rate estimation algorithms, such as employing the least squares [19], linear predictor [26], weak solutions [9]. In a recent study, Zhang et al. [25] attempted to calculate the network's difficulty by using a two-layer neural network model. However, it is challenging to implement the concept because it only provides a model without an approach to working with blockchain systems.

2.2   Energy-Recycling Consensus

In terms of energy recycling, researchers used useful work to replace the hash search task in the Nakamoto Consensus (NC). Primecoin [12] was the first proposed solution, requiring miners to search for long prime number chains. However, the Cunningham chains discovered by miners had no real applications. Subsequently, several similar problems have been applied to consensus algorithms, including matrix computation [24], orthogonal vector solutions, the 3SUM problem, and all-pairs shortest path (APSP) [4] as proof-of-work puzzles. However, these methods show some innate non-deployable problems.

In addition to incorporating mathematical problems into consensus algorithms, many scholars have attempted to address the issue through other types of tasks. Permacoin [20] look into file or file fragment storage and memory using Proof-of-retrievability (PoR), where mining is not based on computing but rather is linked to storage resources. PieceWork [8] separates proof-of-work into internal and external puzzles in order to divert wasted effort toward other goals through outsourcing, such as spam protection and DoS mitigation. PoNW [11] utilizes incremental verifiable computing (IVC) to apply the computational power consumed by proof-of-work to assist in system verification. Huang et al. [10] propose Proof-of-Data (PoD) in a mobile crowdsourcing-aware scenario, using computational power for valuable data quality verification tasks. The computational abilities of miners used in the mining process are applied to diverse sectors in the above research.

Several studies recently looked into the use of blockchain and machine learning to utilize energy for model training and prediction. Li et al. [16] integrated biomedical image segmentation tasks with blockchain systems. PoDL [7] combined deep learning with blockchain, requiring miners to complete a given task to generate blocks; PoLe [18] built on this approach to improve dataset privacy. Coin.AI [3] proposed a proof-of-storage scheme to reward users for providing storage for deep learning models. In the context of federated learning, PoFL [23] is a consensus algorithm based on federated learning, introducing two roles-data provider and requester-allowing miners to contribute their computational power to training models. These studies were able to leverage wasted computing resources, but they also made major modifications to the entire blockchain system, such as adding users, and did not completely secure the privacy of training and testing dataset.

3   PoI Design

In this section, we will introduce the design of PoI. The PoI model will be briefly introduced initially, and then the data structure, mining and verification procedure, difficulty adjustment algorithm, and reward mechanism will be thoroughly discussed.

3.1   Overview and Notaions

As mentioned above, there are many studies proposing the integration of deep learning, federated learning, and other technologies with blockchain systems. However, all of these solutions have major changes to the blockchain structure. In our design, we want to integrate deep learning and blockchain naturally and minimally invasively to support nodes using data of the chain for deep learning training and prediction during the mining process.

Therefore, our system structure remains consistent with NC without adding external participants. This unique design allows the blockchain to improve its performance with deep learning. On top of this, a new difficulty adjustment algorithm is produced to address changes in the network's computational power. Additionally, deep learning technology gets improved on a daily basis. We believe that the deep learning models used in blockchain must be unrestricted for the integration of blockchain with deep learning to be able to adapt to the trend. The PoI algorithm is introduced in more detail below, and the notations used are shown in Table 1.

Table 1. Summary of notations

Notation	Description
V	Version number of the blockchain
$Hash_\alpha$	Hash of α
B	the B-th Block
i	# of miners
Tx	A set of transactions
τ	The header of the block
M	The model in the block
T_{expect}	Expect block time
P_t	A set of parameters for deep learning tasks
E_m	Evaluation baseline for deep learning tasks
m	Size of the dataset fragment
S_t, S_v, S_p	Dataset size for training, validation and testing
D_t, D_v, D_p	Dataset for training, validation and testing
H_c	Combinatorial hash rate

3.2 Data Structure

The block structure of PoI essentially follows the block structure of NC in order to maximize compatibility. However, the current block structure lacks any model-related parameters. In order to realize the mining and verification process based on deep learning, PoI replaces the Nonce number field in the original block header with the hash value of the model. The data structure of PoI is shown in Fig. 1. The block header structure of PoI is as follows:

- $Hash_{prev}$: A hash of previous block.
- $Version$: A version number of the block.
- $Height$: Block's height of the blockchain.
- $Hash_{tx}$: A hash of the root of the merkle tree of this block's transactions.
- $Timestamp$: Unix timestamp.
- $Target$: Difficulty target for this block.
- $Hash_m$: A hash of deep learning model.

To save storage, deep learning models are stored on distributed storage systems such as IPFS [5]. There is no need for extra space to store addresses as distributed storage systems use content addressing, also known as CID, to identify locations.

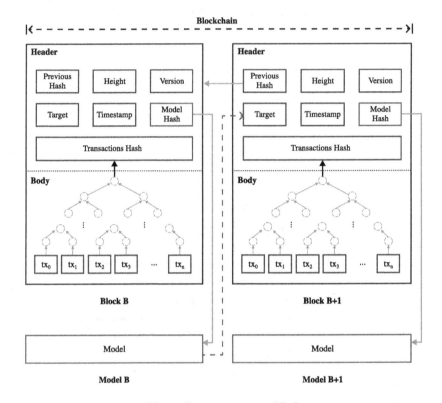

Fig. 1. Data structure of PoI

3.3   Mining Process

Define the system parameters before the mining process starts, such as the following: A version number V to track protocol upgrades; expected block time T_{expect} (e.g. 10 min for Bitcoin); a set P_t of parameters for deep learning tasks, such as model structure, hyperparameters, the size of the dataset and the evaluation metric; evaluation baseline E_m of the model.

These parameters outline the models that are used to train the nodes and the criteria used for evaluating the models' performance after receiving blocks. Deep learning tasks in PoI must be related to the blockchain system itself and require only data from the chain to complete the training and prediction process. In this paper, PoI is stated with the example task of predicting the network-wide computations. For a given task, there are multiple methods to choose from. There are many options for evaluation metrics depending on the type of model, such as accuracy and MSE (accuracy is used as an example in this paper). Similar to Bitcoin, the blockchain maintainers decide and update system parameters, which are following synced to all participants as version upgrades.

Algorithm 1 The block mining process

1: $Tx \leftarrow$ getTransactions()
2: $\tau \leftarrow$ setHeaderInfo(B, Tx)
3: $M \leftarrow$ buildModels(P_t)
4: $D_t \leftarrow$ getPrevBlocks($B - S_t$,$B - S_v$)
5: $D_v \leftarrow$ getPrevBlocks($B - S_v$,$B - 1$)
6: **while** $Hash_{\tau'} > Target$ **do**
7:     $M \leftarrow$ trainModel(D_t)
8:     $E \leftarrow$ validateModel(D_v)
9:     **if** $E < E_m$ **then**
10:        Continue
11:     **else**
12:        $Hash_M \leftarrow$ hash(M)
13:        $\tau' \leftarrow$ setHeaderInfo(τ,$Hash_M$)
14:        $Hash_{\tau'} \leftarrow$ hash(τ')
15:     **end if**
16: **end while**
17: $Block \leftarrow$ createBlock(τ');
18: Broadcast($Block$)

Algorithm 1 gives the pseudo-code of the mining process in PoI. Miners train the model and try to find a block that meets $Target$. Specifically, before mining the block, the miner first selects a set of transactions Tx and fills the information in the block header (Line 1–2). After that, the miner will perform deep learning model training until reaching the minimum model accuracy E_m. Next, the miner needs to keep training and update the $Hash_m$ in the block header while maintaining accuracy until the block's hash meets the difficulty $Target$ (Line 6–16). Finally, the found blocks are broadcasted to the network (Line 17–18). The node that finds the block first will get the bookkeeping rights and receive a reward.

In the mining process, miners need to train a deep learning model and make it meet three requirements:

1. Training with model parameters P_t and the specified dataset (described later).
2. Achieve the minimum model accuracy E_m.
3. $Hash_m$ can make the hash of the block meet $Target$.

Besides, there are some differences compared to the general deep learning training and validation process. First, when building models, to enhance security and prevent model pre-training or sharing, we add a secure mapping layer

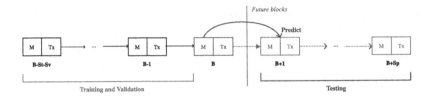

Fig. 2. Overview of model and datasets in PoI

(SML) in the front of the model, which is detailed in [18]. This results in everyone's training process being on the same main road, but with slight differences. Because of this and the difficulty target, the mining process is random rather than deterministic. Second, in terms of the dataset, the nodes will use only the data on the chain. Because each bit of data on the public chain is transparent and available to all, We design an approach to evaluate models as shown in Fig. 2. When the training dataset size is S_t, the validation dataset size is S_v, and the test dataset size is S_p, miner i needs to use at least $S_t + S_v$ closest blocks prior to block B for training and self-validation when mining block B. After the block is verified, the model in block B will be used in the next mining epoch. Node i will validate the performance of the model in block B against the next S_p blocks and receive a training reward for doing so, as described in Sect. 3.5. Because block data are public, all nodes are able to reconstruct the dataset from these $S_t + S_v$ blocks. When the training dataset is undersized, the consensus algorithm of the blockchain is temporarily rolled back to PoW. Finally, in order to make the hash of the block match the difficulty $Target$, miners need to keep searching for suitable models. With the above requirements satisfied, miners can use any way to find it, such as adding the training epoch while maintaining accuracy, expanding the size of the training dataset, etc.

It is difficult for miners to find a model that meets all the requirements, but in contrast, it is easier for other nodes to validate the model. It complies with the norms of proof-of-useful-work algorithms. After a block is received by the full node, the block needs to be verified according to Algorithm 2. Initially, the node needs to check the block's validity, which includes verifying the hash satisfies the difficulty $Target$, its parent block is locally accessible and the transactions are valid (Line 1–5). Second, the node needs to construct the validation dataset (Line 6–12). The validation dataset will be composed of 3 parts from the $S_t + S_v$ blocks in front of the current block, each part has m data. The first two parts are the beginning and ending data, while the remaining part is chosen at random according to the hash of the block. The nodes then use these data to validate that the accuracy of the model in the block satisfies the baseline E_m (Line 13). The model should produce highly accurate prediction results given that these data are actually a part of the training dataset, thus it has to be taken into consideration while setting the accuracy baseline. Finally, the model is used to predict the metrics of the next mining epoch (Line 17). In the example task, the difficulty target for the next mining epoch is adjusted based on the model's output.

Algorithm 2 The block verification process

Input: B: Recieved block; m: The size of the dataset fragment
Output: True or False
1:   verifyTransactions(B)
2:   verifyBlockTarget(B)
3:   **if** any above verification fails **then**
4:       **return** False
5:   **end if**
6:   $M \leftarrow$ getModel(B)
7:   $Hash_B \leftarrow$ hash(B)
8:   $\alpha \leftarrow$ getNonce($B - S_t$, $B - 1$, m, $Hash_B$)
9:   $D_1 \leftarrow$ getPrevBlocks($B - S_t$, $B - S_t + m$)
10: $D_2 \leftarrow$ getPrevBlocks($B - 1 - m$, $B - 1$)
11: $D_3 \leftarrow$ getPrevBlocks($B - \alpha - m$, $B - \alpha$)
12: $D' \leftarrow$ createDataset(D_1, D_2, D_3)
13: $E \leftarrow$ validateModel(M, D')
14: **if** $E < E_m$ **then**
15:      **return** False
16: **else**
17:      predict(M)
18:      **return** True
19: **end if**

3.4   Deep Learning-Based Difficulty Control

In this paper, PoI is instantiated to adjust the difficulty to cope with computing power fluctuations. The task of the model is to predict the computing power for the next epoch. The input of the model is the information of the previous blocks and the output is the computing power prediction for the next mining epoch, represented by the hash rate H^{est}. PoI does not restrict the structure of the model, in other words, the blockchain network can choose any block structures. The choice of models is beyond the scope of this paper.

A hash attempt consists of generating a random nonce and performing two SHA-256 processes in NC. But in PoI, a hash attempt involves an epoch of model training and two SHA-256 operations, which we refer to as the combinatorial hash. In this paper, the task of the model is also to predict the combinatorial hash rate (H_c) for the next mining epoch.

Based on the mining and validation processes mentioned above, nodes utilize the model's output, the estimated hash rate H_c^{est}, for calculating the difficulty of the next mining epoch. The calculation of the difficulty target for the n-th round is shown as (1), where $Target^n$ is the difficulty target for the n-th round, $Target_{max}$ is the maximum output value of the hash function(for SHA-256, $Target_{max}$ is a 256-bit binary string consisting of all ones), and t_{expect} is the expected block time (e.g., 10 min for Bitcoin).

$$Target^n = \frac{Target_{max}}{H_c^{est} \times t_{expect}} \tag{1}$$

In the difficulty adjustment process, we assume that the hash rate and FLOPs change in direct proportion. Since deep model training is incorporated into the consensus mechanism, GPU machines do not have an advantage over ASIC machines. We believe that the above assumption is reasonable when mining with GPUs. In addition, PoI follows the longest chain rule in NC when dealing with forks.

3.5   Reward Mechanism

PoI requires a reward mechanism to incentivize participants to comply with the specified protocol and include models with sufficiently high accuracy in the blocks, rather than just meeting the minimum accuracy requirements of the network. Similar to public blockchains, the miner i generating block B will receive a fixed reward and transaction fees.

Furthermore, to encourage miners to include models with sufficiently high accuracy in the blocks, we design a delayed reward mechanism and distributed more than half of the total reward amount to this reward. The delayed reward will be given to the miner based on the actual performance of the model in the future, and the amount of reward will be correlated with the accuracy of the model. These delayed rewards can be used once a block is confirmed by the network based on the longest chain principle.

In the task of predicting hash rates, nodes will use the next S_t blocks after the block as a test set to evaluate the models in B, and the amount of reward that can be used will be determined based on the accuracy.

4   Simulation Experiment

In this section, PoI is evaluated through simulations based on real-world data. First of all, we evaluate the performance of PoI in coping with fluctuating computing power by using historical data from Bitcoin. Then, we simulate the behavior of cheaters to analyze the effectiveness of our cheat detection approach.

A computer with an Intel Xeon CPU (2.00 GHz), Nvidia V100 GPU, and 16 GB RAM is used to simulate mining processes based on historical data. We randomly select real data of Bitcoin in its history and test the performance of the consensus algorithm under hash rate fluctuations by simulating the operation of PoW and PoI. The final data chosen for the experiment is the block data of Bitcoin with a height between 629775 and 636775 (7000 blocks in total).

For model selection, CEEMDAN-GRU [27] is used with a batch size of 8 and a dropout rate of 0.1. It is a time series prediction model, the input is the time of past mining epochs and the estimated computing power, and the output is the prediction of computing power for the next epoch. Figure 3 shows the performance to predict the hash rate. We selected the first 50 records to check the predictions in detail. It is observed that the model fits the overall trend well, but there are still some gaps with the real values in the specific values.

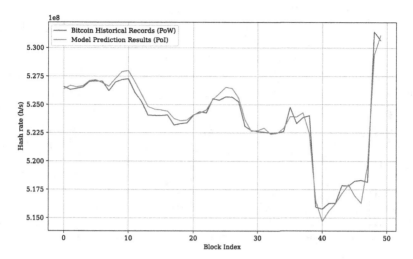

Fig. 3. Hash rate predict results with deep learning.

Difficulty Adjustment with PoI. The change in hash rate during the time period that corresponds to the above-mentioned historical data is illustrated in Fig. 4. For example, there are specific instances where the hash rate of all miners experiences a sudden and significant increase. These instances can be observed near the 1000th, 3000th, and 5500th blocks.

To make it easier to see the changes in the data, we sliding average the data with a sliding average window of 100. Figure 5 shows the PoW and PoI block time under fluctuating hash rate. It can be seen that PoI has stronger stability compared to PoW.

To quantify the stability of block time, we calculated the average and variance of block time, as shown in Table 2. It is evident that in terms of average block time, PoW also reaches the expected level of 10 min. There is not much difference between PoI and PoW in terms of average block production time. However, in terms of the stability of block time, PoW cannot cope well with fluctuations in hash rate, resulting in a large variance. PoI exhibits better stability because it can use deep learning models to predict the entire network computing power for the next mining epoch, adjusting difficulty targets in advance to adapt to changes.

Table 2. The average and variance of the block time (min)

Algorithm	Average of block time	Variance of block time
Proof-of-Work	10.2232	145.5152
Proof-of-Improvement	10.0001	8.2032

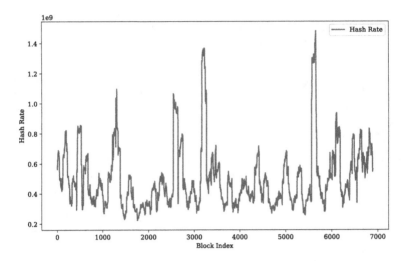

Fig. 4. Hash rate of the data.

Detection of Miners' Cheating. Malicious miners may not use the specified parameters during the mining process to train the model, which can give them an unfair advantage and impact the effectiveness of PoI. Due to the uniformity of the global parameters, nodes can easily detect cheating behavior by miners in terms of model structure and hyperparameters. To address cheating behavior by miners on the training dataset, the paper proposes a method to verify whether miners have used the specified dataset during the model training process based on the fragmentation of the training data in the PoI verification process. In this section, we will experimentally validate the effectiveness of this cheating detection method. In the experiment, the CIFAR-10 [14] dataset is selected, which is a widely used dataset in deep learning. It consists of 60,000 32 × 32-pixel images divided into 10 different object categories, serving as a benchmark for evaluating image classification algorithms. The AlexNet [15] model is used in this experiment.

The experiment simulates both honest miners and malicious miners. Honest participants participate in PoI mining according to the system's specifications. Conversely, malicious miners train using the specified training dataset. The dataset is divided into two non-intersecting parts, one considered as a compliant dataset and the other not. Honest miners use the compliant dataset for training, while malicious miners use the other part of the data for training. Finally, we verify both parties' models using the PoI verification algorithm, and the results are shown in Table 3. It can be observed from the results that the accuracy of the malicious miner's model during the verification process is significantly lower than that of the honest model, enabling the blockchain network to easily detect cheating behavior.

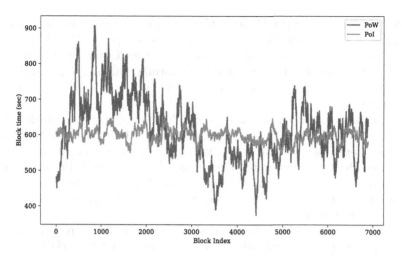

Fig. 5. Performance of PoI and PoW in terms of block time

Table 3. Model accuracy under honesty and cheating

Model	Accuracy
Model (the honest participant with compliant dataset)	99.2756%
Model (the malicious participant with cheating dataset)	71.5733%

5 Discussion

In this section, the applications of PoI beyond enhancing the stability of block chain are discussed. According to our analysis, PoI possesses the following characteristics:

1. Model pluggability: The models used by miners in the mining process are pluggable. As deep learning models continue to improve, the models in the system can also be upgraded to enhance the performance of the system for specific individuals.
2. Task compatibility: PoI's system models are flexible to support any task that is directly related to the blockchain. Its system architecture is generic and can be adapted to different tasks by adjusting the system parameters.
3. System non-invasiveness: In terms of PoI system model architecture, it matters to note that there are no extra participants required for its implementation. Basically, this means that the current commercial blockchain that is in use may be effortlessly upgraded to the PoI consensus without requiring any changes to the underlying business model. As a result, there will be a smooth transition and the integrity of the current system will be preserved, allowing stakeholders to continue working effectively and efficiently within the established framework.

As research into the combination of blockchain technology and deep learning continues, it is becoming clear that many different aspects of blockchain could benefit considerably from the application of the deep learning approach. In this paper, an instance of PoI is presented by performing the task of predicting hash rates. Nevertheless, it is important to note that it is only a subset of what PoI can achieve.

For instance, certain studies made use of deep learning methods to detect illegal activities within the Bitcoin network [22]. In order to evaluate the validity of transactions, they used a deep learning model to extract 19 essential features from the Bitcoin network. This approach has the potential to be implemented within the blockchain system via PoI, allowing the energy used during the blockchain mining process to be redistributed toward improving the financial security of the blockchain.

In a different scenario, Baek et al. [2] proposed a deep learning-based detection method for network-level distributed denial-of-service (DDoS) attacks against Bitcoin. DDoS attacks may target Bitcoin networks, possibly by faking messages with Transmission Control Protocol (TCP) serial numbers. This study uses Bitcoin block data and transaction records to identify DDoS attack data based on the multi-layer perceptron. The proposed model can be used in combination with PoI to boost the blockchain system's robustness in opposition to attacks.

Meanwhile, some limitations of PoI are also noticed. Firstly, PoI can only be used on blockchain-related tasks and requires that the task can complete the training and prediction process using only on-chain data. Secondly, the complexity of the model has restrictions. The nodes need to download the model during the validation process, and the complexity of the model affects the communication overhead. These topics are the direction of our future work.

We are positive that PoI will provide a larger range of application possibilities as the body of research in this field continues to expand and change. It is feasible to open up new avenues for blockchain technology by utilizing deep learning, which will ultimately improve efficiency, security, and adaptability across the board.

6   Conclusion

In this paper, we proposed a novel consensus algorithm called Proof of Improvement (PoI) that integrates deep learning into the mining process of blockchains. It recycles the energy used to mine blocks in order to enhance the blockchain itself. A difficulty adjustment technique is also designed in this paper using PoI to improve block time stability while energy recycling. The performance and security of PoI and its corresponding DAA are evaluated in experiments using real-world data. The results demonstrate that PoI exhibits greater stability compared to PoW in scenarios with fluctuating hash rates.

The integration of deep learning with blockchain continues to evolve, and PoI is expected to find broader applications. We plan to keep on this research in the future, optimize the features of PoI and extend it to more scenarios.

Acknowledgements. This work was supported in part by the National Key Research and Development Program of China (Grant No. 2022YFB2701400), in part by the National Natural Science Foundation of China (Grant No. 62132005, 62172162, 62172161, U22B2029, 62272228).

References

1. Map of coins: BTC Map. https://mapofcoins.com/bitcoin. Accessed 09 May 2023
2. Baek, U.J., Ji, S.H., Park, J.T., Lee, M.S., Park, J.S., Kim, M.S.: DDoS attack detection on bitcoin ecosystem using deep-learning. In: 2019 20th Asia-Pacific Network Operations and Management Symposium (APNOMS), pp. 1–4 (2019)
3. Baldominos, A., Saez, Y.: Coin.AI: a proof-of-useful-work scheme for blockchain-based distributed deep learning. Entropy **21**(8), 723 (2019)
4. Ball, M., Rosen, A., Sabin, M., Vasudevan, P.N.: Proofs of useful work. Cryptology ePrint Archive (2017)
5. Benet, J.: IPFS - Content Addressed, Versioned, P2P File System (2014)
6. Bissias, G., Thibodeau, D., Levine, B.N.: Bonded mining: difficulty adjustment by miner commitment. In: Pérez-Solà, C., Navarro-Arribas, G., Biryukov, A., Garcia-Alfaro, J. (eds.) DPM/CBT -2019. LNCS, vol. 11737, pp. 372–390. Springer, Cham (2019). https://doi.org/10.1007/978-3-030-31500-9_24
7. Chenli, C., Li, B., Shi, Y., Jung, T.: Energy-recycling blockchain with proof-of-deep-learning. In: 2019 IEEE International Conference on Blockchain and Cryptocurrency (ICBC), pp. 19–23 (2019)
8. Daian, P., Eyal, I., Juels, A., Sirer, E.G.: (Short Paper) PieceWork: generalized outsourcing control for proofs of work. In: Brenner, M., et al. (eds.) FC 2017. LNCS, vol. 10323, pp. 182–190. Springer, Cham (2017). https://doi.org/10.1007/978-3-319-70278-0_11
9. Feng, W., Cao, Z., Shen, J., Dong, X.: RTPoW: a proof-of-work consensus scheme with real-time difficulty adjustment algorithm. In: 2021 IEEE 27th International Conference on Parallel and Distributed Systems (ICPADS), pp. 233–240 (2021)
10. Huang, J., et al.: BlockSense: towards trustworthy mobile crowdsensing via proof-of-data blockchain. IEEE Trans. Mob. Comput. 1–17 (2022)
11. Kattis, A., Bonneau, J.: Proof of necessary work: succinct state verification with fairness guarantees. Cryptology ePrint Archive (2020)
12. King, S.: Primecoin: Cryptocurrency with prime number proof-of-work. July 7th **1**(6) (2013)
13. King, S., Nadal, S.: PPCoin: peer-to-peer crypto-currency with proof-of-stake. self-published paper, August **19**(1) (2012)
14. Krizhevsky, A.: Learning multiple layers of features from tiny images (2009)
15. Krizhevsky, A., Sutskever, I., Hinton, G.E.: Imagenet classification with deep convolutional neural networks. Commun. ACM **60**(6), 84–90 (2017)
16. Li, B., Chenli, C., Xu, X., Jung, T., Shi, Y.: Exploiting computation power of blockchain for biomedical image segmentation. In: 2019 IEEE/CVF Conference on Computer Vision and Pattern Recognition Workshops (CVPRW), pp. 2802–2811 (2019)
17. Li, J., Li, N., Peng, J., Cui, H., Wu, Z.: Energy consumption of cryptocurrency mining: a study of electricity consumption in mining cryptocurrencies. Energy **168**, 160–168 (2019)

18. Liu, Y., Lan, Y., Li, B., Miao, C., Tian, Z.: Proof of learning (PoLe): empowering neural network training with consensus building on blockchains. Comput. Netw. **201**, 108594 (2021)
19. Meshkov, D., Chepurnoy, A., Jansen, M.: Short paper: revisiting difficulty control for blockchain systems. In: Garcia-Alfaro, J., Navarro-Arribas, G., Hartenstein, H., Herrera-Joancomartí, J. (eds.) ESORICS/DPM/CBT -2017. LNCS, vol. 10436, pp. 429–436. Springer, Cham (2017). https://doi.org/10.1007/978-3-319-67816-0_25
20. Miller, A., Juels, A., Shi, E., Parno, B., Katz, J.: Permacoin: repurposing bitcoin work for data preservation. In: 2014 IEEE Symposium on Security and Privacy, pp. 475–490. IEEE (2014)
21. Nakamoto, S.: Bitcoin: a peer-to-peer electronic cash system, p. 9 (2008)
22. Nerurkar, P.: Illegal activity detection on bitcoin transaction using deep learning. Soft Comput. **27**(9), 5503–5520 (2023)
23. Qu, X., Wang, S., Hu, Q., Cheng, X.: Proof of federated learning: a novel energy-recycling consensus algorithm. IEEE Trans. Parallel Distrib. Syst. **32**(8), 2074–2085 (2021)
24. Shoker, A.: Sustainable blockchain through proof of exercise. In: 2017 IEEE 16th International Symposium on Network Computing and Applications (NCA), pp. 1–9. IEEE (2017)
25. Zhang, S., Ma, X.: A general difficulty control algorithm for proof-of-work based blockchains. In: ICASSP 2020–2020 IEEE International Conference on Acoustics, Speech and Signal Processing (ICASSP), pp. 3077–3081 (2020)
26. Zheng, K., Zhang, S., Ma, X.: Difficulty prediction for proof-of-work based blockchains. In: 2020 IEEE 21st International Workshop on Signal Processing Advances in Wireless Communications (SPAWC), pp. 1–5 (2020)
27. Zhou, F., Huang, Z., Zhang, C.: Carbon price forecasting based on CEEMDAN and LSTM. Appl. Energy **311**, 118601 (2022)

SIOCEN: Secure Integrity Verification of Outsourced Data in Cloud Storage using Blockchain

Ajay Chandra Korlapati[1], Sanjeet Kumar Nayak[1(✉)] [ID],
Partha Sarathi Chakraborty[2][ID], and Somanath Tripathy[2][ID]

[1] Department of Computer Science and Engineering, IIITDM Kancheepuram,
Chennai, India
{ced18i029,sanjeetn}@iiitdm.ac.in
[2] Department of Computer Science and Engineering, IIT Patna, Patna, India
{partha_1921cs26,som}@iitp.ac.in

Abstract. Storing large volumes of data is a bottleneck on edge devices. Thus, Cloud Storage Technologies have emerged as a viable alternative for large-scale data storage. However, the data owner loses control of the file (once uploaded), which may lead to data integrity issues. Even though there are existing schemes to check the integrity of the files using a third-party auditor, they rely on the unrealistic assumption that the auditors are completely trustworthy. It has been reported in many works of literature that auditors sometimes collude with the cloud server to cheat the system. In this paper, we propose a scheme named secure integrity verification of outsourced data in cloud storage using blockchain (SIOCEN) which protects the system from entity collusion. Using smart contract, we enforce the incentive mechanism in the scheme, which is the most appealing feature of the SIOCEN that increases fairness. The security of the proposed scheme is analysed and proved to be secure. We implement the SIOCEN system on Ethereum network and do a performance analysis, showing the effectiveness of the proposed system.

Keywords: Integrity Verification · Auditing · Cloud Storage · Blockchain · Outsourced Data · Security

1 Introduction

One of the most crucial resources for every organization is data. Regardless of whether you're an individual or a business, data storage has grown to be a critical concern. There has been an increasing trend in the usage of on-demand Cloud Storage Systems. Data is sent over a network, usually the Internet, and kept on distant storage systems where it is maintained, managed, backed up, and made accessible to users as part of a cloud storage service model. Users just pay a per-consumption monthly fee for their cloud data storage.

© The Author(s), under exclusive license to Springer Nature Singapore Pte Ltd. 2023
W. Meng et al. (Eds.): ISPEC 2023, LNCS 14341, pp. 595–613, 2023.
https://doi.org/10.1007/978-981-99-7032-2_35

Though Cloud Storage technologies have many benefits like cost-saving, accessibility, usability, synchronization and sharing benefits, they also have several security threats and privacy concerns. Once a file is uploaded by the data owner/consumer, the control of the file is lost by the owner. The server/cloud service provider, if malicious, can read the contents of the data, can delete parts of the file or can also tamper with the data.

To ensure integrity of the data once uploaded, cryptographic algorithms called Proofs of Retrievability (PoR) were proposed [1]. These schemes are used to guarantee that the server has not tampered the uploaded file. A third person, called Auditor, is introduced into the scheme, who sends a set of challenges to the server, and the server has to response with the correct solution to prove that it has actually stored the file. It monitors the issues of the integrity of the stored files, but it also has other security issues which need to be solved. The Auditor, who is newly introduced into the system, may not be completely trustworthy, and this could lead to a loss of privacy for the owner. This is why we need to choose/devise a proper algorithm that not only solves the file integrity problem but also takes care of other problems like the confidentiality of the file.

Even if we consider that the PoR schemes are completely secure, the basic assumption of such schemes is that the Owner and Auditor are completely trustworthy. This may not be the case in real-life situations. If we assume a Real-Life system of a File Owner, Cloud Service Provider (Server) and Auditor, there is a possibility of one cheating the other for monetary purposes. Hence, we use blockchain technology to try and implement a system where all the parties may not trust each other but have to work together.

Blockchain, a tamper-resistant distributed ledger, has seen several use cases. Blockchain increases trust, security, transparency, and the traceability of data shared across a network. Several works have used blockchain as a judge to settle disputes among involved parties [2,6]. With the support of smart contracts, we can reduce fraudulent activity using preset conditions coded into the smart contract. This also results in the design of fault-tolerant systems, since a single person cannot control the whole system. Smart Contracts also make the whole system autonomous, i.e. there is no single control point or need for intermediaries. In this paper, we propose a blockchain based auditing protocol for cloud storage, named as SIOCEN. Also, we analyse and show that the system is secure and privacy-preserving. We consider all the corrupt cases and argue that the designed system is secure in all cases.

Our contributions can be summarized as:

- We design a blockchain based auditing protocol for any outsourced data stored in a cloud storage system.
- We ensure that the privacy of the data being stored in the cloud is preserved.
- We use a blockchain based payment service as an incentive for the parties involved in the system.
- We analyse the security of our proposed system.
- We implement a prototype version of SIOCEN on Ethereum Network and also do performance analysis, showing effectiveness of the proposed system.

The rest of this paper is organised as follows. Section 2, describes the related work on integrity verification of outsourced data which stored in the cloud and presents the preliminaries in Sect. 3. The proposed SIOCEN system model and its design goals are present in Sect. 4. We describe the construction of our proposed scheme and its correctness proof in Sect. 5. Subsequently, in Sect. 6, we present the security analysis of the scheme. Section 7 presents the implementation result of SIOCEN and Sect. 8 gives the performance evaluation of our proposed model in terms of computation cost. This paper finally concludes in Sect. 9 with discussion on future improvements.

2   Related Work

Many new technologies and frameworks have been developed using Blockchain Technology. Numerous review articles were published to demonstrate the advantages of blockchain for existing applications. Blockchain has also been incorporated into Cloud Computing Technologies which addresses many security concerns [3,19]. Blockchain has also been used in the healthcare and medical fields [12,18,22].

There are many existing systems and frameworks which use Blockchain Technology for Data Storage. Different protocols involving Cryptographic Techniques [5], Data Deduplication Scheme [15], Data Integrity Checking Schemes [28] were proposed on this topic. Bitcoin, which is based on Blockchain, was also used to develop Cloud Storage Technologies, with the payment modes and transactions being done on the bitcoin network [23].

With regard to Proof of Retrievability Schemes, Shacham and Waters [20] propose protocols based on the idea of using homomorphic authenticators for file blocks. Due to the use of integrity values for file blocks, their scheme can use a more efficient erasure code to encode the file; the block authenticators transform the erasure code into an error-correcting code. Their scheme supports an unlimited number of verifications.

Golle, Jarecki, and Miranov [9] propose techniques that enforce a minimum storage complexity on the server responsible for storing file $\mathscr{F}$. This involves a minimum requirement for the size of the file to be stored, so as to meet the security standards put forward by them. They describe protocols that ensure dedicated use by a server of storage at least $|\mathscr{F}|$, but do not enforce requirements on what data the server actually stores. Filho and Barreto [8] describe a POR scheme that relies on the knowledge-of-exponent assumption. Shah et al. [21] consider a symmetric key variant of full-file processing to enable external audits of file possession. The scheme only works for encrypted files, and auditors are required to maintain long-term state.

3   Background and Preliminaries

In this section, we discuss the background of the components involved in SIOCEN.

3.1   Blockchain

Blockchain is a distributed, decentralized tamper-resistant digital ledger that is used to record transactions in blocks. It was first introduced by Satoshi Nakamoto in Bitcoin [16], as a hash-linked chain of blocks, with each block made up of multiple transactions. Each block is made up of the main data block i.e. the transactions and the header part which contains metadata of the present block and the hash value of the previous block. Since all the blocks in the chain are linked through their hash values, transactions once committed cannot be changed or modified, hence, the system is tamper-resistant. Any attempts towards tampering with the data already present is nullified, since a change in the main data of the block leads to the change in the hash value of that corresponding block. The whole chain is maintained by a network of nodes/systems. All the nodes come together to decide on the block to be committed to the chain. Generally, all the participants elect a leader to decide on the block to be committed and there are various mechanisms or algorithms to pick the above-mentioned leader.

3.2   Ethereum and Smart Contracts

Ethereum [25] is one such flavour of Blockchain, where the leader is elected based on the Proof-of-Work(PoW) Algorithm. In this system, the nodes that are part of the network, called miners, are asked to solve a hash based challenge, and whoever solves it first gets elected as the leader. This is done for each and every block. The leader is rewarded with cryptocurrency called Ethers which act as the incentive for potentials' miners to be part of the network.

Apart from being a non-tamperable register, blockchain technology has the capability to execute and perform arbitrary operations in the form of Smart Contracts [14]. Certain Functions are executed when previously set conditions are met and verified while running on the blockchain network. Because of the digital and automated nature of these Smart Contracts, and also no necessity for a mediator, they are very important in designing secure and privacy based systems for real life applications.

Ethereum is one of the most popular blockchain network which supports Smart Contract Execution. The contracts are executed in Ethereum Virtual Machines (EVMs) which is uniform across all nodes, to have the same output on all the nodes across the network. The amount of work done, in terms of the number of operations performed is calculated in terms of gas. A user submits transactions along with ethers (as the transaction fee) to compensate for the work done by the miners. Ethereum is also open source with a large community.

3.3   Bilinear Pairings

We have $\mathcal{G}_1$ and $\mathcal{G}_2$ which are two multiplicative groups made of prime order 'p' [17]. In this case, a pairing is a mapping of a function $e : \mathcal{G}_1 \times \mathcal{G}_2 \to \mathcal{G}_3$. For a pairing to be bilinear, the following conditions must be satisfied

- Bilinearity: $\forall \alpha, \beta \in Z_p^*, \forall U \in \mathcal{G}_1, \forall V \in \mathcal{G}_2$
$$e(\alpha U, \beta V) = e(U, V)^{\alpha\beta}$$
where $Z_p^* = 1 \leq \alpha \leq p - 1 : \gcd(\alpha, p) = 1$ with group operation of multiplication modulo p.
- Non-Degeneracy: $e \neq 1$
- Computability: To calculate e, $\exists$ an effective algorithm.

3.4 Privacy Preserving Proof of Retrievability Scheme

PoR schemes, also called Auditing Protocols, are a set of mathematical schemes that are used to guarantee that the server/storage provider has indeed stored the file and not deleted it for his selfish purposes. They were first introduced by Juels and Kaliski [11]. Normally, a third-party Auditor sends a set of challenges to the server, and the server responds with the appropriate response to prove that it has indeed stored the file uploaded by the owner. Our proposed system is inspired from Yang et al. [27] scheme.

4   SIOCEN: System Model and Design Goal

4.1   System Model

In this section, we describe the construction of SIOCEN in multiple stages and describe each stage. The system model diagram of SIOCEN is shown in Fig. 1. The system model comprises four parties: Data Owner(DO), Cloud Server(CS), Auditor or Third Party Auditor(TPA) and Blockchain.

- *Data Owner*: They are the entities who own the data, but do not have the adequate infrastructure to store the data.
- *Cloud Server*: It is an entity that saves and stores the data of various data owners and processes it accordingly. It is semi-trusted and might delete or alter the data sometimes and hide this information from the data user to maintain its reputation causing chaos, hence, verification of the integrity of data that is stored in cloud server is necessary, which is done by the auditor.
- *Auditor*: It is an entity that checks the data integrity of the outsourced data which is stored in the cloud. The auditor can be a trustworthy organization, may manage by a government, capable of delivering impartial audit outcomes for data owners and cloud servers. It forwards a challenge to the cloud server, expecting proof of possession in return based on the challenge sent. Then it verifies the data integrity by confirming if the proof is valid or not.
- *Blockchain*: We utilize blockchain services to log records of each data transfer and data verification transaction. If any dispute arises between the parties, then we resolve it using these valid records of transaction.

The workflow diagram is shown in Fig. 2 with detail explanation in the below Sect. 5. From Fig. 2 represents during system initialization, the owner generates the public parameters and also generates the keys and the tags for the data.

Once the data is stored on the server, the owner requests the auditor to perform confirmation auditing in order to verify the accurate storage of their data. Once the confirmation is received, the owner has the option to delete the local copy of the data. Subsequently, the auditor performs periodic sampling audits to ensure data integrity.

4.2   Design Goals

Using the above designed system, we will try and achieve the following design goals:

- *Anti Collusion:* Parties in SIOCEN will not be able to collude and work together to compromise the system.
- *Anti-Forgery:* Server will not be able to forge false responses for a given challenge set and cheat the protocol.
- *Public Auditability:* The Auditing process is publicly verifiable and any person can generate challenges and verify the integrity of the stored data.
- *Privacy Preserving:* The data of the owner is kept safe from the Auditor, since the audit process is publicly verifiable and we have to safegaurd the data from random auditors.

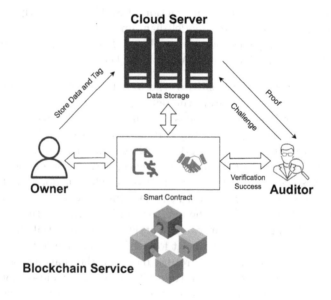

Fig. 1. System Model

5   SIOCEN: The Protocol

5.1   File Processing

To enhance the efficiency of an auditing scheme, we implement *data fragment technique*. Data owners have a file $\mathscr{F}$ to be uploaded and stored in the server. The owner first pays the necessary fee for the services provided by the cloud storage provider/server and the auditor. The smart contract collects this fee. The owner first splits the file into $\mathbb{B}$ data components. Let $\mathscr{F}$ be divided into $f_1, f_2, f_3, \ldots, f_{\mathbb{B}}$. Then, data components f_k divided into n_k blocks $\mathbb{B}_{k1}, \mathbb{B}_{k2}, \mathbb{B}_{k3}, \ldots, \mathbb{B}_{kn_k}$, where each data blocks made up of 's' sectors, i.e. Each block is divided into multiple constant size sectors using data fragment technique, to be encrypted. The encrypted data component is denoted as $\mathscr{F} = \{\mathbb{B}_{ij}\}_{i\in[1,n], j\in[1,s]}$. The data block size should be limited for security purposes based on the security parameter. The number of data blocks for a data component $\mathbb{B}_i$ can be calculated as $n = \frac{sizeof(\mathbb{B}_i)}{s \cdot logp}$, where p is a large prime number, and the size of each sector is constant and equal to p.

5.2   Key Generation and Registration with Smart Contract

Consider two multiplicative groups $\mathcal{G}_1$ and, $\mathcal{G}_2$ with z_1 and z_2 being their generators. Let $\mathcal{H}$ be a collision resistant secure hash function $\mathcal{H} : \{0,1\}^* \to \mathcal{G}_1$ maps $\mathscr{F}_{\mathbb{B}ab}$(abstract information of $\mathscr{F}_{\mathbb{B}}$) to a point in $\mathcal{G}_1$. The key generation algorithm (**KEYGEN**) takes input λ (security parameter) and it picks two random numbers $\rho, \mu \in Z_p$ and considers $X_\tau = \rho$ as its private tag key and $X_\eta = \mu$ for a private hash key. It calculates a publicly available tag key $Y_\tau = z_2^{X_\tau}$. It finally outputs the key set (X_τ, X_η, Y_τ).

The server first submits a random number Y_s to the smart contract as its public key for its digital signature. The owner submits the private hash key X_η and public tag key Y_τ to the auditor. The auditor submits a random number Y_a to the smart contract as its public key.

5.3   File Processing and Tag Generation

Owner uses tag generation algorithm (**TAGGEN**) that chooses random values $r_1, r_2, \ldots, r_s \in Z_p$ where s is the number of sectors. It takes each data component $\mathbb{B}$, X_τ, and X_η as input parameters. Then, calculates $o_j = z_1^{r_j}$ where $o_j \in \mathcal{G}_1$ for all $j \in [1, s]$ and also calculates a tag τ_i for each block as,

$$\tau_i = \left(\mathcal{H}(X_\eta, \mathcal{E}_i) \cdot \prod_{j=1}^{s} o_j^{\mathbb{B}_{ij}} \right)^{X_\tau} \tag{1}$$

where $\mathcal{E}_i = FID\|i$ and FID = number of blocks n and i represents the block number in consideration. Finally, outputs Tag Set $\mathcal{T} = (\tau_1, \tau_2, \ldots, \tau_n)$. Data Owner sends the encrypted message set $\mathbb{B}$ and tag set $\mathcal{T}$ to the cloud server for storage.

The Cloud server signs the Tag Set $\mathcal{T}$ using its private key and sends the signed message back to the data owner. Data owner then verifies the signed tag message sent by the server using the server's public key. The owner then counter-signs the tag message with its own private key, and commits the resultant message to the blockchain. In this case, the tag set is signed by both the owner and server and then committed to the blockchain. After this process, owner submits abstract information $\mathscr{F}_{\mathbb{B}ab}$ about the file (metadata of the file), the private hash key X_η, public tag key Y_τ to the auditor for the audit process.

5.4 Challenge Message Generation

The Auditor collects all information committed by the data owner on the smart contract. Auditor uses a challenge set generation algorithm (**CSETGEN**) that takes $\mathscr{F}_{\mathbb{B}ab}$ as input. It chooses a random number of data block numbers $\mathbb{B}_i$ ($i \in \mathbb{C}$) from the total number of blocks of the file to construct *the Challenge Set* $\mathbb{C}$. For every value of chosen $\mathbb{B}_i$, auditor generates a random value $\theta_i \in Z_p^*$. It then calculates the challenge stamp $\mathscr{S} = (Y_\tau)^\varphi$ where $\varphi \in Z_p^*$ is a random number. Then, it outputs the challenge $\mathscr{C}$ and sends this to the server. The challenge is computed as

$$\mathscr{C} = \left([i, \theta_i]_{i \in \mathbb{C}}, \mathscr{S}\right) \tag{2}$$

5.5 Response Generation by Server

Server receives the challenge set $\mathscr{C}$ sent by the Auditor, and generates the following the Tag Proof $(\mathcal{T}_p)$ and the Data Proof $(\mathcal{D}_p)$ using the response generation algorithm (**RESPONSEGEN**). The tag proof is computed as

$$\mathcal{T}_p = \prod_{i \in \mathbb{C}} \tau_i^{\theta_i} \tag{3}$$

To generate the Data Proof, it first computes the message proof $\mathcal{M}$ for each sector as

$$\mathcal{M}_j = \sum_{i \in \mathbb{C}} \theta_i \mathbb{B}_{ij} \tag{4}$$

Using this, it generates the data proof as

$$\mathcal{D}_p = \prod_{j=1}^{s} e\left(o_j, \mathscr{S}\right)^{\mathcal{M}_j} \tag{5}$$

The server sends this response set $\mathscr{P} = (\mathcal{T}_p, \mathcal{D}_p)$ to the auditor for further validation.

5.6 Verification by Auditor

In this stage, the Auditor calls verification algorithm (**VERIFY**) that takes input the challenge $\mathscr{C}$, response set $\mathscr{P}$, private hash key X_η, public tag key Y_τ

and $\mathscr{F}_{\mathbb{B}ab}$. It first computes the challenge hash $\mathcal{H}_{\mathbb{C}}$ as

$$\mathcal{H}_{\mathbb{C}} = \prod_{i \in \mathbb{C}} \mathcal{H}\left(X_\eta, \mathcal{E}_i\right)^{\varphi\theta_i} \tag{6}$$

Then, runs the final verification equation, which is given in Eq. (7).

$$\mathcal{D}_p . e(\mathcal{H}_{\mathbb{C}}, Y_\tau) = e\left(\mathcal{T}_p, z_2^{\varphi}\right) \tag{7}$$

If the above verification equation is successful, i.e. it outputs 1, the Audit process is successful. Else, the Audit Process has failed, if output 0. The Auditor commits the challenge $\mathscr{C}$, response set $\mathscr{P}$, challenge hash $\mathcal{H}_{\mathbb{C}}$ and the output of the verification process (either 0 or 1) to the smart contract. According to result r, blockchain gives incentive i or penalizes p to entities. In case of dispute, the blockchain has the ability to perform verification by verifying the committed data.

5.7 Correctness

Auditor can verify the integrity of data correctly if Eq. (7) holds. R.H.S. of the Eq. (7) can be simplified as

$$
\begin{aligned}
& e(\mathcal{T}_p, z_2^{\varphi}) \\
&= e(\textstyle\prod_{i \in \mathbb{C}} \mathcal{T}_i^{\theta_i}, z_2^{\varphi}) \\
&= e\left(\prod_{i \in \mathbb{C}} \left(\mathcal{H}\left(X_\eta, \mathcal{E}_i\right) \cdot \prod_{j=1}^{s} o_j^{\mathbb{B}_{ij}} \right)^{X_\tau \theta_i}, z_2^{\varphi} \right) \\
&= e\left(\prod_{i \in \mathbb{C}} \left(\mathcal{H}\left(X_\eta, \mathcal{E}_i\right) \cdot \prod_{j=1}^{s} o_j^{\mathbb{B}_{ij}} \right)^{X_\tau \theta_i \varphi}, z_2 \right) \\
&= e\left(\prod_{i \in \mathbb{C}} \left(\mathcal{H}\left(X_\eta, \mathcal{E}_i\right) \cdot \prod_{j=1}^{s} o_j^{\mathbb{B}_{ij}} \right)^{\theta_i \varphi}, z_2^{X_\tau} \right) \\
&= \prod_{j=1}^{s} e\left(o_j, z_2^{X_\tau \varphi} \right)^{\sum_{i \in \mathbb{C}} \theta_i \mathbb{B}_{ij}} e\left(\prod_{i \in \mathbb{C}} \mathcal{H}\left(X_\eta, \mathcal{E}_i\right)^{\varphi\theta_i}, z_2^{X_\tau} \right) \\
&= \prod_{j=1}^{s} e\left(o_j, (Y_\tau)^{\varphi} \right)^{M_j} e\left(\prod_{i \in \mathbb{C}} \mathcal{H}\left(X_\eta, \mathcal{E}_i\right)^{\varphi\theta_i}, z_2^{X_\tau} \right) \\
&= \prod_{j=1}^{s} e\left(o_j, \mathscr{P} \right)^{M_j} e(\mathcal{H}_{\mathbb{C}}, Y_\tau) \\
&= \mathcal{D}_p . e(\mathcal{H}_{\mathbb{C}}, Y_\tau) \\
&\therefore \text{L.H.S.} = \text{R.H.S.}
\end{aligned}
$$

5.8 Payment by Smart Contract

Once the smart contract receives the information from the auditor after the auditing process, it cross-checks by running the same final verification algorithm. This way, it can find out if the server or auditor has tried to cheat the system. If the smart contract successfully verifies all the audit process, it pays the Auditor and the Server with the necessary fees they were promised. If the smart contract finds fault with any of the parties of the protocol, it promptly penalizes the party.

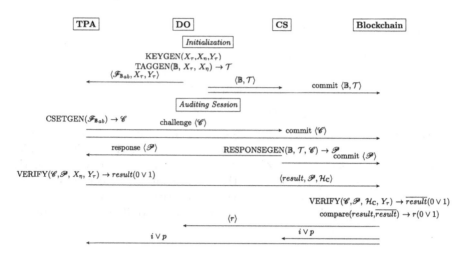

Fig. 2. Flow of Protocol

6   SIOCEN: Security Analysis

Before analysing the security aspects of the proposed system, we will do the following assumptions :

- *Honest Party:* A given party is known to be honest as long as he/she does not deviate from the above-mentioned protocol.
- *Attacker/Adversary:* Any attacker is assumed as a polynomial time algorithm that can attack and take control of any party from the protocol. But the adversary can never break cryptographic primitives like Hash Functions and Digital Signatures.
- *Emolument:* We also assume that the adversary does not do anything to harm the protocol, without any certain motivation like money.

We assume the auditor is trustworthy but inquisitive or *honest-but-curious*. Throughout the entire auditing process, it acts with honesty but maintains a sense of curiosity regarding the received data. Conversely, the cloud server has the potential to be untrustworthy and may initiate the attacks such as *Forge attack*. A forge attack means, depending on the previous response message, the server may generate the response message without retrieving the actual data of the owner.

6.1   Anti-forgery

In this section, SIOCEN is analysed against anti-forgery.

Theorem 1. *For CS, it is computationally infeasible to cheat TPA by constructing a forgery response message without having equated data.*

Proof. CS can successfully construct a forgery response message for the challenge message if it wins the following *security game.*

TPA send a challenge $([i, \theta_i]_{i \in \mathbb{C}}, \mathscr{S})$ to CS. The original response message $\mathscr{P}$ is $(\mathcal{T}_p, \mathcal{D}_p)$ where $\mathcal{T}_p = \prod_{i \in \mathbb{C}} \tau_i^{\theta_i}$ and $\mathcal{D}_p = \prod_{j=1}^{s} e(o_j, \mathscr{S})^{\mathcal{M}_j}$. In-place of generating a correct response message, CS generates a forgery response message $\overline{\mathscr{P}}$ over corrupt data $\overline{\mathbb{B}}$ as $\{\mathcal{T}_p, \overline{\mathcal{D}_p}\}$ where $\overline{\mathcal{D}_p} = \prod_{j=1}^{s} e(o_j, \mathscr{S})^{\overline{\mathcal{M}_j}}$ and $\overline{\mathcal{M}_j} = \sum_{i \in \mathbb{C}} \theta_i \overline{\mathbb{B}_{ij}}$. Define $\Delta \mathcal{M} = \overline{\mathcal{M}} - \mathcal{M}$. Here $\Delta \mathcal{M}$ is non-zero, as θ_i's are random numbers and $\overline{\mathbb{B}} \neq \mathbb{B}$. CS will win this *security game* if the forgery response message on $\overline{\mathbb{B}}$ clears the verification Eq. (7) at the TPA. Else, it loses the game.

Let us assume CS wins the above *security game* and hence corrupt response $\overline{\mathscr{P}}$ passes the verification Eq. (7). So,

$$\overline{\mathcal{D}_p} = e(\mathcal{T}_p, z_2^{\varphi}) \div e(\mathcal{H}_{\mathbb{C}}, Y_\tau) \tag{8}$$

But, according to the proposed scheme SIOCEN, the correct response $(\mathcal{T}_p, \mathcal{D}_p)$ also passes the verification Eq. (7). Hence,

$$\mathcal{D}_p = e(\mathcal{T}_p, z_2^{\varphi}) \div e(\mathcal{H}_{\mathbb{C}}, Y_\tau) \tag{9}$$

Now, from the Eqs. (8) and (9) it is clear that

$$\mathcal{D}_p = \overline{\mathcal{D}_p}$$
$$\Rightarrow \prod_{j=1}^{s} e(o_j, \mathscr{S})^{\mathcal{M}_j} = \prod_{j=1}^{s} e(o_j, \mathscr{S})^{\overline{\mathcal{M}_j}}$$
$$\Rightarrow \prod_{j=1}^{s} e(o_j, \mathscr{S})^{\Delta \mathcal{M}} = 1$$
$$\Rightarrow \gamma^{\Delta \mathcal{M}} = 1$$

In Z_p, for two elements $\alpha, \beta \in Z_p, \exists \omega \in Z_p | \beta = \alpha^\omega$. Hence, given $m, n \in Z_p$, $\gamma = \alpha^\theta \beta^\eta$, where θ and η are random numbers in Z_p. So,

$$\gamma^{\Delta \mathcal{M}} = 1$$
$$\Rightarrow (\alpha^\theta \beta^\eta)^{\Delta \mathcal{M}} = 1$$
$$\Rightarrow (\alpha^{\theta \Delta \mathcal{M}} \beta^{\eta \Delta \mathcal{M}}) = 1$$
$$\Rightarrow \beta^{\eta \Delta \mathcal{M}} = \alpha^{-\theta \Delta \mathcal{M}}$$

Now taking the logarithm and solving the above equation, we get

$$\Rightarrow \beta = \alpha^{-\frac{\theta \Delta \mathcal{M}}{\eta \Delta \mathcal{M}}}$$

Hence, the DL problem solution is $\omega = -\frac{\theta \Delta \mathcal{M}}{\eta \Delta \mathcal{M}}$ unless $\eta \Delta \mathcal{M}$ is zero. However, it is clear that $\Delta \mathcal{M}$ cannot be zero, and according to security game $\Delta \mathcal{M}$ is non-zero as θ_i's are random numbers. As η is a random element in Z_p, so $\eta \Delta \mathcal{M}$ is zero with probability $\frac{1}{p}$ where p is a large prime. Hence, a solution to the DL problem can be found with a probability $1 - \frac{1}{p}$. Therefore, it implies CS has less probability of winning the game. If CS wins the game, then we have the solution of DL problem with a probability of $1 - \frac{1}{p}$, which is quite high. But, it contradicts the DL assumptions[1]. Hence, it is impossible for CS to cheat the TPA in SIOCEN.

6.2   Privacy Preserving

One Party Corrupt Cases. A corrupt owner can upload a file $\mathscr{F}$ but can claim not to have sent the file in the first place. This cannot occur since the owner must first sign the hashed blocks of the file before committing the file to the blockchain. There is only one possibility that the owner has somehow found a collision in the Digital Signature Algorithm, which only occurs with negligible probability. There is no way of denying payments to the server since the smart contract first takes money from the owner before executing the protocol.

A corrupt server might have received a file $\ddot{\mathscr{F}}$, but it can claim to have received a completely different file. This can also happen due to communication problems. This is impossible since the server signs the hash array of the file before it gets committed to the blockchain. If the server signs a different file block (say $\ddot{f}_i$) and sends it back to the owner, the owner will check the hash values anyway. Once a file is committed, the server cannot tamper with the file anyway because of the usage of Blockchain Technology.

During the verification process, the server can try to forge a false response to the queries sent by the auditor. But without the file, the verification process cannot be completed. If the malicious server fails to complete the verification process, the smart contract can easily deny the payment to the server.

A corrupt auditor can say that the verification has failed after an honest server has submitted the appropriate response. But the smart contract can also check for the verification process given the appropriate values. Hence, it will punish the auditor by denying the payment it was promised.

Multi Party Collusion Cases. The cloud server and data owner can work together to deny the payment to the auditor. But since the smart contract handles the payment and can also do the verification process, this cannot happen.

The data owner and auditor are never in contact with each other with respect to the protocol. Even if they collude together, the smart contract ensures a fair process and algorithm execution.

The cloud server and auditor also cannot collude and cheat since the smart contract also checks the challenge and response pairs itself before making the payments.

---

[1] Let $\psi \in Z_p^*$, given h and $h^\psi \in \mathcal{G}$, it is computationally infeasible to determine ψ for a polynomial time adversary $\mathcal{A}_{dl}$. Mathematically,

$$|Pr[\mathcal{A}_{dl}(h, h^\psi) = \psi : \psi \in Z_p^*]| \leq \epsilon \qquad (10)$$

where ϵ is negligible.

6.3   Security of Ethereum Network

The Ethereum Network, which uses Proof-of-Work as its consensus protocol, is vulnerable to the 51% attack. When a group of miners can control more than 50% of the network's mining hash rate, they get the power to alter the blockchain, prevent new transactions, and halt all kinds of payments, thereby compromising the whole network. We will assume that an Adversary does not have the capability to take control of the whole network.

7   Result

Based on the above designed system, we try and develop a prototype on Ethereum Network made up of 50 nodes. The code is written in Golang while the smart contract is written using Solidity. We use one of the popular Ethereum Implementations, Go Ethereum, also known as geth, which is also written in Golang.

For the mathematical operations, mostly involving bilinear pairings, we use the PBC Library available in Golang. The whole prototype has been implemented on a Private Ethereum Network, which is deployed on a computer which runs on i5-8265U CPU with 8 GB RAM. Do note that the Private Ethereum Network, on which we have deployed our prototype, uses Proof-of-Work as it's consensus protocol.

First, we analyse the File Tag Generation and Upload Time taken by the owner for sending the file and the tags to the cloud server (refer Fig. 3). We can see that even though the time taken increases with the increase in number of blocks, the average tag calculation time for each block is almost the same and is approximately 5 s.

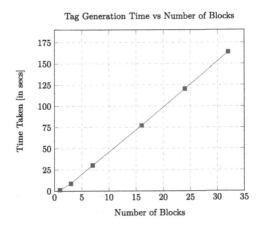

Fig. 3. Tag Generation Time by the Owner

The Proof Set Generation Time taken by the server to respond to the challenges set by the Auditor is shown in Fig. 4. The Algorithm takes approximately 5 s to calculate the Proof Set for each block. We can safely assume that the Proof Generation Time will not depend on the File challenged.

Finally, we check the verification time taken by the Auditor, given a proof set and the query set and the same is shown in Fig. 5. This process seems to be much quicker, taking milliseconds to finish the job by the Auditor. We have also compared SIOCEN with another existing model Li [13], and found that our system takes less time in terms of Verification Time by Auditor.

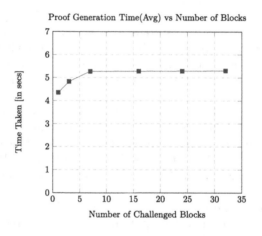

Fig. 4. Proof Generation Time by the Server

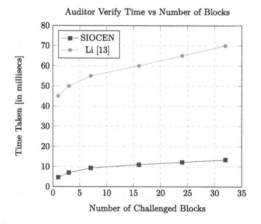

Fig. 5. Verification Time by the Auditor

8   Performance Analysis

In this section, we discuss the performance of SIOCEN and compare it with four other existing works, i.e., Wang [24], Chen [4], Huang [10] and Dredas [7]. With this comparision and analysis, we want to show that the model that we proposed is performing better than the existing works in one or other factors. In Table 1, we provided all the notations used subsequently for discussing performance analysis.

Table 1. Nomenclature used for Performance Analysis

Notations	Meaning
p	A pairing operation
m	A multiplication operation
e	An exponentiation operation
h	A hash operation
n	Number of Blocks of File
q	Number of Challenged Blocks

Table 2. Comparison of Computation Cost at different entity

Schemes	Data Owner	Cloud Server	Auditor
Wang [24]	$(m + 2e + h)n$	$p + e(1 + q) + h(1 + mq)$	$2m + 2p + 2e(1 + hmq)$
Li [13]	$(e + h + 2m)n$	$2p + (q + 1)(e + h) + m(2q - 1)$	$p + e + m(q + 1) + h(2q + 1)$
Chen [4]	$n(nm + ne + h + e)$	$q((2q - 2)m + qe)$	$2p + q(qm + (q + 1)e + h)$
Huang [10]	$(m + 2e + h)n$	$(2q - 1)m + qe$	$3p + qm + (q + 1)e + qh$
Dredas [7]	$(m + 2e + h)n$	$2e + m(q + h) + qe(1 + h)$	$3e + m(2 + q + h) + 2p$
SIOCEN	$(me + h + e)n$	$qe + qm + ep$	$heq + m + 2p$

A comparison with the existing scheme is done in Table 2. We did the comparison in terms of the computation cost incurred for each party i.e. Data Owner, Cloud Server and Auditor. It consists of cost for data proof and tag generation, for proof generation and for verification. It is clearly shown in Table 2 that our scheme SIOCEN performs fewer computations compared to Chen [4], Dredas [7], Huang [10], Li [13], and Wang [24] for each participant to generate the proof and to perform verification. The Huang [10] scheme comparatively takes the same amount of computation time as SIOCEN to generate proof messages at the cloud server, but it requires relatively higher computation in verification at the auditor. Whereas scheme Li [13], Huang [10], Dredas [7], and Wang [24] perform better and consume less computation in data proof and tag generation at the data owner side compared to SIOCEN.

In Fig. 6, the comparison time of each party in SIOCEN is shown. It shows a fast auditing process executes in less than a second. Table 3 gives the analysis summary among a comparison of some related outsourced data integrity checking schemes in terms of security analysis, privacy-preserving, cloud server proof generation, computation cost during verification, computation cost-effectiveness, blockchain services, and the incentive mechanism is considered to perform among the participating parties in blockchain. The ✓ represents the comparison parameter considered in the scheme, and × represents the comparison parameter not considered in the given scheme. From Table 3, we can find that PDP [1] and [4] are not privacy-preserving and not considered as applied to cloud storage systems. Xie [26] and Wang [24] are not performed the incentive mechanism, only develop a scheme with blockchain. Further, Wang [24] is still vulnerable to situations where multiple parties in the protocol collude together to cheat the system. Having a third-party auditor is not possible using their system. Huang [10] and Dredas [7] also use similar models which fulfill the minimum requirements of privacy and security, but they incur more computation costs and take more time during the auditing and verification phases. Whereas SIOCEN is also a blockchain initiative scheme with an incentive mechanism and privacy-preserving that consumes less computation to perform scheme proof generation and verification to form it as a computation cost-effectiveness scheme.

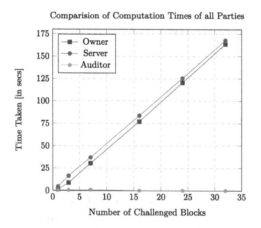

Fig. 6. Computation Time of all Parties

Table 3. Summary and Comparison of Outsourced Data Integrity Checking Schemes.

System Design	SA	PP	CPG	VCP	BS	IM	CCE
PDP [1]	✓	×	✓	✓	×	×	×
IPDP [29]	✓	✓	✓	✓	×	×	×
Li [13]	✓	✓	✓	✓	×	×	×
Xie [26]	✓	✓	✓	✓	✓	×	×
Wang [24]	✓	✓	✓	✓	✓	×	×
Chen [4]	✓	×	✓	✓	✓	✓	×
Huang [10]	✓	✓	✓	✓	✓	✓	×
Dredas [7]	✓	✓	✓	✓	✓	✓	×
SIOCEN	✓	✓	✓	✓	✓	✓	✓

SA: Detail Security Analysis, PP: Privacy Preserving, CPG: Cloud Server Proof Generation, VCP: Verification Computation Cost, BS: Blockchain Services, IM: Incentive Mechanism, CCE: Computation Cost Effective

✓: It is examined in the work; ×: It is not examined in the work.

9 Conclusion

In this paper, we have proposed a data auditing scheme using blockchain for outsourced data stored in cloud storage (SIOCEN). We include blockchain in our proposed scheme to show that it is secure, privacy-preserving, ensures correct execution of the protocol, and it's feasibility. Using Smart Contracts, we enforce the incentive mechanism of the system for fairness. We implement a prototype of the SIOCEN system, and we do a security analysis of the proposed system, which analyses all possible malicious and collusion cases. We also successfully achieve the design goals we set earlier. In future work, we will try to integrate batch auditing for multi-owner and multi-cloud in our proposed model.

References

1. Ateniese, G., et al.: Provable data possession at untrusted stores. In: Proceedings of the 14th ACM Conference on Computer and Communications Security, CCS 2007, pp. 598–609. Association for Computing Machinery, New York (2007). https://doi.org/10.1145/1315245.1315318
2. Bentov, I., Kumaresan, R.: How to use bitcoin to design fair protocols. In: Garay, J.A., Gennaro, R. (eds.) CRYPTO 2014. LNCS, vol. 8617, pp. 421–439. Springer, Heidelberg (2014). https://doi.org/10.1007/978-3-662-44381-1_24
3. Bodi, B., Chiu, W.Y., Meng, W.: Towards blockchain-enabled intrusion detection for vehicular navigation map system. In: Su, C., Gritzalis, D., Piuri, V. (eds.) ISPEC 2022. LNCS, vol. 13620, pp. 3–20. Springer, Cham (2022). https://doi.org/10.1007/978-3-031-21280-2_1

4. Chen, R., Li, Y., Yu, Y., Li, H., Chen, X., Susilo, W.: Blockchain-based dynamic provable data possession for smart cities. IEEE Internet Things J. **7**(5), 4143–4154 (2020). https://doi.org/10.1109/JIOT.2019.2963789

5. Do, H.G., Ng, W.K.: Blockchain-based system for secure data storage with private keyword search. In: 2017 IEEE World Congress on Services (SERVICES), pp. 90–93 (2017). https://doi.org/10.1109/SERVICES.2017.23

6. Dziembowski, S., Eckey, L., Faust, S.: FairSwap: how to fairly exchange digital goods. In: Proceedings of the 2018 ACM SIGSAC Conference on Computer and Communications Security, CCS 2018, pp. 967–984. Association for Computing Machinery, New York (2018). https://doi.org/10.1145/3243734.3243857

7. Fan, K., Bao, Z., Liu, M., Vasilakos, A.V., Shi, W.: Dredas: decentralized, reliable and efficient remote outsourced data auditing scheme with blockchain smart contract for industrial IoT. Futur. Gener. Comput. Syst. **110**, 665–674 (2020). https://doi.org/10.1016/j.future.2019.10.014

8. Filho, D.L.G., Barreto, P.S.L.M.: Demonstrating data possession and uncheatable data transfer. Cryptology ePrint Archive, Paper 2006/150 pp. 1–9 (2006). https://eprint.iacr.org/2006/150

9. Golle, P., Jarecki, S., Mironov, I.: Cryptographic primitives enforcing communication and storage complexity. In: Blaze, M. (ed.) FC 2002. LNCS, vol. 2357, pp. 120–135. Springer, Heidelberg (2003). https://doi.org/10.1007/3-540-36504-4_9

10. Huang, P., Fan, K., Yang, H., Zhang, K., Li, H., Yang, Y.: A collaborative auditing blockchain for trustworthy data integrity in cloud storage system. IEEE Access **8**, 94780–94794 (2020). https://doi.org/10.1109/ACCESS.2020.2993606

11. Juels, A., Kaliski, B.S.: PORs: proofs of retrievability for large files. In: Proceedings of the 14th ACM Conference on Computer and Communications Security, CCS 2007, pp. 584–597. ACM, New York (2007). https://doi.org/10.1145/1315245.1315317

12. Khezr, S., Moniruzzaman, M., Yassine, A., Benlamri, R.: Blockchain technology in healthcare: a comprehensive review and directions for future research. Appl. Sci. **9**(9) (2019). https://doi.org/10.3390/app9091736

13. Li, X., Liu, S., Lu, R., Khan, M.K., Gu, K., Zhang, X.: An efficient privacy-preserving public auditing protocol for cloud-based medical storage system. IEEE J. Biomed. Health Inform. **26**(5), 2020–2031 (2022). https://doi.org/10.1109/JBHI.2022.3140831

14. Liu, J., Liu, Z.: A survey on security verification of blockchain smart contracts. IEEE Access **7**, 77894–77904 (2019). https://doi.org/10.1109/ACCESS.2019.2921624

15. Liu, X.L., Sheu, R.K., Yuan, S.M., Wang, Y.N.: A file-deduplicated private cloud storage service with CDMI standard. Comput. Stand. Interfaces **44**, 18–27 (2016). https://doi.org/10.1016/j.csi.2015.09.010

16. Nakamoto, S.: Bitcoin: a peer-to-peer electronic cash system. Decent. Bus. Rev. 21260 (2008)

17. Nayak, S.K., Tripathy, S.: SEMKC: secure and efficient computation over outsourced data encrypted under multiple keys. IEEE Trans. Emerg. Top. Comput. **9**(01), 414–428 (2021)

18. Ng, Z.Y., Salam, I.: Blockchain-based multi-keyword search on encrypted COVID-19 contact tracing data. In: Su, C., Gritzalis, D., Piuri, V. (eds.) ISPEC 2022. LNCS, vol. 13620, pp. 75–92. Springer, Cham (2022). https://doi.org/10.1007/978-3-031-21280-2_5

19. Park, J.H., Park, J.H.: Blockchain security in cloud computing: use cases, challenges, and solutions. Symmetry **9**(8) (2017). https://doi.org/10.3390/sym9080164

20. Shacham, H., Waters, B.: Compact proofs of retrievability. In: Pieprzyk, J. (ed.) ASIACRYPT 2008. LNCS, vol. 5350, pp. 90–107. Springer, Heidelberg (2008). https://doi.org/10.1007/978-3-540-89255-7_7

21. Shah, M.A., Baker, M., Mogul, J.C., Swaminathan, R.: Auditing to keep online storage services honest. In: Proceedings of the 11th USENIX Workshop on Hot Topics in Operating Systems, HOTOS 2007, pp. 1–6. USENIX Association, USA (2007). https://doi.org/10.5555/1361397.1361408

22. Siyal, A.A., Junejo, A.Z., Zawish, M., Ahmed, K., Khalil, A., Soursou, G.: Applications of blockchain technology in medicine and healthcare: challenges and future perspectives. Cryptography 3(1) (2019). https://doi.org/10.3390/cryptography3010003

23. Wang, H., Wang, X.A., Xiao, S., zhou, Z.: Blockchain-based public auditing scheme for shared data. In: Barolli, L., Xhafa, F., Hussain, O.K. (eds.) IMIS 2019. AISC, vol. 994, pp. 197–206. Springer, Cham (2020). https://doi.org/10.1007/978-3-030-22263-5_19

24. Wang, H., Qin, H., Zhao, M., Wei, X., Shen, H., Susilo, W.: Blockchain-based fair payment smart contract for public cloud storage auditing. Inf. Sci. 519, 348–362 (2020). https://doi.org/10.1016/j.ins.2020.01.051

25. Wood, G., et al.: Ethereum: a secure decentralised generalised transaction ledger. Ethereum Proj. Yellow Pap. 151(2014), 1–32 (2014)

26. Xie, G., Liu, Y., Xin, G., Yang, Q.: Blockchain-based cloud data integrity verification scheme with high efficiency. Secur. Commun. Netw. 2021, 1–15 (2021). https://doi.org/10.1155/2021/9921209

27. Yang, K., Jia, X.: An efficient and secure dynamic auditing protocol for data storage in cloud computing. IEEE Trans. Parallel Distrib. Syst. 24(9), 1717–1726 (2013). https://doi.org/10.1109/TPDS.2012.278

28. Yue, D., Li, R., Zhang, Y., Tian, W., Peng, C.: Blockchain based data integrity verification in P2P cloud storage. In: 2018 IEEE 24th International Conference on Parallel and Distributed Systems (ICPADS), pp. 561–568 (2018). https://doi.org/10.1109/PADSW.2018.8644863

29. Zhu, Y., Ahn, G.J., Hu, H., Yau, S.S., An, H.G., Hu, C.J.: Dynamic audit services for outsourced storages in clouds. IEEE Trans. Serv. Comput. 6(2), 227–238 (2013). https://doi.org/10.1109/TSC.2011.51

Author Index

W. Meng et al. (Eds.): ISPEC 2023, LNCS 14341, pp. 615–616, 2023.
https://doi.org/10.1007/978-981-99-7032-2